Intercultural
Communication

6th Edition

6 EDITION

Intercultural
Communication

A CONTEXTUAL
APPROACH

JAMES W. NEULIEP
St. Norbert College

Los Angeles | London | New Delhi
Singapore | Washington DC

Los Angeles | London | New Delhi
Singapore | Washington DC

FOR INFORMATION:

SAGE Publications, Inc.
2455 Teller Road
Thousand Oaks, California 91320
E-mail: order@sagepub.com

SAGE Publications Ltd.
1 Oliver's Yard
55 City Road
London EC1Y 1SP
United Kingdom

SAGE Publications India Pvt. Ltd.
B 1/I 1 Mohan Cooperative Industrial Area
Mathura Road, New Delhi 110 044
India

SAGE Publications Asia-Pacific Pte. Ltd.
33 Pekin Street #02-01
Far East Square
Singapore 048763

Printed in the United States of America

Library of Congress Cataloging-in-Publication Data

Neuliep, James William, 1957–

Intercultural communication : a contextual approach / James W. Neuliep, St. Norbert College. — 6th Edition.

pages cm
Includes bibliographical references and index.

ISBN 978-1-4522-5659-7 (pbk.)

1. Intercultural communication. 2. Culture. I. Title.

HM1211.N48 2014
303.48'2—dc23   2013046952

This book is printed on acid-free paper.

Acquisitions Editor: Matthew Byrnie
Associate Editor: Nancy Loh
Assistant Editor: Katie Guarino
Editorial Assistant: Gabrielle Piccininni
Production Editor: Jane Haenel
Copy Editor: Megan Granger
Typesetter: C&M Digitals (P) Ltd.
Proofreader: Jen Grubba
Indexer: Terri Corry
Cover Designer: Scott Van Atta
Marketing Manager: Liz Thornton

14 15 16 17 18 10 9 8 7 6 5 4 3 2 1

Brief Contents

129770

Detailed Contents

5 The Perceptual Context

8 The Nonverbal Code   279

9 Developing Intercultural Relationships   329

10 Intercultural Conflict

Preface to the Sixth Edition

*I*ntercultural Communication: A Contextual Approach (sixth edition) is designed for undergraduate students taking their first course in intercultural communication. The purpose of the book is to introduce students to the fundamental topics, theories, concepts, and themes at the center of the study of intercultural communication.

The overall organizational scheme of the book is based on a *contextual model of intercultural communication.* The model is based on the idea that whenever people from different cultures come together and exchange verbal and nonverbal messages, they do so within a variety of contexts, including a cultural, microcultural, environmental, sociorelational, and perceptual context. The model is conceptually and graphically consistent and is presented in Chapter 1.

The overall organizational scheme of the sixth edition is consistent with the earlier editions, but many substantive revisions have been incorporated. Each chapter has been revised and updated to include the most recent research in the field. A continuing and exciting feature of this edition is Student Voices Across Cultures. Each chapter includes at least one essay from a student applying a concept from that chapter to his or her life experiences. Students from China, Saudi Arabia, the Faroe Islands, Mexico, Germany, Colombia, Sweden, and the United States have contributed to this feature. Many of the U.S. students discuss their study-abroad experiences. These essays provide the reader with real-life applications of theoretical concepts. The sixth edition includes five new Student Voices Across Cultures essays. The role of modern technology and its impact on intercultural communication has also been added to many chapters. A few chapters contain a new feature called Developing a Skill Set to help students apply what they have learned in the chapter.

Chapter 1 alerts students to the importance and necessity of intercultural communication in the 21st century. A revised discussion of the role of modern technology is included here. The argument is that modern technology has decentralized information. This means that billions of people across the planet now have access to information that was not available to them only a few years ago. Such information empowers them. In addition, the most current data from the U.S. Census Bureau are reviewed and point to the growing diversity of the U.S. population. The chapter continues with extended discussions of the nature of human communication and culture. An interesting case study has been added in the section on "The Need for Intercultural Communication." While reading Chapter 1, students can complete and score the Personal Report of Communication Apprehension, the Generalized Ethnocentrism Scale, and the Personal Report of Intercultural Communication Apprehension. The chapter closes with a delineation of five fundamental assumptions of intercultural communication. The Student Voices Across Cultures profile in this chapter presents one young woman's experiences with cultural differences while studying abroad in Spain.

In Chapter 2, culture is defined as an accumulated pattern of values, beliefs, and behaviors shared by an identifiable group of people with a common history and verbal and nonverbal code system. The outer circle of the contextual model of intercultural communication represents the cultural context. This is the largest circle because culture permeates every aspect of the communicative exchange, even the physical geography. All communicative exchanges between persons occur within some cultural context. The cultural context is the focus of Chapter 2. Well-recognized topics such as individualism–collectivism, high–low context, weak–strong uncertainty avoidance, value orientations, and small–large power distance are discussed. Self-report scales measuring each of these topics are included in the chapter, and a new scale that measures vertical and horizontal individualism and collectivism has been added. Although most textbooks present individualism and collectivism as opposite dimensions of cultural variability, they are not mutually exclusive; that is, they can coexist within a person of any culture. However, there is an argument that both individualistic and collectivistic ideals serve the self, or are pancultural. The discussion of the pancultural self has been updated and extended. The section on Schwartz's value system also has been completely revised with additional and updated citations. Two Student Voices Across Cultures profiles are included in this chapter: one from a Chinese student who discusses collectivism in China and the other from a Saudi Arabian student who explains power distance in his family.

The focus of Chapter 3 is the microcultural context. Within most cultures are groups of people that differ in some significant way from the general macroculture. These groups are sometimes called minorities, subcultures, or co-cultures. In this book, the term *microculture* is used to refer to those identifiable groups of people that share a set of values, beliefs, and behaviors, and possess a common history and verbal and nonverbal symbol system that is similar to, but systematically varies from, the larger, often dominant cultural milieu. Microcultures can be different from the larger culture in a variety of ways—most often because of race, ethnicity, language, religion, or even behavioral practices. Such microcultures develop their own language for communicating outside the dominant or majority culture's context or value system. The revised Chapter 3 includes an updated discussion of five U.S. microcultures: Hispanics, African Americans, Amish, Hmong, and LGBT (lesbian, gay, bisexual, and transgender) groups. In this new edition, a sixth group—Asian Americans—is also profiled. Included in this chapter is a Student Voices Across Cultures profile written by a gay college professor, who discusses personal examples of being silenced as a member of a microculture.

Chapter 4 focuses on the environmental context. Whereas culture prescribes the overall rules for communication, the environmental context prescribes when and what specific rules apply. The environmental context includes the physical geography, architecture, landscape design, housing, perceptions of privacy, time orientation, and even climate of a particular culture. A discussion of the Japanese phenomenon of microhomes, or ultra-small homes, has been added to this chapter. These environmental factors play a key role in how people communicate. In this chapter, students are given the opportunity to assess their privacy preferences and monochronic/polychronic time orientations. Chapter 4 includes coverage of the nature of privacy in the United States, with a special focus on the perceptions of privacy among U.S. students. The section on online privacy has been revised, now including a summary of an interesting report issued by Privacy International. A new discussion of natural disasters as cultural and social events has been added as well, including a discussion of the

2011 tsunami in Japan. Although natural disasters are triggered by natural events (e.g., tsunamis, earthquakes, floods, etc.), the effects of such disasters vary considerably across cultures because they take place within particular social and cultural systems of laws and values. In the Student Voices Across Cultures profile included in this chapter, a young man from Germany discusses his country's monochronic time orientation. A new chart summarizing characteristics of monochronic and polychronic time orientations also has been added.

Chapter 5 focuses on the perceptual contexts of the interactants and includes a revised and simplified model of human information processing. The perceptual context refers to the individual characteristics of the interactants, including their cognitions, attitudes, dispositions, and motivations. How an individual gathers, stores, and retrieves information is uniquely human but also culturally influenced. An individual's attitudes about others, including stereotypes, are culturally influenced. Also included in Chapter 5 is a discussion of American racism as a parallel to ethnocentrism. The geography of thought—that is, how geographical differences among cultures have a dramatic influence on how humans in those distinct geographical areas perceive the world—is discussed. Here, the focus is on how Asians (Eastern cultures) and Westerners think differently, and why. Another feature of this chapter is a fascinating discussion of the Stereotype Content Model, which explains how and why people stereotype and the essential content of those stereotypes. This model is applicable across cultures. A new feature of this chapter is a discussion of media's influence on stereotypes, including an application of Gerbner's cultivation theory. The chapter applies cultivation theory to three microcultural groups in the United States, examining how they are depicted on television and the resulting stereotypes associated with them. Three specific groups studied are African Americans, Hispanics/Latinos, and Asian Americans. A new look at how Americans are stereotyped is also included here. In one of the Student Voices Across Cultures profiles in this chapter, a young woman who has won beauty pageants discusses the long-held stereotypes applied to beauty queens. In another profile, a student from the United States discusses being stereotyped while studying abroad in Ecuador.

The sociorelational context is the focus of Chapter 6. Whenever two people come together and interact, they establish some sort of social relationship based on their group memberships. Within such relationships, each person assumes a role. Roles prescribe with whom, about what, and how to communicate. Roles vary from culture to culture. For example, in just about every culture, there are student and teacher role relationships, but how student–teacher roles are defined varies significantly from culture to culture. For example, the U.S. American definition of *student* varies significantly from the Japanese definition of *student*. What it means to be a mother or father varies considerably from one culture to another as well. One's roles prescribe the types of verbal and nonverbal symbols exchanged. This revised Chapter 6 contains a new discussion of matriarchy and patriarchy and an updated discussion of family groups that now includes families in Israel and China's Mosuo group. A new section on sex roles in Israel has been added. In the Student Voices Across Cultures profile in this chapter, a young woman from Saudi Arabia discusses sex roles in her family and culture.

Chapter 7 focuses on the verbal code and human language. Throughout much of the book, cultural *differences* are highlighted. In Chapter 7, however, language is characterized as essentially *human* rather than cultural. Based on the ideas of Noam Chomsky and other contemporary linguists, Chapter 7 points out that regardless of culture, people are born with the capacity for language. Humans are born with universal grammar and, through culture, are exposed to a subset that constitutes their particular culture's language (e.g., English, French, and so on). The language of a particular culture is simply a subset of universal language. To be sure, culture certainly affects how we use language. Thus, Chapter 7 outlines several styles of language and how they vary across cultures. Along with a new set of chapter objectives, a new discussion and comparison of sex differences in verbal language in Japan, China, and India is provided here. A discussion of uniquely American accents, including a section addressing whether or not such a thing as a Midwestern accent exists, closes the chapter. In this chapter's Student Voices Across Cultures profile, a student from China explains how her native language emphasizes nonverbal tones that dramatically change the meanings of words.

Chapter 8 focuses on the nonverbal code. After a discussion of the relationship between verbal and nonverbal codes, eight channels of nonverbal communication are discussed: kinesics, paralanguage, occulesics, proxemics, haptics, olfactics, physical appearance/dress, and chronemics. In the section on kinesics, the use of gestures across cultures and an extended discussion of affect displays across cultures are presented. In the coverage of paralanguage, cultural uses of silence, accents, and tonal languages are discussed. A new feature of this chapter is a discussion of the cross-cultural differences in eye contact (i.e., occulesics). Cultural variations of space are covered in the section on proxemics. High- and low-contact cultures are the focus of the section on haptics. An extended discussion of olfactics across cultures is presented, and students can assess their perception of smell by completing the Personal Report of Olfactic Perception and Sensitivity. A discussion of physical appearance and dress looks at cultural variations in India and Japan, among other cultures. The discussion of chronemics reviews Edward T. Hall's monochronic/polychronic distinction, in addition to a discussion of the use of calendars across cultures. Finally, the chapter closes with a cross-cultural application of nonverbal expectancy violations theory. In one of this chapter's Student Voices Across Cultures essays, a U.S. student discusses her trip to Zambia, Africa, and her experience with haptics/touch. A new Student Voices Across Cultures essay, written by a student from Saudi Arabia, describes nonverbal behavior in his country. Another new Student Voices Across Cultures essay, written by a U.S. student, describes the nonverbal behavior of people in England, especially in mass transit contexts.

Chapter 9 discusses the development of intercultural relationships. This chapter focuses on five factors that affect relationships: uncertainty reduction, intercultural communication apprehension, sociocommunicative style, empathy, and similarity. Each factor is discussed, with an emphasis on intercultural relationships. The discussion of anxiety/uncertainty management theory has been completely revised, with the addition of new graphics. A substantially revised and updated section on the Internet and relational maintenance, including how Facebook is used in several different cultures, has been added. The chapter also presents an expanded and updated discussion of relationship differences between Eastern and Western cultures, marital relationships across cultures, interethnic and interracial relationships, arranged marriages, mate selection practices across cultures, and divorce. Also included is a discussion of the research associated with lesbian and gay relational maintenance. In this chapter, students can complete the Sociocommunicative Orientation/Style and Factors in Choosing a Mate instruments and compare their preferences with other cultures. In the two Student Voices Across Cultures profiles, a young man from Saudi Arabia discusses marriage in his country, and a young woman explains relationship building in Colombia. A skill set has also been included at the end of the chapter.

Chapter 10, which focuses on intercultural conflict, has been significantly expanded. The chapter begins with a definition of intercultural conflict and outlines three levels of conflict as described by Young Kim's model. The chapter includes two new models of conflict, including John Oetzel and Stella Ting-Toomey's revised Culture-Based Social Ecological Model of Conflict and Benjamin Broome's Model of Building a Culture of Peace. Then, an example of intercultural conflict is applied to all three models. Through these three applications, students can see how the models might work in practice. The chapter also includes an extended discussion of face-negotiation theory, where students can assess their degree of self-face, other-face, and mutual-face concerns after exposure to a conflict situation. The chapter also includes a discussion of facework and facework strategies and a discussion of the Intercultural Conflict Style Inventory. This inventory is a theoretical model and assessment tool used by professional mediators and trainers to diagnose and manage intercultural conflicts. The chapter closes with a discussion of conflict communication styles and how culture affects one's preference for conflict styles. In the Student Voices Across Cultures profile, a young man from Mexico describes how people in his culture approach interpersonal conflict.

Chapter 11 has also been significantly revised to include a new title, updated and new objectives, a revised section on how the contextual model's contexts affect business, and an updated section on management across cultures. A new Student Voices Across Cultures essay has been added, written by a student from Sweden who discusses business practices in his country. The chapter now includes a completely new section on health communication in intercultural contexts, along with a new section on intercultural communication between patients and providers that highlights some of the issues faced by both sides in health care contexts. A new Student Voices Across Cultures essay has been added to this section as well. The student is from the Faroe Islands, where health care is handled much differently than in the United States. Another new section on intercultural communication in educational settings—containing a section on learning styles across cultures and a graphic of a learning style model, a section on teacher immediacy across cultures, and a series of pedagogical recommendations for teachers in intercultural classrooms—has been added. There is also a revised chapter summary, five new discussion questions, and about 50 additional sources, mostly in the new sections on health care and education.

Chapter 12 presents a discussion of acculturation, culture shock, and intercultural competence. The central theme of this chapter is the practical aspect of traveling or moving to a new culture. A model of assimilation/acculturation is presented, along with factors that influence the acculturation process, such as perceived similarity and host culture attitudes. A four-stage U-curve model of culture shock is outlined. In addition, the chapter includes a discussion of the W-curve model of reentry culture shock. The chapter also includes a variety of self-report inventories to help students prepare for a journey abroad. The chapter closes with a model of intercultural competence as four interdependent components—knowledge, affective, psychomotor, and situational features. The chapter also includes a discussion of Lily Arasaratnam's integrated model and measure of intercultural communication competence. Like others, Arasaratnam maintains that being a competent intercultural communicator involves knowing about other cultures, an approach tendency, and the application of appropriate and effective communication behaviors. A scale that measures intercultural competence is also included.

A new feature of this chapter is an extended discussion of Kim Zapf's Culture Shock Scale, including a checklist of additional culture shock symptoms. A new section titled "Indicators of Success in the Intercultural Context" has been added. This material is based on some current research coming out of the Netherlands. The first Student Voices Across Cultures profile features a young woman's experiences with culture shock during her semester in Spain. A new Student Voices Across Cultures profile based on reentry shock (the W-curve model) has been added. This will nicely complement the earlier essay on culture shock. Many of my students comment that coming back to the United States after a semester abroad (i.e., reentry shock) is more difficult than actually traveling abroad (i.e., culture shock).

As mentioned above, most chapters contain a number of self-assessment instruments. These are designed to help students learn about themselves as they learn about important concepts in intercultural communication. The instruments included are documented as being valid and reliable. As in the earlier editions, most of the chapters in this newly revised edition of the book contain *intercultural conversations*. These hypothetical scripts illustrate how the various concepts discussed in the chapters manifest in human interactions. Each chapter also includes a set of learning objectives, a chapter summary, key terms, discussion questions, and an extensive reference list.

A number of people have been instrumental in the revision of this book. I am blessed, truly blessed, with the professionals at SAGE Publications. That only my name appears on the cover of this book is misleading. My editorial and production staff at SAGE deserve much of the credit for what is good in this book. They have been incredibly helpful, and I wish to express my gratitude publicly. A genuine and sincere thanks goes to my editor, Matt Byrnie, whose expertise, patience, and counsel are so very much appreciated. Thanks, Matt. I hope we continue to work together for a long time. Many thanks to Associate Editor Nancy Loh, who has been working very hard arranging and analyzing reviews. Her behind-the-scenes work is much appreciated. Thanks to my freelance photo researcher Elise Frasier, who endured my missed deadlines without complaining, and to Katie Guarino and Gabrielle Piccininni, editorial assistants who stayed in contact with me throughout the production of the book, provided valuable feedback on a number of issues, and kept me up to date on everything. A special thanks to my production manager, Jane Haenel, who did so much to make the book look so good. Like the others, Jane has been so helpful and tolerant of my missed deadlines and my alleged "sense" of humor.

Once again, a very, very personal and warm thanks goes to Megan (Ms. Meg) Granger, copy editor extraordinaire, who spent so many hours editing the manuscript. As with the fifth edition of this book, I hope Meg is aware of how much I appreciate her late-night/early-morning e-mails, her razor-sharp wit, her relentless pursuit of excellence, and this time, her personal counsel. Thanks, Meg, for enduring me again. Promise me that we'll meet someday.

Although they may not have been directly linked to this new edition, I'd like to thank four exceptional colleagues of mine at St. Norbert College for their support during some trying times during the course of this revision. Thanks to Tom Kunkel, president of St. Norbert College; Jeff Frick, vice president for academic affairs; Bridget Krage-O'Connor, vice president for communications; and Mike Counter, director of media relations. You are my heroes, and you know why.

Speaking of trying times, a very warm and heartfelt thank you to my friends who have supported me in the past year. Your support means more to me than you will ever know. Thank you for holding me up. Thanks to Jeff Zahn, Gary and Karen Wyman, Debbie Faase,

Joanne Wilson, Anna Herrman, Kelly Krummel, Stacey Wanta, Tom Lemorande, Jesse Pagel, and Gene Lannoye.

Thanks also to the following reviewers of the book, whose many suggestions were incorporated into the revision. I very much appreciate their constructive comments and recommendations: Kathryn J. Akiyama, Mount Angel Seminary; Donna M. Allen, Northwest Nazarene University; Angela Cooke-Jackson, Emerson College; Leonard M. Edmonds, Arizona State University; Donna L. Halper, Lesley University; Barbara Houger, Northwest University; Kimberly Huff, Florida Gulf Coast University; Shaughan A. Keaton, Louisiana State University; Edmund Kellerman, University of Florida; Janice Kelly, Molloy College; Ulrich Luenemann, California State University, Sacramento; Marilyn J. Matelski, Boston College; Ann Neville Miller, University of Central Florida; Heidi J. Schara, Riverland Community College; Dan Warren, Bellevue University; and Eva Rose B. Washburn-Repollo, Chaminade University.

As I enter my fourth decade of teaching at the collegiate level, a genuine and sincere thank you goes to my students at St. Norbert College, from whom I have learned a great deal about culture and so much more about life. One of the greatest pleasures of my life is the relationships I have initiated and maintained with my students. In the case of this new edition, the students who contributed to the Student Voices Across Cultures essays deserve a special thanks. Those students are Hussam Almoharb, Carl Ekstrom, Viviann Hansen, Hillary Hubertz, and Anna Shircel.

—*J.W.N.*
DePere, WI

CHAPTER 1

The Necessity of Intercultural Communication

After reading this chapter, you should be able to

1. list and discuss the benefits of intercultural communication;

2. recognize the increasing racial and ethnic diversity in the U.S. population;

3. identify and discuss the eight dimensions of communication;

4. assess your degree of communication apprehension;

5. define and discuss the nature of culture;

6. identify and discuss the five contexts of intercultural communication;

7. discuss the relationship between intercultural communication, uncertainty, and anxiety;

8. assess your degree of intercultural communication apprehension;

9. identify and discuss the five fundamental assumptions of intercultural communication; and

10. assess your degree of ethnocentrism.

The history of our planet has been in great part the history of the mixing of peoples.

—Arthur M. Schlesinger, Jr.[1]

In 1804, the number of people on planet Earth was 1 billion. In 1927, 123 years later, it was 2 billion. By 1960, 33 years later, it was 3 billion. By 1974, 14 years later, it was 4 billion. Currently, there are just over 7 billion (i.e., 7,100,000,000) people on planet Earth. One human is born every 8 seconds and dies every 12 seconds, for a net gain of one person every 13 seconds. Of the 7 billion people on the planet, about 1.4 billion, or nearly 20%, are Chinese, and 1.2 billion, just over 17%, are East Indian. About 317 million, or about 4.5%, reside in the United States; about 3.5% are Indonesian; and just under 3% are Brazilian. The next largest countries, in order, include Pakistan, Nigeria, Bangladesh, Russia, and Japan. The annual world population growth rate has declined in the past few decades and now hovers at about 1.1%. Over the past 200 years, the growth rate, distribution, and density of the world population have not been spread equally. Certain regions of the world have grown disproportionately in terms of the number of people, while other regions vary considerably in terms of population density (i.e., number of people per square mile). As seen in the above statistics, China and India account for nearly 40% of the world's population. African countries make up nearly 15% of the world's population, while Europe constitutes about 11%. Monaco, Singapore, Vatican City, Maldives, and Malta are the world's five most densely populated countries. Monaco, for example, has nearly 43,000 people per square mile, while the United States has about 76 people per square mile and Canada just over 9 people per square mile.[2]

The purpose of the above paragraph is to point out that the world's population is growing disproportionately. Along with that, something else has grown disproportionately—technology and its decentralizing role in information dissemination. In 1948, the painter and writer Wyndham Lewis wrote about a "global village" in his book *America and Cosmic Man*. Several years later, his friend Marshall McLuhan also used the term to describe how technological advances of mass media would eventually disintegrate the natural time and space barriers inherent in human communication. McLuhan predicted that through the elimination of such barriers, people would continue to interact and live on a global scale—but one virtually transformed into a village.[3]

Fourteen years into the 21st century, McLuhan's vision of a global village is no longer considered an abstract idea but a near certainty. Technological changes have made Earth a smaller planet to inhabit. The technological ability of mass media and the Internet to bring events from across the globe into our homes, businesses, and schools dramatically reduces the distance between people of different cultures and societies. Telecommunication systems, including e-mail, texting, and social networking sites such as Facebook, connect people throughout the world via satellites and fiber optics. Skype links people from across the planet in seconds.

The essential effect of this technology is its decentralizing role in disseminating information across local, regional, national, and international borders. This means that billions of people across the planet now have access to information not available to them only a few years ago. Information empowers people. The ease and speed with which people of differing cultures can now communicate is stunning. In 1780—some 230 years ago—when John Adams, the second president of the United States, corresponded with his European counterparts in France, it would take as long as 6 months to send and receive letters, as they traveled by ship across the Atlantic Ocean. Imagine sending a text message to a friend that takes half a year to arrive! Today, it takes less than a second. Moreover, the sheer frequency and quantity of messages sent is baffling compared with only a few years ago. Some sources estimate that in 2013 there were 4.5 billion e-mail accounts worldwide from which 144 billion e-mails were sent each day, of which nearly 70% were spam.[4]

Of course, e-mail is only one of the technological advances facilitating communication across cultures. The technological revolution has reached even remote places such as rural India. Writing for Bloomberg, Pankaj Mishra noted that in 2012, India had 925 million (i.e., nearly 1 billion) cell phone subscribers, which is more than any other country on the planet. There are 3 times as many cell phone subscribers in India as there are people in the United States. Mishra noted that people in India have greater access to mobile phone connections than they do to working toilets. In addition, in India where more than 700 million people (more than twice the number of people in the United States) live on less than $2 a day, the cost of calling is among the lowest in the world. Writing for the *New York Times*, Anand Giridharadas maintained that cell phones play a socially significant role in India, more so than in the wealthy countries where they were invented. Why? Because they give quick and easy access to the rest of the world in a place where 40% of the 1.3 billion people are illiterate and unbelievably poor. More important, cell phone technology has reached into historically impoverished slums and small towns and villages where communicating with outsiders was virtually impossible only a few years ago. According to Mishra and Giridharadas, cell phones allow a class of people to cross the barriers of a rigid caste system where communicating with others outside one's level in the social hierarchy is heavily restricted. The majority of subscribers are now outside the major cities and wealthiest states. Indeed, so valued is the technology that the average cell phone bill of less than $5 per month, which represents 7% of the average Indian's income, is well worth the economic sacrifice to most Indians. If these trends continue, in 5 years, every Indian will own a cell phone.[5] And while many may think that the United States is the cell phone capital of the world, it actually ranks 72nd among 212 countries in terms of the number of cell phones per capita. The top 10 countries for number of cell phones per capita are, in order, the United Arab Emirates, Bahrain, Macau, Hong Kong, Estonia, Qatar, Israel, Lithuania, Bulgaria, and Italy.[6] Technology has linked the world.

Many college students in the United States have a Facebook account or are at least familiar with the social networking site. But unlike e-mail or cell phones, social networking sites such as Facebook are intentionally designed to establish and maintain relationships. So initiating a relationship with someone from across the globe is much easier now than it was only a few years ago. According to its own records, as of June 2013, there were 700 million daily active Facebook users and more than 1 billion active monthly users. About 80% of Facebook daily active users live outside of the United States and Canada.[7]

Although the technological advances mentioned above facilitate the initiation and maintenance of cross-cultural relationships, the late noted historian and Pulitzer Prize winner Arthur Schlesinger warned us that history tells an ugly story of what happens when people of diverse cultural, ethnic, religious, or linguistic backgrounds converge in one place. The hostility of one group of people against another, *different* group of people is among the most instinctive of human drives. Xenophobia—the fear or contempt of that which is foreign or unknown, especially of strangers or those perceived as foreigners—is believed by many to be an innate biological response to intergroup competition. Indeed, Schlesinger contended that unless a common goal binds diverse people together, tribal hostilities will drive them apart. By replacing the conflict of political ideologies that dominated in the 20th century, ethnic, religious, and racial strife will usher in the new millennium as the explosive issue.[8]

Throughout the first decade of the new century, we have witnessed ethnic, racial, and religious conflict and intolerance around the globe. In France, the French Senate voted overwhelmingly to ban the wearing of Islamic headscarves in public buildings and schools. Moreover, by a margin of 4 to 1, the French people agreed with the ban. In October of 2010, German Chancellor Angela Merkel was greeted by a standing ovation from a crowd of supporters after she asserted:

> The approach [to build] a multicultural [society] and to live side by side and to enjoy each other . . . has failed, utterly failed. . . . We feel tied to Christian values. Those who don't accept them don't have a place here.

That same month, the premier of Bavaria and a member of Merkel's ruling coalition called for a halt to Turkish and Arab immigration. The results of a survey of native Germans showed that about one third of them believed the country was overrun by foreigners and more than half believed Arabs are unpleasant people. In her speech, Merkel said the education of unemployed Germans should take priority over recruiting workers from abroad. U.K. Prime Minister David Cameron also criticized state multiculturalism in a recent speech. At a February 2011 security conference in Germany, he argued that the United Kingdom needed a stronger national identity to prevent people from turning to all kinds of extremism. These are just a few instances of the ethnic, racial, and religious conflicts across our planet.[9] But the good news is that, through intercultural communication, such conflict can be managed and reduced. To be sure, only by competently and peacefully interacting with others who are different from us can our global village survive.

THE NEED FOR INTERCULTURAL COMMUNICATION

International tensions around the globe are striking examples of the need for effective and competent intercultural communication. As mentioned above, such conflicts are often fueled by political, ethnic, and religious differences. For example, not too long ago, an international incident with potentially global consequences occurred between the People's Republic of China and the United States, stressing the need for competent intercultural communication. The incident began on April 1, 2001, when a U.S. Navy surveillance plane collided with a Chinese fighter jet in international airspace over the South China Sea. As a result of the collision, the U.S. plane—an EP-3 electronic warfare and surveillance aircraft—was damaged and nearly crashed. However, because of heroic efforts on the part of the crew, the plane landed safely at a Chinese air base. The 24-member crew of the U.S. plane was detained by the Chinese military. China and the United States disagreed as to the cause of the collision, each side blaming the other.

In the days and weeks following the incident, contentious negotiations took place between Chinese and U.S. officials over the release of the U.S. crew. For their release, China demanded that the United States accept responsibility and apologize for the collision. The United States refused, arguing that the collision was the fault of the Chinese pilot. In the meantime, public pressure was mounting on the president of the United States to secure the crew's release. On April 4, the U.S. secretary of state expressed "regret" over the collision and the disappearance of the Chinese pilot. Although Chinese officials acknowledged the statement as a move in the right direction, they insisted that the United States apologize for the incident. On April 8, the vice president of the United States and the secretary of state rejected China's demands for an apology but expressed "sorrow" for the disappearance of the Chinese pilot. They also drafted a letter of sympathy to the pilot's wife. The Chinese continued to demand an apology. On April 10, U.S. officials said that the president would be willing to offer the Chinese a letter expressing regret over the incident, including a statement admitting that the U.S. aircraft landed in Chinese territory without seeking permission. The Chinese continued to demand an apology.

Finally, on April 11, the United States issued a letter to the Chinese foreign minister asking him to "convey to the Chinese people and to the family of Pilot Wang Wei that we are very sorry for their loss." The letter continued, "We are very sorry the entering of China's airspace and the landing did not have verbal clearance." To be sure, the word *apology* did not appear in the letter. But in their announcement of the letter to the Chinese people, Chinese officials chose to translate the double "very sorry" as "*shenbiao qianyi*," which, in Chinese, means a deep expression of apology or regret not used unless one is admitting wrongdoing and accepting responsibility for it. Based on that letter and the subsequent translation, China agreed to release the U.S. crew. John Pomfret, of the *Washington Post* Foreign Service, asserted, "In the end, it was a matter of what the United States chose to say and what China chose to hear." Apparently, such delicacies in communication are common during U.S.–China negotiations. According to Bates Gill, who was then the director of the Center for Northeast Asian Policy Studies at the Brookings Institution, U.S. negotiators often use words such as *acknowledge* that, when translated into Chinese, mean *admit* or *recognize* so that the Chinese can interpret such wordings as an admission of U.S. guilt.[10]

Indeed, national conflicts within our own borders, often ignited by racial and ethnic tensions, underscore the necessity for skillful intercultural communication. But perhaps more important, the need for competent intercultural communication is felt intrapersonally, within our own personal, social, and professional lives and relationships. Consider the following situations that Jim, an undergraduate student at a Midwestern university, has faced in the past few days.

Situation #1

Jim has just met Bridget, an exchange student from England. They are talking in Jim's dorm room.

Jim: So, Bridget, are you enjoying your first few days in the U.S.?

Bridget: Yes, but I am a bit paggered, you know. Got pissed last night.

Jim: Oh . . . sorry . . . are you having problems with someone? Can I help?

Bridget: Not a'tall, oh no, nothing traumatic—just farty things, you know. Nothing to have a dicky fit over.

Jim: Ah, yeah, right.

(Jim's girlfriend, Betsy, enters the room.)

Betsy: Hello.

Jim: Hi, Betsy! Hey, this is Bridget. She's from England.

Betsy: Hi, Bridget.

Bridget: Hello. Nice to meet you. Jim and I were just having a bit of intercourse. Won't you join us?

Betsy: You were what?! (Leaves the room.)

Jim: (Running after her) No! Betsy, that's not true! We were just talking! I swear!

Situation #2

Later that same day, Jim is trying to explain to Betsy that nothing was happening between him and Bridget when Jahan, an exchange student from India, enters the room unannounced.

Jahan: Hello, Jim. Who is this with you?

Jim: Oh, hi, Jahan. This is Betsy. Betsy, this is Jahan. He lives just down the hall.

Betsy: Hi, Jahan.

Jahan: Is this your girlfriend, Jim?

Jim: Ah . . . yeah, she is.

Jahan: Are you two going to marry? Have children?

Jim: Ah, well . . .

Betsy: Uh . . . we really haven't discussed that.

Jahan: Oh, I see. Is your family not wealthy enough for her, Jim? What is your father's occupation?

Jim: What?

Unfortunately, Jim has found himself in some rather awkward situations here. The misinterpretations in each of the situations above are due mostly to cultural and linguistic differences. In Bridget's England, for example, the word *paggered* means tired. The colloquialism *pissed* means to get drunk, *farty* refers to something insignificant, a *dicky fit* is an emotional outburst, and *intercourse* simply means to have a conversation. Translated in terms Jim can understand, Bridget was tired because she had been drunk the night before, but she did not think it significant enough to complain. Upon meeting Betsy, she simply invited her into the conversation.

The second conversation is a bit more complicated. The late Dr. Pittu Laungani, the well-known Indian-born psychologist, wrote extensively about the culture of his native India. In his writings, Laungani asserted that Indians tend to initiate social conversations with complete strangers quite easily. According to Laungani, Indians often ask, without embarrassment, very personal and delicate questions concerning one's age, marital status, occupation, income, religious beliefs, and so on. Laungani professed that Westerners need to learn that these questions are not to be taken with any offense.[11]

Benefits of Intercultural Communication

Although the challenges of an increasingly diverse world are great, the benefits are even greater. Communicating and establishing relationships with people from different cultures can lead to a whole host of benefits, including healthier communities; increased international, national, and local commerce; reduced conflict; and personal growth through increased tolerance (see Table 1.1).

Healthy Communities

Joan England argues that genuine community is a condition of togetherness in which people have lowered their defenses and learned to accept and celebrate their differences. England contends that we can no longer define equality as "sameness" but, instead, must value our differences—whether they be in race, gender, ethnicity, lifestyle, or even occupation or professional discipline.[12] Healthy communities are made up of individuals working collectively for the benefit of everyone, not just their own group. Through open and honest intercultural communication, people can work together to achieve goals that benefit everyone, regardless of group or culture, including the global community in the home, business, or neighborhood. Healthy communities support all community members and strive to understand, appreciate, and acknowledge each member.

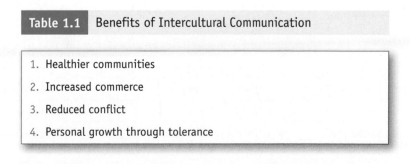

Table 1.1 Benefits of Intercultural Communication

1. Healthier communities
2. Increased commerce
3. Reduced conflict
4. Personal growth through tolerance

Increased Commerce

Our ability to interact with persons from different cultures, both inside and outside our borders, has immense economic benefits. In 2012, the top 10 countries with which the United States traded—in terms of both imports and exports—were, in order, Canada, China, Mexico, Japan, Germany, the United Kingdom, South Korea, Brazil, Saudi Arabia, and France. In 2012, U.S. trade with these countries accounted for nearly $3 trillion (i.e., $3,000,000,000,000). Only through successful intercultural communication can such economic potentials be realized.[13]

Reduced Conflict

Conflict is inevitable; we will never be able to erase it. We can, however, through cooperative intercultural communication, reduce and manage conflict. Often, conflict stems from our inability to see another person's point of view, especially if that person is from a different culture. We develop blatant negative generalizations about the person, which are often incorrect and lead to mistrust. Table 1.2 summarizes some of the most common stereotypes of different racial and ethnic groups in the United States, documented by researchers.[14] Such feelings lead to defensive behavior, which fosters conflict. If we can learn to think and act cooperatively by engaging in assertive (not aggressive) and responsive intercultural communication, we can effectively manage and reduce conflict with others.

Personal Growth Through Tolerance

As you communicate with people from different cultures, you learn more about them and their way of life—including their values, history, and habits—and the substance of their personality. As your relationship develops, you start to understand them better, perhaps even empathizing with them. One of the things you will learn (eventually) is that although your cultures are different, you have much in common. As humans, we all have the same basic desires and needs; we just have different ways of achieving them. As we learn that our way is not the only way, we develop a tolerance for difference. This can be accomplished only when we initiate relationships with people who are different from ourselves. We could learn far more about Japanese culture by initiating and maintaining a relationship with a Japanese student at our college or university than we could by traveling to Japan for a 2- or 3-week vacation. Moreover, although this may sound contradictory, the more we learn about others and other cultures, the more we begin to learn about ourselves. When we observe how others conduct their lives, we begin to understand how we conduct our own lives.

Table 1.2   Common Stereotypes

. . . About Blacks	. . . About Whites	. . . About Asians
"They're lazy."	"They think they know everything."	"They're sneaky."
"They live on welfare."	"They're all arrogant."	"They're good at math."
"They like to dance."	"They're all rich."	"I wouldn't trust them."
"They smoke crack."	"They're materialistic."	"They're really shy."

Diversity in the United States

One need not travel to faraway countries to understand the need for and experience the benefits of intercultural communication. Largely because of immigration trends, cultural and ethnic diversity in the United States is a fact of life. Immigrants, in record numbers, are crossing U.S. borders. According to the latest available U.S. government statistics (i.e., 2010), just over 37 million persons living in the United States, or about 12.5%, were not U.S. citizens at birth. More than half these people were born in Latin America (i.e., the Caribbean, Central America, Mexico, and South America).[15]

Every 10 years, at the beginning of a new decade, the U.S. Department of Commerce conducts a census. The results of the 2010 census, although still being analyzed, profile the remarkable racial and ethnic diversity that has been a hallmark of American society. In 2010, there were about 308 million people in the United States (i.e., roughly 4.5% of the world's population). Of these people, just over 65% were White non-Hispanics, about 15.5% were Hispanic (any race), 12% were Black non-Hispanic, 4% were Asian or Pacific Islander and 1% were American Indian.[16]

Both the 2000 and 2010 censuses point out that different racial and ethnic groups in the United States grow at different rates. For example, in 2000, White non-Hispanics made up nearly 70% of the U.S. population. In 2010, White non-Hispanics made up 65%. By the year 2050, the non-Hispanic White population will shrink to about 50% of the population. Conversely, the Hispanic population in 2000 made up 12.5% of the population, while in 2011, it grew to 16.7%. The Black population has remained stable at 12% in both 2000 and 2010.[17]

One of the most significant population trends in the United States is the growth of the Hispanic population. In 2011, there were 52 million Hispanics living in the United States, of which 33 million were native born. The federal government uses the terms *Hispanic* and *Latino* interchangeably and classifies Hispanics/Latinos as an ethnic group but *not* a racial group. According to the U.S. Census Bureau, Hispanics are a heterogeneous group composed of Mexicans, Cubans, Puerto Ricans, persons from Central and South America, and persons of other Hispanic origin. Mexicans account for 64% of all Hispanics in the United States. In 2011, about 30 million of all Hispanics in the United States lived in just three states— California, Texas, and Florida. Just over 8% lived in the Midwest, and about 14% lived in the Northeast. But that trend is likely to change in the upcoming decades as the Hispanic population expands geographically.[18]

In addition to the rapid growth of non-White populations in the United States, another trend is emerging: An increasing number of groups are revitalizing their ethnic traditions and promoting their cultural and ethnic uniqueness through language. Language is a vital part of maintaining one's cultural heritage, and many people are protective of their native language. For example, in July 2002, in Brown County, Wisconsin—a county with a sizable Hmong and Hispanic community—the county board of commissioners made English the official language of its government and called for more spending to promote English fluency. The all-White Brown County board voted 17 to 8 to approve the measure. "It's saying this is our official language. This is what we believe in, and we should encourage English," said then–Board Supervisor John Vander Leest. On the other hand, in August 2004, the Texas border town of El Cenizo—whose population is heavily Hispanic—adopted Spanish as its official language. Mayor Rafael Rodriguez said that he and most of the town's residents speak only Spanish. According to Rodriguez, "In past administrations, the meetings were done in English and they did not explain anything." The vote means that town business will be conducted in Spanish, which then will be translated into English for official documents to meet the requirements of Texas law. Rodriguez said the city council's intent was not to usurp English or create divisions but to make local government more accessible to the town's residents. "What we are looking for is that the people of the community who attend the meetings and who only speak Spanish be able to voice their opinions," Rodriguez said.[19]

According to 2009 data, nearly one in five people in the United States speaks a language other than English at home. Interestingly, more than half these people report that they speak English very well. When combined with those who speak only English at home, the overwhelming majority of the U.S. population has no difficulty speaking English.[20]

Although the United States prides itself on being a nation of immigrants, there is a growing sense of uncertainty, fear, and distrust among different cultural, ethnic, and linguistic groups. These feelings create anxiety that can foster separatism rather than unity. Schlesinger alerted us that a cult of ethnicity has arisen both among non-Anglo Whites and non-White minorities to denounce the idea of a melting pot; to challenge the concept of "one people"; and to protect, promote, and perpetuate separate ethnic and racial communities.[21] Many Americans are frustrated, confused, and uncertain about these linguistic and definitional issues. Only through intercultural communication can such uncertainty be reduced. Only when diverse people come together and interact can they unify rather than separate. Unity is impossible without communication. Intercultural communication is a necessity.

Human Communication

Communication is everywhere. Every day, everywhere, people are communicating. Even when alone, people are bombarded with communication. Communication professor Charles Larson estimated that, in 2010, most Americans were exposed to more than 5,000 persuasive messages every day.[22] Most people would be miserable if they were not allowed to communicate with others. Indeed, solitary confinement is perhaps the worst form of punishment inflicted on humans. Human communication—that is, the ability to symbolize and use language—separates humans from animals. Communication with others is the essence of what it means to be human. Through communication, people conduct their lives. People define themselves via their communication with others. Communication is the vehicle by which people initiate, maintain, and terminate their relationships with others. Communication is the means by which people influence and persuade others. Through communication, local, regional, national, and international conflicts are managed and resolved.

Ironically, however, communication—and particularly one's *style* of communication—can be the source of many problems. Marriage counselors and divorce lawyers indicate that a breakdown in communication is one of the most frequently cited reasons for relational dissolution in the United States.[23] A specific kind of communication—that is, public speaking—is one of the most frequently cited fears, even more feared than death.

This book is about the ubiquitous subject labeled "communication." Specifically, this is a book about *intercultural* communication—that is, communication between people of different cultures and ethnicities. Throughout the course of this book, you will be introduced to a whole host of concepts and theories that explain the process of people of differing cultural backgrounds coming together and exchanging verbal and nonverbal messages. Chapter 1 is designed as an introductory chapter and is divided into four parts. The first part outlines and discusses the nature of communication. This part will examine communication variables that apply to everyone, regardless of cultural background. The second part outlines and discusses culture. Culture is seen as a paradox; that is, culture is simultaneously a subtle and clearly defined influence on human thought processes and behavior. The third part of the chapter presents a brief history of the study of intercultural communication. The last part of the chapter introduces a contextual model of intercultural communication that will serve as the organizing scheme for the rest of this book.

The Nature of Human Communication

Because of its ubiquitous nature, communication is difficult to define. If you were to go to your university library and select 10 different introductory communication texts, each would probably offer a different definition of communication. Although there is no universally agreed-on definition of communication, most communication scholars agree on certain dimensions of communication that describe its nature. Outlined below are eight of these dimensions, along with eight definitions of communication (see Table 1.3).[24] These definitions come from a variety of scholars with diverse backgrounds in the communication field.

Table 1.3   Eight Dimensions and Definitions of Communication

1. Process	"Communication theory reflects a process point of view . . . you cannot talk about the beginning or the end of communication." (Berlo)
2. Dynamic	"Communication is a transaction among symbol users in which meanings are dynamic, changing as a function of earlier usages and of changes in perceptions and metaperceptions. Common to both meanings is the notion that communication is timebound and irreversible." (Bowers and Bradac)
3. Interactive–transactive	"Communication occurs when two or more people interact through the exchange of messages." (Goss)
4. Symbolic	"All the symbols of the mind, together with the means of conveying them through space and preserving them in time." (Cooley)
5. Intentional	"Communication has as its central interest those behavioral situations in which a source transmits a message to a receiver(s) with conscious intent to affect the latter's behavior." (Miller)
6. Contextual	"Communication always and inevitably occurs within some context." (Fisher)
7. Ubiquitous	"Communication is the discriminatory response of an organism to a stimulus." (Stevens)
8. Cultural	"Culture is communication . . . communication is culture." (Hall)

Dimension 1: Process

Almost all communication scholars concur that communication is a process. A process is anything that is ongoing, ever changing, and continuous. It does not have a specific beginning or ending point. A process is not static or at rest; it is always moving. The human body is a process; it is always aging. Communication is always developing; it is never still or motionless. There is no exact beginning or ending point of a communication exchange. Although individual verbal messages have definite beginning and ending points, the overall process of communication does not. For example, José and Juan meet in the hallway and greet each other. José says, "What up, Juan?" and Juan says, "Not much, man." Both José's and Juan's verbal messages have exact beginning and ending points, but to determine exactly when and where their nonverbal communication begins and ends is virtually impossible. They may not be verbally communicating with each other, but they are still communicating nonverbally. Even if they walk away from each other, they are communicating that they are no longer talking with each other. A process is something that continues to develop and change; it does not stop, nor can it reverse itself. Because communication is irreversible, it affects future communication. How José and Juan interact with each other today is very much influenced by how they interacted yesterday, last week, or even years ago. Think about your own relationships with your friends and how what you have said to one another in the past influences what you say today. Imagine the most recent argument with your boyfriend or girlfriend, for example. You may have said some things you now regret. Such interaction influences your relationships and how you interact today.

Dimension 2: Dynamic

Inextricably bound to the notion that communication is a process is that communication is dynamic. The terms *process* and *dynamic* are closely related. Part of what makes communication a process is its dynamic nature. Something that is dynamic is considered active or forceful. Unfortunately, communication is typically discussed as if it were some physical entity that people can hold or touch. Because communication is a dynamic process, it is impossible to capture its essence in a written definition or graphic model. This problem is not unlike that faced by a photographer who tries to capture the dynamic essence of a running horse. Certainly, the photograph can be informative about the horse, but the camera cannot make a complete reproduction. The relationship between the fore and hind legs, the beautiful "dynamic" muscular motions, cannot be truly represented in a photograph. Any discussion of communication as a dynamic process is subject to the same kinds of limitations.[25] To fully appreciate the process, one must be a part of it or witness it in motion. As a dynamic process, communication is flexible, adaptive, and fluid; thus, it is impossible to identically replicate in a picture, drawing, or model.

Dimension 3: Interactive–Transactive

Communication is interactive and transactive because it occurs between people. While some might argue that people can communicate with themselves (what is called intrapersonal communication), most scholars believe that interaction between people is a fundamental dimension of communication. Communication requires the active participation of two people sending and receiving messages. Active participation means that people are consciously directing their messages to someone else.[26] This means that communication is a two-way process, or interactive. Likewise, to say that communication is transactional means that while José is sending messages to Juan, Juan is simultaneously sending messages to José. Juan's eye contact, facial expression, and body language are nonverbal messages to José informing him how his message is being received. Each person in an interactional setting simultaneously sends (encodes) and receives (decodes) messages. For example, when you listen to your friends talk about the great party they went to last night, it is obvious to you that they are sending you messages. At the same time as they describe the party to you, you are sending messages to them, too. Your eye contact, smiles, and other nonverbal reactions are communicating to them your interest in their story. Hence, both you and your friends are sending and receiving messages at the same time.

Dimension 4: Symbolic

That communication is symbolic is another fundamental assumption guiding most communication scholars. A symbol is an arbitrarily selected and learned stimulus that represents something else. Symbols can be verbal or nonverbal. They are the vehicle by which the thoughts and ideas of one person can be communicated to another person. Messages are constructed with verbal and nonverbal symbols. Through symbols, meanings are transferred between people. Symbols (i.e., words) have no natural relationship with what they represent (they are arbitrarily selected and learned). For example, the verbal symbols "C-A-T" have no natural connection with cute, fuzzy animals that purr and like to be scratched. These particular symbols have no meaning in any languages besides English (see Figure 1.1).

| Figure 1.1 | Different languages use different codes. |

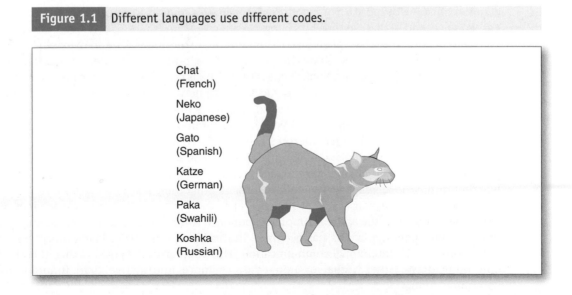

Chat
(French)

Neko
(Japanese)

Gato
(Spanish)

Katze
(German)

Paka
(Swahili)

Koshka
(Russian)

Nonverbal symbols are arbitrary as well. Showing someone your upright middle finger may not communicate much in some cultures. Verbal and nonverbal symbols are meaningful only to people who have learned to associate them with what they represent. People can allow just about any symbols they want to represent just about anything they want. For example, you and your friends probably communicate with one another using private symbols that no one else understands. You have your own secret code. You have words, phrases, gestures, and handshakes that only you and your friends know, understand, and use. This allows you to communicate with one another in your own "foreign" language. Drug dealers and users, for example, have an elaborate and highly rule-governed language that allows them to communicate about their illegal activities. In drug language, the phrase "blow a spliff" is symbolic code for "smoke a marijuana cigarette." Any verbal language (e.g., English, Chinese, Russian) is a code made up of symbols. The letters of the English alphabet (e.g., *A, B, C, . . .*) are a set of symbols that represent sounds. When we combine the individual symbols (e.g., *C + A + T*), they become meaningful. By using symbols, people can represent their thoughts and ideas through writing or speaking. Once an idea has been encoded with symbols, it becomes a message. During communication, people encode their thoughts and send them to someone else. The other person listens to the message and translates or decodes it. When José saw Juan, he encoded a greeting. Juan decoded (i.e., translated) the message and encoded a response. Interaction, then, is the process of encoding and decoding messages. People who speak different languages are simply using different codes.

Dimension 5: Intentional

Perhaps one of the most debated issues regarding the communication process centers on intentionality. On one side of the debate are those who argue that communication is intentional. On the other side are those who insist that communication can occur unintentionally. Intentional communication exists whenever two or more people consciously engage in interaction with some purpose.[27] For example, if Kyoko says to Akira, "Hey, you wanna go out to eat tonight?" and Akira responds by saying, "Yeah, that sounds like a good idea!" intentional communication surely has taken place. Unintentional communication may exist, however. For example, at a party, Kyoko thinks that Akira is consciously ignoring her because he interacts with several other people. Kyoko senses that Akira is consciously sending her a message when, in fact, Akira's intention is simply to talk with new friends. Akira is not intentionally ignoring Kyoko, but she thinks that he is sending her a message (i.e., a nonverbal message). Since a response has been elicited in Kyoko, some communication scholars argue that communication has occurred. Three interpretations can be drawn from the above discussion. To many communication scholars, intentionality is a central property of the communication process. Others insist that any message interpreted by a person qualifies as communication, whether or not the message was intentionally sent. Still others insist that all behavior, intentional or not, is informative and meaningful and, thus, is communicative. So whenever a person (e.g., Kyoko in the above example) responds to some stimulus (e.g., Akira talking with other people), communication has occurred. In this book, the type of communication that will be discussed is intentional communication. This book takes the position that intentional communication, either verbal or nonverbal, is more informative than unintentional communication.

Dimension 6: Contextual

Communication is dependent on the context in which it occurs. The effects and outcomes, styles and fashions, and the resulting meaning are all dependent on the context. In this book, context is the cultural, physical, relational, and perceptual environment in which communication occurs. In many ways, the context defines the meaning of any message. For example, the context of the classroom defines the kind of communication that will occur. Most students sit quietly while the professor psychologically stimulates them with a brilliant lecture. Essentially, four different kinds of context influence the process of communication: (a) the cultural and microcultural context, (b) the physical context, (c) the sociorelational context, and (d) the perceptual context. The cultural context includes all the factors and influences that make up one's culture. This context will be discussed in detail in the next section of this chapter. The physical context is the actual geographical space or territory in which the communication takes place. For example, communication between Juan and José will be different when they are interacting on a busy street in a big city compared with when they are in their university library. The sociorelational context refers to social roles and group memberships (e.g., demographics). Sex, age, religious affiliation, education level, and economic status affect how one communicates and relates with others. Finally, the perceptual context includes all the motivations, intentions, and personality traits people bring to the communication event. When you are interacting with your professor about an examination you just failed, you have a very different set of motivations and intentions than when you are asking someone out on a date.

Dimension 7: Ubiquitous

That communication is ubiquitous simply means it is everywhere, done by everyone, all the time. Humans are constantly bombarded with verbal and nonverbal messages. Wherever one goes, some communication is happening. In fact, some scholars in the field of communication argue that it is impossible *not* to communicate. In their classic writings, Paul Watzlawick, Janet Beavin, and Don Jackson have argued that *one cannot not communicate.* The logic of their argument is that (a) behavior has no opposite—one cannot not behave; (b) in an interactional setting, all behavior has informational value or message value; (c) behavior is informative, and since it is informative, it is communicative; and (d) if behavior is communicative and one cannot not behave, then one cannot not communicate.[28]

Dimension 8: Cultural

Culture shapes communication, and communication is culture bound. People from different cultures communicate differently. The verbal and nonverbal symbols we use to communicate with our friends and families are strongly influenced by our culture. Perhaps the most obvious verbal communication difference between two cultures is language. Even cultures speaking the same language, however, have different meanings for different symbols. For example, although English is the dominant language spoken in the United States and England, many words and phrases have different meanings between these two cultures. In England, to "bomb" an examination is to have performed very well. When in London, do not bother to ask for directions to the nearest bathroom or restroom; in England, it is called the "water closet" or "WC." Australians also speak English but use a variety of colloquialisms not well understood by persons from the United States (see Table 1.4).

Table 1.4   Australian Colloquialisms

Amber fluid = beer

Bag of fruit = slang for men's clothing

Barbie = barbeque

Bickie = cookie

Bottler = expression for a person who performs well

Off = to describe rotten food

Tucker = food

Culture also has a dramatic effect on nonverbal communication. Nonverbal symbols, gestures, and perceptions of personal space and time vary significantly from culture to culture. In the United States, for example, people generally stand about 2 1/2 feet, or an arm's length, away from others when communicating. In many Middle Eastern cultures, people stand very close to each other when interacting, especially men (see Figure 1.2).

Figure 1.2   In many Middle Eastern cultures, men typically stand very close to one another when interacting.

Communication, then, is the dynamic process of encoding and decoding verbal and non-verbal messages within a defined cultural, physiological, sociorelational, and perceptual context. Although many of our messages are sent intentionally, many others—perhaps our nonverbal messages—can unintentionally influence other people.

Human Communication Apprehension

Although communication is difficult to define, we know that people begin to communicate at birth and continue communicating throughout their lives. We also know that many people experience fear and anxiety when communicating with others, particularly in situations such as public speaking, class presentations, a first date, or during a job interview. The fear or anxiety people experience when communicating with others is called communication apprehension. In the past 40 years, a substantial body of research has accumulated regarding the nature and prevalence of communication apprehension. The late Jim McCroskey, considered the father of this concept, believed that nearly everyone experiences some kind of communication apprehension sometimes, but roughly one in five adults in the United States suffer from communication apprehension every time they communicate with others. McCroskey said that experiencing communication apprehension is normal; that is, all of us experience it occasionally. McCroskey argued that there are four types of communication apprehension: traitlike, context based, audience based, and situational. Traitlike communication apprehension is an enduring general personality predisposition where an individual experiences communication apprehension most of the time across most communication situations. Of all adults in the United States, 20% experience traitlike communication apprehension.

Context-based communication apprehension is restricted to a certain generalized context, such as public speaking, group meetings, or job interviews. Persons with context-based communication apprehension experience anxiety only in certain contexts. Audience-based communication apprehension is triggered not by the specific context but by the particular person or audience with whom one is communicating. Hence, persons with audience-based communication apprehension may experience anxiety when communicating with strangers or their superiors, for example. College students with audience-based communication apprehension may experience anxiety when communicating with professors but not when communicating with other students. Finally, situational-based communication apprehension, experienced by virtually everyone, occurs with the combination of a specific context and a specific audience. For example, students may feel anxious interacting with professors only when they are alone with the professor in the professor's office. At other times, perhaps in the hallways or in the classroom, interacting with the professor may not be a problem.[29] To repeat, virtually everyone experiences communication apprehension at some time; if you experience such anxiety, it does not mean you are abnormal or sick. What follows is the Personal Report of Communication Apprehension (PRCA-24), a scale designed to measure your degree of communication apprehension. Take a few moments and complete the scale in Self-Assessment 1.1.

The Nature of Culture

Like communication, culture is ubiquitous and has a profound effect on humans. Culture is simultaneously invisible yet pervasive. As we go about our daily lives, we are not overtly conscious of our culture's influence on us. How often have you sat in your dorm room or classroom, for example, and consciously thought about what it means to be an American? As

Self-Assessment 1.1

Personal Report of Communication Apprehension

Directions: This instrument is composed of 24 statements concerning your feelings about communicating with other people. Please indicate in the space provided the degree to which each statement applies to you by marking whether you (1) strongly agree, (2) agree, (3) are undecided, (4) disagree, or (5) strongly disagree with each statement. There are no right or wrong answers. Many of the statements are similar to other statements. Do not be concerned about this. Work quickly; just record your first impressions.

_____ 1. I dislike participating in group discussions.

_____ 2. Generally, I am comfortable while participating in group discussions.

_____ 3. I am tense and nervous while participating in group discussions.

_____ 4. I like to get involved in group discussions.

_____ 5. Engaging in group discussion with new people makes me tense and nervous.

_____ 6. I am calm and relaxed while participating in group discussions.

_____ 7. Generally, I am nervous when I have to participate in group discussions.

_____ 8. Usually, I am calm and relaxed while participating in meetings.

_____ 9. I am very calm and relaxed when I am called upon to express an opinion at a meeting.

_____ 10. I am afraid to express myself at meetings.

_____ 11. Communicating at meetings usually makes me uncomfortable.

_____ 12. I am very relaxed when answering questions at a meeting.

_____ 13. While participating in a conversation with a new acquaintance, I feel very nervous.

_____ 14. I have no fear of speaking up in conversations.

_____ 15. Ordinarily, I am very tense and nervous in conversations.

_____ 16. Ordinarily, I am very calm and relaxed in conversations.

_____ 17. When conversing with a new acquaintance, I feel very relaxed.

_____ 18. I am afraid to speak up in conversations.

_____ 19. I have no fear of giving a speech.

_____ 20. Certain parts of my body feel very tense and rigid while giving a speech.

_____ 21. I feel relaxed while giving a speech.

_____ 22. My thoughts become confused and jumbled when I am giving a speech.

_____ 23. I face the prospect of giving a speech with confidence.

_____ 24. While giving a speech, I get so nervous I forget facts I really know.

Scoring: The PRCA-24 allows you to compute a total score and four subscores. The total score represents your degree of traitlike communication apprehension. Total scores may range from 24 to 120. McCroskey argued that any score above 72 indicates general communication apprehension. Scores above 80 indicate a very high level of communication apprehension. Scores below 59 indicate a very low level of communication apprehension.

Total PRCA Score:

Step 1. Add what you marked for Items 1, 3, 5, 7, 10, 11, 13, 15, 18, 20, 22, and 24.

Step 2. Add what you marked for Items 2, 4, 6, 8, 9, 12, 14, 16, 17, 19, 21, and 23.

Step 3. Subtract the score from Step 1 from 84 (i.e., 84 minus the score of Step 1). Then add the score of Step 2 to that total. The sum is your PRCA score.

The subscores indicate your degree of communication apprehension across four common contexts: group discussions, meetings, interpersonal conversations, and public speaking. For these scales, a score above 18 is high and a score above 23 is very high.

Subscores for Contexts:

Group Subscore: 18 + scores for Items 2, 4, and 6, minus scores for Items 1, 3, and 5.

Meeting Subscore: 18 + scores for Items 8, 9, and 10, minus scores for Items 7, 10, and 11.

Interpersonal Subscore: 18 + scores for Items 14, 16, and 17, minus scores for Items 13, 15, and 18.

Public Speaking Subscore: 18 + scores for Items 19, 21, and 23, minus scores for Items 20, 22, and 24.

SOURCE: McCroskey, James, *Introduction to Rhetorical Communication* (4th ed), © 1982. Printed and electronically reproduced by permission of Pearson Education, Inc., Upper Saddle River, New Jersey.

you stand in the lunch line, do you say to yourself, "I am acting like an American"? As you sit in your classroom, do you say to yourself, "The professor is really acting like an American"? Yet most of your thoughts, emotions, and behaviors are culturally driven. One need only step into a culture different from one's own to feel the immense impact of culture.

Culture has a direct influence on the physical, relational, and perceptual contexts. For example, the next time you enter your communication classroom, consider how the room is arranged *physically,* including where you sit and where the professor teaches, the location of the chalkboard, windows, and so on. Does the professor lecture from behind a lectern? Do the students sit facing the professor? Is the chalkboard used? Next, think about your *relationship* with the professor and the other students in your class. Is the relationship formal or informal? Do you interact with the professor and students about topics other than class material? Would you consider the relationship personal or impersonal? Finally, think about your *perceptual disposition*—that is, your attitudes, motivations, and emotions about the class. Are you happy to be in the class? Do you enjoy attending? Are you nervous when the instructor asks you a question? To a great extent, the answers to these questions are contingent on your culture. The physical arrangement of classrooms, the social relationship between students and teachers, and the perceptual profiles of the students and teachers vary significantly from culture to culture.

Like communication, culture is difficult to define. To be sure, more than 50 years ago, two well-known anthropologists, Alfred Kroeber and Clyde Kluckhohn, found and examined 300 definitions of culture, no two of which were the same.[30] Perhaps too often, people think of culture only in terms of the fine arts, geography, or history. Small towns or rural communities are often accused of having no culture. Yet culture exists everywhere. There is as much culture in Willard, New Mexico (population 240), as there is in New York City, New York (population 8,400,197). The two cultures are just different. Simply put, culture is people.

Although there may not be a universally accepted definition of culture, there are a number of properties of culture that most people would agree describe its essence. In this book, culture is defined as *an accumulated pattern of values, beliefs, and behaviors shared by an identifiable group of people with a common history and verbal and nonverbal symbol systems.*

Accumulated Pattern of Values, Beliefs, and Behaviors

Cultures can be defined by their value and belief systems and by the actions of their members. People who exist in the same culture generally share similar values and beliefs (see Table 1.5). In the United States, for example, individuality is highly valued. An individual's self-interest takes precedence over group interests. Americans believe that people are unique. Moreover, Americans value personal independence. Conversely, in Japan, a collectivistic and homogeneous culture, a sense of groupness and group harmony, is valued. Most Japanese see themselves as members of a group first and as individuals second. Where Americans value independence, Japanese value interdependence. The values of a particular culture lead to a set of expectations and rules prescribing how people should behave in that culture. Although many Americans prefer to think of themselves as unique individuals, most Americans behave in similar ways. Observe the students around you in your classes. Although you may prefer to think that you are very different from your peers, you are really quite similar to them. Most of your peers follow a similar behavioral pattern to your own. For example, on a day-to-day basis, most of your peers attend classes, take examinations, go to lunch, study, party, and write papers.

Table 1.5 Values Across Cultures

Saudi Arabia	Maori (New Zealand)
Islam	Land
Hospitality	Kinship
Cleanliness	Education
India	Yemen
Family lineage	Islam
Supernatural guidance	Self-respect and honor
Sexual inequality	Family

Americans share a similar behavioral profile. Most Americans work an average of 40 hours a week, receive some form of payment for their work, and pay some of their earnings in taxes. Most Americans spend their money on homes and cars. Almost every home in the United States has a television. Although Americans view themselves as unique individuals, most of them have similar behavioral patterns.

An Identifiable Group of People With a Common History

Because the members of a particular culture share similar values, beliefs, and behaviors, they are identifiable as a distinct group. In addition to their shared values, beliefs, and behaviors, the members of a particular culture share a common history. Any culture's past inextricably binds it to the present and guides its future. At the core of any culture are traditions passed on to future generations (see Figure 1.3). In many cultures, history is a major component of the formal and informal education systems. To learn a culture's history is to learn that culture's values. One way children in the United States develop their sense of independence, for example, is by learning about the Declaration of Independence, one of this country's most sacred documents. Elementary school children in Iran learn about the historical significance of the political and religious revolution that took place in their culture in the 1970s and 1980s. Russian children learn about the arts in Russian history—for example, famous Russian composers, including Tchaikovsky, Rachmaninoff, and Stravinsky. The art of the past helps Russians remember their culture and history as they face disruptive social and political crises. Such historical lessons are the glue that binds people together.

Figure 1.3	Children learn the values, norms, and behaviors of their culture at an early age.

Verbal and Nonverbal Symbol Systems

One of the most important elements of any culture is its communication system. The verbal and nonverbal symbols with which the members of a culture communicate are culture bound. Seeing the difference between the verbal codes of any two cultures is easy. For instance, the dominant verbal code in the United States is English, whereas the dominant verbal code in Mexico is Spanish. But although two cultures may share the same verbal code, they may have dramatically different verbal styles. Most White Americans, for example, use a direct, instrumental, personal style when speaking English. Many Native Americans who also speak English use an indirect, impersonal style and may prefer the use of silence over words.[31]

Nonverbal code systems vary significantly across cultures as well. Nonverbal communication includes the use of body language, gestures, facial expressions, voice, smell, personal and geographical space, time, and artifacts (see Figure 1.4). Body language can communicate a great deal about one's culture. When an adult interacts with a young child in the United States, for example, it is not uncommon for the adult to pat the child's head. This nonverbal gesture is often seen as a form of endearment and is culturally acceptable. In Thailand, however, where the head is considered the seat of the soul, such a gesture is unacceptable. Belching during or after a meal is viewed by most Americans as rude and impolite, perhaps even disgusting. But in China, slurping and making belching noises during a meal simply means one is enjoying the food.[32]

Figure 1.4   Nonverbal communication, including body language, can communicate a great deal about one's culture.

People communicate nonverbally through smell also. Americans, in particular, seem obsessed with the smell of the human body and home environment. Think of all the products you used this morning before you left for class that were designed to mask the natural scent of your body, including soap, toothpaste, mouthwash, deodorant, and cologne and/or perfume. Persons from other cultures often complain that Americans tend to smell antiseptic.

Microcultural Groups

Within most cultures, groups of people—or microcultures—coexist within the mainstream society. Microcultures exist within the broader rules and guidelines of the dominant cultural milieu but are distinct in some way, perhaps racially or linguistically, or via their sexual orientation, age, or even occupation. In some ways, everyone is a member of some microcultural group. Microcultures often have histories that differ from the dominant cultural group. In many cases, microcultural groups are subordinate in some way, perhaps politically or economically.

In the United States, Native American tribes might be considered microcultures. The Amish of Lancaster County, Pennsylvania, also can be considered a microcultural group. Although the Amish are subject to most of the same laws as any other group of citizens, they have unique values and communication systems that differentiate them from mainstream American life. For example, Amish children are exempt from compulsory attendance in public schools after eighth grade. Although almost all Amish speak English, when they interact among themselves, they speak German. During church services, a form of High German is used. Hence, most Amish of Lancaster County speak three languages.

The Study of Intercultural Communication

Ideally, we now have an understanding of the word *communication* and the idea of culture.[33] So what happens when people from different cultures come together and communicate with one another? We call that process "intercultural communication." Compared with many other academic disciplines, the study of intercultural communication is young. The histories of other academic fields such as math, biology, philosophy, and psychology date back hundreds and, in some cases, thousands of years. But the academic discipline of intercultural communication can be traced back only a few decades—specifically, to the year 1959 and the publication of Edward T. Hall's book *The Silent Language*. Hall is generally recognized as the founder of the academic discipline we call intercultural communication. Although the term *intercultural* had been used prior to Hall's work, it is thought that Hall was the first to use the term *intercultural communication*.

Hall held three university degrees (i.e., BA, MA, and PhD) in anthropology. Anthropology is the study of the origin; behavior; and physical, social, and cultural development of humans. Hall earned his doctorate in anthropology in 1942 when the United States was involved in the Second World War. During this period, traditional approaches in anthropology focused on studying a single culture at a time. So a particular anthropologist might focus his or her studies on, say, the Navajo or Hopi Indians of the American Southwest, as did Hall. Hall often referred to this as a macrolevel approach to culture. Among the many significant influences on Hall's approach to his studies was anthropologist Franz Boas. The term *cultural relativism* is often attributed to him.

Boas believed, as did Hall, that humans are inherently ethnocentric (i.e., believing that one's native culture is the standard by which other cultures are observed and judged) and that our observations of other cultures are necessarily biased in favor of our native cultural background. For example, a child raised in Germany, Iran, or China is taught that his or her cultural traditions, values, and customs are the preferred and accepted standards by which one should conduct one's life. Consequently, an individual from a particular culture cannot draw conclusions about some other culture's traditions, values, and customs without some inherent bias. Moreover, Boas believed that any particular culture is an adaptation to and a distinctive product of a unique set of historical, social, and environmental conditions. As these conditions vary, cultures vary accordingly—and in this sense, there is no correct culture.

Following World War II, the U.S. Congress established the Foreign Service Institute (FSI). FSI is the federal government's primary training institution for officers and support personnel of the U.S. foreign affairs community, preparing American diplomats and other professionals to advance U.S. foreign affairs interests overseas and in Washington. In the early 1950s, Hall taught at FSI and soon discovered that the traditional ways of teaching about macrolevel culture, from an anthropological perspective, were not effective in training FSI personnel how to interact with persons from different cultures. So Hall and others began to rethink how to teach about culture and soon developed a new curriculum that eventually became known as intercultural communication.

In this new curriculum, scholars focused on intercultural communication—that is, how people from different cultures interact *with one another*—rather than on how members of a particular culture interact within their culture. This new curriculum also emphasized the nonverbal elements of intercultural communication. Hall was especially interested in the study of how cultures manage the nonverbal channels of time (chronemics), space (proxemics), and body language (kinesics). One of Hall's most fascinating insights was how *invisible* culture is to its own members—that is, how most people are so unaware of their own cultural ways of living. This new approach also embraced Boas's idea of cultural relativism, in that cultures should be judged only from within their specific cultural context, and cultural traditions, beliefs, and behaviors are to be evaluated on that culture's unique set of historical, social, and environmental conditions.

In 1959, Hall published *The Silent Language,* which sold more than 500,000 copies in its first 10 years and is considered the seminal work in the field. In the book, Hall asserted that *culture is communication.* By the late 1960s, we saw the first intercultural communication courses being offered at universities. In 1970, the International Communication Association established a Division of Intercultural Communication. L. S. Harms's 1970 book, *Intercultural Communication,* is thought to be the first textbook on the subject. By 1975, the Speech Communication Association established the Division of Intercultural Communication, and in 1977, the *International Journal of Intercultural Relations* began publication.

A Contextual Model of Intercultural Communication

Intercultural communication occurs whenever a minimum of two persons from different cultures or microcultures come together and exchange verbal and nonverbal symbols. A central theme throughout this book is that intercultural communication is contextual. A contextual model of intercultural communication is presented in Figure 1.5. According to the model, intercultural communication occurs within and between a variety of interconnected contexts, including cultural, microcultural, environmental, perceptual, and sociorelational contexts.

Figure 1.5 A contextual model of intercultural communication.

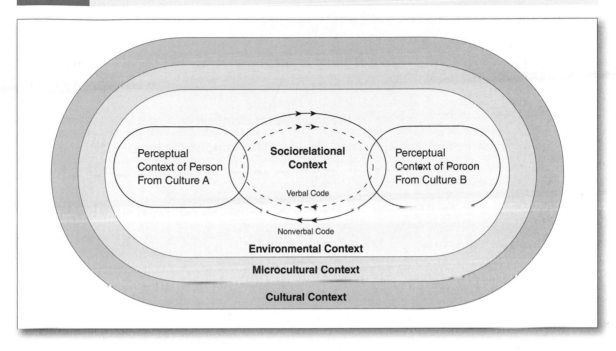

The term *context* refers to the setting, situation, circumstances, background, and overall framework within which communication occurs. For example, when you interact with your friends, you interact in some *physical context,* such as your dorm room. You also interact within a *social context*—that is, friend to friend. You also interact within a *psychological context*—your thoughts and emotions about your friend. The contextual model of intercultural communication attempts to identify the various contexts that define what happens when a person from Culture A communicates with a person from Culture B. As we walk through the contextual model of intercultural communication, please note that the model is both conceptually and graphically consistent.

The largest, outer circle of the model represents the cultural context. All communicative exchanges between persons occur within some culture. The cultural context represents *an accumulated pattern of values, beliefs, and behaviors shared by an identifiable group of people with a common history and verbal and nonverbal symbol systems.* So whenever you and someone from a different culture come together and interact, you are within a cultural context. In this textbook, the cultural context is the focus of Chapter 2.

The next largest circle in the model is the microcultural context (Figure 1.6). As mentioned earlier, within most cultures, separate groups of people coexist. These groups, called microcultures, are in some way different from the larger cultural milieu. Sometimes the difference is via ethnicity, race, or language. Conceptually, microcultures exist within a larger culture; notice that in the model, the microculture is within the cultural context. Often, microcultures are treated differently by the members of the larger culture. Some people refer to microcultural groups as *minority groups* or *subcultures,* but those terms will not be used here. Microcultures are the focus of Chapter 3.

Figure 1.6 The cultural and microcultural contexts.

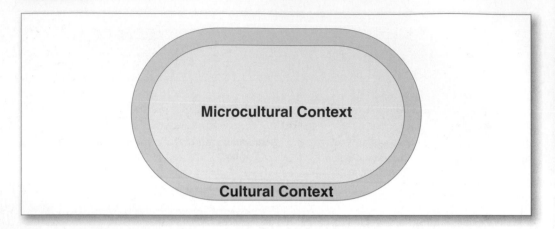

The next largest circle in the model is the environmental context (Figure 1.7). This circle represents the physical, geographical location of the interaction. While culture prescribes the overall rules for communication, the physical location indicates when and where the specific rules apply. For example, in the United States, there are rules about yelling. Depending on the physical location, yelling can be prohibited or encouraged. In a church, yelling is generally prohibited, whereas at a football game, yelling is the preferred method of communicating. The environmental context includes the physical geography, architecture, landscape design, and even climate of a particular culture. All these environmental factors play a key role in how people communicate. In the model, the environmental context is within the microcultural and cultural contexts. Conceptually, this is because one's culture and membership in microcultural groups significantly influence how one perceives the environment. For example, temperatures below 32 degrees (i.e., freezing) are not thought of as extreme to a person raised in International Falls, Minnesota. But to a person raised in Tucson, Arizona, such temperatures may seem unbearable. In this book, the environmental context is discussed in Chapter 4.

Figure 1.7 The cultural, microcultural, and environmental contexts.

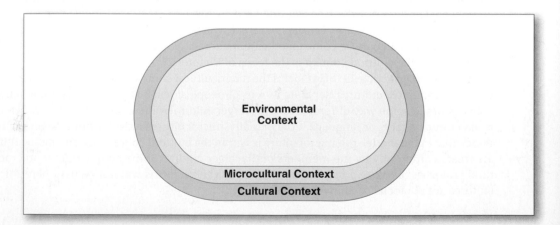

The two circles within the environmental context represent the perceptual context(s) (Figure 1.8). The perceptual context refers to the individual characteristics of each interactant, including cognitions, attitudes, dispositions, and motivations. Specifically, the perceptual context refers to how an individual gathers, stores, and retrieves information. Humans gather information via their senses—that is, through sight, sound, taste, touch, and smell. We then store the information in our memories and retrieve it for later use. Although the ability to gather, store, and retrieve information is fundamentally human, it is also affected by culture. Many of the attitudes, beliefs, and values you hold were taught to you by your culture. For example, what smells good to you is cultural. The music you listen to is also largely a cultural by-product. Moreover, how an individual develops attitudes about others, including stereotypes, varies from culture to culture. The perceptual context is the emphasis of Chapter 5.

 Figure 1.8   The environmental and perceptual contexts.

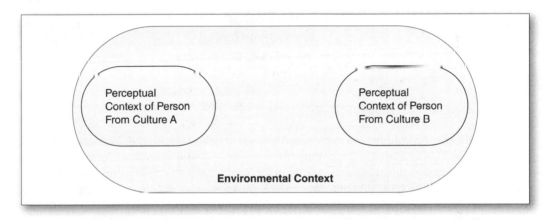

The circles connecting the perceptual contexts in the model form the sociorelational context (Figure 1.9). This refers to the relationship between the interactants. Whenever two people come together and interact, they establish a relationship. Within this relationship, each person assumes a role. Right now, you are assuming the role of student; the person teaching your communication class is assuming the role of teacher. So, in a very real sense, you are having a relationship with your teacher—that is, a student–teacher relationship. Roles prescribe how people should behave. Most of the people with whom you interact are related to you via your role as student. The reason you interact with so many professors is because you are a student. What you interact about—that is, the topic of your interaction—is also defined by your role as student; you and your professors interact about courses. How you interact with your professor—that is, the style of talk (e.g., polite language)—is also prescribed by your role as student. The language and style of your talk with your professor is probably very different from the language and style of talk you use when you go back to your dorm room and interact with your friends. Probably the 10 people with whom you most recently interacted were directly related to you via your role as student. When you go back to your hometown during semester break and step into the role of son/daughter or brother/sister, you are assuming a different role, and your interaction changes accordingly. Your interaction varies as a function of what role you are assuming.

Figure 1.9   A contextual model of intercultural communication.

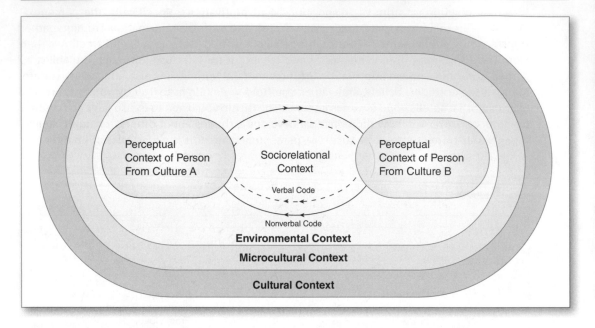

Roles vary from culture to culture. Although in just about every culture there are student and teacher role relationships, how those roles are defined varies significantly. What it means to be a student in the United States is very different from what it means in Japan. In Japan, for example, many students go to school 6 days a week. Japanese teachers are highly respected and play an influential role in the Japanese student's life. What it means to be a mother or father also varies considerably from one culture to another. In the Masai culture of Kenya, a woman is defined by her fertility. To be defined as a mother in Masai culture, a woman must endure circumcision (i.e., clitoridectomy), an arranged marriage, and wife beating.[34] Conceptually, people (i.e., perceptual contexts) are connected to one another via their relationships. The model shows this connection via the sociorelational context (see Figure 1.9). The sociorelational context links the two perceptual contexts. One's roles prescribe the types of verbal and nonverbal symbols that are exchanged. In this book, the sociorelational context and role relationships are the focus of Chapter 6.

All our relationships are defined by the verbal and nonverbal messages we send to our relational partners. What differentiates one relationship from another is the verbal and nonverbal things we do with each other. For example, what differentiates your relationship with your teacher from your relationship with your best friend is the verbal and nonverbal things you do with each other. Notice that in the contextual model, the sociorelational context is graphically represented by two circles labeled nonverbal and verbal code (see Figure 1.9). Again, the verbal and nonverbal messages define the relationship, and the relationship connects the perceptual contexts.

The nonverbal circle is the larger of the two and is represented by a continuous line. The verbal circle is smaller and is represented as a series of dashes in the shape of a circle. The nonverbal message circle is larger than the verbal message circle because the majority of our communicative behavior is nonverbal. Whether we are using words or not, we are communicating nonverbally through eye contact, body stance, and space. In addition, our nonverbal behavior is ongoing; we cannot *not* behave. The verbal message circle is formed by a series of dashes to represent the *digital* quality of verbal communication.[35] By digital, we mean that, unlike our nonverbal communication, our verbal communication is made up of words that have recognizable and discrete beginning and ending points. A word is like a digit. We can start and stop talking with words. However, our nonverbal behavior goes on continuously. Chapter 7 concentrates on verbal communication codes, and Chapter 8 addresses nonverbal codes.

The general theme of this book, as represented in the model, is that intercultural communication is defined by the interdependence of these various contexts. The perceptual contexts combine to create the sociorelational context, which is defined by the verbal and nonverbal messages sent. The sociorelational context is influenced by the environmental context and defined by the microcultural and cultural contexts. These contexts combine in a complex formula to create the phenomenon of intercultural communication.

Intercultural Communication and Uncertainty

When we interact with someone from a different culture, we are faced with a lot of uncertainty. We may not know anything about the person's culture, values, habits, behavior, dress, and so on. We may not know what to say or do in such circumstances. This uncertainty about the other person may make us feel nervous and anxious. Communication theorist Charles Berger contends that the task of interacting with someone from a different culture who may look, act, and communicate differently presents the intercultural communicator with some complex predictive and explanatory problems. To some extent, to effectively interact with someone from a different culture, we must be able to predict how our interaction partner is likely to behave and, based on those predictions, select our appropriate verbal and nonverbal messages.[36]

Berger theorizes that whenever we come together and interact with a stranger, our primary concern is to reduce uncertainty, especially when the other person is someone with whom we will interact again. Often, when we are faced with high levels of uncertainty, we experience anxiety. In high-uncertainty situations, our primary goal is to reduce uncertainty and increase the predictability of the other. This can be accomplished via specific verbal and nonverbal communication strategies such as question asking and appropriate nonverbal expressiveness.[37]

Some types of communication situations may be more anxiety producing than others. For example, Arnold H. Buss argues that novel, unfamiliar, or dissimilar situations lead to increased anxiety. Those situations containing new, atypical, or conspicuously different stimuli are likely to increase our sense of anxiety. Based on these criteria, initial interaction with someone, or interacting with someone from a different culture, may produce heightened anxiety.[38]

Intercultural communication experts William Gudykunst and Young Kim have argued that when we interact with people from different cultures, we tend to view them as strangers. Strangers are unknown people who are members of different groups. Anyone entering a relatively unknown or unfamiliar environment falls under the rubric of "stranger." Interaction with people from different cultures tends to involve the highest degree of "strangerness" and the lowest degree of familiarity. Thus, there is greater uncertainty in initial interaction with strangers than with people with whom we are familiar. According to Gudykunst and Kim, actual or anticipated interaction with members of different groups (e.g., cultures or ethnic groups different from our own) leads to anxiety.[39] If we are too anxious about interacting with strangers, we tend to avoid them. Communication researchers Jim Neuliep and Jim McCroskey state that this type of communication anxiety can be labeled intercultural communication apprehension—that is, the fear or anxiety associated with either real or anticipated interaction with people from different groups, especially different cultural or ethnic groups.[40]

Intercultural Communication Apprehension

Successfully interacting with someone from a different culture requires a degree of communication competence. According to Brian Spitzberg, most models of communication competence include cognitive, affective, and behavioral components. The cognitive component refers to how much one knows about communication. The affective component includes one's motivation to approach or avoid communication. The behavioral component refers to the skills one has to interact competently. An interculturally competent communicator is *motivated* to communicate, *knowledgeable* about how to communicate, and *skilled* in communicating. In addition, an interculturally competent communicator is *sensitive* to the expectations of the context in which communication occurs. Competent communicators interact effectively by adapting messages appropriately to the context. Competent communicators understand the rules, norms, and expectations of the relationship and do not significantly violate them. Communicators are effective to the degree that their goals are accomplished successfully.[41]

STUDENT VOICES ACROSS CULTURES

Jennifer Seidemann

St. Norbert College, 2010

Elementary Education and Spanish

Studied Abroad in Toledo, Spain, Fall 2008

During my experience in Spain, I learned a lot about the Spanish culture and how it compares and contrasts with my own culture in the United States. I found that Spanish natives tend to avoid eye contact and relations with people they do not know. Back at home, I was used to being able to walk down the street and smile or say hello to anybody who walked by, regardless of whether or not I knew them personally. In Spain, this was not the common custom. Eye contact was diverted from the unknown. I found that if I did smile or say hello to people I did not know, the response from them was somewhat cold and confused. The only time eye contact was acceptable was if the person was familiar or if the eye contact was made with a sexual intention. It was not that the people were unfriendly, because if I asked a question about locations or directions, they always seemed helpful. But my initial attempts at interaction through eye contact and greetings were met with skepticism and insecurity.

After studying abroad and taking the course about intercultural communication, I learned that the differences in willingness to make eye contact and communicate with the unknown are based on the given culture's level of uncertainty avoidance. Here in the United States, we have a much weaker uncertainty avoidance than they do in Spain. We better tolerate the unknown or uncertain aspects of our lives compared with those in cultures with a strong uncertainty avoidance. The experience both in Spain and in the course taught me how to embrace and understand the differences between cultures in our world, and I feel much more comfortable in my relationships with people from abroad as a result.

According to Neuliep and McCroskey, a person's affective orientation toward intercultural communication involves the individual's degree of motivation to approach or avoid a given intercultural context or person. Communication studies indicate that at least 20% of the U.S. adult population experience high levels of fear or anxiety even when communicating with members of their own culture. Other studies indicate that 99% of Americans experience communication apprehension at some time in their lives, perhaps during a job interview, a first date, and so on. One outcome of communication apprehension is to avoid communication. When people feel anxious about communicating with others, they tend to avoid such situations.

Given that intercultural communication may be more anxiety producing than other forms of communication, the number of people suffering from intercultural communication apprehension is likely considerable. Identifying such individuals may be the first step toward more effective and successful intercultural communication. Self-Assessment 1.2 is an instrument called the Personal Report of Intercultural Communication Apprehension (PRICA). This scale was developed by communication researchers Neuliep and McCroskey. PRICA is similar to the Personal Report of Communication Apprehension (PRCA-24) you completed earlier in this chapter. The difference between these two scales is that PRICA assesses your degree of apprehension about communicating with someone from a culture different from yours. After completing each scale, you can compare your scores from both instruments.

The PRICA instrument is composed of 14 statements concerning your feelings about communication with people from other cultures. Please indicate in the space provided the degree to which each statement applies to you by marking whether you (1) strongly agree, (2) agree, (3) are undecided, (4) disagree, or (5) strongly disagree with each statement. There are no right or wrong answers, and many of the statements are designed to be similar to other statements. Do not be concerned about this. Work quickly and record your first impressions. Responding to these statements as honestly as possible is very important; otherwise, your score will not be valid.

To the degree that you answered the items honestly, your score is a fairly reliable and valid assessment of your motivation to approach or avoid intercultural communication. Spitzberg argues that as your motivation increases, so does your confidence. As confidence increases, intercultural communication competence also is likely to increase. People who are nervous and tense about interacting with people from different cultures are less likely to approach intercultural communication situations and probably are not confident about encountering new people from different cultures.[42]

FUNDAMENTAL ASSUMPTIONS ABOUT INTERCULTURAL COMMUNICATION

A central premise of this book is that intercultural communication is a complex combination of the cultural, microcultural, environmental, perceptual, and sociorelational contexts between two people who are encoding and decoding verbal and nonverbal messages. Because of the complexity of this process, a fundamental assumption about intercultural communication is that, during intercultural communication, the message sent is usually not the message received.

Self-Assessment 1.2

Personal Report of Intercultural Communication Apprehension

(1) strongly agree, (2) agree, (3) undecided, (4) disagree, or (5) strongly disagree

_____ 1. Generally, I am comfortable interacting with a group of people from different cultures.

_____ 2. I am tense and nervous while interacting in group discussions with people from different cultures.

_____ 3. I like to get involved in group discussions with others who are from different cultures.

_____ 4. Engaging in a group discussion with people from different cultures makes me tense and nervous.

_____ 5. I am calm and relaxed when interacting with a group of people who are from different cultures.

_____ 6. While participating in a conversation with a person from a different culture I feel very nervous.

_____ 7. I have no fear of speaking up in a conversation with a person from a different culture.

_____ 8. Ordinarily, I am very tense and nervous in conversations with a person from a different culture.

_____ 9. Ordinarily, I am very calm and relaxed in conversations with a person from a different culture.

_____ 10. While conversing with a person from a different culture, I feel very relaxed.

_____ 11. I'm afraid to speak up in conversations with a person from a different culture.

_____ 12. I face the prospect of interacting with people from different cultures with confidence.

_____ 13. My thoughts become confused and jumbled when interacting with people from different cultures.

_____ 14. Communicating with people from different cultures makes me feel uncomfortable.

Scoring: To score the instrument, reverse your original response for Items 2, 4, 6, 8, 11, 13, and 14. For example, for each of these items 1 = 5, 2 = 4, 3 = 3, 4 = 2, and 5 = 1. If your original score for Item 2 was 1, change it to a 5. If your original score for Item 4 was a 2, change it to a 4, and so on. After reversing the score for these 7 items, sum all 14 items. Scores cannot be higher than 70 or lower than 14. Higher scores (e.g., 50–70) indicate high intercultural communication apprehension. Lower scores (e.g., 14–28) indicate low intercultural communication apprehension.

SOURCE: Neuliep, J. W., & McCroskey, J. C. (1997). The Development of Intercultural and Interethnic Communication Apprehension Scales. *Communication Research Reports, 14,* 145–156.

Assumption #1: During intercultural communication, the message sent is usually not the message received. Whenever people from different cultures come together and exchange messages, they bring with them a whole host of thoughts, values, emotions, and behaviors that were planted and cultivated by culture. As we have said, intercultural communication is a symbolic activity where the thoughts and ideas of one person are encoded into a verbal or nonverbal message format and then transmitted through some channel to another person who must decode it, interpret it, and respond to it. This process of encoding, decoding, and interpreting is filled with cultural noise. Noted intercultural communication scholar Gudykunst has asserted that, during intercultural communication, culture acts as a filter through which all messages, both verbal and nonverbal, must pass. To this extent, all intercultural exchanges are necessarily, to a greater or lesser extent, charged with ethnocentrism. Hence, during intercultural communication, the message sent is not the message received.[43]

Ethnocentrism refers to the idea that one's own culture is the center of everything and all other groups (or cultures) are scaled and rated with reference to it. Sociologist W. G. Sumner argued that ethnocentrism nourishes a group's pride and vanity while looking on outsiders, or out-groups, with contempt.[44] Although culture may mediate the extent to which we experience ethnocentrism, it is thought to be universal. One of the effects of ethnocentrism is that it clouds our perception of others. We have a tendency to judge others, and their communication, based on the standards set by our own culture. Neuliep and McCroskey have argued that the concept of ethnocentrism is essentially descriptive and not necessarily pejorative. Ethnocentrism may serve a valuable function when one's in-group is under attack or threatened. Moreover, ethnocentrism forms the basis for patriotism, group loyalty, and the willingness to sacrifice for one's own group. To be sure, however, ethnocentrism can be problematic. In not looking past their own culture, people see little importance in understanding other cultures. At high levels, ethnocentrism is an obstacle to effective intercultural communication.[45]

Neuliep and McCroskey have developed the GENE (Generalized Ethnocentrism) Scale, which is designed to measure ethnocentrism. This scale and the directions for completing it are presented in Self-Assessment 1.3.

Assumption #2: Intercultural communication is primarily a nonverbal act between people. Some foreign language teachers might have us believe that competency in a foreign language is tantamount to effective and successful intercultural communication in the culture that speaks that language. To be sure, proficiency in a foreign language expedites the intercultural communication experience, but intercultural communication is primarily and fundamentally a nonverbal process. The expression of intimacy, power, and status among communicators is typically accomplished nonverbally through paralinguistic cues, proxemics, haptics, oculesics, and olfactics. In Korea, for example, one's hierarchical position is displayed via vocal tone and pitch. When a subordinate is offered an important piece of paper, such as a graded exam from a respected professor, he or she grasps it with both hands (not just one) and accompanies this action with a slight nod of the head and indirect eye contact—all nonverbal signs of deference.

The well-known anthropologist Hall has argued that people from different cultures live in different sensory worlds. Hall claims that people from different cultures engage in a selective

Self-Assessment 1.3

GENE (Generalized Ethnocentrism) Scale

Directions: The GENE Scale is composed of 22 statements concerning your feelings about your culture and other cultures. In the space provided to the left of each item, indicate the degree to which the statement applies to you by marking whether you (5) strongly agree, (4) agree, (3) are neutral, (2) disagree, or (1) strongly disagree with the statement. There are no right or wrong answers. Some of the statements are similar. Remember, everyone experiences some degree of ethnocentrism. Fortunately, as we will see in Chapter 5, ethnocentrism can be managed and reduced. Be honest! Work quickly and record your first response.

_____ 1. Most other cultures are backward compared to my culture.

_____ 2. My culture should be the role model for other cultures.

_____ 3. People from other cultures act strange when they come into my culture.

_____ 4. Lifestyles in other cultures are just as valid as those in my culture.

_____ 5. Other cultures should try to be more like my culture.

_____ 6. I'm not interested in the values and customs of other cultures.

_____ 7. People in my culture could learn a lot from people of other cultures.

_____ 8. Most people from other cultures just don't know what's good for them.

_____ 9. I respect the values and customs of other cultures.

_____ 10. Other cultures are smart to look up to our culture.

_____ 11. Most people would be happier if they lived like people in my culture.

_____ 12. I have many friends from other cultures.

_____ 13. People in my culture have just about the best lifestyles of anywhere.

_____ 14. Lifestyles in other cultures are not as valid as those in my culture.

_____ 15. I'm very interested in the values and customs of other cultures.

_____ 16. I apply my values when judging people who are different.

_____ 17. I see people who are similar to me as virtuous.

_____ 18. I do not cooperate with people who are different.

_____ 19. Most people in my culture just don't know what is good for them.

_____ 20. I do not trust people who are different.

_____ 21. I dislike interacting with people from different cultures.

_____ 22. I have little respect for the values and customs of other cultures.

Scoring: To determine your ethnocentrism score, complete the following steps:

Step 1: Add your responses to Items 4, 7, and 9.

Step 2: Add your responses to Items 1, 2, 5, 8, 10, 11, 13, 14, 18, 20, 21, and 22.

Step 3: Subtract the sum from Step 1 from 18 (i.e., 18 minus Step 1 sum).

Step 4: Add the results of Step 2 and Step 3. This sum is your generalized ethnocentrism score (note that not all items are used in scoring). Higher scores indicate higher ethnocentrism. Scores above 55 are considered high ethnocentrism.

SOURCE: Originally called Ethnocentrism Scale, from Neuliep, J. W., & McCroskey, J. C. (1997). The Development of a U.S. and Generalized Ethnocentrism Scale. *Communication Research Reports, 14,* 385–398. Co-created by Neuliep and McCroskey. Permission granted by Neuliep and on McCroskey's website (http://www.jamescmccroskey.com/measures/).

screening of sensory information that ultimately leads to different perceptions of experience.[46] Regarding olfactics (smell), most cultures establish norms for acceptable and unacceptable scents associated with the human body. When people fail to fit into the realm of olfactic cultural acceptability, their odor alerts others that something is wrong with their physical, emotional, or mental health. In the United States, we are obsessed with masking certain smells, especially those of the human body. In Western and Westernized cultures, body odor is regarded as unpleasant and distasteful, and great effort is expended in its removal. As we will see in Chapter 8, our nonverbal messages complement, augment, accent, substitute for, and repeat our verbal messages.

Assumption #3: Intercultural communication necessarily involves a clash of communicator style. In the United States, talk is a highly valued commodity. People are routinely evaluated by their speech. Yet silence—that is, knowing when not to speak—is a fundamental prerequisite for linguistic and cultural competence.[47] The use and interpretation of silence varies dramatically across cultures. In many collectivistic cultures, such as Japan and Korea, silence can carry more meaning than words, especially in the maintenance of intimate relationships. In fact, the Japanese and some Native American tribes in the United States believe that the expression of relational intimacy is best accomplished nonverbally. They believe that having to put one's thoughts and emotions into words somehow cheapens and discounts them.

In the United States, we value, and employ, a direct and personal style of verbal communication. Personal pronouns are an essential ingredient in the composition of just about any utterance. Our mottos are "Get to the point," "Don't beat around the bush," "Tell it like it is," "Speak your mind." Many cultures, however, prefer an indirect and impersonal communication style. In these cultures, there is no need to articulate every message. True understanding is implicit, coming not from words but from actions in the environment, where speakers provide only hints or insinuations. The Chinese say, "One should use the eyes and ears, not the mouth," and "Disaster emanates from careless talk." The Chinese consider the wisest and most trustworthy person to be the one who listens, watches, and restricts his or her verbal communication.[48]

Assumption #4: Initial intercultural communication is a group phenomenon experienced by individuals. Whenever we interact with a person from a different culture, especially early in our relationship with him or her, we carry with us assumptions and impressions of that other person. The specific verbal and nonverbal messages we exchange are usually tailored for the person based on those assumptions and impressions. Often, these are based on characteristics of the other person by virtue of his or her membership in groups related to culture, race, sex, age, or occupation, for example. In other words, we have a tendency to see others not as individuals with unique thoughts, ideas, and goals but, rather, as "an Asian" or "a woman" or "an old person" or "a cab driver." In other words, we do not see the person—we see the groups to which the person belongs. The problem with this is that group data may not be a reliable source on which to construct our messages. Because someone belongs to a specific racial, ethnic, sex, or age group does not necessarily mean that he or she takes on the thoughts, behaviors, and attitudes associated with that group. Thus, the potential for miscommunication is great. So, during initial intercultural communication, we have to be mindful that, while the person with whom we are interacting is from a different cultural group, he or she is also an individual. Once we further develop a relationship with that person, we will start to see the relationship as interpersonal rather than intercultural. We will discuss this more in Chapter 9.[49]

Assumption #5: Intercultural communication is a cycle of stress and adaptation. As mentioned earlier in this chapter, when we come together with a person from a different culture, we may feel uncertain, apprehensive, and anxious. Such feelings are stressful. Hence, sometimes intercultural communication is stressful. The good news is that we can learn and adapt to such stress and eventually grow. During intercultural communication, we have to be mindful that the communication strategies we use with persons with whom we are familiar may not be effective with persons from other cultures. Thus, we have to learn to adapt and adjust our communication style. We have to recognize that we will make mistakes, learn from them, adapt, and move on. A good beginning point is to recognize that people from different cultures are different—not better or worse but simply different. Once we are able to do this, we can adjust and adapt our verbal and nonverbal messages accordingly and become competent interactants.[50]

THE ETHICS OF INTERCULTURAL COMMUNICATION

A recurring theme throughout this book is ethics. Ethics involve judgments about what is right and wrong in the course of human conduct. Ethics set a standard by which judgments of right and wrong are decided. Although some scholars distinguish between ethics and morals, we will treat the two terms interchangeably. Ethics become salient (i.e., particularly relevant) whenever human behavior and decision making are conscious, voluntary, and impact others. Ethics should not be confused with, nor are they necessarily linked to, religion. While most religions profess and advocate strict ethical standards, ethics apply to nonreligious people as well as religious people. One need not be religious to act ethically. Moreover, ethics are not synonymous with whatever is legal. While legal codes integrate ethical standards into laws that guide and control the behavior of citizens, they may not necessarily be ethical. For example, slavery was legal in the United States for more than a hundred years.[51]

If we define culture as an accumulated pattern of values, beliefs, and behaviors held by an identifiable group of people, and if we assume that cultures are different from one another, then intercultural communication takes on a necessary ethical dynamic, because communication is a conscious, voluntary act that influences others. Consider the following situation.

AN INTERCULTURAL CONVERSATION: WHERE SHOULD WE EAT DINNER?

Tommy is from the Chicago suburbs. He is studying abroad in Seoul, South Korea. His host-national friend, Kwan, is a native South Korean student and is serving as his mentor. They are joined by another fellow student, Dinesh, their friend from India.

Tommy:	Hey, guys, I'm starved. Where should we eat dinner?
Kwan:	I know a great place not far from here where they serve *poshintang*. You guys should try it.
Tommy:	*Poshintang*? What's that?
Kwan:	It's dog meat soup. A lot of people eat it in the summer.
Tommy:	Seriously?
Kwan:	Yeah, for sure.
Tommy:	No way am I eating dog.
Dinesh:	Me either. I don't eat any meat anyway. Is there a vegetarian restaurant nearby?
Tommy:	I'm not doing vegetarian, either. I have to have meat, but not dog.
Kwan:	Why don't you just try *poshintang* and see what you think. You'll probably like it.
Tommy:	No way, man. Not me.
Dinesh:	I can't. My parents would be very disappointed in me if I did.
Kwan:	Listen, you guys, you are in Korea now. You need to adapt, ya know . . . *when in Rome?* Do as we do!
Tommy:	No way.

(Continued)

(Continued)

Dinesh: No, I can't.

Kwan: If I were in the U.S. now, you'd probably make me eat something I don't like.

Dinesh: Yeah, would you make me eat beef, Tommy?

Tommy: Sure, you should eat beef, it's natural, and it's full of iron and protein. It's good for you.

Here's a simple example of the ethics involved in communicating with people from different cultures. Although we may not think about it much, people express and create meaning through the shared food they eat. In any culture, food serves a communicative function. Many important cultural and social rituals are conducted around and with food. In the United States, for example, Thanksgiving is a food-centered holiday. Meals are a central feature of birthday parties, weddings, and funerals. First dates often occur in restaurants. Sporting events (e.g., the Super Bowl) are regularly thought of as much as eating events as sporting ones. In her research on the food and eating habits in South Asian cultures, Jennifer B. Saunders observes that in many, the preparation, serving, and consumption of food are often enacted in heightened contexts that create symbolic meanings for both the performers and the audience. Saunders maintains that in Indian culture, the substance and symbol of the food one eats are clearly defined. She notes that the act of eating reveals participants' ethics and character. Each bite of food, she argues, communicates how that person understands himself or herself and how the food will contribute to his or her moral and emotional state.[52]

In 2009, in the United States, nearly 27 billion pounds of beef were consumed—the retail equivalent value of $73 billion. Americans like to eat beef. On the other hand, many Hindus regard cows as sacred and abstain from eating beef, although buffalo beef is consumed by some. And while Americans enjoy eating beef, most are disgusted by the thought of eating a horse, dog, or cat. Yet in parts of South Korea, people still eat dog—although selling dog meat has been illegal in South Korea since 1984. Some statistics show that dog is the fourth most popular meat in South Korea after pork, beef, and chicken. According to a British Broadcasting Corporation report, as many as 6,000 restaurants across South Korea may be selling dog meat soup, or what is called *poshintang,* using up to 8,500 tons of dog meat a year. According to the same report, another 94,000 tons is used to produce a medical tonic called *kaesoju.*[53]

So Tommy, Kwan, and Dinesh are faced with an ethical dilemma within the social/communicative ritual of eating a meal. All three young men have their own cultural ethics guiding their eating habits. Kwan wants Tommy and Dinesh to eat dog meat soup. Neither wants to eat it. Dinesh wants to eat vegetarian. Tommy admits that if they were in his native culture, he would sway them to eat beef. Who is right?

A central question about intercultural ethics is whether the same ethical principles apply to all cultures, a concept sometimes referred to as meta-ethics, or whether unique ethical standards apply to each culture individually, sometimes referred to as cultural relativism.

There is no easy answer to this question. If we argue from a culturally relativistic perspective, then we must be willing to tolerate behaviors that many of us would find abhorrent, such as dowry deaths. In India, marriages are often arranged between the parents of the future bride and groom. In virtually all marital arrangements, the bride's family is required to pay a dowry—that is, a gift of some sort or financial grant to be paid to the groom's family. If the bride's family cannot meet the dowry arrangements, or if the groom's family sees the given dowry as unacceptable, the bride suffers; she is often abused, beaten, and sometimes murdered. The typical cause of dowry deaths is particularly brutal: The bride is chained to the kitchen stove, doused in kerosene, and set afire. Official Indian government agencies estimate the number of dowry deaths at 6,000 every year. And this is believed to be an underestimation. Legislation outlawing dowries in India was enacted in 1961, but such laws are typically ignored. The point here is that few persons would condone the practice of dowry deaths. There is likely not a single anthropologist who, after immersing himself or herself in Indian culture, would come away and justify or excuse such a custom under the guise of cultural relativism.[54]

On the other hand, are there universal standards that everyone on the planet must obey? And who decides on these standards? If Tommy decides, then Dinesh must eat beef. If Kwan decides, then Tommy and Dinesh must eat dog. Historically, scholars from across a variety of academic fields have recognized five approaches to determining which behaviors are ethical: the utilitarian approach, the rights approach, the social justice and fairness approach, the common good approach, and the virtues approach.[55]

The utilitarian approach, sometimes called utilitarianism, posits that ethical actions are those that provide the greatest balance of good over evil. Some act is deemed ethical if it provides the greatest good for the greatest number (of people). To apply such an approach, one must first identify the courses of action available, determine who is affected by such actions in terms of who benefits or who is harmed, and then select the action that produces the greatest benefit and least harm. This approach is called utilitarianism because it emphasizes the consequences of actions on the well-being—that is, the utility—of all persons directly or indirectly benefiting from or harmed by the act.[56]

The rights approach focuses on an individual's right to choose for herself or himself. Advocates of a rights approach maintain that humans are distinct from other living beings on the planet because they have the free will to choose their course of action, and that such free will leads to dignity. Moreover, humans have a basic moral right to have their free choices respected, and it is a violation of human dignity to use people (e.g., hurt, manipulate) in ways they do not freely choose. Other fundamental human rights include the right to the truth, the right to privacy, the right not to be injured, and the right to what is agreed on. From this perspective, all humans have the right to be respected and treated as free, rational, and capable of making their own decisions. Thus, in this view, acts are ethical to the extent that they respect the rights of others. Acts are wrong to the extent that they violate the rights of others.[57]

The fairness or social justice approach is based on the Aristotelian dictum that "equals should be treated equally and unequals unequally." In this case, the ethical question is whether an act treats everyone in the same way or whether it shows favoritism and/or discrimination—that is, treats some unequally. Advocates of this approach maintain that favoritism benefits some people without a justifiable reason. Discrimination burdens people who should be treated equally. Hence, an act that shows favoritism and/or discrimination is unethical. This approach requires that people be treated with consistency.[58]

The common good approach is based on the idea that community life is, in and of itself, good and that people within the community and their subsequent actions should contribute to the community good. This approach has a more societal orientation than does utilitarianism in that it emphasizes that one's actions affect everyone's welfare, including a society's system of just laws, public safety, affordable health care, an effective education system, a clean environment, and even public recreation areas. Thus, an ethical act is one that ensures that such social policies are not violated, especially those that may inordinately affect vulnerable members of the society. This approach differs from the rights approach in that, while respecting and championing the rights of societal members to follow their individual goals, the common good approach also challenges societal members to recognize and advance the goals shared by the community.[59]

The virtues approach asserts the idea that there are certain ideals, principles, or standards (i.e., virtues) toward which every individual should strive to reach his or her highest potential. Individuals realize such virtues through conscious reflection on what kinds of people they have the potential to become. Virtues such as truth, beauty, honesty, courage, compassion, generosity, tolerance, love, fidelity, integrity, fairness, self-control, and prudence are encouraged. Actions manifested in such virtues are considered ethical. In dealing with an ethical problem using the virtue approach, individuals should ask themselves, "What kind of person should I be? What will promote the development of character within me and my community?"[60]

Although the five approaches to ethics listed above are applicable to a large group of people and an array of different cultures, all of them have their roots in Western ideology and philosophy and may not be applicable to all cultures. To be sure, Robert Shuter asserts that many of the fundamental tenets of the above five approaches are, in fact, not a part of the ethics that guide many Eastern cultures.[61] For example, Shuter states that implicit in most of these classical approaches is the tenet that human acts are considered ethical to the extent that they contribute to the happiness and general well-being of the individual—that truthfulness, equality, choice, and fairness are paramount in defining an ethical act. Moreover, Shuter argues that these perspectives place the free will of the individual at the center of ethics, above all else. Such focus assumes that humans are naturally reasonable and intellectual. But, as Shuter points out, the ethical principles of some major Eastern ethical codes do not follow the same assumptions. Two traditions, including Confucianism and Hinduism, have very different perspectives on what is ethical.

Confucianism prescribes an ethical and philosophical scheme of living developed from the writings of Confucius. Cultures and countries strongly influenced by Confucianism include China, Korea, Japan, Taiwan, and Vietnam. Unlike many of the Western approaches to ethics that stress free choice and equality, Confucianism prescribes a set of rituals and conventional social habits to guide humans to appropriate and ethical acts. The wisest of humans is competent at ritual and practicing ritual in all circumstances. By definition, rituals restrict, rather than free, human action. In addition, where many of the Western approaches elevate humans above all else, Confucianism prescribes social rituals designed so that the natural world, social institutions, and humans all flourish interdependently.[62] In Confucianism, there are five basic virtues: *ren* (benevolence/altruism), *yi* (integrity/sense of rightness), *li* (rite and propriety), *chi* (moral understanding), and *shin* (trust).[63] Within these five virtues is the recurring theme that humans are defined by their obedience to their place in the social hierarchy of relationships. By definition, social hierarchies rank order people and prescribe rules for proper conduct within each level of the hierarchy. In Confucianism, the five principal relationships are (1) ruler and subject, (2) parent and child, (3) husband and wife, (4) older sibling and younger sibling, and (5) friend and friend. Peace and harmony can be achieved only if people know, understand, and practice their proper place in society.[64] Some scholars maintain that Confucianism fosters inequality. Yeanmi You states that Confucianism has fostered gender biases by promoting the belief that a son is preferred over a daughter and a man is inherently superior to a woman in society. A woman who is as talented and educated as a man faces great discrimination in society because of the portrayal of a man as superior to a woman, which is deeply rooted in Confucianism.[65]

Hinduism is an inegalitarian, practice-based religion and is the third-largest religion after Christianity and Islam, with more than 1 billion followers. Unlike Christianity and Islam, Hinduism is not monotheistic (i.e., purporting belief in a single god) and has no organized worship. Hinduism is practice based rather than faith based, which means that practices—which are often social—are more important than beliefs. Jeff Spinner-Halev writes:

> Hinduism is concerned with legitimizing hierarchical social relationships and mollifying deities, not with faith or belief. A Hindu may be a theist, pantheist, atheist, communist and believe whatever he likes, but what makes him into a Hindu are the ritual practices he performs and the rules to which he adheres, in short, what he does.[66]

Unlike most of the Western approaches to ethics, Hinduism categorically denies that people are equal and practices a rigid caste system. A caste is a social-ordering hierarchical system in which people are ranked. Hinduism prescribes strict rules and regulations about how one is to act within one's caste level. In some cases, the lower caste may not be allowed even to interact with the higher caste. In India's caste system, there are four levels: (1) Brahmins—the learned, educated elites, and priests; (2) Kshatriyas—the noble and warriors; (3) Vaishyas—the traders, businessmen, and farmers; and (4) Sudras—those who serve the needs of the upper-caste members. The Sudras are further divided into the touchables and untouchables. The touchables take on positions considered demeaning and polluting by the upper caste, such as barbers, hairdressers, or cleaners. The untouchable Sudras are considered spiritually polluting and perform jobs such as garbage collecting. Hinduism prescribes that one is born into a caste level and it is virtually impossible to move from one caste level to the next—that is, from lower to higher levels. In Hindu society, men and women are clearly not equal. The birth of a son is a blessing, while the birth of a daughter is met with misgivings. She is a financial burden to the family.[67]

So we can see from the above discussion that Tommy, Kwan, and Dinesh have themselves an ethical dilemma. The answer to where they will lunch is not an easy one, since each comes from a very different set of ethical standards.

CHAPTER SUMMARY

The purpose of this chapter is to emphasize the necessity of intercultural communication and to define and clarify the terms *communication, culture,* and *intercultural communication.* The first part of this chapter argued that recent technological, political, and sociological advancements have created a global village only dreamed about 25 years ago. The essential effect of this technology is its decentralizing role in disseminating information across local, regional, national, and international borders. This means that billions of people across the planet now have access to information not available to them only a few years ago. Information empowers people. While the dream of a global village holds great promise, the reality is that diverse people have diverse opinions, values, and beliefs that clash and too often result in violence. Although the challenges of an increasingly diverse world are great, the benefits are even greater. Communicating and establishing relationships with people from different cultures can lead to a whole host of benefits, including healthier communities; increased international, national, and local commerce; reduced conflict; and personal growth through increased tolerance. Only through intercultural communication can such conflict be managed and reduced.

The second part of this chapter offered some definitions of *communication* and *culture.* Both terms are difficult to define. Communication is a dynamic, intentional, interactive, transactive, contextual, and cultural process that involves the simultaneous encoding and decoding of verbal and nonverbal messages with someone else, within some relational context. Culture, in part, can be defined as an accumulated pattern of values, beliefs, and behaviors shared by an identifiable group of people with a common history and verbal and non-verbal symbol system. Intercultural communication is essentially contextual. The cultural, microcultural, and environmental contexts surround the communicators, whose sociorelational contexts are defined by the exchange of verbal and nonverbal messages encoded and decoded within each interactant's perceptual context.

The third part of this chapter let you discover something about yourself—in this case, your intercultural communication apprehension. When we interact with someone from a different culture, we are faced with a lot of uncertainty. We may not know anything about the person's culture, values, habits, behavior, dress, and so on. We may not know what to say or do in such circumstances. This uncertainty about the other person may cause us to feel nervous and anxious, and may lead us to avoid such circumstances. Competent intercultural communicators are willing to approach intercultural situations and are sensitive to the differences in those situations. This part of the chapter also outlined some fundamental assumptions about intercultural communication.

The final part of this chapter took a look at ethics. Ethics become salient (i.e., particularly relevant) whenever human behavior and decision making are conscious, voluntary, and impact others, such as during intercultural communication.

Visit the student study site at www.sagepub.com/neuliep6e for e-flashcards, web quizzes, web resources, and more.

DISCUSSION QUESTIONS

1. In what ways is the United States changing demographically? What will the population look like in 50 years?

2. Why are so many people afraid of communication?

3. Why are so many people afraid to communicate with people from cultures different from their own?

4. Using the definition of culture presented in this chapter, how would you describe your culture?

5. How do the various contexts of the contextual model of intercultural communication relate to one another?

6. Why is it that "the message sent is rarely the message received"?

KEY TERMS

communication   17

communication apprehension   17

context   15

cultural context   15

culture   20

dynamic   12

environmental context   26

ethnocentrism   33

GENE (Generalized Ethnocentrism) Scale   33

intentionality   14

intercultural communication   24

intercultural communication apprehension   30

microculture   25

perceptual context   15

Personal Report of Communication Apprehension (PRCA-24)   17

physical context   15

process   12

sociorelational context   15

symbol   13

transactional   13

uncertainty   29

NOTES

1. Schlesinger, A. M. (1993). *The Disuniting of America: Reflections of a Multicultural Society.* New York: Norton, p. 10.

2. These data come from a couple of sources: Rosenberg, M. (2011, March 2). Population Density. Retrieved from http://geography.about.com/od/populationgeography/a/popdensity.thm; U.S. Census Bureau, U.S. Department of Commerce. (n.d.). *U.S. and World Population Clock.* Retrieved from http://www.census.gov/popclock/

3. Lewis, W. (1948). *America and Cosmic Man.* London: Nicholson & Watson.

4. Internet 2012 in Numbers. (2013, January 16). Retrieved from http://royal.pingdom.com/2013/01/16/

internet-2012-in-numbers/; Internet World Users by Language: The Top 10 Languages. (2010). *Internet World Stats: Usage and Population Statistics.* Retrieved from http://www.internetworldstats.com/stats7.htm

5. Giridharadas, A. (2009, May 9). A Pocket-Size Leveler in an Outsize Land. *New York Times.* Retrieved from http://www.nytimes.com/2009/05/10/weekinreview/10giridharadas.html; Mishra, P. (2013). Mobile Phones Disrupt India, for Better and Worse. *Bloomberg.* Retrieved from http://www.bloomberg.com/news/2013-01-27/mobile-phones-disrupt-india-for-better-and-worse.html

6. Media Statistics: Telephones—Mobile Cellular (per Capita) (Most Recent) by Country. (2011, March 28). Retrieved from http://www.nationmaster.com/graph/

med_tel_mob_cel_percap-telephones-mobile-cellular-per-capita

7.   Facebook. (2013). *Key Facts*. Retrieved from https://newsroom.fb.com/Key-Facts

8.   Schlesinger, *The Disuniting of America;* van den Berghe, P. L. (1987). *The Ethnic Phenomenon*. New York: Praeger; Waller, J. (2002). *Becoming Evil: How Ordinary People Commit Genocide and Mass Killing*. New York: Oxford University Press.

9.   Carroll, J. (2010, October 25). The Rising Tides of Xenophobia. *Boston Globe*. Retrieved from http://www.boston.com/bostonglobe/editorial_opinion/oped/articles/2010/10/25/the_rising_tides_of_xenophobia/; Schwirtz, M., & Barry, E. (2010, December 13). Medvedev Warns Against Ethnic Attacks. *New York Times*. Retrieved from http://www.nytimes.com/2010/12/14/world/europe/14russia.html; State Multiculturalism Has Failed, Says David Cameron. (2011, February 5). *BBC News: UK Politics*. Retrieved from http://www.bbc.co.uk/news/uk-politics-12371994

10.   Pomfret, J. (2001, April 12). Resolving Crisis was a Matter of Interpretation. *Washington Post,* p. A1; Ruppe, D. (2001, April 11). China, U.S., Win-Lose in Plane Standoff. *ABC News*. Retrieved from http://abcnews.go.com/International/story?id = 81250&page = 1

11.   Laungani, P. (2007). *Understanding Cross-Cultural Psychology*. London: Sage.

12.   England, J. T. (1992). *Building Community for the 21st Century*. Ann Arbor, MI: ERIC Clearinghouse on Counseling and Personnel Services. (ERIC Document Reproduction Service No. ED347489)

13.   U.S. Census Bureau. (2012). *Top Trading Partners: Total Trade, Exports, Imports*. Retrieved from http://www.census.gov/foreign-trade/statistics/highlights/top/top1212yr.html

14.   These stereotypes are reported in the following sources: Credit Union National Association. (n.d.). *Credit Unions Serving Hispanics: A National Perspective*. Retrieved from www.cuna.org/initiatives/download/hisp_bndr1.pdf; Lee, Y. T., Vue, S., Seklecki, R., & Ma, Y. (2007). How Did Asian Americans Respond to Negative Stereotypes and Hate Crimes? *American Behavioral Scientist, 51,* 271–293; Welch, K. (2007). Black Criminal Stereotypes and Racial Profiling. *Journal of Contemporary Criminal Justice, 23,* 276–288.

15.   U.S. Census Bureau. (2009). *Statistical Abstract of the United States: 2010* (129th ed.). Washington, DC: Author. Retrieved from http://www.census.gov/statab/www/ and http://www.census.gov/compendia/statab/2010/tables/10s0043.pdf

16.   Ibid.

17.   Pew Hispanic Center. (2013). *Statistical Portrait of Hispanics in the United States, 2011*. Washington, DC: Author; Pew Research Center. (2010). *Fact Sheet 2010:*

Hispanics of Mexican Origin in the United States, 2008. Washington, DC: Author; U.S. Census Bureau. (2008). *American Community Survey*. Retrieved from http://www.census.gov/acs/www/

18.   Ibid.

19.   County: English Is Official Language. (2002, July 18). Associated Press; Shin, H. B., & Bruno, R. (2003). *Language Use and English-Speaking Ability: 2000*. Washington, DC: U.S. Department of Commerce, U.S. Census Bureau; Texas Town Adopts Spanish as Official Language. (2004, August). Reuters News Service.

20.   U.S. Census Bureau. (2009). *Language Spoken at Home: 2005–2009 American Community Survey*. Retrieved from http://factfinder.census.gov/servlet/STTable?_bm = y&geo_id = 01000US&-qr_name = ACS_2009_5YR_G00_S1601&-ds_name = ACS_2009_5YR_G00_&-redoLog = false

21.   Schlesinger, *The Disuniting of America,* p. 15.

22.   Larson, C. U. (2010). *Persuasion: Reception and Responsibility* (12th ed.). Boston: Wadsworth.

23.   McCloud, L. (2006). *Top Reasons People Divorce: Is Divorce on the Back of Your Mind as You Are Saying "I Do."* Retrieved from http://voices.yahoo.com/top-reasons-people-divorce-41260.html

24.   Berlo, D. K. (1960). *The Process of Communication*. New York: Holt, Rinehart, & Winston, p. 24; Bowers, J. W., & Bradac, J. J. (1982). Issues in Communication Theory: A Metatheoretical Analysis. In M. Burgoon (Ed.), *Communication Yearbook 5* (p. 3). New Brunswick, NJ: Transaction Books; Goss, B. (1983). *Communication in Everyday Life*. Belmont, CA: Wadsworth; Cooley, C. (1909). *Social Organization*. New York: Scribner, p. 61; Miller, G. R. (1966). On Defining Communication: Another Stab. *Journal of Communication, 16,* 92; Fisher, B. A. (1994). *Interpersonal Communication: Pragmatics of Human Relationships*. New York: Random House, p. 22; Stevens, S. S. (1950). Introduction: A Definition of Communication. *Journal of the Acoustical Society of America, 22,* 689; Hall, E. T. (1959). *The Silent Language*. New York: Doubleday.

25.   Berlo, *The Process of Communication*, p. 24.

26.   Motley, M. T. (1990). On Whether One Can(not) Not Communicate: An Examination via Traditional Communication Postulates. *Western Journal of Communication, 54,* 1–20.

27.   Ibid.

28.   Watzlawick, P., Beavin, J., & Jackson, D. (1967). *Pragmatics of Human Communication: Patterns, Pathologies, and Paradoxes*. New York: Norton.

29.   McCroskey, J. C. (2006). *An Introduction to Rhetorical Communication* (9th ed.). Boston: Allyn & Bacon.

30.   Kroeber, A. I., & Kluckhohn, C. (Eds.). (1954). *Culture: A Critical Review of Concepts and Definitions.*

New York: Random House; Seelye, H. N. (1993). *Teaching Culture: Strategies for Intercultural Communication*. Lincolnwood, IL: National Textbook Company.

31. Basso, K. (1990). "To Give Up on Words": Silence in Western Apache Culture. In D. Carbaugh (Ed.), *Cultural Communication and Intercultural Contact* (pp. 303–320). Hillsdale, NJ: Erlbaum.

32. China: Language, Culture, Customs and Etiquette. (n.d.). *Kwintessential*. Retrieved from http://www.kwintessential.co.uk/resources/global-etiquette/china-country-profile.html; Facts for Traveler. (2011). *Thailand.com: Gateway to Southeast Asia*. Retrieved from http://www.thailand.com/travel/facts/fact_dodont.htm

33. This discussion of the history of intercultural communication is based on the following sources: Boas, F. Retrieved from www.nnnd.com/people/861/000097570/; Hall, *The Silent Language*; Kitao, K. (1985). *A Brief History of Intercultural Communication in the United States*. Education Resources Information Center. (ERIC Document Reproduction Service No. ED278212); Leeds-Hurwitz, L. (1990). Notes in the History of Intercultural Communication: The Foreign Service Institute and the Mandate for Intercultural Training. *Quarterly Journal of Speech, 76, 262–281*, Neuliep, J. W. (2010). Ethical and Cultural Relativism. In R. L. Jackson II (Ed.), *Encyclopedia of Identity* (pp. 252–254). Thousand Oaks, CA: Sage; Rogers, E. M., Hart, W. B., & Miike, Y. (2002). Edward T. Hall and the History of Intercultural Communication: The United States and Japan. *Keio Communication Review, 24*, 3–26.

34. Angeloni, E. (Ed.). (1995). *Mystique of the Masai*. Guilford: Dushkin.

35. Watzlawick et al., *Pragmatics of Human Communication*.

36. Berger, C. R. (1992). Communicating Under Uncertainty. In W. B. Gudykunst & Y. Y. Kim (Eds.), *Readings on Communicating With Strangers* (pp. 5–15). New York: McGraw-Hill.

37. Berger, C. R., & Calabrese, R. (1975). Some Explorations in Initial Interaction and Beyond. *Human Communication Research, 1*, 99–112.

38. Buss, A. H. (1980). *Self-Consciousness and Social Anxiety*. San Francisco: W. H. Freeman.

39. Gudykunst, W. B., & Kim, Y. Y. (1997). *Communicating With Strangers: An Approach to Intercultural Communication*. New York: McGraw-Hill.

40. Neuliep, J. W., & McCroskey, J. C. (1997). The Development of Intercultural and Interethnic Communication Apprehension Scales. *Communication Research Reports, 14*, 145–156.

41. Spitzberg, B. H. (1997). A Model of Intercultural Communication Competence. In L. A. Samovar & R. E. Porter (Eds.), *Intercultural Communication: A Reader* (8th ed., pp. 379–391). Belmont, CA: Wadsworth.

42. Spitzberg, A Model of Intercultural Communication Competence.

43. Gudykunst, W. (1997). Cultural Variability in Communication: An Introduction. *Communication Research, 24*, 327–348.

44. Sumner, W. G. (1906). *Folkways*. Boston: Ginn.

45. Neuliep, J. W., & McCroskey, J. C. (1997). The Development of a U.S. and Generalized Ethnocentrism Scale. *Communication Research Reports, 14*, 385–398.

46. Hall, *The Silent Language*.

47. Braithwaite, C. (1990). Communicative Silence: A Cross-Cultural Study of Basso's Hypothesis. In D. Carbaugh (Ed.), *Cultural Communication and Intercultural Contact* (pp. 321–328). Hillsdale, NJ: Erlbaum.

48. Gudykunst, W. B., & Ting-Toomey, S. (1988). Verbal Communication Styles. In W. B. Gudykunst & S. Ting-Toomey (Eds.), *Culture and Interpersonal Communication* (pp. 427–441). Newbury Park, CA: Sage.

49. Gudykunst & Kim, *Communicating With Strangers*; Kim, Y. Y. (2005). Association and Disassociation: A Contextual Theory of Interethnic Communication. In W. B. Gudykunst (Ed.), *Theorizing About Intercultural Communication* (pp. 323–350). Thousand Oaks, CA: Sage.

50. Kim, Y. Y. (2005). Adapting to a New Culture: An Integrative Communication Theory. In W. B. Gudykunst (Ed.), *Theorizing About Intercultural Communication* (pp. 375–400). Thousand Oaks, CA: Sage.

51. Velasquez, M., Andre, C., Shanks, T., S. J., & Meyer, M. J. (1987). What is ethics? *Issues in Ethics, 1*, N1.

52. Saunders, J. B. (2007). "I don't eat meat": Discourse on food among transnational Hindus. *Contributions to Indian Sociology, 41*, 302–323.

53. South Korea's dog day. (1999, August 17). *BBC News*. Retrieved from http://news.bbc.co.uk/2/hi/asia-pacific/422338.stm

54. Hitchcock, A. (2001). Rising number of dowry deaths in India. *World Socialist Web Site*. Retrieved from http://www.wsws.org/en/articles/2001/07/ind-j04.html

55. This discussion of the five classical approaches to ethics is based largely on Velasquez, M., Andre, C., Shanks, T., S. J., & Meyer, M. J. (1996). Thinking Ethically: A Framework for Moral Decision Making. *Issues in Ethics, 7*(1), 2–5.

56. Ibid.

57. Ibid.

58. Ibid.

59. Ibid.

60. Ibid.

61. Shuter, R. (2003). Ethics, Culture, and Communication: An Intercultural Perspective. In L. A. Samovar & R. E. Porter (Eds.), *Intercultural Communication: A Reader*

(10th ed., pp. 449–455). Belmont, CA: Wadsworth/Thomson.

62.   Billington, R. (1997). Chinese Philosophy III: Confucianism. In R. Billington (Ed.), *Understanding Eastern Philosophy* (pp. 118–133). New York: Routledge.

63.   Cua, A. S. (2000). Confucian Philosophy, Chinese. In E. Craig (Ed.), *Concise Routledge Encyclopedia of Philosophy* (pp. 162–163). New York: Routledge.

64.   Park, M., & Chesla, C. (2007). Revisiting Confucianism as a Conceptual Framework for Asian Family Study. *Journal of Family Nursing, 13*(3), 293–311.

65.   You, Y. (2009). Injustice: It Is Confucianism. *Qualitative Inquiry, 15*(7), 1290–1292.

66.   Spinner-Halev, J. (2005). Hinduism, Christianity, and Liberal Religious Toleration. *Political Theory, 33,* 28–57.

67.   Laungani, *Understanding Cross-Cultural Psychology.*

CHAPTER 2

The Cultural Context

CHAPTER OBJECTIVES

After reading this chapter, you should be able to

1. recognize that cultures are dynamic, fluid, and not static entities;

2. compare and contrast individualism and collectivism;

3. identify some cultures that are individualistic and some that are collectivistic;

4. recognize that no culture is purely individualistic or purely collectivistic;

5. compare and contrast high- and low-context cultures;

6. identify some cultures that are high context and some that are low context;

7. compare value orientations among cultures;

8. compare and contrast large– and small–power-distance cultures;

9. identify some cultures that are large power distance and some that are small power distance;

10. compare and contrast large– and small–uncertainty-avoidant cultures;

11. identify some cultures that are weak uncertainty avoidant and some that are strong uncertainty avoidant; and

12. assess your degree of individualism/collectivism, vertical and horizontal individualism/collectivism, high/low context, and power distance.

Cultural Context

Culture hides more than it reveals, and strangely enough what it hides, it hides most effectively from its own participants.

—Edward T. Hall[1]

The cultural context in which human communication occurs is perhaps the most defining influence on human interaction. Culture provides the overall framework wherein humans learn to organize their thoughts, emotions, and behaviors in relation to their environment. Although people are born into a culture, it is not innate. Culture is learned. Culture teaches one how to *think,* conditions one how to *feel,* and instructs one how to *act,* especially how to *interact* with others—in other words, how to communicate. In many respects, the terms *communication* and *culture* can be used interchangeably. Yet the influence of culture on human interaction is paradoxical. As we conduct our daily lives, most of us are unaware of our culture; however, culture influences our every thought, feeling, and action. As the late internationally recognized anthropologist Edward T. Hall asserted in the quote at the beginning of this chapter, culture hides more than it reveals, particularly from its own members. Australian anthropologist Roger Keesing argues that culture provides people with an implicit theory about how to behave and how to interpret the behavior of others. People from different cultures learn different implicit theories. These theories are learned through socialization. And through socialization, individuals also learn the dominant values of their particular culture and their self-identities.[2]

We often think of a culture in terms of its geography; for example, we think of Saudi Arabia as a hot, desert culture and of Siberia as a cold, mountainous one. But culture is more a human phenomenon than a geographic one. And while geography certainly affects how people live within a particular culture, the people, more than the geography, are what constitute culture. So when you think of a culture, think about the people. That being said, it is also important to understand that cultures of people are not static but, rather, dynamic. This means that cultures change; they are fluid, always moving. For example, a dramatic change we have seen in China is the implementation of the one-child policy, which was established in 1979 to limit that country's population explosion (recall from Chapter 1 that China has 1.4 billion people). Although originally intended to be a temporary measure, the policy limiting couples to one child continues today. Fines, taxes, forced abortions, and sterilization may result if a couple violates the policy. This policy has dramatically changed China's culture; to be sure, it is thought to have reduced the population growth by as many as 300 million people since its inception. To provide some perspective on that change, there are about 314 million people in the United States.[3]

Over the past few decades, anthropologists, communication researchers, psychologists, and sociologists have isolated several dimensions of cultural variability that can be used to differentiate cultures. This chapter will focus on five dimensions of cultural variability: individualism–collectivism, high–low context, value orientations, power distance, and uncertainty avoidance. Each of these dimensions affects how people communicate.

The five dimensions of cultural variability will be presented along cultural continua:

Low [_____] High

The cultural continua allow us to represent the dimensions of cultural variability as continuous and varying in magnitude by degree. In other words, no culture is purely and absolutely individualistic or collectivistic. Instead, a culture may be more individualistic or more collectivistic than some other culture. Another important point to make is that these cultural dimensions of variability are not opposites; that is, a culture where a large power distance is practiced should not be thought of as the opposite of a culture where small power distance is practiced. In some cases, dimensions of cultural variability may coexist in cultures. In addition, as mentioned above, cultures are not static or fixed in time; many cultures are in a state of great transition. Thus, a culture that was once considered collectivistic may now be considered individualistic. For example, Japan is considered a collectivistic, group-oriented society. However, since the 1950s, Japan has been strongly influenced by Western culture. Many Japanese scholars have observed that the younger generation of Japanese, while still considered collectivistic, is more individualistic than their parents and especially their grandparents. Likewise, although the United States is considered very individualistic, many U.S. businesses and corporations employ collectivistic management models in the workplace, focusing on teamwork and cooperation.

Finally, and this is an important point, when we label a culture as individualistic—or large power distance and so forth—that does not mean that every person in that culture is an individualist. The United States, for example, is considered an individualistic culture, yet groups within the United States are collectivistic. While reading through this chapter, remember that cultures are not static. Cultures are dynamic, continuously developing and evolving.

INDIVIDUALISM–COLLECTIVISM

Perhaps the single most studied dimension of cultural variability used to compare and contrast cultures and microcultures is individualism–collectivism (see Figure 2.1).

Figure 2.1 Individualism–collectivism.

Individualism ←————————————→ Collectivism

Cultures falling on one side of the continuum are individualistic, while those falling toward the other side are collectivistic. Cultures falling at the midpoint might possess both individualistic and collectivistic characteristics. Gayle R. Avant and Karen Patrick Knutson write that Norwegians, for example, possess both individualistic and collectivistic tendencies. Norwegians are taught to put the needs of society above their own and to embrace a classless society. Simultaneously, however, Norwegians value personal independence. While they conform to social norms, the individual Norwegian rebuffs traditional rules and standards. They strive for independence yet do not depend on others to recognize their individual achievements. They believe that they must recognize their own good qualities to gain self-esteem.[4]

Perhaps Norway is unusual in that its people carry collectivistic and individualistic tendencies, but regardless of culture, most persons carry both individualistic and collectivistic tendencies to some degree. The difference is that in some cultures individualistic tendencies dominate, while in others collectivistic tendencies dominate.[5]

Individualism

Researchers at the University of Michigan analyzed more than 250 studies that investigated individualism, collectivism, or both.[6] They found that the most relevant feature of individualism, as defined in the majority of the studies they reviewed, was valuing personal independence. Researchers at the University of Auckland in New Zealand point out that valuing personal independence involves putting an emphasis on personal responsibility and freedom of choice, personal autonomy, and achieving self-fulfillment. Moreover, individualists strive to maintain distinctive personal attitudes and opinions and prefer self-directed behavior and independence of groups. Individualists tend to see themselves as unique from others.[7]

Harry C. Triandis, from the University of Illinois, is well known for his work on individualism and collectivism. Triandis discusses four defining attributes of individualism–collectivism:

1. How individuals perceive themselves (e.g., "I am distinct and unique" vs. "I am a member of a family, tribe")

2. How individuals relate to others (e.g., "How/what do I gain from this act?" vs. "How will this act affect others?")

3. The goals individuals follow (e.g., "I want to win" vs. "I'm a team player to help the group win")

4. What drives individuals' behavior (e.g., "It is my right to do this" vs. "My duty is to my group")

Triandis writes that in individualistic cultures, emphasis is placed on individuals' goals over group goals. Social behavior is guided by personal goals, perhaps at the expense of other types of goals. Individualistic cultures stress values that benefit the individual person. The self is promoted because each person is viewed as uniquely endowed and possessing distinctive talent and potential. Individuals are encouraged to pursue and develop their abilities and aptitudes. In many individualistic cultures, people are taught to be creative, self-reliant, and assertive.[8]

Triandis and others have pointed out that an important ingredient of individualistic cultures is that the individual is emotionally disconnected from in-groups such as the family. Because the individual has been taught to be independent, social control depends more on personal guilt than on shame or other social norms or conformity. Ironically, members of individualistic cultures tend to belong to many groups, but their affiliation with those groups is short-lived. Many of the groups to which an individualist belongs are designed to enhance self-worth. Such groups might include self-help groups, therapy groups, or occupational groups.[9]

The origins of individualism have been traced to ancient Greece, where literature (e.g., *The Iliad* and *The Odyssey*) celebrates the accomplishments of individuals. Daphna Oyserman, Heather M. Coon, and Markus Kemmelmeier point out that the term *individualism* may have its roots in the French Revolution (1789–1799), where the word was used to describe the negative influence of individual rights on the well-being of the French commonwealth.[10] Triandis also notes that ecology (i.e., features of geography, resources, and the history of a society) can shape the level of individualism in a culture. For example, modern, industrial–urban, fast-changing cultures tend to be individualistic.

In many cases, individualistic cultures are highly complex and affluent. Complex cultures have heterogeneous populations and economies based on occupational specialization, where individuals do different jobs. Cultural complexity also occurs in cultures where people are separated from one another either geographically or through migration patterns. Many individualistic cultures have a history of colonization, for example.[11]

Collectivism

Oyserman, Coon, and Kemmelmeier point out that the central ingredient of collectivism is the assumption that groups bind and mutually obligate individuals.[12] In their extensive review of literature, they found that collectivism is linked to a sense of duty to group, interdependence, harmony, and working with the group. Triandis asserts that in collectivistic societies, group goals take precedence over individual goals. Collectivistic cultures stress values that serve the in-group by subordinating personal goals for the sake of preserving the in-group. Collectivistic societies are characterized by extended primary groups such as the family, neighborhood, or occupational group in which members have diffuse mutual obligations and expectations based on their status or rank. In collectivistic cultures, people are not seen as isolated individuals. People see themselves as interdependent with others (e.g., their in-group), where responsibility is shared and accountability is collective. A person's identity is defined by his or her group memberships.[13]

Triandis points out that while collectivistic cultures stress the importance of the group over the individual, their members tend to belong to fewer groups than do persons in individualistic cultures. Unlike the individualist, the collectivist is emotionally connected to the in-group. A collectivist's values and beliefs are consistent with and reflect those of the in-group. Moreover, a collectivist's association with his or her in-groups may last a lifetime. In many collectivistic cultures, the primary value is harmony with others. Triandis observes that because group harmony is so highly valued, obedience to and compliance with in-group pressures is routine. One's behavior is role based, and deviations from the prescribed role are discouraged and often negatively sanctioned. In this sense, a person's behavior is guided more by shame than by personal guilt. A collectivist who stands out from the group disrupts the harmony and may be punished. Most collectivistic cultures value social reciprocity, obligation, dependence, and obedience. But by far, the primary value stressed by many collectivistic cultures is harmony.[14]

STUDENT VOICES ACROSS CULTURES

Personal Understanding of Collectivism in China

My name is Pengfei Song, and I'm a 25-year-old guy from China. I was raised in Qiqihaer, a city located in the northeast part of the country. Before I came to the United States to get my bachelor's degree, I had received my education in China from kindergarten through the first 2 years in university.

As far as I can recall, the idea of collectivism was introduced to me when I was in elementary school. I was told that serving your country and people should be your priority, regardless of what you want to do in the future. The reason for this is that we, as Chinese, believe that individuals, to a large extent, cannot have a peaceful life without the prosperity of our nation. Put in another way, our nation is defined as the big family, whereas each household is a small family within that big family. As a result, it is very common for the Chinese people to emphasize group goals over individual goals and to think more in terms of "we."

Dating back to a sports meeting in my high school, I remember that I signed up to compete in the 200-meter race with other students from other classes in my grade. I decided to do it not because I had the ability to win but because my class needed someone to represent it, and I wanted to be that person. To me, the reputation of my class meant more than anything. I could feel that I was not just myself; I stood for all my classmates. So if I failed, my class failed. Fortunately, I won the competition, which meant victory for the whole class. So the repute apparently belonged to my class, not to me.

Individualism Versus Collectivism?

Although they sound as though they're opposite dimensions of cultural variability, individualism and collectivism are not mutually exclusive; that is, they can coexist within a person of any culture. Eva G. T. Green, Jean-Claude Deschamps, and Dario Páez point out that the degree of individualism or collectivism within someone may be triggered by the social context and one's social relations. They suggest that individuals can be characterized by specific combinations of individualistic and collectivistic tendencies. For example, a person may find that individualistic relations are motivated in particular situations, such as in business relationships, whereas with family members, the relationship is collectivistic.[15] To be sure, C. Harry Hui has shown variation in individualistic and collectivistic attitudes in different types of relationships, such as with one's spouse, parent, neighbor, or coworker.[16]

Competitiveness often has been associated with individualism. Instruments that measure individualism often include items that tap into one's competitive nature (e.g., "It's important to me that I win"). Recent research suggests, however, that competitiveness is not a necessary feature of individualism. In their research, Oyserman, Coon, and Kemmelmeier found that Americans generally score higher in individualism than do Japanese. But when competitiveness is included in the measurement of individualism, the difference between Americans and Japanese disappears (i.e., they score the same on measures of individualism).[17] Green, Deschamps, and Páez note that, in any culture, people compete for scarce resources in economically adverse contexts and that scarcity triggers competitiveness, which leads to active individualism aimed at achieving economic success and material well-being. In contexts of affluence, in contrast, other individualistic values such as individual freedom, personal development, quality of life, and relational interdependence become salient.[18] In a Taiwanese sample, An Bang Yu and Kuo Shu Yang found that achievement motivation as a form of competitiveness can be driven by individual or collective concerns. These findings support the idea that competitiveness is associated with individualism as well as with collectivism.[19]

So, Who's an Individualist and Who's a Collectivist?

Because there can be considerable within-country variation, labeling a particular country or culture as individualistic or collectivistic is difficult and may lead to overgeneralizations. However, in their landmark analysis of more than 250 research articles on individualism and collectivism, Oyserman and her colleagues were able to draw some conclusions.[20] The central focus of this study was to answer the question, Are Americans (i.e., European Americans) more individualistic and less collectivistic than others groups? In general, the answer was yes, Americans are more individualistic and less collectivistic than other groups. In comparison with nearly 50 other countries, European Americans were more individualistic than all but 12. European Americans were generally lower in collectivism as well. There were exceptions, though; Americans were higher in collectivism than were people in New Zealand, France, Singapore, Tanzania, Egypt, Costa Rica, and Venezuela. Oyserman et al. note that one of the most remarkable findings was that Americans were slightly more collectivistic than Japanese, and no difference was observed between Americans and Koreans on collectivistic measures.

However, in her recent research, Toshi Imada found that the stories in American textbooks highlighted themes of individualism, such as self-direction and achievement, whereas Japanese stories highlighted themes of collectivism, such as conformity and group harmony. Her study also found cultural differences in story characteristics (e.g., the narrator, attribution of the outcome, picture content) that are related to individualism and collectivism.[21] Oyserman and colleagues have pointed out that although as a group East Asians were simultaneously lower in individualism and higher in collectivism than were Americans, there was notable variety within East Asian countries regarding individualism and collectivism. For example, Chinese were highest in collectivism but lowest in individualism, whereas Japanese were highest in individualism but lowest in collectivism. South Koreans were between Chinese and Japanese on these measures. This may be because South Korean culture has unique features that distinguish it from traditional Confucian-based collectivistic cultures—that is, a strong emphasis on family. In a more recent study, Ronald Fischer and a number of his colleagues examined 11 countries and found that among these countries, the United States ranked highest in overall individualism.[22]

Overall Individualism

1. United States

2. Germany

3. India

4. Lebanon

5. New Zealand

6. Peru

7. Brazil

8. Taiwan

9. Saudi Arabia

10. United Kingdom

11. Argentina

Individualism and collectivism also have been studied among Middle Eastern and African cultures. Shifra Sagy, Emda Orr, Dan Bar-On, and Elia Awwad found that both Israeli-Jewish and Palestinian-Arab groups were more collectivistic than individualistic. However, the Palestinians scored higher than the Israeli group on items measuring and emphasizing an in-group collectivistic orientation (e.g., my nationality, my country). Anna-Maija Pirttilä-Backman, B. Raul Kassea, and Terhi Ikonen found that Cameroonians were shown to be more collectivistic than individualistic. They also found that Cameroonian women were more individualistic than were the men. Cameroon provides an interesting context for the study of individualism and collectivism because of the vast ethnic differences there. For example, although the country is officially bilingual—with about 20% speaking English and the rest speaking French—more than 200 languages are spoken there. Religious diversity abounds as well, with indigenous beliefs held by about 40% of the population, Christian beliefs held by another 40%, and Muslim beliefs by about 20%.[23]

An Intercultural Conversation:
Individualistic and Collectivistic Cultures

To be sure, one's individualistic or collectivistic disposition will affect communication. In the following exchange, Mr. Patterson, an American manager working in Korea, is meeting with his supervisor, Mr. Wyman, who is also American. The United States is considered more individualistic than Korea. In this scenario, Mr. Patterson reports to Mr. Wyman about some changes he has made within several of his sales teams. Later, Park Young Sam, their Korean counterpart, enters into the dialogue.[24]

Mr. Patterson: Good morning, Mr. Wyman. Thanks for meeting with me this morning. As you know, our division has been doing very well this quarter. In fact, our numbers are up across the board.

Mr. Wyman: Yes, I've seen your quarterly reports. Nice job!

Mr. Patterson: Thanks. To recognize their hard work, I've made some changes in our sales teams. I've created team leaders in each group. In our product group, I promoted Lee Young-sam. In the marketing group, I promoted Chun Tae-woo, and in the technology group, I promoted Choi Mino. All of them have been real leaders. I think this idea will really motivate them. In fact, I met with the groups individually and announced the promotions.

Mr. Wyman: Good job, Patterson. I can see you're really on top of things. Good work.

Two Months Later

Mr. Patterson, Mr. Wyman, and Park Young Sam, a Korean manager, are discussing the poor performance of Mr. Patterson's sales teams.

Mr. Wyman: Well, just look at these dismal results. The numbers for this quarter are way down from last quarter. What's happened?

Mr. Patterson: I don't know. Ever since I introduced the team leader concept, the groups' productivity has really plummeted. I thought it was a great idea. I guess I chose the wrong people to lead the teams. I'll assign new leaders tomorrow.

Park Young Sam: Well . . . you may select new leaders if you desire, but the men you chose were all very capable. However, by elevating them, you made them stand out and disrupted the harmony of each group. In Korea, we all work hard for the group . . . not just one person.

Mr. Patterson: I guess I should have just left things as they were.

Following their individualistic orientations, Mr. Patterson and Mr. Wyman were perfectly comfortable with the idea of appointing team leaders within the individual sales groups. However, as Park Young Sam mentioned, doing so upset the harmony of the groups, which in turn led to poor performance. In the United States, workers are often motivated by the opportunity for promotion and advancement, as this serves the individualistic drive for personal achievement. In less individualistic cultures, however, workers may be motivated by being a part of a cohesive and productive team. Mr. Patterson and Mr. Wyman could have consulted with Mr. Sam prior to making the promotions. He probably would have advised against it.

Patterns of Individualism and Collectivism Across the United States

As mentioned above, although the United States is considered individualistic, considerable regional variation exists. Because of ecological, historical, and institutional practices, the Deep South is the most collectivistic region of the United States. Defeat in the Civil War, the institution of slavery, relative poverty, and the prominence of religion all contribute to the collectivistic tendencies of the South. In addition, the Southwest, having been settled by Mexican and Spanish populations before White settlers entered the area, is also considered fairly collectivistic. Hawaii, too, has a culture different from the rest of the United States, with about 65% of its population coming from Asian cultures. Hence, much of the culture has collectivistic characteristics, and Hawaii would be considered collectivistic. On the other hand, the Mountain West and Great Plains is thought to be the most individualistic region in the United States.[25]

In their research, Joseph A. Vandello and Dov Cohen created an index designed to measure collectivism in different regions of the United States. Their index was composed of eight items, including the percentage of people living alone, percentage of elderly people living alone, percentage of households with grandchildren in them, divorce-to-marriage ratio, percentage of people with no religious affiliation, average percentage of those voting Libertarian over the past four presidential elections, ratio of people carpooling to work to people living alone, and percentage of self-employed people. Their index showed a general pattern of relative collectivism in the South, particularly in the former slave states, with maximum individualism in the Great Plains and Mountain West. Montana was the most individualistic state, and Hawaii was the most collectivistic (see Table 2.1).[26]

Table 2.1 The Most Collectivistic States and the Most Individualistic States

Most Collectivistic States	Most Individualistic States
Hawaii	Montana
Louisiana	Oregon
South Carolina	Nebraska
Mississippi	Wyoming
Maryland	South Dakota
Utah	Colorado
Virginia	North Dakota
Georgia	Washington
California	Kansas
New Jersey	Iowa

The point has been made several times now that variations of individualism and collectivism can be seen within any culture. No culture is purely and entirely individualistic or collectivistic. To account for this phenomenon, Triandis and other cross-cultural researchers distinguish between individualism and collectivism at the *cultural* level and idiocentrism and allocentrism at the individual *psychological* level. Many cross-cultural researchers believe that individualism–collectivism cannot be measured at the cultural level. We should not label entire cultures as individualistic or collectivistic, because persons within those cultures may vary considerably. We can, however, measure an individual degree of individualism–collectivism.

When people carry individualistic tendencies, we call them *idiocentric*. When people carry collectivistic tendencies, we call them *allocentric*. Idiocentrism and allocentrism are the individual equivalents of cultural individualism–collectivism. Allocentrics tend to define themselves with reference to social entities (e.g., families, hometowns) more so than do idiocentrics. Allocentrics internalize the norms of the in-group and enjoy behavior along in-group expectations. Allocentrics are less likely to be lonely than idiocentrics. The self-esteem of allocentrics tends to be based on getting along with others, compared with idiocentrics, whose self-esteem is often based on getting ahead of others.[27]

Communication Consequences of Individualism–Collectivism

A given culture's orientation toward individualism or collectivism has important behavioral consequences for that culture's members. Among collectivists, social behavior is guided by the group. Along with group membership come prescribed duties and obligations. Among individualists, social behavior is guided by one's personal attitudes, motivations, and other internal processes. To be sure, individualistic cultures value and reward an individual's uniqueness. The United States, for example, is replete with contests and ceremonies that recognize individual accomplishment. People are publicly rewarded for being the most beautiful, thinnest, strongest, fastest, tallest, smartest, youngest, oldest, funniest, or "best" at whatever they aspire to do. Collectivistic cultures, on the other hand, stress harmony and cooperation. Collectivists strive for the approval of the in-group, which is accomplished not by standing out but by conforming to the group's norm. From the collectivist's perspective, an individual who stands out from the group disrupts harmony. In the United States, "the squeaky wheel gets the grease," but in Japan, "the tallest nail gets hammered down."[28]

Triandis maintains that a culture's individualistic or collectivistic orientation will likely affect child-rearing practices. In individualistic cultures, child rearing emphasizes independence, exploration, creativity, and self-reliance. Individualistic parents encourage their children to be unique, express themselves, and be independent. The children of individualistic parents understand that they are to leave home once they reach a certain age or education level. In fact, it is thought odd or unusual if children past the age of about 21 still live at home with their parents. Though rank order exists in the individualist's family, decisions are often made democratically. In collectivistic cultures, child rearing emphasizes conformity, obedience, security, and reliability. Collectivistic parents teach their children the importance of family lineage and ancestry. Typically, the father dominates the collectivist's home, where rank in the family is often determined by sex and age.[29]

Collectivists are more conscious of in-group/out-group distinctions than are individualists. According to William B. Gudykunst and his colleagues, individualists tend to initiate and maintain specific friendships based on desirable qualities of the other person. Collectivists form friendships that are determined by their hierarchical role in society. Collectivists perceive and rate their in-group friendships as more intimate than do individualists. On the other hand, individualists tend to apply the same value standards to all, whereas collectivists tend to apply different value standards to members of their in-groups and out-groups. For example, collectivists are likely to use the equality norm (i.e., equal distribution of resources) with in-group members and the equity norm (i.e., unequal distribution of resources) with out-group members.[30]

Finally, in their exhaustive review of studies, Oyserman, Coon, and Kemmelmeier summarized behavioral traits that have been shown to be associated with individualism and collectivism (Table 2.2).[31]

Table 2.2   Behavioral Traits Associated With Individualism and Collectivism

Individualism	Collectivism
Optimism	Social self-concept
High self-esteem	Need for affiliation
Lower social anxiety	Sensitivity to rejection
Emotional expression	Sensitivity to embarrassment
Satisfaction with self	In-group relationship preferences
Satisfaction with freedom	Indirect communication style
Ease of interacting with strangers	Valuing of social networks
Direct communication style	
Lower relational commitment	
Preference to work alone	

Measuring Individualism–Collectivism

Over the past decades, cross-cultural researchers have spent considerable effort developing instruments designed to measure one's relative degree of individualism and collectivism. Researchers at the University of Auckland in New Zealand recently developed the Auckland Individualism and Collectivism Scale.[32] (See Self-Assessment 2.1.)

Vertical and Horizontal Individualism and Collectivism

While it is clear that individualistic cultures differ from collectivistic cultures, individualistic cultures can, and do, differ from other individualistic cultures. The same can be said of

Self-Assessment 2.1

Individualism and Collectivism Scale

Directions: Below are 20 statements that may or may not reflect how you act within your relationships with others. For each statement, indicate the *frequency* with which you engage (or not) in the behaviors described.

5 = always, 4 = usually, 3 = sometimes, 2 = rarely, 1 = never

_____ 1. I discuss job or study-related problems with my parents.

_____ 2. I consult my family before making an important decision.

_____ 3. Before taking a major trip, I consult with most members of my family and many friends.

_____ 4. It is important to consult close friends and get their ideas before making a decision.

_____ 5. Even when I strongly disagree with my group members, I avoid an argument.

_____ 6. I hate to disagree with others in my group.

_____ 7. In interacting with superiors, I am always polite.

_____ 8. I sacrifice my self-interest for the benefit of my group.

_____ 9. I define myself as a competitive person.

_____ 10. I enjoy working in situations involving competition with others.

_____ 11. Without competition, it is impossible to have a good society.

_____ 12. Competition is the law of nature.

_____ 13. I consider myself as a unique person, separate from others.

_____ 14. I enjoy being unique and different from others.

_____ 15. I see myself as "my own person."

_____ 16. It is important for me to act as an independent person.

_____ 17. I take responsibility for my own actions.

_____ 18. Being able to take care of myself is a primary concern for me.

_____ 19. I consult with my superior on work-related matters.

_____ 20. I prefer to be self-reliant rather than depend on others.

Scoring: To compute your *collectivism* score, sum your responses for Items 1 through 8. Your sum must be between 8 and 40. Higher sums (e.g., > 30) indicate a prevalence for collectivism. To compute your *individualism* score, sum your responses for Items 9 through 20. Your sum must be between 12 and 60. Higher sums (e.g., > 45) indicate a prevalence for individualism.

collectivistic cultures. Some individualistic cultures, for example, link self-reliance with competition, while other individualistic cultures do not. Some collectivistic cultures emphasize in-group harmony above all else, while other collectivistic cultures do not. To account for some of these finer distinctions among individualistic and collectivistic cultures, Triandis and his colleagues differentiate between vertical and horizontal individualism and collectivism.

According to Theodore M. Singelis, Harry C. Triandis, Dharm P. S. Bhawuk, and Michele J. Gelfand, horizontal individualism is a cultural orientation where an autonomous self is valued but the individual is more or less equal in status to others. The self is perceived as independent but nevertheless the same as others. Vertical individualism is the cultural orientation where an autonomous self is also valued but the self is seen as different from and perhaps unequal to others. Status and competition are important aspects of this orientation. The United States and France are examples of vertical individualism, whereas Sweden and Austria are examples of horizontal individualism.[33] Horizontal collectivism is the cultural orientation where the individual sees the self as a member of an in-group whose members are similar to one another. The self is interdependent and the same as the self of others. Equality is expected and practiced within this orientation. China is probably a good example of horizontal collectivism. Theoretical communism is an example of extreme horizontal collectivism. Vertical collectivism is the cultural orientation in which the individual sees the self as an integral part of the in-group but the members are different from one another, some having more status than others. The self is interdependent, and inequality within the group is valued. In this orientation, serving and sacrifice are important. Japan, India, and rural traditional Greece are examples of vertical collectivism.

In a recent comparison of U.S., Thai, and Japanese students on horizontal and vertical individualism and collectivism, Robert M. McCann, James M. Honeycutt, and Shaughan A. Keaton found significant differences among the three groups and within each group. Regarding horizontal individualism, the U.S. students scored higher than the Japanese, who scored higher than the Thai students. Interestingly, there were no significant differences among the three groups on vertical individualism, where we might have expected the U.S. students to score higher than the other groups. Finally, the Japanese scored higher on horizontal and vertical collectivism than the U.S. and Thai students. Within each culture, the U.S. students scored highest on horizontal individualism, then, in order, horizontal collectivism, vertical collectivism, and vertical individualism. The Japanese students scored highest on horizontal collectivism, virtually the same on vertical collectivism and horizontal individualism, then lowest on vertical individualism. Finally, the Thai students scored highest on horizontal collectivism, then, in order, horizontal individualism, vertical individualism, and vertical collectivism.[34]

There are advantages and disadvantages to being an individualist, just as there are to being a collectivist. Neither approach is "better" than the other; they are simply different orientations. The goal is to recognize and understand the differences, thereby increasing your intercultural competence. To be sure, the individualism–collectivism dimension of cultural variability has been used extensively in describing cultural differences—perhaps too much. Asian cultures, in particular, are often branded as collectivistic. Recently, the individualism–collectivism dichotomy has been the subject of criticism. In her analysis of the Chinese, Hui-Ching Chang argues that by describing cultures as only collectivistic—which focuses on the structure of society—much of the creativity of individual Asian cultures, including rich histories, has been ignored. As Chang asserts,

MEASURING HORIZONTAL AND VERTICAL INDIVIDUALISM–COLLECTIVISM

Consider the following situations. Place a check next to the response that most closely fits how you would act.

1. You and your friends decided spontaneously to go out to dinner at a restaurant. What do you think is the best way to handle the bill?

    A. _____ Split it equally, without regard to who ordered what.

    B. _____ Split it according to how much each person makes.

    C. _____ The group leader pays the bill or decides how to split it.

    D. _____ Compute each person's charge according to what that person ordered.

2. Which of these four book topics are you more likely to find interesting?

    A. _____ How to make friends

    B. _____ How to succeed in business

    C. _____ How to make sure you are meeting your obligations

    D. _____ How to enjoy yourself inexpensively

3. When you buy clothing for a major social event, you would be most satisfied if . . .

    A. _____ your friends like it.

    B. _____ it is so elegant it will dazzle everyone.

    C. _____ your parents like it.

    D. _____ you like it.

4. When people ask me about myself, I . . .

    A. _____ talk about my friends and what we like to do.

    B. _____ talk about my accomplishments.

    C. _____ talk about my ancestors and their traditions.

    D. _____ talk about what makes me unique.

5. Suppose your boyfriend/girlfriend and your parents do not get along very well. What would you do?

    A. _____ Tell my boyfriend/girlfriend that he/she should make a greater effort to "fit in with my family"

    B. _____ Tell my boyfriend/girlfriend that I need my parents' financial support and he/she should learn to handle them

(Continued)

(Continued)

   C. ____ Remind my boyfriend/girlfriend that my parents and family are very important to me and he/she should submit to their wishes

   D. ____ Nothing

6. Suppose you had one word to describe yourself. What would it be?

   A. ____ Cooperative

   B. ____ Competitive

   C. ____ Dutiful

   D. ____ Unique

7. Happiness is attained by . . .

   A. ____ linking with a lot of friendly people.

   B. ____ winning in competition.

   C. ____ gaining a lot of status in the community.

   D. ____ keeping one's privacy.

8. You are at a pizza restaurant with a group of friends. How should you decide what kind of pizza to order?

   A. ____ We select the pizza that most people prefer.

   B. ____ We order the most extravagant pizza available.

   C. ____ The leader of the group orders for everyone.

   D. ____ I order what I like.

Scoring: Indicate the number of times you selected letters A, B, C, and D. The frequency that is the highest represents your general HC, VI, VC, or HI orientation.

   A. ____ Horizontal collectivism (HC)

   B. ____ Vertical individualism (VI)

   C. ____ Vertical collectivism (VC)

   D. ____ Horizontal individualism (HI)

SOURCE: This scale for measuring horizontal and vertical individualism and collectivism is adapted from Triandis, H. C., Chen, X. P., & Chan, D. K. S. (1998). Scenarios for the Measurement of Collectivism and Individualism. *Journal of Cross-Cultural Psychology, 29,* 275–289.

Although it is through the lens of the metaphor "collectivism" that we are allowed to focus on group membership and patterns of relationships in Asian cultures, at the same time, we lose sight of other aspects of delicate cultural reasoning that underlie manifested behavior patterns.[35]

The essence of Chang's argument is that we cannot rely on single metaphorical distinctions such as individualism–collectivism if we really want to accurately describe and ultimately understand other cultures.

THE PANCULTURAL SELF

As mentioned above, in individualistic cultures, emphasis is placed on individual goals over group goals, values that benefit the self are championed, the self is promoted, and individuals are encouraged to pursue and develop their individual abilities and aptitudes. In these cultures, people are taught to be creative, self-reliant, competitive, and assertive. The *individual self* is the most fundamental basis for self-definition. In contrast, in collectivistic cultures, group goals take precedence over individual goals, values that serve the in-group are stressed, and people are not seen as isolated individuals but as interdependent with others. In these cultures, the *collective self* is the most fundamental basis of self-definition.

Yet a growing body of literature suggests that the individual self is pancultural—that is, that the individual self is more fundamental to self-definition across cultures than is the collective self. Constantine Sedikides and her colleagues have spent the past decade studying the idea that, across cultures, people are motivated to enhance and protect their self-worth. She and her associates maintain that two factors play a key role here—*self-enhancement* and *self-protection*. Self-enhancement refers to the idea that people desire to maintain and enhance positive self-views. Self-protection is conceptually the opposite—that is, to minimize negative self-views. Sedikides maintains that self-enhancement and self-protection significantly influence how people think, feel, and act in communicative situations across cultures.[36]

According to Sedikides, to preserve *self-enhancement,* individuals engage three communicative strategies: positivity embracement, favorable construals, and self-affirming reflections. Positivity embracement refers to those communicative tactics whereby people approach and interact with others who are likely to provide them with positive feedback. When the positive feedback is given, the individual then takes credit for it. For example, individuals approach and interact with people who think highly of them and ask for feedback when they expect a positive response. Another example of positivity embracement is attributing positive outcomes to personal–individual effort. For example, when students receive good grades, they assume it was due to their abilities. Favorable construal strategies involve individuals creating self-serving cognitions about the world around them. Sedikides argues that, during communication, most people compare themselves with others and believe they are better than average on important traits, and often interpret ambiguous feedback from others as flattering. For example, a student may believe that he or she is changing, growing, and improving as a student more than his or her peers. When faced with threats, however, individuals engage in self-affirming reflections. Here, individuals reflect on their past successes to counter possible threats. For example, a student might recall significant hardships he or she has overcome to achieve success in college.

On the other hand, during *self-protection* communication, the individual proactively prepares for negative feedback. For example, Sedikides asserts that people often self-handicap before potentially evaluative situations to provide an excuse for failure. They often attribute negative feedback to external causes, rather than to their own failures, and discount such feedback. For example, when students perform poorly on an exam, they may attribute it to poor instruction or to the exam being loaded with "trick questions."[37]

Considerable debate surrounds the idea of whether self-enhancement and self-protection motivation is equally forceful across cultures. Some scholars maintain that collectivistic values are in direct opposition to self-enhancement and self-protection—that the group is primary. Others maintain that self-enhancement and self-protection are universally held across cultures but are practiced differently according to specific cultural norms and values. Most of the current research suggests that both individualistic and collectivistic cultures sanction and even endorse self-enhancement and self-protection but via different means. Collectivism is just another way to promote the self. For example, in individualistic cultures of the West (i.e., the United States, Canada, Great Britain), it is accepted and tolerated to show off one's success. In Eastern cultures (e.g., Japan, Korea, China), it is accepted and tolerated to expect reciprocity based on seniority. In other words, in both types of cultures, a person's motivations for behavior and self-definition stem primarily from personal identity and an independent sense of self. Moreover, research demonstrates that on self-description tasks, people generate more aspects of their individual self than their collective self, regardless of their cultural individualism or collectivism. Some researchers have even suggested that social harmony—a primary value among collectivists—often serves as a means through which to accomplish individual goals. Other researchers have argued that collectivism is explainable not in terms of a fundamentally different cognitive organization of the self but because it is advantageous to the self in the long run. Still others maintain that in collectivistic cultures, individuals may temporarily sacrifice their self-interest for the group as long as they expect to receive rewards from the group eventually (e.g., being perceived as a good team member). Finally, in both individualistic and collectivistic cultures, self-enhancement is sanctioned through upward mobility, status seeking, and general promotions of the self. In both types of cultures, people engage in strategic efforts to self-enhance.[38]

Nao Oyama points out that collectivism has long been used to describe Japanese culture. But, as Oyama asserts, Japanese society is changing and Japanese values also have changed, especially since World War II. Oyama argues that the Japanese collectivistic orientation has been decreasing and that many Japanese now have an individualistic orientation. To be sure, collectivism remains as a cultural system in Japan, especially in decision making in companies or government and in cases of company loyalty or village exclusiveness, but such an expression of collectivism is sometimes just a means of achieving an individually oriented goal. In such circumstances, Oyama contends, seeming collectivistic is a false appearance produced by individually oriented people using collectivistic methods for the realization of personal goals. For example, to value hard work to get rich or to study hard to make a name for oneself indicates an individual orientation that depends on a social system. People are obedient to the social system as a means to get money or honor. In behavioral terms, obedience to a social system resembles the behavior of persons with a collective orientation, but the real value orientation underlying the behavior is individual. According to Oyama, this means that individualism and collectivism, at least as practiced and valued in Japan, are not so different.[39] As Lowell Gaertner, Constantine Sedikides, and Kenneth Graetz note,

Given a choice, however, most persons would opt to stay home rather than go to war, save their hard-earned money rather than pay taxes, and relax in the company of their favorite music than engage in community volunteer work. At the same time, most persons would cherish the protection of the group when attacked individually, seek the financial support of the group when experiencing individual financial troubles, and call on the aid of the community in times of individual disaster. The individual self is the primary basis for self-definition.[40]

AN INTERCULTURAL CONVERSATION:
THE PANCULTURAL SELF ON EXAMINATION DAY

In the following intercultural conversation, undergraduate students Gary, Karen, and Quan are discussing their performance on a recent exam. Gary and Karen are from the United States, and Quan is an exchange student from China.

Gary: Hey, Quan, we're walking over to the library. Want to join us?

Quan: Sure, thanks.

Karen: Guess what? Gary got an A on that exam.

Quan: That's great! Wow, Gary, you are so smart!

Gary: Yeah, I studied my butt off for that exam. That's why I did so well. How did you do, Quan?

Quan: I got an A, too. My parents will be so proud of me! They taught me good study habits. I can't wait to tell them of my success. I think the instructor is excellent as well. How did you do, Karen?

Karen: I got a D. I think the professor sucks, and I think a lot of the questions on that exam were pretty tricky. I think he just wants us to do poorly.

Gary: I don't know about that. I worked really hard to do well. I think I've become a pretty good student in the past few years. Maybe you just need to study more.

Karen: He just doesn't like me.

Quan: I have honored my parents. That is a very good thing in my country.

Notice how all three attribute their performance on the exam to different causes, but each can be seen as a dimension of self-enhancement or self-protection. In the conversation, Gary asks Quan to join him and Karen. Quan offers positive feedback to Gary, and Gary attributes his success on the exam to his study habits. Both are examples of positivity embracement. Quan attributes his success to his upbringing and the professor's excellent instruction, but he recognizes that the success is his own and feels good about himself. Honoring his parents brings him a great deal of personal satisfaction. The instructor and his parents have or will provide him with positive feedback. This is another example of positivity embracement. Karen, on the other hand, engages in self-protection by suggesting that her poor performance on the exam was not her fault but, rather, was due to poor instruction and tricky exam questions.

HIGH- AND LOW-CONTEXT COMMUNICATION

Human communication is dependent on the context in which it occurs. In addition to the verbal and nonverbal codes exchanged between interactants, the salient features of a communicative context include the cultural, physical, sociorelational, and perceptual environments (see Table 2.3).

Table 2.3   Human Communication Is Dependent on the Context in Which It Occurs

Contextual Features	Communication Decisions→Message
Culture (race, language)	Verbal choices
Physical environment (office, church)	Nonverbal choices
Sociorelational (superior/subordinate)	
Perceptual (attitudes, emotions)	

The cultural context includes, among myriad other variables, such features as individualism and collectivism. The physical environment includes the actual geographical location of the interaction (e.g., office, classroom, bedroom). The sociorelational environment encompasses the relationship between the interactants (e.g., superior/subordinate, teacher/student, husband/wife). The perceptual environment consists of the attitudes, motivations, and cognitive dispositions of the interactants. Each of these contexts provides a wealth of information to the interactants about how to communicate. Here's the important point: *The degree to which interactants focus on these contexts while communicating varies considerably from culture to culture.*

Depending on contextual features present during communication, some persons choose to focus more on the verbal codes than on the nonverbal elements, while others actively monitor the nonverbal elements of the context. Hall described the former as low context and the latter as high context. Hall asserted that

> a high-context (HC) communication or message is one in which most of the information is either in the physical context or is internalized in the person, while very little is in the coded, explicit, transmitted part of the message. A low-context (LC) communication is just the opposite; i.e., the mass of information is vested in the explicit code.[41]

Like individualism and collectivism, high–low context is best conceptualized along a cultural continuum (see Figure 2.2). No culture exists exclusively on one end of the continuum.

Figure 2.2   High- and low-context continuum.

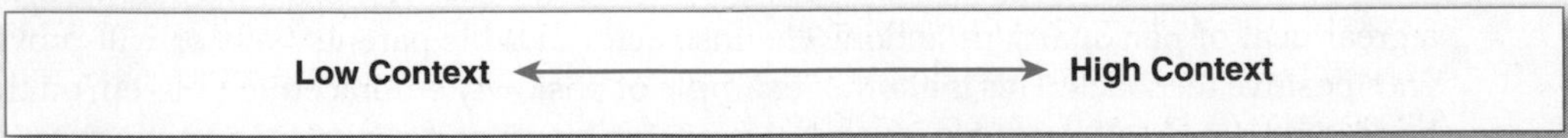

Low Context ⟵⟶ **High Context**

Characteristics of High- and Low-Context Cultures

Hall argued that the environmental, sociorelational, and perceptual contexts have an immense impact on communication. High-context cultures generally have restricted code systems. Users of a restricted code system rely more on the contextual elements of the communication setting for information than on the actual language code. In restricted-code cultures, communication is not general in content across individuals but is specific to particular people, places, and times. Within a high-context transaction, the interactant will look to the physical, sociorelational, and perceptual environment for information. Of particular importance is the social relationship between the interactants, especially their statuses. As Hall noted,

> Twins who have grown up together can and do communicate more economically (HC) than two lawyers in a courtroom during a trial (LC), a mathematician programming a computer, two politicians drafting legislation, two administrators writing a regulation, or a child trying to explain to his mother why he got into a fight.[42]

Because interactants in a high-context culture know and understand each other and their appropriate roles, words are not necessary to convey meaning. One acts according to one's role. Words and sentences may be collapsed and shortened. In this sense, restricted codes are not unlike local dialects, vernacular, or even jargon used by a well-defined group. Users of restricted codes interpret messages based on their accumulation of shared experiences and expectations.

Hall contended that persons communicating in high-context cultures understand that information from the physical, sociorelational, and perceptual environment already exists and need not be codified verbally. Therefore, high-context communication is fast, proficient, and gratifying. Unlike low-context communication, the burden of understanding in high-context communication rests with each interactant. The rules for communication are implicit, and communicators are expected to know and understand unspoken communication. High-context communication involves using and interpreting messages that are not explicit, minimizing the content of verbal messages, and being sensitive to the social roles of others. Although there are exceptions, many high-context cultures have collectivistic tendencies, including China, Japan, North and South Korea, Vietnam, and many Arab and African cultures.[43]

According to Hall, in a low-context transaction, the verbal code is the primary source of information. Low-context cultures generally rely on elaborated codes. Unlike users of restricted codes, users of elaborated codes rely extensively on the verbal code system for creating and interpreting meaning. Information to be shared with others is coded in the verbal message. Although persons in low-context transactions recognize the nonverbal environment, they tend to focus more on the verbal context. Moreover, the rules and expectations are explicitly outlined. Users of elaborated codes are dependent on words to convey meaning and may become uncomfortable with silence. In low-context transactions, the communicants feel a need to speak. People using low-context communication are expected to communicate in ways that are consistent with their feelings. Hence, low-context communication typically involves transmitting direct, explicit messages. Although there are exceptions, many low-context cultures are individualistic, including Switzerland, Germany, Scandinavia, the United States, France, and the United Kingdom.[44]

Communication Consequences of Low- and High-Context Cultural Orientations

Members of high- and low-context cultures communicate differently, especially with the use of silence. Charles Braithwaite argues that one of the fundamental components of cultural and linguistic competence is knowing how and when to use silence as a communicative tactic.[45] During a high-context communicative exchange, the interactants generally are content with silence because they do not rely on verbal communication as their main source of information. Silence, in fact, communicates mutual understanding. Much of the meaning in communication is expected to be interpreted by the receiver. In communicative exchanges between persons of differing status, the person with lower status may recognize the higher status of the other through silence. Steven Pratt and Lawrence Weider contend that many Native American tribes use silence as a way of recognizing "Indianness." A "real" Indian recognizes another real Indian with silence rather than speech. A recognizable Indian knows that neither he nor the others have an obligation to speak and that silence on the part of all conversants is permissible.[46] In her book on the contemporary Japanese woman, Sumiko Iwao writes that most Japanese feel that expressing especially personal or intimate details is best done nonverbally or intuitively—that is, without words. Iwao writes,

> There is an unspoken belief among the Japanese in general that putting deep feelings into words somehow lowers or spoils their value and that understanding attained without words is more precious than that attained through precise articulation.[47]

Unlike in high-context communication, during most low-context transactions, silence is uncomfortable. Persons who do not talk are often perceived negatively. When someone is quiet in a low-context transaction, others may suspect that something is amiss. Silence somehow communicates a problem. Low-context communicators are expected to be direct and to say what they think. Persons in low-context cultures typically separate the issue of communication from the person with whom they are interacting. A manager might say to an employee, "Don't take it personally," as he or she reprimands the person. High-context cultures, on the other hand, tend to see the topic of communication as intrinsic to the person. A person is seen as a role. If the issue is attacked, so is the person. This results in low-context cultures that deliver a direct style of communication, whereas a high-context person prefers indirectness typified by extreme politeness and discretion.

An Intercultural Conversation: High- and Low-Context Cultures

In the following exchange, Mr. Hutchinson is the head of Information Technology within his organization. Mr. Wong is lead computer programmer. Mr. Wong was born and raised in Malaysia, a high-context culture. The two are discussing when Mr. Wong will put a computer program into production. Note that Mr. Hutchinson's speech is direct and to the point, while Mr. Wong's is indirect and subtle. In simple frequency, Mr. Hutchinson uses four times as many words as Mr. Wong.[48]

Mr. Hutchinson:	The program looks good and passed the test run with only minor errors. When do you think you can put it into production? I don't see any production schedule here. The changes need to go into the system by the end of the month. Is that possible? When do you want to go with this?
Mr. Wong:	Maybe I should review the requirements.
Mr. Hutchinson:	The errors were minor. Quality Control needs to know when it will go into production. Let's set the production date now. Just tell me when you'll fix the errors. I'll tell QC.
Mr. Wong:	Perhaps I can e-mail you an estimate. I'll talk to the team.
Mr. Hutchinson:	Couldn't you just tell me when you'll have them fixed? Here, it's no big deal. (Hands Mr. Wong the program.) Don't they seem like easy fixes?
Mr. Wong:	(Looks at the program but says nothing—as if not hearing Mr. Hutchinson's suggestion.)
Mr. Hutchinson:	Mr. Wong? Just give me a date.
Mr. Wong:	Yes. Whenever you prefer is fine. (Hands the program back to Mr. Hutchinson.)
Mr. Hutchinson:	I don't need this. (Hands it back to Mr. Wong.) Well, it's got to go in by the first of next month. OK?
Mr. Wong:	Yes, that is fine.

In the above dialogue, Mr. Hutchinson misses the hint that Mr. Wong is unable to set a production date. When Mr. Wong indicates that setting a date is difficult and will require some expertise, he is indirectly telling Mr. Hutchinson that he is not in a position to make the decision on his own and would prefer to discuss it with the team. Mr. Wong further signals his discomfort by telling Mr. Hutchinson that he could e-mail him the date.

Mr. Hutchinson ignores Mr. Wong's status in the organization and further complicates the issue by handing Mr. Wong the program. Trying to avoid any disagreement, Mr. Wong simply asks Mr. Hutchinson to set the date for production and agrees to whatever he says.

Assessing High- and Low-Context Communication

Communication researcher Gudykunst and his colleagues have developed a survey designed to measure low- and high-context communication styles. The instrument that follows in Self-Assessment 2.2 is an adaptation of Gudykunst's scale.[49]

Self-Assessment 2.2

Low- and High-Context Communication Scale

Directions: Below are 32 statements regarding how you feel about communicating in different ways. In the blank to the left of each item, indicate the degree to which you agree or disagree with each statement. If you are unsure or think that an item does not apply to you, enter a 5 in the blank.

Strongly Disagree	1	2	3	4	5	6	7	8	9	Strongly Agree

_____ 1. I catch on to what others mean, even when they do not say it directly.

_____ 2. I show respect to superiors, even if I dislike them.

_____ 3. I use my feelings to determine whether to trust another person.

_____ 4. I find silence awkward in conversation.

_____ 5. I communicate in an indirect fashion.

_____ 6. I use many colorful words when I talk.

_____ 7. In an argument, I insist on very precise definitions.

_____ 8. I avoid clear-cut expressions of feelings when I communicate with others.

_____ 9. I am good at figuring out what others think of me.

_____ 10. My verbal and nonverbal speech tends to be very dramatic.

_____ 11. I listen attentively, even when others are talking in an uninteresting manner.

_____ 12. I maintain harmony in my communication with others.

_____ 13. Feelings are a valuable source of information.

_____ 14. When pressed for an opinion, I respond with an ambiguous statement/position.

_____ 15. I try to adjust myself to the feelings of the person with whom I am communicating.

_____ 16. I actively use a lot of facial expressions when I talk.

_____ 17. My feelings tell me how to act in a given situation.

_____ 18. I am able to distinguish between a sincere invitation and one intended as a gesture of politeness.

_____ 19. I believe that exaggerating stories makes conversation fun.

_____ 20. I orient people through my emotions.

_____ 21. I find myself initiating conversations with strangers while waiting in line.

_____ 22. As a rule, I openly express my feelings and emotions.

_____ 23. I feel uncomfortable and awkward in social situations where everybody else is talking except me.

_____ 24. I readily reveal personal things about myself.

_____ 25. I like to be accurate when I communicate.

_____ 26. I can read another person "like a book."

_____ 27. I use silence to avoid upsetting others when I communicate.

_____ 28. I openly show my disagreement with others.

_____ 29. I am a very precise communicator.

_____ 30. I can sit with another person, not say anything, and still be comfortable.

_____ 31. I think that untalkative people are boring

_____ 32. I am an extremely open communicator.

Scoring. Reverse your score for Items 4, 6, 7, 10, 16, 19, 21, 22, 23, 24, 25, 28, 29, 31, and 32. If your original score was 1, reverse it to a 9; if your original score was a 2, reverse it to an 8; and so on. After reversing the scores for those 15 items, simply sum the 32 items. Lower scores indicate low-context communication. Higher scores indicate high-context communication.

SOURCE: Reprinted from Gudykunst, Matsumoto, Ting-Toomey, Nishida, Kim, & Heyman, "The Influence of Cultural Individualism–Collectivism, Self Construals, and Individual Values on Communication Styles Across Cultures," in _Human Communication Research, 22,_ 1996, pp. 510–543. Reproduced with permission of John Wiley & Sons, Inc. via Copyright Clearance Center.

At this point in the chapter, you have been given the opportunity to assess your own level of individualism–collectivism and the degree to which your communication style is high or low context. Whatever the outcome on these surveys, one style is not better than the other; they are simply different. The goal is for you to have a better understanding of yourself and those persons with different cultural backgrounds. Individualism–collectivism and high/low context are two dominant ways cultures differ. But perhaps what guides cultural behavior more than anything else is the values held by large collectives.

VALUE ORIENTATIONS

In his seminal book on values, Milton Rokeach argues that

the value concept, more than any other, should occupy a central position across all social sciences. . . . It is an intervening variable that shows promise of being able to unify the apparently diverse interests of all sciences concerned with human behavior.[50]

Values affect intercultural communication. When people from different cultures come together to interact, their messages are guided by and reflect their fundamental value orientations. People who strongly value individuality will likely interact differently than will people who strongly value collectivism. An understanding of cultural value systems can help identify similarities and differences between people from different cultures, from which intercultural communication can proceed. Like culture, values are learned; they are not innate or universal. Rokeach argues that values guide us in the selection and justification of social behavior. Values prescribe what is preferred or prohibited. Values are the evaluative component of an individual's attitudes and beliefs. Values guide how we think about things in terms of what is right/wrong and correct/incorrect. Values trigger positive or negative emotions. Values also guide our actions.[51]

Well-known for his research on values, Shalom Schwartz asserts that values are concepts or beliefs that pertain to outcomes and behaviors, guide the selection and evaluation of behaviors, and are rank ordered according to their relative importance to the individual.[52] Although any individual probably has a unique set of values, there are also sets of values that are representative of a particular culture. Francis Hsu, an anthropologist who has lived much of his life in China and the United States, has outlined what he thinks are the nine basic values of Americans. His list was generated from his personal experiences, American literature and prose, social science research, and studies of criminal behavior in the United States.[53]

HSU'S POSTULATES OF BASIC AMERICAN VALUES

1. An individual's most important concern is self-interest, self-expression, self-improvement, self-gratification, and independence. This takes precedence over all group interests.

2. The privacy of the individual is the individual's inalienable right. Intrusion into it by others is permitted only by invitation.

3. Because the government exists for the benefit of the individual and not vice versa, all forms of authority, including government, are suspect. Patriotism is good.

4. An individual's success in life depends on acceptance among his or her peers.

5. An individual should believe in or acknowledge God and should belong to an organized church or other religious institution. Religion is good. Any religion is better than no religion.

6. Men and women are equal.

7. All human beings are equal.

8. Progress is good and inevitable. An individual must improve himself or herself (minimize efforts and maximize returns); the government must be more efficient to tackle new problems; institutions such as churches must modernize to make themselves more attractive.

9. Being American is synonymous with being progressive, and America is the utmost symbol of progress.

Most of the values listed above reflect America's individualistic tendencies. In addition, they echo our emphasis on equality (discussed later under "Power Distance") and our determination to push toward the future.

An interesting contrast to the values of America—an individualistic, low-context culture—are those of China—a collectivistic, high-context culture. A group of cross-cultural researchers calling themselves the Chinese Culture Connection (CCC) constructed a list of 40 dominant Chinese values. The CCC is an international network of social scientists under the direction of Michael Bond, a professor in the Department of Management and Marketing at Hong Kong Polytechnic University. The members of the CCC approached a number of Chinese social scientists and asked each of them to prepare a list of 10 fundamental and basic Chinese values. Although their procedure resulted in considerable overlap, they were able to eliminate redundancy by creating a master list of 40 values.[54]

THE CHINESE VALUE SURVEY

1. Filial piety (obedience to parents, respect for parents, honoring of ancestors)

2. Industry (working hard)

3. Tolerance of others

4. Harmony with others

5. Humbleness

6. Loyalty to superiors

7. Observation of rites and social rituals

8. Reciprocation of greetings, favors, and gifts

9. Kindness

10. Knowledge (education)

11. Solidarity with others

12. Moderation, following the middle way

13. Self-culturation

14. Ordering relationships by status and observing this order

15. Sense of righteousness

16. Benevolent authority

17. Non-competitiveness

18. Personal steadiness and stability

(Continued)

(Continued)

19. Resistance to corruption

20. Patriotism

21. Sincerity

22. Keeping oneself disinterested and pure

23. Thrift

24. Persistence

25. Patience

26. Repayment of both the good and evil that another person has caused you

27. A sense of cultural superiority

28. Adaptability

29. Prudence (carefulness)

30. Trustworthiness

31. Having a sense of shame

32. Courtesy

33. Contentedness with one's position in life

34. Being conservative

35. Protecting your "face"

36. A close, intimate friend

37. Chastity in women

38. Having few desires

39. Respect for tradition

40. Wealth

In related research, Jianxin Zhang and Michael Harris Bond affirmed the dominance of filial piety in China. They argue that filial piety surpasses all other cultural ethics in Chinese culture. Specifically, filial piety prescribes how children should behave toward their parents, living or dead, as well as toward their ancestors. Chinese children are taught to provide for their parents' material and mental well-being, perform ceremonial ancestral worship, ensure the continuity of the family line, and conduct themselves in a way that brings honor to and avoids shaming the family name. Zhang and Bond assert that Chinese filial piety extends beyond the limits of one's direct nuclear family. Chinese filial piety prescribes not only absolute parental authority over children but also, by extension, the authority of those senior in rank (i.e., age) over those junior in rank. Zhang and Bond maintain that Chinese filial piety influences myriad social behaviors—even in modern China, where Western, individualistic culture has been introduced.[55]

In their research on Chinese values in work organizations, Henry S. R. Kao and NG Sek-Hong discovered that the Chinese values of trust, fidelity, altruism, and unspecified obligations of reciprocity norms are an important source of strategic advantage, giving Chinese corporations resilience and flexibility to cope with change.[56] Researchers George Domino and Mo Therese Hannah argue that Chinese values are taught early and can be seen in the stories told by Chinese children. In comparison with stories told by American children, the Chinese stories demonstrated greater social orientation, greater emphasis on public shame, fewer interpersonal confrontations, more instances of teamwork, more concern for the role of authority, greater preoccupation with moral and ethical rectitude, more expressions of sorrow and happiness, fewer instances of physical aggression, and less economic orientation.[57]

Schwartz Theory of Basic Values

Schwartz, Professor Emeritus at the Hebrew University of Jerusalem, has studied human value systems for nearly 30 years and developed the Schwartz theory of basic human values. Schwartz's theory describes the nature of values and identifies characteristics common to all values and those that differentiate one value from another. Perhaps the most debated aspect of this theory is that Schwartz identifies 10 basic personal values that he argues are universal and recognized across cultures. These 10 values are considered universal because they are based on what Schwartz believes are three universal requirements of human existence: (a) the needs of individuals as biological organisms, (b) the fundamentals of coordinated social interaction, and (c) survival and welfare needs of groups. Schwartz's theory has been tested in a number of studies, and most of them reveal a remarkable consistency in these 10 values across the world's cultures.[58]

As we have seen in this chapter, scholars from across a wide range of academic disciplines have studied human value systems, and many of them tend to treat values as a way to distinguish and characterize the uniqueness of a particular culture. Schwartz argues that although his typology of 10 basic human values is universal, individuals and groups may differ significantly in terms of the relative importance of a specific value. Regarding the nature of values, Schwartz outlines six characteristics he believes are true for all values. First, Schwartz points out that values are beliefs linked to affect; that is, people are emotionally connected to values and become aroused (positively or negatively) if a value is triggered. Second, Schwartz maintains that values are linked to goals that motivate people to act. For example, people who value benevolence are prompted to help others in need. Third, values transcend (exceed or go beyond) specific actions and situations. The value of benevolence, for example, will motivate the individual at home, work, school, etc. Fourth, values serve as a standard or criteria, or a kind of barometer, for deciding what is good or bad, right or wrong. Fifth, an individual's values are ranked hierarchically. Individuals across cultures order and prioritize their values. Sixth, attitudes and behavior are typically motivated and driven by more than one value; that is, multiple values guide social action. Once again, Schwartz argues that these six features are true for all values, but what distinguishes one value from another is the type of goal or motivation it expresses.[59]

SCHWARTZ'S 10 BASIC HUMAN VALUES

1. *Self-direction:* The defining goal of this value type is independent thought and action. (Freedom, creativity, independence, choosing own goals, curiosity, self-respect)

2. *Stimulation:* The goal is derived from the need for variety and stimulation to maintain an optimal level of activation. Some of these needs are biological, while others are learned/cultural. (An exciting life, a varied life, daring)

3. *Hedonism:* The goal here is the need and motivation for pleasure. (Pleasure, enjoying life)

4. *Achievement:* The need and value of personal success and prestige. (Ambition, influence, capability, success, intelligence, self-respect)

5. *Power:* Attainment of social status. (Social power, wealth, authority, preserving my public image, social recognition)

6. *Security:* The goal here is the need for safety, harmony, and the stability of society and relationships. (National security, reciprocation of favors, family security, sense of belonging, social order, health, cleanliness)

7. *Conformity:* Restraint of actions, inclinations, and impulses. (Obedience, self-discipline, politeness, honoring of parents and elders)

8. *Tradition:* The value of religious rites, beliefs, and norms of behavior that, over time, are valued and passed on by a collective. (Respect for children, devotion, acceptance of my portion in life, humility, moderation)

9. *Benevolence:* The need and motivation for positive interaction and affiliation. (Helpfulness, responsibility, forgiveness, honesty, loyalty, mature love, true friendship)

10. *Universalism:* The value of understanding, appreciation, tolerance, and protection for the welfare of all people and for nature. (Equality, unity with nature, wisdom, a world of beauty, social justice, broad-mindedness, protection of the environment, a world at peace)

In earlier typologies, Schwartz included an 11th value of spirituality. Here, the defining goal is meaning, coherence, and inner harmony. In a number of studies, however, this value did not appear consistently across cultures.

As mentioned above, while individuals and groups may differ in how they rank the 10 values, most studies demonstrate remarkable consistency among cultures and their rankings of these values. Studies by numerous scholars have gathered data from hundreds of diverse geographic, cultural, linguistic, religious, age, gender, and occupational groups from more than 80 countries. These studies show that benevolence, universalism, and self-direction are typically ranked highest, whereas power and stimulation are ranked lowest.[60]

In trying to explain why these 10 values are pancultural (across cultures), Schwartz points to two factors: (a) human nature and (b) maintaining societies and social order. Simply put, values that conflict with human nature are unimportant across most cultures. But, according to Schwartz, the social function of values is to motivate and control the actions of group members for the sake of the group. Here, two points are critical. First, Schwartz contends that values function as guides for individuals and their social behavior in that they mitigate the necessary and constant monitoring of the individual by the group. Second, these values prescribe specific behaviors that are appropriate and discourage those that thwart the goals of the group. For example, Schwartz maintains that the high ranking of benevolence across cultures stems from the importance of cooperative social relations in the family—where children learn the values of the larger society and culture that surrounds them. Universalism (which often ranks second among cultures) also motivates positive social interactions, especially among those perceived as different, such as in school, work, or social settings. Self-direction values cultivate creativity and innovation, which satisfy individual needs without necessarily hurting the group. Schwartz notes that power often ranks low among cultures because it often leads to exploitation of others. On the other hand, power is in the top 10 because it motivates people to work for group interests, such as seeking out a high-ranking political or religious position whose function is to help the group.[61]

Kluckhohn and Strodtbeck's Value Orientations

In the early 1960s, Florence Kluckhohn and Fred Strodtbeck developed the concept of value orientations. They argued that every culture has universal problems and conditions that must be addressed. For example, every culture must deal with the natural environment. All cultures must feed themselves. All cultures must face the issues of child rearing. For a given culture, however, there are a limited number of solutions to these problems. These possible solutions are motivated by the values of the culture. Initially, Kluckhohn and Strodtbeck created five sets of value orientations.[62] Several years later, communication researchers John Condon and Fathi Yousef extended the set to a total of 25 value orientations. Condon and Yousef organized the value orientations around six dominant themes: the self, the family, society, human nature, nature, and the supernatural.[63]

The Condon and Yousef set of value orientations provides a structure and vocabulary that can be used to compare cultures. Although there are exceptions, many of the values on the left of the continuum are representative of individualistic, low-context cultures, while those on the right are representative of collectivistic, high-context cultures (see Table 2.4).

| Table 2.4 | The Condon and Yousef Set of Value Orientations |

	Individualistic Low Context		Collectivistic High Context
THE SELF			
1. Individualism	Individualism	Individuality	Interdependence
2. Age	Youth	Middle years	Old age
3. Sex	Equality of sexes	Female superiority	Male superiority
4. Activity	Doing	Being-in-becoming	Being

(Continued)

(Continued)

	Individualistic Low Context		Collectivistic High Context
THE FAMILY			
1. Relational orientations	Individualistic	Collateral	Lineal
2. Authority	Democratic	Authority centered	Authoritarian
3. Positional role behavior	Open	General	Specific—prescribed
4. Mobility	High mobility	Phasic mobility	Low mobility—stasis
SOCIETY			
1. Social reciprocity	Independence	Symmetrical—obligatory	Complementary—obligatory
2. Group membership	Many—brief membership	Balanced	Few—prolonged membership
3. Intermediaries	Few	Specialist only	Essential
4. Formality	Informal	Selective formality	Pervasive formality
5. Property	Private	Utilitarian	Communal
HUMAN NATURE			
1. Rationality	Rational	Intuitive	Irrational
2. Good/evil	Good	Mixture	Evil
3. Happiness/pleasure	Happiness as goal	Inextricable bond of happiness and sadness	Life is mostly sad
4. Mutability	Change, growth, learning	Some change	Unchanging
NATURE			
1. Relationship between humans and nature	Humans dominate nature	Harmonious	Nature dominates humans
2. Ways of knowing nature	Abstract	Circle of induction and deduction	Specific—direct
3. Structure of nature	Mechanistic	Spiritual	Organic
4. Concept of time	Future	Present	Past
THE SUPERNATURAL			
1. Relationship between humans and the supernatural	Humans as God	Pantheism	Humans controlled by supernatural
2. Meaning of life	Physical/material goals	Intellectual goals	Spiritual goals
3. Providence	Good is unlimited	Balance of good and misfortune	Good in life is limited
4. Knowledge of cosmic order	Order is comprehensible	Faith and reason	Mysterious and unknowable

SOURCE: Based on Condon, J. C., & Yousef, F. (1975). *An Introduction to Intercultural Communication.* New York: Macmillan.

The Self

In all cultures, people develop their self-identity. How that identity is fostered is influenced by the culture's values. For example, people in individualistic societies, such as the United States, tend to view their accomplishments and failures personally. Conformity is viewed negatively. Hsu notes that in China, however, conformity and cooperation are highly valued. In the United States, a person is seen as a unique individual and strives for independence from others. When individuals succeed or win, they receive a great deal of attention and adulation, as in the case of winning an Olympic gold medal or an Academy Award. The individual is "put on a pedestal," sometimes literally. Likewise, when individuals lose, they are often left to suffer alone. No one wants to be seen with a loser. Whether on the top or on the bottom, the individual experiences intense emotions. Hsu contends that strong emotions are unavoidable because they are concentrated in one individual. The Chinese, however, are interdependent with others, and for them, responsibility and accountability are shared and divided among the group members. If the group wins, everyone in the group wins; there is no "most valuable player," so to speak. Therefore, the intense emotions experienced by winning or failing are tempered and moderated because they are shared.[64]

The second variation on the self continuum is age. Western, individualistic, low-context cultures tend to value youth. Conversely, old age is valued in many cultures, such as Nigeria, where it is associated with wisdom. According to Philip R. Harris and Robert T. Moran, in Nigeria the elderly are respected because they have much experience and can pass on family history and tradition. Harris and Moran suggest that when conducting business with Nigerians, a company would be wise to send an older person to meet with prospective business partners, as this will show a certain amount of respect for Nigeria's emphasis on age.[65]

The third variation on the self is activity. Americans identify themselves in terms of their activities, usually professions and occupations. Condon and Yousef hold that many English names indicate "doers," such as Baker, Smith, and Carpenter. In the United States, people are often asked about what they "do" for a living. Some non-Western cultures emphasize *being*, a form of self-actualization. In this view, life is an organic whole; it is human to embrace life and to become one with the universe and oneself.[66]

The Family

Familial relationships differ across cultures. Harris and Moran write that in Nigeria, for example, the family is the core group of society. Nigerians value their family lineage through the male head of the household. A Nigerian is known by his or her family lineage and may have privileges and responsibilities based on family name. Furthermore, marriage is seen as a way of producing more children to contribute to this lineage. If one's spouse is sterile, it is grounds for divorce. Nigerians also practice polygamy. Wives are often acquired through the payment of a bride price to the bride's parents.[67]

Positional role behavior within families refers to how strictly roles are prescribed among family members. The Guatemalan Ladinos (a term used to refer to people born through interracial relationships or those who have Spanish and Indian blood) define a man's and woman's role within the family quite differently. Mike Keberlein, who grew up in Guatemala, argues that *machismo* is a Spanish concept that deals mainly with how male and female roles are performed in the home. Ladinos view the men as protectors and providers and women as child rearers and homemakers. Children are taught early by their mother to recognize their responsibilities as men and women. A boy as young as 5 years old may be sent to work in the fields. A girl might start household chores at the same age, where she is taught to care for younger children of the house and to cook. Young boys are expected never to cry or show signs of pain, whereas young girls are taught to show emotion whenever appropriate.[68]

Society

According to Condon and Yousef, social reciprocity refers to the mutual exchanges people make in their dealings with others. What is perceived as a relatively innocuous request in one country may be interpreted quite seriously in others. In the United States, a request for a favor (e.g., "Can I borrow your car?") may imply no necessary reciprocity. In other cultures, one is required to return favors and obligations in kind. Equal exchanges are expected and obligatory.[69]

The second value orientation, group membership, differs greatly among individualistic and collectivistic cultures. According to Condon and Yousef, members of individualistic cultures tend to join many groups throughout their lifetimes, yet their affiliation with any particular group may be quite brief. The group is subordinate to the individual's needs. In the United States, for example, people join political groups, social groups, hobby groups, occupational groups, self-help groups, fraternal groups, and so on. In collectivistic cultures, people tend to belong to fewer groups (e.g., family and occupational) but belong to those groups for a lifetime.[70]

An intermediary is a go-between; intermediaries are more common in collectivistic than in individualistic cultures. Many Chinese prefer to work through an intermediary. The concept of *mian-zi,* or "face," is a critical ingredient for Chinese. The Chinese believe that respect for others binds society together. *Mian-zi* is a sort of social status, or how a person is ranked in relation to others. This is sometimes referred to as one's "face." A person's face is determined by such things as wealth and power. Chinese are very conscious of their face as well as the face of others. The higher in rank a person is, the more critical the concern with face. In business dealings and in personal relationships, it is important to the Chinese that they maintain face and avoid offending the face of others. Hence, it is difficult for the Chinese to be straightforward and open in their daily interactions with others. Intermediaries are, therefore, essential in both personal and business relationships. Accordingly, the notion of losing face means that an individual loses his or her social position or prestige in front of others. When local senior executives perceive the local staff to be incompetent, they may feel that they risk "losing face" vis-à-vis headquarters' management and expatriates. To save face, these executives may think about quitting or involving an intermediary.[71]

Human Nature

The human nature orientation deals with how cultures perceive human character and temperament. In Western cultures such as the United States, people are viewed as essentially rational. American children are taught to "use their heads" when making decisions. Americans frequently tell their friends to "stop being so emotional," as if being emotional implied some character flaw. Japanese children, on the other hand, are often taught to follow their intuition or to lead with their hearts. Condon and Yousef note that in the United States, happiness is viewed as a practical goal, even the primary goal—hence the popular song titled "Don't Worry, Be Happy." Moreover, the Declaration of Independence states that people "are endowed by their creator with certain inalienable rights, that among these are life, liberty, and the pursuit of happiness." Other societies and cultures view happiness and sadness as inseparable, as in the yin–yang philosophy of many Asian cultures. A Chinese proverb reads, "If a man's face does not show a little sadness, his thoughts are not too deep." Another one reads, "One should not miss the flavor of being sick, nor miss the experience of being destitute."[72]

Nature

In the United States, high school students learn about the structure of nature in their biology, geography, and physics classes, among others. Students learn about things they may never actually see, such as the structure of DNA. The models they see are not literal reproductions but, rather, dramatic abstractions. Much of the education taught in the United States is based on abstract concepts and constructs. Condon and Yousef maintain that in other cultures, perhaps those with little formal education, what a person knows about nature is learned through direct experience. Many Western cultures view nature as mechanistic, meaning that nature is structured much like a machine or clock. The brain, for example, is explained using computer analogies. Models of DNA look like double helixes. The organic orientation likens nature to a plant, where nature is seen as an organic whole that is interdependent with all other natural forces.[73]

The Supernatural

Condon and Yousef assert that a culture's perspective on the cosmos reflects its philosophy about its people's relationship with the supernatural and spiritual world. In many Western cultures, the supernatural is studied almost scientifically. Scientists study the structure of space and seek, through scientific means, to find the origins of the universe. We send out satellites equipped with printed messages and recordings in an (perhaps vain) attempt to communicate with extraterrestrials. Most Western cultures believe that the order of the cosmos is knowable. Conversely, other cultures view the cosmos with a great deal of fear and uncertainty. Condon and Yousef point to a farmer in Peru who relies on the phases of the moon and the cycles of the seasons to tell him when to plant or harvest his fields. The farmer thinks of the cosmos with a great deal of superstition and fear. To him, these mysteries are unexplainable.[74]

The organization of the value orientations presented above is neither mutually exclusive nor exhaustive. They are representative of the kinds of values held by cultures and the differences in those values. They also serve as a starting point for researchers to compare and contrast the myriad cultures that cohabit the planet.

POWER DISTANCE

According to Geert Hofstede, while many cultures declare and even legislate equality for their members, all cultures must deal with the issue of human inequality. A fundamental tenet expressed in the beginning of the Declaration of Independence, the document on which the United States was founded, states that "we hold these truths to be self-evident, that all men are created equal." In the United States, we generally try to treat others as equal, in both our personal and professional lives. Although some cultures, such as the United States, affirm equality for their members, some form of inequality exists in virtually every culture. Inequality can occur in areas such as prestige, wealth, power, human rights, and technology, among others. Issues of inequality fall within the rubric of what Hofstede calls "power distance." In his landmark survey research, Hofstede defined power distance as "the extent to which the less powerful members of institutions and organizations within a country expect and accept that power is distributed unequally."[75] Power distance can be seen in families, in bureaucracies, and even in friendships. Inequality of power within organizations is inevitable and desirable in many cases for organizations to function effectively. For example, military organizations are defined by power distance.

Hofstede categorizes cultures as possessing either large or small power distance. Cultures with a smaller power distance emphasize that inequalities among people should be minimized and that there should be interdependence between less powerful and more powerful people. In cultures with small power distance (e.g., the United States, Canada, Austria), family members are generally treated as equal and familial decisions are reached democratically. According to Hofstede, in small–power-distance schools, teachers expect a certain amount of initiative and interaction with students. The overall educational process is student oriented. In class, students are expected to ask questions and perhaps even challenge their teachers. In organizations, decentralization is popular, where subordinates engage in participative decision making. The organizational power hierarchy is mostly for convenience, where the persons who occupy powerful roles may change regularly. In fact, workers are expected to try to "climb the ladder of success" to more power and prestige. In this sense, persons in small–power-distance cultures may recognize "earned" power—that is, power people deserve by virtue of their drive, hard work, and motivation. Moreover, small–power-distance cultures tend to resent those whose power is decreed by birth or wealth (i.e., positional power).[76]

Hofstede maintains that in cultures with a larger power distance, inequalities among people are both expected and desired. Less powerful people should be dependent on more powerful people.

In larger–power-distance cultures (e.g., the Philippines, Mexico, India), children are expected to be obedient. In many such cultures, there is a strict hierarchy among family members in which typically the father rules authoritatively, followed by the eldest son and moving down the ladder by age and sex (see Figure 2.3). In educational settings, teachers, especially older teachers, are treated as parents—with respect and honor. Students who disobey may be punished severely. In the workplace, power is usually centralized, and workers and bosses are treated unequally. In many large–power-distance cultures, Hofstede observed, workers are generally uneducated and superiors are entitled to special privileges and status—in some cultures, by law.[77]

There appears to be a direct link between power distance and the latitude of the country. In a study conducted at 40 universities in the United States, Peter A. Andersen and his colleagues found a strong correlation between latitude and authoritarianism. Residents in the northern U.S. states were less authoritarian than those in the southern states. The population of a country may be another predictor of power distance. Generally, larger cultures tend to have larger power distance (see Table 2.5). As the size of any group increases, it becomes unwieldy and difficult to manage informally.[78]

| Figure 2.3 | In many cultures, there is a strict hierarchy among family members. |

| Table 2.5 | Small- and Large–Power-Distance Cultures |

Small–Power-Distance Cultures	Large–Power-Distance Cultures
Austria	Malaysia
Denmark	Guatemala
New Zealand	Panama
Ireland	Philippines
Sweden	Mexico
Norway	Venezuela
Finland	Ecuador
Switzerland	Indonesia
Great Britain	India
Germany	Brazil

Cultures with large and small power distance may value different types of power. Large–power-distance cultures tend to emphasize positional power. Positional power is based on formal authority (e.g., family rank). Persons with positional power have control over rewards, punishments, and information. Small–power-distance cultures recognize and respect earned power. Earned power is based on an individual's accomplishments, hard work, and effort.

STUDENT VOICES ACROSS CULTURES

Power Distance

My name is Ahmed I. Alshaya, and I am from Riyadh, Saudi Arabia. I graduated from St. Norbert College with a major in business administration.

Saudi Arabia is a large–power-distance country for reasons concerned with favorability of outcomes. The culture focuses on the outcomes that do not disturb the harmony of the people. Power distance in Saudi Arabia is defined by age and sex. There is a hierarchical structure in almost all families. In a typical Saudi family, because of this hierarchical structure, the father is the head of the house. He is the one in charge of the house in all aspects. The father has some responsibilities to his house. For example, the father is responsible for teaching his offspring moral traits. That is, the family must obey the father and treat him with respect and honor. The role then goes to the elder son if the father is not available. There is, of course, dependence on the one in charge, and usually the family looks to him in making decisions.

Moving to a larger scale, society plays a big role in shaping the people of Saudi Arabia. The elderly are always seen as being wise and capable of leading the community to prosperity. Usually, people are expected to treat the elderly with respect. For example, at a time of conflict, the elderly will always step in to resolve a problem, and all the parties involved will have to acknowledge the issue and show some respect for the decision made. The "self-face" and the "other-face" are concerns for the people involved. The "face" is a concern because, if not properly maintained, it will bring disgrace to the family. The "face" is recognized in many ways. For example, it is present during all social gatherings; the elderly are always treated with respect because the host and his sons must save their "self-face" by making the elderly feel comfortable.

In the workplace, Saudi is considered to be power-distance oriented, especially in the relationship between subordinates and their employees. There is a strong hierarchical structure. Employers must be treated with respect because they have authority in the organization. Different organizations have different approaches, but most commonly, employees do not participate in the decision-making role.

Measuring Power Distance

If we know the position of a culture on the power-distance scale relative to our own culture, then we have a starting point from which to proceed in our understanding of that culture. In large–power-distance cultures, subordinates are extremely submissive, whereas in small–power-distance cultures, subordinates are confrontational. Power distance tells us about dependence relationships in a given culture. In those countries where a small power distance is observed (e.g., Austria, Norway), dependence is limited. Workers in these cultures prefer managers who consult with them in decision making. Here, subordinates are generally comfortable approaching and interacting with their superiors. In cultures with large power distance (e.g., Malaysia, Mexico, India), subordinates are considerably dependent on superiors.

Self-Assessment 2.3

Power Distance Scale

Directions: Below are 10 statements regarding issues we face at work, in the classroom, and at home. Indicate in the blank to the left of each statement the degree to which you (1) strongly agree, (2) agree, (3) are unsure, (4) disagree, or (5) strongly disagree with the statement. For example, if you strongly agree with the first statement, place a 1 in the blank. Work quickly and record your initial response.

_____ 1. Within an organization, employees should feel comfortable expressing disagreements to their managers.

_____ 2. Within a classroom, students should be allowed to express their points of view toward a subject without being punished by the teacher/professor.

_____ 3. At home, children should be allowed to openly disagree with their parents.

_____ 4. The primary purpose of a manager is to monitor the work of the employees to make sure they are doing their jobs appropriately.

_____ 5. Authority is essential for the efficient running of an organization, classroom, or home.

_____ 6. At work, people are more productive when they are closely supervised by those in charge.

_____ 7. In problem-solving situations within organizations, input from employees is important.

_____ 8. Generally, employees, students, and children should be seen and not heard.

_____ 9. Obedience to managers, teachers, and parents is good.

_____ 10. Managers, teachers, and parents should be considered equal to their workers, students, and children.

Scoring: For Items 4, 5, 6, 8, and 9, reverse your responses. That is, if your original response was a 1, reverse it to a 5. If your original response was a 2, reverse it to a 4, and so on. Once you have reversed your responses for these items, sum your 10 responses. This sum is your power-distance score. Lower scores equal smaller power distance.

SOURCE: ©Geert Hofstede B.V. Quoted with permission.

Communication and Power Distance

Power distance affects the verbal and nonverbal behavior of a culture. Several studies have investigated power distance and communication during conflict. In their research, Tom R. Tyler, E. Allan Lind, and Yuen J. Huo found that power distance influences the way people react to third-party authorities in conflict situations. Specifically, they found that when making evaluations of authorities, persons in small–power-distance cultures placed more value on the quality of their treatment by authorities. In contrast, those with larger–power-distance values focused more strongly on the favorability of their outcomes. Tyler, Lind, and Huo suggest that the degree to which authorities can gain acceptance for themselves and their decisions through providing dignified, respectful treatment is influenced by the cultural values of the disputants. Specifically, they found that dispute resolution methods, such as mediation, are more likely to be effective among those who have small–power-distance values.[79]

In another study, Peter B. Smith, Shaun Dugan, Ark F. Peterson, and Wok Leung examined how managers handled disagreement with their subordinates. Their results showed that the larger the power distance, the more frequent the reports of out-group disagreements; the smaller the power distance, the more likely managers were to ask peers to handle disagreements and to use subordinates to handle disagreements. The authors conclude that in small–power-distance cultures, managers minimize status differences during conflict and rely on peers and subordinates to assist in mediating conflict.[80]

Stella Ting-Toomey has examined power distance and the concepts of *face* and *facework* in conflict situations. Ting-Toomey and others argue that persons in all cultures have face concerns. Face represents an individual's sense of positive self-image in the context of communication. According to Ting-Toomey, everyone, in all cultures, has face concerns during conflict. *Self-face* is the concern for one's own image, *other-face* is concern for another's image, and *mutual-face* is concern for both parties. *Facework* is used to manage these face concerns during conflict. Ting-Toomey's research has shown that small–power-distance cultures have a greater self-face concern, have lesser other- and mutual-face concerns, use more dominating facework, and use less avoiding facework.[81]

Other research has investigated how power distance affects reactions to messages about alcohol warnings. Anna Perea and Michael D. Slater examined the responses of Mexican American and Anglo young adults to four televised drinking and driving warnings. The messages were manipulated into large– and small–power-distance appeals by attributing or not attributing them to the surgeon general—that is, an authority with power. Anglos (small power distance) rated the warnings without the surgeon general as more believable than warnings with the surgeon general; the opposite was true for Latinos (large power distance).[82]

Student–teacher relationships exist in virtually every culture. Generally, teachers possess more legitimate and expert power than do their students (see Figure 2.4). In an interesting examination of student–teacher relationships in cultures with small (i.e., Britain) and large (i.e., China) power distance, Helen Spencer-Oatey found that Chinese students reported a larger power differential between themselves and their Chinese teachers than did the British students with their British teachers. Yet the Chinese reported their relationships with their teachers to be interpersonally closer than did the British. Moreover, the Chinese students reported that the power differential between them and their teachers was acceptable. Consistent with their value of filial piety, one Chinese student commented that one should "treat teachers as you would treat your elders." On the other hand, the British students were significantly less accepting of the power differential between them and their teachers, even though that differential was small. One British student reported that teachers "certainly have these powers, but shouldn't have."[83]

Figure 2.4 In many cultures (especially those with large power distance), teachers may hold more power over students than do parents.

In another interesting study, Bond and his colleagues found that persons in large–power-distance cultures respond differently to verbal insults than do persons in small–power-distance cultures. In their comparison of Chinese and American students, they found that the Chinese were less critical of an insulter as long as the insulter had higher status than the in-group. Americans, on the other hand, made no distinction as a function of the insulter's status.[84]

Power distance also affects the nonverbal behavior of a culture. In many large–power-distance cultures, persons of lower status are taught not to give direct eye contact to a person of higher status. Indirect eye contact from a subordinate signals to the superior that the subordinate recognizes his or her lower status. In large–power-distance cultures, when a person of high status hands something to a person of lower status (e.g., a book), the lower status person will often use both hands to receive the item, again recognizing his or her lower status. Peter A. Andersen, Michael Hecht, Gregory D. Hoobler, and Maya Smallwood have observed that many large–power-distance cultures prohibit interclass dating, marriage, and contact. They also suggest that persons of lower power must become skilled at decoding nonverbal behavior and that persons of lower status must show only positive emotions to those of higher status. Moreover, in large–power-distance cultures, persons of lower status smile more in an effort to appease those of higher status.[85]

An Intercultural Conversation: Large- and Small-Power-Distance Cultures

Different power-distance orientations manifest themselves in interaction. In the dialogue below, Jim Neuman is a U.S. high school exchange student in Guatemala. Coming from a smaller–power-distance culture, Jim is accustomed to interacting with his teachers. Raising one's hand in a U.S. classroom is not only acceptable but encouraged. In Guatemala, a larger–power-distance culture, the classroom is teacher centered. In Mr. Gutierrez's classroom, there is to be strict order, with Mr. Gutierrez initiating all communication. Teachers are to be treated with deference.

Mr. Gutierrez: This morning, I will be discussing some points about Guatemala's geography. Guatemala is the northernmost country of Central America. (Jim Neuman raises his hand.) To the north it borders the countries of El Salvador and Honduras. To the west, its natural border is the Pacific Ocean. In the east is another natural border, the Atlantic Ocean, as well as the country of Belize.

Jim Neuman: (Raising his hand and waving it slightly) Mr. Gutierrez?

Mr. Gutierrez: Guatemala is called the "Land of the Eternal Spring." It has all the same kinds of natural land forms as Mexico, but they are— (Jim Neuman interrupts.)

Jim Neuman: Mr. Gutierrez, I have a question.

Mr. Gutierrez: Jim, stop interrupting, please.

Jim Neuman: May I ask a question?

Mr. Gutierrez: No! If you continue to disobey, I will punish you! Be quiet!

In the above dialogue, Jim does not understand Mr. Gutierrez's harsh reprimand. Coming from a small–power-distance culture, Jim recognizes that teachers have more power than students but does not see their power as absolute. Jim sees himself as an active participant in the class. After all, for most of his life Jim's teachers have encouraged him to speak up in class. Mr. Gutierrez, on the other hand, sees the classroom as his domain, one he rules absolutely. By raising his hand, Jim demonstrates his insolence toward Mr. Gutierrez. To some extent, a certain degree of power distance is essential if cultures are to survive. Legitimate power is a necessity of civil life. Yet independence from power, liberation, and freedom of choice are politically attractive alternatives. Perhaps the ideal situation is one where individual families operate with internally driven, large power distances while the wider cultural milieu restricts overbearing, omnipotent, and intimidating governments.

UNCERTAINTY AVOIDANCE

William Gudykunst and Young Yun Kim state that communicating with someone from an unknown culture can be uncomfortable because such situations are replete with uncertainty and unpredictability. When uncertainty is high, anxiety is usually high, and communication can be difficult and awkward. This may account for why some people avoid interacting with people from other cultures. By reducing uncertainty, however, anxiety can be reduced, which, in turn, facilitates effective and successful communication. Although uncertainty is probably a universal feature of initial intercultural communication, one's level of tolerance for uncertainty and ambiguity varies across cultures. In addition, argue Gudykunst and Kim, the communicative strategies for reducing uncertainty also vary across cultures. Persons in high-context cultures, for example, look to the environmental, sociorelational, and perceptual contexts for information to reduce uncertainty. People in low-context cultures tend to rely on verbal information-seeking strategies, usually by asking lots of questions.[86]

Hofstede asserts that although the extent to which an individual experiences uncertainty and the subsequent strategies for reducing it may be unique to that person, a general orientation toward uncertainty can be shared culturally. According to Hofstede, tolerance for uncertainty is learned through cultural socialization. Hofstede notes that a culture's technology, system of laws, and religion are markers for how that culture addresses and attempts to avoid or reduce uncertainty. For example, some kinds of technology help a culture manage natural uncertainty (e.g., weather), systems of law are designed to prevent and account for behavioral uncertainties (e.g., crime), and religion can help a culture cope with supernatural uncertainty (e.g., death). A culture's technology, law, and religion are ingrained in the individual through socialization, education, and occupation. Hence, they lead to collective patterns of tolerance for ambiguity and uncertainty.[87]

Uncertainty avoidance is the degree to which the members of a particular culture feel threatened by uncertain or unknown situations. Hofstede contends that this feeling is expressed through nervous stress and as a felt need for predictability and for written and unwritten rules. Cultures possess either a weak or strong uncertainty-avoidance orientation. In cultures with a weak uncertainty-avoidance orientation, uncertainty is seen as a normal part of life, where each day is accepted as it comes. The people are comfortable with ambiguity and are guided by a belief that what is different is curious. In school settings, students are comfortable with open-ended learning situations and enjoy classroom discussion. In the workplace, time is needed only as a guide, not as a master. Precision and punctuality are learned because they do not come naturally. Workers are motivated by their achievements and personal esteem or belongingness. There is also a high tolerance for innovative ideas that may conflict with the norm.[88]

Conversely, cultures with a strong uncertainty-avoidance orientation sense that uncertainty in life is a continuous threat that must be fought. Life can be stressful, where a sense of urgency and high anxiety are typical. Hofstede maintains that strong–uncertainty-avoidant cultures are guided by the belief that what is different is dangerous. Uncertainty-avoidant cultures evade ambiguity in most situations and look for structure in their business organizations, home life, and relationships. At school, students are most comfortable in structured environments. The teachers are supposed to have all the right answers. On the job, time is money; punctuality and precision are expected. There is generally resistance to innovative ideas, and workers are motivated by job security.[89]

A THEORY OF UNCERTAINTY ORIENTATION

Related to Hofstede's concept of uncertainty avoidance is the theory of uncertainty orientation. According to this variation of Hofstede's ideas, some individuals are considered uncertainty oriented and others certainty oriented. Uncertainty-oriented individuals have a weak uncertainty-avoidance tendency, while certainty-oriented individuals have a strong uncertainty-avoidance tendency. Uncertainty-oriented persons' preferred method of handling uncertainty is to seek out information and engage in activity that will directly resolve the uncertainty. These people try to understand and discover aspects of the self and the environment about which they are uncertain.

Certainty-oriented people, on the other hand, develop a self-regulatory style that circumvents uncertainty. Given the choice, persons who are certainty oriented will undertake activity that maintains clarity; when confronted with uncertainty, they will tend to rely on others or on heuristic devices rather than more direct methods of resolving uncertainty (see Figure 2.5).

Figure 2.5   Uncertainty and certainty orientations.

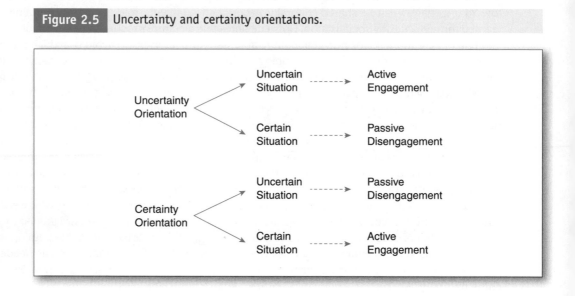

Generally, Eastern cultures have a preference for certainty, whereas Western cultures are uncertainty oriented (see Table 2.6). The tendency to be individualistic or self-oriented in Western populations exists because uncertainty-oriented people like to find out new information about the self. The more personally relevant or uncertain the situation, the more uncertainty-oriented persons will be actively engaged in it. Certainty-oriented people, however, are more group oriented, as the group provides a clear standard for norms and behavior, a standard that can be embraced by the certainty oriented. Western societies tend to be more uncertainty oriented because of their self-oriented and individualistic approaches to life, compared with people in Eastern societies, who, in turn, should be more certainty oriented as a function of their heavy reliance on groups.[90]

Table 2.6	Certainty- and Uncertainty-Oriented Cultures

Certainty-Oriented Cultures	Uncertainty-Oriented Cultures
Japan	United States
Guatemala	Canada
Portugal	New Zealand
Peru	Sweden
El Salvador	Ireland
Panama	Great Britain
Chile	Denmark
Spain	South Africa
Uruguay	Norway

AN INTERCULTURAL CONVERSATION:
WEAK AND STRONG UNCERTAINTY AVOIDANCE

One's uncertainty-avoidance orientation may manifest itself in interaction in any number of ways. In the dialogue presented below, Kelly and Keiko are discussing a dinner invitation. Kelly, from the United States, possesses a relatively weak uncertainty-avoidance index, while Keiko, from Japan, comes from a culture with a relatively strong uncertainty-avoidance index.

Keiko: Hey, Kelly, let's do something tonight.

Kelly: All right.

Keiko: Please come over to my house, and I'll cook dinner for you.

Kelly: I have invited some friends over to my house for dinner tonight, but I don't know if they're coming.

Keiko: Well . . . as soon as you know if they're coming, let me know.

Kelly: I won't know until tonight.

Keiko: What time?

Kelly: I won't know until they call me. They'll probably call later this afternoon.

Keiko: How will you know whether or not to cook enough for everyone?

Kelly: Oh, I'll make up something on the spot. I like to cook. I'll whip up something fast.

Keiko: But . . . what if they don't come? Won't they call and let you know?

Kelly: No . . . if they don't come, I'll know that something else came up. I'll let you know as soon as I can.

Keiko: Maybe we should plan my dinner for some other night.

In the above dialogue, Keiko is confused by Kelly's easygoing attitude toward the evening's plans. Coming from a strong uncertainty-avoidant culture, Keiko would prefer to plan ahead to avoid uncertainty and prepare her script for the evening. Kelly, on the other hand, is perfectly comfortable making plans based on how the evening progresses. Without a plan, how will Keiko know how to act? Although the feelings associated with uncertainty are personal and subjective, they can be shared by whole cultures. Although anxiety creates the same physiological responses in humans, what triggers anxiety and one's level of tolerance for it is learned. A culture's orientation toward uncertainty can be found in its families, schools, and institutions. But uncertainty avoidance ultimately manifests in human interaction.

CHAPTER SUMMARY

In the contextual model of intercultural communication, culture is the largest context, surrounding all the other contexts. This chapter has presented the paradox of culture. On one hand, culture is amorphous; it is shapeless, vague, and nebulous. Most of us are not aware of its influence on our daily behaviors. On the other hand, culture is arguably the strongest influence on an individual's cognitive, affective, and behavioral choices. Over the past few decades, anthropologists, psychologists, and sociologists have isolated several dimensions of cultural variability by which cultures can be compared. This chapter has focused on five of these dimensions, including the extent to which we place individual goals over those of the group (i.e., individualism) or the degree to which we see ourselves as members of a group first, then as individuals (i.e., collectivism). Another dimension is high–low context, which refers to the extent to which we gather information from the physical, social, and psychological context (i.e., high context), or the extent to which we gather information from the verbal code (i.e., low context). One of the most influential features of our lives is our value orientation. A culture's values guide its decisions as to what is right or wrong, decent or indecent, moral or immoral. Cultures also differ regarding the extent to which people accept and expect that power is distributed unequally (i.e., large power distance) or believe that people are inherently equal (i.e., small power distance). And, finally, cultures differ in the extent to which people accept and tolerate uncertainty and unpredictability in their lives (i.e., weak uncertainty avoidance) or the extent to which uncertainty should be fought and conquered (i.e., strong uncertainty avoidance). These dimensions provide a starting point for our future examination of intercultural communication.

Visit the student study site at www.sagepub.com/neuliep6e for e-flashcards, web quizzes, web resources, and more.

DISCUSSION QUESTIONS

1. Do you feel that you belong to an individualistic or collectivistic culture? Why? What are the signs?

2. What are some of the ways you use high-context communication? What are some of the ways you use low-context communication? Which do you prefer?

3. Is your relationship with your professors indicative of large or small power distance?

4. Is your relationship with your parents indicative of large or small power distance?

5. If you have no plans for the upcoming weekend, does that make you feel anxious, or are you comfortable with not knowing? Depending on your answer, are you certainty or uncertainty oriented?

ETHICAL CONSIDERATIONS WITHIN THE CULTURAL CONTEXT

If you were born and raised in the United States, you are probably relatively individualistic, low context, small power distance, and have a weak uncertainty-avoidance tendency. Seeing the various dimensions of cultural variability discussed in this chapter, consider the following situations and how you might address them.

1. A Saudi working in the United States wakes up ill. He sends his younger brother to work for him that day. The U.S. employer sends the brother home. What happened?

   The Saudi has not yet learned that in the United States, relatives usually cannot substitute for each other. Perhaps in other cultures, it is acceptable to have one's siblings or even friends fill in on the job. If the job is done, what difference does it make? What would you do? How would you handle the situation?

2. You are at a social gathering and meet Dr. Dinesh Mammen, a local physician from India who has been living and practicing medicine in the United States for many years. You meet his wife, who has her bachelor's degree in biology and a master's degree in chemistry. You ask about her career and what she does for a living. Dr. Mammen pauses, smiles, and asserts that she stays home and takes care of his needs. How do you react? Do you think Mrs. Mammen should be following a career path related to her college degrees?

KEY TERMS

collectivism   51

high context   67

horizontal collectivism   60

horizontal individualism   60

individualism   50

low context   67

power distance   82

uncertainty avoidance   89

vertical collectivism   60

vertical individualism   60

NOTES

1. Hall, E. T. (1959). *The Silent Language*. Greenwich, CT: Fawcett, p. 39.

2. Keesing, R. M. (1974). Theories of Culture. In B. J. Siegel (Ed.), *Annual Review of Anthropology* (pp. 73–97). Palo Alto, CA: Annual Reviews.

3. Rosenberg, M. (2011, March 2). *China's One Child Policy: One Child Policy in China Designed to Limit Population Growth*. Retrieved from http://geography.about.com/od/populationgeography/a/onechild.htm

4. Avant, G. R., & Knutson, K. P. (1993). Understanding Cultural Differences: Janteloven and Social Conformity in Norway. *Et Cetera, 49,* 449; Yurkovich, D., Pliscott, K., & Halverson, R. (1996). *The Norwegian Culture.* Unpublished student manuscript, St. Norbert College, De Pere, WI.

5. Triandis, H. C. (1990). Cross-Cultural Studies of Individualism and Collectivism. In J. J. Berman (Ed.), *Nebraska Symposium on Motivation: 1989* (pp. 41–133). Lincoln: University of Nebraska Press; Triandis, H. C. (1993). Collectivism and Individualism as Cultural Syndromes. *Cross Cultural Research, 27,* 155–180; Triandis, H. C. (1995). *Individualism and Collectivism.* Boulder, CO: Westview; Triandis, H. C. (2001). Individualism–Collectivism and Personality. *Journal of Personality, 69,* 907–924.

6. Oyserman, D., Coon, H. M., & Kemmelmeier, M. (2002). Rethinking Individualism and Collectivism: Evaluation of Theoretical Assumptions and Meta-Analyses. *Psychological Bulletin, 128,* 3–72.

7. Shulruf, B., Hattie, J., & Dixon, R. (2005). Development of a New Measurement Tool for Individualism and Collectivism. *Journal of Psychoeducational Assessment, 25,* 385–401.

8. Triandis, *Individualism and Collectivism;* Triandis, Individualism–Collectivism and Personality.

9. Shulruf, Hattie, & Dixon, Development of a New Measurement Tool for Individualism and Collectivism; Triandis, *Individualism and Collectivism;* Triandis, Individualism–Collectivism and Personality.

10. Oyserman, Coon, & Kemmelmeier, Rethinking Individualism and Collectivism; Triandis, *Individualism and Collectivism;* Triandis, Individualism–Collectivism and Personality.

11. Triandis, *Individualism and Collectivism;* Triandis, Individualism–Collectivism and Personality.

12. Oyserman, Coon, & Kemmelmeier, Rethinking Individualism and Collectivism.

13. Hsu, F. L. K. (1986). *Americans and Chinese: Passage to Differences.* Honolulu: University of Hawai'i Press; Triandis, *Individualism and Collectivism.*

14. Triandis, Cross-Cultural Studies of Individualism and Collectivism.

15. Green, E. G. T., Deschamps, J.-C., & Páez, D. (2005). Variation of Individualism and Collectivism Within and Between 20 Countries. *Journal of Cross-Cultural Psychology, 36,* 321–339.

16. Hui, C. H. (1988). Measurement of Individualism–Collectivism. *Journal of Research in Personality, 22,* 17–36.

17. Oyserman, Coon, & Kemmelmeier, Rethinking Individualism and Collectivism.

18. Green, Deschamps, & Páez, Variation of Individualism and Collectivism Within and Between 20 Countries.

19. Yu, A.-B., & Yang, K.-S. (1994). The Nature of Achievement Motivation in Collectivist Societies. In U. Kim, H. C. Triandis, C. Kâğitçibaşi, S.-C. Choi, & G. Yoon (Eds.), *Individualism and Collectivism: Theory, Method, and Applications* (pp. 239–250). Thousand Oaks, CA: Sage.

20. Oyserman, Coon, & Kemmelmeier, Rethinking Individualism and Collectivism.

21. Imada, T. (2010). Cultural Narratives of Individualism and Collectivism: A Content Analysis of Textbook Stories in the United States and Japan. *Journal of Cross-Cultural Psychology, 41,* 1–16.

22. Fischer, R., Ferreira, M. C., Assmar, E., Redford, P., Harb, C., Glazer, S., et al. (2009). Individualism–Collectivism, as Descriptive Norms: Development of a Subjective Norm Approach to Culture Measurement. *Journal of Cross-Cultural Psychology, 40,* 187–213.

23. Pirttilä-Backman, A. M., Kassea, B. R., & Ikonen, T. (2004). Cameroonian Forms of Collectivism and Individualism. *Journal of Cross-Cultural Psychology, 35,* 481–498; Sagy, S., Orr, E., Bar-On, D., & Awwad, E. (2001). Individualism and Collectivism in Two Conflicted Societies: Comparing Israeli-Jewish and Palestinian-Arab High School Students. *Youth Society, 33,* 3–30.

24. This dialogue is adapted from a scene in Copeland, L. (Producer). (1983). *Managing the Overseas Assignment* [Motion picture]. San Francisco: Copeland Griggs.

25. Vandello, J. A., & Cohen, D. (1999). Patterns of Individualism and Collectivism Across the United States. *Journal of Personality and Social Psychology, 77*(2), 279–292.

26. Ibid.

27. Triandis, *Individualism and Collectivism;* Triandis, Individualism–Collectivism and Personality.

28. Hsu, *Americans and Chinese: Passage to Differences;* Triandis, *Individualism and Collectivism.*

29. Triandis, *Individualism and Collectivism;* Triandis, Individualism–Collectivism and Personality.

30. Gudykunst, W. B., Matsumoto, Y., Ting-Toomey, S., Nishida, T., Kim, K. S., & Heyman, S. (1994, July). *Measuring Self-Construals Across Cultures.* Paper presented at the International Communication Association Convention, Sydney, Australia; Gudykunst, W. B., Matsumoto, Y., Ting-Toomey, S., Nishida, T., Kim, K. S., & Heyman, S. (1996). The Influence of Cultural Individualism–Collectivism, Self Construals, and Individual Values on Communication Styles Across Cultures. *Human Communication Research, 22,* 510–543.

31. Oyserman, Coon, & Kemmelmeier, Rethinking Individualism and Collectivism.

32. Shulruf, Hattie, & Dixon, Development of a New Measurement Tool for Individualism and Collectivism.

33. Singelis, T. M., Triandis, H. C., Bhawuk, D. P. S., & Gelfand, M. J. (1995). Horizontal and Vertical Dimensions of Individualism and Collectivism: A Theoretical

and Measurement Refinement. *Cross-Cultural Research, 29,* 240–275; Triandis, Cross-Cultural Studies of Individualism and Collectivism.

34. McCann, R. M., Honeycutt, J. M., & Keaton, S. A. (2010). Toward Greater Specificity in Cultural Value Analyses: The Interplay of Intrapersonal Communication Affect and Cultural Values in Japan, Thailand, and the United States. *Journal of Intercultural Communication Research, 39*(3), 157–172; Singelis et al., Horizontal and Vertical Dimensions of Individualism and Collectivism.

35. Chang, H.-C. (1996). *"Collectivism" or "Competitive Bidding": An Alternative Picture of Chinese Communication.* Paper presented at the annual convention of the Speech Communication Association, San Diego, CA, p. 10.

36. Hepper, E. G., Sedikides, C., & Cai, H. (2013). Self-Enhancement and Self-Protection Strategies in China: Cultural Expressions of a Fundamental Human Motive. *Journal of Cross-Cultural Psychology, 44*(1), 5–23; Sedikides, C., & Alicke, M. D. (2012). Self-Enhancement and Self-Protection Motives. In R. M. Ryan (Ed.), *Oxford Handbook of Motivation* (pp. 303–322). New York: Oxford University Press; Sedikides, C., Gaertner, L., & Toguchi, Y. (2003). Pancultural Self-Enhancement. *Journal of Personality and Social Psychology, 84,* 60–79.

37. Ibid.

38. Chang, H., & Holt, R. (1991). More Than a Relationship: Chinese Interaction and the Principle of Kuanhis. *Communication Quarterly, 39,* 251–271; Gaertner, L., Sedikides, C., Vevea, J. L., & Iuzzini, J. (2002). The "I," the "We," and the "When": A Meta-Analysis of Motivational Primacy in Self-Definition. *Journal of Personality and Social Psychology, 83,* 574–591; Mortenson, S. T. (2005). Clarifying the Link Between Culture and Self-Construal Through Structural Equation Models. *Journal of Intercultural Communication Research, 34,* 1–22; Oyama, N. (1990). Some Recent Trends in Japanese Values: Beyond the Individual–Collective Dimension. *International Sociology, 5,* 445–459; Sedikides et al., Pancultural Self-Enhancement; Voronov, M., & Singer, J. A. (2002). The Myth of Individualism–Collectivism: A Critical Review. *Journal of Social Psychology, 142*(4), 461–480; Yamaguchi, S. (1994). Collectivism Among the Japanese: A Perspective From the Self. In U. Kim, H. C. Triandis, C. Kâğitçibaşi, S. H. Choi, & G. Yoon (Eds.), *Individualism and Collectivism: Theory, Method, and Applications* (pp. 175–188). Thousand Oaks, CA: Sage.

39. Oyama, Some Recent Trends in Japanese Values.

40. Gaertner, L., Sedikides, C., & Graetz, K. (1999). In Search of Self-Definition: Motivational Primacy of the Individual Self, Motivational Primacy of the Collective Self, or Contextual Primacy? *Journal of Personality and Social Psychology, 76,* 5–18.

41. Hall, E. T. (1976). *Beyond Culture.* Garden City, NY: Anchor Press/Doubleday, p. 79.

42. Ibid.

43. Ibid.

44. Ibid.

45. Braithwaite, C. A. (1990). Communicative Silence: A Cross-Cultural Study of Basso's Hypothesis. In D. Carbaugh (Ed.), *Cultural Communication and Intercultural Contact* (pp. 321–328). Hillsdale, NJ: Erlbaum.

46. Weider, D. L., & Pratt, S. (1990). On Being a Recognizable Indian Among Indians. In D. Carbaugh (Ed.), *Cultural Communication and Intercultural Contact* (pp. 45–64). Hillsdale, NJ: Erlbaum.

47. Iwao, S. (1993). *The Japanese Woman: Traditional Image and Changing Reality.* Cambridge, MA: Harvard University Press, p. 98.

48. Although different, the model for this dialogue is adapted from Storti, C. (1994). *Cross-Cultural Dialogues: 74 Brief Encounters With Cultural Differences.* Yarmouth, ME: Intercultural Press.

49. Gudykunst et al., The Influence of Cultural Individualism–Collectivism, Self Construals, and Individual Values on Communication Styles Across Cultures.

50. Rokeach, M. (1973). *The Nature of Human Values.* New York: Free Press, p. 3.

51. Ibid.

52. Schwartz, S. H. (1992). Universals in the Content and Structure of Values: Theoretical Advances and Empirical Tests in 20 Countries. In M. P. Zanna (Ed.), *Advances in Experimental Social Psychology* (Vol. 25, pp. 1–66). San Diego, CA: Academic Press.

53. Hsu, F. L. K. (1969). *The Study of Literate Civilizations.* New York: Holt, Rinehart, & Winston; Hsu, F. L. K. (1970). *Americans and Chinese: Reflections on Two Cultures and Their People.* Garden City, NY: Doubleday; Hsu, *Americans and Chinese: Passage to Differences;* Seelye, H. N. (1993). *Teaching Culture Strategies for Intercultural Communication.* Lincolnwood, IL: National Textbook Company.

54. Chinese Culture Connection. (1987). Chinese Values and the Search for Culture-Free Dimensions of Culture. *Journal of Cross-Cultural Psychology, 18,* 143–164.

55. Zhang, J., & Bond, M. H. (1998). Personality and Filial Piety Among College Students in Two Chinese Societies: The Added Value of Indigenous Constructs. *Journal of Cross-Cultural Psychology, 29,* 402–417.

56. Kao, H. S. R., & Sek-Hong, N. (1995). Chinese Values in Work Organization: An Alternative Approach to Change and Development. *Journal of Human Values, 1,* 173–189.

57. Domino, G., & Hannah, M. T. (1987). A Comparative Analysis of Social Values of Chinese and American Children. *Journal of Cross-Cultural Psychology, 18,* 58–77.

58. Schwartz, S. H. (1994). Are There Universal Aspects in the Content and Structure of Values? *Journal of Social Issues, 50,* 19–45; Schwartz, S. H. (2012). An Overview of the Schwartz Theory of Basic Values. *Online Readings in Psychology and Culture, 2*(1). Retrieved from http://dx.doi.org/10.9707/2307-0919.1116; Schwartz, S. H., & Boehnke, K. (2004). Evaluating the Structure of Human Values With Confirmatory Factor Analysis. *Journal of Research in Personality, 38,* 230–255; Schwartz, S. H., Cieciuch, J., Vecchione, M., Davidov, E., Fischer, R., Beierlein, C., et al. (2012). Refining the Theory of Basic Individual Values. *Journal of Personality and Social Psychology, 103,* 663–688.

59. Ibid.

60. Ibid.

61. Ibid.

62. Condon, J. C., & Yousef, F. (1975). *An Introduction to Intercultural Communication.* Indianapolis, IN: Bobbs-Merrill; Kluckhohn, F., & Strodtbeck, F. (1961). *Variations in Value Orientations.* Evanston, IL: Row, Peterson.

63. Condon & Yousef, *An Introduction to Intercultural Communication;* Hsu, *Americans and Chinese: Passage to Differences.*

64. Hsu, *Americans and Chinese: Reflections on Two Cultures and Their People;* Hsu, *Americans and Chinese: Passage to Differences.*

65. Harris, P. R., & Moran, R. T. (1996). *Managing Cultural Differences* (4th ed.). Houston, TX: Gulf.

66. Condon & Yousef, *An Introduction to Intercultural Communication.*

67. Harris & Moran, *Managing Cultural Differences.*

68. Keberlein, M. (1993). *A Cultural Profile of the Guatemalan Ladinos.* Unpublished student manuscript, St. Norbert College, De Pere, WI.

69. Condon & Yousef, *An Introduction to Intercultural Communication.*

70. Ibid.

71. De Menthe, B. (1992). *Chinese Etiquette and Ethics in Business.* Lincolnwood, IL: NTC; Zhang, Y., George, J. M., & Chan, T.-S. (2006). The Paradox of Dueling Identities: The Case of Local Senior Executives in MNC Subsidiaries. *Journal of Management, 32,* 400–425.

72. Condon & Yousef, *An Introduction to Intercultural Communication.*

73. Ibid.

74. Ibid.

75. Hofstede, G. (1980). *Culture's Consequences: International Differences in Work-Related Values.* Beverly Hills, CA: Sage; Hofstede, G., Hofstede, G. J., & Minkov, M. (2010). *Cultures and Organizations: Software of the Mind.* New York: McGraw-Hill.

76. Ibid.

77. Ibid.

78. Andersen, P. A., Hecht, M. L., Hoobler, G. D., & Smallwood, M. (2003). Nonverbal Communication Across Cultures. In W. B. Gudykunst (Ed.), *Cross-Cultural and Intercultural Communication* (pp. 73–90). Thousand Oaks, CA: Sage; Andersen, P. A., Lustig, M. W., & Andersen, J. F. (1990). Changes in Latitude, Changes in Attitude: The Relationship Between Climate and Interpersonal Communication Predispositions. *Communication Quarterly, 38,* 291–311; Lustig, M. W., & Koester, J. (2003). *Intercultural Competence.* Boston: Allyn & Bacon.

79. Tyler, T. R., Lind, E. A., & Huo, Y. J. (2000). Cultural Values and Authority Relations: The Psychology of Conflict Resolution Across Cultures. *Psychology, Public Policy, and Law, 6*(4), 1138–1163.

80. Smith, P. B., Dugan, S., Peterson, M. F., & Leung, K. (1998). Individualism–Collectivism and the Handling of Disagreement: A 23 Country Study. *International Journal of Intercultural Relations, 22,* 351–367.

81. Oetzel, J., Ting-Toomey, S., Chew-Sanchez, M. I., Harris, R., Wilcox, R., & Stumpf, S. (2003). Face and Facework in Conflicts With Parents and Siblings: A Cross-Cultural Comparison of Germans, Japanese, Mexicans, and U.S. Americans. *Journal of Family Communication, 3,* 67–93; Ting-Toomey, S., & Oetzel, J. G. (2003). Cross-Cultural Face Concerns and Conflict Styles. In W. B. Gudykunst (Ed.), *Cross-Cultural and Intercultural Communication* (pp. 127–147). Thousand Oaks, CA: Sage.

82. Perea, A., & Slater, M. D. (1999). Power Distance and Collectivistic/Individualistic Strategies in Alcohol Warnings: Effects by Gender and Ethnicity. *Journal of Health Communication, 4,* 295–310.

83. Spencer-Oatey, H. (1997). Unequal Relationships in High and Low Power Distance Societies: A Comparative Study of Tutor–Student Role Relations in Britain and China. *Journal of Cross-Cultural Psychology, 28,* 284–302.

84. Bond, M. H., Wan, K.-C., Leung, K., & Giacalone, R. A. (1985). How Are Responses to Verbal Insult Related to Cultural Collectivism and Power Distance? *Journal of Cross-Cultural Psychology, 16,* 111–127.

85. Andersen et al., *Nonverbal Communication Across Cultures.*

86. Gudykunst, W. B., & Kim, Y. Y. (1997). *Communicating With Strangers: An Approach to Intercultural Communication.* New York: McGraw-Hill.

87. Hofstede, *Cultures and Organizations: Software of the Mind.*

88. Ibid.

89. Ibid.

90. Shuper, P. A., Sorrentino, R. A., Otsubo, Y., Hodson, G., & Walker, A. M. (2004). A Theory of Uncertainty Orientation: Implications for the Study of Individual Differences Within and Across Cultures. *Journal of Cross-Cultural Psychology, 35,* 460–480.

C · H · A · P · T · E · R   3

The Microcultural Context

Microcultural Context

Cultural Context

For those of us who live in/between, being required, on the one hand, to cast off our cultural selves in order to don the worldview and ethos of an alien culture, on the other hand to cast off the influences of the alien culture as a means of purification and identification is more than a personal dilemma; it is always and most of all a condition of living in/between.

—Richard Morris[1]

Within most cultures, there are groups of people who differ from the general societal culture in some custom, habit, or practice. These groups are sometimes called minorities, subcultures, or co-cultures. In this book, the term microculture is used to refer to those identifiable groups of people who share the set of values, beliefs, and behaviors of the macroculture, possess a common history, and use a common verbal and nonverbal symbol system. In some way, however, the microculture varies from the larger, often dominant cultural milieu. Most microcultural groups are made up of individuals who have much in common with the larger macroculture yet are bonded together by similar experiences, traits, values, or, in some cases, histories. Hence, the term *microculture* includes different types of groups that could be classified by age, class, geographic region, sexual preference, disability (e.g., the deaf), ethnicity, race, size, or even occupation. Most people, regardless of culture, are likely members of some kind of microcultural group.

Microcultures can be different from the larger culture in a variety of ways, often because of race or ethnicity. In the United States, for example, about 65 % of the population is classified as

White or Caucasian.[2] In this context, African Americans, Hispanics, and Hmong might be considered microcultural groups. Microcultures can also differ from the larger culture on account of language or religion. For example, Protestants, Catholics, and Jews might be considered microcultural groups. Finally, persons might be classified as members of microcultures because of their behavioral practices. Persons who use drugs are often said to belong to a "counter-" or "drug" culture, not because of their race, ethnicity, or religion but because they use drugs. Gays or lesbians could be considered a microculture because of their sexual orientation.

In any culture, microcultural groups often develop their own language for communicating outside the dominant or majority culture's context or value system. Indeed, deaf persons, who communicate using sign language, can be considered a microculture. Though not always, microcultural groups generally have less power than the majority or "macro" culture. The majority group's power may be legal, political, economic, or even religious. The group with the most power is considered the dominant or majority group, while the less powerful groups have been known as minority groups. Sociologist Richard Schaefer argues that the term *minority group* is a misnomer, however, in that it does not refer to the relative size of a group. According to Schaefer, a minority group is a subordinate group whose members have significantly less power and control over their own lives than do members of the dominant or majority group.[3] Although defined as a minority, such groups may actually be larger (in population) than the majority group. A classic example is South Africa. From 1948 to 1994, Whites, who were greatly outnumbered by Blacks, ruled in South Africa under the political system of apartheid. In many countries colonized by Europeans, the indigenous people outnumbered the dominant Europeans. And in parts of the United States, certain ethnic/cultural groups outnumber the "dominant" group.

The term *subculture* is sometimes used to refer to microcultural groups. Like *minority group,* the term *subculture* carries negative connotations. By definition, *sub-* means "beneath," "below," and "inferior." The perspective of this book is that no cultural group is beneath or below any other cultural group. To be sure, some cultures are subordinate to (i.e., have less power than) other groups, but such groups should not be considered inferior. Hence, for the reasons cited above, the term *microcultural group* has been chosen as the most appropriate label for these groups.

MICROCULTURAL GROUP STATUS

In many cultures, including the United States, microcultural group status is determined by one's membership in sex, racial, ethnic, or religious groups. Schaefer notes that social scientists generally recognize five characteristics that distinguish microcultural groups from the dominant culture. The first characteristic is that members of the group possess some physical or cultural trait that distinguishes them from others. Two obvious physical properties that distinguish one group from another are skin color and sex. In the United States, for example, Blacks and women are considered minorities (even though women constitute about 51% of the population). White males are considered the most powerful political and economic group in the United States. Blacks are also considered a minority in Brazil, which depended on slave trading much more than did the United States. In fact, Brazil imported 8 times the number of African slaves brought to the United States.[4]

Other traits that can distinguish a microcultural group include language or distinctive dress habits. A microcultural group in Jamaica is the Rastafarians. According to Leonard E. Barrett, the Jamaican Rastafarian movement is the largest, most identifiable indigenous group in Jamaica. Rastas are recognizable by their dreadlock hair and unique dress habits. Barrett argues that their appearance is the most distinguishing mark of the Rastafarians.[5] Regardless of culture, the dominant group decides, perhaps arbitrarily, on what characteristics afford a group its microcultural status. Such traits vary considerably across cultures.

The second distinguishing characteristic is that minority group/microcultural membership is usually not voluntary. Though not always, people are generally born into their microculture. For example, people cannot choose to be of a certain race, ethnicity, or gender. Although people can choose their religion, most people are born into a religion and find it difficult to leave. In tracing its history, Schaefer notes that the roots of the violence in Northern Ireland are based in religion. Northern Ireland is two-thirds Protestant and one-third Catholic. The Catholics in Northern Ireland, a minority in both numbers and power, complain of inadequate housing and education, low income, and high unemployment. They often blame the Protestant majority for their problems. Armed conflict has been the result. Pittu D. Laungani notes that a unique feature of India's society is the caste system—that is, a rigid social hierarchy. In India, one is born into a given caste level, and it is virtually impossible to move from one caste level to another.[6]

The third property that distinguishes a microcultural group from the macroculture is that microcultural group members generally practice endogamy (i.e., marrying within the ingroup). In many cultures, the dominant group staunchly discourages or even prohibits exogamy (i.e., marrying outside one's own group). Ethnologist Suzan Ilcan of the University of Windsor writes that majority groups believe that endogamy strengthens familial ties, preserves family property through inheritance, and upholds cultural and group traditions. Ilcan's work has focused on marital practices in Turkey, where endogamous marriages are viewed as a family or community affair. According to Ilcan, in the village of Sakli in the northwestern region of Turkey, spousal selection and all aspects of marriage are controlled by certain members of the family. Couples have little to do with the arrangements. Moreover, any meaningful romance between unmarried persons is not valued. Love and mutual attraction are expected to come after marriage and, even then, are not considered necessities. In Sakli, people are considered suitable marriage partners based on the compatibility of their families. Familial reputation and comparable economic and social classes are the crucial elements of a marriage.[7] In cultures such as those of Pakistan, China, India, and Laos, among others, endogamous marriages are often arranged.

The fourth characteristic that distinguishes a microcultural group from the dominant group is that the group members are aware of their subordinate status. Because they know they are less powerful within a particular culture, some microcultural groups are very cohesive. In the United States, for example, Blacks have gained significant political and economic strength and are arguably the most powerful microcultural group in the country.

Finally, perhaps the most disturbing aspect of microcultural group membership is that such groups often experience unequal treatment from the dominant group in the form of segregation and discrimination.[8]

MUTED MICROCULTURAL GROUPS

Another type of power that most microcultural groups lack is linguistic power—that is, the power of language. In all cultures, language is the vehicle for representing and expressing experience. And the experiences and perceptions of subordinate microcultural groups are often different from those of the dominant cultural group. For example, microcultural groups often are not able to communicate as freely as the dominant group does. In the United States, for example, historically, women and Blacks could not vote or join the armed services. Only since 1994 have Black South Africans been allowed to vote in their country; for decades, they had no legal voice or representation.[9]

In many cultures, the subordinate microcultural groups do not contribute to the construction of the language of the dominant group. In this sense, the language of a particular culture does not benefit its members equally. Yet the language of the dominant group may not provide the words and symbols representative of the microcultural group's perceptions and experiences. Thus, because such groups are forced to communicate within the dominant mode of expression, they become "muted." In essence, the language of the dominant cultural group, which is the preferred language, contributes to the microcultural group's subordination. This idea is known as the muted group theory.[10]

The manifestation of the muted group theory is that microcultural groups' speech and writing are not valued by the dominant cultural group. Moreover, microcultural groups experience difficulty expressing themselves fluently within the dominant mode of expression; that is, they may not speak the same language as the dominant group; hence, "micro–macro" interaction is difficult. However, because microcultural groups must communicate within the dominant mode, they must achieve some level of linguistic competence to survive. The same is not true of the dominant group, however. In fact, the dominant cultural group experiences more difficulty than microcultural groups in understanding those groups' communication, because the dominant group is not required to learn the microcultural groups' codes. Indeed, the dominant group often considers the communication style of a microcultural group substandard or inferior and rejects it as a legitimate form of communication.

Shirley Weber contends that microcultural groups may respond to the dominant mode of expression in two ways. Some will refuse to live by the standards set forth by the dominant group and will try to change the dominant mode of expression. In the United States, for example, the replacement of words such as *chairman* with simply *chair* or *mailman* with *mail carrier* is demonstrative of this phenomenon. Another way subordinate groups respond is by using their own private language. They create symbols that are not understood or used by the dominant group. They use their own language to express their unique experiences. Weber argues that sometimes the language of the subordinate group serves as a political statement that the microcultural group has not relinquished or abandoned its political or social identity. The group's ability to sustain a living language indicates that the members have control over a certain aspect of their lives and are determined to preserve their culture. As Weber notes, one's language is a model of that culture's adjustment to the world.[11]

Many social scientists consider the hip-hop/rap music generation a microcultural group that has been muted by mainstream culture. Christopher Tyson argues that hip-hop/rap has been the defining African American cultural movement in the United States over the past 35 years.[12] Terri Adams and Douglas Fuller of Howard University point out that rap music emerged as an artistic cultural expression of urban African American youth in the Bronx, New York, in the late 1970s. They describe rap as the poetry of the youth who are often disregarded as a result of their race and class status—that is, as members of a microcultural group. Adams and Fuller maintain that rap has gone through a number of phases and has been used as a primary outlet for microcultural groups to express a variety of ideas, feelings, and emotions. They argue that hope, love, fear, anger, frustration, pride, violence, and misogyny (i.e., hatred of or strong prejudice against women) have all been expressed through the medium of rap.[13]

As most college students know, rap is a fast, rhythmical, and accentuated singing and speaking style. Tyson contends that rap music reflects the growing flux of nonconformity among young African Americans (and, now, other microcultural groups) in mainstream culture and the backlash against middle-class values.[14] Aino Konkka asserts that one of the most recognized styles of rap music is called "gangsta" rap. This style originated on the West Coast, where inner-city gangs are prominent. Gangsta rap lyrics often tell the story of the desperate situation faced by many inner-city youths who feel rejected and alienated by the dominant culture. Because the lyrics of gangsta rap are often profane—dealing with drugs and violence, especially violence against women and law enforcement—gangsta rap music has received a great deal of criticism from mainstream cultural critics.[15]

To be sure, Edgar Tyson, a professor at Florida State University, agrees that a major criticism of some rap music is its noticeable appetite for violent, sexist, and misogynistic images, and what many view as glorification of drugs and alcohol. Tyson argues that such a negative perception of rap music could be explained by the disproportionate media attention given to gangsta rap. He posits that with a similar level of exposure on radio and television to that currently devoted to its negative counterpart, greater awareness of "positive and constructive" rap music would create a more balanced public perception of rap music.[16] Finally, Konkka argues that this music features the language young African Americans understand. According to Konkka, "using language that children can relate to, added with humor and catchy rhythms, helps getting the message through."[17] Consistent with the tenets of the muted group theory, rappers have created and developed a unique vocabulary that they use in their music and to communicate with one another. Although rappers speak English, the vocabulary and its meanings differ considerably from mainstream culture. Table 3.1 lists some examples of rap vocabulary.

Another example of a microcultural group is the Amish. Many Amish groups in the United States are trilingual. They speak low German at home, high German at church, and English at school or with outsiders. High German is more formal, whereas low German is a relaxed oral dialect spoken at home. In Canada, the people of Quebec define themselves as culturally unique from the rest of the country because they speak French. In Quebec, the language debate is so great and emotional that many Quebecers are pushing for sovereignty. Quebecois (those who speak French) use French as a model and insist on keeping French in the home and on the street signs throughout the province.[18]

MICROCULTURES IN THE UNITED STATES

Many microcultures exist in the United States. The formation of microcultural groups is often the result of immigration, annexation, or colonization.[19] In this chapter, six U.S. microcultures

Table 3.1 Rap Vocabulary

Rap Vocabulary	Meaning
"Ace boon coon"	Your best friend, your nigga. But it is rude (and grounds for a beatdown in some circles) for someone of another ethnicity to use it.
"All that"	In possession of all good qualities
"Ay yo trip"	Phrase to seek attention, similar to "check this out"
"Bang"	To fight or kill
"Be geese"	To leave: "Yo, we be geese."
"Bitch"	Label generally used for females but not necessarily derogatory and not necessarily limited to women, as in "All yo niggas be bitches."
"Biscuit"	Genitals: "Gals, if you see a man you like, just grab him in the biscuits . . . and doowutchalike."
"Bone"	To have sexual intercourse: "Your aim is to bone."
"Cave boy"	A White person
"Chill"	To relax
"Coconut"	An Hispanic person trying to be White (like a coconut, they are "brown" on the outside but "white" on the inside)
"Homeboy"	Close friend
"Hood"	The neighborhood, usually a poor community
"Nigga"	Originally considered racist and profane, now used by rappers to express pride; my friend, as in "my nigga"
"Peckerwood"	Derogatory term for a White person
"Roll up"	To arrive on the scene
"Shank"	A custom-made knife used in prisons
"Strawberry"	Someone who willingly exchanges sexual services for drugs
"Tag"	The act of writing graffiti, as in "tagging up"
"Tight"	Feeling really good at the moment

SOURCE: Atoon, P. "Tricky." (2010). *The Rap Dictionary*. Retrieved from www.rapdict.org.

will be explored, with particular attention paid to the communication of each and how it differs from the dominant macroculture.

The first microcultural group to be examined is the Hispanic/Latino group. Hispanics/Latinos represent the largest microcultural group in the United States. The second group consists of African Americans, whose ancestors were brought to the United States mainly as slaves. This group was selected because it represents perhaps the most powerful microcultural group in the United States. And although African Americans have made strides in social, legal, economic, and political power in the United States in the past century, they remain socially disenfranchised by many in the dominant culture. The third microcultural group to be discussed is Asian Americans. Asian Americans now represent the fastest growing microculture in the United States. The fourth group to be explored is the Laotian Hmong (pronounced "mung"), who began their immigration to the United States after the end of the Vietnam War in 1975. Although classified by the U.S. Census Bureau as a part of the Asian American microculture, this group was chosen because its members represent perhaps the newest microculture. They are also a relatively powerless group who lack social, political, and economic power. The fifth group is the Amish. The Amish immigrated to the United States from Europe to escape religious persecution. The Amish were chosen for this discussion because, perhaps more than any other microcultural group, they have maintained their cultural traditions in the face of immense pressure from the dominant culture to conform and yet have managed to coexist successfully within the dominant cultural milieu. The sixth and final microculture to be discussed is lesbian, gay, bisexual, and transgender (LGBT) persons. A debate continues over the rights of LGBT persons and whether they have a unique communication system.

Hispanics/Latinos

Hispanics/Latinos are the largest microcultural group in the United States. According to the 2010 U.S. Census Bureau, just over 50 million people—about 16% of the U.S. population—are of Hispanic or Latino origin. The Hispanic population increased by more than 15 million people between the years 2000 and 2010, accounting for more than half the increase in the total population of the United States during that decade. Moreover, between 2000 and 2010, the Hispanic population grew by 43%—4 times the growth in the total population, which hovered at about 10%. However, according to the U.S. Census Bureau, the population growth between 2000 and 2010 varied by Hispanic group. The Mexican origin population increased by 54%, Puerto Ricans grew by 36%, and the Cuban population increased by 44%. In 2010, the median household income for Hispanics was $37,000, which is considerably lower than for Whites and Asian Americans.[20] Recall from Chapter 1 that the U.S. government distinguishes between race and Hispanic origin, considering the two to be separate and distinct. Hence, Hispanics are not considered a racial group. Specifically, the government defines Hispanic or Latino as "a person of Cuban, Mexican, Puerto Rican, South or Central American, or other Spanish culture or origin regardless of race." According to census data, nearly half of all Hispanics reported their race as White. From the other half, 6% reported they were of two or more races, 2% reported their race as Black or African American, and just over 1% indicated they were American Indian or Alaska native. The rest, 42% of Hispanics, indicated "some other race."[21]

So, Who Is Hispanic?

Given the above discussion, the term *Hispanic* is confusing to many. Ned Crouch argues that the label is a cultural reference, a way of identifying people that is neither racial nor geographic. According to Crouch, persons who consider themselves Hispanic may be Black, as in the Dominican Republic; White, as in Argentina; or of mixed racial heritage, as in Mexico. Crouch argues that *Hispanic* is a cultural reference to people from any Spanish-speaking country except Spain (where people insist that they are Spanish, not Hispanic). In addition, Crouch argues that the term *Latino* is a cultural reference more or less interchangeable with *Hispanic*.[22]

The various groups represented under the Hispanic label include Mexicans, Puerto Ricans, Cubans, Central and South Americans, and Dominicans.[23] See Table 3.2 for some facts about U.S. Hispanics/Latinos. Like other microcultural groups, Hispanics are concentrated in certain geographical areas in the United States. In fact, nearly half of all Hispanics live in California and Texas. Other states with concentrated Hispanic populations include Arizona, Florida, Illinois, New Jersey, and New York. On the other hand, many states have small Hispanic populations, such as Alabama, Kentucky, Maine, Mississippi, New Hampshire, North Dakota, South Dakota, Vermont, and West Virginia.[24] In addition to its overall population trends, the Hispanic population has unique demographics compared with the rest of the United States.

Cultural Values of Hispanics

Although diverse, the Hispanic microculture is united by values, language, and religion. Consultants Anne Marie Pajewski and Luis Enriquez argue that, in Hispanic society, the family or group needs take precedence over individual needs. Hispanics seem collectivistic across a variety of contexts, including academics. According to Pajewski and Enriquez, in school settings, Hispanic students tend to be cooperative, whereas White students tend to be competitive and individualistic. When Hispanic students work in groups, not everyone is expected

Table 3.2	Facts About U.S. Hispanics/Latinos

More than one in eight people in the United States are of Hispanic origin.

Hispanics are more geographically concentrated than non-Hispanic Whites.

Hispanics tend to live inside the central cities of metropolitan areas.

Hispanics are more likely than Whites to be under the age of 18.

Three out of five Hispanics were born in the United States.

Hispanics tend to live in households that are larger than those of non-Hispanic Whites.

Nearly 40% of Hispanics over the age of 25 have not graduated from high school.

Hispanics are more likely than Whites to work in service occupations.

Hispanics are more likely than Whites to live in poverty.

SOURCE: Adapted from *Statistical Portrait of Hispanics in the United States, 2008*. Pew Hispanic Center (http://www.pewhispanic.org/2010/01/21/statistical-portrait-of-hispanics-in-the-united-states-2008/).

to do an equal share; a group member who does not work is not sanctioned. In an Anglo group, however, each student is expected to do his or her share.[25]

Perhaps nowhere is the Hispanic group orientation more prevalent than in the family, or *familia*.[26] Commitment to the family is a dominant cultural value among virtually all Hispanics. Indeed, Crouch argues that

> the group bonding process begins the minute Mexican children are brought home from the hospital and put into the children's room—not their own, separate little pink or blue nursery. Their families tend to congregate in one large room. They are taught to play nicely with each other. Toys are toys and are played with by all the children. They are not owned by boy number one or girl number three. In Anglo culture, the more we misbehave with our siblings, the more attention we get . . . but beyond the conflicting pressures of adolescence, we seem to emerge as individualists . . . unlike the Mexicans, who believe that the more they conform, the more they will all prosper.[27]

In general, Hispanics are a very religious people, with as many as 90% of all Hispanics belonging to the Roman Catholic faith. Ann W. Clutter and Ruben D. Nieto point out that the church is a strong influence on Hispanic family life. In addition, many Hispanic communities celebrate their patron saint's day with more importance and ceremony than individuals do their own birthdays. Although Hispanics are generally religious, they tend to believe in supernatural powers beyond their religious teachings. Many Hispanics believe in witchcraft and the *curadora* (i.e., healers), as well as the healing powers of women and certain herbs.[28]

Spanglish: The Language of Hispanic Americans

The communication style of most Hispanics is more formal than that of the dominant U.S. American culture. Hispanics are sensitive to rank and customarily make use of formal titles. Hispanics tend to demonstrate affection nonverbally through touching, hugging, pats on the back, and cheek kissing.[29] Verbally, many Hispanics speak Spanglish, a combination of Spanish and English. Linguists have noted that when groups of people from different cultures who speak different languages come together and live in the same society, a hybrid language sometimes evolves. This new language will take some of the phonological features (i.e., sounds) and syntactic structures (i.e., grammar) from each group's language and blend them, creating a hybrid language that serves as a vehicle for communication between the groups. This very phenomenon is happening in the United States.

According to Ilan Stavans, Spanglish is the intersection, perhaps the marriage (or divorce), of English and Spanish. Hispanics have taken English words and "Spanish-ized" them and taken Spanish words and "English-ized" them. The result is what linguists call "Spanglish"—part Spanish and part English. Alfredo Ardila notes that Spanglish may be interpreted in different ways: as a pidgin, or Creole language; an interlanguage; or an Anglicized Spanish dialect. Although Spanglish appears to be a fairly recent phenomenon, Ardila argues that it has been around for more than 150 years and traces its origins to the U.S. annexation of Mexican territories in the early to mid-19th century. Ardila points out that in the mid-19th century, the Mexican–American War resulted in ceding about half of the Mexican territory to the United States, but millions of Spanish speakers remained in close contact with the American English speakers. During the late 19th century and early 20th century, an important amount of Latin Americans and Spaniards migrated to the United States.[30]

Scholars and laypeople alike agree that Spanglish unites the Hispanic community. Jane Rifkin of *Hispanic Times Magazine* points out that Spanglish is a widely accepted communication tool used by Spanish-speaking immigrants and native-born Americans. Although some reject Spanglish as intellectually unsophisticated, Rifkin believes that the hybrid language is an expression of friendship, acceptance, and approval. Rifkin refers to Spanglish as the new national slang and contends that Spanglish is "truly a form of communicating among people that has a warmth about it and an inviting expression meant to be non-threatening to people who come together in spite of language barriers."[31]

Stavans argues that there are many variations of Spanglish, depending on the nationality, age, and class of its users. He contends that the Spanglish spoken by Cuban Americans (i.e., Cubonics) is different from that spoken by Dominicans, which is different still from the Ganga Spanglish used by urban Hispanic gangs.[32]

Although there may be many variations of Spanglish in the United States, Bill Cruz and Bill Teck—editors of *Generation ñ,* a magazine primarily targeting Cuban American youths—argue that authentic Spanglish is heard when a speaker switches from English to Spanish, or from Spanish to English, within the same sentence. They argue that Spanglish is commonplace in the homes of Hispanics who, as children, were educated in American schools but spoke Spanish at home. In their defense of Spanglish as a legitimate language, Cruz and Teck maintain that often there are no words in English (or Spanish) that accurately express the speaker's intent. In such cases, the blending of the two languages allows the speaker to capture the essence of one culture in the language of the other. Cruz and Teck have compiled what they call *The Official Spanglish Dictionary.* Table 3.3 shows some examples of Spanglish, taken from their work.[33]

Table 3.3	Examples of Spanglish

Spanglish	English Example
No creo que voy on the trip with you.	"I don't think I'm going on the trip with you."
Lonchando (having lunch)	"I'm lonchando, I don't wanna talk to him now."
Bacuncliner (vacuum cleaner)	"Aye! I think the bacuncliner just swallowed my earring!"
Tiempo is money.	"Time is money."
Frizando (to make frozen, or freezing)	"Turn up the heat, estoy frizando!"
El autopar	Local auto parts store
Guarejaus	A warehouse
Pisa Ho	Pizza Hut restaurant
Macdonal	McDonald's fast-food restaurant
Sebenileben	7-Eleven convenience store
Guendis	Wendy's fast-food restaurant

SOURCE: Cruz, B., & Teck, B. (1998). "The Official Spanglish Dictionary," *Hispanic, 11,* 34–36. These examples of Spanglish can be found in B. Cruz, B. Teck, and the Editors of Generation ñ, "The Official Spanglish Dictionary: Un User's Guia to More Than 300 Words and Phrases That Aren't Exactly Espanol or Ingles," New York: Fireside, 1998.

Chicano English

As immigrants from Mexico settled in California and other parts of the Southwest, they soon formed communities of people who spoke only Spanish. As usual, many of these people began learning English, and, as is typical of immigrants, they took phonological and grammatical complexes from each language and combined them. But the children of these immigrants grew up using both Spanish and English, and as the communities began to grow, a new dialect of English, called Chicano English, evolved. Carmen Fought, a professor of linguistics, studies Chicano English. Fought maintains that Chicano English is neither Spanglish nor a version of nonstandard Spanish but, rather, a unique dialect used by speakers who are typically not bilingual. In fact, Fought argues that most speakers of Chicano English do not know any Spanish at all.[34] Fought maintains that Chicano English is spoken only by native English speakers. She argues that the central myth about Chicano English is that it is spoken by people whose first language is Spanish and whose Spanish introduces mistakes into their English.

Fought asserts that Chicano English

> is one of the English dialects available in the United States for native speakers to learn, like Appalachian English or AAE [African American English] or the English spoken by professors at Harvard University, or by used car dealers in Houston. Chicano English cannot possibly be just a non-native variety spoken by second-language users of English if it is only spoken by people who *only* know English.[35]

Fought notes that because of its origins, Chicano English shares many of the phonological features of Spanish. But, she maintains, Chicano English is not Spanglish. For example, in endings for words such as *going* or *talking,* Chicano English speakers tend to have a higher vowel, more like the Spanish *i* (as in *sí*); so the words sound like "goween" and "talkeen." According to Fought, people who hear Chicano English typically assume that they are hearing the "accent" of a native Spanish speaker. But Fought maintains that many speakers of Chicano English are not bilingual and may not know any Spanish at all. To be sure, notes Fought, these Mexican American speakers have learned English natively and fluently, like most children growing up in the United States. They just happen to have learned a nonstandard variety that retains indicators of contact with Spanish.[36]

Stereotypes of Hispanics

In most cultures, microcultural groups are often stereotyped by the dominant cultural group. In the United States, the Hispanic microculture has been the target of several unfortunate stereotypes. Perhaps the most common, and the most hotly debated, stereotype about Hispanics revolves around the construct of male gender identity called *machismo.* Machismo centers on the notion of Hispanic masculinity and male superiority and dominance in the traditional patriarchal Hispanic society. Stereotypical characteristics associated with macho males include aggressiveness, violence, dominance and supremacy over women, infidelity, and emotional insensitivity.[37]

Manuel Roman, a Puerto Rican psychiatrist, argues that the concept of machismo is power based. He says,

Men are physically more powerful than women. And machismo is derived from the natural state of being bigger, more muscular. It has to do with dominance, autocracy, having power over others. A macho man is somebody who is expected to be sexually knowledgeable and aggressive with women, and to be fearless in his interactions with other males.[38]

To be sure, scholars disagree about the uniqueness of machismo in Hispanic culture. Counseling psychologist J. Manuel Casas and his associates argue that machismo has never been a uniquely Hispanic phenomenon. Instead, they argue that many of the traits associated with machismo can be found in virtually every culture. They note, however, that differences may exist in how the equivalent of the machismo construct is defined across cultures.[39] In other words, many cultures may associate male gender identity with aggressiveness, male supremacy, infidelity, and so on. Although there has not been a substantial amount of research conducted on the machismo identity, some data indicate that at least one characteristic associated with machismo—infidelity—is not unique to Hispanic males. University of Chicago sociologists Robert Michael, John Gagnon, Edward Laumann, and Gina Kolata—authors of the widely publicized "Sex in America" study—found that the infidelity rate among Hispanics in the United States is about the same as for the general U.S. population.[40]

U.S. media, especially advertisers, have been particularly culpable in the dissemination of Hispanic stereotypes. Octavio Nuiry points out that one of the earliest images of Hispanics, and particularly Mexicans, is that of the ruthless bandito. This image has been depicted in all sorts of media, from movie Westerns to a famous advertising campaign for Frito corn chips. In 1967, Frito-Lay Corporation launched this advertising campaign for its brand of corn chips. The ads featured a cartoon character called the Frito Bandito, whose persona was replete with a thick Spanish accent, a long handlebar mustache, a sombrero, and a pair of six-shooters. In the ads, the bandito was described as "cunning, clever, and sly." Contemporary ads for Taco Bell encourage taco lovers to "Run for the Border!" in an apparent reference to the immigration issue. Interestingly, in what advertisers call a crossover commercial, a Miller Lite beer advertisement features boxing champion Carlos Palomino encouraging viewers to "Drink Miller Lite, but don't drink the water."[41]

The influences of the Hispanic microculture in the United States are growing. Now more than ever, Hispanics are noticed by the dominant culture. We see images of Hispanics in television and movies. Hispanic cuisine is popular across the country. Although their unemployment rates are high and their incomes are low, as a microcultural group, Hispanics are increasing their political and economic power. Soon, their voices will not be muted.

African Americans

According to Schaefer, the history of African Americans in the United States dates as far back as the history of Euro-Americans (persons of European descent). Blacks arrived in the new world with the first White explorers. Schaefer reports that in 1619, 20 Africans arrived in Jamestown as indentured servants. At that time, their children were born free people. By the 1660s, however, the British colonies passed laws making Africans slaves for life.[42]

According to Schaefer, the proportion of Blacks in the United States has varied over the centuries and actually declined until the 1940s, primarily because White immigration (mostly from Europe) far outdistanced population growth among Blacks. In 1790, Africans represented a little more than 19% of the total population of the United States. That percentage declined to 9.7% in 1910.[43] According to the 2010 census, there are 42 million African Americans in the United States, representing about 13.6% of the population. The Black population grew by 15.4% from 2000 to 2010. According to the U.S. Census Bureau, nearly 60% of all Blacks live in just 10 states: New York (3.3 million), Florida (3.2 million), Texas (3.2 million), Georgia (3.1 million), California (2.7 million), North Carolina (2.2 million), Illinois (2.0 million), Maryland (1.8 million), Virginia (1.7 million), and Ohio (1.5 million). Among these states, four experienced substantial growth between 2000 and 2010. The Black population grew by 29% in Florida, 28% in Georgia, 27% in Texas, and 21% in North Carolina. They are the second largest microcultural group in the United States. Currently, Blacks and Hispanics compose nearly 30% of the U.S. population. Unlike the rapid and disproportionate growth of the Hispanic population since 1990, the rate of Black population growth remains relatively stable.[44]

African Americans made great progress in the 20th century due mostly to the civil rights movement. Although significant gaps remain between Blacks and Whites in such areas as income, education, employment, and housing, Blacks have come a long way in the past 65 years. For example, in 2005, nearly 30% of all Black families earned annual incomes of $50,000 or more. In 2010, the median household income among Blacks was $32,000. Politically, the number of Black elected officials has increased nearly 300% since 1972. Schaefer notes also that an interesting phenomenon is developing: an ever-growing proportion of the Black population consists of Blacks that are foreign-born. Since 1984, the percentage of Blacks in the United States born outside the country (mostly in the Caribbean) has almost doubled.[45]

Black English, Dialect, and Ebonics

Some linguists maintain that 80% to 90% of African Americans engage in what is frequently labeled Ebonics.[46] To begin, it needs to be clear that both linguistically and functionally, Ebonics serves all communication functions. The term Ebonics (from the combination of the words *ebony* and *phonics*) was first coined in 1973 and refers to a grammatically complex African American speech pattern. Ebonics, or Black language, is uniquely derived from the language of descendents of slaves. Many linguists recognize Black language as a Creole that developed as a result of contact between Africans and Europeans; a new language was formed that was influenced by both languages and took on a variety of forms, depending on whether the influence was French, Portuguese, or English. According to Weber, there is evidence that these languages were spoken on the western coast of Africa as early as the 1500s. Some linguists believe that Africans responded to the English language as do all other nonnative speakers—that is, from the phonological and grammatical constructs of their native language.[47]

One of the primary ways members of cultural groups define themselves and establish in-group and out-group identities is through verbal and nonverbal language—that is, through conversation. Language is the foundation of individual and group construction. In a recent study, researchers at Stanford University explored the meanings of racial identity for African American students in a predominantly African American urban high school. The authors viewed racial identity as both related to membership in a racial group and as a fluid and dynamic disposition maintained by students in the local school context. After interviewing students in focus groups for 9 weeks, their findings showed that students had different meanings of African American racial identity and that these meanings were linked to academic achievement and engagement. Their findings also demonstrated that both high-achieving and low-achieving students considered language patterns to be important for their African American identity. The researchers noted that all the students they interviewed consistently used Ebonics and felt that its use was a part of African American racial identity.[48]

According to Ebonics scholar John Rickford, typical Ebonic pronunciations include the omission of the final consonant in words such as *past* (i.e., "pas") or *hand* (i.e., "han"), the pronunciation of the "th" in *bath* as "t" (i.e., "bat"), and the pronunciation of the vowel in words such as *my* and *ride* as long "ah," as in "mah rahd." According to Rickford, Ebonics pronunciations are systematic and the result of regular rules and restrictions found in any and all languages. For instance, speakers regularly produce sentences without present tense *is* and *are,* as in "Joe trippin'" or "They all right." But they don't omit present tense *am.* Instead of the ungrammatical "Ah walkin'," Ebonics speakers would say, "Ahm walkin'." Ebonics speakers use an invariant *be* in their speech (e.g., "They be goin' to school every day"); however, this *be* is not simply equivalent to *is* or *are.* Invariant *be* refers to actions that occur regularly or habitually rather than on just one occasion.[49]

In addition to its phonological and syntactic elements, Black language includes other communication dimensions that distinguish it from other languages and mark its speakers as members of a unique group (see Figure 3.1). Thomas Kochman argues that African American expression is characteristically "emotionally intense, dynamic, and demonstrative," whereas Euro-American expression is "more modest and emotionally restrained."[50]

Figure 3.1 Black language, including Ebonics, includes many different communication dimensions that distinguish it from other languages.

In comparing African American and Euro-American modes of expression, Kochman asserts that when engaging an issue, Euro-Americans use a detached and unemotional form of "discussion," whereas African Americans use an intense and involving form of "argument." Kochman maintains that Euro-Americans tend to understate their talents, whereas African Americans tend to boast about theirs. In essence, African American speech acts and events are more animated, lively, and forceful than Euro-American speech acts. According to Kochman, the animation and vitality of Black communication is due to the emotional force and spiritual energy Blacks invest in their public presentations and the functional role that emotions play in realizing the goals of Black interactions, activities, and events. For example, a common goal of many African American speech events is to energize the audience into an emotional and spiritual release. Such speech events require a strong speaker, a medium that facilitates the emotional and spiritual release, and active participation from the audience. One type of communication that captures the essence of such revitalization is the "call-and-response" pattern involving reciprocal speech acts between speaker and audience. In the typical call-and-response mode, a speaker begins by calling—that is, making some point or assertion to which the audience responds.

African studies professor Weber describes an instance of call and response while teaching:

> During the lecture, one of my more vocal black students began to respond to the message with some encouraging remarks like "all right," "make it plain," "that all right," and "teach." She was soon joined by a few more black students who gave similar comments. I noticed that this surprised and confused some of the white students. When questioned later about this, their response was that they were not used to having more than one person talk at a time, and they really could not talk and listen at the same time. They found the comments annoying and disruptive. As the lecturer, I found the comments refreshing and inspiring.[51]

African Americans often engage in call-and-response modes in a variety of formalized settings, such as church meetings, and during informal, everyday gatherings.

Origins of Black Language

The origins of many of these African American communicative modes can be traced to ancient African philosophies about the relationship between humans, the spoken word, and the fostering of community. According to African scholar Janheinz Jahn, the traditional African view of the world is one of extraordinary harmony. All being, all essence, in whatever form it is conceived, is subsumed under one of four categories: (a) *muntu,* or human being; (b) *kintu,* or thing; (c) *hantu,* or place and time; and (d) *kuntu,* or modality. Everything that exists must necessarily belong to one of these four categories and is conceived of not as some tangible substance but as a force that affects and is affected by the other forces. All the forces are interrelated and work together to accomplish a common goal. For example, "scholar" belongs in the *muntu* category, "pen" in the *kintu* category, "university" in *hantu,* and "knowledge" in *kuntu.* Anything that exists has distinct characteristics that combine and relate with characteristics in the other categories. For example, the most distinguishing characteristic of *muntu* is the possession of *nommo*—that is, the magic power of the word. Through *nommo,* humans establish their mastery over the other things. According to Jahn, *nommo* is the life force, is the fluid as such, a unity of spiritual-physical fluidity, giving life to everything, penetrating everything, causing everything. . . . And since man has the power over the word, it is he who directs the life force. Through the word he receives it, shares it with other beings, and so fulfills the meaning of life.[52]

Nothing exists without *nommo*; it is the force that fosters the sense of community between speaker and audience wherein they become one as senders and receivers.

Weber argues that the philosophy of *nommo* has been carried into contemporary African American society, where the audience listening and responding to a message is equally as important as the speaker. One of the foremost goals within any African American communicative context is to bring speaker and audience together as one, hence the call-and-response mode. In contemporary and traditional African American speech contexts, the speaker and audience share the platform.[53]

The above discussion suggests that there are differences in the language use of African Americans and Euro-Americans and that the reason for such differences may lie in the language's purpose. African Americans tend to use language to establish and maintain a sense of community. The use of a language that expresses their unique history, bridges social and economic gaps, and helps build their future is a critical ingredient in African American communication and membership in their microcultural group.

Cultural Attitudes About Ebonics

Over the decades, numerous studies have shown that speakers using Ebonics are perceived as less credible than speakers using Standard American English (SAE). Consistent with the tenets of the muted group theory, members of the dominant cultural group prefer their language to that of microcultures. In a recent study, Andrew Billings sought to further test the hypothesis that speakers using Ebonics will be perceived as less competent and trustworthy than speakers using SAE. In his study, a total of nine video clips were produced. Three of the nine clips featured White people speaking SAE; three more featured Black people speaking SAE; the final three featured Black people (the same Black speakers as in the second group) speaking Ebonics. In essence, six speakers were used, with the three Black speakers appearing twice (once speaking SAE and once speaking Ebonics). After watching the videos, participants in the study completed scales that measured competence and trustworthiness. The results reveal that Black speakers of SAE were actually preferred to White speakers of SAE. Andrews maintains that these differences are the result of what he calls a novelty effect; that is, people expected that a Black speaker would use Ebonics, thus leading them to rate Blacks more favorably when they instead spoke SAE. Additional results showed clearly lower ratings of the Ebonics speakers in terms of intelligence, articulation, aggression, education, and qualification (all five measures of competence). Interestingly, the scales measuring trustworthiness—particularly honesty, likability, and attractiveness—did not differ between White and Black speakers. In addition to these results, Andrews reports that Whites preferred speakers of their own race in several measurements of character (e.g., likability, believability, honesty). Moreover, Blacks found White speakers of SAE to be more attractive, kind, and articulate. Finally, Andrews notes that Black participants were much harsher critics of Ebonics than were Whites. Thus, he concludes that within almost all variables, the dialect used and the race of the person who is speaking can significantly alter ratings of speaker perception.[54]

Asian Americans

Asian Americans are now the fastest growing microcultural group in the United States. According to a 2013 Pew Research Center report,

> Asian Americans are the highest-income, best-educated and fastest-growing racial group in the United States. They are more satisfied than the general public with their lives, finances and the direction of the country, and they place more value than other Americans do on marriage, parenthood, hard work and career success.[55]

In 1965, Asian Americans accounted for less than 1% of the total U.S. population. Today, Asian Americans make up nearly 6% of the U.S. population, totaling just over 18 million. And, contrary to popular belief, Asians are the largest group of new immigrants to the United States. For example, in 2000, about 60% of new immigrants to the United States were Hispanic, while about 20% were Asian. In 2010, just over 30% of new immigrants were Hispanic, while about 36% were Asian. More than 60% of Asian American adults who have immigrated from abroad are college educated, which is twice the amount of any other non-Asian group of immigrants. Moreover, about half of Asian Americans indicate that they speak English very well. The 2010 median household income among Asian Americans was $64,000, the highest among all racial groups in the United States, including Whites.[56]

Compared with African Americans and Hispanics (discussed above), Asian Americans do not see discrimination against their group as a major problem. Specifically, only 13% see discrimination as a problem, whereas 48% see it as only a minor problem and 35% say discrimination is not an issue with their group.[57]

Asian Americans are a diverse microcultural group. According to the U.S. Census Bureau, *Asian* refers to a person having origins in any of the original peoples of the Far East, Southeast Asia, or the Indian subcontinent.[58] The majority of persons classified as Asian American either are immigrants from Asia (about 60%) or descendants of Asian immigrants (about 40%). The majority (i.e., 83%) of the Asian American population is from six countries: China, India, Japan, Korea, the Philippines, and Vietnam. But there are more than 25 groups with ethnic Asian backgrounds living in the United States. Of the 18 million Asian Americans, just over 4 million are from China, 3.5 million are from the Philippines, just over 3 million are from India, 1.7 million are from Vietnam, 1.7 million are from Korea, and 1.3 million are from Japan.[59]

Bryan Kim and his colleagues have conducted a number of studies on Asian Americans, and they caution against a "homogenized" view of Asian Americans that distorts important differences among the various Asian American ethnic groups. For example, Kim notes that the per capita income among these groups differs considerably, with Japanese earning the most and Hmong earning the least. Education levels differ as well; for instance, far more Japanese and Chinese Americans hold college degrees compared with Laotian and Hmong Americans.[60]

Asian American Values

For more than a decade, Kim and his colleagues have focused most of their work on Asian American values. They agree that while Asian Americans share many cultural values, the various ethnic groups differ in their adherence to these values. They also have studied how Asian American acculturation into U.S. culture affects behavioral adherence to the values held by Asian Americans.[61] Based on their studies, Kim and his colleagues have identified six dominant values held by most Asian Americans, including collectivism, conforming to norms, emotional self-control, family recognition through achievement, filial piety, and humility.[62]

ASIAN AMERICAN VALUES

Collectivism: The importance of thinking about one's group before oneself; considering the needs of others before one's own needs

Conforming to norms: The importance of conforming to familial and social expectations; following role expectations such as gender roles and family hierarchy; being concerned about bringing disgrace to one's family reputation

Emotional self-control: The importance of having the ability to control one's emotions, having inner resources to solve emotional problems; understanding yet not openly expressing parental love

Family recognition through achievement: The importance of not bringing shame to the family by avoiding occupational and educational failures and by achieving academically

Filial piety: The importance of taking care of one's parents when parents are unable to take care of themselves; not placing parents in retirement homes; recognizing that elders have more wisdom than younger people

Humility: The importance of being humble, not being boastful, and having modesty

---

SOURCE: These value definitions are taken directly from Kim, B. S. K., Yang, P. H., Atkinson, D. R., Wolfe, M. M., & Hong, S. (2001). Cultural Value Similarities and Differences Among Asian American Ethnic Groups. *Cultural Diversity and Ethnic Minority Psychology, 7,* 343–361.

In subsequent work, Kim's research group found that while most Asian Americans relate and attribute similar meaning to these six values, individual groups differ in their level of adherence to them—that is, the extent to which the values are reflected in group members' behavior. In one study comparing Chinese, Japanese, Korean, and Filipino groups, Kim and his colleagues found that Chinese, Japanese, and Koreans indicated greater behavioral adherence to the six values than did Filipinos. And they found that across the four groups, Japanese scored higher on values than did the other three groups.[63]

Asian American Values and Communication Styles

Recall from Chapter 2 that cultures tend to prefer (along a continuum) either high- or low-context communication. Recall also that collectivistic cultures often prefer high-context communication. In some of his research, William Gudykunst found that collectivistic values predict the use of indirect communication. Thus, to the extent that Asian Americans value collectivism, we would expect them to prefer an indirect communication style, where the speaker's intentions are hidden or only hinted at during interaction. The use of ambiguity and vagueness is also characteristic of an indirect style.[64] Park and Kim also studied the relationship between cultural values and communication styles among Asian American and European American college students. In their study, they found that European American students preferred a more open style of communication than did Asian American students, who preferred a more indirect communication style. Interestingly, they found no differences between the two groups in preferences for a contentious, dramatic, interpersonal sensitivity, or inferring meaning style of communication. But they found that as adherence to the Asian American value of humility increased in both groups, the preference for the contentious and dramatic styles decreased while the preference for inferring meaning style increased.[65]

In related research, researchers at the University of Michigan administered the Family Expressiveness Questionnaire (FEQ) to a group of Asian American and European American college students. The FEQ measures the frequency of dominant and submissive communicative behaviors within families, which can be further classified as positive (e.g., happy, affectionate) and/or negative (e.g., sad, angry). They found that European Americans were more likely to engage in both positive and negative dominant and submissive family expressiveness than were Asian Americans and that Asian Americans were emotionally restrained when dealing with family expressiveness.[66]

Normative Communication Styles of African Americans, Asian Americans, and Hispanics/Latinos

In combination, African Americans, Asian Americans, and Hispanics/Latinos constitute about 36% of the U.S. population and are increasing in numbers annually. In the above paragraphs, we reviewed the fundamental values associated with these microcultural groups and their corresponding communication styles. Candia Elliot of Diversity Training Associates in Portland, Oregon; R. Jerry Adams of the Evaluation and Development Institute, also in Portland, Oregon; and Suganya Sockalingam of the Office of Multicultural Health in the Department of Human Resources of the State of Oregon have put together a summary of the normative communication styles and values of African Americans, Asian Americans, and Hispanics/Latinos. This summary is based on their review of the literature associated with these microcultures, as well as focus-group interviews with members of these microcultural groups. Their work was, in part, funded by the U.S. Office of Minority Affairs. The authors argue that many of these communication style differences are "invisible" and create difficulties and conflict in communication when they are wrongly assumed to be based on an individual's personality rather than a culturally learned style. See Table 3.4 for an abridged version of their summary.[67]

Table 3.4   Normative Communication Styles and Values

Communication Style	Very Little	Little	Medium	Much	Very Much
1. Emotional expression	Asian American		Hispanic		African American
2. Gestures	Asian American			Hispanic	African American
3. Vocalics (vocal pitch variation)	Hispanic	Asian American			African American
4. Vocal volume	Asian American	Hispanic			African American
5. Directness	Asian American	Hispanic			African American
6. Eye contact	Asian American	Hispanic			African American
7. Haptics (touching)	Asian American				Hispanic African American
8. Emphasis on hierarchy	African American				Asian American Hispanic
9. Proximity (closeness while interacting with others)	Asian American		African American		Hispanic
10. Formality		Hispanic African American			Asian American
11. Self-promotion	Asian American	Hispanic			African American

The Hmong

While most students in the United States learn about America's involvement in the Vietnam War, some never learn of the "Secret War" fought on behalf of the United States during this time. This "Secret War" refers to the thousands of Hmong who were recruited by the U.S. military through the Central Intelligence Agency (CIA) to help fight the war against Communism in Southeast Asia. According to Daphne Winland, the Hmong belong to the Sino-Tibetan language family. They are culturally similar to the Chinese, and Hmong origins can be traced back to China, where they lived peacefully for hundreds of years. About 150 years ago, Chinese rulers began a campaign of persecution to extinguish the Hmong language. The Hmong moved southward and westward out of China and organized communities in Burma, Thailand, North Vietnam, and the mountains of

Laos. Winland points out that the Hmong, which means "free people" or "mountain people," were singled out by the CIA during the Vietnam War because of their geographically strategic location in the mountains of Laos.[68] In the 1960s, the CIA began secretly enlisting Hmong to prevent North Vietnamese troops from entering and moving supplies to South Vietnam through Laos. The Hmong also set up navigational aids for American bombers and fought to protect them when they were attacked by the North Vietnamese. In addition, Hmong soldiers were highly skilled in the operations required to rescue American pilots shot down over Laos (the United States flew more tactical missions over Laos than it did over Vietnam).[69] The Hmong were fierce fighters yet suffered devastating losses estimated at more than 100 times greater (proportionately) than those of the United States. Although estimates vary, most experts agree that more than 25,000 Hmong lost their lives fighting for the United States during the Vietnam War.[70]

Due to intense political pressures at home, the United States had vowed not to escalate the war into Laos. Hence, the Hmong became known as the "Secret Army," and their participation in the war was called the "Secret War."[71] In 1975, the United States withdrew its forces from Vietnam. Concurrently, a Communist-backed government supported by the Vietnamese and Soviets assumed power in Laos. One of the foremost goals of the new Laotian government was to annihilate the Hmong people because of their alliance with the United States. The Communists tortured, raped, and murdered thousands of Hmong. They napalmed their villages and slaughtered their cattle. There is evidence that the Communists used chemical and biological weapons in their attempt to wipe out the Hmong. With the United States having withdrawn from Vietnam, the Hmong were left without any allies in the midst of their enemies and a new war.[72]

More than 200,000 Hmong fled to Thailand, where they were housed in prison-like conditions in refugee camps. Many Hmong immigrated to the United States, Australia, and France. About 100,000 made it to the United States. Today, about 150,000 Hmong reside in the United States, with large concentrations in California, Wisconsin, and Minnesota. Although they were hired and paid by the United States, Hmong soldiers have received little or no recognition for their efforts and do not receive veteran's benefits. In May 1997, the United States finally acknowledged Hmong veterans with a granite marker in Arlington National Cemetery that reads, "The U.S. Secret Army in the Kingdom of Laos 1961–1973." In both the Laotian and Hmong languages, the marker also reads, "You will never be forgotten." In 1995, as many as 40,000 Hmong were still residing in refugee camps in Thailand.[73]

John Duffy alleges that life in the United States has been very difficult for many Hmong. For the most part, Hmong immigrants have not been welcomed. Unfortunately, many people inaccurately associate the Hmong with the "enemy" in the Vietnam War. To add to their strained situation, many stereotypes preceded their immigration to the United States. News coverage of the Hmong often referred to them as a "pre-literate," "primitive," "hilltribe" group.[74] Moreover, writes Winland, during this time period, just about anything associated with the Vietnam War was anathema. Hence, the Hmong entered the United States bearing the doubt and distrust of many and facing the straightforward bigotry of others. The Hmong find themselves in a situation of relative dependency on U.S. culture while simultaneously experiencing a real sense of cultural isolation.[75]

Unlike the African Americans or the Amish, who have been in the United States for centuries, the Hmong are unique in that they are first-generation immigrants. Their values, customs, and modes of communication have collided head-on with mainstream American culture. For example, the Hmong are traditionally a collectivistic culture. According to Katie Thao, a native Hmong who immigrated to the United States when she was a teenager, the most important group is the family clan. Hmong family clans are patrilineal. Hmong males are given two names—one in childhood and the other when they reach adulthood. When children are born, they are given their father's clan name. When women marry, they keep their father's clan name and do not adopt their husband's, even though they become formal members of his clan. Conversely, Hmong women do not receive an adult name but become known by their husband's clan name. There are between 20 and 30 clan names. The most common clan names in the United States include Cha, Hang, Her, Kong, Kue, Moua, Lee, Lo or Lor, Thao or Thor, Vang, Vue, Xiong, and Yang.[76]

Role Relationships and Marriage

According to Ray Hutchison and Miles McNall, many of the Hmong customs associated with clan membership that have been imported to the United States include sex-role relationships and marriage practices (see Figure 3.2). For the most part, these practices clash with American customs. For example, in traditional Hmong culture, women maintain clearly subordinate roles. Their responsibility is to bear children, maintain the household, and be subservient to their husbands. One way Hmong women demonstrate their subordinate status is by walking directly behind their husbands when in public. Moreover, they have little or no say in the decision making or political affairs of their clans. Some husbands refuse to allow their wives to learn English, hence keeping them muted and powerless in American culture. For the most part, first-generation Hmong women are not allowed an education and are expected to marry early, between the ages of 13 and 18 (whereas men marry between the ages of 18 and 30). Although the practices are gradually changing in the United States, many Hmong marriages are still arranged. Many communities report that a high percentage of Hmong girls drop out of high school to get married. Indeed, Hmong women have the youngest average marriage age of all Southeast Asian refugee groups. Moreover, Hmong fertility rates in the United States are much higher than those of any other refugee or immigrant group.[77]

Figure 3.2	Many customs are imported to the United States, such as sex-role relationships and marriage practices.

Thao participated in an arranged marriage. She did not meet her husband-to-be until the day of her wedding. To many Americans, an arranged marriage seems ridiculous and absurd; but Thao asserts that she was completely comfortable with the idea because she had confidence in her parents, especially her father, to negotiate a good husband for her. Thao contends that an arranged Hmong marriage is a matter of considerable maneuvering and bargaining. Typically, each family selects an elderly male spokesman. These spokesmen, usually the fathers, then negotiate and bargain a bride price that is to be paid to the bride's parents. The philosophy behind "buying a wife" is to ensure that she will be highly valued by her new family. In many cases, the bride's parents hold a feast of roasted pig in their home in celebration of the wedding. After the wedding ceremony, the souls and good fortune of the bride and groom are symbolically wrapped in an umbrella that is carried in procession to the groom's home, where another feast is held. If the bride is entering the groom's home for the first time (which is usually the case because the bride and groom are strangers), a rooster is waved over the bride to symbolize her membership in the groom's clan. In most cases, a Hmong marriage is seen not as a bonding of two people but as a union of two family clans. In some cases, if a married Hmong woman's husband dies, she automatically becomes the wife of his younger brother.[78]

Communication Patterns of the Hmong

Like most microcultural groups, the Hmong share some unique verbal and nonverbal communication patterns. The overwhelming majority of the first Hmong immigrants entering the United States did not speak English. Historically, because the Hmong migrated so often, their written language was eventually lost. Not until the 1950s were orthographies of the written language developed. Well over half of the Hmong who immigrated to the United States could not read or write. For the Hmong who immigrated to Laos, they were taught in Buddhist temples in the Lao language and Lao alphabet. In Laos today, there are two major dialects of Hmong language. One is *Hmoob Dawb,* meaning "White Hmong," and the other is *Hmoob Ntsuab,* meaning "Blue Hmong." Because the White Hmong are in the majority, *Hmoob Dawb* is spoken more frequently.[79]

According to Thao, the phrase "playing a flute into a water buffalo's ear" is used by the Hmong when someone is trying, without success, to explain something to another who simply does not understand. Often, the Hmong will refer to someone who does not understand a message as some kind of animal, often a water buffalo. The idea of a flute is significant because in traditional Hmong culture, the flute communicates emotions such as sorrow, love, and even anger or depression. Another saying, "The grinder doesn't taste salty," is used to refer to a person who is bankrupt. Salt is a valuable ingredient to the Hmong, and when there is no salt, it is an indication that the family is out of money.

The Hmong are animistic, meaning they believe that everything has a spirit. According to Thao, the supernatural is a real part of Hmong life. Evil spirits are thought to exist in unpopulated areas; therefore, many Hmong are afraid to travel alone in uninhabited places. The saying, "The devil will not eat or chew anyone for it," is used when an act or crime is committed wherein no one will be caught or found guilty. The Hmong believe that evil spirits, such as the devil, are omnipresent and can hear and see everything. If the devil will not eat anyone, then the act will go unpunished. "Go check the mousetrap" is said in reference to a meal shared by an entire clan or village. The saying is used to compare someone going to a meal to a mouse going to a trap in search of food. When a person goes to a meal, he or she gets trapped in the company of the clan or family. Many of the Hmong sayings and colloquialisms are indirect expressions. The Hmong believe that if the truth is spoken directly, evil spirits or unwanted guests can overhear it. Thao says that a Hmong farmer might call out to his family, "Come sharpen your knives," rather than saying, "It's time to eat," because the latter might attract evil spirits or animals who will eat the meal.[80]

One of the most significant forms of nonverbal communication for the Hmong is their *paj ntaub*, pronounced "pandoa." *Paj ntaub*, meaning "flower cloth," are sophisticated stitched quilts embroidered with bright threads. They often feature picturesque geometric designs that occasionally include animals or other creatures. Since their immigration to the United States, *paj ntaub* have evolved into "story cloths," often depicting the history and life experiences of the Hmong culture. Emerging from the Thai refugee camps, story cloths were a means to teach written language to Hmong children and others. Now they are treated as works of art and a vehicle for the Hmong to document their history and retain their cultural identity. Created exclusively by Hmong women, the cloths carry much significance. The quality of the needlework communicates the skill and creativity of the women who make them and may bring the women a higher bride price at the time of marriage bargaining.[81]

Another nonverbal gesture used in Hmong culture is twitching the eyes to communicate contempt for another. Twitching the eyes during a long stare is very offensive and may lead to a physical confrontation. Slapping oneself on the buttocks is a nonverbal way of saying, "Kiss my ass" or "Lick my ass." Kneeling is done only by men when they want to express their thanks or to ask another for mercy and forgiveness. A woman's kneeling has little or no value because of her low rank and position in Hmong clans.[82]

Elliot Barkan writes that acculturation in the United States has been difficult for the Hmong. The first-generation Hmong, arriving in the United States in the mid-1970s, have tried hard to preserve their culture, whereas their children, exposed to the values and communication system of the dominant culture, are caught between two cultures. The older Hmong try to preserve the traditional ways, while contemporary culture—including the educational system—encourages their assimilation. Acculturation for the elderly Hmong has been particularly difficult. The age and sex hierarchies that prescribed their superior status are gone. In Laos, women have few, if any, rights; in the United States, of course, women have equal rights. Language has played a key role as well. A Hmong child's quick acquisition of English almost reverses traditional family roles. Contrary to their traditional roles, the parents are now dependent on the child's communication skills to get along. Many parents feel that the learning of such skills undermines their authority; hence, some parents develop a sense of loss and worthlessness and fall into a deep depression.[83]

The Amish

One microcultural group that continues to fascinate much of America is the Amish. John Andrew Hostetler is a former Amish member who left his community and is considered the country's leading expert on Amish custom. Hostetler describes them as "a church, a community, a spiritual union, a conservative branch of Christianity, a religion, a community whose members practice simple and austere living, a familistic entrepreneuring system, and an adaptive human community."[84]

The Amish, sometimes called "the plain people" or "Old Order Amish," are an Anabaptist religious group that emigrated from Europe to the United States in the early 1700s. Currently, no Amish communities remain in Europe. Amish groups today have settled in about 22 states and Ontario, Canada. Historically, the Amish immigrated to the United States to escape religious persecution. Their name is derived from one of their earliest leaders, Jacob Amman, a young Alsatian bishop and farmer who held a strong Bible-centered faith and was staunchly conservative. To his followers, Amman advocated nonresistance, adult baptism, disciplinary dress standards, and separatism from worldly fashion and influence.

From 1730 through 1770, between 50 and 100 Amish families arrived in the United States and initially settled in Pennsylvania. Since then, several groups of Amish have moved farther west to settle in Ohio, Indiana, Illinois, Iowa, and Wisconsin, among other areas. The greatest concentration of Amish is in Holmes and adjoining counties in Northeast Ohio. Next in size is a group of Amish people in Elkhart and surrounding counties in Northeastern Indiana. Then comes the Amish settlement in Lancaster County, Pennsylvania. The Amish population in the United States numbers more than 150,000 and counting, due to large family size (seven children on average) and a church-member retention rate of about 80%.[85]

An Isolated Microculture

Perhaps more than any other microcultural group, the Amish have been relatively successful at isolating themselves from the influences of the dominant culture. The Amish follow five basic tenets: adult baptism; separation of church and state; excommunication from the church for those who break moral law; living life in accordance with the teachings of Christ; and refusal to bear arms, take oaths, or hold political office. Living what they call nonresistant lives, they do not serve in the U.S. military. According to Rich Huber, who was raised a Mennonite in Lancaster County, Pennsylvania, the Amish follow the Bible as literally as possible, citing "Be ye not conformed to the world" (Romans 12:2) as their fundamental principle. Based on their interpretation of this Biblical passage, the Amish believe that true followers of Christ are to be separate from the world. Hence, to evade worldliness and the corruption and sin associated with it, the Amish have drawn strict boundaries between themselves and the dominant cultural milieu.[86]

Although they are generally successful at avoiding contemporary American society, the Amish are considered American citizens and observe most U.S. laws. Hostetler notes that the Amish pay income, property, and sales taxes along with everyone else. They do not pay Social Security taxes, nor do they receive Social Security benefits or any other type of government aid (e.g., food stamps, welfare). In addition, they avoid the courts in settling disputes, are forbidden to take oaths, do not serve on juries, and do not collect settlements from the courts.[87] Moreover, they take full responsibility for the education of their children and generally do not send them to public schools. In fact, in 1972, the Supreme Court heard the case of *Wisconsin v. Yoder,* wherein the court exempted the various Amish sects from compulsory school attendance laws beyond eighth grade. *Wisconsin v. Yoder* represented the first time conflicts over education between the Amish and the government had been argued before the Supreme Court. This is significant because most Amish follow a "turn the other cheek" mentality and do not defend themselves. William MacKaye notes that, when confronted, many Amish simply pack up their belongings and move somewhere else to be left alone.[88]

Today, most Amish children are taught in one-room schoolhouses by teachers with no more than an eighth-grade education. Amish children attend school until the eighth grade, after which they are educated at home and go to work on the family farm. The Amish consider their society as a form of schooling; they train their children vocationally. Almost exclusively, Amish boys become farmers, carpenters, or tradesmen, and girls become homemakers. Beginning on their 16th birthdays, Amish youth enter a kind of decision-making phase, called a "simmie" period, wherein they are to contemplate whether or not they will maintain or renounce their Amish identity. During this time, they are exposed to deviant behaviors and attitudes. The Amish believe that exposing their youth to deviance sifts out those who might not be fit to be adult Amish. Professor Denise Reiling, of Eastern Michigan University, argues that many of the behaviors considered deviant among the Amish would be considered relatively harmless in many other cultural contexts. Such behaviors include being an annoyance, acting irresponsibly, hurting another person's feelings, telling lies, excluding another person from a group activity, or just acting in an unwise, reckless, or impractical fashion. Reiling reports that at the end of their simmie period, the teens announce their decision to either reject or adopt Amish identity. About 20% of youths eventually defect from the Amish. Although the simmie period often results in depression and anxiety for the youth, Reiling notes that most Amish youth remain in the simmie period for 2 to 3 years, whereas others take as long as 8 to 10 years to make a decision. Those who defect are immediately excommunicated, resulting in ostracism and physical separation from their families and the entire Amish settlement.[89]

The Amish have virtually no unemployment.[90] As in other religiously oriented microcultural groups, the Amish believe that God is the absolute power in the universe. They believe that their life on Earth is preparation for their afterlife in heaven. As a result, many of the values and behaviors of the Amish may be similar to those of mainstream America, but for very different reasons. By the time they die, the Amish want their earthly sins settled; hence, every day is to be lived well so as to please God. The Amish do not believe that entrance to heaven is guaranteed, however.[91] As Hostetler notes, complete assurance of heaven is seen as obnoxious because it smacks of pride and boasting. Humility, self-denial, and submissiveness are at the core of Amish values.[92]

Because the Amish want their group to remain much as it was in the 17th century, they are slow to change. They choose to examine change carefully before they accept it. If a new idea or change does not help them keep their lives simple and their families together, they will probably reject it. Hence, the Amish eschew most modern technologies, such as electricity, automobiles, and other conveniences (see Figure 3.3).[93] Also, based on the Biblical passage, "Thou shalt not make unto thee any graven image, or any likeness of anything that . . . is in the earth" (Exodus 20:4), the Amish do not allow anyone to photograph them.[94]

Figure 3.3 The Amish eschew many modern technologies.

Unlike mainstream American society, the Amish are a collectivistic community—what they call *Gemeinde,* which translates to "redemptive community." From this perspective, individuals depend on their community for their identity. The Amish believe that a person's self-worth is defined by his or her role in the community. Individual achievement, self-ambition, power, and worldly acquisitions are not valued. Sharing, community effort, and trading are the core values of most Amish communities. The Amish believe that community service gains one access to God and eternal life.[95] Because of their collectivistic orientation, each member of the group has a well-defined role. For example, sex roles among Amish men and women are clearly prescribed. Patterns of dress and a strict division of labor separate men and women in Amish society. Exclusively, Amish women are homemakers and Amish men are farmers, with the small exception of those men who join the ministry.[96]

Verbal Communication of the Amish

Most Amish are trilingual; that is, they speak three languages. They speak a dialect of German, called high German, during church services. At home or during informal gatherings, they speak low German, sometimes called Pennsylvania Dutch (the term derived from non-Amish mispronunciation of *Deutsche*). They also learn and speak English at school and use it when interacting with non-Amish persons. Like all other microcultures, the Amish frequently use phrases and sayings that carry particular meaning to them. In their study of Amish verbal phrases and colloquialisms, Moellendorf, Warsh, and Yoshimaru report that one traditional Amish saying in German is "*Das alt Gebrauch ist besser*," which translates to "The old way is the better way." According to Moellendorf and her colleagues, the Amish believe that past traditions and the old way of living are superior to the conveniences of modern life and its new technologies. Occasionally, outsiders look to the Amish as an idyllic community. They see the Amish lifestyle as free from the pressures of the modern world. To this, the Amish say, "It's not all pies and cakes"—meaning that the life of the Amish may appear simple and serene, but in reality, it is hard, disciplined, and strenuous. Although it happens only infrequently, sometimes an individual will leave the Amish community and join a less demanding church, such as the Mennonites, or another community. About this, the Amish say, "He got his hair cut," as a polite way of communicating that the individual was unable to meet the rigorous standards of the Amish lifestyle. The saying also suggests that the person has lost his masculine tie (i.e., his long hair) to the community. Another way of communicating a similar phenomenon is to say, "He went English," which is used when an Amish member has left the community to become a part of mainstream American culture.[97]

To enforce church order and discipline, the Amish engage in a form of excommunication called "the ban" or "shunning." Shunning includes prohibiting attendance at church and, in its most extreme form, most types of involvement with members of the community. The ban is particularly difficult for members of the shunned person's family. In such cases, they are expected to cut off all communication with that family member.[98]

Nonverbal Communication of the Amish

Moellendorf and her colleagues also studied the nonverbal communication of the Amish and found that they have a distinct nonverbal communication system. According to Moellendorf, one's role in an Amish community is nonverbally communicated by his or her physical appearance and dress. For example, the style of hat worn by an Amish man communicates his age and marital status. A black hat with three or more inches of brim is given to Amish boys at about the age of 2. The larger brim communicates the young boy's innocence. A bridegroom's hat has a crease around the top and a wide seam along the brim signaling his marriage. Amish fathers wear hats with flat crowns. An Amish woman's bonnet is her way to communicate her marital status. All Amish women wear bonnets over the back part of their hair. Young girls wear colored bonnets and begin to wear black bonnets at about the age of 9. Married Amish women wear white bonnets.[99]

In addition to hats and bonnets, Amish hairstyles communicate status. Young girls wear braids that are fastened around their foreheads. At about the age of 10, their hair is arranged into a bun. Adult Amish women never cut their hair; they part it in the middle and wear a bun. Most Amish women do not shave their legs or trim their eyebrows, as such behavior is seen as interfering with God's work. Amish men shave until marriage, at which time they grow beards, which are analogous to wedding rings. If a single man reaches the age of 40, he may grow a beard. In all cases, married or not, the beard is left untrimmed, and mustaches are not allowed because of their long association with the military.[100]

To communicate submissiveness and pride, enhance group unity, and indicate their desire to be separate from the rest of the contemporary world, the Amish wear only plain clothing. To the Amish, their manner of dress is a statement of conformity to group values. A man's shirts are pocketless, and his trousers do not have hip pockets and are worn loose with suspenders. For women, ribbons, bows, makeup, and jewelry are forbidden, as they are seen as haughty and vain. The dresses of older Amish women close in front, and their hems touch the tops of their shoes. Women are never allowed to wear pants, and they typically wear aprons over their dresses. Generally, the colors of both men's and women's clothing are restricted to white, green, blue, or purple.[101]

Another nonverbal dimension of the Amish culture is the horse and buggy. Donald Kraybill argues that the horse and buggy serve as the prime symbol of Amish life. To the Amish, the horse communicates tradition, time, and proof that they have not succumbed to the conveniences of modern life. The buggy, which is typically gray, communicates *Gelassenheit,* which means a surrender to communal values and modesty. Moreover, because the buggies all look alike, they serve as a kind of equalizer among the Amish.[102]

Amidst incredible societal and technological change, the Amish have maintained their lifestyle for more than 200 years. Although they are generally a quiet and reserved microculture that prefers to be isolated from the dominant culture, some Amish recently have become the targets of hate crimes. Their unassuming appearance and subdued behavior, along with their horses and buggies and refusal to adopt modern technologies, have rendered the Amish easy targets. Several years ago, a young man shot at an Amish buggy full of children and then raped a young Amish woman. The assailant was quoted as saying that he wanted the Amish to know that they do not own this world and that there are other people in the world.[103]

Father J. Mahoney, a priest who has studied various religious groups, argues that the Amish have tried to freeze their culture in the late 17th century. Throughout the centuries, as the mainstream culture of the United States has progressed technologically, the Amish have tried to preserve their lifestyle, creating a disparity between them and the dominant culture. That disparity, and disagreements as to how far they should go in accommodating it, will remain the major challenge for the Amish in the coming decades.[104] As Hostetler notes:

> Over the past three centuries the Amish and other Anabaptist groups have been suspended between two opposing forces: the political forces that would eliminate ethnicity from the face of the earth and the human communities who regard ethnicity as a natural and necessary extension of the familial bonds that integrate human activities. Caught between these forces the "plain" people have sometimes prospered and sometimes suffered for their faith.[105]

Lesbian, Gay, Bisexual, and Transgender Microcultural Groups

Of the six microcultural groups discussed in this chapter, the lesbian, gay, bisexual, and transgender (LGBT) microcultural group is the most difficult to define and characterize. To be sure, LGBT issues are some of the most controversial and most politically contested areas of cultural diversity facing us today. Of the five characteristics that define microcultural groups presented at the beginning of this chapter, LGBT groups seem to meet all of them, but not definitively. First, LGBT groups have a distinguishing cultural trait—that is, their sexual orientation. Beyond that, however, members of the LGBT microculture belong to myriad other demographic, educational, occupational, and social groups. Moreover, one's sexual orientation is not as overtly distinct as, say, skin color or style of dress. LGBT persons can be of any sex, race, ethnicity, nationality, occupation, or other demographic group.

Second, membership in this microculture appears to be involuntary—although some might disagree. In their recent book on LGBT studies, Deborah Meem, Michelle Gibson, and Jonathan Alexander point out that, for more than a century, scientists and scholars have sought to identify the factors that make certain people feel sexual desire for someone of the same sex.[106] Meem and her colleagues chronicle decades of research that has tried to answer the question of whether one's sexual orientation is innate or learned. Some research suggests that it is learned, while other research points to an innate hypothesis. Meem and her colleagues point out that both sides have strengths and weaknesses in their arguments. They conclude:

> Methodological weaknesses have been perceived in both biological and psychological research, not the least of which is that both still assume heterosexuality as the default position. We can see heteronormativity at work in scientific inquiry; researchers look for a "gay gene," but why do they not attempt to isolate a "straight gene"? Presumably, only the nonnormative—the queer—needs to be explained, while the normative goes unremarked as obviously and unquestionably natural.[107]

So while the question of whether one's sexuality is innate or learned goes unanswered, most members of the LGBT microculture maintain that their membership is involuntary. In a recent survey of sexual behavior in the United States, scholars at the Center for Sexual Health Promotion at Indiana University surveyed nearly 6,000 individuals ranging in age from 14 to 94 years old. They found that among adolescent males, 96% indicated they were heterosexual and just under 4% indicated they were gay or lesbian, bisexual, or other. Among adolescent females, just over 90% indicated they were heterosexual, while just under 10% reported that they were gay or lesbian, bisexual, or other. Among adult males, just over 92% reported being heterosexual; thus, just under 8% indicated that they were gay or lesbian, bisexual, or other. Among adult women, 93% reported being heterosexual, while just under 7% indicated being gay or lesbian, bisexual, or other.[108]

Researchers note that estimating who is gay or lesbian, bisexual, or transgender is fraught with difficulty. For example, does a person consider him or herself gay or lesbian after just one same-sex encounter? Two encounters? Three? Or what about the person who has had no same-sex encounters but considers him or herself gay? Like other microcultural groups, LGBT members tend to live in certain geographical regions of the United States, primarily large urban areas. For example, the 10 U.S. cities with the largest percentage of LGBT inhabitants are as follows:[109]

City and Proportion of LGBT Inhabitants

1.	San Francisco	15.4%
2.	Seattle	12.9%
3.	Atlanta	12.8%
4.	Minneapolis	12.5%
5.	Boston	12.3%
6.	Sacramento	9.8%
7.	Portland	8.8%
8.	Denver	8.2%
9.	Washington, D.C.	8.1%
10.	Orlando	7.7%

The third characteristic defining microcultural groups is endogamy. Addressing endogamy among LGBTs in the United States is impossible because same-sex marriage between LGBT persons is illegal in most states. But, as of October 2013, 14 states—California, Connecticut, Delaware, Iowa, Maine, Maryland, Massachusetts, Minnesota, New Hampshire, New Jersey, New York, Rhode Island, Vermont, and Washington—as well as the District of Columbia and three Native American tribes, including the Coquille Indian Tribe in Oregon, have legalized gay marriage.

The fourth and fifth defining characteristics of microcultures are their awareness of their subordination and unequal treatment by the larger dominant group. Clearly, the LGBT microculture is aware of its subordination and is treated unequally, even legally. For example, Title VII of the Civil Rights Act of 1964 was the landmark piece of legislation signed by President Johnson that legally banned discrimination against African Americans and women, including segregation based on race and/or sex. The act banned racial segregation in schools, in the workplace, and by those facilities that serve the general public. But as Julie Gedro points out in her review of the legal environment for LGBTs, noticeably absent from the Civil Rights Act is any mention of sexual orientation. Gedro highlights that there are no federal prohibitions against employment discrimination for LGBT persons in the United States. Indeed, Gedro notes that currently, in 29 states, it is legal to discriminate in the workplace based on sexual orientation. More recent legislation, titled the Employment Non-Discrimination Act, would prohibit employment discrimination, preferential treatment, and retaliation on the basis of sexual orientation or gender identity by employers with 15 or more employees. The act has been introduced to the U.S. Congress nine times— in 1994, 1995, 1996, 1997, 1998, 1999, 2002, 2003, and 2009—and has yet to pass. Yet Gedro identifies no fewer than 30 other countries across the globe that prohibit discrimination on the basis of sexual orientation.[110]

In addition to the lack of federal prohibition against discrimination, a number of organizations across the United States actively protest against the equal rights of LGBTs. Not only do many of these groups actively try to subordinate LGBT groups, but they also advocate violence against LGBT persons and strive for their complete eradication. In 2010, the Southern Poverty

STUDENT VOICES ACROSS CULTURES

Stephen Rupsch

Living as an openly gay man and working as a professor for a Catholic college has been an illuminating experience. Before I arrived here in the Midwest to take a teaching position, I lived most of my adult life on the West Coast and in larger cities, such as San Francisco. I also work in the theatre as a director and teacher. Within those geographic and social groups, the fact that I am gay was, for the most part, a non-issue. San Francisco has a large LGBT community, and the theatre world historically has been a refuge for all sorts of people from fringe groups. I am also 50 and have been out since I was 17. I know what direct silencing looks like and how it feels. What I was surprised with when I arrived for my new job was the amount of indirect silencing. This is what I now call *soft discrimination*.

Example 1: I am speaking with a colleague about minor personal matters. My colleague tells me all about his or her husband or wife, his or her kids, and his or her parents but never asks about my partner, Brett (whom he or she has met). I wouldn't use this as an example if it did not happen *frequently*.

Example 2: I meet a new colleague at a college social function. We have some polite conversation about general life on and off campus. As soon as that person realizes that I am gay, he or she says something like, "I have a friend who is gay" or "I love gay people." I know when people do this, they are trying to connect with me, but seriously, making a big deal about my gayness just makes me feel as though they are *not* really OK with it. Again, this has happened several times.

Example 3: My partner, Brett, and I are grocery shopping. Brett loves big, beautiful rings and wears them often. I hear a man behind me make a strange "disgusted" sound and turn to look at him staring at Brett's ring, then at Brett, and then at me. I turn (probably rolling my eyes) and hear the sound of someone spitting and turn again to see the "loogie" at our feet and the man huffing away. And yes, this has happened a few times.

What is happening when one of your bosses speaks about diversity to a small group but doesn't look you in the eye? Am I imagining it? What is happening when you teach your class about a play with a gay character, but none of the students can look at you when you are speaking about it?

I direct plays for a living and teach acting. I know that you can convey a lot of meaning with very subtle actions. Maybe it is involuntary, but maybe sometimes it's not. And sometimes it silences.

Law Center asserted that LGBTs are the group of people most targeted by hate crimes. The center profiled 18 organized groups, many of which are religiously oriented, whose primary goal was to thwart LGBT progress and equal rights. For example, Abiding Truth Ministries of Springfield, Massachusetts, sponsors an international anti-LGBT campaign. The founder, Scott Lively, coauthored the book *The Pink Swastika: Homosexuality in the Nazi Party,* which accuses homosexuals of running the Nazi Party and is widely cited by gay-bashers. Lively has taken his anti-LGBT rhetoric to Eastern Europe, Africa, and Russia. Americans for Truth About Homosexuality was formed in 1996 by Peter LaBarbera, who reorganized it in 2006 as a much more serious and influential, if often vicious, operation. The Christian Anti-Defamation

Commission (CADC) is focused on the evils of homosexuality and has called the idea of allowing gays to serve openly in the military "evil." The CADC opposes hate crimes legislation and has written that "homosexuals have turned away from humbly worshipping the true and living God and his transcendent moral order in order to make an idol out of their sexual perversion and chaos."[111]

Gayspeak: Communication of the LGBT Microculture

In 1981, *Gayspeak: Gay Male/Lesbian Communication* was published. The book was the first scholarly volume devoted to gay and lesbian communication.[112] With a few exceptions, the book is a collection of essays articulating the thesis that the gay community uses language differently than does the heterosexual community. But the assertion that the LGBT microculture communicates in ways that distinguish it as a unique linguistic community is misleading because the LGBT community is so demographically diverse. For example, in one essay in *Gayspeak,* Joseph Hayes asserts that gayspeak serves three functions: (1) It is a language that protects against detection of one's homosexual status, (2) it facilitates the expression of gay and lesbian roles within gay culture, and (3) it is a vehicle for political identity and activism. While these claims seem reasonable and certainly may apply to LGBT communication, they are not unique to this microculture. Any number of demographic, political, or social groups use language in this way.[113]

Unfortunate stereotypes abound that gay men speak like heterosexual women and lesbians sound like heterosexual men. The classic stereotype that gay men speak with overly careful pronunciation, a high and rapidly changing pitch, a breathy tone, and use of sexual and erotic references, and that lesbians use a lower pitch than do heterosexual women is not supported by any sound empirical research. To be sure, virtually all legitimate scholarly research in this area rejects these stereotypes. Andrea Sims notes that a distinctive communication style unique to LGBT has not been identified because the LGBT microculture does not represent a single unified or delineable social or demographic group.[114]

On the other hand, some scholars have argued that members of the LGBT community may, at times, use a specialized vocabulary, particularly when interacting among themselves. For example, in 1972, *The Queen's Vernacular: A Gay Lexicon* was published, and it is thought to be the first published dictionary of gay slang.[115] Examples from the book include the term *chicken,* referring to a young boy, or *package,* referring to a man's genitalia. Critics have maintained that many of the terms in the book are outdated and no longer used or recognized by LGBT groups. In his well-known book *Word's Out: Gay Men's English,* William Leap has argued that gay men's speech is a gendered approach to communication that may include a specialized vocabulary but may not. In fact, Leap has maintained that much gay communication is subtle, due to the stigmatized nature of being gay. Leap describes openly gay communication as a language of risk. He also points to several functions of gay men's speech, including a language of desire, release of shame (from parents, society, religious institutions), cooperation, and a format for display (e.g., compliments, flirting, etc.).[116] So scholars from across a variety of academic disciplines disagree about whether the phenomenon of gayspeak exists. The communication patterns of the LGBT microculture are only beginning to be identified and understood. But, as Sims notes, the topic is a growing and promising area of research.[117]

CHAPTER SUMMARY

Within most cultures, there are groups of people who differ in some significant way from the general societal culture. In this book, the term *microculture* is used to refer to those identifiable groups of people who share a set of values, beliefs, and behaviors and who possess a common history and a verbal and nonverbal symbol system that is similar to the dominant culture but varies in some way, perhaps subtly. Microcultures can be different from the larger culture in a variety of ways, most often because of race, ethnicity, language, or behavior. But one's age group or occupation might also render one a member of a microcultural group. Perhaps every member of a culture is also a member of a microcultural group.

In this chapter, Hispanics, African Americans, Asian Americans, Hmong, Amish, and LGBT people were profiled as microcultural groups in the United States. Mostly because of immigration and high fertility rates, Hispanics are now the largest microcultural group in the United States. Like many microcultural groups, Hispanics experience lower incomes, higher poverty, and higher unemployment rates than do non-Hispanic White groups. The U.S. government estimates that the Hispanic population will continue to grow through the first half of the 21st century. By then, Hispanic economic influence will be significant. As an economic, political, and socially powerful group, African Americans have maintained an important part of their history—that is, their language. African American history is expressed in the language games African Americans play and in their daily communication with others, for some in the form of Ebonics. Asian Americans have become a powerful microcultural group in the United States. They are the best educated and fastest growing racial group in the country, and they also have the highest average income. Possibly the newest microcultural group in the United States is the Hmong. The Hmong are a group of people who fought alongside American troops in the Vietnam War, only to be abandoned when the war was lost. The Hmong who have immigrated to the United States try desperately to adapt to U.S. culture while simultaneously maintaining some aspects of their traditional culture. Like African Americans, the Hmong face a great deal of racism and resentment.

The Amish were also profiled in this chapter. More than any other microcultural group, the Amish have preserved their traditional culture while peacefully coexisting within the rule structure of the dominant cultural milieu. Unlike any other microcultural group, the Amish have successfully isolated themselves from most of mainstream American culture. Finally, the LGBT group was highlighted. This group is the most difficult to define and characterize. To be sure, LGBT issues are some of the most controversial and most politically contested areas of cultural diversity facing us today. Of the five characteristics that define microcultural groups presented at the beginning of this chapter, LGBT people seem to meet all of them, but not definitively.

Although each microcultural group portrayed in this chapter is obviously different from the others, they all share at least one major feature—that is, language. Each group, while adapting and accommodating to the dominant cultural surroundings, has successfully preserved a part of its original culture through communication. The verbal and nonverbal language of its cultural group maintains its heritage and allows its people to pass along their ancestry for future generations.

Visit the student study site at www.sagepub.com/neuliep6e for e-flashcards, web quizzes, web resources, and more.

DISCUSSION QUESTIONS

1. To what microcultural groups do you belong?

2. Whom do you know who is a member of a microcultural group?

3. How are microcultural group members in your community treated differently than other members?

4. What are some of the common stereotypes in your community of microcultural group members?

5. How might members of your community assist microcultural groups in becoming fully engaged in the culture?

ETHICAL ISSUES AND MICROCULTURES

1. There has been considerable debate among Americans, and even among members of the U.S. Congress and Senate, that English should be declared the official language of the United States and that members of the above-profiled microcultures should be required to speak English, especially when engaged in civil and legal affairs. What do you think? Should English be the official language of the United States?

2. Some people argue that most members of the above microcultures are not doing enough to assimilate, take in, absorb, and become a part of American culture. Do you think microcultures should do more to assimilate to the dominant U.S. culture? Or should microcultures hold on to the traditions and customs of their native cultures?

KEY TERMS

African Americans   109

Amish   121

Ebonics   110

Hispanic   104

Hmong   117

LGBT   126

muted groups   101

Spanglish   106

NOTES

1. Morris, R. (1997). Living in/between. In A. Gonzales, M. Houston, & V. Chen (Eds.), *Our Voices: Essays in Culture, Ethnicity, and Communication* (pp. 163–176). Los Angeles: Roxbury.

2. U.S. Census Bureau. (2009). *Statistical Abstract of the United States: 2010* (129th ed.). Washington, DC: Author. Retrieved from http://www.census.gov/statab/www/ and http://www.census.gov/compendia/statab/2010/tables/10s0043.pdf.

3. Schaefer, R. T. (2012). *Racial and Ethnic Groups* (13th ed.). Upper Saddle River, NJ: Prentice Hall.

4. This discussion of the defining characteristics of minority groups is based on the following sources: Meyers, B. (1984). Minority Group: An Ideological

Formulation. *Social Problems, 32,* 1–15; Schaefer, *Racial and Ethnic Groups;* Wagley, C., & Harris, M. (1958). *Minorities in the New World: Six Cases.* New York: Columbia University Press.

5. Barrett, L. E. (1997). *The Rastafarians.* Boston: Beacon Press.

6. Laungani, P. D. (2007). *Understanding Cross-Cultural Psychology.* London: Sage; Schaefer, *Racial and Ethnic Groups.*

7. Ilcan, S. M. (1994). Marriage Regulation and the Rhetoric of Alliance in Northwestern Turkey. *Ethnology, 33,* 273–297.

8. Schaefer, *Racial and Ethnic Groups.*

9. Ibid.

10. The muted group theory was first articulated by Shirley and Edwin Ardener. The sources used for this discussion are Ardener, S. (Ed.). (1975). *Perceiving Women*. London: Malaby; Kramarae, C. (1981). *Women and Men Speaking*. Rowley, MA: Newbury House.

11. Weber, S. N. (1991). The Need to Be: The Sociocultural Significance of Black Language. In L. A. Samovar & R. E. Porter (Eds.), *Intercultural Communication: A Reader* (6th ed., pp. 277–283). Belmont, CA: Wadsworth.

12. Tyson, C. (2001). Exploring the Generation Gap and Its Implications on African American Consciousness. *Doula: The Journal of Rap Music and Hip Hop Culture*.

13. Adams, T. M., & Fuller, D. B. (2006). The Words Have Changed but the Ideology Remains the Same: Misogynistic Lyrics in Rap Music. *Journal of Black Studies, 36*, 938–957.

14. Tyson, Exploring the Generation Gap and Its Implications on African American Consciousness.

15. Konkka, A. (1998). *Power, Pride, and Politics in Rap Music*. Unpublished manuscript, Department of Translation Studies, University of Tampere, Finland. Retrieved from http://www.universalmetropolis.com/city/threads.php?threadid = 10420

16. Tyson, E. H. (2006). Rap-Music Attitude and Perception Scale: A Validation Study. *Research on Social Work Practice, 16*, 211–223.

17. Konkka, *Power, Pride, and Politics in Rap Music.*

18. Canadian Broadcasting Corporation. (2009, October). *Speaking Out: Quebec's Debate Over Language Laws*. Retrieved from http://www.cbc.ca/news/canada/speaking-out-quebec-s-debate-over-language-laws-1.860189

19. Schaefer, *Racial and Ethnic Groups.*

20. Ennis, S. R., Rios-Vargas, M., & Albert, N. G. (2011). *The Hispanic Population: 2010*. Washington, DC: U.S. Department of Commerce, Economics and Statistics Administration, U.S. Census Bureau. Retrieved from http://www.census.gov/prod/cen2010/briefs/c2010br-04.pdf

21. U.S. Census Bureau. (2008). *Monthly Resident Population Estimates by Age, Sex, Race, and Hispanic Origin for the United States: April 2000 to July 1, 2008*. Retrieved from www.census.gov/popest/national/asrh/2008-nat-res.html; Velasco, G., & Dockterman, D. (2010, January 21). *Statistical Portrait of Hispanics in the United States, 2008*. Retrieved from http://www.pewhispanic.org/2010/01/21/statistical-portrait-of-hispanics-in-the-united-states-2008/

22. Crouch, N. (2004). *Mexicans and Americans: Cracking the Cultural Code*. Yarmouth, ME: Intercultural Press.

23. Velasco & Dockterman, *Statistical Portrait of Hispanics in the United States, 2008.*

24. Ibid.

25. Pajewski, A., & Enriquez, L. (1996). *Teaching From a Hispanic Perspective: A Handbook for Non-Hispanic Adult Educators*. Phoenix: The Arizona Adult Literacy and Technology Resource Center.

26. Crouch, *Mexicans and Americans.*

27. Ibid., p. 102.

28. Clutter, A W., & Nieto, R. D. (2000). *Understanding Hispanic Culture: Ohio State University Fact Sheet*. Columbus: Ohio State University Extension.

29. Rodrigo Villalobos Arevalo, personal communication, January 20, 2010.

30. Ardila, A. (2005). Spanglish: An Anglicized Spanish Dialect. *Hispanic Journal of Behavioral Sciences, 27*, 60–81; Stavans, I. (2000, October 13). The Gravitas of Spanglish. *Chronicle of Higher Education, 47*, B7–B10; Stavans, I. (2003). *Spanglish: The Making of a New American Language*. New York: Rayo (HarperCollins).

31. Rifkin, J. M. (1990). No Problema—Spanglish Language Abounds. *Hispanic Times Magazine, 11*, 30–31.

32. Stavans, The Gravitas of Spanglish.

33. Cruz, B., & Teck, B. (1998). The Official Spanglish Dictionary. *Hispanic, 11*, 34–36. These examples of Spanglish can be found in Cruz, B., Teck, B., & the editors of *Generation ñ*. (1998). *The Official Spanglish Dictionary: Un User's Guia to More Than 300 Words and Phrases That Aren't Exactly Español or Inglés*. New York: Fireside.

34. Fought, C. (2001). Facts and Myths About Chicano Language. *Language Magazine, 1*, 3.

35. Fought, C. (2003). *Chicano English in Context*. Houndmills, Basingstoke, Hampshire, UK: Palgrave MacMillan, p. 4.

36. Ibid.

37. Casas, J. M., Wagenheim, B. R., Banchero, R., & Mendoza-Romero, J. (1994). Hispanic Masculinity: Myth or Psychological Schema Meriting Clinical Consideration. *Hispanic Journal of Behavioral Sciences, 16*, 315–332; Mayo, Y. Q., & Resnick, R. P. (1996). The Impact of Machismo on Hispanic Women. *Journal of Women and Social Work, 11*, 257–278.

38. This quote was included in Anders, G. (1993). Machismo: Dead or Alive? *Hispanic, 6*, 14–18.

39. Casas et al., Hispanic Masculinity.

40. Michael, E. T., Gagnon, J. H., Laumann, E. O., & Kolata, G. (1995). *Sex in America: A Definitive Survey*. New York: Warner.

41. Nuiry, O. E. (1996). Ban the Bandito! *Hispanic, 9*, 26–31.

42. Schaefer, *Racial and Ethnic Groups.*

43. Ibid.

44. Rastogi, S., Johnson, T. D., Hoeffel, E. M., & Drewery, M. R., Jr. (2011). *The Black Population: 2010*. Washington, DC: U.S. Department of Commerce, Economics and Statistics Division, U.S. Census Bureau. Retrieved from http://www.census.gov/prod/cen2010/briefs/c2010br-06.pdf

45. Schaefer, *Racial and Ethnic Groups.*

46. Smitherman, G., & Cunningham, S. (1997). Moving Beyond Resistance: Ebonics and African American Youth. *Journal of Black Psychology, 23,* 227–232.

47. Weber, S. N. (1994). The Need to Be: The Sociocultural Significance of Black Language. In L. A. Samovar & R. E. Porter (Eds.), *Intercultural Communication: A Reader* (7th ed., pp. 221–226). Belmont, CA: Wadsworth.

48. Nasir, N. S., McLaughlin, M. W., & Jones, A. (2009). What Does It Mean to Be African American? Constructions of Race and Academic Identity in an Urban Public High School. *American Educational Research Journal, 46*(1), 73–114.

49. Rickford, J. C. (2004). *What Is Ebonics (African-American Vernacular English)?* Washington, DC: Linguistic Society of America.

50. Kochman, T. (1990). Cultural Pluralism: Black and White Styles. In D. Carbaugh (Ed.), *Cultural Communication and Intercultural Context* (pp. 219–224). Hillsdale, NJ: Erlbaum.

51. Weber, The Need to Be (6th ed.), p. 279.

52. Jahn, J. (1961). *Muntu: An Outline of the New African Culture.* New York: Grove Press, p. 124.

53. Weber, The Need to Be.

54. Billings, A. (2005). Beyond the Ebonics Debate: Attitudes About Black and Standard American English. *Journal of Black Studies, 36,* 68–81.

55. Pew Research Center. (2013). *The Rise of Asian Americans.* Washington, DC: Author. Retrieved from http://www.pewsocialtrends.org/files/2013/04/Asian-Americans-new-full-report-04-2013.pdf (Quote on p. 1)

56. Ibid.

57. Ibid.

58. U.S. Census Bureau. (2010). *Asian Population.* Washington, DC: U.S. Census Bureau, U.S. Department of Commerce. Retrieved from http://www.census.gov/newsroom/minority_links/asian.html

59. Ibid.

60. Kim, B. S. K., Yang, P. H., Atkinson, D. R., Wolfe, M. M., & Hong, S. (2001). Cultural Value Similarities and Differences Among Asian American Ethnic Groups. *Cultural Diversity and Ethnic Minority Psychology, 7,* 343–361; Pew Research Center, *The Rise of Asian Americans.*

61. Kim et al., Cultural Value Similarities and Differences Among Asian American Ethnic Groups.

62. Kim, B. S. K., Atkinson, D. R., & Yang, P. H. (1999). The Asian Values Scale: Development, Factor Analysis, Validation, and Reliability. *Journal of Counseling Psychology, 46,* 342–352; Kim, B. S. K., Li, L. C., & Ng, G. F. (2005). The Asian American Values Scale-Multidimensional: Development, Reliability, and Validity. *Cultural Diversity and Ethnic Minority Psychology, 11,* 181–201; Kim, B. S. K., & Omizo, M. M. (2003). Asian Cultural Values, Attitudes Toward Seeking Professional Psychological Help, and Willingness to See a Counselor. *The Counseling Psychologist, 31,* 343–361; Kim et al., Cultural Value Similarities and Differences Among Asian American Ethnic Groups.

63. Ibid.

64. Gudykunst, W. B., Matsumoto, Y., Ting-Toomey, S., Nishida, T., Kim, K., & Heyman, S. (1996). The Influence of Cultural Individualism–Collectivism, Self Construals, and Individual Values on Communication Styles Across Cultures. *Human Communication Research, 12,* 525–549.

65. Park, Y. S., & Kim, B. S. K. (2008). Asian and European American Cultural Values and Communication Styles Among Asian American and European American College Students. *Cultural Diversity and Ethnic Minority Psychology, 14,* 47–56.

66. Kao, E. M., Nagata, D. K., & Petersen, C. (1997). Explanatory Style, Family Expressiveness, and Self-Esteem Among Asian American and European American College Students. *Journal of Social Psychology, 137,* 435–444.

67. Elliott, C., Adams, R. J., & Sockalingam, S. (2010). *Summary of Normative Communication Styles and Values.* Retrieved from http://www.awesomelibrary.org/multiculturaltoolkit-styleschart-normative.html

68. Winland, D. N. (1992). The Role of Religious Affiliation in Refugee Resettlement: The Case of the Hmong. *Canadian Ethnic Studies, 24,* 96–120.

69. Tyson, J. L. (1994). Congress and State Department Ignore Persecution of Hmong. *Human Events, 50,* 12–14.

70. Fenyvesi, C. (1997, May 26). Honoring the Secret Warriors. *U.S. News and World Report, 122,* 13.

71. Duffy, J. (1996). *Who Are the Hmong? Legends of Literacy, History of Struggle.* Retrieved from www.adone.com/ttj/news/050296/ent3.htm

72. Thao, K. (1995). *The Hmong Culture.* Unpublished student manuscript, St. Norbert College, De Pere, WI.

73. Fenyvesi, Honoring the Secret Warriors.

74. Duffy, *Who Are the Hmong?*

75. Winland, The Role of Religious Affiliation in Refugee Resettlement.

76. Thao, *The Hmong Culture.*

77. Hutchison, R., & McNall, M. (1994). Early Marriage in a Hmong Cohort. *Journal of Marriage and the Family, 56,* 579–591.

78. Thao, *The Hmong Culture.*

79. Ibid.

80. Ibid.

81. Guensburg, C. (1996, June 16). The Fabric of Their Lives. *Milwaukee Journal Sentinel;* Lee, J. H. (1998). *Hmong Quilts—Pa Ndau—Reflect Hmong History.* Retrieved from www.stolaf.edu/people/cdr/hmong/culture/pandau2.html

82. Thao, *The Hmong Culture.*

83. Barkan, E. R. (1995). Out of Carnage and Into the Crucible: Southeast Asian Refugees' Journey From

Old Worlds to a New One. *Journal of American Ethnic History, 14,* 53–58.

84. Hostetler, J. A. (1993). *Amish Society.* Baltimore, MD: Johns Hopkins University Press. (Quote on p. 4)

85. Pennsylvania Dutch Country Welcome Center. (1998). *The Amish, the Mennonites, and "the Plain People."* Retrieved from www.800padutch.com/amish.html; Powell, K., & Powell, A. (2008). *Amish 101: Amish Beliefs, Culture and Lifestyle: History of the Amish in America.* Retrieved from http://pittsburgh.about.com/cs/pennsylvania/a/amish.htm; Schlabach, D. (1998). *An Amishman's Personal Expression.* Retrieved from www.amish-heartland.com

86. Huber, R. (1997). *Be Ye Not Conformed to This World.* Retrieved from www.columbia.edu/cu/sipa/PUBS/SLANT/SPRING97/huber.html

87. Hostetler, *Amish Society;* Pearce, S., Suminski, S., & Tschudy, K. (1996). *The Amish: Simple Values in a Complex World.* Unpublished manuscript, St. Norbert College, De Pere, WI.

88. MacKaye, W. R. (1971, December 9). High court hears Amish school case. *Washington Post.*

89. Reiling, D. M. (2002). The "Simmie" Side of Life: Old Order Amish Youths' Affective Response to Culturally Prescribed Deviance. *Youth and Society, 34,* 146–171.

90. *Origins of the Old Order Amish.* (1997). Retrieved from http://amishreligiousfreedom.org/origin.htm

91. S. A. (1998). *Influences of World View on Individual Life and Culture.* Retrieved from http://web.missouri.edu/~hartmanj/rs150/papers/sall.html

92. Hostetler, *Amish Society.*

93. Pennsylvania Dutch Country Welcome Center, *The Amish, the Mennonites, and "the Plain People."*

94. Huber, *Be Ye Not Conformed to This World.*

95. S. A., *Influences of World View on Individual Life and Culture.*

96. P. D. (1998). *Gender, Work, and Worldview: Reflections on Amish and American Society.* Retrieved from http://web.missouri.edu/~hartmanj/rs150/papers/pdun.html

97. Hostetler, *Amish Society;* Kraybill, D. B. (1989). *The Riddle of Amish Culture.* Baltimore, MD: Johns Hopkins University Press; Moellendorf, S., Warsh, H., & Yoshimaru, K. (1997). *The Amish Culture: A Closer Look at the People of Lancaster County.* Unpublished student manuscript, St. Norbert College, De Pere, WI.

98. Mahoney, J. (1998). *European Free-Church Family.* Retrieved from www.jmahoney.com/european

.htm; Ontario Consultants on Religious Tolerance. (1998). *The Amish.* Retrieved from http://religioustolerance.org/amish.htm

99. Buch, B. B. (1997). *The Nonverbal Cues of Amish Dress.* Unpublished manuscript, St. Norbert College, De Pere, WI; Hostetler, *Amish Society;* Kraybill, *The Riddle of Amish Culture;* Mocllendorf et al., *The Amish Culture.*

100. Ibid.

101. Ibid.

102. Ibid.

103. P. D. (1998). *Amish and Mainstream Culture Clash.* Retrieved from http://web.missouri.edu/~hartmanj/rs150/papers/pd4.html

104. Mahoney, *European Free-Church Family.*

105. Hostetler, J. A. (1992). An Amish Beginning. *American Scholar, 61,* 552–563. (Quote on p. 562)

106. Meem, D. T., Gibson, M. A., & Alexander, J. F. (2010). *Finding Out: An Introduction to LGBT studies.* Los Angeles: Sage.

107. Ibid., pp. 135–136.

108. Herbenick, D., Reece, M., Schick, V., Sanders, S. A., Dodge, B., & Fortenberry, J. D. (2010). Sexual Behavior in the United States: Results From a National Probability Sample of Men and Women Ages 14–94. *Journal of Sexual Medicine, 7*(5), 255–265.

109. Gates, G. J. (2006). *Same-Sex Couples and the Gay, Lesbian, Bisexual Population: New Estimates From the American Community Survey.* Los Angeles: Williams Institute on Sexual Orientation Law and Public Policy, UCLA School of Law.

110. Gedro, J. (2010). Understanding, Designing, and Teaching LGBT Issues. *Advances in Developing Human Resources, 12*(3), 352–366.

111. Schlatter, E. (2010, Winter). 18 Anti-Gay Groups and Their Propaganda. *Southern Poverty Law Center Intelligence Report,* (140).

112. Chesebro, J. (1981). *Gayspeak: Gay Male/Lesbian Communication.* New York: Pilgrim.

113. Cameron, D., & Kulick, D. (2003). *Language and Sexuality.* Cambridge, UK: Cambridge University Press.

114. Sims, A. (2004). Gayspeak. In C. J. Summers (Ed.), *glbtq: An Encyclopedia of Gay, Lesbian, Bisexual, Transgender, and Queer Culture.* Chicago: glbtq.

115. Rodgers, B. (1972). *The Queen's Vernacular: A Gay Lexicon.* San Francisco: Straight Arrow. (This book was published in 1979 by Paragon, New York, under the title *Gay Talk.*)

116. Leap, W. (1996). *Word's Out: Gay Men's English.* Minneapolis: University of Minnesota Press.

117. Sims, *Gayspeak.*

CHAPTER 4

The Environmental Context

After reading this chapter, you should be able to

1. compare and contrast high- and low-load environments;

2. discuss the relationship between culture and the natural, built, and perceptual environments;

3. recognize and discuss that natural disasters are cultural and social, as well as natural, events;

4. identify and describe fixed-feature, semifixed-feature, and informal built environments;

5. compare and contrast the housing patterns of Japanese, Navaho, and Marakwet cultures;

6. compare and contrast cultural preferences for privacy;

7. assess your orientation toward privacy;

8. compare and contrast monochronic and polychronic time orientations; and

9. assess your monochronic/polychronic orientation.

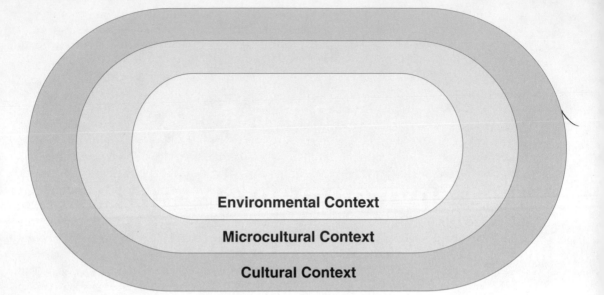

Environment is heir to psyche.

—Howard F. Stein[1]

Consider the following two scenarios:[2]

Scenario #1: It is early evening, and you are alone in your dorm room. You're sitting on your bed reading a chapter in your excellently written intercultural communication textbook. Some quiet music that helps you concentrate is playing in the background. The room is quiet, as is the rest of the dormitory. Most of your friends are studying in their rooms as well.

Scenario #2: You are walking through the international terminal of a major airport. The terminal is crowded with people rushing to and from the various ticket counters and speaking in languages you have never heard. Announcements are coming in over the airport intercom system in two languages. The airport is very noisy, with people conversing, yelling, and laughing. You can hear the various jets landing and taking off as you rush to your gate. The lights are bright.

How would you compare these two environments? How might your verbal and nonverbal communication differ in each scenario? Would you feel and react the same in Scenario #1 as in Scenario #2?

All human communication occurs within a natural/physical, built, and perceptual environment. The environmental context refers to the actual natural/physical geographical place or location where communication occurs. This includes the terrestrial environment (e.g., the natural physical location). The environmental context also refers to the built environment, which includes the human adaptations to the physical environment, such as architecture, landscaping, and housing. The environmental context also refers to how humans perceive and think about the natural and built environments. This perceptual environment is culturally learned. For example, people who were raised and live in International Falls, Minnesota, think nothing of a snowstorm that produces 12 inches or more of snow. To people born and raised in Phoenix, Arizona, such weather is unthinkable.

These environments (i.e., the natural, built, and perceptual) have a pervasive influence on the nature of communication. The purpose of this chapter is to explore the environmental context of intercultural communication. In the contextual model of intercultural communication presented in Chapter 1, the environmental context is the third-largest circle surrounding the interactants. Recall that, in the model, the cultural and microcultural contexts encircle the environmental context. How humans perceive the physical, built, and perceptual environment is significantly affected by their culture and microculture. Furthermore, like the cultural and microcultural contexts, the influence of the physical, built, and perceptual environments is generally outside our conscious awareness.

How we see the environment around us is influenced by our individual psychological perceptions, which, in turn, are shaped by culture. People from all cultures project their mental perceptions onto the physical and built environments and act as though what is projected is, in fact, the true quality of the physical and built world. In other words, even the physical and built environment is subject to cultural interpretation. As Stein notes, far from being a passive component of culture, the environment is an active ingredient of the human experience.[3] In addition, the environment has a considerable impact on our communication. As we move from one physical location to another, our verbal and nonverbal messages adapt accordingly. The types of messages we send and receive in the classroom differ significantly from those we exchange in our dorm rooms or when we are shopping in the mall. As the environment changes, our messages change. And we do this without much thought.

In this chapter, several aspects of the natural, built, and perceptual environment will be discussed, including the information load of an environment; the relationship between cultures and their natural environment; the *built* dimension of the physical environment; crosscultural comparisons of housing; dimensions of privacy, including online privacy; and perceptions of time, including monochronic and polychronic time orientations. Each of these environmental dimensions affects how we communicate with others, and each varies considerably across cultures.

ENVIRONMENTS AND INFORMATION LOAD

Albert Mehrabian is well-known for his work in environmental psychology. According to Mehrabian, there are a number of ways to compare one environment with another (e.g., Scenario #1 and Scenario #2 above). One way is to calculate the information rate—that is, the amount of information contained or perceived in the environment per some unit of time. According to Mehrabian, the more information available to process, the greater the information rate. An environment that has a high information rate has a high load, whereas one with a low information rate has a low load. Mehrabian and his colleagues developed a list of adjectives to describe the load of any given environment (see Table 4.1).[4]

Table 4.1   High Versus Low Load Descriptors

Environment Type	
High Load	**Low Load**
Uncertain	Certain
Varied	Redundant
Complex	Simple
Novel	Familiar
Large-scale	Small-scale
Contrasting	Similar
Dense	Sparse
Intermittent	Continuous
Surprising	Usual
Heterogeneous	Homogeneous
Crowded	Uncrowded
Asymmetrical	Symmetrical
Immediate	Distant
Moving	Still
Rare	Common
Random	Patterned
Improbable	Probable

SOURCE: Adapted from Mehrabian, A. (1976). *Public Places and Private Spaces: The Psychology of Work, Play, and Living Environments.* Basic Books, New York.

An environment containing several of the left-hand adjectives has a high load, whereas one that can be described with the right-hand terms has a low load. Some environments might contain a blend of both the left- and right-hand terms. In comparing Scenario #1 with Scenario #2, many of the right-hand terms apply to Scenario #1, including *simple, small-scale, sparse, uncrowded, homogeneous, symmetrical, still, patterned,* and *probable.* On the other hand, Scenario #2 could be described using several of the left-hand terms, such as *varied, complex, large-scale, contrasting, dense, surprising, heterogeneous, crowded, asymmetrical, moving, random,* and *improbable.* Based on this comparison, Scenario #1 has a low information load and Scenario #2 has a high information load.[5]

Mehrabian argues that, to some extent, information load is equivalent to the level of uncertainty in a particular environment. The higher the information load, the higher the uncertainty, especially in novel and complex environments. The more familiar we are with a situation, the less uncertainty we experience. Of all the environmental factors, people are perhaps the greatest source of uncertainty. This is especially true of strangers, including people from different cultures. Hence, a crowded room of strangers contains high levels of uncertainty and a heavy information load. For this reason, when we are interacting with people from a different culture (especially in their environment), the information load probably will be high.[6]

Mehrabian contends that the information load of a particular environment can affect people's feelings in three ways: arousal–nonarousal, pleasure–displeasure, and dominance–submissiveness.[7] The arousal dimension refers to your level of stimulation and excitability. Pleasure refers to your degree of happiness and satisfaction. Dominance refers to your feelings of control or command of the situation. These emotional responses cause people either to approach or to avoid the environment. Generally, lower load environments produce less negative arousal, are more pleasant, and are controllable. Hence, we're likely to approach these kinds of environments. Conversely, the heavily loaded environments produce anxiety (e.g., negative arousal), are unpleasant, and are less controllable. We may be more likely to avoid such situations.[8] Consider Scenario #1 and Scenario #2 from the beginning of this chapter. If you had the chance to choose one of the two scenarios, which would you choose? Of the two, which produces the most positive arousal, which is more pleasant, and which is more controllable? Likewise, how do you feel about approaching or avoiding communication situations with people from different cultures? Because such situations may be highly loaded, you may prefer to avoid them.

CULTURE AND THE NATURAL ENVIRONMENT

Jon T. Lang, Emeritus Professor of architecture at the University of New South Wales in Sydney, Australia, has written extensively about the relationship between people, their culture, and their environment. Lang explains that the natural, or terrestrial, environment includes the physical geography of the Earth, its climate, and its natural processes. The terrestrial environment for every person is the planet Earth.[9] Environmental psychologist Richard Knopf maintains that the natural environment is valued differently by different people. A culture's relationship with nature is culture bound. According to Knopf, culture influences how much people value nature and the symbols they use to communicate about it. Aivilik Eskimos, notes Knopf, have more than a dozen different terms to describe the winds and various snow conditions. People perceive and create symbols of their environment based on their cultural experiences with it. Knopf argues that it is not the natural environment per se that generates affect but, rather, the verbal and nonverbal symbols we use to communicate about nature. Moreover, how a culture values and treats the natural environment can change quickly, especially if that culture experiences shifts in religion or dramatic advances in science and technology. The United States in the 20th and 21st centuries, for example, witnessed immense changes in how we treat the natural environment. Recycling plastic water bottles, glass containers, cardboard boxes, and paper was unheard of just 30 years ago. Unleaded gasoline is also a relatively new phenomenon. Just 30 years ago, most automobiles averaged about 15 miles per gallon of gas. In June 2013, the International Energy Agency reported that in the United States, a switch from coal to gas in power generation helped reduce energy-related carbon dioxide (CO_2) emissions by 200 million metric tons, bringing them back to the level of the mid-1990s. Because of scientific and technological progress, we now see the environment as something we can control and dominate.[10]

Although all cultures exist within specific terrestrial contexts, unique features of the terrestrial environment exist in every culture. Gravity, for example, exists everywhere on Earth; however, oceans, lakes, streams, mountain ranges, deserts, valleys, trees, and forms of vegetation vary considerably across cultures. Indonesia, for example, is composed of more than 13,000 islands covering more than 700,000 square miles. The vegetation in Indonesia is diverse, with more than 40,000 species of flowering plants, including 5,000 species of orchids.[11] The country of Laos in Southeast Asia has a monsoonal climate wherein heavy rainfall sometimes averages 90 inches a year.[12] Conversely, in some areas of South Yemen, which lies in the southwest corner of the Arabian peninsula, only 4 inches of rain fall in a given year. Some northern and eastern sections of the country can go without rain for years.[13] Russia is the largest country in the world (i.e., geographically) with a land mass of more than 6.5 million square miles and dramatic climate extremes. Northern Siberia, for example, is covered with permafrost, where snow drifts can reach as high as 60 feet and little vegetation is found.[14] Norway's land mass is just more than 100,000 square miles—slightly larger than Arizona—and only 3% of the land is usable as farmland.[15] As the physical environment of a culture varies, so will the vocabulary of the culture. Cultures with different environments create verbal and nonverbal symbols that enable them to adapt to and communicate about their environment.

Lang asserts that the natural environment of any culture influences life in that culture. Physical and climatic aspects of the environment can restrict the kinds of activities that occur.[16] In many cultures, the pace of daily activities reflects the natural climate of the area. A quick example may help illuminate this point. In some Southern European countries (e.g., Spain, Southern Italy), during the warm-weather season, many shop owners close their stores from about midday until late afternoon. They do this to avoid working through the hottest part of the day, when the temperatures can rise above 100 degrees Fahrenheit, because most of the stores in these countries are not air-conditioned. Visitors from other countries, particularly the United States, may interpret this custom as laziness on the part of the shop owners, but in reality, they are simply adjusting to the conditions of their natural climate.

Worldviews of the Natural Environment

Harvard University sociologist Florence Kluckhohn says that cultures can be described as having one of three orientations toward nature, depending on what their members believe: that people are subjugated to nature, that they are an inherent part of nature, or that they are dominant over nature.[17] A culture's orientation toward nature affects how people within that culture communicate about nature and organize their daily activities. Knowing and understanding a particular culture's orientation toward nature is a helpful step in becoming a competent intercultural communicator.

Irwin Altman and Martin Chemers argue that in cultures where nature is viewed as supreme, people believe they are at the mercy of an omnipotent nature. According to Altman and Chemers, in such cultures, nature is perceived as a dominant and unmanageable power. In Biblical times, and even more recently, the natural environment and nature were viewed as threatening and dangerous. Altman and Chemers note that Western fairy tales are replete with references to such environmental features as "dark forests," where danger lurks around every corner.[18] In her research on East India, Rebecca Jo Bishop found that many East Indians believe that the elements of the natural environment dictate the health and well-being of the people. Indeed, astrologers play an important role in India, as the people believe that nothing in nature is accidental and the universe and all living components conform to a fundamental order over which they have no control.[19]

Kluckhohn claims that many cultures attempt a balancing act with nature and try to live in harmony with it. Indeed, argue Altman and Chemers, in these types of cultures, the natural environment is seen as orderly and cyclical. The days and seasons recur regularly, and natural events repeat themselves in consistent patterns. People and environment are viewed as one, changing together, in what Altman and Chemers describe as a timeless mutual relationship.[20] Reick and Ogura hold that in many Eastern societies, nature is perceived as an ally that people draw on for spiritual support. The people of the island nation of Sri Lanka, which sits 20 miles off the southern coast of India, attempt this alliance with nature. According to Reick and Ogura, the source of their belief has its roots in Buddhism, which professes equality among all living things.[21] The Japanese are well known for their attempts to harmonize with nature, which can be seen in Japanese art forms such as gardening and flower arrangements and Haiku poetry (which makes reference to the seasons).

Kluckhohn's third orientation is seen in many Western societies, where people believe that nature is something to be controlled, domesticated, and subjugated.[22] According to Altman and Chemers, some scholars attribute this view to Judeo-Christian doctrine, in which God, who is seen as the creator of the universe, is said to have put humans on Earth to do His will. People are not just part of the environment, like trees, plants, or animals, but are of divine origin. Such philosophies have led to a separation between humans and the environment. When the scientific revolution developed, nature was seen as mechanistic, further separating people from nature. Through technology, buildings, and modern agricultural methods, humans were able to dominate their natural setting to their liking. In the United States, people separate themselves from nature and believe they have the power, even the right, to dominate it in just about any way they can. Many of our proudest achievements (e.g., moon landings, dams, indoor sports facilities) are based on conquering or exploiting nature. As in other countries where European settlement has occurred, the environment is seen as an entity to be conquered. Much of Australia's economic activity is based on the extraction of natural resources such as timber, minerals, natural gas, and oil.[23]

Natural Disasters as Cultural and Social Events

A culture's relationship with nature can be seen in how the culture deals with natural disasters. Whether they be drought, tornadoes, hurricanes, tsunamis, floods, or earthquakes, natural disasters occur in all cultures. How people manage such disaster is shaped by the culture and its view of nature. Moreover, many times when natural disasters strike, people from all over the world come together to help. Understanding the stricken culture's relationship with nature can facilitate communication among those directly affected and those offering aid and comfort. The Red Cross, for example, has people stationed around the world to help in times of need. Natural disasters provide an opportunity for intercultural communication.

Although natural disasters are triggered by natural events (e.g., tsunamis, earthquakes, floods, etc.), the effects of these disasters vary considerably across cultures because they take place within particular social and cultural systems of laws and values. Hence, an individual's vulnerability to a disaster is grounded in the social system and hierarchy within which that individual exists. In this sense, natural disasters are as much social phenomena as they are natural ones. In her extensive review of literature in this area, Sarah Fisher maintains that women are disproportionately affected by disasters because of the unequal power distance between men and women that is evident in many cultures.[24] To be sure, Fisher argues that other social factors also come into play, including one's age, ethnicity, social class standing, and disability. Even within sex groups, some women are disproportionately affected, such as widows, women of low income, and those belonging to marginalized groups. Fisher points out that in most cultures, women take on responsibilities—such as reproductive health needs and caring for children—for which the burden becomes heavier following a natural disaster. Of particular concern is violence against women following natural disasters. Fisher notes that there is considerable evidence that domestic and sexual violence against women increases in the wake of natural disasters. Much of this evidence is based on the reported increase of calls to violence intervention centers located in disaster-stricken areas. Fisher also notes that factors such as the considerable economic loss suffered by disaster-hit areas and the accompanying stress and trauma may account for the increase in violence against women in such situations.

Fisher also points out the many factors that may increase violence against women, including the idea that the daily routines of families are upset and, thus, the responsibilities for income generation and the typical household jobs may shift across sexes. Most families will be faced with economic needs that create strain and stress in relationships. Extreme economic hardship may lead some women to sexual exploitation and prostitution, often with men in positions of authority, such as police officers, members of the military, and humanitarian workers. Moreover, Fisher maintains that men and women cope with the impacts of disasters differently. Women, she argues, are more likely to communicate grief with others and seek assistance from other women, whereas men are more likely to hold back their emotions and express anger and frustration through aggression, violence, and alcoholism. To make matters even worse, overcrowded disaster centers often leave women and children vulnerable to sexual violence. Fisher points to research that indicates women are often assaulted when using such facilities. To aid women in these hard times, Fisher calls for implementation of a gender-based violence prevention and response program in government and humanitarian programs.[25]

On March 11, 2011, a massive earthquake occurred off the coast of Tohoku, Japan. Considered the most powerful earthquake ever to hit Japan and the fifth most powerful earthquake in recorded history, it triggered a devastating tsunami that killed nearly 16,000 Japanese and injured many thousands more. Hundreds of thousands of buildings were either completely destroyed or heavily damaged. The resulting tsunami caused nuclear accidents (i.e., meltdowns) at three reactors in the Fukushima Daiichi Nuclear Power Plant. But the Japanese response to the disaster befuddled many around the world. Under the headline, "Japan Faces Potential Nuclear Disaster as Radiation Levels Rise," the March 14, 2011, *New York Times* reported: "Japan's nuclear crisis verged toward catastrophe on Tuesday after an explosion damaged the vessel containing the nuclear core at one reactor and a fire at another spewed large amounts of radioactive material into the air."[26]

Yet such dramatic headlines were markedly absent from Japanese media. Likewise, official statements from the Japanese government were ostensibly and comparatively calm and understated. Alexander Liss, who lived in Japan for many years, wrote for Australia's *Business Insider*:

> The Japanese government's response to the March 11 earthquake, tsunami, and subsequent nuclear crisis has shown some uniquely Japanese cultural traits. . . . The concepts of *gaman* (enduring deprivation and making sacrifices), *ganbare* (trying your best, no matter how difficult a situation), and *shoganai* (it can't be helped) are common themes running through Japanese language and social customs, which combine to create a sense of determination that is often interpreted in the West as fatalism. This approach leads (and has led) to perseverance in difficult conditions, whether it is the long working hours of a traditional Japanese corporate environment or, on a macro level, the country's impressive rebuilding effort in the aftermath of World War II.[27]

Unlike the looting and crime that accompany the aftermath of disasters in many places around the globe, CNN's Marnie Hunter reports that such responses did not occur in Japan. She maintains that the Japanese's primary motive is to be responsible to the community, rather than to the individual. In her reporting of the tsunami, Hunter interviewed Gregory Pflugfelder, director of the Donald Keene Center of Japanese Culture at Columbia University, who asserted that

> social order and discipline are so enforced in ordinary times that I think it's very easy for Japanese to kind of continue in the manner that they're accustomed to, even under an emergency. . . . Order is seen as coming from the group and from the community as a sort of evening out of various individual needs.[28]

To reiterate, a culture's relationship with nature can be seen in how it deals with natural disasters. Whether they be drought, tornadoes, hurricanes, tsunamis, floods, or earthquakes, natural disasters occur in all cultures. How people manage such disasters is largely shaped by their culture's dominant value orientations.

THE BUILT ENVIRONMENT

Lang explains that the built environment of any culture consists mainly of adaptations to the terrestrial environment, including architecture, housing, lighting, and landscaping (see Figure 4.1). The built environment artificially changes natural patterns of behavior, heat, light, sound, odor, and human communication. Hence, the built environment affects the interaction between people and the natural environment. Moreover, many of these changes are specifically designed to facilitate or restrict human interaction. The built environment is not random; it is an intentionally designed pattern of spatial relationships between objects and objects, objects and people, and people and people. The built environment organizes and manages human communication between people, and it varies considerably across cultures.[29]

Figure 4.1 The architecture of different cultures affects the interaction between people and the natural environment.

Lang notes that, while sometimes designed for purely aesthetic reasons, the built environment is typically structured for specific activities. Classrooms, for example, are designed for a particular kind of communication. The size of the room, the positioning of the blackboards, and so on are all fashioned to facilitate interaction between the teacher and students. Culture affects how the built environment is designed. Amos Rapoport argues that the interior of any given built environment influences and directs the way activities are carried out, how the family is structured, how gender roles are played, attitudes toward privacy, and the overall process of social interaction. Moreover, says Rapoport, how the built environment is planned and constructed reflects the values, motivations, and resources of the culture wherein it exists. The overall economic, political, and legal system of a particular culture affects how that culture designs its built environment, including homes, schools, government facilities, and private business buildings. As the built environments of cultures differ, so do communication patterns.[30]

Lang argues that the degree of ease or difficulty afforded by the built environment when moving from one place to another is a major predictor of human communication patterns. People are more likely to communicate with one another in those environments where access to others is facilitated by the built environment than they are in environments where such access is restricted.[31] Anthropologist Edward Hall has identified three fundamental types of layout patterns in built environments: fixed-feature space, semifixed-feature space, and informal space. **Fixed-feature space** is defined by immoveable or permanent fixtures, such as walls, floors, windows, and so on. **Semifixed-feature space** includes that which is moveable (usually within fixed-feature space), such as furniture. **Informal space** is perceptual and varies according to the movement of the interactants. Informal space lasts only as long as the interactants communicate; it is not stated space and is usually outside the awareness of the people interacting.[32]

The variability of fixed, semifixed, or informal space influences human communication. Some environments must be restructured for certain kinds of activities, whereas others need not be adjusted at all. According to Lang, these kinds of environments are called *adaptable* or *flexible*. For example, in an adaptable fixed-feature space such as a gymnasium, many kinds of activities—such as sporting events, gym classes, commencement ceremonies, dances, plays, speeches, and so on—can occur without any changes to the fixed features. In a flexible semifixed-feature space, changes are made to accommodate certain kinds of activities. Some schools and office buildings, for example, have portable walls. Informal (or dynamic) space between people is controlled, regulated, and managed by the nature of the relationship between the interactants.[33]

In addition to classifying fixed, semifixed, and informal space, Hall also developed a four-level classification of social distances. Hall argues that the physical environment guides behavior and the way people define the space between themselves and others. Hall's classification scheme was modeled after the findings of ethologists (i.e., people who study animal behavior), who observed the various distances animals maintain in their environments. Hall maintains that spatial distance between people is a vehicle for communication, much like sight, sound, smell, and touch. As distance decreases, people can see, hear, touch, and smell others differently than when distance increases. As the distance between interactants increases, the available visual, auditory, olfactic, thermal, and kinesthetic information decreases. As distance increases, the privacy of the individual increases but the privacy of the interaction decreases.[34]

Hall's four-level classification specifies intimate, personal, social–consultative, and public distances. Intimate distance is reserved for close intimate contact, including touching. This distance allows for much visual, auditory, and olfactic sensation. In the United States, intimate distance is 9 to 18 inches and is usually reserved for highly personal relationships. The second type, personal distance, is 1.5 to 4 feet. This is sometimes called "arm's-length" distance because a comfortable distance between interactants is literally about the length of one human arm. Social–consultative distance is the spacing people practice at casual gatherings and in working situations. In the United States, this distance is 4 to 12 feet. In social distance, there is a more formal atmosphere. Public distance is used for talking across a room and for public speaking situations. In the United States, this distance extends from 12 feet and beyond. There is little olfactic sensation at this distance.[35]

To be sure, intimate, personal, social, and public distances vary by culture, and Hall's classifications may not be universal. Hall argues that other factors, such as the relationship between interactants or external environmental factors, may influence distances between people. In addition, the built environment plays a key role in how space is used. Smaller, more confined spaces, insists Hall, increase interaction distances, whereas larger environments motivate people to adopt smaller distances. Myron Lustig and Jolene Koester note, for example, that people in so-called high-contact cultures (e.g., Arabs, Latin Americans, Southern Europeans) tend to use closer interaction distances than do people from low-contact cultures. People in the United States, for instance, prefer greater distances between themselves and others than do persons living in many Latin American cultures. People from colder climates have a tendency to use large physical distances when they communicate. Conversely, people from warm-weather climates tend to use small physical distances. Northern Europeans (e.g., England, Germany, Scandinavia) are said to have larger personal-space "bubbles" than do Southern Europeans (e.g., Greece, Italy, Spain).[36] In some Middle Eastern cultures, people stand close enough to smell each other's breath.

John Aiello has reviewed several studies and found that Indonesians used less space than did Australians and were more likely to initiate a conversation with a stranger. Other studies comparing Americans with other cultures have found no differences; that is, they have found common spatial behavior patterns. American, Australian, British, and South African young adults placed figures representing mental patients at about the same distances apart. In a comparable study, American, British, Scottish, Swedish, and Pakistani subjects similarly rated different seating distances for intimacy level. In an interesting study, it was found that when bilingual Japanese subjects spoke in their native tongue, they sat farther from a same-sex, same-nationality confederate than did both Americans and bilingual Venezuelans. But when all subjects spoke English, the three groups approximated the American seating pattern.[37]

CROSS-CULTURAL COMPARISONS OF HOUSING

The use of space is an integral part of every human being's communication. Decisions about where and when to perform our daily activities are based on spatial patterns that are learned culturally. We become so accustomed to our spatial definitions and boundaries that many of us experience anxiety when forced to interact in novel or unusual environments. Many people complain that they do not sleep well when outside their regular home environments. How we organize space within the built environment says much about our culture—its values and way of life. Perhaps more than any other aspect of the built environment, the home presents a particularly rich source of information about a culture's perception and use of space.

Japanese Housing

The population density of Japan is 836 persons per square mile—about 10 times that of the United States, which has a population density of 84 persons per square mile. In Tokyo, the population density is 36,000 people per square mile. Given Japan's high population density and limited geographical space, housing becomes a problem for Japanese families.

In the past 150 years, much has been written in the West about Japanese architecture, especially the Japanese home. Since World War II, great changes have occurred in Japanese housing. Many of the traditional Japanese homes, where most daily activities occurred in one room, have been replaced by Western-style homes and high-rises, where space is defined by walls.[38] But a relatively new housing phenomenon has emerged in the past 20 years: *kyosho jutaku*, also called microhomes or ultra-small homes. Some of these microhomes are built on lots literally the size of a parking space—some homes as tiny as 300 square feet. For comparison, the average size of a dormitory room in the United States is around 150 to 170 square feet. Thus, a Japanese family of four may be living in a space just twice the size of a dorm room. And, of course, the Japanese home includes a bath, kitchen, living room, bedrooms, etc.[39]

In a report about microhomes, National Public Radio correspondent Lucy Craft discovered that Japanese microhomes conserve space by eliminating many features of conventional homes, such as hallways, entranceways, and closets. A bathroom, writes Craft, may be separated from the rest of the home by only a curtain. She reports that furniture can be folded into the walls. In Japan, vertical space, rather than horizontal space, has become the focus. Often, microhomes are asymmetrical and seem unbalanced so they can fit into compact places. Persons in the United States measure the size of a home in terms of floor space, but Japanese architects tend to think of homes in 3-D.[40]

Houses of various types and styles can be found side by side in contemporary Japan. Shanna Freeman notes that most Japanese still live in traditional single-family homes.[41] In their well-known work, Kiyosi Sieke and Charles Terry indicate that a fair number of homes still reflect traditional Japanese architecture dating back to the 18th century. Other homes reveal clear European influences. Many others, perhaps the majority, have almost completely adopted a Western look. Sieke and Terry believe that the design of contemporary Japanese homes has been influenced by the breakdown of the traditional family system in Japan. Many young people are leaving the traditional multigeneration family home situation and moving to apartments or small houses of their own, such as the microhomes discussed above. In homes where two or three generations still live together, the main part of the house is intended for the second-generation husband and wife. A special section of the house might be designated for the family elders and another section for the children. In many homes like this, the elders' section is organized and decorated in traditional Japanese style, the children's section is completely Western, and the husband and wife's section is a combination of the two styles. This type of home was unheard of before the war.[42]

Although many contemporary Japanese houses reflect a Westernized design, the Japanese attitude about life has not changed. Charles Terry, past editor of *The Japan Architect,* asserts that an essential aspect of Japanese houses and Japanese culture is the gap between the public and private Japanese person. According to Terry, the impression that a Japanese person presents to society may be very different from how that person actually thinks or feels. In public settings, Japanese act according to clearly prescribed social rules. In private, they think and act as they please. This philosophy is reflected in the contemporary Japanese home and its Western influence. According to Terry, most Japanese who build Western-style homes do so because it is fashionable and expected of them. Terry alleges that most Japanese probably prefer the traditional style.[43] Atsushi Ueda, a Japanese author and scholar of traditional

Japanese urban architecture, argues that the contemporary Japanese house is caught between tradition and modernism.[44]

Tetsuro Yoshida, one of Japan's leading contemporary architects, writes that because the Japanese believe in harmony with nature, the traditional Japanese home fits unobtrusively into the landscape, not appearing human-made (as do the microhomes). The traditional Japanese home is a detached house with a garden. Yoshida states that among traditional Japanese, the house and garden are intimately related.[45]

Since ancient times, the Japanese garden has been considered more a work of art than a simple plot of land where flowers and vegetables are cultivated. The Japanese garden is treated as a painting or sculpture to be appreciated from some distance (see Figure 4.2). Yoshida describes the Japanese garden as a quiet monochrome compared with the colorful European or American garden.[46] In contrast, writes Ueda, one seldom encounters anything resembling a proper Japanese garden in contemporary Japanese homes. Instead, one of the most visible features of the modern Japanese home is a car or a garage.[47]

Figure 4.2   A traditional Japanese garden.

In traditional Japanese homes, writes Ueda, rooms are separated by *shoji* or *fusuma,* which are opaque sliding screens. A shoji panel is usually made of cedar lattice with translucent paper stretched over it. Shoji panels are lightweight and easy to slide open or closed with one finger. The purpose, and major advantage, of shoji is that they can be removed easily to convert the entire floor of a house into a single open room. The traditional Japanese house is fundamentally a one-room home partitioned by shoji. Because of the versatility of shoji, the plan of a house is flexible and the divisions of the rooms easily changed. According to Ueda, this is the major characteristic of space allocation in the Japanese home.[48]

Ueda alleges that, regardless of how Westernized they may have become, the Japanese have not abandoned the customs of taking off their shoes before entering a house and of sitting on the floor. The Japanese *yuka* (i.e., floor) developed as a result of this custom. The *yuka* is actually a raised floor and was developed out of a need to maintain sanitary conditions. Even contemporary homes have a raised floor. According to Ueda, the size of a room in a Japanese home is measured by its number of *tatami* mats. The *tatami* mat is a modular floor mat made from straw that is used to cover the floor and on which one sits or sleeps. The principal room in a traditional Japanese home is the reception room, also called the sitting room. The average size of the room is 8 to 10 mats. The room usually faces the garden and incorporates an alcove, called the *tokonoma*. According to Ueda, the *tokonoma* is a recess arranged with staggered shelves, artistic ornaments, hanging scrolls, and perhaps a flower arrangement. It is the most sacred place in the home, holding a sort of spiritual or moral significance. The space immediately in front of the *tokonoma* is the most honored place in a traditional Japanese home.[49]

Two rooms not often discussed but of primary importance in the Japanese home are the kitchen and bathroom. The kitchen, even in modern Japanese homes, is the wife's domain. The kitchen is her place, not to be disturbed by other household members and not to be entered or even observed by guests. The kitchen is a private place. In both traditional and contemporary Japanese homes, the bath is of utmost importance and is thought of as a place of recuperation and solitude. The bathroom, which is separate from the toilet, consists of two distinct areas, one for bathing and another for soaking. Initially, the Japanese will wash with soap under a shower next to the bathtub. Following the shower, they will crouch in the tub, which is designed for sitting, not lying. The water is warmed and sometimes scented with flowers or lemons. The purpose of the tub is to relax and soothe the body. This water is kept for several days and used by all family members.

Japanese architect and author Ueda maintains that the traditional Japanese house is a thing of the past. However, the contemporary Japanese house, he writes, is "nervously confessing its own insecurity."[50] Though dramatic changes have occurred in Japan in the past 50 years, much of the psychology driving the design of the traditional Japanese house still lives in the contemporary population.

American Navajo Housing

Susan Kent, an ethnoarchaeologist, has extensively studied the use of space in Native American Navajo housing. In her pioneering work, Kent compared the use of space across three American co-cultural groups: Native American Navajos, Spanish Americans, and Euro-Americans. Of particular interest is her work with Navajos. According to Kent's studies, many of the Navajos live in remote parts of reservations and have limited contact with White Americans. Traditional Navajo families speak mostly Navajo and live in aboriginal dwellings called hogans. Hogans typically consist of three large converging support posts that interlock at the top with smaller support posts. The hogan is covered with earth. In addition to the hogan, the Navajo camp may consist of a wooden ramada, a wood-chip storage area, a horse corral, and small fields of corn. The hogan is occupied in the winter, and the ramada is used in the summer (see Figure 4.3).[51] The hogan is used for storage during the summer months. Water is hauled in from tribal wells. There is no outhouse. Some camps will have a sweat house.[52]

Figure 4.3 Navajo hogan and ramada.

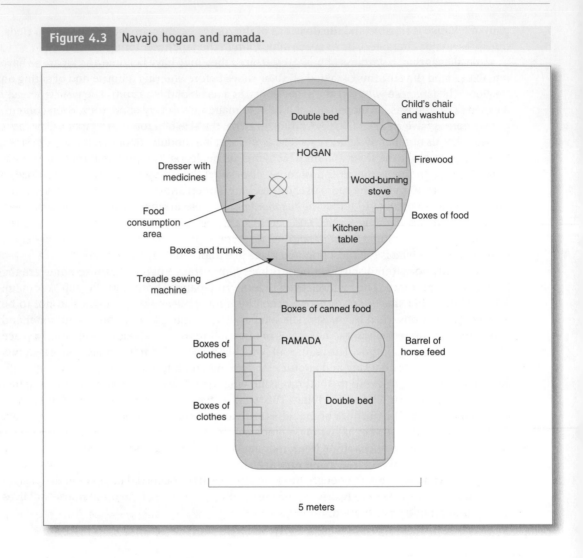

Navajo Hogan and Ramada

In her research, Kent discovered that the space inside the hogan was used differently by the occupants according to their sex. The men stayed almost exclusively in one half of the hogan, while the women and children used the other half. Food preparation always took place in the half occupied by the women and children, but the food was consumed in the half occupied by the men.[53]

Kent writes that in contrast to the sex-defined spaces inside the hogan, both sexes of all ages performed activities at the same locale out-of-doors and in the ramada. Not only did both sexes use the same activity area outside the hogan, but different types of activities were performed in the same location, including stripping hides, weaving, butchering, and washing. An individual's mood and the season seemed to be the only factors affecting the activity areas of the Navajo camp.[54]

Kent observed that the use of space within the ramada differed significantly from that in the hogan. The men were active in all parts of the ramada. The women and children also used most of the ramada without restriction. Chairs and beds were used by each family member regardless of sex or age. Kent also observed that the Navajos seemed to place little emphasis on the differences between the sexes and did not prescribe a traditional division of labor, as seen in many Euro-American homes. Moreover, asserts Kent, the Navajos had only a few sex-specific activities or sex-specific artifacts and very few single-function activity areas or artifacts. In fact, the only sex-specific activity areas used by the Navajos, observed Kent, were in the hogan, where traditional Navajos segregate space into sex-specific areas. In the ramada, there were no sex-specific areas, although identical activities of daily living occurred in both. Kent speculates that the reason for this is that the hogan is perceived as a sacred dwelling, whereas the ramada is not. According to Kent, the hogan is mentioned in important myths and prayers, and specific ceremonies must be conducted only in a hogan. Kent suggests that the circular hogan symbolizes the circular cosmos, whereas the rectangular ramada and out-of-doors do not. The round, sacred hogan is divided into the same male and female areas as is the round, sacred cosmos.[55]

Marakwet Housing

The Marakwet people are a part of the Kalenjin tribe, who live in Western Kenya. Prior to 1900, very little had been written about this group. In 1986, Henrietta Moore published an extensive anthropological study of the Marakwet people, focusing specifically on their use of space. The following discussion of the Marakwet is based on Moore's analysis.[56]

According to Moore, Marakwet country is one of the most secluded parts of Kenya. The Marakwet are divided into a number of villages called *kor*. The village is composed of family compounds consisting of a family house, store, and goat house. According to Moore, the Marakwet people are emotionally attached to the land and see themselves and the land they occupy as inseparable.[57]

Marakwet houses and their associated structures (i.e., stores and goat houses) are the only forms of built environment in the Marakwet village. There is no physically constructed space outside the family compound. According to Moore,

> The nature of village organisation is an interlocking set of social units which are also territorial units. At every moment, the life of the villages focuses down on the household, and that of the household expands out to meet the world of the village: a world where social relations are also spatial relations.[58]

The Marakwet insist that a house must never face out over the valley. In addition, the houses within a particular compound must always face one another. The majority of Marakwet houses are subcircular, with a single entrance and a window, and are made of wattle and daub. Wattle is a fabrication of poles interwoven with branches or reeds. Daub is a covering of some type, usually earth. The houses have thatched roofs. In the dry season, the houses are virtually indistinguishable from the natural terrain.

In her study, Moore observed that each house is divided into three areas, including the sleeping area, the cooking area, and the area beneath the roof store. The bed is typically placed behind the door and is considered the most private place in the house (see Figure 4.4).[59] The fireplace/cooking area is just behind and to the side of the center post. The area beneath the roof store, then, is on the side opposite the bed. Most family compounds within villages contain at least one house and a store or goat house. Like the houses, the stores are made of wattle and daub and are always elevated on stone stilts and have thatched roofs. Stores must always be placed to the back of the family compound. Every Marakwet man starts with one house. After he marries, he may build a second house. Ideally, the second house would be for his wife.[60]

Figure 4.4 The interior of a traditional Marakwet house in the Sibou village.

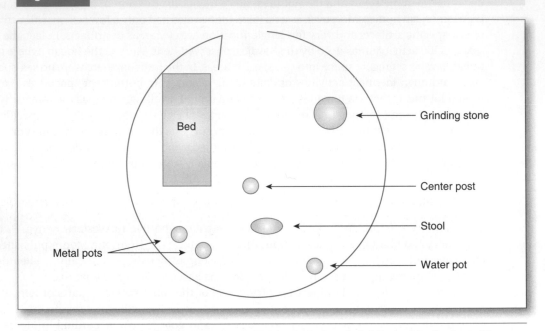

SOURCE: Based on Moore, H. L. (1986). *Space, Text and Gender: An Anthropological Study of the Marakwet of Kenya.* Cambridge, UK: Cambridge University Press.

Based on her observations, Moore concluded that the internal organization of the Marakwet houses is based on the social relationships between family members. In terms of the space, men and women are segregated. In Marakwet society, women are subordinate to men. Men spend the majority of their time away from the house, while women spend the majority of their time within the family house and compound. Men use the house primarily for sleeping and storage, while women use the house for cooking, child bearing and rearing, entertaining, and family maintenance. Men spend most of their time tending to the herds or attending meetings with the other men in the village. Moore notes that because the women spend most of their time in the house, they exert considerable control over its possessions. For example, fellow villagers must ask for and receive permission to enter a house or to remove something from it. Although Marakwet women are subordinate to Marakwet men, they wield a great deal of power within the boundaries of the household.[61]

Moore explains that of particular importance to the Marakwet are the organization and disposal of refuse, which she argues also reflects a clear male–female dichotomy. The majority of refuse for the Marakwet is made up of ash, animal dung, and chaff (i.e., seed coverings). The three types of refuse hold symbolic meaning and have distinct disposal locations. Ash is the result of cooking and burning—that is, a woman's job; hence, ash is associated with womanness and female fertility. Ash, then, is always thrown behind the house. Chaff is placed in front of the compound, and dung is placed near the animal compound. Women are buried near the chaff because their work is to dig and remove chaff; men are buried near the animal dung because their work is to herd the cattle. Goat dung is symbolic of male fertility. The Marakwet are adamant about not mixing the three types of refuse because of their relationship to burial locations and their symbolic meanings.[62]

PRIVACY

Most social scientists agree that human beings, regardless of culture, are a social species with an innate propensity to affiliate and communicate with other human beings. At the same time, however, human beings cannot tolerate extended physical contact with other humans and need privacy.[63] According to Alan Westin, these same competing needs are found in the animal kingdom. Westin maintains that virtually all animals sometimes desire the company of other animals and other times seek individual seclusion.[64]

Although the need for privacy is innate and universal, the degree to which an individual human feels the need for seclusion varies considerably across cultures. For example, Americans value privacy so much that they have made it law. Junior high school students learn that Article 4 of the Bill of Rights of the Constitution of the United States guarantees every citizen the right to be secure in their persons, houses, papers, and effects against unreasonable searches and seizures. Americans literally believe that they have *a right to privacy.* Anthropologists contend that individuals in virtually all cultures engage in a continuous process of seeking privacy at some times and companionship at others (see Figure 4.5). In this sense, privacy is culture bound and is considered a learned response to particular social situations. Irwin Altman argues that privacy is a "boundary control" process whereby people sometimes make themselves accessible to others and sometimes close themselves off from others. The behavioral and environmental strategies people use to accomplish this process are defined by culture.[65]

Figure 4.5 People of all cultures seek privacy at some times and companionship at others.

Westin maintains that privacy is a necessary condition for acceptable social behavior. In some circumstances, privacy is literally required in order not to violate cultural norms. Most cultures specify (sometimes legally) that certain behaviors must be enacted in private. Such rules and norms vary from culture to culture.[66] Even within cultures, microcultural groups have different perceptions of privacy. In the United States, for example, African American opinions and policy preferences regarding privacy differ from those of the White majority. In comparison with Whites, African Americans are more concerned and believe others are more concerned with invasions of privacy.[67]

Lang states that privacy is closely linked to the built environment because it can be designed or maneuvered in a number of ways to promote, encourage, or restrict communication with others.[68] In his seminal work on privacy, Westin identified four types of privacy: (a) solitude, or the state of being free from observation of others; (b) intimacy, or the state of being with another person but free from the outside world; (c) anonymity, or the state of being unknown even in a crowd; and (d) reserve, or the state in which a person employs psychological barriers to control unwanted intrusion.[69] These different forms of privacy serve different purposes, including personal autonomy, release of emotions, self-evaluation, and communication. Westin argues that the type and degree of privacy desired depends on the type of behavior in which one engages, the culture, and the individual's personality traits. The location of sexual intercourse, for example, may vary from culture to culture. In cultures such as the United States, where the nuclear family resides in a walled house that provides for privacy, sexual intercourse is likely to occur within the household. In cultures where the extended family lives together in a communal dwelling without clear spatial divisions, sexual intercourse probably occurs outside the built environment.[70]

Expanding on Westin's four categories of privacy, Darhl Pedersen identified six types of privacy: (a) reserve, (b) isolation, (c) solitude, (d) intimacy with family, (e) intimacy with friends, and (f) anonymity. Reserve indicates an *unwillingness* to be with others, especially strangers. Isolation is defined as total separation and detachment from others. Solitude implies an absence from others. Intimacy with family is being alone with members of one's own family. Intimacy with friends is being alone with friends. Anonymity is a desire to go unnoticed in a crowd. With the exception of isolation and solitude, these types of privacy are independent; that is, one type of privacy does not necessarily go with another. A privacy profile may be expected to be unique for a particular person or culture.[71]

Assessing Dimensions of Privacy

In his work on privacy, Pedersen developed a questionnaire for measuring the types of privacy preferred by individuals. This questionnaire has been used in cross-cultural comparisons. It contains 30 statements regarding the "privacy sphere" and is presented in Self-Assessment 4.1.[72]

Perceptions of Privacy in the United States

Although the United States literally legislates privacy, perceptions of privacy differ throughout the country and among microcultural groups. Moreover, attitudes about privacy have changed dramatically in the past decade or so. Clay Calvert, a professor who holds degrees in communication and law, argues that Americans live in a "voyeur nation." A voyeur is one who

Self-Assessment 4.1

Dimensions of Privacy Questionnaire

Directions: To complete the questionnaire, indicate how often you engage in the activity or state represented in each statement by marking whether it (1) never, (2) rarely, (3) occasionally, (4) sometimes, (5) often, or (6) usually applies. Scoring procedures are outlined following the scale.

_____ 1. I sometimes need to be alone and away from anyone.

_____ 2. I would be reluctant to engage in a prolonged conversation with someone I had just met.

_____ 3. I like to go on vacation with just my family.

_____ 4. I like my friends to sympathize with me and to cheer me up when I am depressed.

_____ 5. I have to be encouraged to put on a stunt at a party even when others are doing the same sort of things.

_____ 6. I want my thoughts and ideas to be known by others.

_____ 7. I'd like to work on a farm all by myself for a summer.

_____ 8. I like to be the center of attention in my group.

_____ 9. I like living in an apartment house because it prevents me from being alone.

_____ 10. I do not like to be disturbed when I am at home engaged in a family activity.

_____ 11. It would be fun to be alone on a high mountain peak surveying the scene below.

_____ 12. I like to be alone at home where it is peaceful and quiet.

_____ 13. I like to be at home with nobody else around.

_____ 14. I have a special person that I can confide in.

_____ 15. I like to attend meetings if I do not know others.

_____ 16. At parties, I am more likely to sit by myself than to join the crowd.

_____ 17. I would like to have a mountain cabin where my family and I could be alone together.

_____ 18. I like my friends to fuss over me when I am sick.

_____ 19. I like other people to notice me when I am in public.

_____ 20. It pleases me when my accomplishments obtain recognition from my friends.

_____ 21. I reserve displays of physical affection for a select few friends and family.

_____ 22. I'd be happy living all alone in a cabin in the woods.

_____ 23. Sometimes I like to be alone where I cannot be observed by anyone.

_____ 24. I tell my problems only to my family.

(Continued)

(Continued)

_____ 25. My personal relations with people are cool and distant.

_____ 26. I think I'd like the kind of work a forest ranger does.

_____ 27. I prefer doing things with only my family.

_____ 28. I like to meet new people.

_____ 29. Whenever possible, I avoid being in a crowd.

_____ 30. I like being in a room by myself.

Scoring: Reverse your score for Items 6, 8, 9, 15, 19, and 28, and then follow the directions below.

Add your responses to Items 1, 12, 13, 23, and 30. This represents your "Solitude" score.

Add your responses to Items 4, 14, 18, 19, and 20. This represents your "Intimacy with Friends" score.

Add your responses to Items 2, 16, 25, 28, and 29. This represents your "Reserve" score.

Add your responses to Items 7, 9, 11, 22, and 26. This represents your "Isolation" score.

Add your responses to Items 3, 10, 17, 24, and 27. This represents your "Intimacy with Family" score.

Add your responses to Items 5, 6, 8, 15, and 21. This represents your "Anonymity" score.

Scores of 20 or higher on these subscales indicate a greater preference for the specific type of privacy.

SOURCE: Reproduced with permission of author and publisher from Pedersen, D. M. (1979). Dimensions of Privacy. *Perceptual and Motor Skills, 48*, 1291–1297. © Perceptual and Motor Skills 1979.

seeks sexual stimulation by visual means or is a prying observer of sordid or scandalous material. Calvert maintains that voyeurism has become a central theme of American entertainment and culture. Calvert argues that the American public has access to information not originally intended for public consumption, made available via television and the Internet in what he calls "mediated voyeurism." Calvert categorizes four types of mediated voyeurism.[73] The first type is video vérité voyeurism—that is, unrehearsed and unscripted moments of actual events filmed by a video camera or smartphone. Nearly half of all Americans own smartphones. NBC reporter Emily Feldman notes that much has changed since the terror attacks on the World Trade Center in New York City on September 11, 2001, when just 1% of Americans learned of the attacks from the Internet and/or cell phones. Since then, social media and the prevalence of smartphones, now used by nearly 150 million Americans, have given news organizations, law enforcement officials, and the public more information to work with as a crisis unfolds. Feldman notes that within hours of the bombing at the finish line of the Boston Marathon in April 2013, news organizations relied heavily on reports from bystanders who captured on their smartphones some of the first images from the horrific scene.[74] The second type of mediated voyeurism is reconstruction voyeurism, where some actual event is dramatized for the benefit of the viewer. The television show *America's Most Wanted* is an example of reconstructed voyeurism. The third type, tell-all/show-all voyeurism, is typical of television shows such as *Jerry Springer*. Finally, the fourth type is sexual voyeurism, characterized by explicit Internet sites where hidden cameras are placed in bathrooms, bedrooms, up women's skirts, and so on. Calvert maintains that the American voyeur mentality has serious implications for an individual's constitutional right to privacy. Frankly, Calvert is not particularly sanguine (optimistic) about the future of privacy rights in the United States.

Different groups of people throughout the United States have different concerns about privacy. Many college students, for example, are concerned about what types of information, and how much, their college or university can disclose about them. The 1974 Family Educational Rights and Privacy Act, also known as the Buckley Amendment, forbids colleges from disclosing academic records without student approval. In October 1998, the U.S. Congress passed an amendment to the Family Educational Rights and Privacy Act that allows colleges and universities to inform parents any time a student under the age of 21 violates drug or alcohol laws. The privacy act still prohibits colleges and universities from releasing students' grades, but many colleges and universities are routinely calling parents and informing them of drug and alcohol policy violations. Moreover, colleges are not required to alert students when they have notified their parents. The new laws also allow colleges to disclose information regarding any violent crimes committed by students, and the new amendment now permits a college to release a student's grades to a court.[75]

African Americans seem to have different views on privacy compared with Whites. For example, Oscar Gandy reports that educated African Americans extend broad privacy rights to individuals and, unlike Whites, do not view information-gathering techniques used by businesses as invasions of privacy. In addition, when African Americans are concerned about privacy, it is because they sense that a loss of control over personal information renders them more susceptible to discrimination, especially in terms of employment, insurance, and credit. According to Gandy, African Americans are most concerned about privacy issues as they relate to relationships between individuals and the government, but not more so than other groups (e.g., Whites).[76]

Cross-Cultural Variations on Privacy

Pedersen's privacy questionnaire can be useful in determining the privacy preferences of a variety of cultural groups. Knowing a culture's preferences about privacy can help you determine when and where communication can and should take place. For example, if you know when and how a culture desires privacy, you will know when to restrict communication with persons from that culture. Invasions of privacy are negatively perceived across cultures and will be interpreted as a sign of incompetent communication.

Darhl Pedersen and Shelia Frances found that within the United States, men tend to score higher on isolation, while women score higher on intimacy with family and friends. They also found three consistent trends in the privacy choices of people across various regions of the United States. People from the mountain states tend to score higher than do those on the West Coast in their preferences for isolation, anonymity, and solitude. People from the Southwest are like those on the West Coast in their low preference for isolation and like those in the mountain states in their high preference for anonymity. Those on the West Coast score lower than all others on solitude.[77]

A culture's definition and perception of privacy are often based on its history and dominant cultural values. China is a fascinating case study of how cultural values associated with privacy have changed over the years. In her studies of Chinese culture, Orna Naftali traces the history of privacy in China.[78] She notes that in traditional Chinese culture, the basic unit of privacy was not the individual but the extended family. An individual's privacy was held only within the social hierarchy of the family, where higher-ranked individuals enjoyed privacy from the lower ranked but not vice versa. Furthermore, children were seen as the private property of the higher-ranked family members. Naftali also notes that in traditional Chinese culture, the term *private* carried negative connotations and was associated with selfishness and immorality. During the socialist revolution in the mid-20th century, individual privacy was disdained. Private property was banned, and the desire for personal privacy, including one's own physical private space, was despised by the people.

But these cultural values have changed. Naftali argues that even though most Chinese do not benefit from the privacy that persons in Western cultures enjoy, for the past 30 years or so, the Chinese people have witnessed a return of a relative private and personal social life. Recall from Chapter 2 that in 1979 China imposed a one-child policy, which was established to limit that country's population explosion. Couples are allowed to have only one child each. That's quite an imposition of privacy. Naftali notes that with the recent reduction of socialist-era welfare policies and the introduction of market reforms, the Chinese government is shifting its focus from reliance on the state to reliance on the self. Given the one-child policy, privacy has become a major focal point in child rearing. In fact, in 1992, China enacted the Law of Protection of Minors, which, among other things, legislated a child's right to privacy. This change in both attitude and policy has led to dramatic changes in education and housing. Urban Chinese houses now provide children with private spaces. In public areas, too, distinct areas are partitioned for children. This is a dramatic change from when there were few or no doors between rooms in traditional Chinese homes and parents had unconditional rights to enter their child's private space. In her study of urban Chinese homes, Naftali observed that most children had a room of their own.[79]

In a related study, Shengming Tang and Xiaoping Dong explored parents' and children's perceptions of privacy in China.[80] They maintain that unlike most Western cultures—where privacy is achieved primarily by means of space manipulation—in China, privacy is often defined in abstract ethical terms. But they agree that privacy issues have changed dramatically in China. In their study, Tang and Dong examined privacy in three areas: spatial, physical, and mental. Spatial privacy issues would include children being allowed to close the door when in a room with a group of friends. Physical privacy would include parents refraining from hugging or kissing their teenage children when in public if the children do not like it. Mental privacy is about parental access to what children watch on the Internet, their exam scores, e-mails to friends, etc. Tang and Dong surveyed both Chinese parents and children about these privacy areas. Their results showed that parents and children were consistent (with each other) in their ratings. Overall, both parents and children ranked spatial and physical privacy as important; that is, the children felt that they deserved this privacy, and Chinese parents respected their children's privacy—although, interestingly, fathers rated these privacy areas higher than did mothers. The lowest-rated areas were those of mental privacy. Rated lowest of these were Internet, letter, and e-mail privacy. Tang and Dong note that this may be due to the Chinese government's strict control over the Internet. Based on their findings, Tang and Dong conclude that Chinese children have strong desires for privacy and their parents generally respect those desires. They note that the concept of privacy once associated mainly with Western cultures seems to exist in China as well.[81]

Ahmet Rustemli and Dogan Kokdemir administered Pedersen's privacy questionnaire to Turkish students, and the results of their study are comparable to those for Americans. The overall preferences for solitude, isolation, anonymity, and intimacy are virtually the same for Americans and Turks. Preferences for reserve and intimacy with family differed across cultures, however. Unlike American subjects, the Turkish subjects demonstrated a lower preference for reserve and intimacy with family members. The Turkish subjects preferred intimacy with friends over intimacy with family. This may be due to the family structure in Turkish culture, where the family is an intact group with intense care for children. In the typical Turkish family, the children develop an intimate and dependent, but restricted, relationship with their parents. That is, the children become dependent on their parents but have limited intimate communication with them. Thus, issues of personal identity and intimacy are directed toward peers rather than parents.[82]

In referring to a paper delivered by Clifford Geertz, Westin describes the living arrangements of the people living in Java. According to Westin, the Javanese live in small, bamboo-walled houses that have no interior walls or doors. Except for the bathroom, there are no truly private areas. Westin claims that because the Javanese have no physical privacy, they have developed a kind of psychological privacy in their everyday behaviors and communication. They speak softly, conceal their feelings, are emotionally restrained, and are indirect in their verbal and nonverbal communication.[83]

Altman has reviewed the privacy behaviors of several groups, including the Mehinacu Indians, a tribal culture in Central Brazil. According to Altman, the Mehinacu live in communal villages where they have virtually no privacy in their houses. Instead of achieving privacy within their homes, the Mehinacu create privacy by leaving the village for extended periods of time, even years. Newly born children and their parents are isolated from the village in their homes for several weeks or months. Young boys are required to stay within the home behind a wooden partition, where they have virtually no communication with anyone. Food and bathing materials are brought to them. Altman states that during their seclusion, the boys are taught to speak quietly, are not allowed to play, and must abstain from emotional displays. Young women go through a similar seclusion after their initial menstruation. Other forms of seclusion occur after the death of a spouse. Altman notes that the typical Mehinacu Indian may spend 7 to 8 years of his or her life in isolation from others.[84]

While the Javanese and Mehinacu cultures may be characterized by minimal daily privacy, the Balinese and Tuareg cultures desire maximum privacy. According to Altman, the Balinese live in houses surrounded by high walls and narrow doorways. The Tuareg, a Moslem culture in North Africa, wear clothes that cover the entire body except for the eyes. In addition, they wear a sleeveless undergarment and a flowing outer garment that reaches from the shoulder to the ankle. A veil and headdress that cover the forehead and bridge over the nose are worn continuously throughout their lives. Altman suggests that the veil is not unlike a door that allows some to enter and keeps others out.[85]

Hesselink, Mullen, and Rouse have studied privacy in Moroccan culture. They claim that Moroccans value privacy as a way of protecting themselves from the external environment. Moroccans keep private the things they value most. The outside of a Moroccan home, for example, is very plain, so as to expose little information about the people who live there. Hesselink and colleagues note that the walls of the homes are so tall that the only way to see into one is to walk from the rooftop of one house to that of another. Moroccan women are also considered private and are hidden when males who are not a part of the immediate family enter the home.[86]

The built environment is only one way a culture defines its communication with others. The way a particular culture achieves privacy involves a complex formula of environmental, verbal, nonverbal, and cultural factors. Focusing on only one of these dimensions provides a distorted view of the privacy regulation system of any culture.

Online Privacy Across Cultures

Kenneth Farrall of New York University writes: "Globally, privacy is under threat. To many in academia, there is little hope in preserving active domains of seclusion, secrecy or anonymity within an increasingly risk-averse, surveillance-networked, global society."[87]

Sociologist Sherry Turkle argues that there is a tension in American culture between the individual's desire for and right to privacy and the invasion of personal privacy brought on by the computer age.[88] Because so much personal information about people is stored electronically, it is relatively easy to gain access to it, including virtually all of one's financial and medical data. According to Carole Lane, a paid Internet searcher,

> In a few hours, sitting at my computer, beginning with no more than your name and address, I can find out what you do for a living, the names and ages of your spouses and children, what kind of car you drive, the value of your house and how much taxes you pay on it.[89]

In June 2013, the *Washington Post* reported that the U.S. National Security Agency and the FBI were tapping directly into the central computer servers of nine U.S. Internet companies (e.g., Google), extracting audio and video chats, photographs, e-mails, documents, and connection logs that would enable security officials to track U.S. citizens and foreigners.[90] The program, code-named PRISM, was not known to the public until *The Washington Post* published its article. The purpose of the program, according to government officials, was to track potential terrorists. Reactions to the program were mixed but very strong. Many U.S. citizens accused the government of spying, while others believed it was a necessary step in protecting the United States from future terrorist attacks. Dwayne Melancon, chief technology officer of Tripwire, Inc., a leading global provider of IT security and compliance solutions, asserts:

> The PRISM situation has a lot of implications in our world. More and more of our information is being shared in the name of convenience, but we have no idea how it's being used beyond our expectations. I've heard people say they feel violated based on what they are learning about PRISM, but don't know what they can do about it. Unfortunately, the genie is out of the bottle on your past data and you may be limited in how much you can affect how your data is used in the future.[91]

Recall from Chapter 1 the idea that technological advances in areas such as the Internet and cell phones have decentralized information across the globe—meaning that more people than ever before have access to more information. Recall that in India, more people have cell phones than there are people in the United States. Because so many people have access to information, information privacy is becoming a salient issue in our information-saturated global village. Recently, Hichang Cho, Milagros Rivera-Sánchez, and Sun Sun Lim conducted a multinational study of online privacy.[92] Cho and his colleagues argue that the overwhelming majority of consumers are concerned about their privacy and that such concerns limit online commerce. In their review of the research of online privacy issues, they point out that female Internet users are more concerned about their personal privacy than are male users. Older and better-educated persons are also more concerned about privacy, presumably because they are more aware of privacy problems. Research is mixed regarding overall Internet usage and privacy concerns. Some studies show that as Internet usage increases, privacy concerns decrease; other research shows the opposite. These authors hypothesize that two dimensions of cultural variability discussed in Chapter 2 may have implications for online privacy concerns. Specifically, they note that persons from individualistic cultures tend to place more value on private life, while those from collectivistic cultures more easily accept groups' and organizations' intrusion into their private lives.

Power distance, too, may affect privacy concerns. Cho and his colleagues argue that persons from large–power-distance cultures tolerate power inequality but tend to mistrust those in power. Hence, they hypothesized that persons from individualistic cultures and those from large–power-distance cultures would exhibit higher concerns about online privacy. They selected five cities for their study, including Seoul, Singapore, and Bangalore (India), which were chosen because the authors assumed that these are collectivistic and large–power-distance cultures. Sydney and New York were picked because they were assumed to be individualistic and small power distance. They also measured the age, sex, and education level of respondents in these cultures. Their results showed that older, female Internet users were more concerned with online privacy than were younger, male users. More-educated persons were also more concerned with online privacy. Regarding the cultural variables of individualism and power distance, respondents from Sydney and New York—presumably individualistic cities—did report more concerns about online privacy than did respondents from Seoul, Singapore, and Bangalore. Power distance did not play a role, however. The authors reason that individualists desire a private life away from the collective, whereas collectivists (and those in high-context cultures) prefer indirect communication and, thus, do not seek explicit details about privacy protection.

For nearly two decades, the U.S.-based Electronic Privacy Information Center and U.K.-based Privacy International have administered and published a comprehensive survey of global privacy issues called the *Privacy and Human Rights Report*.[93] The report details privacy issues in 70 countries, assessing the state of surveillance and privacy protection. The most recent collection of global country reports was published in 2007.[94] Below is a brief summary of some of their findings:

- The 2007 rankings indicate an overall worsening of privacy protection across the world, reflecting an increase in surveillance and a declining performance of privacy safeguards.
- The 2007 rankings show an increasing trend amongst governments to archive data on the geographic, communications and financial records of all their citizens and residents. This trend leads to the conclusion that all citizens, regardless of legal status, are under suspicion.
- The privacy trends have been fuelled by the emergence of a profitable surveillance industry dominated by global IT companies and the creation of numerous international treaties that frequently operate outside judicial or democratic processes.
- Despite political shifts in the US Congress, surveillance initiatives in the US continue to expand, affecting visitors and citizens alike.
- Surveillance initiatives initiated by Brussels have caused a substantial decline in privacy across Europe, eroding protections even in those countries that have shown a traditionally high regard for privacy.

- The lowest ranking countries in the survey continue to be Malaysia, Russia and China. The highest-ranking countries in 2007 are Greece, Romania and Canada.
- In terms of statutory protections and privacy enforcement, the US is the worst ranking country in the democratic world. In terms of overall privacy protection the United States has performed very poorly, being out-ranked by both India and the Philippines and falling into the "black" category, denoting endemic surveillance.[95]

MONOCHRONIC VERSUS POLYCHRONIC TIME ORIENTATION

In addition to its physical and spatial components, the built environment also contains a perceptual–temporal feature. Human communication occurs in a physical space and *perceptual time*. Hall is well-known for his discussion of time across cultures. Hall asserts,

> Time talks. It speaks more plainly than words. The message it conveys comes through loud and clear. Because it is manipulated less consciously, it is subject to less distortion than the spoken language. It can shout truth where words lie.[96]

Like other components of the environment, the perception and use of time are cultural. Unlike other elements of the built environment, time is not physical or tangible; it is a *psychological* or *perceptual* component of the environment. Regarding time, Hall categorizes cultures as either monochronic or polychronic. Monochronic- and polychronic-oriented cultures organize time and space differently. According to Hall, people with a monochronic time (or M-time) orientation emphasize schedules—the compartmentalization and segmentation of measurable units of time. Conversely, people with a polychronic time (or P-time) orientation see time as much less tangible and stress multiple activities with little emphasis on scheduling. P-time cultures allow the natural context (instead of a clock) to guide behaviors. P-time cultures stress involvement of people and the completion of tasks as opposed to a strict adherence to schedules. Hall maintains that the two orientations are incompatible.[97]

In M-time cultures, such as the United States, time is thought of as almost physical, like something you can touch and hold in your hand. Time is treated like money. We talk of saving, spending, wasting, and losing time. Hall argues that for M-time people, time is linear and compartmentalized into discrete, quantifiable and measurable units (e.g., minutes, hours, days, weeks, years). The schedule is paramount in M-time cultures. In M-time cultures, scheduling dictates just about every activity of every day. In many ways, scheduling is like a computer program, specifying what actions will be performed while prohibiting others. Moreover, asserts Hall, scheduling allows only a limited number of activities to be performed in one place at one time. In M-time cultures, people are concerned with doing only one activity at a time. When stressed or trying to multitask, M-timers can be heard exclaiming, "I can do only one thing at a time!"[98]

Hall explains that by its very nature, scheduling segments people from one another and dictates how they conduct their relationships. Because time is viewed as so valuable, people with the most power and prestige are given the most time (and space) and allowed more flexibility and less accountability with their time. Physicians, for example, are routinely late for appointments without sanction. Late or "no-show" patients, on the other hand, may pay heavily for their inconsideration of the physician's time.

Hall maintains that although an M-time orientation is learned and completely arbitrary, it becomes so ingrained in people that they have no other way of thinking about their world. At an early age, children are taught the importance of time, scheduling, and promptness. Moreover, they are often punished if they fail to adhere. A child learns when to eat, nap, and play. In schools, subjects are taught at certain times of the day for a specific duration. Through compartmentalizing and segmenting time, a person's day is completely planned and scheduled—including sleep, work, leisure, and even sex. Hall notes that tardiness and missed appointments are a source of extreme anxiety for many M-timers. Hall points out that perhaps the most important consequence of M-time is that it *denies the natural context and progression of human communication.* Rather than completing an assignment or finishing a conversation, scheduling forces people into an artificial pattern and sequence of behavior. Scheduling, by its very nature, selects what will and will not be perceived and attended to and permits only a limited number of events within a given time period. Many M-time cultures are low context, including the United States, Germany, Scandinavia, Canada, France, and most of Northern Europe.[99] To the M-time person, the shortest, and most efficient, distance between Point A and Point B is a straight line.

A ————————→ B

On the other hand, Hall argues that in P-time cultures, schedules are less important and are frequently broken. P-time people can do many things at once, and relationships take priority over schedules. P-timers are often distractible and tolerant of interruptions. In P-time cultures, time is not thought of as tangible, and a person may be engaged in several activities, in the same space with several people, simultaneously. Although P-timers obviously can read a clock and understand the idea of a schedule, they are more interested in completing the task at hand than leaving it because of some predetermined, and artificial, schedule. Hall contends that people in P-time cultures are not slaves to schedules and are frequently late for appointments or may not show up at all. The guiding principle behind P-time cultures is that the natural context, *in the present,* guides behavior. Many P-time cultures are high context, including Southern Europe, Latin America, and many African and Middle Eastern countries.[100] To a P-time person, getting from Point A to Point B may take some time, including a few diversions and interruptions, but Point B will eventually be reached.

Consequences of Monochronic and Polychronic Orientations

M-time and P-time cultures organize their space in much the same way as their time. Hence, the M-timer has a specific area set aside for specific activities, and, generally, these are the only activities allowed in that area. In M-time office buildings, for example, people have their own private offices in which to conduct their business. Likewise, in P-time cultures, where multiple activities occur simultaneously, many tasks are conducted in the same place. Keberlein describes the inside of the municipal building in a small Guatemalan town. The building has no interior walls to cordon off people from one another; instead, it is one large room where all the town's municipal needs are handled. There may be one desk surrounded by many people vying for the attention of the local mayor, who seems to be interacting with two or three people simultaneously. No lines are formed, and people compete for the mayor's attention. The mayor probably is a very important and informed person in this town.[101] Hall has observed that many P-time cultures feature a defined centralization of bureaucratic control. This is because the leaders interact with many people, and the people are informed because they interact with one another. Polychronic people tend to be well informed of one another's business. Hall argues that their involvement with one another is the essence of their existence. Consequently, P-time bureaucracies can be slow and difficult to penetrate unless one knows an "insider."[102]

A similar contrast can be seen in the homes of M-time and P-time cultures. In most M-time cultures, the home is carefully planned and organized. It is compartmentalized into individual rooms, each with its specific purpose (e.g., kitchen, dining room, bedroom, laundry room, bathroom). Many P-time homes, on the other hand, may be defined by one large living area. In traditional Japanese homes, for example, the main living area is a single room where the entire family eats, sleeps, and interacts as a group.

Some cultures possess elements of both M-time and P-time. Vandehey, Buerger, and Krueger explain that the Masai, a nomadic culture of Kenya, do not compartmentalize time into seconds, minutes, and hours but, instead, schedule specific periods of the day around the rising and setting sun and the feeding of their cattle. The typical Masai day begins just prior to sunrise, when the cattle go to the river to drink. This period is called "the red blood period" because of the color of the sunrise. The afternoon consists of a period of time when "the shadows lower themselves." The evening begins when the cattle return from the river.[103]

According to Vandehey and her colleagues, the Masai have a unique way of classifying people by age. Rather than using a calendar of years, as most cultures do, the Masai belong to age sets. One's age set determines his or her privileges and responsibilities. Instead of a calendar, the Masai measure time periods by seasons and months, the duration of which is determined by rainfall. Although the Masai compartmentalize time into months, they are not restricted to any set time. For example, a particular month lasts as long as the rains continue. A new month does not begin until the rains have ceased.[104] (See Table 4.2 for a review of the characteristics of monochronic and polychronic cultures.)

Table 4.2 Characteristics of Monochronic Versus Polychronic Cultures

Monochronic Cultures	Polychronic Cultures
Compartmentalize time	Allow the natural context to govern/guide activities
Are schedule oriented	Are context oriented
Perform one activity at a time	Perform multiple activities simultaneously
Concentrate on the job	Are distractible and subject to interruptions
Take time commitments seriously	Consider time commitments as an objective to be achieved if possible
Are low context	Are high context
Adhere tightly to plans	Change plans often and easily
Emphasize promptness	Are committed to people and relationships (often late to appointments)
Are future oriented	Are past oriented

STUDENT VOICES ACROSS CULTURES

Monochronic Time In Germany

Being a German exchange student showed me how important it is to have an understanding of what different perceptions of time mean in nonverbal communication. I, for my part—like most people in Germany—feel strongly committed to a monochronic perception of time. Always being on time, respecting deadlines, and doing one task after another, for example, are important to me and also affect my daily schedule, both at university and in my private life.

Apart from being overly punctual in private or business meetings, a good example to point out the perception of time for most Germans is the public transportation system. Since many people commute to work, they count on the punctuality of the public transportation system. People usually get mad quickly if a train or bus is 5 minutes late because they see time as a precious resource.

Especially when dealing with members of different cultures, one should keep in mind that differences in the perception of time might predominate. While Germany and the United States share a more monochronic perception of time, I realized on a trip to Spain that the people there are committed to more polychronic time systems. Nobody seems to care if the bus is on time or 20 minutes late, which is the result of a less formal perception of time.

Bio:

My name is Sebastian Friedemann. I'm from Düsseldorf, Germany, and I'm currently earning my master's degree in sports, media, and communication at the German Sports University in Cologne. Between 2008 and 2009, I was an exchange student at St. Norbert College in De Pere, WI.

AN INTERCULTURAL CONVERSATION: MONOCHRONIC AND POLYCHRONIC CULTURES

Mr. Paul Bersik is the international sales representative for his computer equipment company. His most recent trip takes him to Saudi Arabia, where he is scheduled to meet with his Saudi counterpart, Abdul Arami. In the following scenario, Mr. Bersik comes face to face with P-time. Mr. Bersik and his training team arrived in Saudi Arabia 3 days ago for a scheduled appointment with Mr. Arami. Mr. Arami has not yet met with Mr. Bersik or his team. Finally, a call to Mr. Bersik's hotel room indicates that Mr. Arami is prepared to meet with him. When he arrives at the location, Mr. Bersik is asked to wait outside Mr. Arami's office. As he waits, he notices many people entering and leaving Mr. Arami's office at a quick pace. The hallways of this building are a hustle and bustle of activity, with people shuffling in and out of many rooms. Finally, after several hours, Mr. Bersik is called in to meet Mr. Arami.[105]

Mr. Bersik:	Ah, Mr. Arami, it's so good to finally see you. Gosh, I've been waiting for days. Did you forget our appointment?
Mr. Arami:	Hello, Mr. Bersik, please sit down. Everything is fine?
Mr. Bersik:	Actually, no . . . (Phone rings.) . . . the problem is . . .
Mr. Arami:	Excuse me . . . (Takes the phone call and speaks in Arabic. After several minutes, he concludes the phone conversation.) Yes, now . . . everything is fine?
Mr. Bersik:	Well, actually, I've got a small problem. You see, the computer equipment you ordered . . . (A staff person enters the room and hands Mr. Arami something to sign.)
Mr. Arami:	Oh, excuse me. (Signs the document.) Yes, now, everything is fine?
Mr. Bersik:	As I was saying . . . all the computer equipment you ordered is just sitting on a ship in the dock. I need your help in getting it unloaded. I mean, it's been there for 2 weeks!
Mr. Arami:	Hmmm. I see . . . this is no problem.
Mr. Bersik:	Well, if it sits in the heat much longer it could be damaged. Could I get you to sign a work order to have it unloaded by Friday?
Mr. Arami:	There is no need for that. The job will get done.
Mr. Bersik:	Well, could we set up some kind of deadline? You see, I have a staff of people here waiting to train your people on the equipment. I need to let them know when it will be ready. How about this Friday? Could we do it then? My people are here now, and they're waiting to begin training.
Mr. Arami:	There is no great rush. We have lived for many generations without this equipment. We can wait a few more weeks, if necessary. This is not a problem. (Two men enter the room and begin a conversation with Mr. Arami.)

There is little chance that Mr. Arami will sign any kind of work order for Mr. Bersik. Within the context of the Saudi culture, Mr. Bersik's behavior is inappropriate. His emphasis on deadlines is perceived by Mr. Arami as either insane or irreligious. For his part, Mr. Bersik is distressed by the constant interruptions. To Mr. Arami, Mr. Bersik is in too much of a hurry. In the future, Mr. Bersik must learn that the Saudis' perception of time is very different from his own. Mr. Bersik is monochronic, whereas Mr. Arami is polychronic. When he does business in Saudi Arabia, Mr. Bersik must understand the temporal feature of the culture. (See Self-Assessment 4.2 for a questionnaire to determine your time orientation.)[106]

Self-Assessment 4.2

Assessing Time Orientation

Directions: Below is a scale created by Charles Phipps. The scale is designed to measure one's monochronic and/or polychronic time orientation. In the blank before each item, indicate the degree to which you (1) strongly agree, (2) agree, (3) are neutral, (4) disagree, or (5) strongly disagree with the statement. There are no right or wrong answers, and many of the statements are similar; this is by design. Work quickly and record your first impression.

_____ 1. I usually feel frustrated after I choose to do a number of tasks when I could have chosen to do one at a time.

_____ 2. When I talk with my friends in a group setting, I feel comfortable trying to hold two or three conversations at a time.

_____ 3. When I work on a project around the house, it doesn't bother me to stop in the middle of one job to pick up another job that needs to be done.

_____ 4. I like to finish one task before going on to another task.

_____ 5. At church, it wouldn't bother me to meet at the same time with several different people who all had different church matters to discuss.

_____ 6. I tend to concentrate on one job before moving on to another task.

_____ 7. The easiest way for me to function is to organize my day with activities with a schedule.

_____ 8. If I were a teacher and had several students wishing to talk with me about assigned homework, I would meet with the whole group rather than one student at a time.

_____ 9. I like doing several tasks at one time.

_____ 10. I am frustrated when I have to start on a task without first finishing a previous one.

_____ 11. In trying to solve problems, I find it stimulating to think about several different problems at the same time.

_____ 12. I am mildly irritated when someone in a meeting wants to bring up a personal topic that is unrelated to the purpose of the meeting.

_____ 13. In school, I prefer studying one subject to completion before going on to the next subject.

_____ 14. I'm hesitant to focus my attention on only one thing because I may miss something equally important.

_____ 15. I usually need to pay attention to only one task at a time to finish it.

(Continued)

(Continued)

Scoring: For Items 2, 3, 5, 8, 9, and 11, reverse your responses: (5 = 1), (4 = 2), (3 = 3), (2 = 4), and (1 = 5). For example, if your response to Item 2 was 5, reverse it to 1. If your response to Item 3 was 4, reverse it to 2. Once you have reversed your responses to those 6 items, sum the scores of all 15 items. Scores of approximately 30 and below indicate a monochronic orientation. Scores of approximately 42 and above indicate a polychronic orientation.

SOURCE: This scale was developed by Charles A. Phipps as a part of his senior honors thesis, titled "The Measurement of Monochronic and Polychronic Cognitions Among Hispanics and Anglos," Abilene Christian University, 1987. Used with permission.

CHAPTER SUMMARY

The relationship between humans and their environment is complex. By its very nature, the environment—natural or built—is loaded with information. How that information is perceived and processed is strongly influenced by culture and can dramatically affect communication. In this chapter, we saw that cultures vary considerably in how they view the natural environment. Some see the environment as a dominating force, one that cannot be harnessed. Other cultures prefer a balancing act between the environment and their needs. These cultures try to coexist with nature peacefully. Still others see nature as a slave and try to control and rule it. Whether dominated by it, living in harmony with it, or treating it as a slave, humans are in constant interaction with their environment.

As the contextual model of intercultural communication shows, all human communication exists within some kind of environment. Most human communication occurs within a built environment. The built environment is specifically designed either to restrict or facilitate human interaction. How a culture designs its built environment says much about how it approaches communication, especially through its housing. Understanding how cultures manage the built and home environments leads one to a better understanding of cultures and to being a more competent intercultural communicator.

This chapter also discussed issues of privacy. People of all cultures have an innate inclination to affiliate and communicate with other human beings. At the same time, however, people cannot tolerate extended physical contact with others and have a need for privacy. The degree to which one senses privacy is learned and varies from culture to culture. Moreover, the issue of online privacy has become a significant concern across the globe.

Finally, this chapter described two orientations toward the perceptual environmental variable of time: monochronic and polychronic. Monochronic time orientations emphasize schedules, the compartmentalization and segmentation of measurable units of time, and promptness. Conversely, polychronic time orientations see time as much less tangible and stress multiple activities at once, with little emphasis on scheduling. Polychronic cultures stress involvement of people and completion of tasks as opposed to a strict adherence to artificial schedules. The natural, built, and perceptual aspects of the environment are pervasive influences on how people communicate with one another. Moreover, our perceptions of the environment are largely molded by our culture.

Visit the student study site at www.sagepub.com/neuliep6e for e-flashcards, web quizzes, web resources, and more.

DISCUSSION QUESTIONS

1. How does the information load of your classrooms change throughout the semester?

2. How does your perception of time (i.e., monochronic or polychronic) affect your daily life? Your study schedule? Your free time?

3. How do you go about securing privacy when you need it? How does your culture facilitate or hinder privacy?

4. How does your physical environment restrict and enhance your sensation; that is, how does it affect what you see, hear, taste, touch, and smell? Give examples.

ETHICS AND THE ENVIRONMENTAL CONTEXT

1. Upon graduation, you've decided to spend a year in the Peace Corps. Your first assignment is to southern provinces of Sri Lanka, where a flood has left thousands homeless. Arriving at the humanitarian aid station, you are stunned to find men assaulting displaced women. No one seems to be helping. Do you intervene?

2. You've just finished a semester at college, where your grades were not as good as you would have liked. When you arrive home for break, you learn that your college has mailed your grades to your parents and they have seen them. What do you do now? Was it fair of your college to mail your grades home?

3. You work for a nonprofit group that brings aid to underdeveloped countries across the world. Presently, you are in South America helping a small tribe build a water works station to bring much-needed fresh water to most of the townspeople. The station can be built at only one location, above a well, and this will require that your team cut down several trees. The locals ask that you not cut down the trees because they hold spiritual value for them. What will you do?

KEY TERMS

built environment   143

fixed-feature space   145

high load   137

informal space   145

information rate   137

low load   137

monochronic time orientation   162

polychronic time orientation   162

semifixed-feature space   145

terrestrial environment   139

NOTES

1. Stein, H. F. (1987). *Developmental Time, Cultural Space.* Norman: University of Oklahoma Press.

2. Although different, the idea to compare two scenarios is adapted from Mehrabian, A. (1976). *Public Places and Private Spaces: The Psychology of Work, Play, and Living Arrangements.* New York: Basic.

3. Stein, *Developmental Time, Cultural Space.*

4. Mehrabian, *Public Places and Private Spaces.*

5. Ibid.

6. Ibid.

7. Ibid.

8. Ibid.

9. Lang, J. (1987). *Creating Architectural Theory: The Role of the Behavioral Sciences in Environmental Design.* New York: Van Nostrand Reinhold.

10. International Energy Agency. (2013, June 10). *Four Energy Policies Can Keep the 2°C Climate Goal Alive.* Retrieved from http://www.iea.org/newsroomandevents/pressreleases/2013/june/name,38773,en.html; Knopf, R. C. (1987). Human Behavior, Cognitions, and Affect in the Natural Environment. In D. Stokols & I. Altman (Eds.), *Handbook of Environmental Psychology* (Vol. 1, pp. 783–826). New York: Wiley.

11. Safra, J. E. (1997). Indonesia. *The New Encyclopedia Britannica* (Vol. 6, pp. 298–299). Chicago: Encyclopedia Britannica.

12. Thao, K. (1995). *The Hmong Culture.* Unpublished student manuscript, St. Norbert College, De Pere, WI; Yang, D. (1993). *Hmong at the Turning Point.* Minneapolis, MN: Worldbridge.

13. Nyrop, R. F. (Ed.). (1986). *The Yemens: Country Studies.* Washington, DC: U.S. Government Printing Office.

14. Shoemaker, M. W. (1996). *Russia, Eurasian States, and Eastern Europe: 1996.* Harpers Ferry, WV: Stryler-Post; Westfahl, G., Koltz, R., & Manders, A. (1996). *Ethnic Russian Culture and Society.* Unpublished student manuscript, St. Norbert College, De Pere, WI.

15. Central Intelligence Agency. (1995). *The World Fact Book.* Washington, DC: U.S. Government Printing Office; Yurkovich, D., Pliscott, K., & Halverson, R. (1996). *The Norwegian Culture.* Unpublished student manuscript, St. Norbert College, De Pere, WI.

16. Lang, *Creating Architectural Theory.*

17. Kluckhohn, F. R. (1953). Dominant and Variant Value Orientations. In C. Kluckhohn, H. A. Murray, & D. M. Schneider (Eds.), *Personality in Nature, Culture, and Society* (pp. 342–357). New York: Knopf.

18. Altman, I., & Chemers, N. M. (1980). Cultural Aspects of the Environment–Behavior Relationship. In H. C. Triandis & R. W. Brislin (Eds.), *Handbook of Cross-Cultural Psychology* (Vol. 5, pp. 335–394). Boston: Allyn & Bacon.

19. Bishop, R. J. (1995). *Cultural Profile, Examination of Value Orientations and Sociocultural Influences, and Verbal and Nonverbal Language Aspects of the East Indian Culture.* Unpublished manuscript, St. Norbert College, De Pere, WI; Harris, P. R., & Moran, R. T. (1996). *Managing Cultural Differences* (4th ed.). Houston, TX: Gulf; Srinivasan, R. (1951). *India.* New York: Marshall Cavendish.

20. Altman & Chemers, Cultural Aspects of the Environment–Behavior Relationship.

21. Borden, G. A., Conaway, W. A., & Morrison, T. (1993). *Kiss, Bow, or Shake Hands.* Holbrook, MA: Bob Adams; Reick, S., & Ogura, M. (1996). *Sri Lanka: The Pearl of the Indian Ocean.* Unpublished student manuscript, St. Norbert College, De Pere, WI.

22. Kluckhohn, Dominant and Variant Value Orientations.

23. Altman & Chemers, Cultural Aspects of the Environment–Behavior Relationship; Thorne, R., & Hall, R. (1987). Environmental Psychology in Australia. In D. Stokols & I. Altman (Eds.), *Handbook of Environmental Psychology* (Vol. 2, pp. 1137–1154). New York: Wiley.

24. Fisher, S. (2010). Violence Against Women and Natural Disasters: Findings From Post-Tsunami Sri Lanka. *Violence Against Women, 16*(8), 902–918.

25. Ibid.

26. Tabuchi, H., Sanger, D. E., & Bradsher, K. (2011, March 14). Japan Faces Potential Nuclear Disaster as Radiation Levels Rise. *New York Times.* Retrieved from http://www.nytimes.com/2011/03/15/world/asia/15nuclear.html?_r = 2&scp = 5&sq = catastrophic % 20radiation % 20 leak&st = cse&

27. Liss, A. (2011, June 9). Crisis Mode: How Cultural Differences Can Shape Perception. *Business Insider Australia.* Retrieved from http://au.businessinsider.com/america-is-too-critical-of-japans-tsunami-and-nuclear-response-2011-6

28. Hunter, M. (2011). Orderly Disaster Reaction in Line With Deep Cultural Roots. *CNN.* Retrieved from http://news.blogs.cnn.com/2011/03/12/orderly-disaster-reaction-in-line-with-deep-cultural-roots/

29. Lang, *Creating Architectural Theory;* Rapoport, A. (1980). Cross-Cultural Aspects of Environmental Design. In I. Altman, A. Rapoport, & J. F. Wohlwill (Eds.), *Human Behavior and Environment: Advances in Theory and Research* (pp. 7–46). New York: Plenum.

30. Rapoport, A. (1969). *House Form and Culture.* Englewood Cliffs, NJ: Prentice Hall.

31. Lang, *Creating Architectural Theory.*

32. Hall, E. T. (1966). *The Hidden Dimension*. New York: Doubleday.

33. Lang, *Creating Architectural Theory*.

34. Altman, I., & Vinsel, A. M. (1977). Personal Space: An Analysis of E. T. Hall's Proxemics Framework. In I. Altman & J. F. Wohlwill (Eds.), *Human Behavior and Environment: Advances in Theory and Research* (Vol. 2, pp. 181–260). New York: Plenum; Hall, *The Hidden Dimension*.

35. Hall, *The Hidden Dimension*.

36. Lustig, M. W., & Koester, J. (1996). *Intercultural Competence: Interpersonal Communication Across Cultures* (2nd ed.). New York: HarperCollins.

37. For an excellent summary of research related to personal space across cultures, see Aiello, J. (1987). Human Spatial Behavior. In D. Stokols & I. Altman (Eds.), *Handbook of Environmental Psychology* (Vol. 1, pp. 389–504). New York: Wiley.

38. Hagino, G., Mochizuki, M., & Yamamoto, T. (1987). Environmental Psychology in Japan. In D. Stokols & I. Altman (Eds.), *Handbook of Environmental Psychology* (Vol. 2, pp. 1155–1170). New York. Wiley.

39. Craft, L. (2010). In Japan, Living Large in Really Tiny Houses. *National Public Radio*. Retrieved from http://www.npr.org/templates/story/story.php?storyId=128953596

40. Ibid.

41. Freeman, S. (2013). How Japanese Traditions Work. *How Stuff Works*. Retrieved from http://people.howstuffworks.com/culture-traditions/national-traditions/japanese-tradition.htm

42. Sieke, K., & Terry, C. S. (1970). *Contemporary Japanese Houses*. Tokyo: Kodansha.

43. Ibid., pp. 11–12.

44. Ueda, A. (1990). *The Inner Harmony of the Japanese House*. Tokyo: Kodansha.

45. Yoshida, T. (1969). *The Japanese House and Garden*. London: Pall Mall.

46. Ibid.

47. Ueda, *The Inner Harmony of the Japanese House*.

48. Ibid.

49. Ueda, *The Inner Harmony of the Japanese House;* Yoshida, *The Japanese House and Garden*.

50. Ueda, *The Inner Harmony of the Japanese House*, p. 9.

51. Though not an exact duplication, this graphic is based on those present in Kent, S. (1984). *Analyzing Activity Areas: An Ethnoarchaeological Study of the Use of Space*. Albuquerque: University of New Mexico Press.

52. Kent, *Analyzing Activity Areas*.

53. Ibid.

54. Ibid.

55. Ibid.

56. Moore, H. L. (1986). *Space, Text, and Gender: An Anthropological Study of the Marakwet of Kenya*. Cambridge, UK: Cambridge University Press.

57. Ibid.

58. Ibid., p. 45.

59. Though not an exact duplication, this figure is based on Moore's *Space, Text, and Gender*.

60. Moore, *Space, Text, and Gender*.

61. Ibid.

62. Ibid.

63. Burgoon, J. K. (1978). A Communication Model of Personal Space Violations: Explication and an Initial Test. *Human Communication Research, 4*(2), 129–142.

64. Westin, A. F. (1967). *Privacy and Freedom*. New York: Atheneum.

65. Altman, I. (1977). Privacy Regulation: Culturally Universal or Culturally Specific? *Journal of Social Issues, 83*(3), 66–84.

66. Westin, *Privacy and Freedom*.

67. Gandy, O. H. (1993). African-Americans and Privacy: Understanding the Black Perspective in the Emerging Policy Debate. *Journal of Black Studies, 42*(2), 178–195.

68. Lang, *Creating Architectural Theory*.

69. Westin, *Privacy and Freedom*.

70. Ibid.

71. Pedersen, D. M. (1979). Dimensions of Privacy. *Perceptual and Motor Skills, 48,* 1291–1297.

72. Ibid. Reprinted by permission.

73. Calvert, C. (2000). *Voyeur Nation: Media, Privacy, and Peering in Modern Culture*. Boulder, CO: Westview; Stepp, C. S. (2001). Playing at Peeping Tom. *American Journalism Review, 23,* 58.

74. Feldman, E. (2013, April 17). Smart Phones, Social Media Color Boston Bombing Response. *NBC Bay Area*. Retrieved from http://www.nbcbayarea.com/news/national-international/NATL-Smart-Phones-Social-Media-Color-Boston-Bombing-Response-203235691.html

75. Burd, S. (2000). Colleges Allowed to Tell Parents About Alcohol Use. *Chronicle of Higher Education, 46,* A31; Reisberg, L. (2001). 2 Years After Colleges Started Calling Home, Administrators Say Alcohol Policy Works. *Chronicle of Higher Education, 47,* A34.

76. Gandy, African-Americans and Privacy.

77. Pedersen, D. M., & Frances, S. (1990). Regional Differences in Privacy Preferences. *Psychological Reports, 66,* 731–736.

78. Naftali, O. (2010). Caged Golden Canaries: Childhood, Privacy, and the Subjectivity in Contemporary Urban China. *Childhood, 17,* 297–311.

79. Ibid.

80. Tang, S., & Dong, X. (2006). Parents' and Children's Perceptions of Privacy Rights in China. *Journal of Family Issues, 27*(3), 285–300.

81. Ibid.

82. Rustemli, A., & Kokdemir, D. (1993). Privacy Dimensions and Preferences Among Turkish Students. *Journal of Social Psychology, 133*(6), 807–814.

83. Westin, *Privacy and Freedom.*

84. Altman, Privacy Regulation; Roberts, J. M., & Gregor, T. A. (1971). Privacy: A Cultural View. In J. R. Pennock & J. W. Chapman (Eds.), *Privacy* (pp. 199–225). New York: Atherton.

85. Altman, Privacy Regulation.

86. Bowles, P. (1993). *Morocco.* New York: Abrams; Hesselink, R. C., Mullen, R. T., & Rouse, J. M. (1996). *Moroccan Culture: An In-Depth Study.* Unpublished manuscript, St. Norbert College, De Pere, WI; *Overview of Islamic Architecture.* Retrieved from http://venture.cob. ohio-state.edu:1111/khalid/pages/archtcre/overview.htm; Seward, P. (1995). *Cultures of the World: Morocco.* New York: Marshall Cavendish.

87. Farrall, K. (2008). Global Privacy in Flux: Illuminating Privacy Across Cultures in China and the U.S. *International Journal of Communication 2,* 993–1030.

88. Quittner, J., & Dowell, W. (1997). Invasion of Privacy. *Time, 150,* 28–36.

89. Ibid.

90. Gellman, B., & Poitraa, J. (2013, June 6). U.S., British Intelligence Mining Data from Nine U.S. Internet Companies in Broad Secret Program. *Washington Post.* Retrieved from http://articles.washingtonpost.com/2013-06-06/news/39784046_1_prism-nsa-u-s-servers

91. Help Net Security. (2013, June 11). Reactions From the Security Community to the NSA Spying Scandal. Retrieved from http://www.net-security.org/secworld .php?id = 15045

92. Cho, M., Rivera-Sánchez, M., & Lim, S. S. (2009). A Multinational Study on Online Privacy: Global Concerns and Local Responses. *New Media and Society, 11*(3), 395–416.

93. Privacy International. (2007, December 31). *Surveillance Monitor 2007: International Country Rankings.* Retrieved from https://www.privacyinternational. org/reports/surveillance-monitor-2007-international-country-rankings

94. Privacy International, *Surveillance Monitor 2007,* Chapter I.

95. Ibid.

96. Hall, E. T. (1959). *The Silent Language.* Greenwich, CT: Fawcett, p. 15.

97. Hall, *The Silent Language;* Hall, E. T. (1983). *The Dance of Life.* New York: Doubleday.

98. Ibid.

99. Ibid.

100. Ibid.

101. Keberlein, M. C. G. (1993). *A Cultural Profile of the Guatemalan Ladinos.* Unpublished manuscript, St. Norbert College, De Pere, WI.

102. Hall, *The Silent Language.*

103. Hollis, A. C. (1995). *The Masai: Their Language and Folklore* (Rev. ed.). New York: Clarendon; Vandehey, K., Buerger, C., & Krueger, K. (1996). *Traditional Aspects and Struggles of the Masai Culture.* Unpublished manuscript, St. Norbert College, De Pere, WI.

104. Ibid.

105. Although different, the model for the dialogue is adapted from Copeland, L. (Producer). (1982). *Managing the Overseas Assignment* [Motion picture]. San Francisco: Copeland Griggs.

106. This scale was developed by Charles A. Phipps as a part of his senior honors thesis, titled *The Measurement of Monochronic and Polychronic Cognitions Among Hispanics and Anglos,* Abilene Christian University, 1987.

CHAPTER 5

The Perceptual Context

After reading this chapter, you should be able to

1. list and discuss the three stages of human information processing,

2. discuss cross-cultural differences in perception,

3. define and discuss short- and long-term memory,

4. discuss cross-cultural differences in memory and recall,

5. define and discuss at least four types of mental categories,

6. define and discuss racial and ethnic stereotypes,

7. identify and discuss at least two reasons why people stereotype,

8. define and discuss the nature of ethnocentrism, and

9. define and discuss the nature of racism.

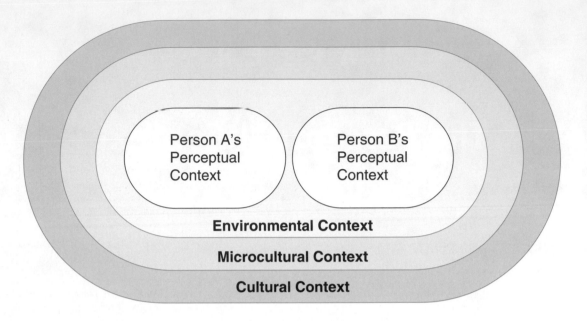

It seems to me that we have sound reasons for thus considering theoretical knowledge as more objective than immediate experience.

—Michael Polyani[1]

Think back to when you were in the second grade. You were about 7 years old then; it was quite a few years ago. Who was your second-grade teacher? Do you remember his or her name? You probably do. Now, think back to last week. What did you have for dinner on Tuesday night? Can't remember? After so many years, you can recall the name of your second-grade teacher almost immediately, but you can't remember what you had for dinner last Tuesday night. What's going on in your head that allows you to recall your second-grade teacher's name in a matter of seconds when you can't recall Tuesday night's dinner choice no matter how hard you try?

Consider the following interaction between Jim, an American college student, and Olga, a Ukrainian exchange student studying at the same college as Jim in the United States.

Jim:	Ya know, Olga, I've been thinking about America's involvement in the war in Afghanistan. I see reports of people starving and dying, and it's just so depressing. I hope this is over soon.
Olga:	Yes, I know, it's a terrible thing. My country has experienced a lot of starvation and war, too.
Jim:	Really?

Olga: Oh, yes. My country has been fought over and suppressed for a long time. We gained our independence from Russia for a short time between 1917 and 1920, but that was followed by ruthless Soviet rule that was responsible for two famines in which over 8 million people died. Can you imagine that, Jim? And then World War II, where the German and Soviet armies killed some 7 million of my people. So in the 20th century alone, over 15 million people died, some say for no good reason.

Jim: I had no idea. I can't imagine how that makes you feel.

Olga: Right, I understand. Our history gives my people a whole different perspective on life and how we see and live our lives. It's almost impossible not to carry a little sadness in our hearts.

Jim: My generation has never experienced anything like that. This is brand new to us. It's very confusing.

Whenever two people come together and interact, as Jim and Olga did, they process great quantities of information. In addition to the cultural, microcultural, and environmental contexts influencing their interaction, Jim and Olga both bring with them their unique perceptual (i.e., psychological) experiences, which affect their observations of the world around them. In this chapter, the perceptual context refers to how the human brain takes in, stores, and recalls information. In their brief conversation, Jim and Olga encode, decode, and interpret a vast amount of information about themselves, their cultures' histories, current events, their surroundings, and each other. Because they come from different cultures, they see the world differently. Their interpretations of world events differ dramatically.

Whenever two people come together and communicate, they do so within a cultural context (Chapter 2), a microcultural context (Chapter 3), and an environmental context (Chapter 4). And each person brings to the cultural, microcultural, and environmental contexts their own unique psychological perspective. So intercultural communication is a process of connecting the perceptual contexts of the two interactants within these other contexts. Although the ability to take in, store, and retrieve information is a universal human phenomenon, it is influenced by one's culture, microculture, and environment. Our knowledge of the world is dependent on our senses. What we see, hear, smell, taste, and touch provides the data from which we construct our world. Yet what we see, hear, smell, taste, and touch is subjective and biased. You might enjoy the smell of hamburgers being grilled, but your Hindu friend from India is repulsed by that same smell. Why? Because our perception of the world is subjective and biased due to the influence of our cultural, microcultural, and environmental contexts.

Dutch sociologist Geert Hofstede argues that culture is the software of the mind.[2] Think of the human brain as a computer where information is entered, stored, and recalled. As you sit at your computer, you type in information (i.e., input data). After a while, you decide to take a break from writing and you hit the "save" button, which stores the information in the computer's memory. Later, when you return to the computer, you recall the information (i.e., open the saved file) and continue writing. The human brain works in the same way. Via our senses, we take in information (i.e., we see, hear, smell, taste, and feel it). We then store the information in memory and recall it later. Who was your second-grade teacher? All human brains, regardless of culture, take in, store, and recall information. Without the brain's ability to take in, store, and recall information, human communication would be impossible.

Following Hofstede's analogy, culture (and microculture) represents the computer's (i.e., the brain's) software. In other words, exactly *how* we take in information, store it, and recall it is based on our culture—that is, our software. We are *born* human. All normal human brains are naturally equipped to take in, store, and retrieve information. But we *become* cultural. Culture teaches and conditions the human brain exactly how to take in, store, and retrieve information. Culture, then, is the software of the mind. And a critical point here is that culture is not objective; it is biased. Humans are not neutral or objective processors of information. Some of our subjectivity is based on the simple physiological differences among humans. No two humans are biologically exactly alike, for example. Many people suffer from astigmatism, an eye disorder in which the cornea (the clear tissue covering the front of the eye) is abnormally curved, causing out-of-focus vision. People are born with astigmatism. It is not cultural. Some of our subjectivity is based on culture. To a degree, culture teaches us what looks good and what looks bad and is not at all related to whether we have astigmatism. Therefore, if you grew up in the United States, you probably enjoy the smell of a hamburger grilling. If you grew up in India, you may be repulsed by that smell. Or if you were raised in a Hindu community in the United States (i.e., a microculture), you may still find the smell of a grilling hamburger disgusting.

This chapter is about the mental activities of the individual that constitute the perceptual context of intercultural communication. In addition to the cultural, microcultural, and environmental contexts, the perceptual context affects how people interact. Every time we enter into a communicative exchange with someone, we bring with us a perceptual frame of reference through which all our messages are filtered. The cultural, microcultural, environmental, and perceptual contexts are interdependent influences that combine in a complex formula and ultimately define our interactions with others.

The first part of this chapter introduces the idea of culture and cognition and outlines a model of human information processing. The second part of the chapter explains a common form of information processing called categorization. The third part of the chapter focuses on two attitudinal dimensions of information processing: stereotyping and ethnocentrism. The overall purpose of the chapter is to explain how the human mind processes information during communication, especially intercultural communication.

CULTURE AND COGNITION

People from different cultures think about different things. The Aleutian Eskimos of Western Alaska and the Marakwet tribe in Western Kenya think about different things because of the extreme differences in their natural environments (i.e., their environmental contexts). Moreover, people from different cultures think differently about their life experiences. The life experiences of a Guatemalan Ladino are markedly different from those of a Ukrainian. Few people question that the content of thought for people in different cultures varies. What is open to speculation, however, is whether higher mental processes, such as perception and remembering, differ across cultures. How much do the cultural, microcultural, and environmental contexts affect how the human brain processes information?

The Geography of Thought

Richard Nisbett, a distinguished professor at the University of Michigan, has researched and written extensively about how humans process information. His central thesis is that geographical differences in culture have a dramatic influence on how humans in those distinct geographical areas perceive the world. Specifically, his focus is on how Asians (Eastern cultures) and Westerners think differently from each other and why. His argument is that peoples from the East and West think differently because of foundations of Eastern and Western philosophies professed 2,500 years ago by the ancient Greeks and Chinese. Professor Nisbett compares the Confucian-influenced Chinese thinking of the collective against the Greek–Western orientation of the individual. The ancient Greeks focused on linear methods of understanding and seeing separate objects in isolation, without much regard for the context in which they existed. Individuals are unique, with distinct attributes and goals. Confucian-driven Chinese philosophies emphasized fluctuation, holism, interdependence, and harmony. All things (e.g., people and objects) are to be understood in terms of their relationships with others, their groupness—including the environment in which they exist. Nisbett contrasts the Western tendency to classify objects into discrete categories based on their similarity with the Eastern preference to classify objects into categories based on their relationships.[3] Consider the photograph in Figure 5.1.

Figure 5.1 How would you describe this photograph?

Describe what you see in the photo (Figure 5.1). When Nisbett asked American students to describe the photo, most of them referred to the fish. When Japanese students described it, they referred to the pond. How did you describe it?

Now, consider the three photos in Figure 5.2. Your task is to group two of the three photos together. Which two photos do you think go together? Nisbett found that American children tend to group the cow and the chicken together, as animals. Chinese children tend to put the cow and grass together, as a relationship, because the cow eats the grass. Obviously, you can see that Nisbett is tapping into the individualism and collectivism dimension of cultural variability discussed in Chapter 2. The essential point here is that these orientations affect the way humans process information. We are not objective or neutral processors; we are biased. One way is not necessarily better than the other, but it is important to understand that not all humans think the same way.

Figure 5.2   Which two photographs go together?

A Model of Human Information Processing

As mentioned above, the human mind is analogous to a computer. Information is entered, stored, and retrieved in a sequence of stages, where each stage involves performing a specific operation on the information.[4] During Stage 1, the input stage, information is taken in via the senses. In Stage 2, the storage stage, information is held in memory. During Stage 3, the retrieval stage, information is recalled. For people to communicate with one another, in any culture, they are required to take in, store, and recall information. Although these stages are probably universal, culture influences the specific strategies and styles of processing information in each stage.

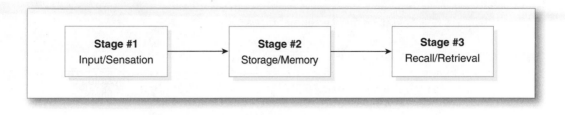

Stage #1: Input/Sensation

The first stage of information processing is the input stage, where raw information is taken in through the senses. This is called perception. Margaret Matlin defines perception as the mental interpretation of external stimuli via sensation.[6] According to Matlin, at any given point in time, especially during human communication, human beings are bombarded with external stimuli. They take in visual stimuli with their eyes, auditory stimuli with their ears, olfactic stimuli with their noses, taste stimuli with their mouths, and tactile stimuli through their skin (see Figure 5.3).

Figure 5.3 Human information processor.

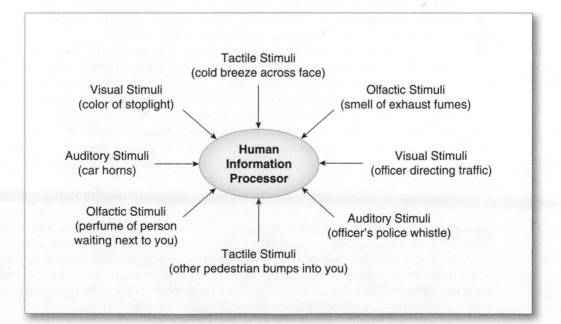

During intercultural communication, many of the stimuli come from the cultural, micro-cultural, and environmental contexts. Once taken in through the senses and prior to being stored in memory, the stimuli are passed through at least three perceptual filters: physiological, sociological, and psychological (see Figure 5.4).[6]

Figure 5.4 Sensation and perceptual filters.

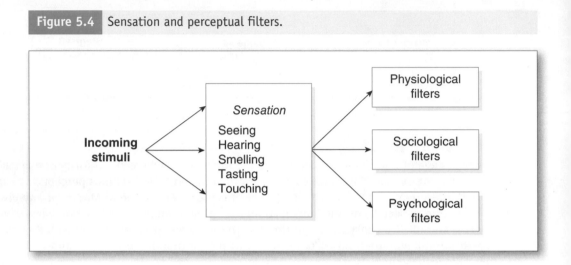

Physiological filters include the natural or genetic differences in how one sees, hears, smells, tastes, or feels. For example, eyesight varies considerably from person to person. Many people are required to wear eyeglasses to accommodate their poor visual sensation. As most people age, they lose some of their hearing. Research has shown that as people age, they also lose some of their sense of smell. So, right away, what you see, hear, smell, taste, or touch, is filtered through your senses, which are physiologically different from your closest friend's. Perhaps you are nearsighted and need glasses to see clearly but your best friend does not.

Sociological filters represent demographic data and one's membership in groups, including one's culture, microculture, and hometown, for example. The groups to which people belong influence how they perceive incoming stimuli. For example, many college-aged persons in the United States enjoy listening to rap music, a form of auditory stimuli. Few octogenarians (persons in their 80s) enjoy listening to such music, however. When President Barack Obama gives a speech, Democrats typically praise it while Republicans typically criticize it. The groups to which you belong (e.g., sex, age, education, political, etc.) affect how you process information.

Psychological filters include the attitudes, beliefs, and dispositions of the individual. A person's likes, dislikes, and beliefs about what is right or wrong filter the perception of incoming stimuli. If someone has a negative attitude about a professor, he or she may perceive that professor's class as especially boring or uninformative. If people believe that abortion is immoral, then they may perceive an abortion rights speaker as unattractive. Although all of us are bombarded with the same visual, auditory, tactile, olfactic, and taste stimuli, our sensations and perceptions of those stimuli will differ considerably, especially if we come from different cultures. Once again, we are biased processors.

Cross-Cultural Differences in Sensation and Perception

In addition to the physiological, sociological, and psychological filters, culture also affects one's ability to perceive incoming information. John Berry and his associates outline four explanations for cross-cultural differences in the perception of sensory stimuli: (a) conditions of the physical environment, (b) indirect environmental conditions, (c) genetic differences, and (d) cultural differences in how people interact with their environment.[7]

Regarding conditions in the physical environment, in the early 1970s, H. Reuning and Wendy Wortley conducted a cross-cultural study on auditory acuity (i.e., sharpness). In their comparison of Kalahari Bushmen, Danish, and American subjects, they found less hearing loss in the Kalahari sample than in the Danish or American samples, particularly among older subjects. Reuning and Wortley attributed their findings to low levels of ambient noise in the Kalahari Desert region. They also cited other studies that found a slower loss of hearing in nonindustrialized societies. This may suggest that environmental noise, such as that heard in industrialized societies, has a negative effect on hearing.[8]

In his study, C. H. Wyndham attributed an indirect environmental factor—specifically, poor nutrition—as the reason for slower dark adaptation among Black South African miners than among Whites. Wyndham found that it took longer for the eyes of Black miners to adapt to the dark than it did for White miners. Wyndham suggests that many of the Black mine workers might suffer from forms of liver ailments, which in turn could be associated with nutritional deficiencies in early childhood.[9]

Berry and his associates argue that genetic factors seem to account for red–green color blindness, taste blindness, and the "alcoholic flush" phenomenon. Many studies have demonstrated that the frequency of red–green color blindness is much lower in non-Caucasian groups than among Caucasians. About 30% of all Caucasians are taste blind to certain substances that taste bitter to Africans and Native American Indians. The alcoholic flush, a reddening of the face after consuming only a few alcoholic drinks, is much more common in Asian populations than in Caucasians.[10]

Socialization and enculturation with the environment play a role in sensory stimulation. Children are taught to pay attention to certain kinds of stimuli. Africans, for example, tend to excel in auditory tasks, whereas Europeans tend to excel in visual tasks. Cultural groups are taught to favor some sensory receptors over others. These people develop a sensotype—that is, the relative importance of one sensory modality over the others.[11]

Marshall Segall and his colleagues have conducted an extensive body of cross-cultural research on perception.[12] Segall believes that repeated experience with certain objects affects how those objects are perceived. His study involved the perception of optical illusions. Almost 2,000 subjects, from 14 non-Western cultures (mostly in Africa) and 3 Western cultures, participated in the study. Each participant was shown a series of optical illusions. Segall argued that optical illusions occur because previously learned interpretations of visual cues are misapplied due to unusual or misleading characteristics of stimuli. One hypothesis that explains vulnerability to illusions is called the carpentered-world hypothesis.

According to Segall and the carpentered-world hypothesis, there is a learned tendency among those raised in an environment shaped by carpenters (e.g., rectangular furniture, houses, right angles) to interpret nonrectangular figures as representations of rectangular figures seen *in perspective*. In most urbanized places, rooms and buildings are typically rectangular, with lots of right angles. Look around the room you are in right now. Look at all the right angles. They are everywhere! The windows, the corner of your desk, the doorway, and where the walls meet the ceiling all form right angles. Being surrounded by such an environment, we learn to depend on depth cues based on a linear perspective more than would people who live in less carpentered (i.e., less built) environments. For example, rural isolated Zulus live in a noncarpentered world, with round huts and round doors. They do not plow their land in straight rows as farmers in the United States would but, instead, tend to plow in curves.

Segall uses the Sander parallelogram to explain the carpentered-world hypothesis (see Figure 5.5). For people living in carpentered societies, the diagonal line bisecting the larger, left-hand parallelogram appears to be considerably longer than the one bisecting the smaller, right-hand parallelogram—but they are, in fact, the same length. In other words, the apparently longer portion of the figure may be interpreted as the corner of a room receding in depth, because the wings of the illusion act as linear perspective cues.[13]

| Figure 5.5 | Sander parallelogram. |

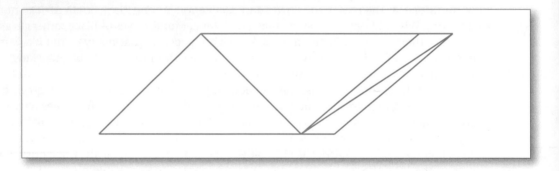

Stage #2: Storage/Memory

Once information has been sensed and passed through the perceptual filters, it is processed into memory. Memory involves maintaining information over time.[14] Memory is required for virtually all human communication. Without the ability to store information over time, we could not communicate with others. Imagine not being able to remember your own name or recognize your family members. Without memory, you could not read this book, nor would you be able to construct a single spoken sentence! The importance of memory is why many cultures regard it as the most crucial component of human intelligence. Generally, cognitive psychologists recognize two types of memory: working memory and long-term memory.[15]

According to Matlin, working memory, sometimes called short-term memory, is brief, immediate memory for information you are processing at the current moment. Working memory coordinates ongoing mental activities, and information is constantly being handled, combined, and transformed. It holds both new and old information that has been retrieved from long-term memory. In some cases, the information is committed to long-term memory, and in many other cases, the information is simply lost.[16] The amount of information stored in short-term memory is quite limited. Although psychologists disagree, many concur with George Miller's conclusion that short-term memory is limited to seven items, plus or minus two. In what is now considered a classic article, Miller coined the phrase "The magical number seven, plus or minus two" in referring to the storage capacity of short-term memory.[17]

In her summary of research associated with working memory, Matlin notes that working memory is relatively fragile and that, unless rehearsed and repeated, information held in working memory is easily lost within about 30 seconds. Although working memory is temporary, limited, and fragile, it is essential for human communication. In any culture, most communicative tasks, such as reading, writing, listening, and speaking, are entirely dependent on the ability to maintain information for short periods of time. In any culture, the ability to finish a spoken or written sentence is contingent on remembering its first words.[18]

Individuals' working memory may be affected by differences in their writing systems, however. In his work, Nader Tavassoli found that memory for the presentation order of written words was better for native English speakers than for native Chinese speakers. This may be because English words rely to a greater degree on sounds than on visual features, which are emphasized in written Chinese. For example, in English, the letters in the alphabet represent sounds. In contrast, Chinese characters represent meanings (what is called a logographic script). There appear to be fundamental processing differences between reading alphabetic and logographic scripts. Whereas reading alphabetic words, as English speakers do, is dominated by phonological cognitive processes, reading logographs, as Chinese speakers do, appears to rely to a greater degree on visual cognitive processes. Readers of Chinese logographs also appear to attend more to visual features of complete written words. For example, compared with readers of alphabetic English words, readers of Chinese logographs were more likely to remember the print color of words.[19]

In addition to working memory, humans possess long-term memory. The essential difference between working and long-term memory is the duration of storage. Unlike working memory, information in long-term memory may be held for a lifetime. People may be able to recall events that took place 40 or 50 years ago. A second major difference between the two stores is their capacity. Whereas the working short-term store may be limited to seven items, plus or minus two, the storage capacity in long-term memory is virtually unlimited. Another difference between the two memories is their method of forgetting. Information in working memory seems to be lost due to decay; that is, if the information is not used, it simply fades away. Although long-term memories also decay, the long-term store seems most disrupted by interference; that is, other information gets in the way of stored information.[20]

Many cognitive psychologists distinguish between three types of long-term memory: episodic or autobiographical memory, semantic memory, and procedural memory.[21] Although these three types of long-term memory appear to be different, they are also highly interconnected and probably operate interdependently. Episodic long-term memory refers to that type of stored information pertaining to the unique experiences of the individual. Episodic memory is autobiographical. One's birthday, first-grade teacher, first date, and so on are different for each person and are representative of the type of information stored in episodic long-term memory.

Qi Wang and Jens Brockmeier suggest that one's cultural background affects autobiographical memory. Remember from Chapter 2 that in individualistic cultures, such as the United States, an independent self is promoted. In many East Asian cultures, such as China, an interdependent self is advocated. Wang and Brockmeier point out that such differences affect the content of autobiographical memory because the relationship between memory and self is built into the culture.[22] In fact, Wang found that, compared with Caucasian Americans, who recalled their earliest autobiographical memories from as young as 3.5 years of age, Asians and Asian Americans reported memories dated more than 6 months later. In related research, Wang asked American and Chinese college students to report their earliest childhood memory. Wang found that the descriptions provided by Americans were mostly individual focused and self-assured, while the descriptions provided by Chinese tended to be group oriented and modest. Wang concluded that an independently oriented self is associated with the earlier establishment of an autobiographical history that is elaborate, specific, emotionally charged, and self-focused. On the other hand, a collectivistic self is associated with the later establishment of an autobiographical memory that is brief, general, emotionally unexpressive, and relationship centered.[23]

Semantic long-term memory preserves a person's general conceptual information, world knowledge, and language abilities unrelated to an individual's experiences. Semantic memory allows humans to communicate with language. How to spell words, count, and construct sentences would be information preserved in semantic long-term memory. In a very interesting study, Ramanand Durga found that bilingual individuals take significantly more time to process verbal information than do monolingual individuals.[24]

Procedural memory refers to one's knowledge about how to do something manually. For example, remembering how to ride a bike and how to send an e-mail message to a friend are accomplished via procedural memory.[25] Although persons from different cultures certainly perform different manual tasks, very little research has investigated specific cross-cultural differences in procedural memory.

Stage #3: Recall/Retrieval

Once information has been stored, it is relatively useless unless it can be retrieved. The human information processor excels at retrieval. Information that has been stored for a lifetime yet is rarely used can be recalled in an instant. Other times, however, recently stored information seems very difficult to recall. Most adults can easily recall the name of their first-grade teacher but cannot remember what they had for dinner three nights ago. Moreover, the quality of human information retrieval is typically approximate rather than literal. People retain global memories of conversations or events rather than verbatim transcriptions. According to Roy Lachman and his colleagues, forgetting is memory failure—the inability to recall or recognize stored information. Although most of us regret it when we forget something, cognitive psychologists now treat long-term memory forgetting as an asset rather than a liability because it is a useful way to prevent long-term memory from getting cluttered with information that is not being used. Forgetting often follows what is called a "negatively accelerated curve." Most forgetting occurs rapidly and then levels off over time. Other researchers contend that information is never really forgotten; people just lose access to it.[26]

Matlin points out that we might forget something for many reasons, including decay, interference, arousal, trauma, and depth of processing. Forgetting that is due to decay occurs when a memory is not rehearsed or used over time. Eventually, the information diminishes or fades from memory. Interference occurs when other information intrudes on stored information. Sometimes, forgetting occurs when old memories interfere with the storage of new information. Other times, forgetting occurs when new information disrupts previously stored "old" memories. Matlin devised a mini-experiment that demonstrates the effect of interference.[27]

INTERFERENCE FORGETTING MINI-EXPERIMENT

Present the following word list to a friend or roommate:

River	Card
Door	Test
Cat	Tree
Plate	Ball
Book	Road

Allow a few moments for your friend to read the list. After he or she finishes, ask him or her either to write down or to recite orally a list of 10 vegetables. When he or she has finished the list of vegetables, ask him or her to recall the words on the list he or she read. See how many he or she recalls and with what degree of accuracy. Repeat the experiment with another friend, but this time delete the vegetable list exercise. Compare their results. Theoretically, the vegetable word list exercise should interfere with your friend's ability to store the word list in memory.

Negative arousal, or anxiety, is also thought to interfere with the retrieval of information from long-term memory.[28] Persons suffering from anxiety often report being unable to recall certain information. Students, for example, often complain that test anxiety prohibits them from performing well on exams. According to Matlin, another form of forgetting may be due to repression. This occurs when people actively, but unconsciously, forget unpleasant material. Similarly, pleasant material may be processed more easily than unpleasant. Refer back to the interference forgetting mini-experiment. After your friend completes the experiment, make a note of the first few and the last few vegetables on the list. Chances are those vegetables listed first are the ones your friend enjoys while those listed toward the end are those he or she dislikes.[29]

Matlin suggests that the effort required to gather and store information may also affect its retrieval. Meaningful information that requires deeper cognitive processing may be easier to recall than information that requires minimal effort to encode. Likewise, the context in which the information is encoded may facilitate recall. In this situation, called *encoding specificity,* the contextual cues present during the gathering and storing of information may serve as cues for the recall of stored information.[30]

Cross-Cultural Differences in Memory and Retrieval

Several studies indicate that culture affects information retrieval. In addition to culture, age and education are two other variables strongly linked to recall. Age and recall are curvilinearly related (see Figure 5.6). Up to a point, one's age facilitates recall. When many people reach a certain age, however, their memory skills deteriorate. Likewise, educated persons seem to employ different kinds of memory strategies. Barbara Rogoff claims that to the extent that cultures have different educational systems and methods, their people may have different memory skills. Persons educated in industrialized cultures have been taught to remember disconnected bits of information, such as names and dates. These persons may be more likely than nonschooled individuals to use memory strategies that facilitate the organization of unrelated items. Moreover, Rogoff asserts that schooled individuals are more likely to classify similar objects together, whereas nonschooled persons classify objects based on their functional similarity. For example, in many memory tests, persons are presented with lists of unrelated pieces of information, not unlike the word list presented in the interference forgetting miniexperiment. This type of information may be remembered better if the person employs some sort of mnemonic (pronounced "neh-monic," meaning a technique for improving memory) device such as rehearsing or classifying. Nonschooled persons, including preschool children, generally do not employ mnemonic strategies and have difficulty with such tasks.[31]

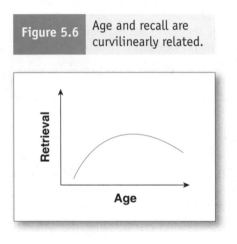

| Figure 5.6 | Age and recall are curvilinearly related. |

With contextually organized information, however, fewer memory differences are observed between schooled and nonschooled persons. In one study reported by Rogoff, for example, Guatemalan Mayan and American 9-year-olds watched an experimenter place 20 miniature objects such as cars, animals, furniture, people, and household items into a panorama model of a town. The 20 items were then removed from the panorama and put into a pool of 80 other objects. The children were then asked to reconstruct the panorama using as many of the original 20 items as they could remember. The Mayan children performed slightly better than the American children. This difference may have been due to the fact that about one third of the American children used rehearsal strategies, such as rehearsing the names of the objects, typical for remembering unrelated bits of information. This type of strategy may be inappropriate for remembering spatially oriented, contextual information.[32]

In related research, Makoto Yoshida, Clea Fernandez, and James Stigler explored Japanese and American students' recognition memory for statements made during a videotaped mathematics lesson. Japanese and American fourth- and sixth-graders watched either a Japanese or English version of the same lesson and then were tested for recognition of teacher statements that were relevant or irrelevant to the content of the lesson. The Japanese and American students were equally successful at recognizing relevant statements, but American students remembered more irrelevant statements than did the Japanese.[33]

Michael Cole and John Gay assert that a culture's language and literacy rate may affect recall. Some evidence indicates that nonliterate societies develop mnemonic skills differently from those of literate societies. In nonliterate societies, there may be no written language to facilitate memory. Imagine studying for an examination for which you have no notes! Cole and Gay note that in nonliterate societies, people must store information in memory rather than on a piece of paper. Likewise, the histories of nonliterate societies must be stored in the memories of their people rather than on paper or in books.[34] In a study conducted by Bruce Ross and Carol Millsom, two groups of university students, one group from Ghana and the other from New York, were read several stories aloud and then asked to recall them. Generally, the Ghanaian students showed better recall of the stories than did the American students.

Researchers in a related study examined the effects of culturally based knowledge on memory of stories about people performing common activities.[35]

In a study by Richard Jackson Harris, Lawrence Schoen, and Deana Hensley, college students from America and Mexico read three brief stories of everyday activities. There were two versions of the same story, consistent with either an American or a Mexican cultural script. The students read each version. Researchers administered memory tests immediately after the students read the story, 30 minutes after they read the story, and 1 week after they read the story. After 1 week, both groups of students mistakenly recalled the stories from the other culture as being more like their own culture than they in fact were.[36]

Other memory research reviewed by In-mao Liu indicates that Chinese persons may have superior memory. For example, in word-pair association memory tasks, Chinese college students usually attain perfect recall within two or three trials compared with students from other cultures, whose accuracy is typically below 70%.[37] Until more is known, final conclusions about the relationship between culture and memory should be made with some degree of caution. Although several studies indicate a connection between culture and memory, these studies may actually be revealing differences in other factors that affect recall, such as socialization or education. Because cultures differ in so many ways, it is difficult to pinpoint culture as the sole mechanism for memory ability.

Categorization and Mental Economy

Humans are constantly bombarded by so many stimuli simultaneously that they cannot possibly process all of it. To manage the enormous quantities of information, humans tend to engage in mental economy strategies. One such strategy is called categorization. Categorization consists of grouping, sorting, or classifying objects, events, or living things into identifiable groups or compartments based on the belief that the category members share certain features or characteristics. Most cognitive psychologists argue that all people, regardless of culture, engage in categorization and that it is a necessary part of everyday life. Categorization is an essential cognitive mechanism by which humans organize and manage the natural and social world that surrounds them.[38] Eleanor Rosch is well known for her work on categorization. She has argued that

> the world consists of a virtually infinite number of discriminably different stimuli. Since no organism can cope with infinite diversity, one of the most basic functions of all organisms is the cutting up of the environment into classifications by which nonidentical stimuli can be treated as equivalent.[39]

Although people categorize just about everything (e.g., plants, cars, events), intercultural communication researchers are interested in the ways people categorize other people. William Gudykunst and Young Kim suggest that categories are useful because they help the information processor reduce uncertainty and increase the accuracy of predictions about others. Moreover, categories help us make attributions about the behavior of others and help us recall and recognize information. Understanding categorization is particularly important for intercultural communication because whenever we interact with someone from a different culture, we are faced with high levels of uncertainty and unfamiliar stimuli to process.[40]

According to Richard Brislin, people often form categories on the basis of perceived conspicuous differences. Conspicuous differences categories are based on easily seen similarities or differences. According to Brislin, these types of categories are formed quickly during initial interaction with someone from a different culture. Conspicuous differences may stem from skin color, dress, language, or occupation. These differences help classify others as members of in-groups and out-groups.[41] Unfortunately, there is evidence to suggest that in-group/out-group categorization is a principal category formed by people that often leads to intergroup discrimination and intergroup bias. David Wilder has argued that intergroup bias and prejudice are unavoidable by-products of categorization. Moreover, Wilder maintains that such bias may have nothing to do with irrational thought processes but is a consequence of people's attempts to organize and simplify their environment (i.e., categorization).[42] Likewise, Bernadette Park and Charles Judd point out that it is probably impossible to eliminate in-group/out-group categorization and may not be possible for human beings to think of one another as "individuals" or as all one and the same. They maintain that most social categorization schemes are correlated with ethnicity and form the basis for intergroup hostilities.[43] To be sure, Charles Ridley and Carrie Hill maintain that categorization is the primary cognitive process associated with racism.[44]

Although people in all cultures categorize, researchers have found that culture affects categorization. In their summary of this research, Sara Unsworth, Christopher Sears, and Penny Pexman found that people from Asian cultures, especially the Chinese, create holistic categories and that Westerners create analytic categories. Unsworth and her colleagues point out that holistic categories focus on context and environmental factors; relationships are explained with reference to how objects are related to their environment, and it is held that a part cannot be separated from the whole. Analytic categories, on the other hand, are characterized by the separation of an object from its context; similarity among objects or people is used to differentiate them into distinct groups, and predictions about people are made based on these categories.[45]

STEREOTYPING

By constructing categories, the human mind processes information more efficiently. Once created, categories are the basis of prejudgment, such as stereotyping. Considered a subset of categorization, stereotyping involves members of one group attributing characteristics to members of another group. These attributions typically carry a positive or negative evaluation. In this sense, stereotypes are categories with an attitude. Stereotypes typically refer to membership in social categories—such as sex, race, age, or profession—that are believed to be associated with certain traits and behaviors. In the United States, race and gender groups are often stereotyped. Richard Schaefer defines stereotypes as exaggerated images of the characteristics of a particular group held by prejudiced people who hold ill feelings toward that group. Gudykunst and Kim define stereotypes as cognitive representations of another group that influence one's feelings about the group. They argue that stereotypes provide the content of social categories.[46]

Although it is hard to admit, we all stereotype. Stereotyping is a natural and universal information-processing strategy. Donald Taylor and Lana Porter maintain that stereotyping should be seen as a normal information-processing tool that is especially useful in diverse societies.[47] The difficulty arises when stereotypes carry a negative valence and are used to overgeneralize negative traits to an entire group of people when, in reality, few members of the group actually possess such traits. In this way, stereotyping can lead to ethnocentrism, prejudice, and discrimination (see Figures 5.7a and 5.7b).

Figure 5.7a What stereotypical traits might be associated with these young men?

Figure 5.7b What stereotypical traits might be associated with these young women?

STUDENT VOICES ACROSS CULTURES

Amanda Garrity

Many are aware of the inescapable shadow of stereotypes that follows a pageant girl no matter what spotlight she stands in. Typical stereotypes of pageant girls are that we are blonde, unrealistically thin, vain, and remarkably unintelligent. As a blonde, slender young woman who wears a crown of my own, I am the target of these stereotypes. However, these misconceptions only give me the satisfying challenge of proving the true image and beauty of my pageant world.

Like most stereotypes, those surrounding women who participate in pageants are limiting and inaccurate, especially when those who hold the stereotypes use media outlets to spread their distorted perceptions. Often, pageants are seen as a pedestal for young women to display their sex appeal, where beauty is equated with vanity and shallowness. Those experienced in the world of pageantry could not disagree more.

I started entering pageants at the age of 13, not in hopes of having people dote on my prettiness but to gain confidence and to accept and express myself. After competing and winning my first title, however, these stereotypes began to loom over me and shook the very confidence I was seeking. When I would wear my crown to community events to spread the news and information about my platform, people would glare negatively, tell my parents that they should be ashamed of themselves, and avoid me. At school, false allegations were made that I had developed an eating disorder, and friends stopped sending me invitations to join them in my favorite activities: four-wheeling, soccer, etc. As fast as the crown was placed on my head, the perceptions of me changed. With these stereotypes weighing on me, there were times I actually believed it would be easier to become the person they saw me as instead of spending all my time and energy defending myself.

There was a short time when I started to believe that these stereotypes may be true. Only when I realized where and how these stereotypes were developed, and that I would only be turning into another statistic if I gave in by becoming who they thought I was, did I begin to recognize and promote the positive effects pageants can have on young women and to debunk the distortions. Through my experiences with pageant organizations, I was able to attend the college of my choice, after receiving many academic scholarships, and graduate debt free.

By featuring stage competitions, such as evening gown, swimsuit, talent, and onstage questions, pageant organizations emphasize the importance of taking care of yourself, leading a healthy lifestyle, promoting and sharing your talents, and forming a strong personal opinion about world events. These are all qualities and standards people should have in their lives to be accomplished and successful.

Because of pageants, I have the confidence to stay true to who I really am. Whether I'm camping with my family and not wearing any makeup for weeks at a time, leaving my heels in the closet to lace up my sneakers for a day full of dirty course, or standing on the grandest stage of all at Miss America, I can stand tall knowing that because of pageants, I am proud of who I have become.

Racial and Ethnic Stereotypes

Social scientists have long been interested in stereotypes and prejudice, two concepts that are often related. The systematic study of racial and ethnic stereotypes in the United States began in the 1930s with a classic study conducted by David Katz and Kenneth Braly. In their study, college students were presented with a list of 84 adjectives (e.g., *lazy*, *ignorant*, *arrogant*, *intelligent*) and were asked to indicate which traits were characteristic of 10 ethnic groups: Americans, Blacks, Chinese, English, Germans, Italians, Irish, Japanese, Jews, and Turks. The results of their study showed that the college students consistently agreed on which traits described which group. The results were particularly consistent for Blacks and Jews.

Traits Associated With Blacks (Katz & Braly, 1933)	Traits Associated With Jews (Katz & Braly, 1933)
Superstitious	Shrewd
Lazy	Mercenary (selfish)
Happy-go-lucky	Sly
Ignorant	Aggressive
Stupid	Industrious
Dirty (physically)	Intelligent
Musical	Ambitious
Religious	

In their original study, Katz and Braly found a high level of consistency in the adjectives respondents associated with the Black stereotype. Moreover, the adjectives selected were generally negative. Since their original work, several other researchers have replicated Katz and Braly's stereotype checklist method using the same 84 adjectives as in the original study—G. M. Gilbert in 1950 and L. Gordon in 1969 and 1982. Patricia Devine and Andrew Elliot replicated the research in 1995.[48]

American Stereotypes

Canadian psychologists Taylor and Porter examined some of the socially desirable aspects of stereotyping and allege that the negative connotation associated with stereotyping may be uniquely American. They argue that, historically, the study of stereotypes in the United States mainly has focused on White stereotypes of African Americans, which have been particularly brutal and negative (see Figure 5.8). Second, Taylor and Porter suggest that the essence of the political doctrine in the United States is modeled after the "melting-pot" metaphor, wherein the peoples of all the different cultures immigrating to the United States get "stirred up in the great pot until cultural differences are boiled away and a single culture remains—American." Because stereotyping, by definition, recognizes and highlights differences among groups, it directly conflicts with the melting-pot image. Third, Taylor and Porter suggest that psychologists studying interpersonal attraction have long understood that perceived similarity is a major determinant in how much people are attracted to and like others. The more we perceive people to be similar to us, the more likely we are to be attracted to and like them. Hence, stereotypes that emphasize group differences essentially block the potential for intergroup friendships. Given these trends, Taylor and Porter assert that there are compelling reasons why Americans view stereotyping as a destructive social force. This, they argue, has led to an enormous investment in human and financial resources to rid people of their stereotypes.[49]

Figure 5.8   Often, White stereotypes of African Americans have been brutal and negative.

Taylor and Porter recognize that people in countries different from the United States are brought up in entirely different cultural contexts where it is perfectly acceptable to categorize people into groups. In Europe and Canada, for example, people presume that society is culturally diverse and are proud of their various group memberships. Taylor and Porter suggest that this philosophy contrasts sharply with the American melting-pot metaphor, which emphasizes cultural homogeneity. In other countries, the significance of cultural diversity is symbolized through metaphors that are very different from the melting pot, such as a mosaic or montage—that is, an assortment of people in the same place but not necessarily blending together.

Taylor and Porter claim that a fundamental feature of any pluralistic society is that ethnic attitudes exist between different groups, particularly in-groups and out-groups. Ethnic attitudes and stereotypes are a part of all cultures, and no one can avoid learning them.[50] In fact, research conducted by Ashton Trice and Kimberly Rush indicates that stereotypes are well established in children's memories long before they acquire the intellectual ability to question or evaluate them. In their study of American 4-year-olds, Trice and Rush found that boys were significantly more likely to accept male-stereotyped occupations (e.g., police officer, truck driver, house builder) than female-stereotyped occupations (e.g., teacher, nurse, secretary). Likewise, girls were significantly more likely to accept female-stereotyped occupations than male-stereotyped occupations.[51]

STUDENT VOICES ACROSS CULTURES

STEREOTYPES

Morgan Leah Johnson

Whether the purpose is academic, service, or leisure oriented, I have always eagerly sought travel to Spanish-speaking locations to help master my second language. In the past few years, I have been fortunate enough to travel to Puerto Rico, Mexico, Costa Rica, Ecuador, and Spain. With each new place comes a unique community that, like any other, internalizes various beliefs, values, attitudes, and ways of life. Naturally, as a stranger entering their environment, members of each community immediately stereotype me. Most frequently, I am categorized as a young, White, American female. By young, they mean I am naïve with little work ethic; by White, affluent; by American, culturally ignorant, demanding, and more focused on financial gain than family tradition; by female, dainty and in need of male assistance. Generally speaking, I am not offended by the stereotypes assigned to me, as our conversations ultimately refute many of them. For example, although young, I have faced many life obstacles, including domestic violence, divorce, poverty, the death of a parent, and health challenges—all of which taught me a great deal about life. I understand the usefulness of stereotypes to provide comfort in an unfamiliar situation; however, if we overlook the opportunities to teach others about who we are as individuals, life-changing experiences will be lost and negative stereotypes will persist.

One specific instance of stereotyping, among many, happened to me while in Ecuador for an internship. I was at a family reunion of the hostess with whom I was living, and throughout the day I found myself isolated; everyone in the family interacted among themselves, not with me. I felt like a child looking in on a perfectly choreographed ballet—wanting to join but fearing I did not possess sufficient skills. At the time, I did not realize that I was being stereotyped by her extended family. Based on their observations that I was young and American, they deduced that I was not family oriented and thus not worth getting to know.

Twenty of us ate dinner that evening, and the topic of my impending return home surfaced. Someone asked me what I loved most about Ecuador. I replied that it was the strength and importance of family, and went on to relate characteristics of their family to mine. As soon as my desire to see my family again became apparent, the discussion shifted to their notions about the values and traditions of the American family: how kids get "kicked out" at 18 years of age, how families move very far away from one another and never see one another, and how we never help one another. I told them quite a different story of family: that I live at home when I am not away at college, how my extended family lives within 30 miles of everyone, and how my mom helped me prepare for my trip. Throughout the night, we dispelled stereotypes by participating in mutual self-disclosure. For example, an aunt brought out a personalized calendar with pictures of her family and shared stories about each member with me as we flipped through the months. I truly felt like part of their family, and I still consider them part of mine.

The Foundations in Area Studies for Translators (FAST) program at the University of Tampere in Finland is a degree program designed for students to study the national cultures of the United States, England, Canada, and Finland. In one of its reference papers is a list of stereotypes of Americans held by Spanish high school students who had never been to the United States or had any American friends (see the following box).[52]

Physical Appearance and Dress

Most Americans are very tall with blue eyes and blond hair.

All American men are as handsome as movie stars.

Men in the U.S. have muscular builds; they resemble Arnold Schwarzenegger or Sylvester Stallone.

American men like to wear short, sleeveless T-shirts to show off their physiques.

American women are either unusually fat or unusually thin, never of normal build.

Work and Leisure

Americans spend almost all day at work; they have very little free time.

Although they are punctual and efficient in their jobs, Americans don't consider their work important; family comes first.

The first two things an American wants to discuss are salary and age.

The two favorite leisure-time activities in the U.S. are movies and rodeos.

Home Life

Most Americans live either in skyscrapers or on farms.

In big cities everyone has a large car like a Cadillac, but outside of cities people usually travel on horseback.

Americans divorce repeatedly and have very complicated private lives.

In marriages in the U.S., the wife always dominates.

American cities are so dangerous that a person has a good chance of being killed in the street; therefore, American men either know kung-fu or carry a gun.

Food

Americans eat almost nothing but hamburgers, hot dogs, popcorn, and Coke.

Americans generally eat fast food Monday through Saturday, but never on Sunday.

American men are always drinking beer, even at breakfast.

American breakfasts are huge. A typical one might consist of eggs, toast, bacon, and pancakes with peanut butter.

Communication and Social Interaction

Americans speak very quickly and very loudly. They use their hands a lot, often gesturing in an exaggerated way when they talk. Their strange intonation makes their speech sound like singing.

American English is extremely difficult to understand because people speak as if they were chewing gum.

The typical American is very rude, often putting his feet on a desk or table and frequently belching in public. He yawns a lot, never trying to hide it.

In international affairs as in personal life, Americans do whatever they want and don't care what other people think.

Media Influence on Stereotypes

So how did the Spanish high school students acquire such stereotypes of Americans, without having been to the United States and without having any U.S. friends? A considerable body of research suggests that media play a significant role in the development of stereotypes. In their stereotypes of Americans, the Spanish students mention Arnold Schwarzenegger and Sylvester Stallone, two well-known film actors in the United States. To be sure, stereotypes are acquired and learned in many ways. There probably is not a single factor responsible for the development of any stereotype. But one theory, called cultivation theory, developed by George Gerbner and his colleagues proposes that long-term exposure to media, especially television, "cultivates" in viewers a perception of social reality that is reflective of the content they view on television.[53] Gerbner describes the thrust of his theory:

> We have used the concept of "cultivation" to describe the independent contribution television viewing makes to viewer conceptions of social reality. . . . When we talk about the "independent contribution" of television viewing, we mean that the development (in some) and the maintenance (in others) of some set of outlooks or beliefs can be traced to steady, cumulative exposure to the world of television.[54]

Although a complete description of cultivation theory is beyond the scope of this chapter, the central thesis of the theory is that the images, characters, news accounts, and especially the stories (e.g., situation comedies, reality shows, dramas, etc.) portrayed on television, whether accurate or not, become the social reality that viewers believe is correct and representative of their society. Gerbner refers to this as symbolic reality and contends that this process begins early in life. He observes that before they can read or even speak, children watch television, much of it designed specifically for them. But Gerbner is careful to point out that viewers are not passive receivers in the cultivation process. Viewers make their desires known, and the producers of television programming are sensitive to them and appeal to them. So the cultivation process is a dynamic, interdependent one that evolves and adapts with each new generation of viewers.[55]

So what does this have to do with stereotypes? Once again, heavy viewers of television believe that the real world is similar to the world they see on television. But, as Mary Beth Oliver asserts, the real world and the television world may be remarkably different. For example, Oliver points out that television tends to overrepresent the pervasiveness of violence in society, and heavy viewers of television overestimate the frequency of violence in their communities. Moreover, the perception of the people associated with the violence—that is, the victims, criminals, and law enforcement officers—is also distorted. Television violence is just one example, but the point here is that how people are portrayed on television affects how they are perceived in reality.[56]

A number of researchers applying cultivation theory have studied microcultural groups in the United States and how they are depicted on television, and the resulting stereotypes associated with them. Three specific groups studied include African Americans, Hispanics/Latinos, and Asian Americans. (Recall that these microcultural groups were profiled in Chapter 3.) Ron Tamborini and his colleagues have traced the history of African American and Hispanic microcultural group representation on fictional television.[57] They report that over the past several decades, the televised images of these two groups have evolved. For example, during the early years of television in the 1940s and '50s, African Americans were rarely seen on television, but when they were, they were presented as "overweight domestic servants" and "lazy simpletons." From the late 1950s through the 1980s, the frequency of African American images in fictional television increased and began to take on professional and intellectual roles. Tracing the history of Hispanics/Latinos, Tamborini and his colleagues observed that they were often portrayed as drug dealers, gangsters, or buffoons who lacked intelligence and ability to speak English. Yet, in their 2007 analysis of more than 100 action/adventure, cartoon, courtroom drama, crime drama, family drama, medical drama, reality-based, science fiction, sitcom, and soap opera programs, Tamborini's research found that "on both a comparative and an absolute basis, the portrayals of Blacks and Latinos were found to be very similar to those of their White counterparts in the roles they held and attributes associated with them."[58] Oliver notes, however, that compared with fictional television, in contemporary news and reality entertainment, Whites, African Americans, and Hispanics/Latinos are portrayed differently. In her analysis of news accounts and reality-based programs (e.g., *America's Most Wanted*), Oliver found that the majority of White characters in programs were portrayed as police officers rather than suspects, while the majority of Black and Latino characters were portrayed as criminal suspects rather than police. She also found that when confronting Black and Latino suspects, White police officers were more likely to employ force than when confronting White suspects.[59]

Asian Americans, too, have been stereotyped in television. But unlike the negative stereotypes of African Americans and Hispanics/Latinos, Asian Americans have been described as the *model minority,* portrayed on television as noncontroversial, polite, and hardworking.[60] Yuko Kawai of Tokai University in Japan has studied stereotypes of Asian Americans and writes that "the model minority is probably the most influential and prevalent stereotype of Asian Americans today."[61] Traits associated with the Asian American model-minority stereotype include close family ties; academic success; white-collar, high-wage employment; law-abiding conduct; discipline; and accountability. Kawai maintains that the model minority stereotype portrays Asian Americans as possessing these traits despite their racial background, which some then use as evidence to deny U.S. institutional racism. Moreover, depicting Asian Americans as the model minority also contrasts with the negative stereotypes of African Americans and Hispanics/Latinos, making them appear as problem minorities. But like African Americans and Hispanics/Latinos, Kawai notes that the early stereotype of Asian Americans was quite negative. Referred to as the Yellow Peril, this stereotype of Asian Americans dates back to the late 19th and early 20th centuries, when Asians immigrating to the United States were perceived to be an economic, political, and military threat to mainstream White America.

Kawai points to the contradiction of these two stereotypes. Asian Americans are stereotyped as the model minority when they outperform other minorities but are perceived as the Yellow Peril when they threaten and outperform Whites.[62]

Consistent with the propositions of cultivation theory, the Yellow Peril stereotype was perpetuated in the media by way of Dr. Fu Manchu, an intellectual but murderous fictional character introduced in a series of novels by British author Sax Rohmer. Writing for the *South China Morning Post*, Canadian reporter Ian Young describes the Fu Manchu character as one of the most racist characters in history, featured extensively in cinema, television, radio, comic strips, and comic books for nearly 100 years. Young references the 1932 film *The Mask of Fu Manchu,* in which the villain tells his followers to "kill the White men and take their women."[63]

So what are the implications of cultivation theory and media representations of microcultural groups? To the extent media portray African Americans, Asian Americans, and Hispanics/Latinos in stereotypical rather than accurate ways, such stereotyping serves to validate, accentuate, and perpetuate hostile, and sometimes benevolent, racism.

STEREOTYPE CONTENT MODEL

For the past 10 years, professors Amy Cuddy and Susan Fiske have embarked on an extensive and extremely productive program of theory and research on stereotypes. They have created a model, called the Stereotype Content Model (SCM), that explains how and why people stereotype and the essential content of those stereotypes. Cuddy and Fiske maintain that the model is applicable across cultures and have presented convincing data to support their claims.[64]

At the core of the SCM is the thesis that individuals' social perceptions (i.e., stereotypes) about others are based on two judgments: (a) warmth and (b) competence. The model posits that people ask two questions upon encountering out-group members: *Do they intend to harm me?* and *Are they capable of harming me?* In the SCM, judgments of warmth and competence stem from two appraisals: (a) the potential harm or benefit of the target's intent and (b) whether the target can effectively enact that intent. Judgments of warmth are based on social perceptions of honesty, trustworthiness, friendliness, sincerity, etc. Judgments of competence are based on social perceptions of skillfulness, knowledge, intelligence, confidence, etc. When stereotyping, competitors lack warmth, while noncompetitors are warm; high-status people are competent, while low-status people are incompetent. While both warmth and competence are core dimensions in all stereotypes, judgments of warmth seem to be primary; that is, warmth is judged before competence, probably because judgments of warmth determine approach–avoidance tendencies (e.g., Is this person safe?). However, according to the SCM, when a person stereotypes someone, that stereotype is based on a combination of both warmth and competence. The stereotyped person could be judged as either high or low on warmth and either high or low on competence.

Cuddy and Fiske agree that some stereotypes may have some idiosyncratic content but that warmth and competence constitute the core of all stereotypes and are universal across cultures. The SCM model posits that some groups, perhaps many, will receive ambivalent judgments—that is, positive on one dimension and negative on another. Some groups may be perceived as warm but not competent, while others may be perceived as competent but not warm. To be sure, some groups may be perceived as warm and competent, while others are perceived as not warm (i.e., cold) and not competent. The SCM proposes that warmth and competence judgments elicit one of four unique emotional responses: admiration, envy, contempt, or pity.

Judgment	Emotion
Low competence–low warmth	Contempt (out-groups)
Low competence–high warmth	Pity (paternalistic stereotype)
High competence–low warmth	Admiration (envious stereotype)
High competence–high warmth	Pride (in-groups)

In addition to these four emotional responses, judgments of warmth and competence elicit active and passive behavioral responses. Perceived warmth predicts active behaviors, while perceived competence predicts passive behaviors.

For example, admired groups (i.e., competent and warm) elicit both active and passive facilitation—that is, both helping and associating. Envied groups (i.e., low competence and cold) elicit both kinds of harm—active attack and passive neglect. The ambivalent combinations are more unpredictable. For example, pitied groups elicit both active helping and passive neglect. Cuddy and Fiske point to the patronizing behavior toward older and disabled people, who are sometimes over-helped yet at other times neglected. On the other hand, envied groups elicit both passive association and active harm—for example, when people shop at the stores of the out-group but then, during social or economic duress, attack and loot those same stores.

Judgment	Behavior
High warmth	Active facilitation (e.g., help)
Low warmth	Active harm (e.g., attack/discriminate)
High competence	Passive facilitation (e.g., obligatory association)
Low competence	Passive harm (e.g., neglect, ignoring)

According to the SCM, the origins of perceived warmth and competence stem from larger social structures seen in all cultures, specifically competition and status. In all cultures, groups compete with one another for resources (e.g., jobs, schools, housing). In all cultures, groups are ranked within some social hierarchy (e.g., microcultures). Noncompetitive groups are seen as warm, while competitive groups are seen as cold. High-status groups are seen as competent, while low-status groups are seen as incompetent. SCM posits a direct link between the larger social structures, stereotypes, prejudice, and discrimination:

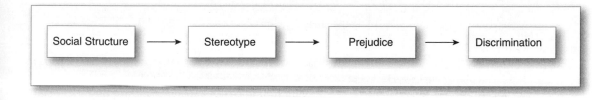

In testing the SCM, Cuddy and Fiske and their associates have surveyed diverse samples of people from across the United States. Participants in their studies were asked to rate a variety of social groups on perceptions of both warmth and competence. The rated groups included occupational groups, nationality, race, ethnicity, socioeconomic status, religion, and gender groups. Participants were not asked to rate the groups according to their own perceptions but, rather, according to how they believed others saw these groups. Some of the results are presented below.

Low Competence–Low Warmth	Low Competence–High Warmth	High Competence–High Warmth	High Competence–Low Warmth
Welfare recipients	Elderly	Americans	Asians
Arabs	Disabled	Christians	Jews
Poor	Retarded	Irish	Rich
Feminists	Black professionals	Whites	
Turks	Middle class	British	
Drug addicts	Housewives		

The authors of the SCM claim its universality across cultures and have tested the model in several cross-cultural studies. In one study, respondents from 17 European countries completed a survey similar to the one reported above, completed by U.S. respondents. The respondents completed survey items measuring warmth and competence of the various cultural groups (all the surveys were translated into the appropriate languages). The results were as follows:

Low Competence–High Warmth	High Competence–Low Warmth	Extreme High Competence–Extreme Low Warmth
Spain	Belgium	Germany
Ireland	Finland	United Kingdom
Italy	Sweden	
Greece	Denmark	
Portugal	Netherlands	
Austria		

Cuddy and Fiske also conducted a study including East Asian samples, arguing that Asian cultures tend to differ from Western cultures on dimensions of cultural variability such as individualism and collectivism. Specifically, they asked Chinese students in Hong Kong to complete surveys similar to the ones described above to rate social groups in Hong Kong.

Low Competence–Low Warmth	Low Competence–High Warmth	Mod Competence–Mod Warmth	High Competence–Low Warmth
Mainlanders	Children	Students	Rich
Filipino maids	Christians	Chinese	Professionals
Unemployed	Mentally ill	Blue-collar	
Immigrants	Elderly	Women	
Pakistanis	Foreigners		
Asians			
Singles			
College grads			
Hong Kong locals			

These researchers recognize that any number of cultural differences could challenge their claim of the universal principles of stereotyping. For example, as we have seen in this chapter, culture affects basic cognitive processes, especially categorization. Culture shapes the ideologies that seem to justify prejudice and discrimination against some groups (e.g., microcultures). As we saw in Chapter 2, cultural values vary considerably. Cuddy and Fiske point out that some societies might not value competence and warmth as strongly as do other cultures. Finally, a culture's political climate influences how people perceive out-groups. In the United States, for example, Cuddy and Fiske note that political correctness might lead some to grant out-groups a positive stereotype.

To be sure, Cuddy and Fiske and their colleagues continue their program research on the SCM. They have produced considerable evidence that social perceptions of warmth and competence, driven by the social structures of competition and status, operate as universal dimensions of stereotypes. Targets perceived as warm and competent elicit uniformly positive emotions. Those lacking both warmth and competence are stereotyped negatively.[65]

Why Stereotype?

In addition to Gerbner's cultivation theory and the logic provided by the SCM discussed above, there are other explanations as to why stereotyping is so common and universal, none of which relate to prejudice. One explanation is called the out-group homogeneity effect. This effect is the tendency for people to see members of an out-group as less diverse and more stereotypic than the members of that group see themselves. We have a tendency to see out-group members as highly similar (i.e., homogeneous) yet view ourselves and our in-group members as unique and individual. For example, students may think that all professors are the same. Likewise, professors may think that all students are alike. Yet neither professors nor students see themselves as "just like" all the others. The out-group homogeneity effect has been observed across a wide variety of different kinds of groups, including national, religious, political, and age groups. The effect is a theoretically important one because differences in the perceived variability of groups can cause differences in the stereotyping of those groups. Taylor and Porter contend that because in-groups and out-groups do not interact much, they may be unable to develop accurate representations of each other.[66]

A second plausible explanation for stereotyping, originally proposed by David Hamilton and Robert Gifford, is called the illusory correlation principle. Hamilton and Gifford argued that negative behaviors are numerically rare and when performed by microcultural group members—who, by definition, are also numerically rare—these behaviors become disproportionately memorable, leading to later impressions that microcultural group members are responsible for more than their fair share of undesirable behavior. Hamilton and Gifford point out that no prior expectation regarding the rare groups is necessary to produce the effects, just the unique memorability of rare-group/rare-behavior pairings due to their relative infrequency. Recently, Jane Risen, Thomas Gilovich, and David Dunning of Cornell University found evidence of one-shot illusory correlations—in which a single instance of unusual behavior by a member of a rare group is sufficient to create an association between group and behavior. As Taylor and Porter explain, when two objects that are unfamiliar or unusual in some way are observed to be connected on some occasion, we have the tendency to believe that they are always connected. For example, if we observe an out-group member participating in some atypical incident or behavior, such as a felony, then out-group members and felonies become associated in our minds. Then the next time we see a member of the same out-group, we will stereotype him or her as a felon. The correlation between the out-group members and felonies is illusory or unreal because the out-group is now linked to felonies on account of only one or relatively few observed occurrences.[67]

Neither the out-group homogeneity effect nor the illusory correlation principle is necessarily wrong or socially "bad." Both are naturally occurring information-processing strategies that are a part of everyone's normal cognitive repertoire. The problem is that they may lead to negative attitudes and subsequent prejudice. If people understand their information-processing functions and are informed of these kinds of strategies, then they can become mindful of the process and ward off any potentially harmful negative consequences that may result.

Schaefer offers two other reasons why stereotypes are so widely held by groups of people. First, he argues that stereotypes may arise out of real conditions. For example, a disproportionate number of people from a particular racial or ethnic group may live in poverty; so members of other groups stereotype all of them as poor or even lazy. A second explanation of stereotypes is their role in self-fulfilling prophecies. The dominant group in a particular culture may construct social or legal obstacles, making it hard for members of the stereotyped group to act differently from the stereotype. Hence, conformity to the stereotype, although forced, validates the stereotype in the minds of the dominant group. For example, members of a subordinate stereotyped group may have difficulty obtaining high-paying, prestigious employment because members of the dominant group refuse to hire them. Hence, they accept low-paying, less prestigious jobs and reinforce the stereotype.[68]

Henri Tajfel contends that another reason why people retain stereotypes is that they help us develop and maintain a positive self-esteem. Our memberships in various groups constitute a major aspect of our self-concept. Our social identities are essentially made up of our group memberships (e.g., husband, professor, colleague, friend, counsel). Tajfel asserts that our sense of esteem is nourished when we differentiate our in-groups from out-groups, usually by assigning traits (i.e., stereotypes) that are favorable to the in-group and negative for the out-group. Typically, we differentiate our in-groups on the basis of power, ancestry, religion, language, culture, race, or a whole host of other variables.[69]

According to Claude Steele and Joshua Aronson, some members of stereotyped groups actually start to believe the stereotype. They call this phenomenon stereotype threat. Stereotype threat occurs when we sense that some aspect of our self (e.g., our behavior, physical characteristics, or social condition) seems to match the stereotype, making it appear valid. Steele and Aronson believe that stereotype threat is experienced essentially as a self-evaluative threat.

In related research, Steele, Spencer, and Aronson assert that whenever there is a negative group stereotype, along with a person to whom the stereotype can be applied and a performance that might confirm the applicability of the stereotype to the person, stereotype threat can emerge. Specifically, stereotype threat is the fear or anxiety people feel when performing in some area in which their group is stereotyped to lack ability—as in test taking, for example. Stereotype threat occurs because individuals are afraid of the implications of confirming the stereotype held by others.

In their research on stereotype threat, Steele and Aronson varied the stereotype vulnerability of African Americans taking a difficult verbal test. In one condition, the participants were told that the test was a valid measure of intellectual ability. In a second condition, they were told that the test was simply a problem-solving activity not designed to measure ability. Their results showed that African Americans performed worse than Whites when the test was presented as a measure of their intellectual ability but improved dramatically, matching the performance of Whites, when the test was presented as less reflective of ability. Steele and Aronson theorize that stereotype threat inhibits efficient information processing in much the same way as other evaluative pressures do. Stereotype-threatened persons alternate their attention between trying to accomplish the task at hand and trying to assess their self-significance. This leads to reduced speed and accuracy.

Other studies have shown a stereotype threat effect on a wide variety of stigmatized groups, including women performing poorly on math exams, elderly people on cognitive tests, and people from low socioeconomic backgrounds on measures of intelligence. Stereotype threat is not limited to stigmatized groups, however. In recent related research, Cynthia Frantz and her colleagues demonstrated that the threat of appearing racist led White students to perform poorly on a test that measures racism; that is, they received scores indicating that they were racist.[70]

In their recent research, Jenessa Shapiro and Steven Neuberg claim that stereotype threat can occur in a variety of ways, including as a threat to one's personal self ("What if this stereotype is true of me?"), one's group membership ("What if this stereotype is true of my group?"), one's standing as perceived by out-group members ("What if out-groups see me as stereotypic?"), one's in-group's standing as perceived by out-group members ("What if out-groups see my group as stereotypic?"), one's own reputation as perceived by in-group members ("What if my in-group sees me as stereotypic?"), and one's in-group's standing as perceived by in-group members ("What if my in-group sees our group as stereotypic?").[71]

In their summary of research related to stereotype, Shapiro and Neuberg note that women have been observed to underperform on quantitative tasks, in comparison with men, when stereotypes about women's math abilities are made explicit but not when these stereotypes are presented as irrelevant to the task. Similarly, Latinos performed less well on tests labeled as predictive of intelligence. But Shapiro and Neuberg maintain that stereotype threat is situational and can emerge in any situation in which negative stereotypes about one's group membership are perceived to apply. They point out that membership in a group with relatively low status (e.g., microcultural groups) is not a prerequisite for the experience of stereotype threat. For example, White men may experience stereotype threat in math performance when Asians' superior mathematical ability is made salient.[72]

Stereotypes and Expectations

Although evidence suggests that stereotyping may be independent of one's attitudes about others, some studies have demonstrated that stereotypes distort social perception of others. Human perception is not necessarily accurate and honest. Perception is influenced by one's needs, wishes, and expectations. In many cases, people perceive what they expect to perceive, regardless of reality. Figure 5.9 is a popular illustration of how expectations affect perception. Most read the words in the triangle as "Paris in the spring," failing to notice the duplication of the word *the*. By definition, stereotyping is categorizing people according to some easily identifiable characteristic and then attributing to them qualities or behaviors believed to be typical of members of that classification. In this sense, stereotyping leads to expectations that, in turn, affect our social perception of others. In what is now considered a classic experiment, Jerome Bruner and Cecile Goodman found that persons of lower socioeconomic status tended to accentuate the size of coins.[73]

Figure 5.9 How many *the*'s are in this graphic?

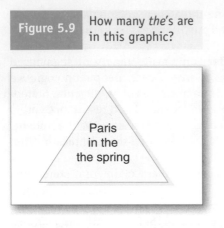

Paris
in the
the spring

In related research, Birt Duncan found that perceptions of an ambiguously aggressive act are strongly influenced by racial stereotypes. In his study, White male college students coded the behaviors observed in what they thought was a live conversation displayed on a television monitor. The conversation ended with an ambiguous shove. About half the students witnessed a Black actor shove another person, whereas the other half observed the identical act by a White actor. Of the 48 observers, 35 coded the shove as violent behavior when it was performed by a Black actor, yet only 6 of the 48 observers coded the identical act as violent behavior when it was performed by a White actor. Duncan argued that because of stereotypes associating Blacks with violence, the violent behavior category is cognitively more accessible to observers viewing a Black perpetrator than to those viewing a White one.[74]

The results of Duncan's study were replicated by H. Andrew Sagar and Janet Schofield, who studied Black and White sixth-graders. The students were shown a variety of ambiguously aggressive acts performed by Black and White actors. Both Black and White students rated the behaviors of Black actors as more mean and threatening than when the identical acts were performed by White actors. Sagar and Schofield argue that stereotypes create expectations and conclude that, "in the existing social order, the stereotype is all too real. To activate it, the person engaging in an ambiguous behavior need only be black."[75]

AN INTERCULTURAL CONVERSATION: STEREOTYPING

Akira is an exchange student from Japan who is spending a semester at an American university. Jim is a student at the same university. Jim was born and raised in Milwaukee. Jim and Akira are meeting for the first time. Below is an excerpt from their initial interaction.

Jim: Hi. (Thinks to himself—"Man, he's so short. He's just like all the other Asians I've seen.")

Akira: Hi. I'm Akira. (Thinks to himself—"Wow, he's pretty tall.")

Jim: I'm Jim. Are you a student here? (Thinks to himself—"He's probably a math major.")

Akira: Yes. (Thinks to himself—"He probably thinks I'm Chinese.")

Jim: Are you from Japan? (Thinks to himself—"He probably wonders if I drive a Honda. I wonder if he realizes how many Americans are unemployed because of all the imported Japanese cars.")

Akira: Yes, I am. (Thinks to himself—"What will he ask me now? These Americans are so impolite.")

Jim: Yeah? That's cool. How do you like it here in the United States? Have you been here before? (Thinks to himself—"He must love it here . . . it's got to be better than his country.")

Akira: I like it here a lot. (Thinks to himself—"I'd better not tell him that the food here is horrible. It might upset him.")

In this brief exchange, both Jim and Akira engage in categorization and stereotyping. Initially, Jim categorizes Akira based on conspicuous differences ("Man, he's short"). Jim seems to experience the out-group homogeneity effect ("He's just like all the other Asians I've seen") and the illusory correlation principle ("He's probably a math major"), and he tries to enhance his in-group's self-esteem ("I wonder if he realizes how many Americans are unemployed because of all the imported Japanese cars"). Akira categorizes and stereotypes Jim in much the same way.

ETHNOCENTRISM

One of the central concepts in understanding out-group attitudes and intergroup relations is ethnocentrism. William Graham Sumner originally defined ethnocentrism as "the technical name for this view of things in which one's own group is the center of everything, and all others are scaled and rated with reference to it."[76] Many scholars maintain that ethnocentricity is a natural condition and that most peoples of the world do not like foreigners and openly display feelings of hostility and fear toward them.[77] At the core of ethnocentrism, asserts Segall, is the tendency for any people to put their own group in a position of centrality and worth while creating and reinforcing negative attitudes and behaviors toward out-groups.[78] As Dutch sociologist Hofstede argues, ethnocentrism is to a people what egocentrism is to an individual.[79] The term comes from the Greek words *ethnos,* which refers to nation, and *kentron,* which refers to center.[80] James Neuliep and James McCroskey assert, however, that the term can also be applied to an ethnic or microcultural group within a country. Similar views can be held based on religion (e.g., Judaism is the only true religion) or a region of origin (e.g., Texans are the only real Americans).[81]

Ethnocentric persons hold attitudes and behaviors toward in-groups that are different from their attitudes and behaviors toward out-groups. Specifically, the attitudes and behaviors of ethnocentric persons are biased in favor of the in-group, often at the expense of the out-group. Although ethnocentrism is generally thought to be a negative trait, it fosters in-group survival, solidarity, conformity, cooperation, loyalty, and effectiveness. In his seminal work, Daniel Levinson argued that ethnocentrism is

> based on a pervasive and rigid in-group–out-group distinction; it involves stereotyped, negative imagery and hostile attitudes regarding out-groups, stereotyped positive imagery and submissive attitudes regarding in-groups, and a hierarchical, authoritarian view of group interaction in which in-groups are rightly dominant, out-groups subordinate.[82]

In related research, Donald Taylor and Vaishna Jaggi introduced a phenomenon called ethnocentric attributional bias. In his research, Thomas Pettigrew referred to this phenomenon as the *ultimate attribution error.* Both labels refer to the idea that when people perceive what they regard as some negative act performed by a member of an out-group, they attribute such behavior to some internal disposition possessed by the out-group member (e.g., he's lazy, he's a thief). Yet when people perceive what they regard as a positive act performed by members of an out-group, they attribute such behavior to situational factors (e.g., she got lucky). Conversely, when people perceive what they regard as some negative act performed by a member of an in-group, they attribute such behavior to situational factors (e.g., it's not his fault). And when people perceive what they regard as a positive act performed by members of an in-group, they attribute such behavior to dispositional factors (e.g., she's so smart).[83]

A Contemporary Conceptualization of Ethnocentrism

Neuliep and McCroskey have offered a contemporary conceptualization of ethnocentrism. We argue that ethnocentrism should be viewed along a continuum—that everyone is, to some extent, ethnocentric. As newborns, humans are entirely, and naturally, egocentric. Eventually, we develop an awareness of others around us. By age 2 or 3, we engage in social perspective taking of those most central to us. These people, our biological or adopted families, are the center of our universe. As we become socialized, we observe that our families coexist with other families and that this culmination of people constitutes some form of neighborhood, clan, tribe, community, city, society, and finally culture. By the time we realize that we are a part of some much larger whole, we are officially enculturated and ethnocentric.[84]

Ethnocentrism is essentially descriptive, not necessarily pejorative. On one end of the continuum, ethnocentrism may serve a valuable function when one's central group is under actual attack or threat of attack. Ethnocentrism forms the basis for patriotism and the willingness to sacrifice for one's central group. On the other end of the continuum, the tendency for people to see their own way as the only right way can be dangerous and lead to pathological forms of ethnocentrism that result in prejudice, discrimination, and even ethnic cleansing (see Figure 5.10).[85]

Figure 5.10   Ethnocentrism continuum.

To the extent that humans are ethnocentric, we tend to view other cultures (and microcultures) from our own cultural vantage point. That is, our culture is the standard by which we evaluate other cultures and the people from those cultures. Most deviations from that standard are viewed negatively and will be used as evidence of the inferiority of people from the other culture.

Ethnocentrism, Intercultural Communication, and Interpersonal Perception

Ethnocentrism negatively influences intercultural communication. Gudykunst points out that one's cultural orientation acts as a filter for processing incoming and outgoing verbal and nonverbal messages. To this extent, all intercultural exchanges are necessarily, to a greater or lesser degree, charged with ethnocentrism.[86] Indeed, most cross-cultural researchers recognize that human communication is replete with cultural noise that interferes with the transmission of information. Shijie Guan points out that ethnocentrism leads to "self-centered dialogue" where interactants use their own cultural standards to evaluate and communicate with others.[87]

Gudykunst and Kim assert that high levels of ethnocentrism are dysfunctional with respect to intercultural communication and expand on Fred Peng's concept of communicative distance and Janet Lukens's concept of ethnocentric speech.[88] Peng alleges that ethnocentric attitudes are reflected in linguistic diversity and create communicative distance between interactants that manifests itself in the expressions, idioms, and words of the speakers.[89] Lukens claims that ethnocentric speech results in three types of communicative distance: indifference, avoidance, and disparagement.[90] The distance of indifference is communicated in speech patterns, such as talking loudly and slowly to a nonnative speaker of the language, including exaggerated pronunciation and simplification. The communicative distance of indifference is also communicated in such expressions as "Jew them down," "top of the totem pole," and "the blind leading the blind." The distance of avoidance communicates that the speaker prefers to minimize or avoid contact with persons from other cultures through the use of in-group jargon or slang that members of other cultures or out-groups do not understand. The distance of disparagement is meant to openly express contempt for persons of different cultures and is communicated through ethnophaulisms such as "nigger," "nip," "chink," and so on.[91]

Neuliep and McCroskey contend that ethnocentrism acts as a perceptual filter that affects not only the perceptions of verbal and nonverbal messages but also perceptions of their source. For the most part, we tend to initiate and maintain communication with those to whom we are attracted. When we interact with someone from another culture, however, our perception of the other's attractiveness is affected by our degree of ethnocentrism.

Moreover, many studies indicate that perceived similarity is related to attraction. Thus, if we perceive someone as similar to ourselves, we are more likely to be attracted to that person. But, by definition, ethnocentrics perceive themselves as dissimilar to out-groups. Specifically, ethnocentrics perceive themselves as superior to out-groups (e.g., ethnic/racial groups). Hence, when interacting with people from a different culture or ethnicity, high ethnocentrics are likely to perceive out-group members as less attractive than in-group members. Judgment of another's credibility is also affected by ethnocentrism. Persons are thought to be credible to the degree that they are perceived to be informed, qualified, trained, intelligent, trustworthy, and so on. However, because they see themselves as superior, ethnocentrics tend to judge out-group members as less competent, less honest, less trustworthy, and so on.[92]

Ethnocentrism and Communication in the Workplace

The effects of ethnocentrism manifest in any social context, including organizational environments where persons of different cultural backgrounds interact in the workplace. In their research, Neuliep, Hintz, and McCroskey investigated the effects of ethnocentrism in an employment interview. In their study, U.S. students watched a videotape of a Korean national student being interviewed for a job in the financial aid office of her U.S. college. The students then completed measures of ethnocentrism, interpersonal attraction, and credibility, and they were asked to give a hiring recommendation. Their results showed that ethnocentrism was negatively and significantly correlated with perceptions of social attraction, competence, character, and hiring recommendations.[93] Their results are consistent with Theresa House, who reports that cultural or ethnic similarity, or both, between interviewee and interviewer may play a role in hiring decisions. House maintains that interviewers are more likely to hire people with whom they feel they have the most in common (e.g., culture or ethnicity). This effect may be enhanced by ethnocentrism.[94]

In additional research, Neuliep, Hintz, and McCroskey investigated the effects of ethnocentrism on manager–subordinate communication. In this study, participants watched a video of an Asian student manager reprimanding a White student worker. A different group of participants watched a nearly identical video of a White student manager reprimanding the same White student worker (the same scripts were used for both videos). After watching the video, each group of participants completed measures of ethnocentrism, interpersonal attraction, credibility, attitudes about the manager, and managerial effectiveness. For the group of participants who watched the Asian student manager reprimanding the White student worker, ethnocentrism was negatively and significantly correlated with perceptions of the manager's physical, social, and task attraction and competence, as well as general attitudes about the manager. For the group of participants who watched the White student manager, there were no significant correlations between ethnocentrism and any of the other variables.[95]

The implications of these results are significant. In an increasingly diverse workplace, managers and subordinates of different cultures and ethnicities are likely to find themselves interacting together. To the extent that such interactants are ethnocentric, interpersonal perceptions and communication will be influenced negatively. In addition to providing leadership functions, one of the primary functions of management, in any organization, is performance appraisal of subordinates. The results of this study suggest that in cases where managers and subordinates are of different cultures or ethnicities, subordinate ethnocentrism may interfere with the interpretation of managerial appraisals. If ethnocentric subordinates perceive managers of different cultures/ethnicities to be less attractive, less competent, and less credible, they may be less likely to accept their appraisal and any of the recommendations contained therein. Moreover, the position of an effective manager is one that fosters a certain level of obedience and compliance by subordinates. To the extent that managers are perceived as credible, subordinates are more likely to comply with them. As Neuliep, Hintz, and McCroskey found, in manager–subordinate transactions, ethnocentrism interferes with perceptions; that is, ethnocentric managers perceive out-group subordinates as less attractive or credible. Similarly, ethnocentric subordinates may perceive out-group managers as less credible or attractive.

Other research has found that the consequences of racial or ethnic differences between managers and subordinates are most clearly evident in performance appraisals. For example, Frank Landy and James Farr, and Kurt Kraiger and Kevin Ford found that African American and White managers consistently gave more positive appraisals to members of their own race. Manager or subordinate ethnocentrism may amplify this effect.[96]

Ethnocentrism and Racism

Although the terms *racism* and *ethnocentrism* are not synonymous, they are related. Ethnocentrism refers to the degree to which one sees his or her culture as superior and the standard by which other cultures should be judged. Racism refers to a belief that one racial group is superior to others and that other racial groups are necessarily inferior. To be ethnocentric but not racist is possible. To be racist and not ethnocentric is unlikely. In other words, you may believe your culture is superior to other cultures but not necessarily believe that your race is superior. However, if you believe that your race is superior, chances are good that you also believe your culture is superior. There is a biological component at the core of racist ideology that does not exist in the concept of ethnocentrism. Racist ideology is a belief in the moral or intellectual superiority of one race over the others. This superiority is biologically based. Because such superiority is biological, rather than social, it cannot be conditioned by culture or education. However, racist ideology asserts that racial–biological superiority does, in fact, translate into cultural or social superiority. Hence, a superior race produces a superior culture. Whereas racism refers to the hierarchical ranking of one race above the others, ethnocentrism refers to the strong preference for one's own culture over other cultures. Just as racism is rooted in biology, ethnocentrism is rooted in ethnicity and culture.

Racial groups are biological. Ethnic groups can be based on blood, common history, nationality, religion, or even geographic region.[97] In addition to their conceptual differences, racism and ethnocentrism have different origins. As mentioned previously, many scholars believe that ethnocentrism is a universal phenomenon that reflects a biologically rooted survival instinct experienced, to some degree, by all people in all cultures. Hence, it is thought that ethnocentrism is innately human; that is, we are born ethnocentric. Racism, on the other hand, is not universal and is thought to be learned. This begs the question, Why would anyone teach others to be racist? One argument, espoused by scholars from across a wide variety of disciplines, is that racism is the by-product of ignorance, fear, and hate.

Although slavery is not unique to the United States, in American history, racism is often associated with the forced immigration and enslavement of Africans. Because the U.S. Constitution was predicated on the tenet that all men are created equal, slavery presented a moral dilemma for the country. The enslavement and brutal treatment of Africans was a blatant violation of any sort of equality creed. But if Whites could define Blacks as biologically inferior, then they could justify slavery and practice it with a clear conscience.[98] Hence, the institutionalization of a flagrantly racist system of unequal treatment was established. Many political scientists offer a socioeconomic–political explanation of the causes of racism, frequently called the frustration–aggression hypothesis. During times of social, economic, or political stress (e.g., depressed economy, mass immigration), the dominant cultural group often will place blame on subordinate racial groups. Racism becomes a way of releasing the stress and frustration associated with difficult social, economic, or political times. In these situations, the dominant group often will act out its frustration against the subordinate racial group via prejudice and discrimination.[99] Racism, stereotyping, prejudice, and discrimination are often linked. When a racial group is labeled inferior, stereotypes emerge, such as those presented earlier in this chapter. Because racial stereotypes are often negative, people become prejudiced toward the racial group and discriminate against it. Prejudice determines how people feel or think about a particular group, and discrimination is the behavioral outcome—that is, action against that group.

CHAPTER SUMMARY

The purpose of this chapter was to describe and explain the perceptual context of intercultural communication, which refers to the human ability to take in, store, and retrieve information. Whenever two people come together and interact, they process immense amounts of information. Whenever two people come together and communicate, they do so within a cultural context, a microcultural context, and an environmental context. And each person brings to these contexts his or her own unique psychological perspective. So humans are not objective processors of information but, rather, biased processors. In this chapter, we have seen that the three stages of information processing (i.e., input, memory, and retrieval), while human, are affected by culture. We also saw that two information-processing strategies that facilitate the input, storage, and retrieval of information are categorization and stereotyping. Although stereotyping is a natural cognitive process, it can lead to misrepresentations of others, which may lead to prejudice and discrimination. Finally, the chapter ends with a discussion of ethnocentrism. Ethnocentrism is the cognitive process of using the standards of one's own group as the basis for judging other groups. Like stereotyping, it is a natural cognitive process, but it, too, can lead to prejudice and discrimination.

Visit the student study site at www.sagepub.com/neuliep6e for e-flashcards, web quizzes, web resources, and more.

DISCUSSION QUESTIONS

1. What are your initial impressions when you think about people from different cultures?

2. When you actually meet someone from a different culture, what do you remember about him or her?

3. Although difficult to admit, what are some of the stereotypes you hold about people from other cultures?

4. What are some of the stereotypes others hold about you and your cultural group?

5. Go back to Chapter 1 and review your score on the GENE (Generalized Ethnocentrism) Scale. Are you ethnocentric? Why or why not?

ETHICS AND THE PERCEPTUAL CONTEXT

1. You are having a party at your dorm/apartment tonight. What groups of people will you not invite because of the stereotypes you hold regarding those groups? Be honest.

2. The author of this book was once at a restaurant in France and asked the waiter how an item on the menu was prepared. The waiter responded in a gruff tone, "Well, you're an American. You know everything, so how would you like it prepared?" How would you explain the waiter's response?

KEY TERMS

carpentered-world hypothesis   181

categorization   187

decay   183

episodic long-term memory   183

ethnocentric attributional bias   205

ethnocentrism   205

illusory correlation principle   201

interference   104

long-term memory   183

memory   182

out-group homogeneity effect   201

perception   179

perceptual filters   180

semantic long-term memory   184

sensation   179

sensory receptors   181

short-term memory   182

Stereotype Content Model   197

stereotype threat   202

stereotypes   188

NOTES

1.   Polyani, M. (1958). *Personal Knowledge: Towards a Post-Critical Philosophy.* Chicago: University of Chicago Press.

2.   Hofstede, G., Hofstede, G.-J., & Minkov, M. (2010). *Cultures and Organizations: Software of the Mind.* New York: McGraw-Hill.

3.   Nisbett, R. E. (2003). *The Geography of Thought: How Asians and Westerners Think Differently and Why.* New York: Free Press.

4.   This discussion of information processing is based on Lachman, R., Lachman, J. L., & Butterfield, E. C. (1979). *Cognitive Psychology and Information Processing: An Introduction.* Hillsdale, NJ: Erlbaum; see also Stillings, N. A., Weisler, S. E., Chase, C. H., Feinstein, M. H., Garfield, J. L., & Rissland, E. L. (1995). *Cognitive Science: An Introduction.* Cambridge: MIT Press.

5.   Matlin, M. (2013). *Cognition* (8th ed.). Hoboken, NJ: Wiley.

6.   Goss, B. (1989). *The Psychology of Human Communication.* Prospect Heights, IL: Waveland.

7.   Berry, J. W., Poortinga, Y. H., Segall, M. H., & Dasen, P. R. (2002). *Cross-Cultural Psychology: Research and Applications* (2nd ed.). Cambridge, UK: Cambridge University Press.

8.   Reuning, H., & Wortley, W. (1973). Psychological Studies of the Bushmen. *Psychologia Africana (Monograph Supplement #7);* cited in Berry et al., *Cross-Cultural Psychology.*

9.   Wyndham, C. H. (1975). Ergonomic Problems in the Transition From Peasant to Industrial Life in South Africa. In A. Chapanis (Ed.), *Ethnic Variables in Human Factor Engineering* (pp. 115–134). Baltimore: Johns Hopkins University Press; see also Berry et al., *Cross-Cultural Psychology.*

10.   Berry et al., *Cross-Cultural Psychology.*

11.   Ibid.

12.   Segall, M. H. (1994). A Cross-Cultural Research Contribution to Unraveling the Nativist–Empiricist Controversy. In W. J. Lonner & R. Malpass (Eds.), *Psychology and Culture* (pp. 135–138). Boston: Allyn & Bacon.

13.   Ibid.; see also Coren, S., Ward, L. M., & Enns, J. T. (2004). *Sensation and Perception* (6th ed.). Hoboken, NJ: Wiley.

14.   Lachman et al., *Cognitive Psychology and Information Processing.*

15.   Matlin, *Cognition.*

16.   Ibid.

17.   Miller, G. A. (1956). The Magical Number Seven, Plus or Minus Two: Some Limits on Our Capacity for Processing Information. *Psychological Review, 63,* 81–97.

18.   Matlin, *Cognition.*

19.   Tavassoli, N. T. (2002). Spatial Memory for Chinese and English. *Journal of Cross-Cultural Psychology, 33,* 415–431.

20.   Howard, R. W. (1995). *Learning and Memory: Major Ideas, Principles, Issues, and Applications.* Westport, CT: Praeger.

21. Matlin, *Cognition*.

22. Wang, Q., & Brockmeier, J. (2002). Autobiographical Remembering as Cultural Practice: Understanding the Interplay Between Memory, Self, and Culture. *Culture and Psychology, 8*, 45–64.

23. Wang, Q. (2001). Cultural Effects on Adults' Earliest Childhood Recollection and Self-Description: Implications for the Relation Between Memory and the Self. *Journal of Personality and Social Psychology, 81*(2), 220–233.

24. Durga, R. (1978). Bilingualism and Interlingual Interference. *Journal of Cross-Cultural Psychology, 9*, 401–415.

25. Matlin, *Cognition*.

26. Howard, *Learning and Memory;* Lachman et al., *Cognitive Psychology and Information Processing*.

27. Matlin, *Cognition*.

28. Goss, B., Neuliep, J. W., & O'Hair, D. (1985). Reduced Conversational Recall as a Function of Negative Arousal: A Preliminary Analysis. *Communication Research Reports, 2*, 202–205.

29. Matlin, *Cognition*.

30. Ibid.

31. Rogoff, B. (1990). *Apprenticeship in Thinking: Cognitive Development in Social Context*. New York: Oxford University Press.

32. Ibid.

33. Yoshida, M., Fernandez, C., & Stigler, J. W. (1993). Japanese and American Students' Differential Recognition Memory for Teachers' Statements During a Mathematics Lesson. *Journal of Educational Psychology, 85*, 610–617.

34. Cole, M., & Gay, J. (1972). Culture and Memory. *American Anthropologist, 74*, 1066–1084.

35. Ross, B. M., & Millsom, C. (1970). Repeated Memory of Oral Prose in Ghana and New York. *International Journal of Psychology, 5*, 173–181.

36. Harris, R. J., Schoen, L. M., & Hensley, D. I. (1992). A Cross-Cultural Study of Story Memory. *Journal of Cross-Cultural Psychology, 23*, 133–147.

37. Liu, I. (1986). Chinese Cognition. In M. H. Bond (Ed.), *The Psychology of the Chinese People* (pp. 73–105). Hong Kong: Oxford University Press.

38. Park, B., & Judd, C. M. (2005). Rethinking the Link Between Categorization and Prejudice Within the Social Cognition Perspective. *Personality and Social Psychology Review, 9*, 108–130; Ridley, C. R., & Hill, C. L. (1999). Categorization as a Primary-Process Cognition in Racism: Implications for Counseling. *The Counseling Psychologist, 27*, 245–255.

39. Rosch, E. (1977). Human Categorization. In N. Warren (Ed.), *Studies in Cross-Cultural Psychology* (Vol. 1, pp. 1–49). New York: Academic. (Quote on pp. 1–2)

40. Gudykunst, W. B., & Kim, Y. Y. (1997). *Communicating With Strangers: An Approach to Intercultural Communication*. New York: McGraw-Hill.

41. Brislin, R. (1981). *Cross-Cultural Encounters*. Elmsford, NY: Pergamon.

42. Wilder, D. A. (1981). Perceiving Persons as a Group: Categorization and Intergroup Relations. In D. L. Hamilton (Ed.), *Cognitive Processes in Stereotyping and Intergroup Behavior* (pp. 213–257). Hillsdale, NJ: Erlbaum.

43. Park & Judd, Rethinking the Link Between Categorization and Prejudice Within the Social Cognition Perspective.

44. Ridley & Hill, Categorization as a Primary-Process Cognition in Racism: Implications for Counseling.

45. Unsworth, S. J., Sears, C. R., & Pexman, P. M. (2005). Cultural Influences on Categorization Processes. *Journal of Cross-Cultural Psychology, 36*, 662–688.

46. Gudykunst & Kim, *Communicating With Strangers*. Schaefer, R.T. (2012). *Racial and Ethnic Groups* (13th ed.). Upper Saddle River, NJ: Prentice Hall.

47. Berry et al., *Cross-Cultural Psychology;* Taylor, D. M., & Porter, L. E. (1994). A Multicultural View of Stereotyping. In W. J. Lonner & R. Malpass (Eds.), *Psychology and Culture* (pp. 85–90). Boston: Allyn & Bacon.

48. Devine, P. G., & Elliot, A. J. (1995). Are Racial Stereotypes Really Fading? The Princeton Trilogy Revisited. *Personality and Social Psychology Bulletin, 21*, 1139–1150; Gilbert, G. (1951). Stereotype Persistence and Change Among College Students. *Journal of Abnormal and Social Psychology, 46*, 245–254; Gordon, L. (1973). The Fragmentation of Literary Stereotypes of Jews and Negroes Among College Students. *Pacific Sociological Review, 16*, 411–425; Gordon, L. (1986). College Student Stereotypes of Blacks and Jews on Two Campuses: Four Studies Spanning 50 Years. *Sociology and Social Research, 70*, 200–201; Katz, D., & Braly, K. W. (1933). Racial Stereotypes of One Hundred College Students. *Journal of Abnormal Sociology and Psychology, 28*, 280–290.

49. Taylor & Porter, A Multicultural View of Stereotyping.

50. Ibid.

51. Trice, A. D., & Rush, K. (1995). Sex-Stereotyping in Four-Year-Olds' Occupational Aspirations. *Perceptual and Motor Skills, 81*, 701–702.

52. FAST Area Studies Program. (2010). *Cultural Stereotypes About Americans* (FAST-US-7 United States Popular Culture Reference File). Tampere, Finland: Department of Translation Studies, University of Tampere. Retrieved from http://www15.uta.fi/FAST/US7/REF/us-stero.html

53. Gerbner, G. (1998). Cultivation Analysis: An Overview. *Mass Communication & Society, 1*(3–4), 175–194.

54. Ibid., p. 180.

55. Ibid.

56. Oliver, M. B. (2003). African American Men as "Criminal and Dangerous": Implications of Media Portrayals of Crime on the "Criminalization" of African American Men. *Journal of African American Studies, 7*(2), 3–18.

57. Tamborini, R., Mastro, D. E., Chory-Assad, R. M., & Huang, R. H. (2000). The Color of Crime and the Court: A Content Analysis of Minority Representation on Television. *Journalism and Mass Communication Quarterly, 77*(3), 639–653.

58. Ibid., p. 649.

59. Oliver, African American Men as "Criminal and Dangerous."

60. Ramasubramanian, S. (2007). Media-Based Strategies to Reduce Racial Stereotypes Activated by News Stories. *Journalism and Mass Communication Quarterly, 84*(2), 249–264.

61. Kawai, Y. (2005). Stereotyping Asian Americans: The Dialectic of the Model Minority and the Yellow Peril. *Howard Journal of Communication, 16*, 109–130. (Quote on p. 109)

62. Ibid.

63. Young, I. (2013, May 3). GM pulls "racist" Chevrolet 'ching-ching, chop suey' ad. *South China Morning Post.* Retrieved from http://www.scmp.com/news/world/article/1227375/exclusive-general-motors-pulls-racist-chevrolet-ad-over-ching-ching-chop

64. This discussion of SCM is based on a number of sources, including the following: Caprariello, P. A., Cuddy, A. J. C., & Fiske, S. T. (2009). Social Structure Shapes Cultural Stereotypes and Emotions: A Causal Test of the Stereotype Content Model. *Group Processes and Intergroup Relations, 12*(2), 147–155; Cuddy, A. J. C., & Fiske, S. T. (2002). Doddering, But Dear: Process, Content, and Function in Stereotyping of Older Persons. In T. D. Nelson (Ed.), *Ageism* (pp. 3–26). Cambridge: MIT Press; Cuddy, A. J. C., Fiske, S. T., & Glick, P. (2004). When Professionals Become Mothers, Warmth Doesn't Cut the Ice. *Journal of Social Issues, 60*, 701–718; Cuddy, A. J. C., Fiske, S. T., & Glick, P. (2007). The BIAS Map: Behaviors from Intergroup Affect and Stereotypes. *Journal of Personality and Social Psychology, 92*, 631–648; Cuddy, A. J. C., Fiske, S. T., & Glick, P. (2008). Warmth and Competence as Universal Dimensions of Social Perception: The Stereotype Content Model and the BIAS Map. In M. P. Zanna (Ed.), *Advances in Experimental Social Psychology* (Vol. 40, pp. 62–150). San Diego: Academic Press; Cuddy, A. J. C., Fiske, S. T., Kwan, V. S. Y., Glick, P., Demoulin, S., Leyens, J.-P., et al. (2009). Is the Stereotype Content Model Culture-Bound? A Cross-Cultural Comparison Reveals Systematic Similarities and Differences. *British Journal of Social Psychology, 48*, 1–33; Cuddy, A. J. C., Norton, M. I., & Fiske, S. T. (2005). This Old Stereotype: The Pervasiveness and Persistence of the Elderly Stereotype. *Journal of Social Issues, 61*, 265–283; Fiske, S. T., & Cuddy, A. J. C. (2006). Stereotype Content Across Cultures as a Function of Group Status. In S. Guimond (Ed.), *Social Comparison Processes and Levels of Analysis.* New York: Cambridge University Press; Fiske, S. T., Cuddy, A. J., & Glick, P. (2002). Emotions Up and Down: Intergroup Emotions Result From Perceived Status and Competition. In D. M. Mackie & E. R. Smith (Eds.), *From Prejudice to Intergroup Emotions: Differentiated Reactions to Social Groups* (pp. 247–264). Philadelphia: Psychology Press; Fiske, S. T., Cuddy, A. J. C., & Glick, P. (2007). Universal Dimensions of Social Cognition: Warmth and Competence. *Trends in Cognitive Sciences, 11*, 77–83; Fiske, S. T., Cuddy, A. J. C., Glick, P., & Xu, J. (2002). A Model of (Often Mixed) Stereotype Content: Competence and Warmth Respectively Follow From Perceived Status and Competition. *Journal of Personality and Social Psychology, 82*, 878–902.

65. Ibid.

66. Judd, C. M., & Park, B. (1988). Outgroup Homogeneity: Judgments of Variability at the Individual and Group Levels. *Journal of Personality and Social Psychology, 54*, 778–700; Park, B., & Judd, C. M. (1990). Measures and Models of Perceived Outgroup Variability. *Journal of Personality and Social Psychology, 59*, 173–191; Rubin, M., & Badea, C. (2007). Why Do People Perceive Ingroup Homogeneity on Ingroup Traits and Outgroup Homogeneity on Outgroup Traits? *Personality and Social Psychology Bulletin, 33*, 31–42; Taylor & Porter, A Multicultural View of Stereotyping.

67. Hamilton, D. L., & Gifford, R. K. (1976). Illusory Correlation in Interpersonal Perception: A Cognitive Basis of Stereotypic Judgments. *Journal of Experimental Social Psychology, 12*, 392–407; Risen, J. L., Gilovich, T., & Dunning, D. (2007). One-Shot Illusory Correlations and Stereotype Formation. *Personality and Social Psychology Bulletin, 33*, 1492–1502; Taylor & Porter, A Multicultural View of Stereotyping.

68. Schaefer, *Racial and Ethnic Groups.*

69. Tajfel, H. (1978). *Differentiating Between Social Groups: Studies in Intergroup Behavior.* London: Academic Press.

70. Croizet, J. C., & Claire, T. (1998). Extending the Concept of Stereotype Threat to Social Class: The Intellectual Underperformance of Students From Low Socioeconomic Backgrounds. *Personality and Social Psychology Bulletin, 24*, 588–594; Frantz, C. M., Cuddy, A. J. C., Burnett, M., Ray, H., & Hart, A. (2004). A Threat in the Computer: The Race Implicit Association Test as a Stereotype Threat Experience. *Personality and Social Psychology Bulletin, 30*, 1611–1624; Hess, T. M., Auman, C., Colcombe, S. J., & Rahhal, T. A. (2003). The Impact of Stereotype Threat on Age Differences in Memory Performance. *Journals of Gerontology: Series B: Psychological Sciences and Social Sciences, 58B*, 3–11; Spencer, S. J., Steele, C. M., & Quinn, D. M. (1999). Stereotype Threat and Women's

Math Performance. *Journal of Experimental Social Psychology, 35,* 4–28; Steele, C. M., & Aronson, J. (1995). Stereotype Threat and the Intellectual Performance of African Americans. *Journal of Personality and Social Psychology, 69,* 797–811; Steele, C. M., Spencer, S. J., & Aronson, J. (2002). Contending With Group Image: The Psychology of Stereotype and Social Identity Threat. In M. P. Zanna (Ed.), *Advances in Experimental Social Psychology* (Vol. 34, pp. 379–440). San Diego, CA: Academic Press.

71. Shapiro, J. R., & Neuberg, S. L. (2007). From Stereotype Threat to Stereotype Threats: Implications of a Multi-Threat Framework for Causes, Moderators, Mediators, Consequences, and Interventions. *Personality and Social Psychology Review, 11,* 107–130.

72. Ibid.

73. Bruner, J. S., & Goodman, C. C. (1947). Value and Need as Organizing Factors in Perception. *Journal of Abnormal Social Psychology, 42,* 33–44.

74. Duncan, B. L. (1976). Differential Social Perception and Attribution of Intergroup Violence: Testing the Lower Limits of Stereotyping of Blacks. *Journal of Personality and Social Psychology, 34,* 590–598.

75. Sagar, A. H., & Schofield, J. W. (1980). Racial and Behavioral Cues in Black and White Children's Perceptions of Ambiguously Aggressive Acts. *Journal of Personality and Social Psychology, 39,* 590–598.

76. Sumner, W. G. (1906). *Folkways.* Boston: Ginn.

77. Lewis, I. M. (1985). *Social Anthropology in Perspective.* Cambridge, UK: Cambridge University Press; Lynn, R. (1976, July). The Sociobiology of Nationalism. *New Society,* pp. 11–14; Rushton, J. P. (1984). Genetic Similarity, Human Altruism, and Group Selection. *Behavioral and Brain Sciences, 12,* 503–559.

78. Segall, A Cross-Cultural Research Contribution to Unraveling the Nativist–Empiricist Controversy.

79. Hofstede, G. (1991). *Cultures and Organizations: Software of the Mind.* London: McGraw-Hill.

80. Klopf, D. W. (1995). *Intercultural Encounters: The Fundamentals of Intercultural Communication.* Englewood, CO: Morton.

81. Neuliep, J. W., & McCroskey, J. C. (1997). The Development of a U.S. and Generalized Ethnocentrism Scale. *Communication Research Reports, 14,* 385–398.

82. Levinson, D. J. (1950). Politico-Economic Ideology and Group Memberships in Relation to Ethnocentrism. In T. W. Adorno, E. Frenkel-Brunswik, D. J. Levinson, & R. N. Sanford (Eds.), *The Authoritarian Personality* (pp. 151–221). New York: Harper & Brothers. (Quote on p. 151)

83. Pettigrew, T. F. (1979). The Ultimate Attribution Error: Extending Allport's Cognitive Analysis of Prejudice. *Personality and Social Psychology Bulletin, 5*(4), 461–476; Taylor, D. M., & Jaggi, V. (1974). Ethnocentrism and Causal Attribution in a South Indian Context. *Journal of Cross-Cultural Psychology, 5,* 162–171.

84. Neuliep & McCroskey, The Development of a U.S. and Generalized Ethnocentrism Scale.

85. Ibid.

86. Gudykunst & Kim, *Communicating With Strangers.*

87. Guan, S. J. (1995). *Intercultural Communication.* Beijing: Peking University Press.

88. Gudykunst & Kim, *Communicating With Strangers.*

89. Peng, F. (1974). Communicative Distance. *Language Science, 31,* 32–38.

90. Lukens, J. (1978). Ethnocentric Speech. *Ethnic Groups, 2,* 35–53.

91. Gudykunst & Kim, *Communicating With Strangers;* Lukens, Ethnocentric Speech; Peng, Communicative Distance.

92. Neuliep & McCroskey, The Development of a U.S. and Generalized Ethnocentrism Scale.

93. Neuliep, J. W., Hintz, S. M., & McCroskey, J. C. (2005). The Influence of Ethnocentrism in Organizational Contexts: Perceptions of Interviewee and Managerial Attractiveness, Credibility, and Effectiveness. *Communication Quarterly, 53*(1), 41–56.

94. House, T. (2001). Equal Hiring a Must. *Computerworld, 35,* 32–34.

95. Neuliep et al., The Influence of Ethnocentrism in Organizational Contexts.

96. Kraiger, K., & Ford, J. K. (1985). A Meta-Analysis of Ratee Race Effects in Performance Ratings. *Journal of Applied Psychology, 70,* 56–65; Landy, F., & Farr, J. (1980). Performance Rating. *Psychological Bulletin, 87,* 72–107.

97. This discussion of racism is based on de Benoist, A. (1999). What Is Racism? *Telos, 114,* 11–49; D'Souza, D. (1995). *The End of Racism: Principles for a Multiracial Society.* New York: Free Press.

98. This slavery argument is found in a variety of sources. The sources used here are Briggs, M. T. (Director & Producer). (1987). *Ethnic Notions* [Motion picture]. Available from California Newsreel, Berkeley, CA; A Learned Behavior. (1996). *Canada and the World Backgrounder, 61,* 4–10.

99. Castle, S. (1993). Explaining Racism in the New Germany. *Social Alternatives, 12,* 9–13; Wolfe, C. T., & Spencer, S. J. (1996). Stereotypes and Prejudice. *American Behavioral Scientist, 40,* 177–187.

CHAPTER 6

The Sociorelational Context

After reading this chapter, you should be able to

1. compare and contrast membership and nonmembership groups,

2. compare and contrast voluntary and involuntary groups,

3. define and discuss the significance of reference groups,

4. define and discuss the concept of group roles,

5. compare and contrast formal and informal roles across cultures,

6. compare and contrast sex roles across cultures, and

7. compare and contrast family roles across cultures.

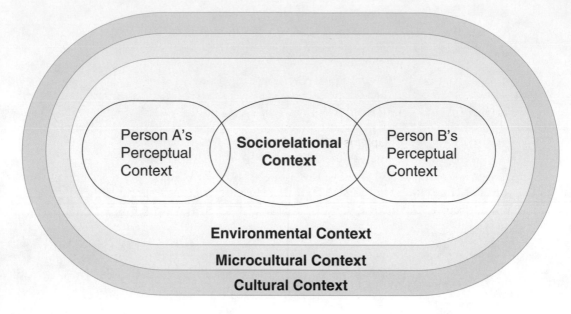

Americans of all ages, all conditions, and all dispositions form associations . . . associations of a thousand different kinds—religious, moral, serious, futile, extensive, or restricted, enormous or diminutive.

—Alexis de Tocqueville[1]

All human beings, regardless of culture, belong to groups. Although some cultures (such as the United States) promote individuality and independence, our survival depends on our interdependency and cooperation with other humans. This, of course, requires human communication. Historians believe that social cooperation, social organization, the initiation of group hunting methods, a system of distributing work, and our ability to share knowledge were what empowered our human ancestors to survive when other related species, such as Neanderthals, became extinct.[2]

As mentioned in Chapter 1, intercultural communication is a group phenomenon experienced by individuals. In other words, when people from different cultures come together to interact, they typically view one another not as unique individuals but as members of different cultural *groups*. Think about your own communication experiences with strangers from different cultures. When you meet a stranger from a different culture, do you see that person as an individual or as a member of a cultural group different from your own? Even intraculturally—that is, within our own culture—when we meet strangers, we typically see them in terms of the groups to which they belong (e.g., sex, race, age). In fact, there is no other way to describe a stranger than by the groups to which he or she belongs.[3]

The sociorelational context, then, refers to how group memberships affect communication. Whenever people from different cultures come together to interact, their verbal and nonverbal messages are defined by, and filtered through, their group memberships. The social relationship they develop is significantly influenced by the groups to which they belong, hence the term *sociorelational context*. Although all people belong to groups, the nature of group membership and group behavior, especially group communication, differs considerably across cultures. The number of social groups to which a person belongs, the length of association with those groups, whether group membership is determined by birth or eligibility, and the purpose of the groups vary from one culture to the next. Our membership in groups represents the sociorelational context of intercultural communication.

The purpose of this chapter is to explore the idea of groupness and how social groups vary across cultures. The first part of this chapter focuses on definitional aspects of group memberships and categories of groups. The second part of the chapter discusses role relationships, social hierarchies, and stratification across cultures. The third part of the chapter looks at family groups, and the final part of the chapter examines gender groups.

DIMENSIONS OF GROUP VARIABILITY

Membership and Nonmembership Groups

Much of what makes each of us human is our membership in social groups. Regardless of our culture, we all belong to groups. For individuals in any culture, there are those groups to which they belong, called membership groups, and those groups to which they do not belong, called nonmembership groups. There are two classes of membership groups: voluntary and involuntary. Involuntary membership groups are those groups to which people have no choice but to belong. Examples of involuntary membership groups include one's age, race, sex, and biological family group. Obviously, we cannot choose our age, race, or sex. Although we may choose to interact or not with our biological family group, we cannot choose our biological father, mother, brother, or sister. Voluntary membership groups are those to which people consciously choose to belong. Examples of voluntary groups include one's political affiliation, religion, occupation, and, to some extent, economic status—among others.[4]

Voluntary and involuntary nonmembership groups are those groups to which people do not belong. Some people may want to belong to a group but are ineligible to join because they do not possess the needed qualifications (e.g., age, education). In other cases, people might be eligible for membership in a group but choose not to join. The distinction is important because people who are eligible to join a group but choose not to may be more likely than ineligible nonmembers to accept and embrace the norms and behaviors of the group. Nonmembers may also differ regarding their ability and motivation to become members. For example, some nonmembers may aspire to membership, some may be indifferent, and others may be motivated to remain unaffiliated.

In India, people are divided into social classes called castes. Dramatic social disparities exist between the different levels of the caste system. Pittu Laungani notes that since one is born into a given caste, it is virtually impossible to move from one caste to another. Usually, members of the lower levels are exploited and treated harshly. The four main castes, from highest to lowest, are Brahmins, Kshatriyas, Vaisyas, and Sudras. As mentioned, a native person is born into a caste and cannot leave it until the beginning of his or her next lifetime. Hence, one's caste level is an involuntary membership group, and a person is ineligible for membership in any other caste.[5]

In-Groups and Out-Groups

In 1906, sociologist William Graham Sumner introduced the concepts of in-group and out-group when he wrote,

> A differentiation arises between ourselves, the we-group, or in-group, and everybody else, or the others-group, out-group. The insiders in a we-group are in a relation of peace, order, law, government and industry, to each other. Their relation to all outsiders, or others-group, is one of war and plunder, except as agreements have modified it. . . . The relation of comradeship and peace in the we-group and that of hostility and war towards the others-group are correlative to each other.[6]

Figure 6.1   In the United States, racist groups such as the Ku Klux Klan are characterized by potent internal cohesiveness among their members and an intense hostility toward out-groups.

Based on Sumner's thesis, an in-group represents a special class of membership group characterized by a potent internal cohesiveness among its members and a sometimes intense hostility toward out-groups (see Figure 6.1). To be sure, however, earnest loyalty to one's membership group does not necessarily mean that you will feel hostility toward nonmembership groups or out-groups. Sumner's dichotomy of in-group/out-group animosity can be seen in cases of extreme nationalism. Nationalists are members of a group, usually ethnic or religious, who believe that their group should dominate and rule a political entity such as a state or nation. A nationalist state, then, is dominated by an ethnic or religious group. The symbols and laws of a nationalist state are reflective of the particular ethnic or religious group. Nationalist groups believe that political organizations within the state or nation should be ethnic or religious in character, and may take extreme measures to see that they are.[7]

Harry Triandis defines an in-group as a group whose norms, aspirations, and values shape the behavior of its members. An out-group, on the other hand, is a group whose attributes are dissimilar from those of the in-group, or one that opposes the accomplishment of the in-group's goals. Triandis maintains that to be classified as an out-group, the group must be perceived as threatening in some way to the in-group and must be relatively stable, impenetrable, and dissimilar. An important point articulated by Triandis is that persons can be perceived as in-group members in one context and as out-group members in another.[8] For example, a White American might view a Black American as a member of an out-group within the boundaries of the United States but see the same person as an in-group member while visiting a foreign country. Furthermore, definitions of in-groups and out-groups differ widely across cultures. In Greece, for example, family and close friends are considered in-group members, whereas other Greeks are considered out-group members.

Marilynn Brewer and Donald Campbell assert that the tendency to distinguish between in-groups and out-groups is universal.[9] As mentioned in Chapter 5, when we meet someone from a different culture for the first time, we immediately categorize that person as an in-group or out-group member. Attributions about in-group and out-group members are typically biased in favor of the in-group, at the expense of the out-group. Some theorists argue that in-group biases function to promote, enhance, protect, and maintain the in-group's self esteem.

Others maintain that in-group biases function to preserve in-group solidarity and justify the exploitation of out-groups. Henri Tajfel and John Turner argue that the mere presence of an out-group is sufficient to provoke intergroup competition or discriminatory responses from the in-group. Moreover, the magnitude of in-group and out-group dissimilarity tends to intensify in-group biases. That is, the more different the groups appear (e.g., in sex, race, religion, status), the greater the extent of in-group bias.[10]

Richard Schaefer points out that in-group bias can manifest in what he calls in-group virtues and out-group vices. The behaviors and practices of the in-group often are perceived by the in-group as virtuous (i.e., in-group virtues), yet when the very same behaviors are practiced by the out-group, they are seen as unacceptable (i.e., out-group vices).[11]

Reference Groups

Another type of group that affects our communication and our relationships with others is the reference group. A **reference group** is a group to which we may or may not belong but with which we identify in some important way. A reference group possesses some quality to which we aspire and, hence, serves as a "reference" for our decisions or behavior. From time to time, we are faced with decisions about matters of which we know very little or for which we need direction. We may not know how to feel about a particular political issue or which way to vote in an upcoming referendum. In these kinds of situations, we often look to others whose opinions we value and trust to help us make our decision. For example, students often look to teachers for guidance. In this way, teachers are a reference group for students. Attorneys may be a reference group for law students. We use the group's position on an issue as a reference, standard, or barometer in developing our own attitudes. Reference groups can be membership or nonmembership and positive or negative. For example, in deciding for which political candidate to cast your vote, you may look to your political party (i.e., a membership group) for guidance. A law student, for example, might view lawyers or judges as a reference group but does not yet belong to that group. Usually, though not necessarily, voluntary membership in-groups serve as positive reference groups, whereas voluntary nonmembership out-groups are seen as negative reference groups.

Rodney Napier and Matti Gershenfeld point out that reference groups serve two functions—a comparative function and a normative function.[12] We often compare ourselves against reference groups in making judgments and evaluations. For example, when professors return examinations, students try to see their peers' grades in an effort to determine their own relative standing. If a student fails an examination but learns that most of the class also failed, then she or he will not feel so bad. A failing grade has less impact if several other students failed as well. Individuals also use reference groups to establish the norms and standards to which they conform. For example, many students on college campuses dress according to how other students dress. Our reference groups influence our self-concept, our self-esteem, and our relationships with others. For example, in most cultures, children look to their elders as a positive reference group. The elders of the Masai culture of Southern Kenya are an important reference group. Social power in Masai culture is based on age; this is called a gerontocracy. In the Masai gerontocracy, wisdom, insight, and sound judgment stem from age and are highly respected. The elders have moral and political authority, and the younger Masai age groups look to them for advice and direction. Through their age-based level in the hierarchy, the elders are the central reference group of their culture.[13]

ROLE RELATIONSHIPS

Whenever we join a group, voluntarily or involuntarily, we assume a role. A role is one's relative position in a group—that is, one's rank. Any group role exists in relation to some other role in that group. In fact, roles cannot exist in isolation; they are always related to some other role. You cannot be a son without a father. You cannot be a student without a teacher. Leaders cannot lead without followers.

With all roles, in all groups, certain behaviors are expected. A role, then, can be defined as one's relative position in a group with an expected set of verbal and nonverbal behaviors. By virtue of our membership in groups, even family groups, we are expected to behave in certain ways, usually according to some set of standards or norms established by the group. In your role as student, for example, you are expected to attend class, write papers, and complete examinations, among other behaviors. Within groups, roles are hierarchically organized, where some roles have more influence and prestige than others. In this sense, our role in a group represents our relative position or rank in the group.[14]

There are two types of roles in most cultures: formal and informal.[15] Formal roles have well-defined, and often contractual, behavioral expectations associated with them. The chief executive officer of a corporation, the president of your college or university, and the president of the United States all have clearly prescribed sets of behaviors they are expected to enact by virtue of their roles. Most fraternities, sororities, and academic organizations have constitutions or charters that specifically spell out the roles of their officers and members. In many cases, the person assuming a formal role takes an oath declaring his or her allegiance to the group and pledging a faithful effort to follow the expectations prescribed. Violations of such prescriptions are often subject to negative evaluation and even removal from the role. An important point about formal roles is that regardless of who assumes the role, the behavioral expectations remain the same. Formal roles and their prescriptions vary across cultures.

Informal roles are learned informally and are much less explicit than formal roles. Unlike formal roles, the behavioral expectations associated with informal roles must be mastered by experience and vary considerably from person to person and group to group. Your role as son or daughter, brother or sister, or even boyfriend or girlfriend, for example, is learned through experience. What it means to be a son or daughter in your family may be quite different from what it means to be a son or daughter in the family of your next-door neighbor. Informal roles and their prescriptions vary across and within cultures.

Roles and communication are integrally linked. Roles prescribe (1) with whom, (2) about what, and (3) how to communicate.[16] Because you are assuming the role of student, most of the people with whom you communicate include teachers, students, resident-hall assistants, librarians, and so on. If not for your role as college student, you probably would not have communicated with any of the people with whom you have already communicated today. In addition to prescribing with whom you communicate, your role prescribes the topic of your communication. With teachers, for example, much of your interaction is about class-related topics and assignments. Finally, your role defines how you communicate, or your style of communication (see Figure 6.2). When you are interacting with your professors about class-related topics, you probably engage in a more formal communication pattern than when you interact with other students. You probably use less slang and perhaps speak more politely with professors than with other students. Although your role as a student is probably your most defining role now, the total combination of all your roles (e.g., brother, sister, boyfriend, girlfriend, coworker, son, daughter) defines your social identity. Your social identity is how the society around you sees you and hierarchically ranks you.

Because the nature and prevalence of formal and informal roles varies so much across cultures, the roles we assume in our native culture may not be practiced or valued similarly in another culture. This would include the roles we assume in our cultural, national, ethnic, demographic, and various other in-groups. Because roles and communication are so closely related, they must be considered cross-cultural; that is, roles vary significantly across cultures. For example, although there are probably teachers and students in every culture, what it means to be a teacher or student in the United States might differ remarkably from what it means in China or Japan.

William Gudykunst and Young Kim argue that there are at least four dimensions on which roles vary across

| Figure 6.2 | How does your communication style shift when interacting with persons in different roles? |

cultures: the degree of personalness, formality, hierarchy, and deviation from the ideal role enactment.[17] According to Gudykunst and Kim, roles can vary from personal to impersonal. Some role relationships are quite close and perhaps intimate, whereas others are distant. The degree of formality between roles varies from formal to informal. In some cases, our role relationships are prim and proper, whereas others are casual and relaxed. The degree of hierarchy refers to how strictly roles are ranked. In some cultures, there may be a very rigid hierarchical distinction between student and teacher, whereas in others, the difference may be quite loose and flexible. The degree of deviation allowed refers to how much a person is permitted to deviate from the prescribed role expectation without significant negative sanction.

The roles of teacher and student in the United States and Korea illustrate how Gudykunst and Kim's four dimensions can be applied. In Korea, an old adage states, "One should not step even on the shadow of one's teacher." This expression, emphasizing the degree of respect accorded teachers, has been a guiding tenet in Korean education for years. Social order in Korea is based on Confucianism, whose central axiom is obedience to superiors. At just about any type of social gathering, who greets whom first, who sits where, who sits first, who speaks first, and so on are of utmost importance. In Korea, special care must be taken not to upset the social order, for to do so is interpreted as uncouth and lacking in social decorum. In Korea, the recognition of one's place in the social hierarchy is communicated via special vocabularies. These vocabularies consist of particular terms and phrases for addressing one who is superior, equal, or of lower status.[18]

In the United States, most students respect their teachers but do not recognize strict adherence to formality and hierarchy to the degree seen in Korea. In Korea, the student/teacher role relationship is quite proper and formal and the communication is scripted. Similarly, the difference in rank between Korean student and teacher is strict and recognized. On the other hand, the student/teacher role relationship in the United States is more personal and usually allows for more deviation from the ideal role prescription. Students and teacher can interact informally and may even engage in activities outside the formal classroom. On the four role dimensions outlined by Gudykunst and Kim, we can see where the student/teacher role relationship might fall in both cultures (see Figure 6.3). In most cases, the student/teacher relationship in Korea is less personal, more formal, and more hierarchical, with less room for deviation from the ideal role enactment than in the United States.

Figure 6.3   Four dimensions of cross-cultural role variation.

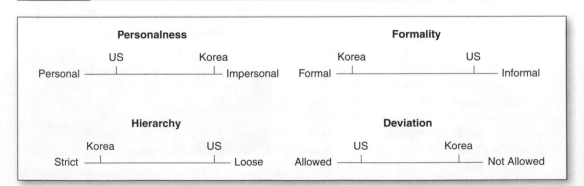

An Intercultural Conversation: Student–Teacher Role Positions

Because roles prescribe with whom, about what, and how people communicate, differences in the four role dimensions manifest in communication. On pages 223–224, there are two cross-cultural interactions between a student and a teacher. Scenario A is between a student and a teacher in the United States. Scenario B is between a student and a teacher in Korea. Note the differences in formality and personalness and the degree to which the students recognize the hierarchical difference between themselves and the teacher. In each case, the student wishes to speak to the teacher about an assignment.

The conversation between Jeff and Dr. Neuliep is generally smooth and coordinated. The situation is informal enough that Jeff shows up unannounced, without an appointment. Jeff uses informal dialect (e.g., "havin'," "ya") and refers to Dr. Neuliep as "Dr. N.," demonstrating a degree of personalness. Dr. Neuliep invites Jeff to sit down, reducing the hierarchical distance between them. Generally, their conversation, though perfectly respectful, is informal. In Scenario B, Mino has set up an appointment with Dr. Choi prior to the meeting, shows up at the appointed time, and asks permission to enter the office. The conversation is rather formal and impersonal. Mino does not engage in any slang or informal vocabulary, does not sit down, and keeps the conversation as short as possible. Unlike Jeff, Mino is prepared to state his choice of subject. To ask the professor for a suggestion, as Jeff did in Scenario A, would be impertinent in Korean culture, where responsibility rests entirely on the student.

Role Differentiation and Stratification

As mentioned earlier, whenever we assume a role in a group, that role represents our rank or relative position within the group. On a much larger scale, our roles are ranked by our culture as well. Some roles are at the top of the hierarchy, while others are at the bottom. In the United States, for example, physicians and attorneys are high-ranked roles, whereas used-car salespeople are low-ranked occupational roles. The rank ordering of roles within a culture is called social stratification.

Scenario A:

Jeff: (Approaches Dr. Neuliep's office unannounced.) Hey, Dr. N., how's it goin'?

Dr. Neuliep: Hey, Jeff, what's up?

Jeff: (Steps into the office.) I thought I would stop by an' see if I could talk to ya about my paper assignment.

Dr. Neuliep: Sure, c'mon in, have a seat. What are you thinking about?

Jeff: Well . . . I'm kinda havin' some trouble coming up with a topic. Do you have any ideas?

(Continued)

(Continued)

Dr. Neuliep: I suggest doing something that's interesting to you; otherwise, the assignment might bore you to death. Stay away from topics that have very little research associated with them. Also . . . you might try doing a search on the Internet. Sometimes you'll find topics that you might not ever have thought of yourself.

Jeff: Yeah . . . that's a good idea. If I find somethin', can I stop by and show it to you before I get started?

Dr. Neuliep: Sure, just stop by or leave a message on my voice mail.

Jeff: OK, yeah. OK, well . . . thanks a lot.

Dr. Neuliep: Sure.

Scenario B:

Mino: (Approaches Dr. Choi's office and knocks on the door.) Good morning, Professor Choi.

Dr. Choi: Hello, Mino.

Mino: I am here for my appointment.

Dr. Choi: Yes.

Mino: May I come in?

Dr. Choi: Yes.

Mino: Thank you (enters Dr. Choi's office). I am here to approve my topic for the research paper assignment, as you requested.

Dr. Choi: Yes, what have you decided?

Mino: I would like to research the natural resources of Northern India, if that is acceptable.

Dr. Choi: Yes, that topic is fine.

Mino: Thank you. Thank you for seeing me this morning.

Dr. Choi: Yes, you are welcome. Good day.

Social stratification varies across cultures, and not all roles are valued the same. The complexity of the role hierarchy varies from culture to culture, too. Some cultures make relatively few distinctions, whereas others make many; this is called role differentiation. For example, a relatively undifferentiated culture might distinguish among only a few roles, such as family, social, and occupational roles. A highly differentiated culture may make numerous role distinctions, such as corporate roles (e.g., owner, vice president, manager, worker, retiree), religious roles (e.g., pope, cardinal, bishop, priest, parishioner), educational roles (e.g., superintendent, principal, teacher, senior, junior, sophomore, freshman), and military roles (e.g., general, colonel, major, captain, lieutenant), among others.

According to cross-cultural researcher John Berry and his colleagues, social stratification exists in a culture with a highly differentiated role hierarchy that is organized in a vertical status structure. As mentioned above, most cultures have some form of role hierarchy that distinguishes between high- and low-ranking roles. Berry maintains that cultural role differentiation and stratification appear to be related to the ecological systems among cultures. For example, nomadic hunter–gatherer cultures tend to have less role differentiation and stratification, whereas industrialized urban cultures are typically quite differentiated and stratified. Sedentary agricultural societies fall somewhere in the middle.[19]

Although it is impossible to generalize across every culture, many collectivistic, high-context, and large–power-distance cultures possess a relatively strict hierarchical role stratification compared with low-context, individualistic, small–power-distance cultures. Recall from Chapter 2 that, generally, individualistic, small–power-distance cultures believe that people are created equal and have inalienable rights. Collectivistic cultures, on the other hand, see people not as individuals but as members of groups. In these cultures, one's level in the role stratification hierarchy often is based on one's membership in sex, age, family, and occupation groups. In such cultures, one person is almost always more powerful than another.

Mike Keberlein points out that the Guatemalan Ladino stratification is vertically shaped, like a pyramid, with the wealthy at the top and the poor at the bottom. Belonging to an upper class means owning a home and having land to work and rent. Members of the upper class have their own social in-groups, such as the International Rotary Club, to which only they are accepted for membership. Lower-class Ladinos are left to work the land. They are also the ones who attend church most often. The upper class, however, establishes the rules for what is considered socially acceptable. Interestingly, according to Keberlein, the lower-class Ladinos practice the values of the culture more than any other social class.[20]

As mentioned earlier, the most notorious system of social stratification is the caste system of India. The caste system—whose origins date back more than 3,500 years—prescribes a strict and practiced code of conduct. A person's social status depends on the caste to which he or she belongs. Although deemed illegal 50 years ago, the caste system still operates in many parts of India today, especially in rural areas. Although the system contains literally thousands of subcastes, there are four or five generally recognized levels. At the top of the castes are the Brahmins. These are priests or seers who possess spiritual power. Next are the Kshatriyas—that is, warriors and rulers. The third level is the Vaishyas, or merchants. The fourth level is the Sudras, whose main function is to serve the needs of the upper three levels. The Sudras are further subdivided into touchables and untouchables. The touchable Sudras engage in occupations that are considered by the upper three to be demeaning, such as barber, hairdresser, cleaner, water carrier, and so on. The untouchables—or as Gandhi termed them, the *Harijan*, meaning "children of God"—are workers who take on the lowest of job roles, which are considered to be spiritually polluting, such as sweepers, butchers, potters, and so on. Also outside the system are tribal groups (called *adivasis*) with unique ethnic, linguistic, and cultural histories.[21]

Because roles prescribe with whom, about what, and how to communicate with others, communication in cultures with a rigid social stratification system is very predictable. Verbal and nonverbal messages are prescribed according to one's role and rank in the social hierarchy. Accepted forms of address, vocabulary, nonverbal behavior such as eye contact, and social manners are defined for practically every social situation. When two strangers interact for the first time, much uncertainty is reduced simply by recognizing role differences. They need only to know each other's roles to communicate appropriately. Although not exclusively, many of these cultures can be found in the East (e.g., China, Japan, India, Korea).

Many individualistic, low-context, small–power-distance cultures profess equality and minimize role stratification. In the United States, for example, children are taught that they are equal to everyone else. In fact, in many of these cultures, equality is legislated. Although role differences are recognized and respected, these cultures believe that a person occupying a role is a unique individual. In this sense, knowing someone's role provides only minimal information about the person. Hence, knowing one's role does not reduce as much uncertainty as it would in a high-context, large–power-distance culture. Many of these cultures can be found in the West, but there are certainly exceptions (e.g., Australia, New Zealand).

Understanding a culture's role differentiation and stratification is important for communication because special vocabularies exist for different roles. Donald Klopf and James McCroskey note, for example, that in Korea, the terms a husband will use to refer to his wife vary depending on with whom he is interacting. She is his *cho* when he is speaking to someone of higher rank, his *chip saram* when speaking to an equal, or his *ago omoni* when speaking to a person of lower rank or status.[22]

Communication problems often result when persons from different cultures do not understand or recognize the role differences between cultures. Many international exchange students may find American teachers rather informal and personal compared with their teachers back home. Students from Eastern cultures, for example, find an American teacher's use of humor quite strange, because teachers in their cultures would never act in such a way.

An Intercultural Conversation: Cross-Cultural Role Positions

In cultures such as the United States, Canada, and Australia, among others, people are accustomed to treating everyone else as equal, regardless of sex, age, occupation, and so on. This can lead to misunderstandings when interacting with people who, in their culture's role hierarchy, are accorded special privileges. In the following cross-cultural interaction, Mr. Mammen, an East Indian living in the United States, has taken his wife and family to a nice restaurant. When he arrives at the restaurant, he expects to be seated even though he has not made dinner reservations. Because of his social standing, he assumes that he will be accommodated.[23]

Because of his cultural role position, in Mr. Mammen's native culture, he probably would have been seated in the restaurant even though he did not have a reservation. In the United States, however, one's occupational role will not ensure any special favors outside of that occupation. The host of this restaurant is simply following his culture's way of treating everyone—that is, equally. As shown in the illustration below, this leads to conflict and misunderstanding.

Mr. Mammen:	(Approaches the host.)
Host:	Good evening, may I help you?
Mr. Mammen:	Yes, my wife and family are here for dinner.
Host:	Certainly, your name please?
Mr. Mammen:	I am Mr. Mammen.
Host:	I'm sorry. I don't see your name on our reservation listing.
Mr. Mammen:	I don't have reservations, but I can make them now.
Host:	I'm sorry, but this evening's dinner reservation list is completely full.
Mr. Mammen:	No . . . I disagree. This restaurant is not full. I see empty tables.
Host:	Yes, but these tables are reserved for those people who have reservations for this evening.
Mr. Mammen:	I will make a reservation right now.
Host:	I'm sorry, but the evening is completely full.
Mr. Mammen:	I can see that it is not full. I want to see a manager right now! I am here to have dinner!

Family Groups

All human beings, regardless of culture, belong to a family. A child's biological or adoptive family is the first and probably most significant socialization influence on that child. The structure of the family and the degree of influence the family has on its children differ notably across cultures. Two terms related to the family structure, which are sometimes confused, are *patriarchy* and *matriarchy*. By definition, *patriarchy* refers to a social system (e.g., familial, political) in which the father, or eldest male, is head of the clan or family unit and descent is traced through the male line. In patriarchal societies, males wield power disproportionately compared with women. To be sure, notes Allan Johnson, this does not mean all men are powerful or all women are powerless. Johnson argues that in patriarchal societies, the most powerful roles are held predominantly by men and the less powerful roles by women.[24]

Matriarchy, on the other hand, is often incorrectly thought to mean the opposite of *patriarchy*. German philosopher Heide Göttner-Abendroth has spent much of her professional career writing about matriarchies. She argues that they are not the opposite of patriarchies, with women ruling over men, but rather are characterized by being equality based and need oriented. According to Göttner-Abendroth, in matriarchal cultures, the natural differences between men and women are acknowledged and respected, but they are not used to create social hierarchies, as in patriarchal societies. Instead, argues Göttner-Abendroth, men and women complement each other, and their natural differences function interdependently to meet societal needs. In such a milieu, writes Göttner-Abendroth, social life is organized in a way that is based on the economic, social, and political needs of the people, inclusive of men and women. Göttner-Abendroth (and others) maintain that societies based on the incorrect use of the term *matriarchy*—that is, societies ruled by women—have never existed. But matriarchal societies based on the contemporary conceptualization of matriarchy as essentially egalitarian have existed in various cultures throughout history.[25]

The nuclear family consists of the father, mother, and children. The extended family consists of the nuclear family plus other relatives, such as grandparents, uncles, aunts, cousins, and in-laws. As a unit, the nuclear family is prevalent in most low-context, individualistic, small–power-distance cultures such as the United States, Canada, and Northern European cultures such as England, Ireland, Germany, and France. Extended families are common in Central and South America, Africa, the Middle East, and throughout Asia, although trends are changing even in these countries. There are clearly exceptions to the above list, such as African American and Latino families in the United States, who have a cultural pattern of a strong extended family interaction and kinship network.

In collectivistic cultures, families are generally cohesive and well integrated. Familial relations are caring and warm but also hierarchical. The decision-making process typically is not democratic. The interests of the family group take precedence over individual family members. Familial role prescriptions are clearly defined not only within the family but also in the larger cultural context. In individualistic cultures, on the other hand, there is less emphasis on hierarchy and more emphasis on individual development. Family decisions may be more participative than in collectivistic cultures. Familial role prescriptions are open and may vary considerably across the cultural context.[26]

Hmong

In the Hmong culture of Laos, the most important sociocultural groups are the family and the clan, both of which are headed by men (i.e., patriarchal). According to Katie Thao, the Hmong clan system combines social, political, economic, and religious dimensions, and is the primary guide for Hmong behavior. Within a clan, each person has certain obligations to others. When one shares with fellow clan members, the act is returned. Clan members of the same generation (but of different biological families) will call one another "brothers" and "sisters." Although the bond is not biological, it is so close that marriages between members of the same clan are seen as almost incestuous, leading to the Hmong practice of clan exogamy.[27] In most cultures, the family group is the most valued social structure.

Korea

Familial role prescriptions, however, differ widely across cultures. For example, two important variables in understanding Korean family structure are family surname and Confucianism. According to Sungjong Paik, there are only about 250 family names in South and North Korea. In fact, more than half the population uses one of five family names: Kim, Yi, Pak, Ch'oe, and Chong. One in five family names in Korea is Kim. Of all Koreans, 15% use Yi, 9% use Pak, 5% use Ch'oe, and 4% use Chong. In comparison, in many other countries, such as the United States, literally hundreds of thousands of family names are used.[28] Many Koreans believe that because of their common family names, they are descended from a common ancestor. Hence, many Koreans belong to formal family name organizations, called *taejong-hoe.* According to Paik, *taejonghoe* are rather formal organizations with head offices in Seoul and hundreds of branch offices throughout the country. They publish newsletters, award scholarships, and sponsor sporting events. Paik argues that *taejonghoe* exercise great influence on Korean social life. For example, one's social status is often determined by membership in a specific family name lineage. Moreover, Paik asserts that many politicians try to use their family names to gain political influence.[29]

As in many cultures, the family is the foundation of Korean society. Historically, and in traditional Korean society, family roles and social interaction were governed by patriarchal Confucianism. Hye-On Kim and Siegfried Hoppe-Graff maintain that since the 14th century, patriarchal Confucianism has been the dominant social force in Korea. They point out that Confucianism imposes a rigid hierarchy and inequality between different age groups and between men and women, especially within families.[30] In traditional families, the husband/father's role is head of the family, and his authority is based on the power derived from his status (as male). His relation to his children is emotionally distant and authority based. The wife/mother's family role is that of the "inner master," whose authority is based on her emotional competence and who is intimate and affectionate with her children. In traditional Confucian families, children are socialized to conform to traditional gender stereotypes and are segregated by sex. Following the father, the eldest son has the highest social status in the family. Communication in Confucian familial relationships requires the use of a restricted code. In the United States, when speaking to a brother or sister, or an aunt or uncle, English speakers use the generic terms *brother, sister, aunt,* or *uncle.* Linguistically, one's age or status is irrelevant. In Korean language (i.e., Hangul), the relationship term used to refer to a familial relative changes based on the sender's and receiver's familial rank, which is based on age and sex.[31]

As in many cultures, however, family life in Korea is changing. Diane Levande, John Herrick, and Kyu-Taik Sung maintain that while filial piety (i.e., loyalty and obedience to parents, the elderly) remains a central value among Koreans, familial relationships between parents and children are changing from duty and obligation to intergenerational affection. Levande, Herrick, and Sung argue that Korean families are moving away from the authoritarian and patriarchal norms of the past to more egalitarian and reciprocal patterns of mutual support between generations.[32] Kim and Hoppe-Graff agree, noting that urban families in Korea typically include family members from only two generations, that marriages are generally no longer arranged, and that the father's role is based on his ability to provide for the family financially. They note that because of the high priority given to education, the mother has gained dominance in the family because of her involvement with the children's education. In addition, more women are employed now than before. The employment rate for South Korean women (ages 15 to 64) has increased from 9% in 1960 to just over 53% in 2011.[33]

Israel

Compared with the cultures discussed above, Israel is relatively young, having been established as a state in 1948. Like the other cultures profiled here, Israel is considered a family-centered society. According to the Israeli Central Bureau of Statistics, family in Israel is defined as "two or more persons who share the same household, and are related to one another as husband and wife, or as an unmarried couple, or as parent and child."[34] Sociologist Noah Lewin-Epstein, a professor at Tel-Aviv University, and his associates point out that Israel is unique in that a strong family orientation is a formal part of Israeli social policy. They point out that throughout much of Israel's turbulent history, a central goal of the Israeli government has been to increase the Jewish population via family. For example, the Israeli income tax system includes tax benefits for families, at least two state programs provide housing assistance for families with children, and various child support and child health programs have been established for families.[35]

There are about 1.73 million families in Israel, with an average size of 3.7 people per family. About 80% of families describe themselves as Jewish, and about 16% as Arab Israelis. Among the Jewish population, the average family size is 3.5, while among Arabs it is 4.8. Jewish families average 2.2 children, and Arab families average 2.9 children per household. More than half of Israeli families comprise two parents and children under the age of 17. Although the majority of Israeli couples are married (i.e., 97%), recent years have seen a sizable increase in the number of single-parent families. Since 2000, there has been a 63% increase in the number of single-parent families—specifically, in the number of single women (without a partner) becoming mothers. Of the nearly 3 million households in Israel in 2010, about 400,000 were households without a family unit—that is, persons living alone.[36]

Mosuo

The Mosuo are one of China's microcultural nationalities. They have a population of about 400,000 and live between the Yongning basin of Ninglang County in Yunnan Province and in the west Yanyuan County in Sichuan Province. In recent years, the Mosuo have become the focus of national and international attention (much of it distorted) because they follow the matrilineal family principle of descent; are thought to be matriarchal; and practice *zou hun*, sometimes called "walking" or "visiting" marriages. To be sure, controversy surrounds the Mosuo because of the exaggerated claims made by popular media and attempts by others, including the Chinese government, to attract tourist dollars to this economically underdeveloped region of China. Two scholars who have tried to accurately describe the Mosuo family structure are Professor Tiplut Nongbri of Jawaharla Nehru University and Professor Eileen Rose Walsh of Skidmore College.[37] Walsh argues that while Mosuo society is matrilineal in that many household heads are women, nearly one third of households are headed by men. She also argues that the term *household head* is misunderstood because the Mosuo believe that all adults, both men and women, should have a say in decision making.

Perhaps one of the most intriguing dimensions of the Mosuo family structure is the idea of the "walking" or "visiting" marriage. Nongbri writes that in Mosuo culture, the primary function of marriage is to satisfy the individual's emotional and biological needs. Indeed, Nongbir observes that both the man and the woman continue to live with their native biological families, rather than with each other, while raising their offspring. In fact, the father does not take any responsibility for the children. The term *walking marriage* or *visiting marriage* stems from the practice of the father visiting the mother only at night, engaging in sexual relations with her, and leaving early in the morning. Nongbri emphasizes that essentially no social or economic commitments are attached to the relationship. Any and all offspring are the custody of the mother.[38]

According to Nonbri, in Mosuo culture, the mother is the foundation of the family lineage. Indeed, asserts Nongbri, the biological father plays no part in rearing the children. And, she observes, the Mosuo house contains little or no physical or symbolic representations of the father. Moreover, the verbal code of Mosuo culture contains no words for paternal relatives, such as the father, father's brother, father's sister, and so forth. However, terms for the mother's relations are common. Nongbri notes that if/when paternity is recognized, either the terms of address for the father and other paternal relatives are borrowed from other Chinese dialects or the terms used for the mother's relatives are applied to them. Nongbri is careful to point out that although women benefit from having full rights over their children and practice marital and sexual independence, such power is restricted to domestic contexts. Within the public/political context of Mosuo culture, power is unequally distributed to men.[39]

Sex and Gender Groups

One group to which every human being belongs, regardless of culture, is determined by biological sex. Biological differences between males and females are universally recognized. But like any other group, to be a member of a sex group is to assume a role—in this case, a sex role. And like any other role, one's **sex role**, or gender, is a set of expectations about how one should behave.

The terms *sex* and *gender* often are used interchangeably, but as Sandra Bem notes, the terms are not synonymous. Bem has done considerable research on sex roles. Like others, Bem recognizes that sex refers to the biological and anatomical classifications of males and females. Gender, on the other hand, is a social and symbolic creation we learn through enculturation and socialization. Whereas sex is innate, gender is learned. In most cultures, however, sex and gender share a close association. That is, most cultures establish norms and expectations that they assign people on the basis of their biological sex. According to Bem, our sex role orientation (i.e., gender) is based on the extent to which we internalize our culture's sex type expectations of desirable behavior for men and women.

In most cases, there is a high correlation between biological sex and sex role orientation. In other words, most people assume the gender roles their culture prescribes. We are taught by our parents, teachers, and peers how we should behave based on our culture's standards. Boys are taught to be masculine (however the culture defines it), and girls are expected to act feminine (however the culture defines it). Thus, when cultures recognize some behaviors as masculine and others as feminine, they are saying that the majority of people taking on this role should be male (for the former) and female (for the latter). Gender, then, can be defined as the behavioral, cultural, and psychological traits typically associated with one's sex. To be sure, as Bem notes, this is not to say that a person of a certain sex cannot fulfill the other role but, rather, that the characteristics of the person assuming the role are associated with that sex. Indeed, some people possess both feminine and masculine traits. These persons may be classified as *androgynous*, a term that combines *andro,* meaning male/masculine, and *gyne,* meaning woman.[40]

The value associated with masculinity and femininity seems to vary across cultures (see Table 6.1). In his seminal cross-cultural survey of more than 50 countries, Dutch sociologist Geert Hofstede asked participants to rate the value of masculinity. According to Hofstede, masculinity stands for a society in which social gender roles are clearly distinct. In masculine cultures, men are conditioned to be assertive, tough, and focused on material success. In these same cultures, women are conditioned to be modest, tender, and concerned with the quality of life. Hofstede argues that feminine-oriented cultures see sex roles as overlapping in some cases.[41]

Table 6.1	Countries and Masculinity Scores

Countries With High Masculinity Scores	Countries With Low Masculinity Scores
Japan	South Korea
Austria	Uruguay
Venezuela	Guatemala
Italy	Thailand
Switzerland	Portugal
Mexico	Chile
Ireland	Finland
Jamaica	Yugoslavia
Great Britain	Costa Rica
Germany (FR)	Denmark
Philippines	Netherlands
Colombia	Norway
South Africa	Sweden
Ecuador	
USA	

When people deviate from their cultural sex role expectations, they are often negatively sanctioned. Some researchers have argued that collectivistic cultures are more traditional than individualistic cultures and are more likely to punish persons who violate cultural sex role expectations. Recall from Chapter 2 that collectivistic cultures stress interdependence, prescribe clear role expectations, and value conforming to the needs of the group. Violating one's role prescription (including sex role) disrupts the harmony of the group. Individualistic cultures, on the other hand, value independence, self-expression, and the pursuit of individual goals over group goals. Promotion of an individual's uniqueness is common in individualistic cultures. Therefore, when an individual violates a cultural sex role expectation, it is likely to be tolerated more in an individualistic culture than in a collectivistic culture.[42]

Gender Stereotypes

In most cultures, men and women carry out different sex roles, yet there is remarkable consistency in how cultures view the roles of men and women. Beginning in 1990, John Williams and Deborah Best, professors of psychology at Wake Forest University, conducted a series of cross-cultural studies investigating gender stereotypes. Williams and Best asked university students in more than 30 countries to consider a list of 300 adjectives and to indicate whether in their culture the adjectives were more frequently associated with men, with women, or equally with both. The responses of the participants in each country were tallied to determine the frequency with which each adjective was associated with men and with women. A surprising degree of cross-cultural agreement was found among 100 of the 300 adjectives. These 100 adjectives are presented in Table 6.2. The countries surveyed included Canada, Finland, England, Italy, Pakistan, Malaysia, Nigeria, Singapore,

India, Japan, the Netherlands, Venezuela, Germany, the United States, New Zealand, Peru, Australia, South Africa, and Brazil. Williams and Best also scored each of the adjectives in terms of its affective meaning (i.e., its favorability, strength, and activity). They found that the characteristics associated with men were generally stronger (e.g., *tough*) and more active (e.g., *robust*) than those associated with women but that the adjectives were equally favorable for both men and women. Williams and Best also concluded that the male stereotypes were more favorable than the female stereotypes in certain countries, such as Japan, South Africa, and Nigeria, whereas the female stereotypes were more favorable in countries such as Italy, Peru, and Australia. They also found that gender stereotypes were more differentiated in Protestant countries than in Catholic countries.[43]

Table 6.2 Adjectives Associated With Sex Stereotypes

Male Associated		Female Associated	
Active	Loud	Affected	Modest
Adventurous	Obnoxious	Affectionate	Nervous
Aggressive	Opinionated	Appreciative	Patient
Arrogant	Opportunistic	Cautious	Pleasant
Autocratic	Pleasure-seeking	Changeable	Prudish
Bossy	Precise	Charming	Self-pitying
Capable	Progressive	Complaining	Sensitive
Coarse	Quick	Complicated	Sentimental
Conceited	Rational	Confused	Sexy
Confident	Realistic	Curious	Shy
Courageous	Reckless	Dependent	Softhearted
Cruel	Resourceful	Dreamy	Sophisticated
Cynical	Rigid	Emotional	Submissive
Determined	Robust	Excitable	Suggestible
Disorderly	Serious	Fault-finding	Talkative
Enterprising	Sharp-witted	Fearful	Timid
Greedy	Show-off	Fickle	Touchy
Hardheaded	Steady	Foolish	Unambitious
Humorous	Stern	Forgiving	Unintelligent
Indifferent	Stingy	Frivolous	Unstable
Individualistic	Stolid (detached)	Fussy	Warm
Initiative	Tough	Gentle	Weak
Interests wide	Unfriendly	Imaginative	Worrying
Inventive	Unscrupulous	Kind	Understanding
Lazy	Witty	Mild	Superstitious

SOURCE: Adapted from Williams, J. E., & Best, D. L. (1994). Cross-Cultural Views of Women and Men. In W. J. Lonner & R. Malpass (Eds.), *Psychology and Culture* (pp. 191–196). Boston: Allyn & Bacon.

In a related study, Williams and Best surveyed 5- and 8-year-old children in 25 countries. In this study, the children were shown silhouettes of a man and a woman and were asked to select between the silhouettes which ones were described in brief stories. The stories were written to reflect the more important features of the adult sex stereotype characteristics. For example, children were asked to select "the person who gets into the most fights" or "the person who cries a lot." Their results indicate that the children in each culture showed at least a beginning knowledge of the adult stereotypes. The stories most frequently associated with the male figures were those involving the strong, aggressive, and cruel characteristics, whereas the stories associated with women were emotional, weak, and softhearted. Pakistani children seemed to show the most developed gender stereotypes, and the Brazilian children showed the least. In each country, stereotype knowledge increased significantly when moving from the 5- to the 8-year-old children.[44]

SEX AND GENDER ROLES ACROSS CULTURES

The variability of sex roles across cultures is dramatic. But many anthropologists and some feminist writers contend that although the customs and practices with which women's subordination is expressed differ from culture to culture, the secondary status of women across the globe is one of the few universal cross-cultural truisms. No book or chapter could possibly describe all the sex role differences between males and females across all cultures. Discussed below is a selection of cultures and their sex roles, with special attention given to women's roles.

| Figure 6.4 | Japanese women enjoy more freedom today than perhaps ever in their history. |

Japan

Sumiko Iwao has written a fascinating book portraying the role of women in contemporary Japan. Iwao notes that the "kimono clad, bamboo parasol–toting, bowing female walking three paces behind her husband" is still seen in some parts of Japan. But she contends that the lives and attitudes of many younger, contemporary Japanese women have undergone dramatic changes in the past 25 years. The postwar Japanese Constitution stipulates that all Japanese are equal under the law and outlaws discrimination on the basis of sex. To be sure, however, most private and political organizations that compose the dominant Japanese culture are controlled by men. But Japanese women enjoy more freedom today than perhaps ever in their history (see Figure 6.4).

Yet, as Miyoko Ui and Yutaka Matsui note in their 2008 survey of Japanese adults' sex role attitudes, a close look at Japanese society shows very few women in parliament or corporate management positions.

Ui and Matsui note that many women, much more so than men, are burdened by household duties and child rearing. In their survey of Japanese adults, Ui and Matsui found that more women than men have egalitarian (i.e., democratic or classless) attitudes toward sex roles, and more men than women have sexist attitudes. Ui and Matsui also point out that such attitudes are linked to the age group being surveyed. Younger Japanese have egalitarian attitudes toward sex roles, whereas older age groups prefer more traditional (i.e., male dominant) sex roles.

To be sure, Iwao remarks that although today's Japanese women are much more outspoken and direct than their mothers, even modern Japanese women recognize their secondary status and have not completely discarded their earmark passivity. Moreover, when asked, many Japanese women acknowledge their fate as a subordinate group. Even the modern Japanese woman's happiness remains tied to her family—so much so that she will repress her personal feelings to an extent many American women would find unendurable. Following their collectivistic histories, most Japanese women continue to sacrifice personal goals for the sake of the harmony of the family. Because they have fewer opportunities than men maintaining interpersonal harmony is of utmost concern for Japanese women.[45]

India

A Reuters poll conducted in 2011 asked more than 200 women's rights experts from five continents to rank the world's countries according to six key risks to women: sexual violence, nonsexual violence, cultural or religious factors, discrimination, lack of access to resources, and trafficking. The results showed that India was the fourth most dangerous country on the planet for women.[46]

In his extensive writing on his native India, Laungani indicates that the socialization processes for boys and girls in India differ significantly. To be sure, writes Laungani, boys are privileged—so much so that in impoverished homes, of which there are many, a larger share of food is given to the male children, and they are also fed first by family members. Laungani notes that the birth of a male child is considered a blessing because it ensures the continuation of the family name. Male children are seen as an economic asset and, when married, bring to their family a nice dowry (i.e., obligatory gift from the bride's family, usually money). The birth of a daughter, on the other hand, is seen as a burden. A daughter is seen as an economic liability, and she never really possesses an identity of her own. Laungani has observed that while boys are pampered and accorded privileges, girls are raised on a strict regime. Girls are made aware of the role they are to play, where "verily is virtue and virginity venerated."[47]

Margot Duley has also written about women in India. According to Duley, the Preamble of the Indian Constitution guarantees all citizens "equality of status." Unfortunately, writes Duley, legal equality remains elusive for most Indian women. She argues that the subordination of women in India is primarily economically based. Most women work in agricultural jobs, but in the past few decades, India has developed a commercial market economy with capital-intensive production. Although laws favoring women's rights have been passed, they have not had much impact. For example, there are no uniform statutes governing marriage and inheritance laws. In most areas, purity and chastity of women are strongly emphasized. Nearly half of all young women marry by the age of 17. The Dowry Prohibition Act of 1961 is largely ignored. The practice of giving a dowry has actually spread in recent years because of the overwhelming pressure on girls to marry.

STUDENT VOICES ACROSS CULTURES

Ala Aldahneem

When I arrived in the United States from Saudi Arabia, I was the first Saudi female at my college. The students, faculty, and staff welcomed me and took into consideration our cultural differences. At the same time, most of the people who first met me would ask questions about a woman's role in Saudi Arabia. They were mostly curious if it was true that women have no voice or opinions. Others would ask if it is hard to move to the United Sates due to the cultures being so different. As the conversations continued, people frequently asked if I wanted to go back to Saudi Arabia or stay in the United States. I saw many surprised faces when they learned that I wanted to finish my schooling first and then go back to Saudi Arabia. I chose that because, in my country, I have respect and my needs will be guaranteed.

Unlike the stereotype that women are not respected and cannot make any choices for themselves in Saudi Arabia, I feel I have more respect than what many Westerners think—just like any mother, wife, or daughter in other families. Take the example of my moving to the United States. My family respects that I am a grown adult, and when I decided to study in the United States, they considered my choice and let me come alone.

These stereotypes are probably the result of some of Saudi's laws. It is true that many laws are restrictive toward women, such as driving or checking into a hotel without a male guardian. I cannot travel without permission. That is, I can travel without a man, but I must have the proper papers/permission to travel out of Saudi Arabia. I traveled with my dad the week I got married, but they did not let me go without his permission. However, it is not how it seems. Regarding driving, most families in Saudi Arabia have drivers who drive women wherever they want to go. Otherwise, the father or brothers are more than happy to give rides.

Another example would be checking into a hotel. I still remember the day when I traveled to Medina in the western part of Saudi Arabia. The receptionist told me that I could not check in without a male family member and that he was sorry for that. Because of the law, I was informed, I had to wait for my family to arrive before I could check in and get comfortable in the hotel after a long day of travel.

Even though there are some restrictions on women, my life is guaranteed. I have a place to live regardless of whether I am working or not. My father or husband is responsible for my housing and other personal needs. It doesn't matter if women are rich, working, or poor. Therefore, in any case, I have someone who will be responsible for me with love and a family orientation.

The phenomenon of dowry deaths, or bride burning, is particularly troubling. A dowry is a financial arrangement (e.g., currency, goods, or land) a woman brings to the marriage via her family. Dr. Rochona Majumdar, a professor of media studies at the University of Chicago and an expert on India, writes that in India a dowry represents a kind of coercive social power placed on the family of the bride that focuses particularly on the social standing and reputation of the bride's father. She argues that there is intense pressure on the bride's family, from the groom's family and Indian society in general, to provide an ample dowry to the groom's family. Majumdar notes that failure to meet dowry demands often results in unbelievable punishment for the bride, oftentimes death. In 2010, for example, 8,391 dowry death cases were reported across India, indicating that a bride was burned to death every 90 minutes. In a typical case, the bride is handcuffed to a stove, doused in kerosene, and lit on fire in an effort to make the murder appear accidental.

The horror of dowry deaths notwithstanding, women also have less access to education than do men, and women's literacy rate (25%) is less than half that among men. Only 13% of women enroll in high school. Duley writes that because of the large dowries required at marriage, daughters receive poor nutrition and health care and less love and nurturance than their brothers. Essentially, women are seen as an economic liability. In some areas, female feticide, the act of aborting a fetus because it is female, is widely practiced. The Reuters poll cited above indicates that as many as 50 million Indian girls have gone missing over the past century (i.e., an average of 500,000 per year) due to female infanticide and feticide.[48]

China

In X. M. Wang's 1993 monograph, "The Storm of a Divorce," the husband of a female student in China says to his wife, "You're such a good person. You'd be an excellent wife if you weren't studying for your doctorate."[49] In a survey of 10,000 Chinese urban men and women, 92% of the men indicated that they wanted a wife who would be aggressive in her career, yet 96% of men desired a virtuous wife who would do most of the household chores. Nearly half the Chinese women surveyed, however, wanted men to share chores more and considered an equal division of labor as important for the development of equality between men and women.[50]

The husbands' sentiments are typical of China's long history of women having little freedom and few rights. According to Gracie Ming Zhao, for most of its history, China has been a feudal society in which the Chinese were under the dictatorial rule of an emperor. About 100 years ago, the Chinese overthrew that system, and about 60 years ago, they established the People's Republic. Since then, the Chinese women's liberation movement has made significant advances toward women's rights. Zhao notes, for example, that the 1954 Constitution stipulated the freedom of marriage and stated that every individual has the right to decide his or her own marriage. Moreover, asserts Zhao, the 1950 Marriage Law abolished all feudal forms of marriage, such as concubines (i.e., where a young woman is in a quasi-matrimonial relationship with a man of higher social status), polygamy, and arranged marriages. Zhao laments, however, that while the Chinese government has enacted several laws and policies that equate women and men legally and socially, they are of little use in abolishing the long-standing preference of males over females.[51]

In her research, Delia Davin notes that Chinese are generally expected to live with their family circle unless there is reason to do otherwise and that such expectations are greater for women than for men. Chinese women, especially single women, are considered more vulnerable and less capable of dealing with the outside world than are men. Davin reports that women are seen as needing the protection and supervision of their families to preserve their virginity and marriageability.[52]

Within marriages, Ellen Efron Pimentel points out, the division of household chores has changed in contemporary Chinese culture. According to Pimentel, fewer young women, compared with older women, take on the entire load of domestic work. Ironically, these same Chinese women are increasingly dissatisfied with the division of labor and less happy in their marriages. Pimentel suggests that the push for women's equality in the family has produced a backlash among men, such that younger Chinese men are actually far less democratic than their older counterparts. Chinese men and women seem to be growing further apart. Because marriage quality is linked to separation and divorce, the communication between Chinese men and women within their homes is extremely important. Moreover, notes Pimentel, the road to women's liberation in China remains a long one. Asking women to achieve their own equality in a male-defined, male-centered world has negative implications for men and women and the relations between them.[53]

Mexico

Celina Melgoza Marquez was born in a small town in Guanajuato, Mexico. In addition to her parents, she has four sisters and five brothers. Recently, Marquez published a book about the role of women in Mexico.[54] In it, she profiles the status of women and the advances they have made in contemporary Mexico. In terms of population, Mexico has about 110 million people, of which women hold a slight majority. Marquez maintains that the marital status of Mexican people represents the rights and responsibilities of men and women because it reflects the population's social levels.

More Mexican women than men are divorced, possibly because Mexican men tend to emigrate once they divorce. Historically, the average marrying age of the population was 16 years old. However, by 1995, both sexes started marrying later, with the national average marrying age being 20 years old for women and a little more than 23 years old for men. The increase in age results from Mexicans pursuing higher education. Marquez says that a Mexican woman's childbearing rate is related to her educational, social, and economic conditions. For example, Marquez notes that in 1976, an average of 5.7 children were born per woman. In 1986, the rate decreased to 3.8; in 1995, to 2.8; and in 2007, to 2.4. Today, Mexican women are more educated than ever. In the past 25 years, the literacy rate of the Mexican population has increased noticeably. In 2004, the literacy rate among men was 92%, and among women it was 89%. Marquez maintains that males and females used to have specific and separate roles. Traditionally, men were the providers and women did the domestic work. During the past few years, however, the roles of men and women have changed noticeably. For example, 35 years ago, 17% of women age 12 years and older worked outside the home. By 1995, that number had increased to 35%. Today, about 42% of Mexican women are in the labor force.[55]

Although women now contribute much in the work world, they also contribute at home with the family. Nearly 93% of women age 12 years and older do domestic work. But, Marquez argues, men and women often work together to maintain the family. As a result, some men do domestic activities while some women work outside the home. Marquez notes that in Mexico, authority and responsibility are given to the father or to the oldest male, or *jefe,* of the household. Few women hold this position. Authority in Mexican society has been held by the men. Men are in charge of the family direction, and women take this responsibility only when the men have left home.[56]

Israel

Since Israel's establishment as a state in 1948, women in Israel have been guaranteed equal rights. In fact, Israel is the only country in the world with a compulsory military service requirement for women and where women constitute a third of all soldiers and just over half of military officers. To be sure, the Israeli Declaration of Independence guarantees equal rights to all Israeli citizens, regardless of religion, race, or sex.[57] But consider the following sequence of events as described by *New York Times* reporters Ethan Bronner and Isabel Kershner:

> In the three months since the Israeli Health Ministry awarded a prize to a pediatrics professor for her book on hereditary diseases common to Jews, her experience at the awards ceremony has become a rallying cry.
>
> The professor, Channa Maayan, knew that the acting health minister, who is ultra-Orthodox, and other religious people would be in attendance. So she wore a long-sleeve top and a long skirt. But that was hardly enough.
>
> Not only did Dr. Maayan and her husband have to sit separately, as men and women were segregated at the event, but she was instructed that a male colleague would have to accept the award for her because women were not permitted on stage.[58]

Bronner and Kershner describe similar instances, including the barring of women from speaking at Israeli professional organizations; a case where ultra-Orthodox men spit on an 8-year-old girl whom they considered immodestly dressed; and the case where ultra-Orthodox protesters carried posters depicting the Jerusalem police chief as Adolf Hitler because he had instructed public bus drivers, whose buses allowed mixed-sex seating, to drive through ultra-Orthodox neighborhoods. Also, in some Jerusalem neighborhoods, vandals routinely black out women's faces on advertising billboards.[59]

Bronner and Kershner note that while Israeli women are guaranteed equal rights under Israeli law, certain fundamental religious groups reject such rights—so much so that a new term, *hadarat nashim*, meaning the exclusion of women, has become common in the Israeli sociopolitical dialogue. At the center of the conflict is Haredi, an ultra-Orthodox Jewish microcultural group of about 1 million Israeli citizens. This group is one of many factions of Orthodox Judaism that reject contemporary, secular Israeli culture. Most male members are physically distinguished by their long black coats, wide-brimmed hats, beards, and side locks. Women wear long skirts and long sleeves, high necklines, and, if they are married, some form of head covering, such as a scarf, hat, or wig. Regarding the sexes, Haredi prescribe strict rules prohibiting/restricting interaction between men and women, and boys and girls. Some men, for example, will not look directly at women other than their wives. Young boys and girls attend separate schools. And while the Israeli Supreme Court ruling has banned sex-segregated seating on buses, many private and public bus lines, especially those that run through traditional neighborhoods, ignore the ban and allow men to sit in the front of the bus and force women to the back. Some Haredi publications will not publish photographs of women. According to a British Broadcasting Corporation report, in 2009 the Haredi newspaper *Yated Ne'eman* digitally altered photographs of the newly elected Israeli cabinet members and replaced two female ministers with photos of men.[60]

DEVELOPING A SKILL SET: TOWARD
INTERCULTURAL COMMUNICATION COMPETENCE

1. Recall from Chapter 1 that one of the fundamental assumptions about intercultural communication is that it is a group phenomenon experienced by individuals. Especially during our initial encounters with people from cultures different from our own, we tend to see them according to their group memberships, rather than as individuals. We tend to see the Saudi guy, rather than Ahmed, or the Japanese woman, rather than Michiko. To an extent, this is fine and appropriate because Ahmed is from Saudi Arabia and Michiko is Japanese, and those data provide us with valuable information by which to reduce uncertainty and interact appropriately. But to become competent interactants and develop meaningful relationships with others, we need to recognize not only the other person's group memberships but also his or her unique individuality. We need to learn how to tailor our messages to that person's cultural and individual identity.

2. Having said the above, keep in mind your own group memberships and how they affect your verbal and nonverbal communication style. When you are interacting with people from different cultures, they see you as a member of a group first; therefore, their impression of you is limited and based on generalizations. So be patient with others as they try to get to know you. Intercultural communication is a two-person process.

3. Be mindful of the variety of roles you play and how you code shift as you move from role to role. Remember also that the roles you play, and especially their prescriptions (i.e., with whom, about what, and how you communicate), differ considerably across cultures. So what it means to be a student in your culture is not necessarily what it means to be a student in another's culture. Take note of how your vocabulary changes and how your nonverbal communication is adjusted as you shift from your role as student to your role as friend.

CHAPTER SUMMARY

Our lives are inextricably tied to our group memberships and the roles we play. How we see ourselves and how our culture treats us is based on the total accumulation of roles we assume. They represent our social standing in our culture. This chapter has focused on the sociorelational context of intercultural communication—that is, the group memberships we assume. All of us belong to any number of groups. Groups to which we belong are called membership groups. Some of these are voluntary, whereas others are involuntary. Voluntary in-groups often serve as reference groups, which help us make decisions about significant issues in our lives. The reference group serves as a standard by which we judge ourselves. As group members, we assume roles that define with whom, about what, and how we communicate with others. Some of our roles are formal, whereas others are informal. Regardless, roles prescribe how we should communicate with others. Roles are a set of expectations that, if violated, are subject to negative sanctions. Roles vary considerably across cultures, especially family and sex roles. To be competent communicators across cultures, we must understand the expectations of the roles we assume. We must also understand and appreciate that the roles we assume in our native culture may be quite different in other cultures.

Visit the student study site at www.sagepub.com/neulicp6e for e-flashcards, web quizzes, web resources, and more.

DISCUSSION QUESTIONS

1. List the number of groups to which you now belong. Include both voluntary and involuntary groups.

2. How do the groups you listed affect the way you think, feel, and act in your society?

3. What is your role within these groups?

4. How does society perceive the groups to which you belong? Favorably or unfavorably? In other words, by virtue of your membership in these groups, how are you treated by others?

5. What are some of the groups to which you would like to belong but do not?

ETHICS AND THE SOCIORELATIONAL CONTEXT

1. You are a member of a sales team that is opening accounts in Egypt and Saudi Arabia. You are to send a representative from your company to Egypt and Saudi Arabia to meet with the Egyptian and Saudi company counterparts and begin a marketing campaign. Your top salesperson is Susan Que. She's young and motivated, and knows and understands the company products well. Should you send her or Tom Smith, the salesperson who has been with the company for 18 years but isn't exactly the best salesperson? Being male, he would probably have better success in both of these countries. Sending Susan might insult your new partners. What will you do?

2. Mino Choi, a friend of yours from South Korea, is an international student at your college/university. He's a senior and will graduate with you this year. In a recent conversation, you asked Mino what he's going to do after he graduates and returns to Korea. You are curious as to what kind of job and career he will pursue. When you ask him, he answers that his father will make that decision for him. What do you think of that idea? Would you be comfortable having your father make such decisions about your life?

KEY TERMS

gender   231

in-group   218

involuntary membership groups   217

involuntary nonmembership groups   217

membership groups   217

nonmembership groups   217

out-group   218

reference group   219

role   220

sex   231

NOTES

1. de Tocqueville, A. (1900). *Democracy in America* (H. Reeve, Trans., Vol. 2). New York: P. F. Collier (Copyright 1900 by the Colonial Press), p. 114.

2. Johnson, D. W., & Johnson, F. P. (2013). *Joining Together: Group Theory and Group Skills* (11th ed.). New York: Pearson.

3. Gudykunst, W. B., & Kim, Y. Y. (2003). *Communicating With Strangers: An Approach to Intercultural Communication* (4th ed.). New York: McGraw-Hill.

4. This discussion of membership, nonmembership, and voluntary and involuntary groups can be found in a number of textbooks. The source used here is Merton, R. K. (1959). *Social Theory and Social Structure.* Glencoe, IL: Free Press.

5. Laungani, P. D. (2007). *Understanding Cross-Cultural Psychology.* London: Sage.

6. Sumner, W. G. (1906). *Folkways.* Boston: Ginn, pp. 12–13.

7. Merton, *Social Theory and Social Structure.*

8. Triandis, H. (1990). Cross-Cultural Studies in Individualism and Collectivism. In J. J. Berman (Ed.), *Nebraska Symposium on Motivation, 1989* (pp. 41–133). Lincoln: University of Nebraska Press.

9. Brewer, M. B., & Campbell, D. T. (1976). *Ethnocentrism and Intergroup Attitudes.* New York: Wiley.

10. Brewer, M. B. (1979). Ingroup Bias in the Minimal Intergroup Situation: A Cognitive Motivational Analysis. *Psychological Bulletin, 86,* 307–324; Tajfel, H., & Turner, J. (1979). An Integrative Theory of Intergroup Conflict. In W. Austin & S. Worchel (Eds.), *The Social Psychology of Intergroup Conflict.* Monterey, CA: Brooks/Cole; Weber, J. (1994). The Nature of Ethnocentric Attribution Bias: Ingroup Projection or Enhancement? *Journal of Experimental Social Psychology, 30,* 482–504.

11. Schaefer, R. T. (2012). *Racial and Ethnic Groups* (13th ed.). New York: Pearson.

12. Napier, R. W., & Gershenfeld, M. K. (2003). *Groups: Theory and Experience* (7th ed.). Boston: Houghton Mifflin.

13. Spear, T., & Waller, R. (Eds.). (1993). *Being Masai.* London: James Currey; Vandehey, K., Buerger, C. M., & Krueger, K. (1996). *Traditional Aspects and Struggles of the Masai Culture.* Unpublished manuscript, St. Norbert College, De Pere, WI.

14. The discussion of roles can be found in any number of group textbooks. The particular one used here is Fisher, B. A., & Ellis, D. G. (1990). *Small Group Decision Making* (3rd ed.). New York: McGraw-Hill.

15. This discussion of formal and informal roles was based on Galanes, G. J., & Adams, K. (2012). *Effective Group Discussion: Theory and Practice* (14th ed.). Boston: McGraw-Hill.

16. Adler, R. B., & Proctor, R. F. (2010). *Looking Out Looking In* (13th ed.). Belmont, CA: Wadsworth.

17. Gudykunst & Kim, *Communicating With Strangers.*

18. This information about Korea was found on the following webpage: *Customs and Traditions in Korea.* (1997). Retrieved from http://www.emb.washington.dc.us/Korea/Scustoms.html

19. Berry, J. W., Poortinga, Y. H., Segall, M. H., & Dasen, P. R. (1992). *Cross-Cultural Psychology: Research and Applications.* Cambridge, UK: Cambridge University Press.

20. Keberlein, M. (1993). *A Cultural Profile of the Guatemalan Ladinos.* Unpublished manuscript, St. Norbert College, De Pere, WI.

21. Laungani, *Understanding Cross-Cultural Psychology.*

22. Klopf, D. W., & McCroskey, J. C. (2006). *Intercultural Encounters: The Fundamentals of Intercultural Communication.* Boston: Allyn & Bacon.

23. Although different, this dialogue is adapted from a scene in Copeland, L. (Producer). (1982). *Managing the Overseas Assignment* [Motion picture]. San Francisco: Copeland Griggs.

24. Johnson, A. G. (2005). *The Gender Knot: Unraveling Our Patriarchal Legacy.* Philadelphia: Temple University Press.

25. Goettner-Abendroth, H. (2004). Matriarchal Society: Definition and Theory. In G. Vaughan (Ed.), *The Gift, Il Dono: A Feminist Analysis.* Rome: Meltemi; Goettner-Abendroth, H. (Ed.). (2009). *Societies of Peace: Matriarchies Past, Present and Future.* Toronto: Inanna and Educations Inc.

26. Condon, J. C., & Yousef, F. (1975). *An Introduction to Intercultural Communication.* Indianapolis, IN: Bobbs-Merrill.

27. Chan, S. (1984). *Hmong Means Free*. Philadelphia: Temple University Press; Thao, K. (1995). *The Hmong Culture*. Unpublished manuscript, St. Norbert College, De Pere, WI.

28. Paik, S. (2000). The Formation of the United Lineage in Korea. *History of the Family, 5*, 75–90.

29. Ibid.

30. Kim, H.-O., & Hoppe-Graff, S. (2001). Mothers' Roles in Traditional and Modern Korean Families: The Consequences for Parental Practices and Adolescent Socialization. *Asia Pacific Education Review, 2*(1), 85–93.

31. Ibid.

32. Levande, D., Herrick, J., & Sung, K. (2000). Eldercare in the United States and South Korea. *Journal of Family Issues, 21*, 632–652.

33. Kim & Hoppe-Graff, Mothers' Roles in Traditional and Modern Korean Families; OECD. (2010). *Labour Force Statistics by Sex and Age: Indicators*. Retrieved from http://www.oecd-ilibrary.org/employment/data/labour-market-statistics/labour-force-statistics-by-sex-and-age-indicators_data-00310-en

34. Central Bureau of Statistics, State of Israel (2011, February 2). *Families and Households in Israel: Family Day* [Press release], p. 2. Retrieved from http://www.cbs.gov.il/hodaot2011n/11_11_025e.pdf

35. Clearinghouse on International Developments in Child, Youth and Family Policies at Columbia University. (n.d.). Israel. Retrieved from http://www.childpolicyintl.org/countries/israel.htm; Lewin-Epstein, N., Stier, H., Braun, M., & Langfeldt, B. (2000). Family policy and public attitudes in Germany and Israel. *European Sociological Journal, 16*(4), 385–401.

36. Central Bureau of Statistics, State of Israel, *Families and Households in Israel;* Eglash, R. (2010, October 2). CBS: Ma, Pa, & Kids Still the Prevalent Family Structure. *Jerusalem Post*.

37. Nongbri, T. (2010). Family, Gender and Identity: A Comparative Analysis of Trans-Himalayan Matrilineal Structures. *Contributions to Indian Sociology, 44*, 155–178; Walsh, E. R. (2005). From Nu Guo to Nu er Guo: Negotiating Desire in the Land of the Mosuo. *Modern China, 31*, 448–486.

38. Ibid.

39. Ibid.

40. Bem, S. L. (1974). The Measurement of Psychological Androgyny. *Journal of Consulting and Clinical Psychology, 81*, 506–520; Wood, J. (2000). Gender, Communication, and Culture. In L. A. Samovar & R. E. Porter (Eds.), *Intercultural Communication: A Reader* (9th ed., pp. 170–179). Belmont, CA: Wadsworth.

41. Hofstede, G. (1991). *Cultures and Organization: Software of the Mind*. New York: McGraw-Hill.

42. Lobel, T. E., Mashraki-Redhatzur, S., Mantzur, A., & Libby, S. (2000). Gender Discrimination as a Function of Stereotypic and Counterstereotypic Behavior: A Cross-Cultural Study. *Sex Roles, 43*, 395–406.

43. Williams, J. E., & Best, D. L. (1990). *Measuring Sex Stereotypes Across Cultures: A Multi-Nation Study*. Newbury Park, CA: Sage.

44. Williams, J. E., & Best, D. L. (1994). Cross-Cultural Views of Women and Men. In W. J. Lonner & R. Malpass (Eds.), *Psychology and Culture* (pp. 191–196). Boston: Allyn & Bacon.

45. Iwao, S. (1993). *The Japanese Woman: Traditional Image and Changing Reality*. Cambridge, MA: Harvard University Press; Sugihara, Y., & Katsurada, E. (1999). Masculinity and Femininity in Japanese Culture: A Pilot Study. *Sex Roles, 40*, 635–646; Ui, M., & Matsui, Y. (2008). Japanese Adults' Sex Role Attitudes and Judgment Criteria Concerning Gender Equality: The Diversity of Gender Egalitarianism. *Sex Roles, 50*, 113–123.

46. TrustLaw. (2011, June 15). *The World's Most Dangerous Countries for Women*. Retrieved from http://www.trust.org/item/20110615000000-hurik/?source = spotlight

47. Laungani, *Understanding Cross-Cultural Psychology*.

48. Bedi, R. (2012, February 27). Indian Dowry Deaths on the Rise. *Telegraph*. Retrieved from http://www.telegraph.co.uk/news/worldnews/asia/india/9108642/Indian-dowry-deaths-on-the-rise.html; Duley, M. I. (1986). Women in India. In M. I. Duley & M. I. Edwards (Eds.), *The Cross-Cultural Study of Women* (pp. 127–236). New York: Feminist Press; India: Actions to Stop Feticide. (2000). *Women's International Network News, 26*, 47; India: Dowry Deaths Still Increasing. (1996). *Women's International Network News, 22*, 67; Majumdar, R. (2004). Snehalata's Death: Dowry and Women's Agency in Colonial Bengal. *Indian Economic Social History Review, 41*, 433–464; Mandelbaum, P. (1999). Dowry Deaths in India. *Commonweal, 126*, 18–21.

49. Wang, X. M. (1993). The Storm of a Divorce. *Chinese Education and Society, 26*, 48.

50. Pimentel, E. E. (2006). Gender Ideology, Household Behavior, and Backlash in Urban China. *Journal of Family Issues, 27*, 341–365.

51. Zhao, G. M. (2003). Trafficking of Women for Marriage in China: Policy and Practice. *Criminal Justice, 3*, 83–102.

52. Davin, D. (2005). Women and Migration in Contemporary China. *China Report, 41*, 29–38.

53. Pimentel, Gender Ideology, Household Behavior, and Backlash in Urban China.

54. Marquez, C. M. (n.d.). *An Introduction to Mexico and the Role of Women*. West Virginia University Extension Service (WP513).

55. McCaa, R., Esteve, A., Gutierrez, R., & Vasquez, G. (2004, January). *Women in the Workforce: Calibrating Census*

Microdata Against Gold Standards Mexico, 1990–2000. Minneapolis: University of Minnesota Population Center.

56. Marquez, *An Introduction to Mexico and the Role of Women.*

57. Israel Defense Forces. (2010, August 25). *Statistics: Women's Service in the IDF for 2010.* Retrieved from http://www.idfblog.com/2010/08/25/statistics-womens-service-in-the-idf-for-2010-25-aug-2010/

58. Bronner, E., & Kershner, I. (2012, January 14). Israelis Facing Seismic Rift Over Role of Women. *New York Times.* Retrieved from http://www.nytimes.com/2012/01/15/world/middleeast/israel-faces-crisis-over-role-of-ultra-orthodox-in-society.html?pagewanted = all&_r = 0

59. Ibid.

60. Bronner & Kershner, Israelis Facing Seismic Rift Over Role of Women; Malkov, T., & Heller, M. (2012, September 19). Haredi Women Attack "Immodest" Women. *Ynet Jewish World.* Retrieved from http://www.ynetnews.com/articles/0,7340,L-4281828,00.html; Papers Alter Israel Cabinet Photo. (2009, April 3). *BBC News.* Retrieved from http://news.bbc.co.uk/2/hi/middle_east/7982146.stm; Shapira-Rosenberg, R. (2010, November). *Excluded, for God's Sake: Gender Segregation in Public Space in Israel.* © Israel Religious Action Center, Israel Movement for Progressive (Reform) Judaism. Retrieved from http://www.irac.org/userfiles//

CHAPTER 7

The Verbal Code

After reading this chapter, you should be able to

1. explain the relationship between language and culture;

2. explain the principles of linguistic relativity and linguistic determinism;

3. define the three levels of language;

4. explain the principle of universal grammar;

5. list and define three universals of language;

6. compare and contrast elaborated and restricted codes;

7. compare and contrast direct versus indirect styles, affective versus instrumental styles, personal versus contextual styles, and elaborate, exacting, and succinct styles of language use across cultures;

8. cogently discuss and compare sex differences in verbal language in Japan, China, and India; and

9. compare and contrast U.S. American dialects.

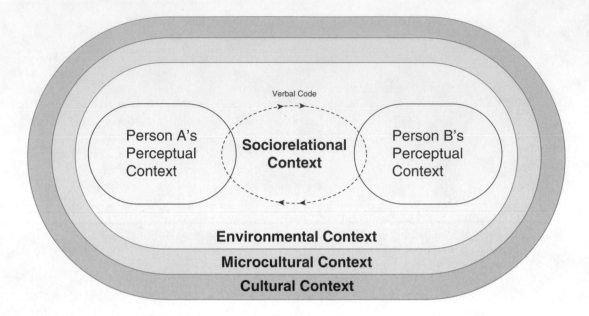

The language faculty is a system, a subsystem of the brain. . . . Its major elements don't appear to exist in other similar organisms. . . . To a large extent it appears to be determined by our biological endowment and is essentially invariant across the species.

—Noam Chomsky[1]

The capacity of the human brain to acquire language may be the most distinguishing feature that separates humans from the rest of the living beings on the planet. Our ability to put thoughts into a code to communicate with someone else empowers us beyond imagination. Other living beings are larger, stronger, faster, and smaller, but no other living being has the capacity for language. Because of their capacity for language, humans have become the most powerful living beings on Earth. The purpose of this chapter is to explore the idea of language and how it varies across cultures. This chapter outlines the relationship between language and culture by first exploring the Sapir–Whorf hypothesis. The second part of the chapter outlines the fundamental structure of language, including a discussion of the concept of a universal grammar that applies to all languages. The third part of this chapter looks at universals of language that are shared across cultures. The fourth part of the chapter focuses on how the use of language differs across cultures, including a look at elaborate and restricted codes and cross-cultural comparisons of language style. The fifth part examines sex differences in language among native speakers of Japanese, Mandarin Chinese, and Hindi. Finally, the chapter closes with a look at various dialects across the United States.

THE RELATIONSHIP BETWEEN LANGUAGE AND CULTURE

Linguist and cultural anthropologist Zdenek Salzmann points out that, historically, anthropologists and linguists often grouped language, culture, and race together as though any one of them automatically implied the other two. Contemporary linguistic anthropologists generally agree, however, that culture, race, and language are historically distinct. In other words, a person's race does not determine what language he or she will speak. As we saw in Chapter 5, however, the language of a particular culture and the thought processes of its people are related.[2]

Sapir–Whorf Hypothesis

In 1929, anthropologist and linguist Edward Sapir published a paper in the journal *Language* that changed the face of the study of language and culture. Sapir's thesis was that the language of a particular culture directly influences how people think. In the paper, he wrote,

> The network of cultural patterns of a civilization is indexed in the language which expresses that civilization. . . . Language is a guide to "social reality." . . . Human beings do not live in the objective world alone . . . but are very much at the mercy of the particular language which has become the medium of expression for their society.[3]

Sapir continued to argue that the ways people perceive the world around them, including their natural and social environments, are essentially dictated by their language. In fact, Sapir argued that the speakers of different languages see different worlds. Strongly influenced by Sapir was one of his students, Benjamin Whorf.[4] Whorf was persuaded by Sapir's writings and further developed this line of thought. In 1940, Whorf wrote,

> The background linguistic system (in other words the grammar) of each language is not merely a reproducing instrument for voicing ideas but rather is itself the shaper of ideas. . . . We dissect nature along lines laid down by our native languages.[5]

Like Sapir, Whorf believed that the people who speak different languages are directed to different types of observations; therefore, they are not equivalent as observers and must arrive at somewhat different views of the world.[6] Sapir and Whorf's ideas received a great deal of attention and have become well-known as the Sapir–Whorf hypothesis. Salzmann contends that the Sapir–Whorf hypothesis delineates two principles. One is the principle of linguistic determinism, which says that the way one thinks is determined by the language one speaks. Taken at its extreme, this principle means that if we don't have a word for it, then we can't think about it. The second is the principle of linguistic relativity, which says that the differences among languages must be reflected in the differences in the worldviews of their speakers.[7]

These principles raise some important issues for cross-cultural communication. If how we think is a reflection of the language we speak, then the speakers of two very different languages must think very differently. This could render effective and successful intercultural communication extremely difficult, if not impossible. The well-known linguist Steven Pinker maintains that the Sapir–Whorf hypothesis is unfounded and that if the principle of linguistic determinism were valid, speakers of one language would find it impossible, or at least extremely difficult, to think in a particular way that comes naturally to speakers of another language. Another reason why Pinker believes that language does not determine thought is because people consistently create new language forms, a topic we will review in this chapter.[8]

Today, most linguists, like Pinker, believe that the reason the vocabulary and grammar of a particular language differ from others is because languages reflect nonverbal elements of culture. In other words, the geographic, climatic, kinesic, spatial, and proxemic aspects of a culture are emphasized and accented in a culture's language. Salzmann notes, for example, that in Pintupi (one of the aboriginal languages of Australia), there are at least 10 words designating various kinds of holes. *Mutara* is a special hole in a spear, *pulpa* refers to a rabbit burrow, *makarnpa* is the burrow of a monitor lizard, and *katarta* is the hole left by a monitor lizard after it has broken the surface after hibernation.

Moreover, linguists believe that the syntactic features of a language influence how speakers of that language categorize and mentally organize their worlds. For example, speakers of English use the personal pronoun *you* whether they are addressing one or several children, adults, old persons, subordinates, or individuals much superior in rank to themselves. Other languages operate differently. When addressing someone, speakers of Dutch, French, German, Italian, Russian, and Spanish must choose between the "familiar" personal pronoun and the "polite" personal pronoun and/or the corresponding verb form. In English, the word *teacher* refers to a person who teaches, whether it is a man or a woman. In German, *Lehrer* is the masculine form of teacher and *Lehrerin* is the feminine form. In this way, speakers of Dutch, French, German, and Italian may be more conscious of the status differences between them and another person because their language requires them to use words designating the power differential.[9] Therefore, most linguists now believe that the users of a particular language may overlook or ignore objects or events that speakers of another language may emphasize.

THE STRUCTURE OF HUMAN LANGUAGE

All languages consist of a systematic set of sounds, combined with a set of rules, for the sole purpose of creating meaning and communicating.[10] Any and all human languages are made up of a set of sounds. These sounds are represented symbolically in the language's alphabet. In English, for example, there are about 40 sounds represented in an alphabet of 26 letters. The Korean script, called Hangul, consists of 16 consonants—of which there are five basic forms—and 10 vowels. The Hebrew alphabet of 22 letters (5 of which have a different form when they appear at the end of a word) consists entirely of consonants. The language is written from right to left without vowels. Thus, the word *kelev* (i.e., dog) appears as the Hebrew equivalents of, from right to left, *k, l,* and *v.* If you are not familiar with Hebrew, it is impossible to know how to pronounce a word from the way it is written.[11]

The written form of Japanese consists of three major alphabets. A fourth alphabet, called *romaji,* is a Romanization using English letters. All four alphabets are used simultaneously

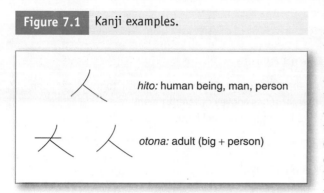

Figure 7.1 Kanji examples.

hito: human being, man, person

otona: adult (big + person)

in any given piece of writing. The first alphabet, called *kanji,* consists of more than 5,000 borrowed characters from Chinese. The word *kanji* means "Chinese character." Kanji are the Chinese characters used in written Japanese. Each kanji character represents an idea or concept, rather than a simple sound. The meaning of the character changes when the combination of characters varies. For an example, see Figure 7.1. To be able to read a Japanese newspaper, you would need to know and understand at least 2,000 basic characters.

Moreover, you would have to learn the different readings or compounds of two or more kanji. There are more than 4,000 kanji compounds. The Japanese also have two phonetic alphabets, called *hiragana* and *katakana. Hiragana* consists of 46 characters. These are phonetic sounds that make up the kanji and are used to change verb tenses. The *katakana* also consists of 46 sounds. The *katakana* sounds coincide with the *hiragana,* but the characters are different. *Katakana* is used for many foreign words coming from outside of Japan.[12]

Sounds and Symbols

The letters of a language's alphabet are symbols representing sounds, called phonemes. Phonemes are the smallest unit of sound in a language. For example, in English, the letter *c* represents the sound "see" or "ka," the letter *a* represents the sound "ah," and the letter *t* represents the sound "tee." When combined, phonemes become words—what linguists call morphemes, the smallest unit of sound that has meaning. When coarticulated, the sounds "ka," "ah," and "tee" create the word/morpheme *cat.*

There is no natural or inherent relationship between the sounds and their accompanying alphabet. That is, there is no intrinsic or immanent relationship between the symbol *c* and the "see" sound, the *a* and the "ah" sound, or the *t* and the "tee" sound. That *c* represents the "see" sound is completely random and arbitrary. Likewise, there is no natural relationship between any word and its referent. In other words, there is no natural or necessary relationship between the word *cat* and that fuzzy little animal that sits on the windowsill and chirps at birds in the yard. In Spanish, for example, that particular fuzzy little animal is called *gato;* in Japanese, *neko;* and in French, *chat.* Each of the different languages uses a different set of sounds to refer to the same referent. Although the letters and the sound systems of any two languages may be different, the function of an alphabet is the same across languages—to symbolize sound. A symbol, then, is an arbitrarily selected and learned stimulus representing something else.[13] The ability to represent sounds with symbols seems to be limited to humans. To be sure, animals can learn to associate sounds with behaviors, as when a dog learns to sit when you say "sit." But they can do so only at a very rudimentary level. Animals do not understand the concept of democracy or freedom, for example.

STUDENT VOICES ACROSS CULTURES

Chen Chen

Chinese is a tonal language. There are four basic tones in common speech. Different tones convey different meanings.

The four tones are represented by the following tone marks:

" – " is the first tone.

" ´ " is the second tone.

" ˇ " is the third tone.

" ` " is the fourth tone.

Besides these four basic tones, there are some variations of the tones, such as third-tone sandhi and neutral tone.

Here are examples of the four tones:

(Chinese character, tone, and English translation)

妈 (mā) mother

麻 (má) hemp

马 (mǎ) horse

骂 (mà) to curse somebody

Syntax and Universal Grammar

Along with a system of sounds, all languages have a set of rules for combining the sounds to create meaning. The set of rules, or grammar, is called syntax. Through syntax, sentences are generated. Through syntax, sound and meaning are connected. Noam Chomsky is perhaps the most recognized linguist in the world. Over the past 60 years, Chomsky has developed a fascinating theory about syntax.[14] Chomsky contends that although the 5,000 or so languages spoken in the world today appear to be very different, they are, in fact, remarkably similar. Moreover, Chomsky asserts that the differences among languages are actually quite trivial. Chomsky maintains that the languages spoken on the planet today are all dialects of one common language—human language—and that it has all the properties of normal physical growth. Thus, in essence, Chomsky and others are arguing that language is biological.[15]

To defend his thesis that language is biological, Chomsky argues that all human languages share a universal grammar that is innate in the human species and culturally invariant. Chomsky and other linguists claim that every normal child is genetically programmed for human language. Just as humans are programmed to walk upright, so are humans programmed with universal grammar (see Figure 7.2). In this sense, language is as much a part of the human brain as the thumb is a part of the human hand. Hence, just as humans do not learn how to see, they do not learn language; they come into the world already equipped with it. But Chomsky points out that humans are not born knowing any specific language, such as English or Spanish. They are born with universal grammar—that is, a deep-seated set of rules (i.e., syntax) that all the languages of the world follow in some way or another. So English and French, German and Italian are all subsets or variations of human language.

| Figure 7.2 | Humans have a need to communicate. |

Humans do, however, learn a specific language. The acquisition of a particular language (e.g., English, Japanese) is influenced by the specific cultural environment in which a child is born.[16] In other words, no individual language is universal to human beings. Children learn their specific language by being exposed to it in their cultural environment. Children born and raised in China learn to speak Chinese, whereas children born and raised in Norway learn to speak Norwegian—not because of their race or ethnicity but because of their cultural environment. So if your parents had given you up for adoption and you were raised by your adoptive parents in China, by about the age of 3 you would have been speaking (relatively fluently) some dialect of Chinese.

The commonalities between different languages (e.g., Chinese and Norwegian) are so striking that Chomsky and other linguists are convinced that the fundamental syntax for all languages is universal and that the particular languages of any given culture are simply dialects or subsets of the universal grammar. For example, all languages the world over rely on word order or inflection to convey meaning. English, for example, relies heavily on word order. "The man is in the car" means something very different from "The car is in the man." English also uses inflection to carry meaning. Inflections are changes to words to indicate grammatical relationships such as number, case, gender, tense, and so on. For example, to indicate the plural of something in English, we add the letter s to the end of a word. A single fuzzy little animal is called a "cat," and two fuzzy little animals are called "cats." The language of the Warlpiri people of Australia relies almost exclusively on inflection rather than word order. Latin also relies heavily on inflection. The point is that word order and inflection are a part of all languages, as are many other grammatical rules. As linguist Dan Slobin asserts,

> In a way [language is] like the human face. A human face is very simple—two eyes, a nose, and a mouth. You can draw a simple sketch of it. But look at the incredible diversity. Each one of us has a uniquely different face. Yet each face is obviously a human face. Languages are the same. Each one is obviously a different language, but they're clearly examples of the same kind of system.[17]

Lila Gleitman puts forward two additional arguments in favor of the universality of language.[18] The first is that language learning proceeds uniformly among children within and across cultures. Chinese children and Norwegian children learn language at the same time in their development. All normal children begin to use language at about the same time, across cultures. Pinker has observed that sometime around their first birthday, all babies start to understand and use words. At about 18 months, children's vocabulary, across all cultures, increases at a rate of about one word every 2 hours and continues to grow through adolescence. Also at about 18 months, two-word strings appear. These two-word combinations are highly similar across cultures. Children announce when objects appear, disappear, and move about. According to Pinker, by the age of 3 years, a child's vocabulary grows dramatically and he or she can produce fluent grammatical conversation. Such sentences, though quite short, illustrate the child's knowledge and competence of the basic structure of language (e.g., appropriate word order). For example, even though he or she has never had a lesson in English grammar, an English-speaking child might say, "I want cookie," but would never say, "Want I cookie." By the age of 5 or so, children in normal learning settings begin to use complex sentences.[19]

Gleitman argues that even in cases where the learning environment changes, children learn language at essentially the same rate. For example, studies indicate that a child's language learning rate is basically unaffected by differences in mothers' speech. Furthermore, deaf and blind children learn language at the same time and rate as children with normal hearing and sight. Gleitman points out that the vocabulary and syntax of sign languages are essentially the same as those of spoken languages. At about the age of 2, deaf children start to put gestures together into elementary two- and three-gesture sentences. By 5 years of age, they are constructing complex, multigesture sentences. In addition, blind children have little trouble acquiring terms that describe visual experiences. Gleitman suggests that because blind children are unable to see, phrases referring to sight (e.g., "Look at that!") might be absent from their speech. Yet such terms are some of the first to appear in blind children's vocabulary. For example, in response to the command "look up," blind children raise their hands instead of their heads. When they are told that they can "look but not touch," blind children very slowly stretch out their hands and cautiously touch the object. When told "go ahead and look," they handle the object with enthusiasm (see Figure 7.3).[20]

The second point supporting the universality of language argument is that children across cultures acquire many linguistic generalizations that experience alone could not have given

| Figure 7.3 | Language acquisition proceeds at a very early age and uniformly among children across cultures. |

them. Children of all cultures say things that no one could have taught them. Chomsky argues that in advance of experience, children of all cultures are already equipped with an understanding of the basic structure of any human language. Like walking or growing hair, language is encoded into the genetic makeup of normal-functioning human beings. By the age of 3, for example, children cannot do any number of things, such as tie their own shoes, perform mathematical computations, or spell most words; they can, however, construct meaningful sentences in ways that no one has ever taught them.[21]

Moreover, as Pinker notes, the sentences children create are grammatically correct. Indeed, asserts Pinker, children never make certain mistakes. For example, a child might ask, "What did you eat your eggs with?" but would never say, "What did you eat your eggs and?" which seems to be a straightforward extension of the statement, "I ate ham and eggs." The interesting point here is that no one has ever taught the child not to end sentences with the word *and*. Pinker and Chomsky argue that children never make such errors because to do so would violate some principle of universal grammar. Below is another example provided by Pinker. In this example, a language learner who hears the (a) and (b) sentences could quite sensibly extract a general rule that, when applied to the (c) sentence, would yield sentence (d). But the resulting sentence (d) is something no one would say.

(a) We expect the bird to fly.
(b) We expect the bird will fly.

(c)   The bird is expected to fly.

(d)   The bird is expected will fly.[22]

The proposition that all languages share a universal grammar innate to humans is widely accepted among contemporary linguists. But these linguists also recognize that all human languages are somewhat different. For example, although virtually all languages rely on some form of word order to construct sentences, the word order may vary across languages. For example, the word order for a sentence in most European languages is subject–verb–object, as in the sentence, "I watch television." In Japanese, however, the order is subject–object–verb, as in the sentence, "I television watch." In addition, Japanese, like other Asian languages, does not contain a grammatical equivalent to plurality, as found in English.[23]

The Swahili alphabet lacks the letters *c, q,* and *x* but contains a number of its own. The letter *dh* is pronounced like the "th" of *this,* and *gh* like the German *ch.* Whereas English grammatical inflections occur at the end of a word, in Swahili everything is done at the beginning. *Kitabu* is the Swahili word for "book," but the word for "books" is *vitabu.* This word falls into the so-called Ki-Vi class, one of eight in the Swahili language. Others include the M-Mi class (e.g., *mkono* = "hand," *mikono* = "hands," *mji* = "town," *miji* = "towns") and the M-Wa class, used mainly to refer to people (e.g., *mtu* = "man," *watu* = "men"; *mjinga* = "fool," *wajinga* = "fools"). Thus, "one big book" in Swahili is *kitabu kikubwa kimoja,* which translates as "book–big–one," but "two big books" is *vitabu vikubwa viwili.* Many languages are read from left to right, as in English. Most languages of the Middle East, however, including Arabic, Hebrew, and Persian, are read from right to left. Korean writing differs considerably from most other languages in that the letters of each syllable are grouped together into clusters, as if the English word *seldom* were written in one of the following ways:

S D   S E L

E O   or   D O M

L M

The point here is that although human languages across the globe have much in common, each is unique in some way.[24]

All human languages have a set of rules that is used to combine the language's sounds into meaningful units. Complex languages exist even in remote parts of the world, where people have yet to be exposed to modern technology and media. Papua, New Guinea, for example, is home to some of the most isolated people on Earth, and yet it is probably the most linguistically diverse country. Among its population of 3 million people, more than 750 languages are spoken—about one fifth of the total number of languages spoken on Earth. Some of the languages in this country are spoken by fewer than 1,000 people. In his longitudinal work with the Menya people of Papua, New Guinea, Carl Whitehead has found that the Menya use a language as complex as any other language. He argues that one of the most remarkable features of the Menya language is its verb system. Some Menya verbs, according to Whitehead, can have as many as 2,000 to 3,000 different forms. Compare that with English, where a verb can have up to five forms. Languages such as Menya are as highly rule governed as any other language. In this sense, there is no such thing as a primitive language.[25]

Universals of Language

Another reason why so many linguists believe that all languages evolved from a universal grammar is their numerous commonalities. All languages are remarkably similar. For example, all languages have some way of labeling objects, places, or things (such as the English noun). All languages have a way of naming action (such as the English verb). All human languages have some way of stating the negative (e.g., "It is *not* raining out"), a way to construct interrogatives, and a way of differentiating between singular and plural.[26]

According to Salzmann, the uniquely human way of communicating via speech shares several other universal features, regardless of culture, race, and particular lexicon. First, Salzmann notes that all human speech is transmitted via a vocal–auditory channel. Conversely, some sounds produced by animals are not vocal or are not received auditorily (e.g., bees have no ears). An important advantage of the vocal–auditory channel for humans is that the rest of the body is left free to carry on other activities. Second, speech sounds are emitted in all directions from their source of origin, making it possible to determine the location of the source. Functionally, this is important because the sender and the receiver do not have to see each other to communicate. This is also important because it enables speakers to communicate without necessarily being face to face—for example, from around corners, or in the dark.

Third, speech sounds are heard within a limited range and only during production. Soon after, they are lost. In this sense, speech is transitory. Fourth, speech is also interchangeable. We are capable of repeating what others say. This is not true of many animal species. Fifth, human speakers are equipped with complete intrapersonal feedback. As speakers, we can hear ourselves and are capable of monitoring our own messages. Sixth, speech is specialized. Human speech has only a single function—that is, to communicate. Seventh, speech can be displaced from time and space. We can talk about something that happened 1,000 years ago or project what we think will happen 1,000 years from now. Eighth, what a person may say can be completely false. Ninth, speech is reflexive. We use language to talk about language. Tenth, and finally, the speakers of any language can learn a second language or even several languages in addition to their native tongue.[27]

Generative Grammar

Recall that, according to the Sapir–Whorf hypothesis, human thought is restricted by the vocabulary of one's language. Yet one of the most remarkable features of any language's rule structure (i.e., syntax) is that it allows the speakers to generate sentences that have never before been spoken. Chomsky refers to this aspect of language as its generative grammar. From a finite set of sounds and a finite set of rules, speakers of any language can create an infinite number of sentences, many of which have never before been uttered, yet are easily comprehended by other speakers of the same language.[28]

Many of the sentences you have produced today have never before been spoken by anyone on the planet, and yet everyone understood them. Linguist George A. Miller contends that any sentence more than 20 words in length has probably never before been spoken. Miller demonstrates this through an example. According to Miller, suppose it is possible for someone to choose the next word he or she is going to say from a list of 10 possible words. Continuing on, assume that the second word someone is going to speak is also one of 10 possible words. At this point, the total number of possible combinations of two-word sentences is 10 times

10, or 100 possible two-word sentences. Now assume that the person is to select a third word out of a possible 10 words. The number of possible three-word sentences is 10 to the third power, or 1,000 possible sentences (see Figure 7.4).

Figure 7.4 Number of possible two- and three-word sentences.

First Word Options	Second Word Options	
Blue	Dog	
Green	Cat	
Yellow	Bird	
Red	Pig	Number of possible two-word
Black	Cow	sentences is 10 × 10 = 100
Brown	Horse	
Orange	Chicken	
Grey	Rat	
White	Mouse	
Violet	Fish	

First Word Options	Second Word Options	Third Word Options	
Stephanie	Ran	Fast	
Jim	Walked	Slow	
Gary	Jumped	Quickly	
Karen	Limped	Rapidly	
Kevin	Opened	Leisurely	Number of possible three-word
Donna	Cried	Gradually	sentences is 10 × 10 × 10 = 1,000
Jeff	Laughed	Briefly	
Judy	Rode	Promptly	
Steve	Drove	Swiftly	
Noreen	Flew	Fashionably	

SOURCE: © James W. Neuliep.

Moving on to a fourth possible word, out of a list of 10 possible words, the number of potential four-word sentences is 10 to the fourth power, or 10,000 possible sentences. The number of possible messages increases rapidly as the length of the message increases. Following this example, the number of possible 20-word sentences is 10 to the 20th power, or 100,000,000,000,000,000,000 possible sentences. Based on this example, Miller alleges that the number of possible sentences in any language is essentially infinite.[29]

In addition to creating new sentences, people routinely create new words to refer to people, places, and events in their world. The academic journal *American Speech,* which is published quarterly, devotes to each issue a section titled "Among the New Words," where the journal's editors highlight new words in the American English lexicon. Consider some of the following entries:[30]

asshole-ocracy, assholocracy, assholeocracy: *n* Government in which power is vested in selfish, uncaring people

bodysnarking: *n* Among women, belittling or criticizing the appearance of another woman

bromance: *n* Strong (platonic) relationship between two men

bunga bunga, bunga-bunga 1a: *adj* (Of a party) characterized by sexual antics

-cation: *suffix* Combining form connoting and derived from *vacation*

break-cation: *n* Taken over short period, not far from home, and with short notice

daycation: *n* Overnight holiday or trip

edu-cation: *n* A vacation taken for the purpose of learning

faux-cation: *n* Vacation during which a person works

mancation: *n* Trip or vacation taken together by men without the company of women

paycation: *n* Discounted vacation offered to travel agents for training as a reward

DWT: *n* Driving While Texting

First Dude, first dude: *n* Male spouse of a female president or governor

FOMO, Fomo: *abbr* [*fear of missing out*] Anxiety caused by the possibility that one might miss an opportunity

Game-Changer: *n* In sports and competitive contests, something or someone that could potentially change, or has changed, the outcome of a match or contest

Hockey-mom: *n* Mother, often portrayed as resilient and capable, who is heavily involved with her child's participation in hockey

humblebrag, humble brag [popularized by the @humblebrag Twitter account created by comedian Harris Wittels to point out faux-humble celebrity tweets] 1: *n* A boastful or self-important expression in the guise of false humility

Kardash, kardash: *n* 72 days; unit of measure defined by the length of Kim Kardashian's marriage to basketball player Kris Humphries

Planking: *vbl n* Lying rigidly face down in unusual places

Tebowing: *vbl n* Posing like quarterback Tim Tebow praying, on one's knee with an elbow perched on that knee and one's head down

Thought-shower: *n* Moment or session of creative thinking; brainstorm

So, as you can see, not only does language not limit or curb our thinking, as the principle of linguistic determinism posits, but its syntax actually frees the mind to create new words and sentences never before heard or spoken, yet readily understood.

ELABORATED AND RESTRICTED CODES

Although the world's 5,000 or so languages have much in common, the style or fashion in which they are used by the people who speak them differs considerably from culture to culture. In fact, speakers of the same language often use it differently. Some of these differences may be explained by Edward T. Hall's concept of high- and low-context cultures. Persons in high-context cultures generally rely more on their nonverbal code than on their verbal code to communicate, whereas members of low-context cultures rely extensively on the verbal code during communication. Basil Bernstein argues that the use of linguistic codes is closely related to the social structure of a particular culture. First, Bernstein differentiates between language and speech. As it is described above, Bernstein agrees that language is a system of sounds and syntax that allows speakers to represent their reality and generate an infinite number of sentences. In fact, he argues that all languages are equal in terms of their ability to represent reality. Speech, on the other hand, is at the mercy of the social circumstances wherein it is employed. Bernstein maintains that whereas language symbolizes what is *possible* to do, speech symbolizes what is actually occurring. The social context of communication sets up the boundaries for the type of speech that is preferred, obligated, or prohibited. As the social context varies, the speakers of the language will generate different kinds of speech, even if they speak the same language. The social system delimits the speaker's options in terms of language use. The speech codes, then, are not defined in terms of lexicon or syntax but by the social structure of the culture.[31]

Broadly speaking, Bernstein identifies two types of linguistic/speech codes: elaborated and restricted. A restricted code is one wherein the options (not necessarily the vocabulary) are limited as to what the speakers can say or do verbally. A restricted code is considered a status-oriented speech system. The code reinforces the social system by restricting or limiting its speakers to a finite number of linguistic options during communication. Restricted codes are most often seen in high-context cultures wherein the status of the interactants dictates who says what to whom and how it is said. When interactants of a high-context, collectivistic culture communicate, their words and phrases are strictly prescribed, leaving them little choice about what to say or how to say it. In this way, their code is "restricted" and is highly predictable.

Bernstein points out that the Chinese, for example, operate with a restricted code but have one of the most complex languages on Earth. Chinese people need to learn several thousand characters to read and write, but they speak with a restricted code because the social system (highly status and group oriented) dictates what can be said to whom in a given social circumstance. Restricted codes also emerge in individualistic cultures as interactants develop close relationships. Restricted codes can be found in what Bernstein calls "closed" communities, such as prison camps and criminal subgroups, but can develop within any social structure where the individuals share social identifications (e.g., spouses, coworkers). In this way, restricted codes show up in both high- and low-context cultures, although they tend to be more salient across the entire culture in a high-context culture.[32]

With an elaborated code, speakers can choose from among a variety of linguistic options to communicate. Bernstein argues that speakers using an elaborated code are able, via the social system, to put their thoughts, intents, and goals into an explicit verbal message. Bernstein argues that elaborated codes develop in circumstances where the speakers' intents are unknown or vary widely, as in individualistic cultures. Because the individual speaker's intent is unclear, the speaker has a variety of linguistic options from which to choose. The speaker must expand and elaborate so his or her intentions are clearly communicated. Any language will allow the speaker to do that, but the social system regulates it. The social structure of an elaborated code user is such that considerable flexibility exists in one's role prescription. To communicate his or her intent, the speaker must be given much linguistic latitude. In this way, it is difficult to predict the vocabulary and syntax of a speaker using an elaborated code. Students in the United States, for example, may have no idea what kinds of things a new professor will say on the first day of class. Students in China, on the other hand, can probably predict quite accurately the kinds of messages their professor will send. In the United States, the culture generally uses an elaborated code, whereas in China, the code is restricted.[33]

CROSS-CULTURAL COMMUNICATION STYLES

Although the capacity for language is universal, the language of a particular culture must be learned by its members. Moreover, cultures seem to have a predominant manner, fashion, or style in which they use their language. Communication theorists William Gudykunst and Stella Ting-Toomey argue that at different language acquisition stages, children learn not only the structure and lexicon of their culture's language but also the various styles of language interaction unique to their culture. Such language style reflects the affective, moral, and aesthetic patterns of a culture. Gudykunst and Ting-Toomey describe a culture's verbal style as its tonal coloring of a message, communicated through shades of tonal qualities. Gudykunst and Ting-Toomey describe four verbal communication styles that have been identified by intercultural theorists. The styles are direct–indirect, elaborate–succinct, personal–contextual, and instrumental–affective. Variations of these styles may exist in any culture, but one style tends to dominate within a given culture.[34]

Direct and Indirect Styles

According to Gudykunst and Ting-Toomey, cultures differ in the degree to which speakers disclose their intentions through precise and candid verbal communication. Persons using a direct style employ overt expressions of intention. In using a direct style, interactants assert self-face needs. Such messages clearly articulate the speaker's desires and needs. Direct styles are often used in low-context, individualistic cultures. Conversely, an indirect style, which is often seen in high-context and collectivistic cultures, is one where the speaker's intentions are hidden or only hinted at during interaction. The use of ambiguity and vagueness is characteristic of an indirect style. In high-context cultures, there is no need to articulate every message. True understanding is implicit, coming not from words but from actions in the environment. Moreover, indirect communication prevents potentially embarrassing moments that might threaten the face of either speaker.[35]

The direct style is preferred in cultures such as the United States, England, Australia, Germany, and Israel, among others. In the United States, we frequently use such phrases as "for sure," "no question," and "without a doubt." We value verbal precision and self-expression. Americans are encouraged to "speak their minds." We are so direct and candid that we will even announce to an entire room when we are going to use the bathroom, as in, "I'll be right back. I have to use the restroom." Gudykunst and Ting-Toomey allege that Israel is also considered a direct culture, perhaps even more so than the United States. Kevin Fedarko points out that many Israelis use the direct style of *dugri* (straight talk) that is quintessentially Israeli. Israelis value communication that is simple, direct, and honest. A speaker displaying *dugri* places substance before style and makes no attempt at pretense or deception. Some have referred to Israel as having an "in-your-face" culture when it comes to interacting.[36] Germans, too, value frankness and directness in their interaction with others and are especially fond of the use of examples. Along with their direct style is an absence of small talk. Edward Hall and Mildred Reed Hall maintain that in their quest for direct and candid talk, Germans avoid social chitchat. Sometimes, Germans are perceived by their European counterparts as brutally frank.[37]

The use of an indirect style of language is seen in many Asian cultures. Indirectness is valued in these cultures because saving face and maintaining harmony in social relationships are highly valued. Directness threatens both of these goals. According to Gudykunst and Ting-Toomey, Japanese speakers, for example, limit themselves to implicit and even ambiguous use of words such as *maybe* and *perhaps*. Children in Japan are taught not to be self-centered, and those who take the initiative are generally not rewarded. Japanese mothers typically use rhetorical questions, tone of voice, and context to express disapproval.

Sumiko Iwao argues that there is an unspoken belief among Japanese that verbalizing deep feelings spoils their value. To the Japanese, being understood without words is far more cherished than precise articulation. Iwao asserts that in Japan, interpersonal communication is based on a great deal of guessing and reading between the lines. Directness is disagreeable and repugnant. The ability to correctly grasp what a person thinks and feels without verbal expression is considered a sign of closeness between two persons. In marital relationships, verbal communication is thought to be unnecessary. Iwao calls Japan "a culture of no words." She alleges that this may be due to the high value placed on masculinity. According to Japanese ideals, the most masculine of men is one of few words who does not disclose personal weakness by complaining or expose his innermost thoughts and feelings, especially not to his wife.[38]

To a certain degree, the French are indirect. Hall and Hall argue that the French often indulge in small talk and prefer some mystery in their interaction with others. They maintain that the French will often talk around the point they wish to make.[39]

An Intercultural Conversation: Direct and Indirect Speaking

To some extent, direct and indirect modes of communication are universal. Indirect modes, for example, are often used out of simple politeness. But direct modes of communication are seen most often in cultures such as the United States, whereas indirect modes are seen in many Asian cultures, such as Japan, Korea, and China. The following dialogue takes place between a young couple who have been dating for a short time. The man is a U.S. student, and the woman is from an Asian culture. Note the misunderstanding that results as a consequence of the use of direct and indirect modes of communication.[40]

In all likelihood, Jim is not going to get much of a direct answer from Michiko. She continues throughout the dialogue to use rather general answers to Jim's very specific and direct questions about her feelings toward the United States. Michiko might believe that Jim is being far too direct and invading her privacy. Besides, the fact that she has traveled halfway around the world should be proof of her desire to be here, right? There must be something about the United States that attracted her. Michiko cannot possibly say something critical about the United States because she would lose face, as would Jim, being a native. She relies on imprecise and indefinite answers.

Jim:	Ya know, Michiko, I really enjoy the time we spend together. I really like you. I've been so happy since we met.
Michiko:	Hmmm, thank you.
Jim:	I mean, I feel like I've learned so much about you and your culture.
Michiko:	Yeah . . .
Jim:	I'm so glad you came to the United States. Do you like it here? What is your favorite thing about us?
Michiko:	Well, it's pretty big. It's nice here.
Jim:	What do you think about Americans?
Michiko:	I don't know. Maybe I haven't been here long enough to know.
Jim:	You must think something!
Michiko:	Well, I'd probably have to think about it.
Jim:	I mean, do you like us?
Michiko:	Well, I don't really know that many Americans yet.

Elaborate, Exacting, and Succinct Styles

According to Gudykunst and Ting-Toomey, the elaborate, exacting, and succinct communication styles deal with the quantity or volume of talk preferred across cultural groups. There are three levels: an elaborate style, which emphasizes flashy and embellished language; an exacting style, where persons say no more or less than is needed; and a succinct style, characterized by the use of concise statements, understatements, and even silence.[41] An elaborate style of communication can be seen in many Arab, Middle Eastern, and Afro-American cultures. Many Middle Easterners tend to use metaphors, similes, and adjectives in everyday conversation. African Americans, too, prefer personalized, often exaggerated, spontaneous styles of interaction. Thomas Kochman writes,

Stylistic self-expression within Black culture is characterized by dramatic self-conscious flair. . . . Black stylistic self-expression is also characterized by inventive (humorously ironic) exaggeration as in the self-promotion of demonstrably capable aspects of self ("If you've got it, flaunt it") or even by less demonstrably positive capabilities ("If you don't have it, flaunt it anyway"), which is all part of Afro-American boasting: the "making of one's noise." As Hollywood Henderson said, "I put a lot of pressure on myself to see if I can play up to my mouth." But exaggeration also serves to characterize (and neutralize the impact of) negative situations, such as poverty ("The soles on my shoes are so thin, I can step on a dime and tell you whether it's heads or tails").[42]

Generally, European Americans prefer an exacting style of interaction consistent with a "just-the-facts" mentality, popularized by the 1960s television series *Dragnet*. A succinct style can be found in Japan, China, and some Native American (e.g., Apache, Navajo) cultures. These cultures value the use of concise talk and silence. To the Chinese, silence is a means to maintain social control in a situation. Jessica Stowell points out that the Chinese, as a rule, do not value verbal skills. In fact, speaking skills in general are considered immoral. The skilled speaker may be labeled as "having a flattering mouth," "an oil mouth," or a "honey mouth." Chinese children are taught to be cautious about the use of words. The Chinese say, "One should use the eyes and ears, not the mouth," and "Disaster emanates from careless talk." The Chinese consider the wisest and most trustworthy person to be the one who talks the least but listens, watches, and restricts his or her verbal communication.[43]

The American Indian tribes of the Navajo and Apache also value the use of silence as a way to deal with ambiguity. Steven Pratt, an actively participating member of the Osage tribe, and Lawrence Weider, a professor of communication, argue,

> To the real Indian, it appears that White Americans who are strangers to each other may freely engage in conversation in such places as the supermarket check-out line. Commercial airlines provide an even more intense opportunity for easy conversation between strangers. Seatmates often disclose their life histories to each other. In the culture of real Indians, these are extraordinary and improper ways to behave, especially when both parties are real Indians. When real Indians who are strangers to one another pass each other in a public space, wait in line, occupy adjoining seats, and so forth, they take it that it is proper to remain silent and to not initiate conversation. Being silent at this point is a constituent part of the real Indian's mode of communicating with others, especially other Indians.[44]

The use of an elaborated, exacting, or succinct style is closely related to Hall's high- and low-context communication and Bernstein's classification of restricted and elaborated codes. Gudykunst and Kim contend that restricted codes resemble jargon or shorthand speech in which speakers are almost telegraphic. This seems to correlate with a succinct style. Conversely, Bernstein asserts that elaborated codes rely heavily on verbal amplification for message transmission, with much less emphasis on the nonverbal code or environmental cues. This seems to correspond with the elaborate style.[45]

Personal and Contextual Styles

Gudykunst and Ting-Toomey define the personal style of communication as one that amplifies the individual identity of the speaker. Such a style stresses and underscores "personhood."

This style is often seen in individualistic cultures. A personal style relies on the use of first-person pronouns in sentence construction. Person-oriented language stresses informality and symmetrical power relationships. For example, English has only one form for the second person—that is, *you*. Regardless of whether they are speaking to someone of higher, equal, or lower status, English speakers use the same form for the second person. For example, if we were to meet the president of the United States, we might say, "It's nice to meet you." If we were to meet a new colleague or neighbor, we could say, "It's nice to meet you." If we were to meet our new colleague's first-grade daughter, we might say, "It's nice to meet you." The personal nature of our language does not distinguish status or rank via pronoun usage.

Moreover, in the United States, we tend to treat one another with informality and forgo the use of formal titles and strict manners. These cultural attitudes are reflected in our personal verbal style. As John Condon notes, two of the most frequently used words in English are *I* and *you*. He points out that for many Americans, it is difficult to talk for any length of time without using pronouns. In Japan, however, there are at least 10 words that might be equivalent to the English *I*.[46] In addition, Craig Storti notes that the Thai language has 12 forms of the pronoun *you*.[47]

On the other hand, assert Gudykunst and Ting-Toomey, a **contextual style** accentuates and highlights one's role identity and status. In cultures that employ a contextual style, the social context dictates word choice, especially personal pronouns. For example, when using the Thai language, one must look carefully at the situation, including the status and intimacy levels among the interactants, to decide what form of pronoun to use. Unlike a personal style, where pronoun usage is consistent across situations, contextual-style language varies across situations. The correct pronoun form is contingent on the context. Storti notes that German and French, for example, have familiar and formal forms of the pronoun *you*. The decision to use one form over another is based on the context of the interactants.[48] To use the familiar form with an unfamiliar interactant would be inappropriate. Germans are well known for their formality and strict use of titles, even among friends. German neighbors who have known each other for years still use the title "Herr" when addressing each other.

June Ock Yum maintains that a fundamental function of many East Asian languages is to recognize the social status, degree of intimacy, age, and sex of the interactants. These types of demographics will influence the degree of formality and the use of honorifics in the language code. Many Asian languages highlight status differences and asymmetrical power relationships. According to Samuel Martin, Korean and Japanese have what he calls two "axes of distinction"—the axis of address and the axis of reference. In the axis of address, the speaker carefully chooses language based on the status role of the other speaker. With the axis of reference, the speaker chooses language based on the other speaker's attitude about the subject of communication. Yum provides the example of the phrase "to eat." In English, "to eat" is "to eat" regardless of with whom one is eating (e.g., a friend, a parent, or the president of the United States). In Korean, however, there are at least three different ways to say "to eat," depending on the role of the speakers: *muka-da* (plain), *du-shin-da* (polite), and *chap-soo-shin-da* (honorific).[49]

The Japanese use a contextual style, and their language includes an elaborate system of honorifics. Honorifics are linguistic forms that communicate respect according to one's rank and the rank of those to whom one is speaking. Honorifics take the form of suffixes to nouns, adjectives, and verbs. For example, the informal form of the verb "to go," *iku,* is used when speaking to someone with whom one is intimate. If the person with whom one is interacting is a stranger or is older, then the politeness marker, *-masu*, appears, as in *iki-masu*. If the person with whom one is interacting is socially superior, then the honorific form of the verb "to go," *irassyaru*, is used.[50] Hooker notes that one cannot learn to speak Japanese without learning the honorific language forms, including syntax and grammar, for defining one's social status. According to Hooker, through most of Japanese history, learning the language meant experiencing and reinforcing the social differences that ordered society. He points out that there was a time in Japanese history when one literally could not construct a sentence without defining one's own social class and the social class of the person to whom one was speaking. In addition, Hooker notes, Japanese honorifics are a gendered system. Women's speech tends to be filled with honorifics and a sense of deference (i.e., honor, regard) to males.[51]

AN INTERCULTURAL CONVERSATION: PERSONAL AND CONTEXTUAL SPEAKING

In the following interaction, Jim is a student at a local university. He was born and raised in the United States. Akira is an exchange student from Japan. Jim and Akira are eating dinner together in a local restaurant. They have known each other for only a short time. Not only is Jim's style of communication overtly personal, but he's also quite direct.

Jim: Hey, buddy, what do you think of this American restaurant? I really like it.

Akira: Yes, Mr. Jim. This is very nice.

Jim: I always prefer restaurants like this, kinda casual but good food. I come here a lot. Do you go out to eat much in Japan?

Akira: Japanese restaurants are nice, too.

Jim: Yeah, but do you go out to eat much?

Akira: Sure, Japanese people like restaurants.

Jim: Whenever I come here, I usually order the same thing. It's kinda funny, but since I like it, I figure I may as well eat it. I have a lot of friends that do that.

Akira: Sure.

Jim: Yeah, I was thinking the other day that since the dorm food sucks so bad, I should go out to eat more often.

Akira: Yes, that's a good idea.

Jim is trying to involve Akira in the conversation by relating to him his personal experiences and preferences. Jim uses the first person "I" no fewer than 11 times and even refers to Akira as "buddy." Akira never refers to himself in the first person. Akira generally defers to Jim and says little, even addressing him as "Mr. Jim." As a foreigner, Akira probably sees Jim as socially superior and uses a formal title. Moreover, rather than talking about his personal preferences, Akira mentions that Japanese people enjoy restaurants.

Instrumental and Affective Styles

Gudykunst and Ting-Toomey define an instrumental style as sender based and goal–outcome based. The instrumental speaker uses communication to achieve some goal or outcome. Instrumental messages often are constructed to persuade and influence others and to maintain one's face. Yum says that users of the instrumental style believe that communication should end after some goal has been attained and outcomes can be assessed, such as friends gained, opponents defeated, or some form of self-fulfillment reached.[52] Julia Wood reports that men in the United States engage in an instrumental style more often than do U.S. women. U.S. women, on the other hand, use collaborative and cooperative talk.[53]

An affective style of communication is receiver and process oriented. The affective speaker is concerned not so much with the outcome of the communication but with the process. In cultures where an instrumental style predominates, the burden of understanding often rests with the speaker. The speaker carefully chooses and organizes his or her messages to be understood by the audience. In cultures where an affective style is used, the responsibility of understanding rests with both parties—that is, the speaker and the listener. Affective speakers carefully watch for the reactions of their listeners. Verbal expressions are insinuated and quite subtle. Affective speakers often operate on an intuitive sense and are nonverbally expressive. Hall and Hall assert that before getting down to business, the French prefer to establish a mood or a feeling, and a certain amount of intuition is required on the listener's part to discover the meaning.[54] Condon argues that where Americans like to talk about themselves, Japanese talk about each other. The Japanese are very conscious of the other person with whom they are interacting; it is an interdependent concern, unlike the American concern for independence. Condon notes,

> The difference in orientations is apparent when friends who have not seen each other for a while happen to meet. Americans are likely to ask about each other and tell each other about where they have been or what they have been doing. Who speaks first does not seem to matter very much. When Japanese friends meet, one is likely to begin by thanking the other for some previous favor or gift or letter that was sent. Most often, a reference to the last time they were together is part of this greeting. Thus, they re-establish a particular continuing relationship.[55]

Samuel Martin contends that the Japanese language has a complex array of polite formulas, or stock phrases, that have a leveling effect in just about any social situation. Martin argues that foreigners traveling in Japan can increase their effectiveness if they memorize these 20 or 30 polite formulas. Martin states that, to some extent, Japanese conversation is all formula and no content.[56] The affective style of the Japanese is perhaps best reflected in Haiku poetry. Haiku is a short form of poetry popular in Japan. Haiku poems always deal with some aspect of the seasons. Japanese Haiku poets are required to communicate a vivid impression using only 17 Japanese characters. The Haiku poem is concise while simultaneously communicating a deep spiritual understanding. From the reader of Haiku, much effort is required. One of the most popular Haiku poets was Basho, who lived some 300 years ago but whose poetry is still used as the definitive model for contemporary Haiku poets.

Waterjar cracks:

I lie awake

This icy night.

Lightning:

Heron's cry

Stabs the darkness

Sick on a journey:

Over parched fields

Dreams wander on.[57]

Chinese communication is also said to be more affective than instrumental. Carl Becker argues that Chinese people reject debate and argumentation during the process of communication.[58] Yum believes that Confucianism has a large impact on Chinese communication and asserts that the Chinese emphasize a process and receiver orientation. According to Confucian philosophy, the primary function of communication is to initiate, develop, and maintain social relationships. Yum states that in China, it is important to engage in small talk before initiating business and to communicate personalized information. The Chinese view communication as a never-ending interpretive process. During a conversation, Chinese do not calculate what they give or receive. To do so, states Yum, would be to think about immediate personal profits, which conflicts with the Confucian notion of mutual faithfulness. The Chinese are disgusted by purely businesslike transactions that are carefully planned and orchestrated.[59] Echoing Yum's seminal work, Stowell contends that Chinese is a listener-responsible language rather than a speaker-responsible language, as is English. In a listener-responsible language, the listener is required to construct the meaning based on his or her relationship with the speaker. The Chinese view communication as an interdependent process whereby both speaker and listener are active participants who, together, create meaning.[60]

An Intercultural Conversation: Instrumental and Affective Speaking

In the following dialogue, Mr. Benton has traveled to China to introduce Mr. Yeh-Ching to a new operating system. Mr. Benton is coming from a culture that values an instrumental style of speaking, so he wants to get right down to business. Mr. Yeh-Ching, on the other hand, wants to establish a relationship before discussing any business possibilities. Mr. Benton and Mr. Yeh-Ching are meeting at a local restaurant in Beijing.[61]

Chances are pretty good that Mr. Yeh-Ching will not buy Mr. Benton's new computer system. To an affective speaker such as Mr. Yeh-Ching, Mr. Benton is too concerned about his business and not concerned enough about the personal side of business—that is, relationships. Affective speakers are sometimes suspicious of people who refuse to get to know each other before striking a deal.

Mr. Benton:	Ah, Mr. Yeh-Ching. I've been waiting awhile. Had you forgotten about our meeting?
Mr. Yeh-Ching:	Good morning, Jerry. It is so nice to see you.
Mr. Benton:	Well . . . I'm glad you're finally here. I have all the material you need to see about the new computers we're installing. Here's our plan . . .
Mr. Yeh-Ching:	Jerry, have you seen much of our city?
Mr. Benton:	Well . . . I really don't have much time for sightseeing. This isn't a vacation, ya know. Business, business, business. My boss expects me to close this deal today and be back in New York by the weekend. So, here's my idea for installation.
Mr. Yeh-Ching:	Our city is so beautiful and full of history. Please allow me to arrange a tour for you. We can go together.
Mr. Benton:	I'd love to, but ya know . . . business is business.
Mr. Yeh-Ching:	Can I arrange a tour for you? My staff would be delighted to get to meet you.
Mr. Benton:	No, thanks, but I'd like to show you something. Look at these new configurations for the computers we're installing. Now . . . notice that—
Mr. Yeh-Ching:	Here is a menu. This restaurant has some very interesting Chinese dishes that I would like for you to try.
Mr. Benton:	Oh, I grabbed a bite to eat at the Hilton. Go ahead and eat, though. I can show you the production schedule.

GENDERED LANGUAGE ACROSS CULTURES

The function of human language goes beyond communicating useful information. As we have seen above, the *style* of one's language communicates a variety of information about the interactants, including their social status and the context in which they are communicating (e.g., formal–informal). The members of any speech community conform to the prescribed rules of their specific language or dialect to establish their social identity. In addition, the language used by men and women differs considerably across most, if not all, cultures. And through language, one's sex and gender are communicated. As we saw in Chapter 6, sex roles vary dramatically across cultures. Recall also from Chapter 6 that sex roles prescribe with whom, about what, and how we communicate with others.

For example, in his classic research, Gerry Philipsen studied male communication styles in Teamsterville, a White, blue-collar, low-income neighborhood in the Near South Side of Chicago. Based on his observations, Philipsen found that presenting oneself as a *man* in Teamsterville requires an implicit understanding of the communication rules of the particular speech community of real men. *Real* men in Teamsterville engage in a variety of communicative strategies that signal their membership in the group. Specifically, they do not rely on speech as their primary mode of self-expression. Only in situations where the interactants are equal (e.g., two *men*) is speaking allowed. Here, speaking serves as a means for expressing solidarity.

In Teamsterville, speaking is restricted when the communicants are unequal, as in cases where a man is interacting with someone of higher or lower status. Moreover, speaking is discouraged when a man must assert his power or influence over others, as in cases where he is responding to an insult to himself or his wife/girlfriend, disciplining children, or asserting himself in political or economic discussions. In these types of contexts, nonverbal communication is preferred. In some cases, men may be silent, but in others, they may react physically, as when responding to an insult. Keep in mind that this research was conducted in a specific geographical location near Chicago and probably is not generalizable to all men across the United States.[62]

Perhaps more so than in the United States, sex roles in Japan are clearly defined and are reflected in the communication of Japanese men and women. Japanese language (spoken by 130 million people) employs an extensive system of politeness, or what are called *honorifics*. Moreover, how Japanese is used in daily interaction differs considerably between men and women. The Japanese speaker must be mindful of his or her place in the Japanese social hierarchy, as well as that of the person with whom he or she is interacting. The specific verbs, adjectives, pronouns, and nouns one uses reflect the status of both the source and the receiver of the message. And all these vary considerably according to the sex of the source and receiver. According to Hillary Brass, Japanese Women's Language (JWL) is a clearly defined subset of Japanese language. JWL, or *joseego*, is considered the ideal form of female communication. Men's language, or *danseego*, is employed by Japanese men. Brass maintains that *joseego* and *danseego* are considered opposites. She notes that while the verbal communication of men and women will vary in any culture, the differences between *joseego* and *danseego* are more explicit and definable than those in most cultures. Brass also points out that verbal communication is closely linked to attractiveness in Japanese culture, especially for Japanese women. Thus, if a Japanese woman wants to be seen as physically attractive, she must engage the proper *joseego*. Youthfulness, too, is a desirable trait for Japanese women. Brass notes that by using a particular speech style, Japanese women may appear younger than they are. For example, she points out that by altering the use of the pronoun *shi* to *si*, a woman may sound as if she has a lisp and, thus, may sound younger. Brass asserts that in doing this, a woman "linguistically reduces her age." Brass also observes that sentence-final particles (i.e., words that occur at the end of a sentence and do not carry much meaning) are also used in JWL. Similar to tag questions in English (e.g., "That's a nice picture, don't you think?"), sentence-final particles tend to be used more by Japanese women than by Japanese men because, as Brass notes, women do not want to be perceived as opinionated or pushy. Brass points out that the sentence-final particles Japanese women tend to use are *wa, na no, yo ne,* and *no ne,* which require a response from the receiver, such as an agreement or confirmation. Japanese men will use *ze, yo, day o, da,* and *dane,* which are perceived as confident and final and typically do not require a response. Brass is careful to point out that some Japanese women do not use JWL, including proponents of women's liberation in Japan and many schoolgirls. But one group of Japanese speakers who use a variant of JWL called *one kotoba,* or older sister speech, includes members of the gay community of Japanese men.[63]

There are nearly 1 billion native speakers of Mandarin Chinese, more than for any other language on the planet. And, as for any other language, numerous linguistic differences exist between men and women. Marjorie Chan, a professor at the Ohio State University, has written extensively about Asian languages and specifically about Chinese language and dialects. Chan has observed that Chinese men and women differ in their pronunciation of standard

Mandarin Chinese. Women, she notes, are more sensitive than men to proper pronunciation because it may elevate their perceived status in the social hierarchy. Chan also notes that those who pay the least attention to proper pronunciation are younger Chinese men who hold positions of power in the Revolutionary Committees of the government. Chan speculates that these men may not need to worry about proper pronunciation given their positions of authority. Young schoolgirls, notes Chan, use what is called a feminine accent, where they use fronted palatals (i.e., consonants articulated with the body of the tongue raised against the middle part of the roof of the mouth) that are perceived to be more fragile and feminine than alveolars (i.e., consonants articulated with the tip of the tongue), which are perceived to be more masculine. Somewhat analogous to Japanese *joseego* discussed above is the *sajiao* style of speaking, which Chan describes as when Chinese women deliberately act like spoiled children to gain affection. Here, the speaker prolongs the pronunciation of vowels and softens the pronunciation of consonants. She notes that *sajiao* is used most often by children with their parents and by females with their male lovers. As in other cultures, Chan notes, the use of profanity is generally more acceptable among men than women and, in general, Chinese women are expected to be polite when they speak. Finally, as we have seen in both U.S. and Japanese culture, Chinese women are more likely than men to use sentence-final particles.[64]

Although estimates vary, about 600 million people speak Hindi as either a first or second language. Hindi is among the five most widely spoken languages in the world and is one of the official languages of India. Unlike many languages that classify words into three categories—masculine, feminine, and neuter—Hindi classifies words as either masculine or feminine. Anjalai Pande writes that the Hindi speaker has to identify his or her gender via specific suffixes and verbal auxiliaries. Pande notes that via the verbal code, Hindi speakers constantly communicate their gender identity. Analogous to what has been discussed above regarding Japanese and Chinese, Pande points out that women are pressured to use correct Hindi language, or what is called "better" language. According to Pande, a woman is expected to talk little, talk in a soft voice, and talk only when necessary, or perhaps not at all. Indian girls, notes Pande, are not to let their voices be heard, not to answer back, not to argue, and not to ask questions. One way this is accomplished linguistically is through the use of the pronoun *we* instead of *I*. This shifts the burden of responsibility to each interactant rather than the speaker.[65]

LANGUAGE AND ETHNIC IDENTITY

As we saw in Chapter 6, a fundamental way groups distinguish themselves from other groups, and thereby maintain their group identity, is through the language they speak. Within groups, status and hierarchy are recognized primarily through the use of language. Often, immigrant groups maintain their cultural heritage and identity by using their native language in their host culture and by teaching it to their children. Other immigrant groups may discourage the use of their native tongue so as to establish themselves as legitimate members of their new culture. Tim McNamara argues that immigrants entering a new culture may have to redefine their former social identity. In a study of Hebrew-speaking Israeli immigrants in Australia, McNamara found that as the Israeli immigrants changed their social identities, there was a corresponding change in their attitudes favoring English over Hebrew. The subjects in McNamara's study were considered *yordin,* a term with negative connotations referring to Israelis living abroad. Among other things, language identified the *yordin* as an out-group in Australia. As with most migrant languages used in Australia, Hebrew had low status. By learning and speaking English and teaching it to their children, the *yordin* were able, to some extent, to manage their negative social identities in their new host culture.[66]

Patricia SanAntonio conducted research on the language practices of an American computer company based in Japan. This particular company required its employees to speak English. Because they wanted to hire native Japanese persons with business expertise and English skills, however, they had trouble attracting high-quality candidates. To compete with other Japanese companies, they hired new college graduates who lacked proficient English skills. The result was that they had a workforce with a great deal of English-speaking variety; that is, some were quite competent, whereas others struggled considerably. Because English was so important to the company, the ability to speak English and to interact with American managers became a real source of power within the company. SanAntonio argued that within the Japanese context, language and identity are inextricably linked and that the ability and willingness of Japanese employees to use English identified them and their desire to integrate into the organization. SanAntonio concluded that the English-only policy created a boundary between the Japanese and Americans such that Japanese input was reduced. The policy essentially circumvented the Japanese hierarchy and allowed the Americans to maintain control within the organization.[67]

Intraculturally, the use of language can mark a person as a member of a particular group. In their analysis, Weider and Pratt argue that among some Native Americans, being silent is fundamental in the "real" Indian's mode of communicating. Moreover, the topic of one's "Indianness" is forbidden; "real" Indians do not discuss it. Real Indians do not engage in casual conversation or idle chitchat with other Indians. Weider and Pratt note that individuals who initiate small talk or openly discuss their Indianness are disqualified from the group of "real" Indians.[68]

Like any other group in the United States, African Americans are identified by their use of language, specifically Ebonics. Moreover, Blacks clearly identify themselves in terms of their use of Ebonics. Geneva Smitherman estimates that 80% to 90% of all African Americans use some form of Ebonics in some situations. Shirley Weber asserts that Ebonics is critical in fostering Black identity in the United States for at least three reasons. First, Weber maintains that because Blacks experience life differently than do other groups, they need a language to express their unique experience. Second, Black language bridges the economic, educational, and social gaps among Blacks. Weber states that Ebonics "is the language that binds, that creates community for blacks, so that the brother in the three-piece Brooks Brothers suit can go to the local corner where folks 'hang out' and say, 'hey blood, what it is?' and be one with them." Finally, Ebonics expresses a political statement that Blacks have not relinquished a vital part of themselves—that is, language—and that they can maintain control over at least one part of their lives.[69]

The controversy over Ebonics is both political and linguistic. Linguists disagree about whether Ebonics is a dialect (of English) or a language by itself. If a language is defined as a set of sounds combined with a set of rules for the purpose of communicating, then Ebonics should be considered a language. A **dialect** is typically thought of as a regional variety, or subset, of a language. Dialects are distinguished from other regional varieties by their variations in vocabulary, grammar, and pronunciation. As Smitherman notes, the labels "language" and "dialect" are equally respectable among linguists. The term *dialect* has, however, taken on negative connotations among the public.[70] Politically, the debate centers on the appropriateness of Ebonics in various social settings, such as schools. Politically, some factions argue that Ebonics is appropriate and should be taught in schools. For example, in December 1996, the Oakland, California School Board wrote,

> BE IT RESOLVED that the Board of Education officially recognizes the existence, and the cultural and historic bases of West and Niger-Congo African Language Systems, and each language as the predominantly primary language of African-American students. . . . BE IT FURTHER RESOLVED that the Superintendent in conjunction with her staff shall immediately devise and implement the best possible academic program for imparting instruction to African-American students in their primary language for the combined purposes of maintaining the legitimacy and richness of . . . "Ebonics" . . . and to facilitate their acquisition and mastery of English language skills.[71]

The resolution prompted an anti-Ebonics movement spearheaded by Peter King (New York), member of the U.S. House of Representatives. On January 9, 1997, King introduced House Resolution 28, which read, in part, that no federal funds should be used to pay for or support any program that is based on the premise that Ebonics is a legitimate language.[72] Linguistic and political arguments notwithstanding, Ebonics is clearly a medium of expression for many African Americans. Ebonics not only serves as a vehicle for communication but also fosters a sense of identity and community among those who speak it.

Do You Speak American?

In 2004, celebrated award-winning author and journalist Robert MacNeil traveled across the United States exploring how the English language is used throughout the various regions of the country. MacNeil wanted to answer the question, What does it mean to "speak American"? Throughout his travels, MacNeil discovered that the English used in the United States differs considerably from region to region, among ethnic and social groups, and by age and gender. In addition, MacNeil found that many people shift from one version of English to another depending on the person with whom they are speaking (see Figures 7.5a and 7.5b).[73]

Linguists often argue over the term Standard English—that is, the variety of English spoken in the United States that is considered correct. Some linguists argue that there is a right and a wrong way to speak English and that certain correct forms should always be used. But most linguists also recognize that different varieties of English exist in different geographical areas. As we move from region to region across the country, we can hear differences in pronunciation, grammatical structures, vocabulary, and pitch. Most people think of such differences as *accents*; hence, "Southern accent" is used to describe the speech of people who live in the Southern United States. Another term often used by sociolinguists (scholars who study language as it is used in various social contexts) is *dialect*—that is, a language variety associated with a particular region or social group. An accent or dialect should not be confused with *slang* or *jargon*. Slang refers to words or expressions typically used in informal communication. Slang words often do not last long, and other slang replaces them. Jargon refers to the specialized or technical vocabulary used by persons in the same group, such as doctors, lawyers, computer specialists, and so on. Many sociolinguists now use the term language variety to refer to the way a particular group of people uses language.[74]

Figure 7.5a & b   American dialects can be found in many different areas of pop culture. The Car Talk guys (from an NPR radio show) speak in a distinct "R-less" dialect (you can hear a portion of their show at http://cartalk.com). The movie *Clueless* focuses on a group of rich kids in Los Angeles who speak in the Valley Girl dialect.

a.

b.

Speakers of a particular dialect often believe that their language variety is the best, correct, and standard way to speak. They may even believe that their language variety is so standard that it is not even considered a dialect. Noted sociolinguist Walt Wolfram argues that everyone speaks some form of dialect. He maintains that it is not possible to speak a language without speaking a dialect of that language. Moreover, he dispels the myth that dialects result from unsuccessful attempts of people to speak the correct form of a language. Instead, Wolfram contends that speakers acquire their dialect by adopting the speech features of those around them, not by failing in their attempts to adopt standard language features. Dialects, like all language systems, are systematic and regular, and they function as any standard language variety.[75]

Estimating the number of dialects in the United States is difficult. Some linguists argue that there may be as few as three, whereas others contend that there are as many as 25 dialects in the United States (which would include Ebonics, Spanglish, and Chicano English, discussed in Chapter 3). Still others maintain that it is impossible to count the possible language varieties in the United States. A few U.S. dialects are discussed below.

Appalachian English

Appalachian English is spoken by people in the Appalachian Mountains from Eastern Pennsylvania to North Carolina. Perhaps the most distinctive feature of this dialect is *a-prefixing*—that is, putting an *a* sound before words that end in -*ing*, as in "I was a-slippin' and a-slidin' on the ice" or "What are you a-doin' here so early?" The a-prefix can occur only with verb complements, not with -*ing* participles that function as nouns. Thus, the sentence "The man went a-sailin'" is appropriate, but the sentence "The man likes a-sailin'" is not.[76]

Cajun English

Cajun English, sometimes called Linguistic Gumbo, is the term that describes the variety of French spoken in South Louisiana. It originates from the language spoken by the French and Acadian people who settled in Louisiana in the 17th century. Five features distinguish Cajun English: vowel pronunciation, stress changes, the lack of the /th/ phonemes, non-aspiration of /p/, /t/, and /k/, and lexical differences. Cajuns talk extremely fast, their vowels are clipped, and French terms abound in their speech.[77]

R-Less or R-Dropping Dialects

Regional differences in how the *r* sound is pronounced distinguish one dialect from another. The *r* sound before a vowel (e.g., *red, bread*) is pronounced much the same way across the United States. But in many dialects of the East Coast (e.g., Boston, New York), the *r* sound before a consonant is dropped and speakers of such dialects lengthen the preceding vowel sound, as in "paahk the caah."[78]

California English

In recent years, much attention has focused on the Valley Girl dialect phenomenon (e.g., "Gag me with a spoon!"). But California is diverse ethnically, with substantial Black and Hispanic populations; thus, the stereotypic Valley Girl dialect is spoken mostly by the White population. In such speech, the vowels of *hock* and *hawk, cot* and *caught,* are pronounced the same—so *awesome* rhymes with *possum*. Also, the vowels in *boot* and *boat* (called "back vowels" because they are pronounced in the back of the mouth) all have a tendency to move forward in the mouth; so the vowel in *dude* or *spoon* (as in "gag me with a . . .") sounds a little like the word *you,* or the vowel in *pure* or *cute*. Also, *boat* and *loan* often sound like *bewt* and *lewn*—or *eeeeuuw*.[79]

Texas English

Pamela Colloff reports on how linguistics professor Guy Bailey studies the regional dialects of Texas. According to Bailey, the Texas dialect began when two populations merged in Texas in the 1850s. Those who migrated from Louisiana, Alabama, and Mississippi brought with them their Lower South Dialect (i.e., drawl), while those from Tennessee and Kentucky brought with them the South Midland Dialect (i.e., twang). Bailey notes that many Texans use a flattened vowel sound that makes the word *night* sound like "naht," an indicator of the Texas twang. In an interesting observation, Bailey maintains that the Texas twang is actually expanding across many socioeconomic groups, particularly among young Texans. Bailey notes that phrases such as "y'all" and "fixin' to" are becoming trendy among young Texans. Another characteristic is that where a Southerner might say "muthuh an' fathuh," a Texan would say "muther an' father." Bailey also identifies the monophthong as the key indicator of a Texas accent. Merging the words *fire* and *far,* the vowel in both becomes a monophthong, as in "The house is on fahr" and "How fahr is it to the next town?" Another characteristic is the vowel merger. The vowel merger is a blending of vowel sounds so that words such as *win* and *when* sound alike, as do *cot* and *caught, feel* and *fill*.[80]

The Midwest Accent?

Many Midwesterners are under the illusion that they speak without an accent. They may even believe that they speak Standard American English. But most linguists understand that there is not a single, correct way to speak English. So, yes, even Midwesterners speak with an accent. Professor of English Matthew Gordon has written about the Midwestern accent. Many Midwesterners, he maintains, mispronounce words and fall victim to a phenomenon known as the "lower back vowel merger," or what many linguists call the *cot/caught* merger. Many Midwesterners pronounce the words *cot* and *caught* the same way, as they would pronounce the words *don* and *dawn* the same way. The vowel sound in *cot* and *don* is supposed to be pronounced with the tongue low and back in the mouth and with the lips spread open. The vowel sound in *caught* and *dawn* is supposed to involve a higher tongue position and a rounding of the lips. But many Midwesterners pronounce the words the same way.

Gordan cites a personal experience with the *don/dawn* merger. He recalls a time when an acquaintance was speaking about a friend named Dawn. The friend's grandmother was confused, asking why Dawn's parents had given her a boy's name (i.e., Don). Gordan also reports that a colleague from Michigan is sometimes asked why his son, Ian, has a girl's name. Apparently, some of his fellow Michiganders hear the name Ann, which they pronounce as "eeyan."[81]

Language has an immense impact on how individuals see themselves and others within any cultural milieu. Language is perhaps the major marker that people use to categorize and group others.

CHAPTER SUMMARY

All human languages are made up of a system of sounds, syntax, and semantics. The sole purpose of language is to communicate. Historically, linguists believed that language was tied to race and culture. Contemporary linguists have discounted that notion in favor of the idea that languages are essentially human and are not unique to any particular race or culture. As humans, regardless of culture, we are born with a universal grammar that allows us to learn the particular language of our culture. Any individual language is simply a subset of the universal grammar that is embedded in our brains. Considerable evidence shows that children (even deaf and blind children) acquire language in the same way at about the same time. Moreover, children are able to construct grammatically correct sentences without ever having been formally taught to do so. Language is a guide to social reality, helping people observe events around them and organize their thoughts. Moreover, language is so powerful that speakers can generate an infinite number of never-before-spoken sentences that are completely comprehensible by speakers of the same language. Although the universal grammar of all languages is similar, persons from different cultures use different styles of language, ranging from direct to indirect, personal to contextual, instrumental to affective, and elaborate to succinct. Direct–indirect style refers to how speakers reveal their intentions. The personal–contextual style refers to the degree to which speakers focus on themselves or their partners during communication. Instrumental styles are goal oriented, whereas affective styles are process oriented. Elaborate and succinct styles refer to the actual quantity or volume of talk that is preferred. These different styles probably reflect cultural values and beliefs.

 Visit the student study site at **www.sagepub.com/neuliep6e** for e-flashcards, web quizzes, web resources, and more.

DISCUSSION QUESTIONS

1. How does your language affect the way you think?

2. When you hear people speak a dialect of English different from yours, how do you feel about them?

3. Do you think your brand of English is better than others? Why or why not?

4. List five words you and your friends use that few other people would recognize.

5. List five of your favorite phrases that you use repeatedly every day. How do these phrases define you?

6. What is your least favorite U.S. dialect? Why?

ETHICS AND THE VERBAL CODE

1. In the United States, there is an English-only movement, also known as the Official English movement. Members of this organization advocate that only the English language should be used in official government operations and that English should be the official language in the United States. What do you think? Should English be the official language of the United States? Or should people be allowed to speak any language they wish? Some business owners across the country have signs in their store windows that read: "Only English spoken here." Does the linguistic variation we hear across the United States erode our country's identity?

2. There is a debate across the country as to whether Ebonics and Spanglish are valid languages. Some argue that they are legitimate languages. Others argue that they are slang or jargon used by groups too lazy to speak Standard English. What do you think?

KEY TERMS

affective style   265

contextual style   263

dialect   270

direct style   259

elaborate style   261

elaborated code   258

exacting style   261

generative grammar   255

indirect style   259

instrumental style   265

language variety   271

languages   248

morphemes   249

personal style   262

phonemes   249

restricted code   258

Standard English   271

succinct style   261

universal grammar   250

NOTES

1. Searchinger, G. (Director & Producer). (1996). *The Human Language Series: Part I: Colorless Green Ideas* [Motion picture]. Available from Ways of Knowing, Inc., 200 West 72nd Street, New York, NY 10023.

2. Salzmann, Z. (1993). *Language, Culture, and Society.* Boulder, CO: Westview.

3. Sapir, E. (1929). The Status of Linguistics as a Science. *Language, 5,* 207–214.

4. Salzmann, *Language, Culture, and Society.*

5. Whorf, B. (1940). Science and Linguistics. *Technology Review, 42,* 229–231, 247–248.

6. Whorf, B. (1940). Linguistics as an Exact Science. *Technology Review, 43,* 61–63, 80–83.

7. Salzmann, *Language, Culture, and Society.*

8. Pinker, S. (2007). *The Stuff of Thought: Language as a Window Into Human Nature.* New York: Viking.

9. Salzmann, *Language, Culture, and Society.*

10. Chomsky, N. (1965). *Aspects of the Theory of Syntax.* Cambridge: MIT Press; Goss, B., & O'Hair, D. (1988). *Communicating in Interpersonal Relationships.* New York: Macmillan.

11. Katzner, K. (1975). *Languages of the World.* New York: Funk & Wagnalls.

12. Tohsaku, C. K. (1997). *Japanese "Kanji."* Retrieved from http://edweb.sdsu.edu/courses/edtec670/cardboard/card/k/kanji.html

13. Goss & O'Hair, *Communicating in Interpersonal Relationships.*

14. Chomsky, N. (1957). *Syntactic Structures.* The Hague, Netherlands: Mouton.

15. Much of this discussion of language is based on interviews with Chomsky and other linguists in Searchinger, *The Human Language Series.*

16. Searchinger, *The Human Language Series.*

17. Ibid.

18. Gleitman, L. R. (1993). A Human Universal: The Capacity to Learn Language. *Modern Philology, 90,* 515–535.

19. Pinker, S. (1995). Language Acquisition. In L. R. Gleitman & M. Liberman (Eds.), *An Invitation to Cognitive Science: Vol. 1: Language* (2nd ed.). Cambridge: MIT Press.

20. Gleitman, A Human Universal.

21. Searchinger, *The Human Language Series.*

22. Pinker, Language Acquisition. Some of these examples are from an interview with Pinker in Searchinger, *The Human Language Series.*

23. Heath, J. (1997). *Super-Quick Overview of Characteristics of the Japanese Language.* Retrieved from http://stripe.colorado.edu/-jheath/faq4.html

24. Katzner, *Languages of the World.*

25. Kulick, D. (1992). *Language Shift and Cultural Reproduction: Socialization, Self, and Syncretism in a Papua New Guinean Village.* Cambridge, UK: Cambridge University Press; Searchinger, *The Human Language Series.*

26. Ibid.

27. Salzmann, *Language, Culture, and Society.*

28. Searchinger, *The Human Language Series.*

29. Ibid.

30. Barrett, G. (2009). Among the New Words. *American Speech, 84*(2), 192–210; Zimmer, B., & Carson, C. E. (2012). Among the New Words. *American Speech, 87*(1), 89–106.

31. Bernstein, B. (1966). Elaborated and Restricted Codes: Their Social Origins and Some Consequences. In A. G. Smith (Ed.), *Communication and Culture* (pp. 427–441). New York: Holt, Rinehart & Winston.

32. Ibid.

33. Ibid.

34. Gudykunst, W. B., & Ting-Toomey, S. (1988). Verbal Communication Styles. In W. B. Gudykunst & S. Ting-Toomey (Eds.), *Culture and Interpersonal Communication* (pp. 99–115). Newbury Park, CA: Sage.

35. Ibid.

36. Fedarko, K. (1995). Man of Israel: Rabin's Stirring Life Story Marks Out the Mileposts in the History of His Nation. *Time, 146*(20), 68–72.

37. Hall, E. T., & Hall, M. R. (1990). *Understanding Cultural Differences: Germans, French, and Americans.* Yarmouth, ME: Intercultural Press.

38. Iwao, S. (1993). *The Japanese Woman: Traditional Image and Changing Reality.* Cambridge, MA: Harvard University Press.

39. Hall & Hall, *Understanding Cultural Differences.*

40. This dialogue is loosely adapted from Storti, C. (1994). *Cross-Cultural Dialogues: 74 Brief Encounters With Cultural Difference.* Yarmouth, ME: Intercultural Press.

41. Gudykunst & Ting-Toomey, Verbal Communication Styles.

42. Kochman, T. (1990). Cultural Pluralism: Black and White Styles. In D. Carbaugh (Ed.), *Cultural Communication and Intercultural Contact* (pp. 219–224). Hillsdale, NJ: Erlbaum.

43. Stowell, J. (1996). *The Changing Face of Chinese Communication: A Synthesis of Interpersonal Communication Concepts.* Paper presented at the annual convention of the Speech Communication Association, San Diego, CA.

44. Weider, D. L., & Pratt, S. (1990). On Being a Recognizable Indian Among Indians. In D. Carbaugh (Ed.), *Cultural Communication and Intercultural Contact* (pp. 45–64). Hillsdale, NJ: Erlbaum.

45. Bernstein, Elaborated and Restricted Codes; Gudykunst, W. B., & Kim, Y. Y. (1997). *Communicating With Strangers: An Approach to Intercultural Communication.* New York: McGraw-Hill.

46. Condon, J. C. (1984). *With Respect to the Japanese: A Guide for Americans.* Yarmouth, ME: Intercultural Press; Gudykunst & Ting-Toomey, *Culture and Interpersonal Communication.*

47. Storti, *Cross-Cultural Dialogues.*

48. Ibid.

49. Martin, S. E. (1964). Speech Levels in Japan and Korea. In D. Hymes (Ed.), *Language in Culture and Society* (pp. 407–415). New York: Harper & Row; Yum, J. O. (1997). The Impact of Confucianism on Interpersonal Relationships and Communication Patterns in East Asia. In L. A. Samovar & R. E. Porter (Eds.), *Intercultural Communication: A Reader* (pp. 78–88). Belmont, CA: Wadsworth.

50. Miyagawa, S. (1995). *The Japanese Language.* Massachusetts Institute of Technology. Retrieved from http://web.mit.edu/jpnet/articles/JapaneseLanguage.html

51. Hooker, R. (1999). *The Japanese Language.* Retrieved from www.wsu.edu:8080/~dee/ANCJAPAN/language.htm

52. Gudykunst & Ting-Toomey, *Verbal Communication Styles;* Yum, The Impact of Confucianism on Interpersonal Relationships and Communication Patterns in East Asia.

53. Wood, J. T. (2011). *Gendered Lives: Communication, Gender, and Culture* (9th ed.). Boston: Wadsworth.

54. Hall & Hall, *Understanding Cultural Differences.*

55. Condon, *With Respect to the Japanese,* p. 50.

56. Martin, Speech Levels in Japan and Korea.

57. *A Haiku Homepage.* Retrieved from http://www.dmu.ac.uk/-pkal/haiku.html; *The Shiki Internet Haiku Salon.* Retrieved from http://www.cc.matsuyama-u.ac.jp/~shiki/

58. Becker, C. B. (1986). Reasons for the Lack of Argumentation and Debate in the Far East. *International Journal of Intercultural Relations, 10,* 75–92.

59. Yum, The Impact of Confucianism on Interpersonal Relationships and Communication Patterns in East Asia.

60. Lustig, M. W., & Koester, J. (2013). *Intercultural Competence: Interpersonal Communication Across Cultures* (7th ed.). New York: Pearson; Stowell, *The Changing Face of Chinese Communication.*

61. This dialogue is adapted from Copeland, L. (Producer). (1983). *Managing the Overseas Assignment* [Motion picture]. San Francisco: Copeland Griggs Productions.

62. Philipsen, G. (1990). Speaking "Like a Man" in Teamsterville: Culture Patterns of Role Enactment in an Urban Neighborhood. In D. Carbaugh (Ed.), *Cultural Communication and Intercultural Contact* (pp. 11–20). Hillsdale, NJ: Erlbaum, p. 17.

63. Brass, H. (2005–2006). Japanese Women's Language: Changing Language, Changing Roles. *Journal of Undergraduate Research.* The University of Notre Dame.

64. Chan, M. K. M. (1998). Gendered Differences in the Chinese Language: A Preliminary Report. In H. Lin (Ed.), *Proceedings of the Ninth North American Conference on Chinese Linguistics* (Vol. 2, pp. 35–52). Los Angeles: GSIL, University of California.

65. Pande, A. (2004). Undoing Gender Stereotypes in Hindi. *Linguistik Online, 21.*

66. McNamara, T. F. (1988). Language and Social Identity: Israelis Abroad. In W. B. Gudykunst (Ed.), *Language and Ethnic Identity* (pp. 59–72). Clevedon, UK: Multilingual Matters.

67. SanAntonio, P. M. (1988). Social Mobility and Language Use in an American Company in Japan. In W. B. Gudykunst (Ed.), *Language and Ethnic Identity* (pp. 35–44). Clevedon, UK: Multilingual Matters.

68. Weider & Pratt, On Being a Recognizable Indian Among Indians.

69. Smitherman, G. (2000). *Talkin That Talk: Language, Culture, and Education in African America.* New York: Routledge; Weber, S. (1994). The Need to Be: The Socio-Cultural Significance of Black Language. In L. A. Samovar & R. E. Porter (Eds.), *Intercultural Communication: A Reader* (pp. 221–226). Belmont, CA: Wadsworth.

70. Smitherman, *Talkin That Talk.*

71. Excerpt taken from Smitherman, *Talkin That Talk,* p. xi.

72. Richardson, E. (1998). The Anti-Ebonics Movement: "Standard" English Only. *Journal of English Linguistics, 26,* 156–170.

73. MacNeil, R., & Cran, W. (2005). *Do You Speak American?* New York: Random House. Available from www.pbs.org/speak

74. MacNeil & Cran, *Do You Speak American?*; Wolfram, W., & Schilling-Estes, N. (2006). *American English: Dialects and Variation* (2nd ed.). Malden, MA: Blackwell.

75. Wolfram & Schilling-Estes, *American English.*

76. Montgomery, M. (2005). A-Prefixing in Appalachian English: Archaism or Innovation? *Do You Speak American?* Retrieved from www.pbs.org/speak/seatosea/americanvarieties/a-prefixing/background

77. Melancon, M. (2005). Stirring the Linguistic Gumbo. *Do You Speak American?* Retrieved from www.pbs.org/speak/seatosea/americanvarieties/cajun/

78. Fought, J. (2005). *Starting With the Coast.* Retrieved from http://www.pbs.org/speak/seatosea/americanvarieties/southern/

79. Eckert, P., & Mendoza-Denton, N. (2002). Getting Real in the Golden State. *Language Magazine, 1*(7), 29–30, 33–34.

80. MacNeil & Cran, *Do You Speak American?*; see also Colloff, P. (2003, June 1). Drawl or Nothin': Did You Think Our Beloved Texas Accent Was Disappearing? Not So Fast, Y'all. Turns Out It's Hotter Than a Two-Dollar Pistol. *Texas Monthly.*

81. Gordon, M. J. (2002). Straight Talking From the Heartland. *Language Magazine, 1*(5), 35–38.

CHAPTER 8

The Nonverbal Code

CHAPTER OBJECTIVES

After reading this chapter, you should be able to

1. define nonverbal communication,

2. compare and contrast verbal and nonverbal codes,

3. define kinesics and provide examples of kinesic behavior across cultures,

4. define occulesics and provide examples of occulesic behavior across cultures,

5. define paralanguage and provide cross-cultural examples of paralinguistic differences,

6. define proxemics and provide cross-cultural examples of proxemic differences,

7. define haptics and provide cross-cultural examples of haptic differences,

8. define olfactics and discuss how smell is perceived across cultures,

9. define chronemics and discuss how time is perceived across cultures, and

10. recount the fundamental assumptions of the nonverbal expectancy violations theory.

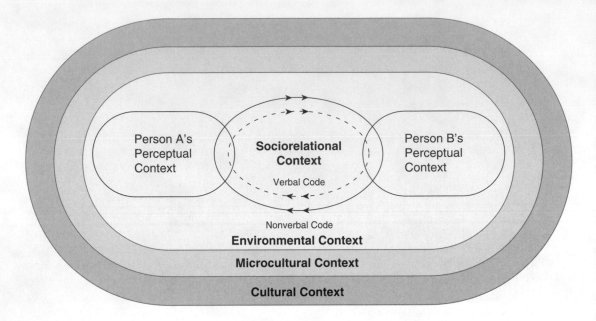

Speakers of every language accompany their words with nonverbal signals that serve to mark the structure of their utterances.

—Peter Farb[1]

Try to imagine what it would be like if you were unable to comprehend the meaning of a nonverbal gesture. Imagine that you have traveled to Japan for a study-abroad semester. You have been in Japan for only a short time. Today, you are out shopping with a Japanese acquaintance in downtown Tokyo. While looking over some expensive designer clothing items, you notice that your Japanese friend takes the index and middle fingers of his right hand, pretends to lick them, and then wipes his eyebrows. He does this several times. Although you suspect this is meaningful in some way, you have no idea what it signifies. Your uncertainty level skyrockets. Are you doing something wrong? Is he trying to tell you something? Is your acquaintance just weird? A native Japanese would not be anxious about this at all, because he or she would understand that your friend is simply trying to tell you that the expensive designer clothing items you are considering are fakes. Do not be too alarmed by what has just happened to you. Research shows that the longer you stay in Japan, or any other culture, the more your ability to recognize gestures—and, hence, your intercultural communication competence—will increase.[2]

When you interact with someone from a different culture, a challenge you will face is learning the implicit rules of interpersonal communication. Becoming interculturally competent requires that you acquire some understanding of the verbal language of the new culture, but even more important is that you become proficient in your host culture's nonverbal system of communication. And, like the verbal system of communication, the nonverbal system not only varies across cultures but also varies between men and women within any culture.

Many linguists, psychologists, and sociologists believe that human language evolved from a system of nonlinguistic (nonverbal) communication. To these scholars, language and communication are not the same. As humans, we possess a host of nonlinguistic ways to communicate with one another through the use of our hands, arms, faces, and personal space. When we combine verbal and nonverbal language, we create an intricate communication system through which humans come to know and understand one another.[3] All animals interact nonlinguistically—that is, nonverbally—through sight, sound, smell, or touch. Moths, for example, communicate by smell and color. Through smell, some species of male moths can detect female moths miles away. Elephants communicate with low-frequency sound waves undetectable to humans. Felines are well-known for rubbing their scent on (marking) people and objects to communicate their ownership of them. This kind of animal or nonlinguistic communication is probably innate and invariant within a particular species. Most scholars also recognize that a significant portion of our nonverbal behavior, such as the facial expressions accompanying certain emotions, is innate and varies little across cultures. Like verbal language, however, much of our nonverbal communication is learned and varies across cultures.

This chapter investigates nonverbal communication and how it differs across cultures. It begins with some definitions of nonverbal communication and a discussion of how verbal and nonverbal codes differ. The chapter then outlines eight channels of nonverbal communication and how cultures differ regarding their use. These channels include kinesics, occulesics, paralanguage, proxemics, haptics, olfactics, physical appearance and dress, and chronemics. The chapter closes with a discussion of nonverbal expectancy violations theory.

DEFINITIONS OF NONVERBAL COMMUNICATION

The study of nonverbal communication focuses on the messages people send to one another that do not contain words, such as messages sent through body motions; eye contact, touch, and vocal qualities; and the use of time, space, artifacts, dress, and even smell. Communication with the body, called kinesics, consists of the use of one's hands, arms, legs, and face to send messages. Haptics, or touch, is one of the most dynamic forms of nonverbal communication, as is occulesics, or eye contact. Paralanguage, or the use of the voice, refers to vocal characteristics such as volume, pitch, rate, and so forth. Through paralanguage, people communicate their emotional state, veracity, and sincerity. Most of us can identify when speakers are confident or nervous by paying attention to their vocal pitch, rate, and pace. Through chronemics, the use of time, people can communicate status and punctuality. We saw in Chapter 3 that cultures differ widely in their monochronic or polychronic orientation. By studying space, or proxemics, we can learn how people express intimacy and power. In the United States, for example, people tend to prefer maintaining an "arm's-length" distance from others during communication. Through smell, called olfactics, a person's ethnicity, social class, and status are communicated. Many cultures establish norms for acceptable and unacceptable scents associated with the human body. To other cultures, for example, people raised in the United States seem obsessed with deodorants, perfumes, soaps, and shampoos that mask natural body odors.

As stated in Chapter 1, intercultural communication is primarily a nonverbal act between people. During intercultural communication, verbal and nonverbal messages are sent simultaneously. Verbal communication represents the literal content of a message, whereas the nonverbal component communicates the style or how the message is to be interpreted. Hence, the nonverbal code often *complements, accents, substitutes, repeats,* or even *contradicts* the verbal message.[4] For example, a speaker might complement the verbal message "This dinner is delicious!" with a smile and increased vocal volume. Politicians often accent their speeches by pounding their fists on the podium. When asked how many minutes are left to complete an exam, the professor might simply raise five fingers to substitute for the words "5 minutes." Persons often repeat their verbal message "Yes" with affirmative head nodding.

Sometimes, however, a person's verbal and nonverbal messages contradict each other. When this happens, we usually believe the nonverbal message. For example, your roommate has been quiet and reserved for a couple of days. Finally, you ask what is wrong. Your roommate replies with a long sigh and says, "Oh . . . nothing." Which do you believe—the verbal or nonverbal message? Most people believe the nonverbal message because, unlike the verbal message, which requires conscious effort to encode, nonverbal messages are often less conscious and are therefore perceived as more honest. Psychologist David McNeill argues that our nonverbal behavior is partly unconscious and represents a sort of visual metaphor or analogue of conscious thought. He states that gestures and other body motions are primitive forms of speech. Whereas verbal language takes thought and puts it into linear digital form— that is, a sentence—gestures and body movements show the instantaneous thought as an analogue of itself.[5] This is why verbal communication is often called **digital communication** and nonverbal communication is called **analogic communication**. Because we have less control over our nonverbal behavior, it tends to be perceived as more honest than our verbal behavior.

In addition to complementing, accenting, substituting, repeating, and contradicting verbal communication, nonverbal communication also regulates and manages our conversations with others. Professors delivering lectures can monitor the reactions of their students through their eye contact, body posture, and other nonverbal behaviors (e.g., yawning), and adapt their lectures accordingly. Students who raise their hands are signaling the professor that they have questions or comments. Such behavior manages the flow of communication in the classroom. Individually, we can regulate the flow and pace of a conversation by engaging in direct eye contact, affirmative head nodding, and stance, thus signaling our conversational partner to continue or stop the communication.

THE RELATIONSHIP BETWEEN VERBAL AND NONVERBAL CODES

By comparing and contrasting the human verbal and nonverbal codes, many linguists have concluded that verbal language evolved from its nonlinguistic predecessor. Noam Chomsky argues that verbal language is an advanced and refined form of an inherited nonlinguistic (nonverbal) system.[6] A key distinction between the two is that the verbal language system is based primarily on symbols, whereas the nonverbal system is signal based. The difference between a symbol and a signal is that a *symbol* is an arbitrarily selected and *learned* stimulus representing something else. A *sign,* or *signal,* however, is a natural and constituent part of that which it represents. For example, when we hear thunder in the distance, it signals us that a storm is approaching. The thunder is a sign of a storm. But the thunder is also an intrinsic part of the storm. Sweating, for example, signals that one may be hot, but sweating is a natural part of being hot, as shivering is a natural part of being cold. Humans do not learn to sweat or shiver. Unlike signals, symbols have no natural relationship with that which they represent; therefore, they are arbitrary abstractions and must be learned. For example, the symbols *c-a-t* have no intrinsic connection with a feline animal. Speakers of any language learn to associate symbols with referents.

Another difference between the verbal and nonverbal code is that the nonverbal signal system is much more restrictive in sending capacity than the verbal code. For example, it is virtually impossible to communicate about the past or future through nonverbal communication. You might be able to signal a friend of impending danger by waving your hands, but you cannot warn your friend of danger that might occur tomorrow or recall danger that occurred yesterday with nonverbal signals. In addition, communication of negation is practically impossible with the nonverbal code system. Try communicating to a friend nonverbally that you are not going to the grocery store tomorrow. The same task is relatively easy through the linguistic system, however.[7]

Formal Versus Informal Code Systems

In Chapter 7, verbal language was defined as a systematic set of sounds combined with a set of rules for the sole purpose of communication. All verbal languages have a formal set of sounds, syntax, and semantics. The degree of formality of verbal language is not found in the nonverbal code, however. The alphabets of most verbal languages in the world represent about 40 sounds. No such formalized alphabet exists for nonverbal codes.

Different types of nonverbal behavior can be categorized, but these categories are much more loosely defined than in the verbal code. All verbal languages have a set of rules, called grammar or syntax, that prescribes how to combine the various sounds of the language into meaningful units, such as words and sentences. Although rules govern the use of nonverbal communication, a formal grammar or syntax does not exist. Nowhere is there a book or guide prescribing exactly what nonverbal behavior should be used when and where. No doubt, certain social contexts prescribe certain nonverbal behaviors, such as a handshake when greeting someone in the United States, but no systematic rule book on the same level of formality as an English grammar book exists for nonverbal communication. The rules for nonverbal communication are learned informally through socialization and vary considerably, even intraculturally.

Finally, the verbal code, when used with the correct syntax, takes on denotative meaning. When using verbal language, if we hear a word we do not understand, we can quickly consult a dictionary and it will define the word for us. The dictionary tells us what the language means. No such device exists for our nonverbal communication. If someone touches us or stands too close or engages in prolonged eye contact, we can only surmise the action's meaning. Popular psychology notwithstanding, we have no dictionary for nonverbal communication. To be sure, nonverbal communication is meaningful—perhaps even more so than verbal communication—but the denotative meaning of the nonverbal act must be inferred.[8]

CHANNELS OF NONVERBAL COMMUNICATION

The closest thing the nonverbal code has to an alphabet is a gross classification system of the various channels through which nonverbal communication is sent. These channels are kinesics, occulesics, paralanguage, proxemics, haptics, olfactics, physical appearance and dress, and chronemics. As we will see later in this chapter, some nonverbal expressions, particularly some facial expressions of emotion, seem to be universal, but much of our nonverbal behavior is learned and is therefore culturally unique.

Kinesics

Kinesics, or body movement, includes gestures, hand and arm movements, leg movements, facial expressions, eye gaze and blinking, and stance or posture. Although just about any part of the body can be used for communicating nonverbally, the face, hands, and arms are the primary kinesic channels through which nonverbal messages are sent. Relative to other body parts, they have a high sending capacity, especially the face. The most widely recognized system for classifying kinesic channels was developed by Paul Ekman and Wallace Friesen. Together, they organized kinesic behavior into five broad categories: (1) *emblems,* (2) *illustrators,* (3) *affect displays,* (4) *regulators,* and (5) *adaptors.* The meaning behind most of these kinesic behaviors varies across cultures.[9]

Emblems and Illustrators

Emblems are primarily (though not exclusively) hand gestures that have a direct literal verbal translation. Illustrators are typically hand and arm movements that accompany speech or function to accent or complement what is being said. In the United States, the hand gesture used to represent "peace" is an example of a widely recognized emblem. Emblems vary considerably across cultures. Pounding your fist on the podium during a speech is an example of an illustrator. Illustrators serve a *metacommunicative function*—that is, they are messages about messages. They are nonverbal messages that tell us how to interpret verbal messages. For example, shaking your fist at someone while expressing anger is an illustrator. For the most part, emblems and illustrators are not taught in school but are learned informally through a child's socialization in his or her culture. There is growing evidence that emblems and illustrators play an important role in language, cognitive development, and communicative development.

Michèle Guidetti and Elena Nicoladis assert that children use such gestures earlier in their communication development than they do words. While words eventually replace gestures as a child's preferred method of communication, children continue to gesture to reinforce and expand their verbal messages and even to replace them. Guidetti and Nicoladis maintain that gestures also offer insight into children's unspoken thoughts.[10] Related research indicates that by 6 months of age, babies in all cultures begin to use gestures to communicate to their parents. Joanna Blake and her colleagues point out that the change in a child's inventory of gestures from 9 to 14 months of age may provide the foundation for verbal language acquisition. Specifically, across cultures, there is a shift at 1 year of age in the types of gestures used by children toward gestural sharing of objects and information. The development of these communicative gestures supports the idea of the universality of language and may form a base for language acquisition across cultures.[11]

Dane Archer maintains that emblems and illustrators are at least 2,500 years old and can be seen in the ancient artwork of various cultures. Archer asserts that the systematic study of gestures began about 400 years ago, during Shakespeare's time. Although cultures differ widely in their use of emblems and illustrators, people in most cultures tend to use them for the same kinds of communication situations. For example, most cultures use emblems and illustrators during greetings and departures, to insult or to communicate obscenities to others, to indicate fight or flight, and to designate friendly or romantic relationships.[12]

Understanding the meanings of nonverbal gestures, especially emblems and illustrators, is a prerequisite to becoming a competent intercultural communicator. Gestures are a part of the lexicon of every culture. The well-known, oft-cited anthropologist Edward Sapir noted that gestures are a part of the secret code of all cultures that is "written nowhere, known by none, and understood by all."[13] In their recent research, Andrew Molinsky, Mary Anne Krabbenhoft, Nalini Ambady, and Y. Susan Choi argue that for individuals to function effectively across cultures, gestures, such as emblems, are a critical feature of interpersonal communication and the navigation of intercultural situations. Indeed, they write that natives of a particular culture have the ability to pilot seamlessly through the maze of the secret code of gestures. Yet nonnatives do not share this same luxury. In their study of native and nonnative members of U.S. culture, Molinsky and his colleagues found that an individual's length of stay in the culture is directly linked to gesture recognition accuracy and perceptions of intercultural communication accuracy. Specifically, nonnative persons in the United States were able to correctly recognize both valid and invalid (i.e., fake) gestures based on their length of stay in the United States. These same persons were perceived by others (i.e., U.S. natives) as more interculturally competent than nonnatives with shorter lengths of stay.[14]

Greeting rituals are an important component in any person's communicative repertoire. Knowing the greetings of different cultures when interacting outside your own culture is a first step toward developing intercultural communication competence. In high-context and collectivistic cultures, greeting rituals often differ according to one's social status. Moreover, in many cultures, men and women have different rules for how to greet someone. Bowing is the customary greeting in Korea and other Asian cultures, such as Japan and Vietnam. When Koreans greet elders, professors, persons of power, and persons of higher status, they bow lower and longer and divert eye contact. When businesspeople or friends meet, the bow is generally not as low and is quicker.[15] In Japan, the appropriate bow is made with the hands sliding down toward the knees, back and neck stiff, and eyes averted (see Figure 8.1). Japanese women should hold their hands flat against the body, with fingers clasped. Japanese men should hold their arms straight against their sides, palms against the legs. As in other Asian cultures, bowing recognizes social stratification. Social subordinates should bow lower and longer than their superiors. Persons of equal status match bows unless one is younger, in which case the younger person should bow a shade lower and longer. One's eyes should always be lowered.[16]

Figure 8.1   Bowing is the customary greeting in Japan.

In addition to bowing as a greeting, Japanese businesspeople typically exchange business cards. Double-sided business cards in Japanese and English are important because they demonstrate to your Japanese partners that you are serious and respect their culture. Typically, business cards are exchanged at the beginning of a meeting while standing. During the exchange, face your counterpart, bow slightly, and offer your card with the Japanese side pointing up, either with your right hand or both hands. The same procedures apply when receiving a card. Do not immediately put the card away; take the time to review it. Japanese tend to exchange business cards routinely.[17]

Microcultural groups in the United States have unique greetings as well. Moellendorf, Warsh, and Yoshimaru note that although most Amish generally will not initiate greetings with strangers or non-Amish persons, many Amish will respond to an outsider's wave by pointing an index finger toward the sky. The raised finger points to heaven and shows respect to the non-Amish while revealing the Amish people's strong religious beliefs.[18]

As in the United States, the handshake is a common gesture/illustrator during a greeting in most parts of developed Kenya. In this case, however, when greeting a person of higher status, such as a teacher, the person of lower status should take the left hand (the hand not being used in the handshake) and grasp his or her own right arm somewhere in the proximity of the forearm during the handshake. Close female friends may hug and kiss once on each cheek instead of shaking hands. In cross-gender greetings, men should wait for a woman to extend her hand first.[19]

According to Roger Axtell, the handshake is a common greeting in China as well. The traditional Chinese greeting is to cup one's hands (left over right), place them about chest high, and raise them while bowing.[20] According to Bishop, when greeting a holy man or priest, East Indians bow slightly or kneel with their hands pressed together palm to palm in front of their chests. This shows ultimate respect for the higher castes.[21]

Philip Harris, Robert Moran, and Sarah Moran report that when greeting male friends in Saudi Arabia, Saudi men kiss each other on both cheeks. They prefer to get very close during the greeting. Amongst Saudis, cross-gender greetings do not usually take place.[22] In traditional Sri Lankan greetings, the hands are placed together, palms touching at the chin level, and the person bows slightly and says, "*Namaste,*" which means, "I salute the Godlike qualities in you."[23]

Archer has observed that many cultures have emblems and illustrators for insulting others and for communicating obscenities. According to Archer, some cultures may have as many as six or seven obscene gestures, whereas some Northern European cultures, such as the Netherlands and Norway, do not have any native obscene gestures.[24] Giving someone "the finger" (making a fist with the hand and extending the middle finger upward) is a widely recognized obscene gesture in many parts of the world, including the United States, Mexico, and much of Europe. Forming a "V" with the index and middle fingers, with the palm facing in, is vulgar in Australia and England, communicating the same intent as "the finger." Creating the very same gesture with the palm facing out is completely acceptable, however, and represents "V for victory."

In the Ladino culture of Guatemala, a hand gesture called *la mano caliente* ("the hot hand") is equivalent to "the finger" and is created by placing the thumb between the first and middle fingers, then squeezing the hand to make a fist (see Figure 8.2). This gesture is considered obscene in other Central and South American cultures as well. In the Ladino culture, however, this gesture is very offensive, and anyone using it should be prepared to fight. If a person were to direct *la mano caliente* toward a military or police officer, the offender could expect to spend time in jail or do hard labor in the army.[25] The same hand gesture is used in Hmong culture to belittle or insult someone. In the Hmong culture, only males use this gesture.[26] In Jamaica, this gesture is called "the fig" and is considered obscene there also.[27]

In Peru, making a pistol gesture with each hand and then pointing the "pistols" at someone from about waist level is considered obscene and may provoke a fight (see Figure 8.3). In Iran, putting an open hand directly in front of and horizontal to one's face with the palm facing in and rubbing the hand down over the face from about the eyes to the chin, almost as if stroking a beard, is considered obscene and is equivalent to saying, "Fuck you" (see Figure 8.4). An obscene gesture recognized in many European cultures, especially France, is taking either hand and putting it palm down on the biceps of the opposite arm while quickly raising the opposite arm and making a fist, all in one fluid motion (see Figure 8.5). This gesture is basically equivalent to "the finger" and to the verbal designate "Up yours" or "Fuck you."[28]

Figure 8.2 In the Ladino culture of Guatemala, this gesture, called *la mano caliente*, is considered offensive.

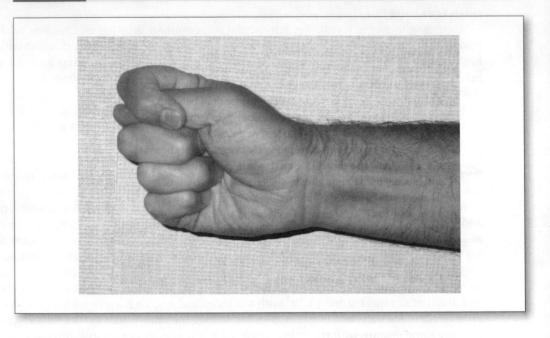

Figure 8.3 This hand gesture is highly offensive in Peru and could provoke a fight.

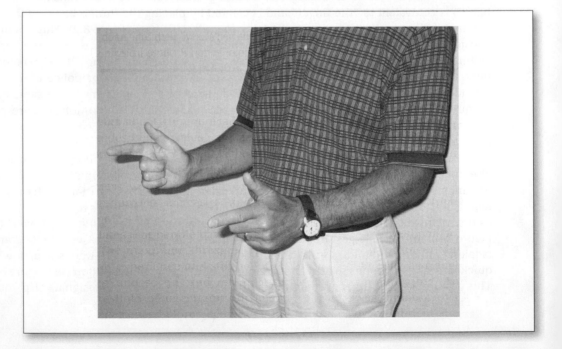

Figure 8.4 This is the Iranian equivalent of "the finger."

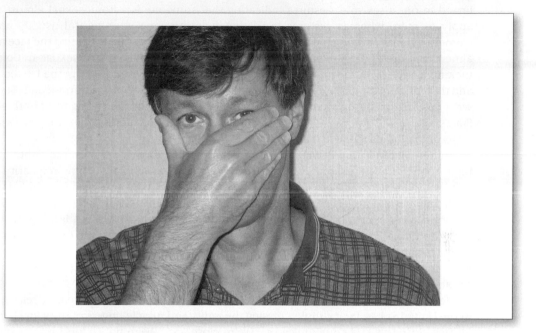

Figure 8.5 In some European cultures, this gesture is similar to "the finger."

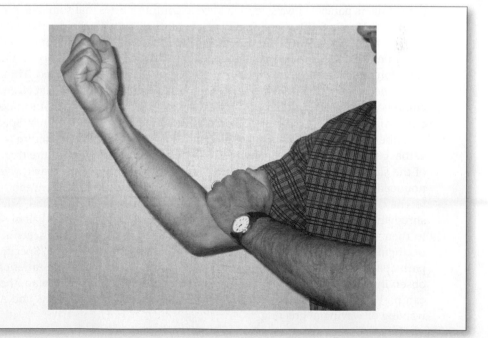

Archer points out that in addition to obscene emblems and illustrators, many cultures have gestures indicating that someone is homosexual or an adulterer. These gestures are strongly linked to one's sex role. Gestures indicating that someone is a homosexual almost always apply to men, whereas gestures indicating that someone is unfaithful usually apply to women. In Japan, putting the hand palm out against the cheek while turning the face away—almost as if pretending to tell a secret—is a sign that someone is homosexual. In Colombia, making a circle with the index finger and thumb (like the "OK" gesture in the United States) and then placing the circle around the nose indicates that someone is homosexual. The limp-wrist gesture, or slight variations of it, to signify homosexuality is recognized in the United States, China, Mexico, and Thailand, among other countries. In Uruguay, four or five quick claps of the hands indicate that a woman is a lesbian.[29]

Archer contends that gestures communicating "I am afraid" or "I want to fight you" (i.e., fight or flight) are uncommon in the United States but occur with some regularity across cultures. In Mexico and Nepal, placing a hand with the palm up and fingers extended upward while moving the fingers in and out, touching the thumb, is an invitation to fight. In Japan, putting the index fingers on the temples of the head, as if making horns, is a sign that one is angry. In China, pretending to pull up one's sleeve with the hand of the opposite arm designates that one is ready to fight.[30] In Hmong culture, clapping one's hands during an argument is a signal to the opponent that it is time to fight. The gesture is usually reserved for intense situations in which someone intends to physically harm someone else.[31]

Most cultures use emblems and illustrators to designate friendly or romantic relationships. In the United States, for example, crossing the index and middle fingers of the same hand designates closeness and communicates, "We're close" or "We're tight." In China, clasping the index fingers from each hand together signals love or romance. In Thailand, pressing the palms of both hands together and placing them against a cheek (as in a "Sleeping Beauty" gesture) is indicative of romance. Tapping the tips of the index fingers together in Japan or extending both index fingers parallel at waist level in Mexico communicates that someone is in love.[32]

Abigail Marsh and her colleagues point out that, as with their verbal code, people have nonverbal accents. Nonverbal accents are tendencies to display nonverbal behaviors in a certain manner, style, or fashion independent of the context. These styles are distinctions or variations in the degree to which the nonverbal gesture is expressed. Think, for example, about the number of different ways people walk or sit. Marsh notes that given all the possible combinations of all the gradations of all the muscle movements that can contribute to the expression of a gesture, there are probably myriad nonverbal accents. Specifically, Marsh describes nonverbal accents as the tendency for the people of one culture to express a nonverbal gesture in a way that is more similar to others' within the culture than to expressions of the same gesture in another culture. This is comparable to the way a given word is pronounced more similarly among members of a given culture than between members of different cultures. All sorts of nonverbal expressions may be accented, such as laughing, shrugging the shoulders, giving the finger, waving, saluting, and one's gait or style of walking. In their research, Marsh and her colleagues found that nonverbal accents helped people distinguish the nationality of other persons displaying the expression. Specifically, American participants accurately determined the nationality of Australian and American adults when observing their emotional expressions but not neutral expressions. In another study, American participants accurately determined the nationality of Australians and Americans seen walking or waving in greeting.[33]

Affect Displays: Facial Expressions of Emotion

Mark Knapp and Judith Hall point out that perhaps more than any other part of the body, the face has the highest nonverbal sending capacity. Through facial expressions, we can communicate our personality, open and close channels of communication, complement or qualify other nonverbal behavior, and, perhaps more than anything, communicate emotional states.[34]

Many linguists believe that our verbal language evolved from a system of nonlinguistic communication that was inherited from our animal past. If this is a valid assumption, then we should expect that some forms of our nonverbal communication are invariant across cultures. Current evidence suggests that some facial expressions of emotion, called affect displays, are universal. Paul Ekman alleges that humans can make more than 10,000 facial expressions and that 2,000 to 3,000 of them have to do with emotion. Ekman is careful to point out that by studying faces, we cannot tell what people are thinking, only what they are feeling about what they are thinking.[35] Initially, Ekman believed that affect displays, like so many other forms of communication, were the result of learning and were culturally unique. He originally agreed with sociologist Ray Birdwhistell, who wrote,

> Just as there are no universal words, no sound complexes, which carry the same meaning the world over, there are no body movements, facial expressions, or gestures which provoke identical responses the world over.[36]

In contrast to Birdwhistell, other scholars have hypothesized that because they were inherited, human nonverbal expressions should be similar, if not universal, the world over. The basis of this argument can be found in the writings of evolutionary scholar Charles Darwin, who wrote,

> We can thus also understand the fact that the young and the old of widely different races, both with man and animals, express the same state of mind by the same movements. . . . I have endeavoured to show in considerable detail that all the chief expressions exhibited by man are the same throughout the world. This fact is interesting, as it affords a new argument in favour of the several races being descended from a single parent-stock, which must have been almost completely human in structure, and to a large extent in mind, before the period at which the races diverged from each other.[37]

The late Harvard University professor Stephen Jay Gould, well-known for his stance on evolution, agreed with Darwin and argued that although universal facial expressions may have been functional for the animals from whom we inherited them, they are not functional for us today. Take, for example, a facial expression of anger, in which a person snarls, grits his or her teeth, and displays the canine teeth (see Figure 8.6a). This facial expression is remarkably similar to expressions of anger in several animal species (see Figure 8.6b). The fact that there is no need for us to display our teeth to express anger (we can simply say how angry we are) suggests that such a gesture must have been inherited.[38]

Ekman was determined to find whether certain elements of facial behavior are universal or culturally specific. He and his colleagues believed that there may be distinctive

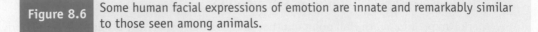

Figure 8.6   Some human facial expressions of emotion are innate and remarkably similar to those seen among animals.

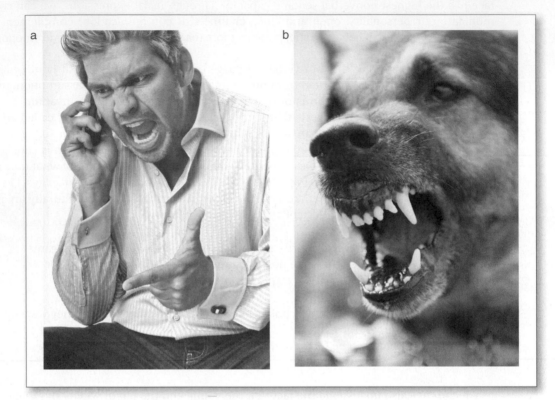

movements of the face for the primary emotions of surprise, fear, anger, disgust, happiness, and sadness that are probably universal. They further argued that while people from divergent cultures may express emotions similarly, what stimulates the emotion and the intensity with which it is expressed is probably culturally specific. In other words, although Germans and Japanese may express fear, surprise, anger, happiness, disgust, and sadness similarly in terms of muscular facial expressions, what *elicits* fear in Germans may be different from what elicits fear in Japanese. Moreover, cultures may differ in how they manage and regulate facial expressions of emotion, particularly in the presence of others. Ekman and Friesen (among others) have conducted numerous studies testing their hypotheses.[39]

In one study, Ekman, Friesen, and a number of their associates had more than 500 participants from 10 different countries look at slides of people expressing the six emotions of fear, anger, happiness, disgust, sadness, and surprise. The participants in the study came from a variety of cultures the world over: Estonia, Italy, Germany, Japan, Hong Kong, Scotland, Sumatra, Turkey, Greece, and the United States. Participants were shown photographs of Caucasians in posed facial expressions of the six different emotions, one at a time for 10 seconds each, and were instructed to indicate which of the six emotions was presented. The participants were also asked to rate the intensity of the presented emotion on a scale of 1 to 8.

The results showed that in an overwhelming number of trials, the emotion rated strongest by the largest number of observers in each culture was the predicted emotion. Where cultures differed was in their ratings of intensity of the emotion. Ekman reasoned that perhaps people judge a foreigner's expressions to be less intense than expressions shown by members of their own culture or that attributions of less intense emotions to foreigners might be due more to uncertainty about the emotional state of a person from an unfamiliar culture.

In interpreting these results, Carroll Izard claims that an evolutionary and biological relationship appears to exist between facial expressions and certain emotional states but that this connection can be uncoupled by the human capacity to exercise voluntary control over innate emotional expressions.[40] Although Ekman's studies provide evidence that facial expressions of primary emotions appear to be universal, other data suggest that cultural influences, such as individualism and collectivism, play a role in the expression of emotion. Walter Stephan, Cookie White Stephan, and Marylin Cabezas De Vargas found that persons from individualistic cultures express emotions affirming independent self-conceptions, such as self-actualized, capable, self-satisfied, and proud of oneself. They also found that persons from collectivistic cultures were less comfortable expressing negative emotions (e.g., indignant, annoyed, distrustful) than were persons from individualistic cultures.[41]

In related research, Ulrich Schimmack found that persons from individualistic cultures are better able to recognize happiness than are collectivists and that persons from high–uncertainty-avoidance cultures were less accurate in the recognition of facial expressions of fear and sadness than were persons with low uncertainty avoidance.[42] David Matsumoto alleges that high–uncertainty-avoidance cultures create social institutions to deal with fear and, therefore, recognize this emotion less well.[43] Along similar lines, Jeffery Pittam, Cynthia Gallois, Saburo Iwawaki, and Pieter Kroonenberg found that Australians were rated as more expressive by Japanese and that Japanese may conceptualize emotions as less intense.[44]

In her ongoing research with nonverbal accents—that is, subtle differences in the appearance of facial expressions of emotion across cultures—Marsh argues that while some facial expressions of emotion seem to be universal, it is reasonable to expect that there will be some "local" (i.e., regional or cultural) variations across cultures. She notes that while Ekman's research is convincing, there is still room for fine distinctions. In one study, Marsh and her colleagues had students judge photographs of Japanese nationals and Japanese Americans posing with emotional facial expressions and neutral facial expressions. With the emotional expressions, the posers' muscle movements were standardized to eliminate differences in expressions. Yet they found that participants were able to guess the nationality of the posers at above-chance levels and with greater accuracy than they judged the nationality of the same posers displaying neutral facial expressions. Marsh argues that these findings demonstrate that facial expressions of emotion include nonverbal accents that identify the expresser's nationality or culture. She maintains that cultural differences are intensified during emotional expressions. Finally, she maintains that her evidence suggests that extreme positions regarding the universality of emotional expressions are incomplete and need further investigation.[45]

Recent research conducted by Rachael Jack of the University of Glasgow also challenges Darwin's assumption that facial expressions of emotion are universal. In the study, Jack and her colleagues had 15 Western Caucasians and 15 East Asians (all living in Glasgow) view emotion-neutral animated faces that were then randomly altered on a computer screen into the six emotions of happiness, sadness, surprise, fear, disgust, and anger. The participants' judgments allowed Jack and her colleagues to identify the expressive facial features that participants associated with each emotion. Their results indicated that the East Asian participants relied on the eyes more to represent facial expressions, while the Western Caucasians relied on the eyebrows and mouth. Jack concludes that these culturally based distinctions could lead to misinterpreted signals about emotions during intercultural communication.[46]

Cross-Racial Recognition of Faces

Most of us have heard statements such as, "I can't tell one Japanese from another . . . they all look alike!" Although this statement smacks of racism and ignorance, scientific evidence indicates that own-race identifications tend to be more accurate, by as much as 10% to 15%, than cross-race identifications. Own-race identifications are those in which we identify someone of the same race as our own. Cross-race identifications are those in which we identify people from a race different from our own.[47] Legal scholars have expressed concern over own-race recognition bias in eyewitness identification for some time. In fact, Gustave Feingold argued 100 years ago that, other things being equal, individuals of a given race are distinguishable from one another in proportion to our familiarity and contact with the race as a whole. Thus, to the uninitiated American, all Asiatics look alike, whereas to the Asiatic, all White people look alike.[48]

Experts in the field of eyewitness memory and about half of potential jurors endorse the belief that cross-racial identifications are less reliable than same-race identifications. This presumption is based on the belief in the existence of an own-race bias—that is, that people recognize others of their own race better than they do those of another race. John Brigham and Roy Malpass note that the own-race recognition bias has been demonstrated among Whites, Blacks, Asians, Latinos, and Hispanics. Explanations for this phenomenon vary. Some evidence shows that persons who have close friends of the other race show less of an own-race recognition bias.[49]

Moreover, Saul Feinman and Doris Entwistle found that children living in mixed-race environments show less of an own-race recognition bias than do children living in a segregated environment.[50] Conversely, other research indicates that the own-race recognition bias is not reduced by frequent contact with the other race and that prejudiced persons are no more likely to exhibit an own-race recognition bias than are nonprejudiced persons.[51] Some evidence indicates that persons who view other-race faces tend to focus on the constituent (individual) features of the face, such as the eyes or lips, whereas observers of same-race faces focus on the face as a whole.[52]

Recent research conducted at the University of Miami offers an alternative explanation for the own-race recognition bias. Researchers there maintain that environmental or contextual cues, such as one's socioeconomic status, bring out a recategorization of same-race individuals as out-group members and thus reduce same-race face recognition but not other-race recognition. Edwin Shriver and his colleagues found that to middle-class White perceivers, presenting White faces on impoverished backgrounds led to significantly worse same-race recognition than presenting those same faces on wealthy backgrounds. Thus, a social context implying that an individual is a poor rather than middle-class White is enough to reduce the recognition advantage of same-race faces. In addition, for White faces on impoverished backgrounds, same-race recognition is about equal to other-race recognition, regardless of whether impoverished White faces are compared with impoverished Black faces or wealthy Black faces. However, the economic status shown by the background had no effect on the other-race recognition of Black faces, regardless of wealthy or impoverished contexts. Thus, when same-race faces were seen on backgrounds that indicated they were out-group members, the accuracy of same-race face recognition was reduced.[53]

Researchers Kareem Johnson and Barbara Fredrickson of Temple University discuss the idea that, when viewing cross-race faces, people focus more on the other's race than on individual identity. They point out that race is one of the most salient features people use to categorize others. In fact, Johnson and Fredrickson note that racial differences are detected faster than other demographics, such as sex and age. To be sure, humans are about 50% faster at responding to racial differences than they are to sex differences. And people are also significantly faster at categorizing cross-race faces as racially different than they are own-race faces as racially similar; that is, own-race bias occurs because encoding information about the other's race interferes with encoding information about the individual. Johnson and Fredrickson maintain that categorizing a face by race alters how that individual's face is represented in memory. For example, if someone initially categorizes a face as *African American*, he or she may recall the person's skin tone as darker than it actually is and facial features as more stereotypically African American. Thus, Johnson and Fredrickson conclude that the perception of cross-race faces due to the categorization process may underlie own-race bias.[54]

Perhaps cross-race identification is not as complicated as we think. Stephen Young and Kurt Hugenberg found that cross-face recognition is most effective when people are motivated to process and recognize cross-race faces. Their model predicts that with very high levels of motivation, even a person with relatively little intergroup interaction will be able to encode and subsequently remember cross-race faces fairly well. But Young and Hugenberg's research shows that the combination of increased intergroup interaction and motivation yields the most accurate perception of cross-race identification.[55]

Regulators

Nonverbal **regulators** are those behaviors and actions that govern, direct, or manage conversation. During conversations in the United States, for example, direct eye contact and affirmative head nodding typically communicate agreement or that a conversant understands what is being communicated. How close one stands to another during a conversation can also signal to the conversant whether to continue the communication. Communicator distance during conversation can also govern the flow of communication (see Figure 8.7). According to Almaney and Alwan, in some Middle Eastern cultures, people stand close together during interaction to smell each other's breath. To smell each other is considered desirable. In fact, to deny someone your breath communicates shame.[56] Harris, Moran, and Moran point out that in many Arab cultures, men hold hands as they converse to demonstrate their trust in each other. During conversation, a raising of the eyebrows or a clicking of the tongue signifies a negative response and a disruption in the flow of communication.[57]

| Figure 8.7 | Communicator distance during conversation often governs the flow of communication and provides cues as to the nature of the relationship. |

Adaptors

Adaptors are kinesic actions that satisfy physiological or psychological needs. Scratching an itch satisfies a physiological need, whereas tapping the tip of your pen on the desk while waiting for the professor to deliver a final exam satisfies a psychological need. Very little, if any, cross-cultural research on adaptors has been conducted. For the most part, adaptors are not learned and probably do not vary much across cultures.

Occulesics

Occulesics is the study of eye contact. Eye contact is one of the most dynamic forms of non-verbal behavior and is an essential biological skill necessary for effective social interactions. Indeed, many researchers believe that basic visual processes, including attraction to the eye region of the face, are not only innate in humans but in animals as well.[58] In humans (and probably animals) both adults and infants prefer to look at the eyes of another over other facial features. For example, in their classic study, Stephen Janik, A. Rodney Wellens, Myron Goldberg, and Louis Dell'Osso found that nearly 45% of the attention time humans pay to another is focused on the other person's eyes.[59] Reginald Adams and Robert Kleck maintain that both eye gaze and affect (i.e., emotion) are closely associated with approach–avoidance tendencies. They assert that direct gaze is associated with approach tendencies, while averted gaze is associated with avoidance tendencies. But Adams and Kleck also point out that direct gaze in both humans and animals can communicate threat or friendliness. Thus, they maintain that contextual cues become important in discerning the meaning of eye gaze within social arenas. This is where culture plays a role.[60]

Although researchers believe that the basic visual processes are innate, many also believe that culture influences eye behavior across social contexts. For example, social rules for direct eye contact and distance during communication vary considerably across cultures and genders. In many Asian cultures, such as South Korea, Vietnam, China, and Japan, direct eye contact is prohibited between persons of differing status. Caroline Blais and her colleagues at the University of Glasgow in Scotland have studied and reviewed the research associated with eye behavior across cultures. In one of their studies, Blais and her colleagues monitored the eye movements of Western Caucasian and East Asian subjects during the learning stages of a facial recognition task, using Western Caucasian and East Asian faces as stimuli. Their results showed that the Western Caucasian subjects fixated on the eye region and partially on the mouths of the stimuli faces, while the East Asian subjects fixated more on the central region of the stimuli faces. They note that direct or excessive eye contact is considered rude in many East Asian cultures and that this cultural norm might have determined the eye behavior in the East Asian subjects in their study.[61] In Korea, for example, a large–power-distance culture, persons with lower status avoid direct eye contact with persons of higher status because doing so is seen as a challenge or conflict, even within the family. In China, also a large–power-distance culture, prolonged direct eye contact is considered rude and disrespectful, especially to persons of higher status. Moreover, recall from Chapter 1 that there are 1.4 billion people in China, and in crowded situations, which are typical in the cities, the Chinese avoid eye contact as a way to give themselves privacy. In a recent study, researchers at the University of Tokyo studied the eye behavior of Japanese and Finnish subjects and measured physiological (i.e., heart rate and gaze duration) and subjective responses to direct and averted eye gaze with another real person. Their results showed that compared with averted eye contact, direct eye contact with a real person elicited stronger heart rate deceleration and shorter looking times in both cultures. But the two groups differed in their subjective ratings. Compared to Finnish subjects, Japanese subjects perceive another's face as being angrier, unapproachable, and unpleasant when making direct eye contact, as opposed to using an averted gaze. These results suggest that cultural differences in eye contact emerge from cultural norms rather than innate physiological responses.[62]

Unlike the cultures discussed above, in other cultures such as Australia, the United States, Germany, Italy, France, and Spain, direct eye contact is seen as appropriate, as demonstrating one's veracity, and as showing interest in the other. Indirect eye contact may be perceived as rude and communicates that one may be hiding something or not being truthful.

Eye contact differs between men and women across most cultures. Audry Nelson writes that in most cultures, women do more to enhance their eyes than men do. She notes that Cleopatra was well-known for eye adornment; she used kohl makeup to outline and accentuate her eyes. Nelson also notes that in India, women place jewels around their eyes to draw attention to them. Among strangers, Saudi men do not make eye contact with Saudi women. In the United States, women have their own methods for enhancing their eyes, including under-eye concealer, false eyelashes, eye shadow, eyeliner, and mascara. Nelson maintains that in the United States, women use eye contact to communicate affiliation and approach tendencies, while men use eye contact as a way to assert status and dominance. She points out that women will also lower their eyes in submission.[63]

Paralanguage

Paralanguage refers to vocal qualities that usually, though not necessarily, accompany speech. Knapp and Hall divide paralanguage into two broad categories: voice qualities and vocalizations. Paralinguistic voice qualities include pitch, rhythm, tempo, articulation, and resonance of the voice. Paralinguistic vocalizations include laughing, crying, sighing, belching, swallowing, clearing the throat, snoring, and so forth. Other paralinguistic vocalizations are intensity and *nonfluencies,* such as *um, ah*, and *uh*.

Silence is also considered within the domain of paralanguage.[64] Often, paralinguistic qualities, vocalizations, and nonfluencies reveal a speaker's emotional state or veracity. Audiences can discern when speakers are nervous or confident by listening to their tone of voice, rhythm, pace, and the number of nonfluencies they utter. Parents often detect a child's deception not so much by what the child says but by how it is said. Through paralanguage, we can tell whether speakers are being genuine, cynical, or sarcastic. Moreover, a person's geographical origin can be determined by listening closely to his or her paralanguage.[65]

In all spoken languages, vocal sounds are carried by vowels; it is impossible to speak words without them. Consonants, on the other hand, function to stop and start sound. Linguist Peter Ladefoged has observed that although there are perhaps as many as 900 consonants and 200 vowels in all the world's languages, many languages tend to use only five vowel sounds. In fact, one in five languages use the same vowel sounds as are used in Spanish and English—*a, e, i, o*, and *u*—although there are variations on their pronunciation. According to Ladefoged, although any human is capable of making literally thousands of speech sounds, only a few hundred have ever been observed among the world's spoken languages. The average language uses only about 40 sounds, and all babies are capable of making all of them.

All babies, the world over, make the same sounds during infancy. Linguists believe that these sounds are the building blocks by which infants construct mature sounds. Although infants have not yet learned the specific language of their culture and have not yet spoken a single word, they practice the sounds of all human languages. All babies regularly produce a small subset of universal syllable types that occur in all the world's languages. This is strong evidence that human language was not invented by humans but, rather, evolved. To be sure, unusual sounds show up in some languages. Clicking sounds, for example, can be heard in South Africa's Zulu and Xhosa languages, and nasal sounds are heard in Eskimo languages. Although these sounds may be unique components of these languages, all human babies, regardless of culture, can be heard making them at some time prior to learning their culture's formal verbal language.[66]

Some languages, called tonal languages, rely on vocalized tones to communicate meaning. In these languages, a rising or falling tone changes the meaning of a word. Thai is a pentatonal language that uses five tones: monotone, low, falling, high, and rising. Modern Vietnamese is a monosyllabic language, meaning that all words are only one syllable long. Like the Thai language, Vietnamese is tonal, and the meaning of the syllable changes with tone. The

Chinese language is tonal also. Mandarin Chinese, the most common language in China, is based on four or five tones. Every syllable in Mandarin has its definite tone. The first tone, called *yinping,* is a high-pitched tone without variation from beginning to end. The syllable is spoken with an even tone, using the highest pitch of the speaker's voice. The second tone, *yangping,* starts from a lower pitch and ends high. The syllable is spoken with a rising tone, not unlike the one used by speakers of English when asking a question. The third tone, *shang-sheng,* is perhaps the most difficult to master. It begins as a middle-level tone, goes down, bounds up, and ends with a relatively higher pitch. The fourth tone, *chyusheng,* is a falling tone that starts high and ends at the lowest range of the speaker's voice. The fifth tone, *ching-sheng,* is often left out of descriptions of Mandarin. This tone is spoken quickly and lightly, as if it has no tone at all. *Chingsheng* is often called the neutral tone.[67]

To be sure, English and other languages have inflections—that is, a change in pitch on certain words and sentences. English speakers can communicate anger or sadness by changing the pitch of their voice. Without the appropriate inflection, the meaning of an English speaker's sentence can be misinterpreted. In Chinese, however, tones completely change the meaning of a word. Take, for example, the word *ma.* In the first tone, *ma* is "mother." In the second tone, *ma* becomes "hemp" or "grass." In the third tone, *ma* becomes "horse," and in the fourth tone, *ma* becomes "to scold" or "to nag." In Mandarin Chinese, the meanings of words are strictly based on the tones, which remain constant in whispering, yelling, or even singing. Mandarin tones are relative to the natural pitch of the speaker. A deep-voiced man's high note may be much lower than the high note of a woman.[68]

As with any other form of communication, some paralinguistic devices are learned and vary across cultures. South Koreans are taught to avoid talking or laughing loudly in any situation; such behavior is seen as rude and unbecoming since it tends to draw attention. Many Koreans, especially women, cover their mouths when laughing.[69] In their study of paralanguage, Miron Zuckerman and Kunitate Miyake introduce the idea of a vocal attractiveness stereotype. They contend that, as with physical attractiveness, individuals perceived to be vocally attractive elicit more favorable impressions than those not perceived to be vocally attractive. The results of their study indicate that attractive voices are those that are relatively loud, resonant, and articulate. Unattractive voices are squeaky, nasal, monotone, and off pitch. Zuckerman and Miyake found some sex differences in vocal attractiveness. For example, throatiness was perceived more negatively among female voices than among male voices.[70]

Perhaps in any culture, as we move from region to region, we can hear differences in paralanguage; that is, we hear differences in the pronunciation and vocal pitch of the people, or in their accents. Agata Gluszek and John Dovidio of Yale University point out that while speakers often do not recognize it in themselves, everyone speaks with an accent.[71] Following the pioneering work of Howard Giles, an accent represents a manner or style of pronunciation and is distinct from a speaker's dialect. According to Giles, dialect refers to differences in grammar and vocabulary among different versions of the same language, whereas an accent is the paralinguistic component combined with the phonological and intonation features of the spoken word—that is, its sound. Hence, speakers with different accents may share the same grammar, syntax, and lexicon but sound very different in their usage.[72] Such paralinguistic differences often prompt social perceptions of others, especially during intercultural communication in which one or more of the interactants speaks with a nonnative accent. A substantial body of research has accumulated in the social sciences regarding the social and psychological impact of speaking with a nonnative accent. Much of this research supports the argument that the manner and style in which one speaks, including one's accent, plays a central role in creating and maintaining one's social makeup while communicating to others meaningful social data.[73] Most researchers in this area agree that a nonnative accent often stigmatizes a person as foreign-born and as someone who does not apply the language competently.[74]

In their review of some of the research in this area, Katherine Kinzler and her associates point out that perceived accent is an initial indicator of in-group/out-group distinctions and that children as young as 5 months old, who have virtually no verbal competence, can discriminate between two languages or dialects, provided that one of the languages/dialects is their own. They also suggest that 5-month-old infants display social preferences based on paralanguage. In their own studies, Kinzler and her colleagues presented 5-year-olds with photographs and voice recordings of children they did not know. The children chose to be friends with native speakers of their native language rather than children with foreign accents. The researchers note that these preferences were not due to the verbal intelligibility of the foreign speakers' speech, as children found the accented speech to be comprehensible; the preferences were based on paralinguistic cues. In addition, they found that children chose same-race children as friends when the target children were silent, but they chose as friends other-race children with a native accent over same-race children with accents. In other words, children use accent more than race as a criterion in choosing friends.[75]

In their recent review of literature on nonnative accents, Gluszek and Dovidio assert that a nonnative accent is one of the most salient characteristics of a person that identifies him or her as an out-group member and that a nonnative accent almost always stigmatizes that person. Gluszek and Dovidio emphasize that a nonnative accent is distinct from verbal language competency. That is, people who are perfectly verbally fluent in a second language may still carry a nonnative accent after many years in a host country because they retain the paralinguistic phonology (i.e., the sounds) of their native tongue. These people, they argue, are usually stereotyped negatively, which carries serious social, professional, and economic consequences. Gluszek and Dovidio stress that nonnative accents are associated with a wide range of negative stereotypes, including perceptions that the people who speak them are less intelligent, less loyal, less competent, and lower in social status. But Gluszek and Dovidio also point out that in some cases, a nonnative accent is associated with positive traits. For example, in the United States, a British accent is often perceived as prestigious. Generally, in the United States, Western European accents are perceived more favorably than Asian or Hispanic accents. So this idea, and the finding that children as young as 5 months old recognize accents as markers during person perception, suggests that there is nothing inherent to accents that renders some more aesthetically pleasing than others. Instead, accents serve as social identity cues, which, in turn, trigger negative or positive perceptions.[76]

In addition to being negatively stereotyped, persons with nonnative accents may face prejudice and discrimination and are unprotected by the courts. Nonnative accent discrimination differs from ethnic or racial discrimination in that the United States Civil Rights Act of 1964 prohibits discrimination on the basis of race or national origin but does not specifically mention accent. Gluszek and Dovidio point to research that has found that nonnative speakers of English face discrimination in housing and employment. They are more likely to be assigned lower-status positions within organizations and to receive lower pay increments. In fact, according to Gluszek and Dovidio, many employers who have been sued by nonnative speakers for discrimination have actually won their cases, especially when they could demonstrate that the nonnative speaker's accent impaired his or her job performance.

Even in the college classroom, perceptions of nonnative accents affect student comprehension. In one study, two groups of students listened to the very same lecture while seeing a photo of either a Japanese or White instructor. The students who saw the Japanese photo actually believed they heard an accent and performed worse on a lecture comprehension test than did those who were exposed to the White instructor's photograph. In another study, conducted in England, researchers manipulated the accent of a British male criminal suspect. They found that when participants listened to a recorded conversation between the British male criminal suspect and a male policeman, they rated the suspect as significantly more guilty when he employed a Birmingham accent rather than a standard British accent.[77]

While one's accent is something that is heard, silence is also a part of the paralinguistic channel. Tomohiro Hasegawa and William Gudykunst maintain that silence is the lack of verbal communication or the absence of sound. Hasegawa and Gudykunst assert that culture influences the meaning and use of silence. In their research, they compared the use of silence among Japanese and Americans and found that, in the United States, silence is defined as a pause, break, empty space, or lack of verbal communication. Hasegawa and Gudykunst maintain that silence generally is not a part of Americans' everyday communication routines. They argue that although silence is acceptable among intimate others, when meeting strangers, Americans are conscious of silence and find it quite awkward. In Japan, however, silence is a space or pause during verbal communication that has important meaning. Pauses, or silence, are to be interpreted carefully. Stylistically, Japanese are taught to be indirect and sometimes ambiguous to maintain harmony. Silence, then, can be used to avoid directness, such as bluntly saying "no" to a request.[78]

Charles Braithwaite has studied silence across cultures and argues that it is a central nonverbal component of any speech community. He argues that some communicative functions of silence may be universal and do not vary across cultures. For example, Braithwaite maintains that among Native American groups, Japanese, Japanese Americans in Hawaii, and people in rural Appalachia, the use of silence as a communicative act is associated with communication situations where the status of the interactants is uncertain, unpredictable, or ambiguous. In addition, Braithwaite argues that silence as a communicative act is associated with communication situations where there is a known and unequal distribution of power among interactants. In other words, when interactants consciously recognize their differential status, they consciously use silence. Braithwaite cites evidence of this in many cultures, including the Anang of Southwestern Nigeria, the Wolof of Senegal, the Maori of New Zealand, the Malagasy in Madagascar, urban African American women, and some working-class White Americans.[79]

Proxemics

Proxemics refers to the perception and use of space, including territoriality and personal space. Territoriality refers to physical geographical space; personal space refers to perceptual or psychological space—sometimes thought of as the "bubble" of space that humans carry with them in their day-to-day activities. College students who live in the very close quarters of a dorm are usually quite sensitive to proxemics and territoriality. Dorm rooms do not allow for much personal space or territoriality. In their comparison of territoriality among Turkish and American students, Naz Kaya and Margaret Weber found that in both cultures, men tended to demonstrate more nonsharing behavior and less personalization of their space than did women. The authors also report that students in both cultures who knew their roommates tended to share their personal belongings and other dimensions of the dorm room more than students who did not know their roommates previously. Interestingly, American students experienced their rooms as more personal and expressive of the self than did Turkish students. Americans are generally very protective of their space.[80]

In Nigeria, the student population in residence halls at colleges and universities has tripled over the past 20 years. In her research, architect Dalapo Amole focused on the coping strategies used by Nigerian college students, gender differences in those coping styles, and the influence of the length of stay. Her results showed that men and women differed in many of the coping strategies. These included (a) rearranging the furniture, used more by males than females; (b) decorating personal place, used more by females than males; (c) generally segregating space in the bedroom, used more by females than males; (d) entertaining and meeting friends elsewhere, used more by males than females; and (e) coming to the room only to sleep, used more by males than females. Staying away from the room, storing some personal items elsewhere, and sleeping elsewhere were strategies used equally by both men and women. Length of stay in the dorm did not appear to be important except with respect to studying and entertaining friends.[81]

In cultures whose population density is high, personal space and territoriality are highly valued. Privacy in densely populated locations is often accomplished psychologically rather than physiologically. In Calcutta, India, for example, there are nearly 80,000 persons per square mile. There is literally not enough room in the city to claim any personal space. Touching and bumping into others while walking through the streets of Calcutta is quite common and to be expected.[82]

Socioeconomic factors can also affect a culture's perception of space. Cramped and insufficient housing is common in much of Sri Lanka. In the 1980s, most housing units were quite small. Of all the homes, 33% had only one room, another 33% had two rooms, and only 20% had three rooms. Moreover, the average number of persons per home was five. (Overcrowding in Sri Lanka is declining, however, since the government initiated intensive housing programs in the 1990s.)[83] The Moroccan perception of space reflects the culture's valuing of community. Personal space during a conversation is typically less than an arm's length. In mosques, worshipers line up shoulder to shoulder to pray. Houses typically have very little space between them as well.[84] Because Kenyan culture values harmony and sharing, Kenyans tend to be less aware of personal territory than are people in the United States. For example, many Kenyans do not designate specific rooms in the home for specific activities, such as a living room or a dining room. In addition, the personal space distance between interactants is much closer than in the United States.[85]

Many other studies support the link between culture and proxemic behavior in comparing Americans with Arabs, Latin Americans, Pakistanis, Germans, Italians, Japanese, and Venezuelans. These examples suggest that culture plays a decisive role in how spatial distances are maintained during communication. Other variables besides culture can affect proxemic distances, however, such as the age and sex of the interactants, the nature of the relationship, the environment, and ethnicity of interactants. Several studies have documented that in most cultures, the need for personal space increases with age. In addition, the use of space as influenced by sex seems to vary significantly by culture.[86]

STUDENT VOICES ACROSS CULTURES

Anna Shircel

I am a 21-year-old St. Norbert College student from Sheboygan, Wisconsin, pursuing a degree in communication and media studies. During the spring semester of my junior year, I studied abroad in London.

Though I did not experience the barrier of a foreign language, my time in London did provide me with countless instances of intercultural communication. I found the most apparent difference to be the nonverbal communication behaviors I encountered on British public transportation. The Underground—or the Tube, as it's known to the British—is a vital part of life in London and serves as a hub of unique nonverbal behaviors.

The British have particular unwritten rules regarding proper Tube etiquette. First, one does not make eye contact with or speak to other passengers. Most passengers tend to read or listen to music, better to avoid communication. This is the rule many tourists fail to follow. Groups of travelers would hop on the Tube, laughing and talking loudly, much to the disdain of the locals trying to get through their daily commute in silence. British passengers would appear visibly annoyed by these individuals.

Another nonverbal behavior difference on the Tube was based on proxemics, or the perception and use of space. During rush hour, the concept of personal space becomes nonexistent. Businessmen and women cram into the cars in an effort to make it to work on time. During parts of my commute, I would ride pushed right up against the door by other bodies. This situation was extremely awkward for me at first, but I gradually became accustomed to the close confines of the Tube during these peak hours.

The concept of space is also important when the Tube is less busy. One never sits directly next to someone when other seats are open. One can choose a seat next to someone only when all other seats have been filled. Again, British individuals seemed rather taken aback whenever an unknowing tourist sat directly next to them when there were other options.

While these nonverbal behaviors and unwritten rules may seem unusual in the United States, accepting them allowed me to feel more integrated into my host country and gave me a more authentic study-abroad experience. In fact, by the end of my time in London, I found myself feeling just as frustrated as the locals by those not partaking in appropriate nonverbal behaviors on the Tube.

Haptics

Skin is the biggest organ of the human body, which not only surrounds the body, but also separates it from the environment. . . . Skin represents a social organ through which humans are able to get in touch with and get close to other human beings.[87]

Haptics, or tactile communication, refers to the use of touch. Knapp and Hall argue that touch may be the most primitive form of communication.[88] Haptic communication varies widely across cultures, and the amount and kind of touch varies with the age, sex, situation, and relationship of the people involved. In his theorizing about culture and touch, Edward Hall distinguishes between contact and noncontact cultures.[89] Contact cultures are those that tend to encourage touching and engage in touching more frequently than do either moderate-contact or noncontact cultures, in which touching occurs less frequently and is generally discouraged. Many South and Central American countries are considered contact cultures, as are many Southern European countries. The United States is regarded as a moderate-contact culture, whereas many Asian countries are considered noncontact. Many Asian cultures have established norms that forbid public displays of affection and intimacy that involve touch. One of the five central tenets of Confucian philosophy is the division between the sexes. Because Confucianism is so central to many Asian cultures, engaging in touch with the opposite sex is considered uncivil.[90]

In their field study of touch patterns among cross-sex couples, Ed McDaniel and Peter Andersen observed the touch behavior of couples in airports. They found that couples from the United States touched most, followed by (in order of most to least touching) couples from Northern Europe, the Caribbean/Latin America, Southeast Asia, and Northeast Asia.[91] In their study, Rosemarie Dibiase and Jaime Gunnoe found that touching behavior at a dance club at night differed among people from Italy, the United States, and the Czech Republic. Italians engaged in the most hand and nonhand touching, while men and women from the United States showed the least touching behavior.[92]

Psychologist Sidney Jourard conducted a study that counted the frequency of body contact between couples as they sat in cafés in different cities and countries. He found that the average number of touches per hour in San Juan, Puerto Rico, was 180; in Paris, 110; in Gainesville, Florida, 2; and in London, 0.[93]

Because we are often taught not to touch others, some people develop touch avoidance. These people feel uncomfortable in situations requiring touch and generally avoid touching when possible. In her study of Americans, Japanese, Puerto Ricans, and Koreans, Beth Casteel found no touch-avoidance differences in same-sex dyads for the Japanese and Americans, in that both were significantly more touch avoidant than were same-sex dyads in Puerto Rico and Korea. In opposite-sex dyads, however, Japanese and Koreans showed much higher levels of touch avoidance than did Americans and Puerto Ricans. Casteel concluded that the Japanese and Americans allow women to touch other women, but men should not touch men. Koreans and Puerto Ricans are just the reverse.[94] In their comparison of high-contact cultures of Southern Europe and low-contact cultures of Northern Europe, psychologists Martin Remland, Tricia Jones, and Heidi Brinkman found that more touch was observed among Italian and Greek dyads than among English, French, and Dutch dyads.[95] The people of Northern Italy have few inhibitions about personal space and touch. Heterosexual men are often seen kissing each other on both cheeks and walking together arm in arm, as are women. East Indians are very expressive with touch. To touch the feet of elders is a sign of respect. Indians demonstrate their trust for each other by holding hands briefly during a conversation or religious activity. When a Hindu priest blesses others at religious gatherings, he gently touches the palms of their outstretched hands.[96] Saudi Arabians tend to value touching also. Saudi businessmen often hold hands as a sign of trust, a form of touch behavior that some Americans often misunderstand. Saudi women, however, are never to be touched in public.[97]

Most cultures prohibit some forms of touch. Harris, Moran, and Moran observe that in Thailand, Sri Lanka, and some other cultures, the head is considered sacred and should not be touched by others. Americans sometimes make the mistake of patting children of other cultures on the top of the head as a sign of affection or endearment. In some cultures, this is seen as a serious breach of etiquette.[98] In many African and Middle Eastern cultures, the use of the left hand is forbidden in certain social situations. In Kenya, Indonesia, and Pakistan, for example, the left hand should not be used in eating or serving food. Harris, Moran, and Moran report that in Kenya, the left hand is considered weak and unimportant. Sometimes, Kenyans intentionally use the left hand when serving food to someone they disrespect. In other cultures, such as Iraq and Iran, the left hand is used for cleaning oneself following the performance of certain bodily functions and, thus, should never be used to give or receive gifts or other objects.[99] Like proxemics, the nature of touch is often mediated by more than culture. The relationship between the interactants, the location and duration of touch, the relative pressure of the touch, the environment in which the touch occurs (public or private), and whether the touch is intentional or accidental influence touch across cultures.

Christina Schut and her colleagues at the University of Gieben in Germany conducted a rather interesting study that investigated the differences in the self-appraisal of one's own skin among persons from Germany, Italy, France, and Syria.[100] In their study, Schut and her colleagues had nearly 3,500 participants complete the Touch-Shame-Disgust-Questionnaire that measures pleasure in touching oneself, touching in a partnership, parental touching during childhood, and skin-related feelings of shame and disgust. Their results showed that Italians had the highest scores on pleasure in touching oneself and touching in a partnership, whereas the German and Italian sample both scored significantly higher on pleasure in parental touching compared with participants from France and Syria. Men and women did not differ significantly concerning physical pleasure in touching oneself, parental touching, or touching in a partnership. In addition, education level had no significant effect on pleasure in touching oneself but did have a significant impact on pleasure in parental touching and touching in a partnership. Participants with a low education level reported less pleasure in touching in a partnership than did those with a higher education level. Participants with an average education level reported more pleasure in parental touching than did participants with a lower or higher education level. Age had a significant effect on pleasure in touching oneself, parental touching, and touching in a partnership. Being older was associated with low pleasure in touching oneself, parental touching, and touching in a partnership. Regarding shame and disgust, Germans scored significantly lower on shame than did French, Italian, and Syrian participants. Syrians had significantly more feelings of disgust than did the French, Germans, and Italians. Germans had more feelings of disgust than did the French and Italians.[101] Significant gender effects were also observed. Across all four cultures, men reported having less feelings of shame and disgust than did women. Education level had no significant impact on feelings of disgust, but participants with a higher education level reported having more feelings of shame than did participants with an average or lower education level. Age also had a significant effect on shame, such that with increasing age, shame decreased and disgust increased.[102]

STUDENT VOICES ACROSS CULTURES

Lindsey Novitzke

 I'm a 20-year-old college student from New Richmond, Wisconsin. In May of 2010, I visited Zambia, Africa, with an organization called The Zambia Project, which works throughout the year doing various fundraising events for Zambian Open Community Schools, a nonprofit that exists to provide education to orphans in Zambia. I had the adventure of a lifetime visiting schools, distributing school supplies, interacting with the people, and experiencing Zambian culture.

Nonverbal communication played a crucial role in my interactions with the people of Zambia. Although the official language is English, many of the people of Zambia speak primarily their own native and cultural languages, in addition to a different kind of English than what we speak in the United States. Oftentimes, the younger children did not know any English; therefore, much of our communication was nonverbal. Most specifically, touch played a considerable role in all our interactions with the Zambian people, and even more so with the children. Zambian culture is a high-contact culture, where even the handshake they use as a greeting involves more touch than a handshake in the United States.

I would often see male and female children of all ages holding hands as they walked to and from school. Zambian social structure, such as the school and the home, promotes a heavy amount of touch, requiring people to sit and work closely together. Young girls and women carry their children or siblings in a sling that hangs off their shoulder, where the baby is constantly touching them—teaching them, from an early age, that touch is essential. Since my verbal communication with the younger children was minimal, I often held their hands or let them sit in my lap as a way to demonstrate my friendship.

For adults to touch one another as they interacted was not uncommon. Their personal space "bubbles" were small, almost nonexistent. Being from a low-contact culture, I felt bombarded by the amount of touch occurring during interactions. Many of the children loved to rub my skin and touch my hair, since many of them had never seen blond hair or a Caucasian person up close. Ironically, after returning to the United States, I actually craved touch and felt that people in the United States were unusually distant. Touch played a major role in my visit to Zambia.

Olfactics

Probably the least understood, yet most fascinating, of all human sensations is olfactics—that is, our sense of smell. Our lack of understanding is certainly not because we lack a sense of smell. According to Boyd Gibbons, humans can detect as many as 10,000 different compounds by smell. Moreover, about 1% of our genes are devoted to detecting odors. Although this may not seem like much, humans have more olfactory genes than any other type of gene identified in human and mammalian DNA. Gibbons suggests that our lack of understanding may be because we lack a vocabulary for smell and are discouraged from talking about smell. Particularly in the United States, we have become obsessed with masking certain smells, especially those of the human body. According to Gibbons, the biggest users of fragrance in the world are U.S.-based companies such as Procter & Gamble, Lever Bros., and Colgate. Some brands of soap use more than 2 million pounds of fragrance a year. In many Western cultures, body odor is regarded as unpleasant and distasteful, and we go to great efforts to mask or remove it.[103]

David Stoddart asserts that in addition to our ability to detect odors, humans are even more adept at producing odors. According to Stoddart, evidence from anatomy, chemistry, and psychology indicates that humans are the most highly scented of all the apes. Human scent comes from two types of glands that lie beneath the skin, the sebaceous glands and the apocrine glands. Sebaceous glands are all over the body, wherever there are hair follicles. They produce an odorous, oily fluid whose original purpose was to protect hair. The apocrine glands are a type of sweat gland. They are most dense in our armpits but are also found in the pubic and anal regions, the face, the scalp, and the umbilical region of the abdomen (the belly button). Women appear to have more apocrine glands than do men, but some evidence suggests that their glands are less active than those in men. The most distasteful odors come from the apocrine glands, which are activated when we are frightened, excited, or aroused. Human saliva and urine also produce scent.[104]

According to James Kohl and Robert Francoeur, research has repeatedly shown that women perceive odors differently at various phases of their menstrual cycles. They tend to be the most sensitive to odors during ovulation. Other studies indicate that when in close proximity to one another over time, as in dormitory living, women synchronize their menstrual cycles. Scientists believe that axillary organ secretions function as odor cues to stimulate their cycles. On a related note, studies have shown that vaginal secretions during ovulation are minimally unpleasant, whereas such secretions before and after ovulation are described as distinctly unpleasant.[105]

Kohl and Francoeur suggest that although preferences for certain smells seem to vary across cultures, there appears to be a universal preference for some kinds of scents that may have biological and evolutionary roots. These preferences are probably mediated by culture to some extent, however. For example, the finest perfumes in the world contain olfactory hints of urine. Scientists allege that these scents function as sex attractants. We know, for example, that sex-attractant pheromones are expelled from the body in urine. These two kinds of smell may mirror those of our humanoid ancestors and unconsciously stimulate the deepest parts of our brains.[106]

In addition to functioning as a sex attractant, smell is also used politically for marking social class distinctions. Constance Classen, David Howes, and Anthony Synnott contend that smell plays a significant role in the construction of power relations in many societies.[107] Annick Le Guérer comments, for example, that idiomatic expressions often employ smell-related terms to voice antagonism and repugnance toward others. People refer to persons they dislike as "stinkers." When we are suspicious of someone, we say we "smell a rat." When something seems wrong or amiss, we comment that "it doesn't smell right" or "smells fishy." Dishonest politicians may "reek of hypocrisy."[108]

Anthony Synnott claims that odor is often used to categorize groups of people into status, power, and moral classes. To be sure, the smells themselves are not intrinsically moral or immoral, but the qualities or thoughts attributed to the specific scents give them moral significance. Synott argues that a person's scent is not only an individual emission and a moral statement but also a perceived social attribute that is especially significant for members of subordinate groups, who are often labeled "smelly." Such labels often foster racial, ethnic, and religious prejudice and hatred. Subordinate and microcultural groups are often described as possessing negative olfactory characteristics. In fact, Synnott argues that perceived foul odors legitimize inequalities and are one of the criteria by which a negative identity is imposed on a particular class or race.[109]

Many cultures establish norms for acceptable and unacceptable scents associated with the human body. When individuals or groups of people fail to fit into the realm of acceptability, their odor signals that something is "wrong" with them, either physically or mentally. Kohl and Francoeur note that the American Puritan tradition of "cleanliness is next to godliness" may explain the American obsession with deodorants, perfumes, soaps, and shampoos.[110] Social class distinctions based on smells are the cultural product of education, religion, parenting, and social pressure from peers. With the exception of those scents that appeal to everyone, people are conditioned to find certain scents attractive and others dirty or foul. Moreover, such distinctions sustain social barriers between groups and even justify a dominant group's persecution of subordinate groups.[111] In the Middle Ages, wealthy people bought perfumes to diminish the scent of the lower classes. Nineteenth-century Japanese described European traders with the term *bata-kusai*—"stinks of butter."[112] Adolf Hitler's hatred of Jews was based partially on olfactics; he claimed that their foul odor was representative of their "moral mildew" and reflected their outer and inner foulness and, therefore, their immorality.[113]

Gibbons reports that during World Wars I and II, German and English soldiers claimed they could identify the enemy by their smell. Similar claims have been made by North Vietnamese and U.S. troops.[114] John Baker reports that in U.S. history, Thomas Jefferson is purported to have said that Blacks have "a very strong and disagreeable odour."[115] John Dollard claims that many White racists used the "disagreeable scent" of Blacks as a final proof of the impossibility of close association between the races.[116] In 1912, sociologist Georg Simmel wrote, "It would appear impossible for the Negro ever to be accepted into high society in North America because of his bodily odor."[117] Indeed, Simmel concluded that "the moral ideal of harmony and equality between the different classes and races runs up against the brick wall of an invincible disgust inspired by the sense of smell."[118]

Classen, Howes, and Synnott maintain that more than any other group, women are stereotyped and classified by their scent. Historically, in many cultures, women were considered the fragrant sex, unless they were prostitutes or suffragettes or challenged the male-dominated social order. The role of fragrance was primarily to entice men. In general, the Western cultural axiom has been that, unless perfumed, women stink. Jonathan Swift's poem "The Lady's Dressing Room" expresses this belief:

His foul imagination links

Each Dame he sees with all her Stinks:

And, if unsav'ry Odours fly,

Conceives a Lady standing by.[119]

Although it may be the least studied of all the senses, social scientists are discovering that olfactory sensation is a potent influence on social interaction. Survey data indicate that a significant percentage of adults are conscious of and influenced by smells in their environment. In their poll of more than 350 American adults, the Olfactory Research Fund found that 64% of respondents indicated that smell greatly influenced the quality of their lives. Specifically,

76% of the respondents reported that the sense of smell was "very important" in their daily relationships with persons of the opposite sex, and 20% indicated that it was "somewhat important." As related to their relationships with their spouses, 74% indicated that smell was "very important," and 22% said that it was "somewhat important." Although the percentages dropped somewhat, 36% of the respondents indicated that smell was "important" in their relationships with friends, and 40% agreed that smell was "very important" in their relationships with coworkers. Of all respondents, 80% reported using environmental fragrances, such as potpourri, room sprays, and scented candles. Well over 60% of respondents believed that particular aromas enhance the quality of life, relieve stress, and help retrieve memories. Of those respondents who used cologne, perfume, or aftershave, 83% said they did so because they liked the scent, 68% said it made them feel better about themselves, 56% said it enhanced their sense of well-being, 51% said they used fragrances to make themselves more romantically attractive to others, and 46% said they used fragrances to make a fashion statement.[120]

This emphasis on smell is often motivated by the pivotal role olfactics play in the maintenance of social relationships. Josephine Todrank, Deidre Byrnes, Amy Wrzesniewski, and Paul Rozin assert that most cultures assign meaning to odors that is often displaced onto the people wearing those odors.[121] This is especially evident in relationships with members of the opposite sex. Although it is widely recognized that odors play a determinant role in the mating practices of many animal species, Kohl and Francoeur argue that odors are also an important ingredient in human mating and bonding, and they cite empirical evidence showing that odors hasten puberty, mediate women's menstrual cycles, and even influence sexual orientation.[122] Extant research indicates that odors help people identify their family members, facilitate the bond between parents and children, and influence how often and with whom individuals mate.

Kate Fox is a social anthropologist and the director of the Social Issues Research Center in Oxford, England. Fox has studied cultural differences in olfactics, with a special emphasis on non-Western cultures. Fox maintains that, unlike in most Western cultures, smell is "the emperor of the senses" in many cultures. For example, Fox describes the importance of smell among the Ongee people of the Andaman Islands, a group of islands off the southeast coast of India. According to Fox, much of Ongee cultural life revolves around smell. For example, their calendar is based on the smell of flowers that bloom at different times of the year. One's personal identity is defined by smell. Fox writes that to refer to himself or herself, an Ongee touches the tip of his or her nose, which is a gesture meaning both "me" and "my smell." Fox also reports that during greetings, Ongee routinely ask, "How is your nose?" rather than "How are you?" Ongee etiquette prescribes that if a person responds that he or she feels "heavy with smell," the greeter should inhale deeply to remove the excess smell. Conversely, if the greeted person indicates that he or she is short on smell energy, Ongee etiquette prescribes that the greeter contribute some extra scent by blowing on him or her.[123]

Fox also describes smell rituals among the Bororo peoples of Brazil and the Serer Ndut of Senegal (Western Africa). Among the Bororo, personal body smell indicates the life force of the individual, whereas one's breath odor indicates the state of one's soul. The Ndut believe that individuals possess a physical smell, defined by one's body and breath odor, and a spiritual smell. The spiritual smell is thought to be a reincarnated smell. For example, the Ndut can tell which ancestor has been reincarnated by associating the smell of a child with that of a deceased person.[124] (Complete Self-Assessment 8.1 to get an idea of your own level of olfactory perception and sensitivity.)

Self-Assessment 8.1

Personal Report of Olfactory Perception and Sensitivity (PROPS)

Directions: The following instrument is designed to assess your level of olfactory perception and sensitivity. On a scale of 1 to 7, indicate the degree to which each statement applies to you.

1 = strongly disagree, 2 = disagree, 3 = slightly disagree, 4 = undecided, 5 = slightly agree, 6 = agree, and 7 = strongly agree.

_____ 1. When interacting with a stranger of the opposite sex, I am typically conscious of the scent of his or her breath.

_____ 2. When interacting with a stranger of the opposite sex, I am typically conscious of the scent of his or her body.

_____ 3. When interacting with a stranger of the opposite sex, I am typically conscious of the scent of his or her cologne or perfume.

_____ 4. When interacting with a stranger of the same sex, I am typically conscious of the scent of his or her breath.

_____ 5. When interacting with a stranger of the same sex, I am typically conscious of the scent of his or her body.

_____ 6. When interacting with a stranger of the same sex, I am typically conscious of the scent of his or her cologne or perfume.

_____ 7. When interacting with a close friend of the opposite sex, I am typically conscious of the scent of his or her breath.

_____ 8. When interacting with a close friend of the opposite sex, I am typically conscious of the scent of his or her body.

_____ 9. When interacting with a close friend of the opposite sex, I am typically conscious of the scent of his or her cologne or perfume.

_____ 10. When interacting with a close friend of the same sex, I am typically conscious of the scent of his or her breath.

_____ 11. When interacting with a close friend of the same sex, I am typically conscious of the scent of his or her body.

_____ 12. When interacting with a close friend of the same sex, I am typically conscious of the scent of his or her cologne or perfume.

_____ 13. When interacting with a stranger of the opposite sex, I am typically conscious of the scent of my breath.

_____ 14. When interacting with a stranger of the opposite sex, I am typically conscious of the scent of my body.

_____ 15. When interacting with a stranger of the opposite sex, I am typically conscious of the scent of my cologne or perfume.

_____ 16. When interacting with a stranger of the same sex, I am typically conscious of the scent of my breath.

_____ 17. When interacting with a stranger of the same sex, I am typically conscious of the scent of my body.

_____ 18. When interacting with a stranger of the same sex, I am typically conscious of the scent of my cologne or perfume.

_____ 19. When interacting with a close friend of the opposite sex, I am typically conscious of the scent of my breath.

_____ 20. When interacting with a close friend of the opposite sex, I am typically conscious of the scent of my body.

_____ 21. When interacting with a close friend of the opposite sex, I am typically conscious of the scent of my cologne or perfume.

_____ 22. When interacting with a close friend of the same sex, I am typically conscious of the scent of my breath.

_____ 23. When interacting with a close friend of the same sex, I am typically conscious of the scent of my body.

_____ 24. When interacting with a close friend of the same sex, I am typically conscious of the scent of my cologne or perfume.

_____ 25. When interacting with someone from a different culture or ethnicity, I am typically conscious of the scent of his or her breath.

_____ 26. When interacting with someone from a different culture or ethnicity, I am typically conscious of the scent of his or her cologne or perfume.

_____ 27. When interacting with someone from a different culture or ethnicity, I am typically conscious of the scent of his or her body.

_____ 28. When interacting with someone in a private environment, I am typically conscious of the scent of the immediate surroundings.

_____ 29. When interacting with someone in a private environment, I am typically conscious of the scent of the furniture.

_____ 30. When interacting with someone in a public environment, I am typically conscious of the scent of the immediate surroundings.

Scoring: To calculate your PROPS score, sum your responses as follows:

1. Perception and sensitivity to others: add Items 1–12 (range = 12–84).

2. Perception and sensitivity to self: add Items 13–24 (range = 12–84).

3. Perception and sensitivity to different cultures: add Items 25–27 (range = 3–21).

4. Perception and sensitivity to environment: add Items 28–30 (range = 3–21).

(Continued)

(Continued)

Higher scores indicate more sensitivity to the particular contexts. For example, scores above 50 for perception and sensitivity to others and/or self would be high, whereas scores below 30 would be considered low sensitivity. Scores above 15 for perception and sensitivity to persons from different cultures would be considered high, whereas scores below 7 would be considered low sensitivity.

SOURCE: J. W. Neuliep and E. L. Groshkopf, Toward a Communication Theory of Olfactics: Explication, Development of the Personal Report of Olfactic Perception and Sensation and Some Initial Tests. Paper presented at the 2001 annual convention of the National Communication Association, Atlanta, GA.

In her olfactic research, Fox has discovered that among those cultures where smell is closely associated with one's personal identity, the exchange or mixing of odors among people is carefully prescribed. For example, among the Amazonian Desana, members of a particular tribal group are thought to share a similar odor. Marriage is allowed only between people of different odors; that is, between members of different tribal groups. Similarly, among the Batek Negrito of the Malay Peninsula, people of similar odor groups are prohibited from engaging in sexual intercourse and even sitting too close to one another. The Batek Negrito believe that the prolonged mixing of similar odors causes illness in the people themselves and any children they may conceive.[125]

Fox also writes that Western smell preferences are not universal. For example, the Dassanetch, a tribal cattle-raising group in Ethiopia, believe that the smell of cows is the most pleasing of all smells. Dassanetch men routinely wash their hands in cattle urine and smear their bodies with cattle manure. Such smells are associated with status and fertility. The Dogon people of Mali find the scent of onions attractive, especially for young men and women, who rub fried onions all over their bodies.[126]

Physical Appearance and Dress

Often, we can identify a person's culture by his or her physical appearance and dress. Communication with another is often preceded by visual observations of the other's physical appearance. Moreover, in most cultures, people consciously manipulate their physical appearance to communicate their identity. Most cultures have strict rules for how their members should present themselves. Violating a culture's prescriptions for appearance may result in negative sanctions. In many cultures, a person's physical appearance and dress communicate the person's age, sex, and status within the culture.

In virtually every culture, men and women dress differently, and in many cultures, the differences begin at birth. In the United States, for example, male infants are traditionally dressed in blue and female infants in pink. In the Masai culture of Kenya, the distinction between young girls and women is communicated through body artifacts. According to Vandehey, Buerger, and Krueger, Masai women wear specific necklaces and earrings to designate their marital status. For a married woman to be seen without her earrings may bring harsh physical punishment from her husband. Masai men wear earrings and arm rings that designate social status. The specific earring distinguishes the man as an elder or warrior. Other body ornaments communicate whether a Masai (male or female) has been circumcised.[127]

Harris, Moran, and Moran observe that in India, businessmen wear a *dhoti,* a single piece of white cloth about 5 yards long and 3 feet wide that wraps around their lower body. Long shirts are worn on the upper part of the body. Most Indian women wear a sari and blouse. A sari consists of several yards of lightweight cloth draped so that one end forms a skirt and the other a head and shoulder covering. It is not acceptable for women to show skin above the knees or a large portion of the back. Wearing clothes that are in any way revealing is discouraged because it may unintentionally communicate that one is "a loose woman."[128] In Japan, the kimono—a long robe with wide sleeves—is the traditional clothing for both men and women; it is traditionally worn with a broad sash, or obi, as an outer garment. The specific design of the kimono varies according to one's sex, age, and marital status, the time of year, and the occasion. In the ancient past, there was no distinction between a man's and a woman's kimono. Today, there are several types of kimonos worn by men, women, and children. Men typically wear kimonos of blue, black, brown, gray, or white. Women's kimonos are the most elaborate and varied in style and design. The fabric, cut, color, sleeve length, and details of the obi vary according to a woman's age, social status, and marital status, as well as the season. During the summer months, women wear *yukatas,* or lightweight cotton kimonos. Many Japanese hotels provide *yukatas* for guests to wear in their rooms. In Japan, on "7–5–3 Day" (November 15), boys who are 3 or 5 years old and girls who are 3 or 7 years old dress in kimonos to pray at the temples. There is also a special day for all girls and all boys to go to the temple: March 3 is Girls' Day and May 5 is Boys' Day. Kimonos are worn on those days as well.[129]

STUDENT VOICES ACROSS CULTURES

Nonverbal Communication in Saudi Culture

My name is Hussam Almoharb. I am 28 years old, and I was born and raised in Riyadh, the capital city of Saudi Arabia. In Riyadh, I went to an associate college to study computer science. In 2009, I came to the United States to finish my degree and to learn English.

In Saudi Arabia, the traditional Saudi clothing for men is called *Thobe.* It is usually white in the summer and can be any color in the other seasons. *Thobe* is the formal wear for Saudi men, but sometimes young Saudi men wear jeans. For Saudi women, *hijab* (an Islamic headscarf) or *niqab* (an Islamic veil) is required in public places. However, In the large cities of Saudi Arabia, it is possible to see some women without *hijab*, especially if they are non-Saudis.

Based on my experience, there are many differences between the Saudi and American cultures, especially in their nonverbal communication. For Saudis, it is impolite not to make eye contact while talking to someone, especially if the other person is older. However, making eye contact without saying, "*As-Salamu Alaykum*" (Peace be upon you) is considered very impolite, too. The other thing is the physical contact. Compared with American culture, Saudis prefer a lot more physical contact during normal conversations. When meeting, Saudis shake hands and say, "*As-Salamu Alaykum*." Sometimes they keep holding hands until the conversation is over. In Saudi Arabia, holding hands means trust and welcome. However, it is inappropriate for a Saudi man to shake hands with a Saudi woman, especially if she is wearing a veil. Also, one should avoid using the left hand for gesturing. In fact, using the left hand for greeting is viewed as disrespectful.

Chronemics

Chronemics refers to the nonverbal channel of time. Recall (from Chapter 4) Hall's description of monochronic and polychronic time-oriented cultures. According to Hall, monochronic (M-time) orientations emphasize schedules and the compartmentalization and segmentation of measurable units of time. Many M-time cultures are low context, including the United States, Germany, Scandinavia, Canada, France, and most of Northern Europe. Conversely, polychronic (P-time) orientations see time as much less tangible and stress multiple activities with little emphasis on scheduling. P-time cultures stress involvement of people and the completion of tasks as opposed to a strict adherence to schedules. Many P-time cultures are high context, including Southern Europe, Latin America, and many African and Middle Eastern countries.[130]

The primary system for organizing time, in just about every culture, is the calendar. According to L. E. Doggett, one of the world's leading authorities on calendars, cultures create and use calendars as a way of organizing units of time to satisfy the needs of the society. Doggett maintains that calendars give people a sense that they can control time. Calendars also provide a link between people and the cosmos, or the supernatural. Doggett asserts that, in many cultures, calendars are considered nearly sacred and serve as a source of social order and cultural identity. In many ways, calendars dictate human communication patterns. When people eat, work, celebrate, worship, engage in leisure, attend school, hunt, rest, and fight wars is often prescribed by the calendar. Social contracts of just about every kind are typically determined by calendars. For example, marriages are deemed successful by the number of years they have lasted. Prison terms are defined in months or years. In most cultures, an individual's age, which is measured by a calendar, is the primary criterion for social and cultural privileges and responsibilities.[131]

According to Doggett, about 40 calendars are used in the world today. Most of these calendars are astronomically based. The primary astronomical cycles include the day, month, and year. Days are defined by the rotation of the Earth on its axis. The month is based on the revolution of the moon around the Earth. The year is based on the revolution of the Earth around the sun. Most cultures use either a solar, lunar, or lunisolar calendar. Many Western cultures, such as the United States, use a solar calendar. The Hebrew and Chinese use a lunisolar calendar.[132]

Doggett points out that the Gregorian calendar (a solar calendar) serves as the international standard. The United States functions under the Gregorian calendar. A common year is 365 days, with leap years of 366 days. Months are either 30 or 31 days, except for February, which has 28 or 29 days depending on whether or not it is a leap year. The Hebrew calendar is lunisolar and is the official calendar of Israel. Each year consists of either 12 or 13 months. Months consist of either 29 or 30 days. The beginning of each month is determined by a new moon. Traditionally, days of the week are designated by number, except for the seventh day, the Sabbath. Days begin and end at sunset. In China, the Gregorian calendar is used for governmental purposes, but the traditional Chinese calendar is used for scheduling cultural festivals and timing agricultural activities. The Chinese calendar is lunisolar, where months are either 29 or 30 days.[133]

Hall has pointed out that perceptions of time differ considerably across cultures. In the United States, for example, time is tangible (i.e., concrete, perceptible). Hall notes that to Americans, time can be bought, sold, saved, spent, wasted, lost, made up, and measured.

Americans are also future oriented in that we take great efforts to plan and schedule what we expect (or want) to happen. Hall also notes that duration is an important component to one's perception of time. According to Hall, duration is what happens between two points. Most Americans view time in this manner and carefully schedule and evaluate cultural events according to their duration (e.g., minutes, hours, days), as in, "Oh, that movie was way too long," "This won't take but a minute," and "When will you get here?" To some Native American groups, time is not thought of as measurable; rather, time is a sequence of events that differs for each set of circumstances.[134]

NONVERBAL COMMUNICATION AND DIMENSIONS OF CULTURAL VARIABILITY

Throughout this book, several dimensions of cultural variability have been discussed, including individualism–collectivism, power distance, and high–low context. Each of these dimensions can help explain cultural differences in nonverbal communication across cultures.

Individualism–Collectivism

In Chapter 2, individualism was defined as a cultural orientation where individuals precede groups in importance. In individualistic cultures, emphasis is placed on individual goals over group goals, and social behavior is guided by personal goals, perhaps at the expense of other types of goals. Individualistic cultures stress values that benefit the individual person. The self is promoted because each person is viewed as uniquely endowed and possessing distinctive talent and potential.

In collectivistic cultures, on the other hand, group goals have precedence over individual goals. Collectivistic cultures stress values that serve the in-group by subordinating personal goals for the sake of preserving the in-group as a whole. Collectivistic societies are characterized by extended primary groups such as the family, neighborhood, or occupational group, in which members have diffuse mutual obligations and expectations based on their status or rank. In collectivistic cultures, people are not seen as isolated individuals but as *interdependent* with others (e.g., their in-group), where responsibility is shared and accountability is collective. A person is seen not as an individual but as a member of a group.

In their review of nonverbal communication in individualistic and collectivistic cultures, Peter Andersen, Michael Hecht, Gregory Hoobler, and Maya Smallwood note that persons in individualistic cultures tend to be distant proximally, whereas persons in collectivistic cultures tend to work, play, live, and sleep in close proximity. In addition, body movements tend to be more synchronized in collectivistic cultures than in individualistic cultures. Facial behaviors (i.e., affect displays) differ as well. Persons in individualistic cultures tend to smile more than persons in collectivistic cultures. Andersen and his colleagues reason that people in collectivistic cultures are more likely to suppress their emotional displays because maintaining group harmony is primary. Finally, individualistic cultures are more nonverbally affiliative (i.e., enlisting nonverbal behaviors that bring people closer together physically and psychologically) than are collectivistic cultures.[135]

Power Distance

A culture's power distance (i.e., large vs. small) may account for nonverbal differences across cultures. Power distance refers to the extent to which less powerful members of a culture expect and accept that power is distributed unequally. Cultures with a smaller power distance emphasize that inequalities among people should be minimized and there should be interdependence between less and more powerful people. In cultures with a larger power distance, inequalities among people are both expected and desired. Less powerful people should be dependent on more powerful people. In high–power-distance cultures, interaction between persons of low and high power may be restricted, thus limiting the amount of nonverbal interaction. Andersen and his colleagues point out that in large–power-distance cultures, people without power are expected to express only positive emotional displays (e.g., smile more) when interacting with those of higher power.[136]

Power distance also affects paralinguistic cues. Persons in small–power-distance cultures are generally less aware of their vocalics (e.g., volume, intensity) than are persons in large–power-distance cultures. Andersen and his colleagues mention that North Americans (small power distance) are often perceived as noisy, exaggerated, and childlike.[137]

Occulesics, the way the eyes are used during communication, is also affected by power distance. In large–power-distance cultures, subordinates are taught to avert eye contact, often as a sign of respect for those in superior roles. For example, in large–power-distance cultures, students rarely give teachers direct eye contact. Direct eye gaze can be interpreted as a threat or a challenge to the person of higher power.

High and Low Context

Recall from Chapter 2 that high and low context refer to the degree to which interactants focus on the physical, social, and psychological (i.e., the nonverbal) context for information. Persons in high-context cultures are especially sensitive to the nonverbal context. Persons in low-context cultures focus less on the social or physical context and more on the explicit verbal code. Persons from low-context cultures are perceived as direct and talkative, whereas persons from high-context cultures are perceived as quiet, shy, and perhaps even sneaky.

Persons in high-context cultures tend to pay a great deal of attention to nonverbal behavior during interaction. Thus, facial expressions, touch, distance, and eye contact serve as important cues. Subtle body movements that may be missed by a low-context person may take on special meaning to a high-context person.

Nonverbal Expectancy Violations Theory

Judee Burgoon has formalized a theory of nonverbal communication called the nonverbal expectancy violations theory (NEV theory).[138] The basic premise of the theory is that people hold expectancies about the appropriateness of the nonverbal behaviors of others. These expectations are learned and culturally driven. For example, in the United States, people expect to shake hands when they are introduced to someone. Burgoon posits that, occasionally, people violate nonverbal expectations. When this happens, the violation produces arousal, which can be physiological or cognitive, positive or negative.

Burgoon maintains that once a violation has been committed and arousal is triggered, the recipient evaluates the violation and the violator. Violations initiated by highly attractive sources may be evaluated positively, whereas those initiated by unattractive sources may be evaluated negatively.[139] The same violation may produce very different evaluations, depending on who committed it. The evaluation of the violation depends on (a) the evaluation of the communicator, (b) implicit messages associated with the violation, and (c) evaluations of the act itself. In presenting the theory, Burgoon outlines several key assumptions (see Table 8.1).

Burgoon bases Assumption 1 on literature from anthropology, sociology, and psychology, indicating that humans are a social species with a biological/survival instinct to be with

Table 8.1 Fundamental Assumptions of NFV Theory
Assumption 1: Humans have two competing needs, a need for affiliation and a need for personal space (or distance). These two needs cannot be satisfied at once.
Assumption 2: The desire for affiliation may be elicited or magnified by the presence of rewards in the communication context. The rewards may be biological or social.
Assumption 3: The greater the degree to which a person or situation is defined as rewarding, the greater the tendency for others to approach that person or situation; the greater the degree to which a person or situation is defined as punishing, the greater the tendency for others to avoid that person or situation.
Assumption 4: Humans are able to perceive gradations in distance.
Assumption 5: Human interaction patterns, including personal space or distance patterns, are normative.
Assumption 6: Humans may develop idiosyncratic behavior patterns that differ from the social norms.
Assumption 7: In any communication context, the norms are a function of three classes of factors: (a) characteristics of the interactants, (b) features of the interaction itself, and (c) features of the immediate physical environment.
Assumption 8: Interactants develop expectations about the communication behavior of others. Consequently, they are able to recognize or at least respond differently to normative versus deviant behaviors on the part of others.
Assumption 9: Deviations from expectations have arousal value.
Assumption 10: Interactants make evaluations of others.
Assumption 11: Evaluations are influenced by the degree to which the other is perceived as rewarding, such that a positively valued message is only rewarding if the source is highly regarded and a negatively valued message is only punishing if the source is not highly regarded.

SOURCE: Reprinted from Burgoon, J. K. (1978). A Communication Model of Personal Space Violations: Explication and an Initial Test. In *Human Communication Research, 4,* 129–142. Copyright © 1978 Blackwell Publishing.

other humans. Conversely, humans cannot tolerate extended physical contact, or excessive closeness, with others; that is, humans have a basic need to insulate themselves from others and a need for privacy. Although this first assumption appears to be universal, the degree to which a person feels the need to be with others or insulated from them is probably culturally driven. An individualist may be more comfortable alone in the same situations in which a collectivist feels uncomfortable being alone. Moreover, the ways people satisfy the need for privacy or affiliation certainly vary across cultures. In the United States and Germany, for example, privacy is often satisfied by physical separation from others (e.g., closed doors), whereas in densely populated cultures such as India, privacy may be fulfilled psychologically.

Assumption 2 indicates that affiliation with others is triggered by rewards within the communicative context. These rewards may be biological (e.g., food, sex, safety) or social (e.g., belonging, esteem, status). Biological needs are no doubt universal, but social needs are often learned and vary across cultures. Belonging needs are felt much more strongly in collectivistic cultures than in individualistic ones. Conversely, esteem needs are more strongly felt in individualistic cultures than in collectivistic ones. Assumption 3 extends Assumption 2 by stating that humans are attracted to rewarding situations and repelled by punishing situations. This phenomenon is probably universal, but it should be noted that what people deem rewarding and punishing varies across cultures.

Assumption 4 asserts that humans have the perceptual ability to discern differences in spatial relationships. We can tell when someone is standing close to us or far away from us. Assumption 5 deals with the establishment of normative nonverbal behaviors. Normative behavior is that which is usual or typical, or that follows a regular pattern. For example, the lecture style of your professor is probably consistent day after day. The professor has established a normative way of delivering his or her material. Many normative behaviors are established by society and culture. In the United States, for example, saying "goodbye" is a normative way of terminating a telephone conversation.

Assumption 6 recognizes that even though most of us follow similar normative rules and regulations for our verbal and nonverbal behavior, we also develop our own personal style of interaction that is unique in some way. Assumption 7 states that norms operate as a function of the interactants, the interaction, and the environment. Characteristics of the interactants might include their sex, age, personality, and race. Characteristics of the interaction itself might include status differences or degree of intimacy between the interactants. Finally, characteristics of the environment may include the physical features of the setting, such as furniture arrangement, lighting, or even temperature.

Assumption 8 deals with the notion of expectancies, a key element of the theory. Burgoon argues that during interaction, interactants develop expectancies and preferences about the behaviors of others. These expectancies are anticipations of others' behavior that are perceived to be appropriate for the situation. Typically, expectancies are based on a combination of societal and cultural norms. For example, students expect that their professors will behave in an appropriate and consistent manner. In certain cases, however, students might expect idiosyncratic deviations from the norms for particular professors (e.g., a certain professor frequently tells jokes in class).

Assumption 9 focuses on two other key ingredients in the theory: violation of expectancies and arousal. Burgoon subscribes to the notion that when a person's nonverbal expectancies are violated, the person becomes aroused. The violation tends to stimulate the receiver/communicator's attention and to arouse either adaptive or defensive reactions. For example, we learned earlier in this chapter that in some cultures (e.g., Korea), touching the top of a child's head is prohibited. Doing so would be a violation of expectancy, and the child or the parents might respond negatively or defensively. In some situations, however, some violations are perceived positively. A shaman may be allowed to touch the top of a child's head, and such behavior may be perceived positively. Assumption 10 states that people make value judgments about others. Assumption 11 extends this notion by specifying how evaluations are made.

Burgoon contends that the first factor influencing the positive or negative evaluation of a violation is the communicator reward valence—that is, how much the violator is perceived as someone with whom interaction is desirable. Thus, communicator reward valence is based on communicator and relationship characteristics (e.g., age, sex, personality, status, reputation, anticipated future interaction) and interactional behaviors (e.g., style, positive feedback). Communicator reward valence influences how one will evaluate the violation of expectancies. Burgoon's theory holds that more favorable evaluations will be given when the violation is committed by a high-reward person as opposed to a low-reward person. If someone to whom you are attracted stands close to you at a party, much closer than is normative, you may interpret this violation positively as a sign of mutual attraction or affiliation. Conversely, if someone whom you find repulsive stands too close to you at a party, you may evaluate this violation quite negatively. Burgoon asserts that positively evaluated violations produce favorable communication patterns and consequences, whereas negatively evaluated violations produce unfavorable communication patterns. In addition, Burgoon contends that even extreme violations, if committed by a high-reward person, can be evaluated positively and produce reciprocal communication patterns. Although a significant number of studies support the assumptions of Burgoon's theory, very few, if any, have investigated its cross-cultural applicability.

Cultural Contexts and Nonverbal Expectancies

As we have seen throughout this book, the cultures of Japan and the United States differ significantly. Japan is a collectivistic, high-context culture, whereas the United States is an individualistic, low-context culture. Individualistic cultures stress the importance of an individual's unique identity. Emphasis is placed on individual goals over group goals. In contrast, American children are taught from an early age that they are individuals with unique abilities and talents. People are rewarded for being "the best," "the one and only," and "number one" in whatever they do. The goal of Americans is to be the best they can be and to strive for the top. A well-known cliché in the United States notes that "the squeaky wheel gets the grease," meaning that to get attention or to have one's needs met, one must draw attention to oneself. In contrast, collectivistic cultures place precedence on group goals over individual goals. Collectivistic cultures emphasize values that serve the in-group by subordinating personal goals for the sake of the in-group. Group activities are dominant and pervasive. Responsibility is shared, and accountability is collective.[140] Japan has an unofficial motto that reads, *"Deru kugi wa utareru,"* or "The tallest nail gets hammered down." Children are taught at a young age that their identity is based on their relationship within the group (family or business). Group leadership, rather than individual initiative, is valued. Especially among Japanese youth, however, a new sense of individualism is growing in Japan.[141]

A high-context culture, such as Japan, is one whose members are highly sensitive to the perceptual, sociorelational, and environmental contexts for information. High-context cultures have a restricted code system (i.e., language). Members do not rely on verbal communication as their main source of information. Silence and nonverbal behavior are most informative. Statements or actions of affection are rare. Members are quite adept at decoding nonverbal behavior. Japanese, for example, expect others (i.e., other Japanese) to understand their unarticulated communication. Cultural members are expected to know how to perform in various situations where the guidelines are implicit.[142]

Members of a low-context culture, such as the United States, are less sensitive to the perceptual, sociorelational, and environmental contexts. That is not to say that they ignore the environment; they are simply less aware of it than are members of a high-context culture. A low-context communication is one in which the mass of information is found in the explicit code. Hence, low-context cultures have an elaborated code system. Verbal messages are extremely important when information to be shared with others is coded in the verbal message. Members of low-context cultures do not perceive the environment as a source of information. Guidelines and expectations are frequently explained explicitly.[143]

In addition to high-context/low-context distinctions between the two countries, Japan is considered a low-contact culture, whereas the United States is considered a moderate-contact culture. Many of the communicative behaviors of high/low-context, individualistic/collectivistic, and high/low-contact cultures are different, and interactants from these cultures will inevitably violate each other's expectations regarding appropriate nonverbal behavior.

AN INTERCULTURAL CONVERSATION: VIOLATION OF NONVERBAL EXPECTANCIES

In the following two scenarios, Jim, Akira, and Mitsuko interact. Akira and Mitsuko are exchange students from Japan who are spending a semester studying at an American college. Jim is an American student at the same college. Notice how each violates the other's expectations without realizing it.

When reading the following scenes, keep in mind the different cultural orientations and the assumptions of NEV theory.

Jim and Akira are at a party.

1. *Jim:*   (Nudges Akira and says loudly) This is a great party, eh?

2. *Akira:*   (Is startled—stands back—tries to put some distance between himself and Jim.) Yes, thank you.

3. *Jim:*   (Leaning forward toward Akira, with direct eye contact) If you want to meet some girls, I could introduce you.

4. *Akira:*   (Shocked by such an offer, he backs away.) But I don't know them. They might be upset.

5. *Jim:*   Well, how else are you going to meet them?

6. *Akira:*   (Uncomfortable) Maybe during a class or something.

Mitsuko, another Japanese exchange student, approaches Jim and Akira. She knows Akira but not Jim.

7. *Mitsuko:*   Hello, Akira. (Bows slightly and looks down.)

8. *Akira:*   Ah, Mitsuko, this is my friend Jim.

9. *Jim:*   Hi! (Leaning forward into her space)

10. *Mitsuko:*   Hi, Jim. (Bows slightly and does not make direct eye contact.)

11. *Jim:*   Are you two friends? (Wonders why she won't look at him, thinks to himself, "Well, I'm not one of them. She probably thinks I'm ugly.")

12. *Akira:*   Yes, we know each other.

A long pause ensues.

13. *Jim:*   (Thinks to himself, "This is going nowhere—I've got to think of something to say." He speaks rather loudly.) Great party, hey guys?

Akira and Mitsuko both jump back.

14. *Akira:*   (Thinks to himself, "This guy is too weird.") Yeah, this is fun.

During this scenario, Jim violates Akira's kinesic, proxemic, paralinguistic, and haptic expectations. Several of the axioms and propositions from Burgoon's NEV theory can be applied to this interaction. Notice in Lines 1 through 4 that Akira perceives that Jim is standing too close and talking too loudly and, thus, backs away. From Akira's point of view, Jim violated his proxemic and paralinguistic expectations. In Line 1, Jim touches Akira, which probably violates Akira's nonverbal expectations regarding haptics. From Jim's vantage point, Akira violates his expectations as well, by not looking at him and not responding to his offer to introduce him to women. According to NEV theory, violations have arousal value (Assumption 9).

Throughout the dialogue, we can see how Akira and Jim become aroused (e.g., shocked, uncomfortable, startled, annoyed) by each other's violations. Both Mitsuko and Akira jump when Jim yells, "Great party, hey guys?" In Lines 13 and 14, we can see how Burgoon's Assumption 10 applies in that the arousal leads to evaluations (e.g., "This is going nowhere," "This guy is too weird"). In this case, the evaluations are negative.

According to the theory, the greater the degree to which a person is perceived as rewarding, the greater the tendency for others to approach that person. Likewise, the greater the degree to which a person is perceived as punishing, the greater the tendency for others to avoid that person. Unfortunately for Akira, because he is in a "foreign" country, he will be the more likely of the two to change his behavior to conform to the expectations of others.

CHAPTER SUMMARY

Many social scientists believe that our verbal language evolved from a system of nonlinguistic communication that we inherited from our animal predecessors. As humans, we possess a host of nonlinguistic ways to communicate with one another through the use of kinesics, occulesics, proxemics, paralanguage, haptics, olfactics, and physical appearance. Our nonverbal communication, when combined with verbal language, creates a complicated communication system through which humans come to know and understand one another.

Our nonverbal behavior is innate and learned. Many of our unconscious behaviors, such as the expression of emotions, are universal. People from all cultures express anger, happiness, and sadness the very same way. Yet other forms of nonverbal communication, such as gestures, are unique manifestations of our culture's distinctive cosmos. We learn how to communicate with our bodies (kinesics), with our eyes (occulesics), through the use of space (proxemics), by touching others (haptics), with our voices (paralanguage), with smell (olfactics), and through the way we dress and present ourselves. Sometimes, our nonverbal behaviors violate the expectations of others. Sometimes, we stand too close or touch too much. When this happens, the other person evaluates the violation as positive or negative depending on whether we are perceived as attractive or unattractive. If we are thought of as attractive, our violation may be welcome. If we are perceived as unattractive, the same violation may be evaluated quite negatively.

Visit the student study site at www.sagepub.com/neuliep6e for e-flashcards, web quizzes, web resources, and more.

DISCUSSION QUESTIONS

1. When you observe the nonverbal behavior of others, what do you notice first?

2. How does your style of dress identify you as a member of a particular culture?

3. What types of gestures have you used today to communicate without words?

4. How do you communicate intimacy nonverbally?

5. Without using words, how do you communicate to someone that you do not understand what he or she is saying?

6. How do you try to manipulate your unique smell?

ETHICS AND THE NONVERBAL CODE

1. Recently, the author of this excellently written text had a female student from Saudi Arabia enrolled in his class. At one of their first meetings, the author extended his hand to her in greeting. She refused to shake his hand and said it was against her culture's rules to shake a male's hand. What do you think? As a visiting international exchange student, should she have shaken hands with the author?

2. Recently, the author of this excellently written text had several male students from Saudi Arabia enrolled in his class. Oftentimes in his class, the author distributes handouts to the students. The Saudi students asked that he not use his left hand to pass them the handouts. What do you think? Is their request unreasonable? Should the author comply?

3. A student recently complained that his roommate, who is an international exchange student, bathes only occasionally and smells bad. What do you think? Should the student say something to his roommate? Perhaps the roommate is just comfortable with the natural scent of the human body.

KEY TERMS

adaptors   296

affect displays   291

analogic communication   282

chronemics   314

denotative meaning   283

digital communication   282

emblems   284

haptics   304

illustrators   284

kinesics   284

nonverbal expectancy violations theory   316

occulesics   296

olfactics   306

paralanguage   298

proxemics   301

regulators   295

NOTES

1. Farb, P. (1973). *Word Play: What Happens When People Talk.* New York: Bantam, p. 234.

2. Molinsky, A. L., Krabbenhoft, M. A., Ambady, N., & Choi, Y. S. (2005). Cracking the Nonverbal Code: Intercultural Competence and Gesture Recognition Across Cultures. *Journal of Cross-Cultural Psychology, 36,* 380–395.

3. Searchinger, G. (Director & Producer). (1996). *The Human Language Series: Part III: With and Without Words* [Motion picture]. Available from Ways of Knowing, Inc., 200 West 72nd Street, New York, NY 10023.

4. Knapp, M. L., & Hall, J. A. (2009). *Nonverbal Communication in Human Interaction* (7th ed.). Belmont, CA: Wadsworth (Thomson Learning).

5. Searchinger, *The Human Language Series.*

6. Ibid.

7. Ibid.

8. Condon, J. C., & Yousef, F. (1975). *An Approach to Intercultural Communication.* Indianapolis, IN:

Bobbs-Merrill; Littlejohn, S. W. (1996). *Theories of Human Communication* (5th ed.). Belmont, CA: Wadsworth.

9. Ekman, P., & Friesen, W. V. (1969). The Repertoire of Nonverbal Behavior: Categories, Origins, Usage, and Coding. *Semiotica, 1,* 49–98.

10. Guidetti, M., & Nicoladis, E. (2006). Gestures and Communicative Development. *First Language, 26,* 346.

11. Blake, J., Osborne, P., Cabral, M., & Gluck, P. (2003). The Development of Communicative Gestures in Japanese Infants. *First Language, 23,* 3–20.

12. Archer, D. (Producer), & Silver, J. (Director). (1991). *A World of Gestures: Culture and Nonverbal Communication* [Motion picture]. Available from University of California Extension, Center for Media and Independent Learning, 2000 Center Street, Fourth Floor, Berkeley, CA 94704.

13. Sapir, E. (1949). The Unconscious Patterning of Behaviour in Society. In D. G. Mendelbaum (Ed.), *Selected*

Writings of Edward Sapir (pp. 544–559). Berkeley: University of California Press. (Quote on p. 554)

14. Molinsky et al., Cracking the Nonverbal Code.

15. Choi, M. (1995). *Cultural Profile of South Korea.* Unpublished student manuscript, St. Norbert College, De Pere, WI.

16. Harris, P. R., Moran, R. T., & Moran, S. V. (2004). *Managing Cultural Differences: Global Leadership Strategies for the 21st Century* (6th ed.). Burlington, MA: Elsevier, Butterworth-Heineman; Kachka, B. (2007). *Etiquette 101: Japan.* Retrieved from http://www.cntraveler.com/travel-tips/travel-etiquette/2007/11/Etiquette-101-Japan

17. Visiting Cards. (2013). *Japan-Guide.com.* Retrieved from http://www.japan-guide.com/e/e2227.html

18. Moellendorf, S., Warsh, H., & Yoshimaru, K. (1996). *The Amish Culture: A Closer Look at the People of Lancaster County.* Unpublished manuscript, St. Norbert College, De Pere, WI.

19. Kenya: Language, Culture, Customs and Etiquette. (n.d.). *Kwintessential.* Retrieved from http://www.kwintessential.co.uk/resources/global-etiquette/kenya.html

20. Axtell, R. E. (1991). *Gestures: The Do's and Taboos of Gestures and Body Language Around the World.* New York: Wiley.

21. Bishop, R. J. (1995). *Cultural Profile, Examination of Value Orientations and Sociocultural Influences, and Verbal and Nonverbal Language Aspects of the East Indian Culture.* Unpublished student manuscript, St. Norbert College, De Pere, WI.

22. Harris et al., *Managing Cultural Differences;* Wolter, A. (1994). *Saudi Arabia and Its Culture.* Unpublished manuscript, St. Norbert College, De Pere, WI.

23. Rieck, S., & Ogura, M. (1996). *Sri Lanka: The Pearl of the Indian Ocean.* Unpublished manuscript, St. Norbert College, De Pere, WI.

24. Archer & Silver, *A World of Gestures.*

25. Keberlein, M. C. (1993). *A Cultural Profile of the Guatemalan Ladinos.* Unpublished manuscript, St. Norbert College, De Pere, WI.

26. Thao, K. (1995). *The Hmong Culture.* Unpublished student manuscript, St. Norbert College, De Pere, WI.

27. Penasa, A. G., Peters, M., & Smits, S. (1996). *Jamaica: Out of Many, One People.* Unpublished manuscript, St. Norbert College, De Pere, WI.

28. These examples are shown in Archer & Silver, *A World of Gestures.*

29. Ibid.

30. Ibid.

31. Thao, *The Hmong Culture.*

32. Archer & Silver, *A World of Gestures.*

33. Marsh, A. A., Anger-Elfenbein, H., & Ambady, N. (2007). Separated by a Common Language: Nonverbal Accents and Cultural Stereotypes About Americans and Australians. *Journal of Cross-Cultural Psychology, 38,* 284–301.

34. Knapp & Hall, *Nonverbal Communication in Human Interaction.*

35. Searchinger, *The Human Language Series.*

36. Birdwhistell, R. L. (1970). *Kinesics and Context: Essays on Body Motion Communication.* New York: Ballantine, p. 42.

37. Darwin, C. (1872). *The Expression of the Emotions in Man and Animals.* London: J. Murray, p. 361.

38. Searchinger, *The Human Language Series.*

39. Ekman, P., Friesen, W., O'Sullivan, M., Chan, A., Diacoyanni-Tarlatzis, I., Heider, K., et al. (1987). Universals and Cultural Differences in the Judgment of Facial Expressions of Emotions. *Journal of Personality and Social Psychology, 53,* 712–717.

40. Izard, C. E. (1994). Innate and Universal Facial Expressions: Evidence From Developmental and Cross-Cultural Research. *Psychological Bulletin, 115,* 288–299.

41. Stephan, W. G., Stephan, C. W., & De Vargas, M. C. (1996). Emotional Expressions in Costa Rica and the United States. *Journal of Cross-Cultural Psychology, 27,* 147–160.

42. Schimmack, U. (1996). Cultural Influences on the Recognition of Emotion by Facial Expressions. *Journal of Cross-Cultural Psychology, 27,* 37–51.

43. Matsumoto, D. (1989). Cultural Influences on the Perception of Emotion. *Journal of Cross-Cultural Psychology, 20,* 92–105.

44. Pittam, J., Gallois, C., Iwawaki, S., & Kroonenberg, P. (1995). Australian and Japanese Concepts of Expressive Behavior. *Journal of Cross-Cultural Psychology, 26,* 451–473.

45. Marsh, A., Elfenbein, H. A., & Ambady, N. (2003). Nonverbal "Accents": Cultural Differences in Facial Expressions of Emotion. *Psychological Science, 14,* 373–376.

46. Jack, R. E., Garrod, O. G. B., Yu, H., Caldara, R., & Schyns, P. G. (2012). Facial Expressions of Emotion Are Not Culturally Universal. *Proceedings of the National Academy of Sciences, 109*(19), 7241–7244.

47. Bothwell, R. K., Brigham, J. C., & Malpass, R. S. (1989). Cross-Racial Identification. *Personality and Psychology Bulletin, 15,* 19–25; Malpass, R. S., & Kravitz, J. (1969). Recognition for Faces of Own and Other Race. *Journal of Personality and Social Psychology, 13,* 330–354.

48. Feingold, G. A. (1914). The Influence of Environment on Identification of Persons and Things. *Journal of Criminal Law and Police Science, 5,* 50.

49. Brigham, J. C., & Malpass, R. S. (1985). The Role of Experience and Contact in the Recognition of Faces of Own- and Other-Race Persons. *Journal of Social Issues, 41,* 139–155.

50. Feinman, S., & Entwistle, D. R. (1976). Children's Ability to Recognize Other Children's Faces. *Child Development, 47*, 506–510.

51. Brigham, J. C., & Barkowitz, P. (1978). Do They All Look Alike? The Effect of Race, Sex, Experience, and Attitudes on the Ability to Recognize Faces. *Journal of Applied Social Psychology, 8*, 306–318; Malpass & Kravitz, Recognition for Faces of Own and Other Race; Ng, W. J., & Lindsay, R. C. L. (1994). Cross-Race Facial Recognition: Failure of the Contact Hypothesis. *Journal of Cross-Cultural Psychology, 25*, 217–232; Teitelbaum, S., & Geiselman, R. E. (1997). Observer Mood and Cross-Racial Recognition of Faces. *Journal of Cross-Cultural Psychology, 28*, 93–106.

52. Rhodes, G., Tan, S., Brake, S., & Taylor, K. (1989). Expertise and Configural Coding in Face Recognition. *British Journal of Psychology, 80*, 313–331.

53. Shriver, E. R., Young, S. G., Hugenberg, K., Bernstein, M. J., & Lanter, J. R. (2008). Class, Race, and the Face: Social Context Modulates the Cross-Race Effect in Face Recognition. *Personality and Social Psychology Bulletin, 34*, 260–274.

54. Johnson, K. J., & Fredrickson, B. L. (2005). "We All Look the Same to Me": Positive Emotions Eliminate the Own-Race Bias in Face Recognition. *Psychological Science, 16*, 875–881; Maclin, O. H., & Malpass, R. S. (2003). The Ambiguous-Race Face Illusion. *Perception, 32*, 249–252.

55. Young, S. G., & Hugenberg, K. (2012). Individuation Motivation and Face Experience Can Operate Jointly to Produce the Own-Race Bias. *Social Psychological and Personality Science, 3*, 80–87.

56. Almaney, A., & Alwan, A. (1982). *Communicating With the Arabs.* Prospect Heights, IL: Waveland.

57. Harris et al., *Managing Cultural Differences.*

58. Adams, R. B., Jr., & Kleck, R. E. (2003). Perceived Gaze Direction and the Processing of Facial Displays of Emotion. *Psychological Science, 14*(6), 644–647.

59. Janik S. W., Wellens, A. R., Goldberg, M. L., & Dell'Osso, L. F. (1978). Eyes as the Center of Focus in the Visual Examination of Human Faces. *Perceptual and Motor Skills, 47*, 857–858.

60. Adams & Kleck, Perceived Gaze Direction and the Processing of Facial Displays of Emotion.

61. Blais, C., Jack, R. E., Scheepers, C., Fiset, D., & Caldara, R. (2008). Culture Shapes How We Look at Faces. *PLoS ONE, 3*(8), e3022. doi:10.1371/journal.pone.0003022

62. Akechi, H., Senju, A., Uibo, H., Kikuchi, Y., Hasegawa, T., & Hietanen, J. K. (2013). Attention to Eye Contact in the West and East: Autonomic Responses and Evaluative Ratings. *PLoS ONE, 8*(3), e59312.

63. Nelson, A. (2010). The Politics of Eye Contact: A Gender Perspective. *Psychology Today*. Retrieved from http://www.psychologytoday.com/blog/he-speaks-she-speaks/201009/the-politics-eye-contact-gender-perspective

64. Knapp & Hall, *Nonverbal Communication in Human Interaction.*

65. Ibid.

66. Searchinger, *The Human Language Series.*

67. Chinese Mandarin Tones. (n.d.). *Qi: The Journal of Traditional Eastern Health and Fitness.* Retrieved from http://www.qi-journal.com/Popups/tones.html; Hsin-Yun, Y. (1998). *The Four Tones in Mandarin Chinese.* Retrieved from www.wellgot.ca/english-fm.html

68. Ibid.

69. Choi, *Cultural Profile of South Korea.*

70. Zuckerman, M., & Miyake, K. (1993). The Attractive Voice: What Makes It So? *Journal of Nonverbal Behavior, 17*, 119–135.

71. Gluszek, A., & Dovidio, J. F. (2010). Speaking With a Nonnative Accent: Perception of Bias, Communication, Difficulties, and Belonging in the United States. *Journal of Language and Social Psychology, 29*(2), 229–234; Gluszek, A., & Dovidio, J. F. (2010). The Way *They* Speak: A Social Psychological Perspective on the Stigma of Nonnative Accents in Communication. *Personality and Social Psychology Review, 14*(2), 214–237.

72. Giles, H. (1970). Evaluative Reactions to Accents. *Educational Review, 22*, 211–227; Gluszek & Dovidio, Speaking With a Nonnative Accent; Gluszek & Dovidio, The Way *They* Speak.

73. Giles, Evaluative Reactions to Accents; Giles, H., & Johnson, P. (1987). Ethnolinguistic Identity Theory: A Social Psychological Approach to Language Maintenance. *International Journal of the Sociology of Language, 68*, 69–99; Gluszek & Dovidio, Speaking With a Nonnative Accent; Gluszek & Dovidio, The Way *They* Speak.

74. Cargile, A. C., & Giles, H. (1997). Understanding Language Attitudes: Exploring Listener Affect and Identity. *Language & Communication, 17*, 195–217; Dixon, J. A., Mahoney, B., & Cocks, R. (2002). Accents of Guilt? Effects of Regional Accent, Race, and Crime Type on Attributions of Guilt. *Journal of Language and Social Psychology, 21*, 162–168; Edwards, J. (1999). Refining Our Understanding of Language Attitudes. *Journal of Language and Social Psychology, 18*, 101–110; Gluszek & Dovidio, Speaking With a Nonnative Accent; Gluszek & Dovidio, The Way *They* Speak; Lippi-Green, R. (1994). Accent, Standard Language Ideology, and Discriminatory Pretext in the Courts. *Language in Society, 23*, 163–198; Stewart, M. A., Ryan, E. B., & Giles, H. (1985). Accent and Social Class Effects on Status and Solidarity Evaluations. *Personality and Social Psychology Bulletin, 11*, 98–105.

75. Kinzler, K. D., Shutts, K., DeJesus, J., & Spelke, E. S. (2009). Accent Trumps Race in Guiding Children's Social Preferences. *Social Cognition, 27*, 623–634.

76. Gluszek & Dovidio, The Way *They* Speak.

77. Dixon et al., Accents of Guilt? Effects of Regional Accents, Race, and Crime Type on Attributions of Guilt; Gluszek & Dovidio, The Way *They* Speak; Rubin,

D. L. (1992). Nonlanguage Factors Affecting Undergraduates' Judgments of Nonnative English-Speaking Teaching Assistants. *Research in Higher Education, 33,* 511–531.

78. Hasegawa, T., & Gudykunst, W. B. (1998). Silence in Japan and the United States. *Journal of Cross-Cultural Psychology, 29,* 668–684.

79. Braithwaite, C. A. (1999). Cultural Uses and Interpretations of Silence. In L. K. Guerrero, J. A. DeVito, & M. L. Hecht (Eds.), *The Nonverbal Communication Reader* (2nd ed., pp. 163–172). Prospect Heights, IL: Waveland.

80. Kaya, N., & Weber, M. J. (2003). Territorial Behavior in Residence Halls: A Cross-Cultural Study. *Environment and Behavior, 35,* 400–415.

81. Amole, D. (2005). Coping Strategies for Living in Student Residential Facilities in Nigeria. *Environment and Behavior, 37,* 201–219.

82. Bishop, *Cultural Profile, Examination of Value Orientations and Sociocultural Influences, and Verbal and Nonverbal Language Aspects of the East Indian Culture.*

83. Rieck & Ogura, *Sri Lanka: The Pearl of the Indian Ocean.*

84. Hesselink, R. C., Mullen, R. T., & Rouse, J. M. (1996). *Moroccan Culture: An In-Depth Study.* Unpublished manuscript, St. Norbert College, De Pere, WI.

85. Ishikawa, Y., & Hashimoto, M. (1996). *The Kenyan Culture.* Unpublished student manuscript, St. Norbert College, De Pere, WI.

86. Argyle, M. (1975). *Bodily Communication.* New York: International Universities Press; Wolter, *Saudi Arabia and Its Culture.*

87. Schut, C., Linder, D., Brosig, B., Niemeier, V., Ermler, C., Madejski, K., et al. (2013). Appraisal of Touching Behavior, Shame and Disgust: A Cross-Cultural Study. *International Journal of Culture and Mental Health, 6*(1), 1–15. (Quote on p. 1)

88. Knapp & Hall, *Nonverbal Communication in Human Interaction.*

89. Hall, E. T. (1963). A System for the Notation of Proxemic Behavior. *American Anthropologist, 65,* 1003–1026.

90. Kim, M. S. (1998). A Comparative Analysis of Nonverbal Expressions as Portrayed by Korean and American Print-Media Advertising. In J. N. Martin, T. K. Nakayama, & L. A. Flores (Eds.), *Readings in Cultural Contexts* (pp. 206–216). Mountain View, CA: Mayfield.

91. McDaniel, E., & Andersen, P. A. (1998). International Patterns of Interpersonal Tactile Communication: A Field Study. *Journal of Nonverbal Behavior, 22,* 59–76.

92. Dibiase, R., & Gunnoe, J. (2004). Gender and Culture Differences in Touching Behavior. *Journal of Social Psychology, 144,* 49–62.

93. Jourard, S. M. (1966). An Exploratory Study of Body Accessibility. *British Journal of Social and Clinical Psychology, 5,* 221–231.

94. Casteel, B. (1995). *A Cross-Cultural Study of Touch Avoidance.* Unpublished master's thesis, West Virginia University. Cited in D. W. Klopf (1995), *Intercultural Encounters: The Fundamentals of Intercultural Communication.* Englewood, CO: Morton.

95. Remland, M. S., Jones, T. S., & Brinkman, H. (1995). Interpersonal Distance, Body Orientation, and Touch: Effects of Culture, Gender, and Age. *Journal of Social Psychology, 135,* 281–298.

96. Bishop, *Cultural Profile, Examination of Value Orientations and Sociocultural Influences, and Verbal and Nonverbal Language Aspects of the East Indian Culture.*

97. Wolter, *Saudi Arabia and Its Culture.*

98. Harris et al., *Managing Cultural Differences.*

99. Ibid.

100. Schut et al., Appraisal of Touching Behavior, Shame and Disgust.

101. Ibid.

102. Ibid.

103. Gibbons, B. (1987). The Intimate Sense of Smell. *National Geographic, 170,* 324–361.

104. Stoddart, D. M. (1990). *The Scented Ape: The Biology and Culture of Human Odour.* Cambridge, UK: Cambridge University Press.

105. Kohl, J. V., & Francoeur, R. T. (1995). *The Scent of Eros.* New York: Continuum.

106. Ibid.

107. Classen, C., Howes, D., & Synnott, A. (1994). *Aroma: The Cultural History of Smell.* New York: Routledge.

108. Le Guérer, A. (1992). *Scent: The Mysterious and Essential Powers of Smell.* New York: Turtle Bay Books.

109. Howes, D., Synnott, A., & Classen, C. (1995). The Anthropology of Odour. In A. N. Gilbert (Ed.), *Compendium of Olfactory Research* (pp. 111–116). Dubuque, Iowa: Kendall-Hunt; Synnott, A. (1996). A Sociology of Smell. *Canadian Review of Sociology and Anthropology, 28*(4), 437–460.

110. Kohl & Francoeur, *The Scent of Eros.*

111. Classen et al., *Aroma: The Cultural History of Smell.*

112. Gibbons, The Intimate Sense of Smell.

113. Synnott, A Sociology of Smell.

114. Gibbons, The Intimate Sense of Smell.

115. Baker, J. R. (1974). *Race.* New York: Oxford University Press.

116. Classen et al., *Aroma: The Cultural History of Smell;* Dollard, J. (1957). *Caste and Class in a Southern Town.* New York: Doubleday.

117. Classen et al., *Aroma: The Cultural History of Smell;* Le Guérer, *Scent: The Mysterious and Essential Powers of Smell;* Simmel, G. (1912). *Mélanges de Philosophie Relativiste.* Paris: F. Alcon, p. 12.

118. Classen et al., *Aroma: The Cultural History of Smell;* Le Guérer, *Scent: The Mysterious and Essential Powers of Smell;* Simmel, *Mélanges de Philosophie Relativiste,* p. 34.

119. This poem was cited in Classen et al., *Aroma: The Cultural History of Smell*. The original source is H. Williams (1937), *The Poems of Jonathan Swift* (Vol. 2). Oxford, UK: Clarendon, p. 529.

120. Olfactory Research Fund. *Enthusiastic Response to Website Sense of Smell Survey (1996–1997)*. Retrieved from www.olfactory.org/response.html

121. Todrank, J., Byrnes, D., Wrzesniewski, A., & Rozin, P. (1995). Odors Can Change Preferences for People in Photographs: A Cross-Modal Evaluative Conditioning Study With Olfactory USs and Visual CSs. *Learning and Motivation, 26,* 116–140.

122. Kohl & Francoeur, *The Scent of Eros*.

123. Fox, K. (2001). *The Smell Report*. Oxford, UK: Social Issues Research Centre.

124. Ibid.

125. Ibid.

126. Ibid.

127. Vandehey, K., Buerger, C., & Krueger, K. (1996). *Traditional Aspects and Struggles of the Masai Culture*. Unpublished manuscript, St. Norbert College, De Pere, WI.

128. Harris et al., *Managing Cultural Differences; Recreational Travel Guide to India*. (1993). Retrieved from www.solutions.mb.ca/rec-traqvel/asia/india/india-guide.html

129. *A History of Kimono*. (n.d.). Retrieved from www.japan.mit.edu/kimono/intro.html. This site is a part of the Japanese Language and Culture Network.

130. Hall, E. T. (1959). *The Silent Language*. New York: Doubleday.

131. Doggett, L. E. (1992). Calendars. In P. K. Seidelmann (Ed.), *Explanatory Supplement to the Astronomical Almanac* (p. 579). Sausalito, CA: University Science Books.

132. Ibid.

133. Ibid.

134. Hall, *The Silent Language*.

135. Andersen, P. A., Hecht, M. L., Hoobler, G. D., & Smallwood, M. (2003). Nonverbal Communication Across Cultures. In W. B. Gudykunst (Ed.), *Cross-Cultural and Intercultural Communication* (pp. 73–90). Thousand Oaks, CA: Sage.

136. Ibid.

137. Ibid.

138. Burgoon, J. K. (1978). A Communication Model of Personal Space Violations: Explication and an Initial Test. *Human Communication Research, 4,* 129–142; Burgoon, J. K., & Jones, S. B. (1976). Toward a Theory of Personal Space Expectations and Their Violations. *Human Communication Research, 2,* 131–146.

139. An excellent review of research associated with NEV can be found in Burgoon, J. K., & Hale, J. L. (1988). Nonverbal Expectancy Violations: Model Elaboration and Application to Immediacy Behaviors. *Communication Monographs, 55,* 58–79.

140. Schwartz, S. H. (1990). Individualism–Collectivism: Critique and Proposed Refinements. *Journal of Cross-Cultural Psychology, 21,* 139–157.

141. Harris et al., *Managing Cultural Differences*.

142. Schwartz, Individualism–Collectivism.

143. Gudykunst, W. B. (Ed.). (1983). *Intercultural Communication Theory: Current Perspectives*. Beverly Hills, CA: Sage.

C H A P T E R   9

Developing
Intercultural Relationships

CHAPTER OBJECTIVES

After reading this chapter, you should be able to

1. recount the fundamental assumptions of the uncertainty reduction theory,

2. discuss the relationship between uncertainty reduction and intercultural communication apprehension,

3. cogently discuss the fundamental assumptions of anxiety/uncertainty management theory,

4. identify assertive and responsive sociocommunicative styles,

5. define relational empathy and third-culture building,

6. compare ratings of relational intimacy across cultures,

7. describe differences in relationships between Eastern and Western cultures,

8. compare marital types across cultures, and

9. compare divorce rates across cultures.

Without others, there is no self.

—Kenneth J. Gergen[1]

———

Before reading this chapter any further, take a moment and think about you. Yes, think about yourself. If someone were to ask you to describe yourself, what would you say? Now, in the space below, list three terms that describe you. Use whatever terms you want.

1. _____

2. _____

3. _____

Next question: How do you know that the terms you wrote above are accurate? Perhaps you wrote that you are a *good student,* a *loyal friend, honest,* or a *fast runner.* How do you know that these descriptors are accurate? The only reason you know these terms are correct is because of *others* around you. Yes, other people (i.e., your relationships) help you define yourself. For example, if you describe yourself as a good student, the only reason you know that is because of your relationships with teachers who have provided you with feedback. If you describe yourself as a fast runner, the only way you know that is by comparing your running with that of other runners. You can describe yourself only in relation to others. You cannot be tall unless someone else is short. You cannot be a fast runner unless someone else is a slow runner. As Kenneth Gergen's quote at the beginning of the chapter states, without others, there is no self.

Initiating and maintaining relationships with others is one of the most necessary and challenging functions of human survival. Our self-concept and self-esteem are sustained largely by the substance of our relationships with others. From our relational partners, we receive feedback that we use to assess ourselves. We compare ourselves to our relational partners. In essence, the only way we know ourselves is through our relationships with others. Our social existence is relative to other people. Regardless of one's cultural origins, relationships provide the substance of life. This chapter focuses on several variables that affect the initiation and maintenance of personal relationships. Much of our communication behavior during the first stage of a relationship is designed to reduce uncertainty about our relational partner. One factor that affects our ability to do that is the degree to which we experience intercultural communication apprehension. Another variable that affects the uncertainty process is our sociocommunicative style—that is, the extent to which we are assertive and responsive with our relational partners.

Two other variables that affect our relations with others are the degree to which we can empathize with others and how similar we perceive ourselves to be to others. Uncertainty reduction, intercultural communication apprehension, sociocommunicative style, empathy, and similarity are experienced differently by each interactant in a relationship. The relationship established by any two people is the result of a complex combination of these factors, as depicted in Figure 9.1.

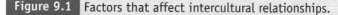

Figure 9.1 Factors that affect intercultural relationships.

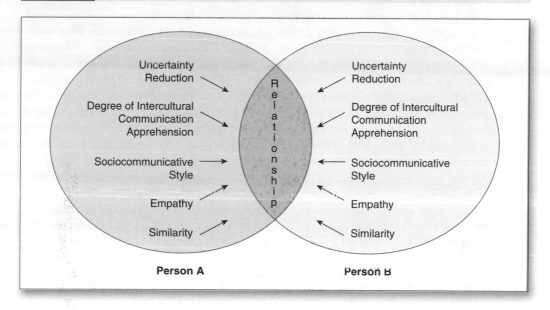

This chapter explores a variety of topics associated with relationships. The first section deals with uncertainty reduction and factors that affect how people go about reducing uncertainty, including intercultural communication apprehension and sociocommunicative style. The next part of the chapter focuses on empathy, third-culture building, and similarity. The third part of the chapter examines how perceptions about relationships vary across cultures, with particular emphasis on how relationships are perceived in Eastern and Western cultures. The final part of the chapter looks at intercultural, interracial, and lesbian/gay relationships, along with mate selection across cultures, arranged marriages, and divorce.

COMMUNICATION AND UNCERTAINTY

All relationships must begin somewhere. The people with whom we are now intimate were at one time strangers. Think about your closest friends. At some point, they were strangers to you. Can you remember the first time you interacted with them? Communication with a stranger, particularly a person from a different culture, can be frightening and full of uncertainty. **Uncertainty** refers to the amount of predictability—that is, what you know about the person with whom you are interacting. When someone is a stranger, we know almost nothing about him or her. Because of the uncertainty, we experience anxiety when interacting with that person for the first time. Uncertainty is cognitive (what we know and think), while anxiety is affective (how we feel). Uncertainty and anxiety are closely linked. Interacting with a person from a different culture probably involves more uncertainty and therefore may be even more anxiety producing. In an attempt to explain our communication behavior during initial communication encounters with others, Charles Berger and Richard Calabrese developed a communication theory called **uncertainty** reduction theory (URT). The major premise of this theory is that when strangers first meet, their primary goal is to reduce uncertainty and increase predictability in their own and the other person's behavior.[2] To accomplish this, they use specific communication strategies.

According to URT, uncertainty can be a proactive, interactive, and retroactive process. That is, we can reduce uncertainty before, during, and after interacting with someone. We can proactively reduce uncertainty when we weigh alternative behavioral options prior to interacting with another. In doing so, we try to figure out ways the other might interact and then select our own communication strategies on the basis of this prediction. For example, if you are about to interact with a person from a different culture, you might anticipate that the other person does not speak English and adjust your speech accordingly. Interactively, during communication, we might try to reduce uncertainty by asking a lot of questions. Retroactively, we may reduce uncertainty by attempting to explain someone's behavior after it has been enacted. For example, after interacting with a South Korean, we may be able to explain why the person did not engage in direct eye contact.

In their original theory, Berger and Calabrese posited seven axioms outlining the theory's fundamental assumptions.[3] Although people in any culture seek to reduce uncertainty, Berger and Calabrese's seven axioms (i.e., fundamental assumptions) are based on communication patterns of people in the United States and may not be generalizable across cultures. Many researchers believe that the verbal and nonverbal communication strategies people use to reduce uncertainty vary from culture to culture.

The Seven Axioms of Uncertainty Reduction Theory

Axiom 1:   Given the high level of uncertainty present at the onset of the entry phase, as the amount of verbal communication between strangers increases, the level of uncertainty for each interactant in the relationship will decrease. As uncertainty is further reduced, the amount of verbal communication will increase.

Axiom 2:   As nonverbal affiliative expressiveness increases, uncertainty levels will decrease in an initial interaction situation. In addition, decreases in uncertainty level will cause increases in nonverbal affiliative expressiveness.

Axiom 3:   High levels of uncertainty cause increases in information-seeking behavior. As uncertainty levels decline, information-seeking behavior decreases.

Axiom 4:   High levels of uncertainty in a relationship cause decreases in the intimacy level of communication content. Low levels of uncertainty produce high levels of intimacy.

Axiom 5:   High levels of uncertainty produce high rates of reciprocity. Low levels of uncertainty produce low reciprocity rates.

Axiom 6:   Similarities between persons reduce uncertainty, whereas dissimilarities produce increases in uncertainty.

Axiom 7:   Increases in uncertainty level produce decreases in liking; decreases in uncertainty level produce increases in liking.

SOURCE: Berger, C. R., & Calabrese, R. J. (1975). Some Explorations in Initial Interaction and Beyond: Toward a Developmental Theory of Interpersonal Communication. *Human Communication Research, 1*, 99–112. Used by permission of International Communication Association and Charles R. Berger.

William Gudykunst and Young Kim maintain that people are more motivated to reduce uncertainty during initial intercultural communication than during communication with someone who is familiar.[4] And one's cultural background affects how one reduces uncertainty. For example, Gudykunst points out that people from high-context cultures try to reduce uncertainty in initial encounters, but the nature of the information they seek seems to be different from that sought by persons from low-context cultures. Because much of the information resides in the context as opposed to the individual, persons from high-context cultures are more cautious concerning what they talk about with strangers. In addition, certain types of information are more important sources of uncertainty for persons in high-context cultures than for people in low-context cultures, including the others' social background, whether others will behave in a socially appropriate manner, whether others understand individuals' feelings, what others mean when they communicate, and whether others will make allowances for individuals when they communicate.[5] So when interacting together for the first time, people from high- and low-context cultures are both trying to reduce uncertainty, but they use different kinds of communication. The low-context person asks a lot of questions verbally, whereas the high-context person focuses on nonverbal aspects, such as status of the interactants.

Axioms 1 and 2 deal with the quantity of verbal and nonverbal communication and its effect on uncertainty—that is, as communication increases, uncertainty decreases. Gudykunst and Tsukasa Nishida found that the frequency of communication predicts uncertainty reduction in individualistic, low-context cultures but not in collectivistic, high-context cultures.[6] In Axiom 2, "nonverbal affiliative expressiveness" refers to nonverbal behaviors that reduce the physiological and psychological distance between interactants. In the United States, direct eye contact, pleasantness of vocal expressions, affirmative head nods, number of head and arm gestures per minute, and closer physical distance between interactants are considered affiliative. In other cultures, these same behaviors may actually increase uncertainty and anxiety. In cultures such as South Korea and Guatemala, for example, persons of lower status do not engage in direct eye contact with parents or people of higher status because doing so communicates a challenge. Judith Sanders and Richard Wiseman found that positive nonverbal expressiveness predicts uncertainty reduction for Whites, Hispanics, and Asian Americans but not for African Americans.[7] These studies indicate that the specific nonverbal behaviors that constitute affiliative expressiveness may vary across cultures.

Axiom 3 is closely related to the first two insofar as information-seeking behavior is defined as the number of questions asked by each interactant. In the United States, people seek information from others by asking questions. In other cultures, particularly high-context cultures, people may seek information through nonverbal means, perhaps with silence or by observing the other's cultural and sociorelational background. In fact, Gudykunst, Lori Sodetani, and Kevin Sonoda suggest that question asking as a form of uncertainty reduction may be limited to Whites.[8]

Axiom 4 refers not to the quantity of communication, as do the preceding axioms, but to the quality of communication. In this case, the lower the level of uncertainty, the higher the level of intimacy in the communication. Intimate communication may be defined as interaction based on issues related to the interactants' attitudes, beliefs, motivations, and dispositions. Cross-cultural research in this area is limited.

Axiom 5 deals with the concept of communication reciprocity, or the mutual exchange of information between interactants. Berger and Calabrese contend that at early stages in a relationship, the interactants are compelled to ask for and give the same kinds of information at the same rate so that neither person gains information power over the other. As the relationship develops and uncertainty is reduced, there is less felt need to reciprocate because the interactants are more comfortable with the relationship.[9] To date, little or no cross-cultural research has examined this hypothesis outside the United States.

Axiom 6 centers on the notion of similarity. Berger and Calabrese argue that as similarity between interactants increases, uncertainty decreases. Likewise, the more dissimilarity present, the more uncertainty. Berger and Calabrese assert that knowledge of dissimilar attitudes leads to a greater number of attributions about why another may hold such attitudes, thus increasing uncertainty about the other.[10] Cross-cultural research on Germany, Norway, Canada, and Japan seems to validate this axiom. People can be similar to one another in a number of ways; for example, two people may share race, language, age, sex, and/or occupation. Linguistic similarity is of particular importance here. Uncertainty can be difficult to reduce if two people speak different languages and have little knowledge of the other's linguistic code.[11]

Finally, Axiom 7 focuses on the concept of liking. Unless we know something about other people, it is difficult to like them. Thus, liking other people is somewhat contingent on knowing something about them. The research on this axiom, even within the United States, is mixed. In some cases, the more we know about another, the less we may like that person.

AN INTERCULTURAL CONVERSATION: UNCERTAINTY REDUCTION AND HIGH- AND LOW-CONTEXT CULTURES

As mentioned above, people in all cultures try to reduce uncertainty when initiating communication with someone. In the conversation below, Andrew Wienke, a tenured communication professor, is interacting with his newly hired colleague from China, Yang Zhang. The two cross paths in the hallway of their academic building during the start of a new semester.

Andrew: Hey, Yang, good to see you! (Approaches him.) How's everything going? All moved in?

Yang: Hello, Dr. Wienke. (Nods.) Nice to see you, too.

Andrew: It's Andy. Everything going OK? (Leans forward and makes direct contact.) How are classes?

Yang: Yes, I'm very busy. (Backs away and diverts eye contact.)

Andrew: Classes OK? Any problems or concerns so far? Anything I can do to help? (Maintains direct eye contact.)

Yang: Classes are very big. Lots of students. (Looks away.)

Andrew: Yeah . . . that's true. My classes are pretty big, too.

Yang: Yes.

Andrew: Are you all moved into your apartment and everything?

Yang: Yes.

Andrew:	So, are you looking forward to the start of the new school year?
Yang:	I think so, yes.
Andrew:	Yeah, me too.
Yang:	OK.
Andrew:	Yeah, well . . . OK. Good to see you. If you have any questions or need anything, don't hesitate to ask.
Yang:	OK. Yes.

In this conversation, Andrew engages in classic uncertainty reduction for a low-context person. He asks Yang no fewer than eight questions as a form of information seeking (Axiom 3). Notice the brevity of Yang's contributions to the conversation. He prefers to reduce uncertainty with silence, allowing the context to inform him. His silence is also influenced by what he perceives as the status difference between himself and Andrew, which leads him to refer to Andrew as "Dr. Wienke." Andrew leans forward and makes direct eye contact, two actions considered nonverbal affiliative expressiveness in low-context cultures. Yang diverts eye contact, which is a nonverbal way of recognizing the perceived status difference between himself and Andrew (Axiom 2). The quantity of verbal talk is also much greater for Andrew than for Yang (Axiom 1).

ANXIETY/UNCERTAINTY MANAGEMENT THEORY OF EFFECTIVE COMMUNICATION

Noted intercultural communication scholar William Gudykunst developed a theory, called anxiety/uncertainty management theory (AUM), to explain the interrelationships among uncertainty, anxiety, mindfulness, and communication effectiveness.[12] According to AUM, the general processes underlying communication between people from different cultures or ethnicities are the same processes underlying communication between people from the same culture. Gudykunst refers to these common properties as *communicating with strangers*. According to AUM, a stranger is someone who is physically near and conceptually distant simultaneously. Thus, interacting with strangers is replete with uncertainty and anxiety.

AUM and URT are similar in that each theory focuses on the effects of uncertainty and anxiety on communication. But AUM differs from URT in that it shifts the focus from uncertainty and anxiety *reduction* to uncertainty and anxiety *management*. To be sure, during initial encounters with strangers, the primary motive is to *reduce* uncertainty. But over time, once uncertainty has been reduced to a tolerable amount, interactants move toward managing the uncertainty. AUM also incorporates the concepts of mindfulness and communication effectiveness.[13] Remember that uncertainty is a cognitive phenomenon. Uncertainty affects the

STUDENT VOICES ACROSS CULTURES

Establishing Relationships in Colombia

My name is Karen Margarita Henao Carbonell, and I am 21 years old. I was born and raised in Bogota, Colombia, a city with a population of about 7 million people. I graduated from high school in Colombia and decided to come to the United States in 2006 to learn English. After I attended high school in Madison, Wisconsin, for a year, I decided to stay and further my education at St. Norbert College.

I'll never forget my first day in an American high school. I was nervous and excited, especially because I wanted to make friends. Of course everyone was staring at me, trying to figure out who I was, but people were friendly overall. As a couple of girls approached me and said: "Hey, you're the new girl from Colombia, right?" I leaned toward them, kissed each one of them on the cheek, and said: "Yes, my name is Karen. Nice to meet you!" They were extremely shocked after that, and they could not believe I had just greeted them by kissing their cheeks, especially since we had met only a minute before.

It seems as though establishing relationships in Latin American countries, particularly in Colombia, is a whole lot easier than here in the United States. When you meet someone for the first time in Colombia, not only do you kiss each other's cheeks, but you jump right into talking about your life, what you do for a living, what neighborhood you live in, and even where you purchased the shoes you are wearing. Once you have become acquainted with someone, it is socially acceptable to allow physical contact and "burst the invisible bubble."

After living in the United States for more than 5 years, I have realized that establishing relationships with people in this country is more difficult. Americans believe that it takes a lot of time for a person to begin trusting and revealing personal information; they are friendly and willing to help, but trust needs to be built before they open the doors into their lives. When such relationships have been established, people confide in each other, but the physical aspect is not an important factor.

way people *think* about communication and involves our ability, or inability, to predict a stranger's attitudes, beliefs, values, and behaviors. People experience more uncertainty when interacting with strangers. Anxiety is the affective equivalent of uncertainty. Anxiety affects the way people *feel* about interacting with someone else and includes a sense of uneasiness, apprehensiveness, worry, and so on. Uncertainty and anxiety are related in that as uncertainty increases, anxiety increases. Anxiety affects one's motivation to approach or avoid communication.[14]

AUM stipulates that people have minimum and maximum thresholds for uncertainty and anxiety. The maximum threshold is the highest amount of uncertainty or anxiety individuals can experience and still believe that they can predict a stranger's attitudes, beliefs, values, and so on, and remain comfortable communicating. An individual's minimum threshold of uncertainty or anxiety is the lowest amount of uncertainty a person can experience before becoming unmotivated or overconfident about predicting the stranger's behavior when interacting. Although it sounds peculiar, too little uncertainty and too much predictability can lead to dull, monotonous, and uninteresting communication. But if our uncertainty is above the maximum threshold, we become too anxious to approach others and cannot communicate effectively; thus, communicating effectively requires that uncertainty and anxiety fall between the minimum and maximum thresholds (see Figure 9.2).

Figure 9.2 Minimum/maximum uncertainty thresholds.

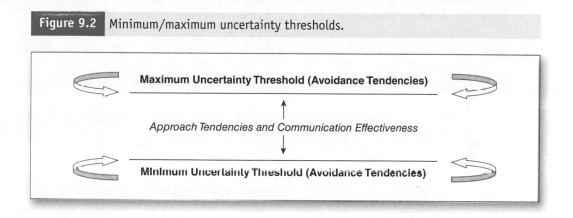

Gudykunst makes an important point that minimum and maximum thresholds vary considerably across cultures.[15]

In addition to uncertainty and anxiety, AUM incorporates the concepts of mindfulness and communication effectiveness. Mindfulness refers to a person's conscious attention to incoming information. A mindful communicator is open to new information and the processing of new categories. Mindful communicators perceive aspects of the self and others that mindless communicators miss. Gudykunst points out that to be mindful, people must recognize that strangers may understand or explain interaction from different perspectives. When we are mindless, we tend to assume that strangers interpret our messages the same way we do. Mindfulness, on the other hand, means *negotiating* meaning with strangers. Communication effectiveness refers to the idea that a person receiving and interpreting a message attaches a meaning to the message that is relatively similar to what the person transmitting the message intended. The result of communication effectiveness is maximum understanding among communicators. Gudykunst maintains that the majority of the time when people are not mindful, communication is ineffective.[16]

Two central concepts of intercultural communication are also relevant to uncertainty/anxiety management and mindfulness during intercultural communication: ethnocentrism and intercultural communication apprehension (ICA). For example, Jim Neuliep recently demonstrated that ICA and ethnocentrism are significantly and negatively related to uncertainty reduction and communication satisfaction. This means that ethnocentric persons approach others less often and thereby reduce less uncertainty. Likewise, persons with high ICA approach others less often and reduce less uncertainty during communication.

As mentioned in Chapters 1 and 5, ethnocentrism refers to the degree to which persons believe that the attitudes and behaviors of their in-group should serve as the standard by which other groups are judged. To the extent that people are ethnocentric, they tend to view other cultures (and microcultures) from their own cultural vantage point. That is, one's own culture is the standard by which other cultures and the people from those cultures are evaluated. Deviations from that standard are viewed negatively. Moreover, because highly ethnocentric persons see themselves as superior to persons from different cultures, they have little or no motivation to communicate effectively with them, approach less, are generally not mindful, and have little or no motivation to reduce uncertainty.

Ethnocentrism acts as a perceptual filter that affects not only the perceptions of verbal and nonverbal messages but also perceptions of their source. Thus, when highly ethnocentric persons enter into an intercultural communicative exchange, few positive outcomes can be expected, including lowering uncertainty to manageable levels. Ethnocentrics prefer *intra*cultural interaction and avoid communicating with persons from other cultures. Such avoidance tendencies inhibit the reduction or management of uncertainty and anxiety and, thus, impede mindfulness.[17]

Recall also from Chapter 1 that ICA is the fear or anxiety associated with either real or anticipated communication with people from different cultural or ethnic groups. People with ICA approach others less often, which inhibits uncertainty reduction and management and hinders mindfulness. Conceptually, like ethnocentrism, ICA interferes with effective intercultural communication. ICA also interferes with the reduction of uncertainty associated with the future behavior of a fellow interactant, the other's behavior, and the participant's feelings about the interaction. Furthermore, other studies claim that ICA and ethnocentrism are negatively related to intercultural willingness to communicate and intentions to engage in intercultural interactions (i.e., affective-approach tendencies). Like high ethnocentrics, individuals with high ICA prefer intracultural interaction and are less likely to approach intercultural strangers, thus inhibiting their reduction and management of uncertainty and anxiety.[18]

UNCERTAINTY REDUCTION AND INTERCULTURAL COMMUNICATION APPREHENSION

Communication researchers Jim Neuliep and Dan Ryan investigated the relationship between ICA and uncertainty reduction during initial intercultural interaction. Imagine that you have just been introduced to someone from a different culture. You have never met this person before and know very little about his or her culture. Chances are good that you will experience a bit of anxiety and apprehension. This is a common response, and you need not feel bad about yourself for having felt it. Neuliep and Ryan argue that because intercultural communication is loaded with novelty and dissimilarity, people may experience inordinate amounts of anxiety, which inhibit the ability to reduce uncertainty.[19]

Many people, regardless of culture, experience anxiety when communicating, or when anticipating communicating, with persons from different cultures or ethnic groups. Often, we tend to avoid those situations that make us feel anxious. In this case, if intercultural communication causes us to feel anxious, we may avoid initiating interaction with people from different cultures. However, unless we interact, we cannot reduce much uncertainty, and, therefore, our anxiety levels remain high. In their theory of uncertainty reduction, Berger and Calabrese maintain that the principal way people reduce uncertainty during initial interaction is through verbal and nonverbal communication.[20]

To the extent that people can reduce uncertainty and anxiety during communication, they can increase their communication effectiveness. In their study, Neuliep and Ryan found a direct relationship between ICA and uncertainty reduction. Specifically, they found that during initial intercultural communication, people who experienced high ICA also experienced high uncertainty. Neuliep and Ryan reasoned that because persons with high ICA may avoid or withdraw from communication with persons from different cultures, they are less likely to engage in communication tactics that reduce uncertainty. Persons who generally do not experience apprehension interacting with persons from other cultures communicate comfortably, thereby facilitating uncertainty reduction. A lesson here is that by increasing our interaction with persons from different cultures, we can reduce our uncertainty about them and reduce our anxiety.[21]

In fact, in related research, Neuliep and Erica Grohskopf found that as individuals reduce uncertainty, their satisfaction with communication increases. Hence, by engaging in intercultural communication, we can reduce uncertainty, which will reduce anxiety and result in more satisfying communication with others. It is a "win–win" situation![22]

Although an individual may face large amounts of uncertainty and anxiety during initial intercultural communication, Neuliep and Ryan reasoned that the person's communication style may enable him or her to reduce uncertainty effectively. Jim McCroskey and Virginia Richmond have outlined two types of communication style—what they call *sociocommunicative orientation*—that affect how one communicates in different situations. These types of communication are assertiveness and responsiveness.[23] Assertiveness refers to one's ability to make requests; actively disagree; express positive or negative personal rights and feelings; initiate, sustain, and terminate conversations; and defend oneself without attacking others. Responsiveness refers to one's ability to be sensitive to the communication of others, be a good listener, engage in comforting communication, and recognize the needs and wants of relevant others.

McCroskey and Richmond note that assertiveness and responsiveness are inversely related to communication apprehension. In other words, persons high in communication apprehension are not likely to engage in assertive or responsive communication behaviors. Because apprehensive persons tend to avoid communication, they are not likely to initiate conversation or advance their position on a topic of communication during conversation.[24] Likewise, a responsive communicator is one who invites others to engage in conversation. In their research, Neuliep and Ryan argued that these tendencies may be highlighted during initial intercultural interaction, in which situational novelty, unfamiliarity, and dissimilarity are prominent. Indeed, in their study, Neuliep and Ryan found that people who were assertive and responsive reported experiencing less ICA.[25]

Neuliep and Ryan contend that the fundamental components of assertiveness and responsiveness are consistent with those behaviors associated with reduced uncertainty. For example, a characteristic of assertiveness is the ability to make requests. In Axiom 3 of URT, Berger and Calabrese point out that as information-seeking behavior (question asking) increases, uncertainty decreases. In addition, assertiveness is associated with initiation and maintenance of conversations. In Axiom 1 of URT, Berger and Calabrese maintain that as verbal communication increases, uncertainty decreases. Responsive communicators invite others to interact, thus increasing verbal communication. Likewise, responsive communicators are nonverbally sensitive to others. Responsiveness is communicated through eye contact, smiling, forward leaning, and touching. Axiom 2 states that as nonverbal affiliative expressiveness increases, uncertainty decreases. From the association of assertiveness and responsiveness with behaviors designed to reduce uncertainty, Neuliep and Ryan predicted that assertive and responsive communicators may be better able to reduce uncertainty. Their results supported their prediction. Persons scoring high on assertiveness and responsiveness instruments reported experiencing less uncertainty during initial cross-cultural interaction.[26]

An Intercultural Conversation: Uncertainty Reduction and Sociocommunicative Style

In the following intercultural conversations, we see how an individual's sociocommunicative style affects uncertainty reduction during initial intercultural communication. In the first conversation, we see Dan, who is from the United States, interacting with Natasha, who is from Ukraine. Dan seems unassertive and unresponsive. In the second conversation, we see Jim, who is from the United States, interacting with Foday, who is from Sierra Leone. In comparison with Dan, Jim seems assertive and responsive. Jim's assertiveness and responsiveness help him reduce uncertainty about Foday and Sierra Leone.

Conversation A

Natasha: Hi, I'm Natasha.

Dan: Oh, hi.

Natasha: What's your name?

Dan: Dan.

Natasha: Hi, Dan.

Dan: Hi.

Natasha: I'm not from here. I'm from Ukraine.

Dan: Oh.

Natasha: You've heard of it?

Dan: Uh, yeah, I think so.

Natasha: Ukraine is in Eastern Europe, between Poland and Russia.

Dan: Oh.

Natasha: Yeah. Have you ever been to Europe?

Dan: Yeah, but I was pretty young.

Natasha: It must have been quite an experience, though.

Dan: Ah . . . do you know what time it is?

Natasha: It's about 3 o'clock.

Dan: I have to go now. Bye.

Natasha: Bye, Dan. Nice meeting you.

Conversation B

Jim: Hi, I'm Jim. I don't believe we've met.

Foday: Hello, Jim. I'm Foday.

Jim: Hi, Foday. Where are you from?

Foday: I'm from Sierra Leone.

Jim: Oh really? Where is Sierra Leone? I know it's on the African continent, but I'm not sure where.

Foday: It's on the western coast between Guinea and Liberia.

Jim: Oh, toward the north? How big is it?

Foday: Yes, that's right. We're about the size of your South Carolina.

Jim: That's interesting. What kind of government do you have in Sierra Leone?

Foday: We have a constitutional democracy.

Jim: Is that based on English law?

Foday: Yes.

Jim: By the way, you speak English very well. Is that your official language?

Foday: English is the official language of my country, but it is spoken only by a minority of about 20% of the population.

Jim: Really? What language do the other 80% speak?

Foday: People in the north speak a vernacular language called Temme, whereas those in the south speak Mende.

Jim: I understand that mining is a major industry in Sierra Leone. I hear you mine diamonds.

Foday: Yes, they are a big export. But many people live by simple subsistence farming, like my father.

Jim: Foday, it has been really nice meeting you. I'd like to introduce you to my girlfriend. She's over there.

Foday: Thank you. I'd like to meet her.

In comparing the two conversations, notice how much more uncertainty Jim reduces in his short conversation with Foday than Dan does with Natasha. Jim is assertive in initiating conversation with Foday and asking him questions about his country. Jim also appears responsive to Foday, using such comments as, "That's interesting." Dan, on the other hand, says very little, even when prompted by Natasha. Natasha is probably more uncertain about Dan after the conversation than before. His lack of assertiveness and responsiveness probably leaves a negative impression on her.

Assessing Sociocommunicative Orientation/Style

In their study of uncertainty reduction during initial intercultural communication, Neuliep and Ryan measured assertiveness and responsiveness using an instrument McCroskey and Richmond developed, presented in Self-Assessment 9.1. These scales have been used successfully in other cultures, including China, Finland, Japan, Korea, and Russia. Note, however, that these scales were designed to measure assertiveness and responsiveness as defined in the United States and may not be generalizable across all cultures. In fact, studies examining assertiveness and responsiveness across cultures have reported differences. American men and women, for example, score higher on the assertiveness dimension than do Finnish and Japanese men and women. Generally, American women score higher on the responsiveness scale than do men and women from other cultures. Within most cultures, however, men generally score higher on the assertiveness scale, whereas women tend to score higher on the responsiveness scale.[27] Complete the scale on the following page to assess your own degree of assertiveness and responsiveness.

EMPATHY AND SIMILARITY IN RELATIONSHIP DEVELOPMENT

The majority of uncertainty reduction occurs during the initial stages of a relationship. To the extent that relational partners are able to reduce uncertainty, they learn more about each other and can further develop their relationship. Once the relationship has been established and the individuals get to know each other, uncertainty management processes begin. Two factors (among others) that have a significant influence on communication and relational development are *empathy* and *similarity*. Empathy and similarity are important in any relationship, but they take on added importance in intercultural relationships. Due to their cultural differences, persons in intercultural relationships may find it difficult to empathize with their relational partners because they are dissimilar.

Empathy

As uncertainty is reduced, people get to know each other more and can work on developing their relationship. The ability to empathize with someone is a crucial ingredient in any relationship. Empathy takes on added importance in intercultural relationships, however. Because persons from other cultures are different from us, it may be difficult

Self-Assessment 9.1

The Sociocommunicative Orientation/Style Instrument

Directions: The following questionnaire lists 20 personality traits. Indicate the degree to which you believe each of these characteristics applies to you, as you normally communicate with others, by marking whether you (5) strongly agree that it applies, (4) agree that it applies, (3) are undecided, (2) disagree that it applies, or (1) strongly disagree that it applies. There are no right or wrong answers. Work quickly; record your first impression.

_____ 1. Helpful

_____ 2. Defends own beliefs

_____ 3. Independent

_____ 4. Responsive to others

_____ 5. Forceful

_____ 6. Has strong personality

_____ 7. Sympathetic

_____ 8. Compassionate

_____ 9. Assertive

_____ 10. Sensitive to the needs of others

_____ 11. Dominant

_____ 12. Sincere

_____ 13. Gentle

_____ 14. Willing to take a stand

_____ 15. Warm

_____ 16. Tender

_____ 17. Friendly

_____ 18. Acts as a leader

_____ 19. Aggressive

_____ 20. Competitive

Scoring: Items 2, 3, 5, 6, 9, 11, 14, 18, 19, and 20 measure assertiveness. Add the scores on these items to get your assertiveness score. Scores above 40 indicate that you see yourself as assertive. Items 1, 4, 7, 8, 10, 12, 13, 15, 16, and 17 measure responsiveness. Add the scores on these items to get your responsiveness score. Scores above 40 suggest that you see yourself as responsive. Being assertive and responsive is not necessarily "good" or "bad." Your sociocommunicative style is a barometer of how you interact with others, not whether you are a good or bad person.

SOURCE: From McCroskey, J. C., & Richmond, V. P. (1996). _Fundamentals of Human Communication: An Interpersonal Perspective._ Copyright © McCroskey.

for us to empathize with them, their ideas, and their style of communication. In these types of relationships, reducing uncertainty becomes essential. In fact, some communication scholars maintain that empathy may be impossible in intercultural communication. However, in general, communication scholars believe that because empathy motivates communication behavior, it is an essential ingredient in effective interpersonal communication. **Empathy** is often defined as the degree to which we can accurately infer another's thoughts or feelings. Benjamin Broome contends that this definition is inadequate for the study of intercultural communication and offers what he calls a model of **relational empathy** (see Figure 9.3). Broome argues that because our thoughts and perceptions are based on our unique personal, cultural, sociocultural, and individual past experiences, we can never completely comprehend or directly know what another is thinking or feeling. Broome argues, "While we can never become another person, it is possible to erect a structure within the framework of which the other's interpretation of the world or us takes shape or assumes meaning."[28]

The model of relational empathy is based on the idea that whenever two people develop a relationship, they create a **third culture** of shared meaning and relational empathy.[29] Broome argues that mutual understanding and shared meaning are a product of the relationship between individuals. Relational empathy is not the ability to accurately reproduce another's perceptions or emotions but, rather, the creation of new perceptions and emotions by the two people interacting. This third culture of relational empathy and shared meaning is the outcome or harmonization of communication in which the interactants share

Figure 9.3 Model of relational empathy.

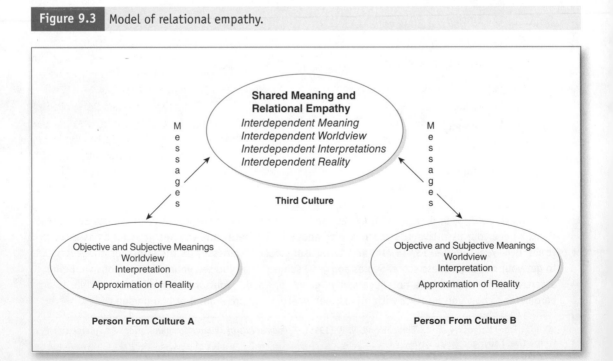

unique values, beliefs, norms, and symbols. For example, think of your closest friends and the verbal and nonverbal language you use with them. You probably have unique words and phrases and even nonverbal gestures that you use with your friends that no one else understands. This sort of private language between you and your friends represents a part of what Broome calls the third culture.

Broome asserts that the third culture emerges when the interactants are open and willing to communicate with others and expose themselves to new meanings. According to the model, persons cannot possess direct, firsthand knowledge of the emotional states or cognitive processes of another person. Instead, people possess objective and subjective meanings. Objective meaning, according to Broome, is one's interpretation of one's own personal experiences. For example, your interpretation of what it meant to grow up in your hometown with your family is a part of your own objective meaning. Subjective meaning, on the other hand, is one's interpretation of the other person's experiences in relation to one's own. For example, a friend's description of what it meant to grow up in his or her hometown and of his or her family experiences would be a part of your subjective meaning.

When two people come together and interact, a product of the third culture is interdependent meaning—that is, new meaning based on the combining of each individual's objective and subjective meanings. People also bring with them a personal worldview largely based on cultural orientation. Hence, a Chinese person brings a collectivistic, high-context worldview, and an American brings an individualistic, low-context worldview. In a relationship, these two different worldviews merge into an interdependent worldview. Because of the individuals' objective and subjective knowledge and worldviews, they have different interpretations of what is real. Through the establishment of relational empathy, an interdependent interpretation and approximation of reality materializes.

Broome asserts that similarity among individuals is not necessary to achieve relational empathy and shared meaning. Instead, Broome's model assumes that the emergence of a third culture creates a medium in which the interactants can relate and similarity becomes moot. Because a third culture has evolved through the verbal and nonverbal messages of the interactants, each is an active participant in its creation. Hence, neither person has to re-create anything, because each is an integral part of the third culture's existence.[30]

Intercultural researcher Donald Klopf maintains that we can approach empathy with others by developing empathic listening skills. Empathic listening means listening more to the meanings than to the words of another person. According to Klopf, empathic listening involves (a) *paraphrasing,* rewording what the other person has said; (b) *reflecting feelings,* relating back to the other the feelings we believe the other is experiencing; (c) *reflecting meanings,* restating what we heard to confirm its meaning; and (d) *summarizing,* briefly restating the major topics the other has communicated.[31]

Although no one can experience complete empathy, by taking Broome's model of relational empathy and Klopf's prescription for empathic listening into account and putting them into practice, we can develop and enhance our relationships with persons from cultures different from our own.

Similarity

Although Broome's model of relational empathy discounts the importance of similarity, a great deal of research (mostly conducted in the United States) has demonstrated that similarity plays a key role in the establishment and development of relationships. As communication researcher Steve Duck states, "All communication and all relationships are likewise founded on a necessary base of similarity of understanding or similarity of meaning that facilitates the development of each."[32] Intercultural communication researchers have found that the more we perceive another as similar to ourselves, the more we are able to reduce uncertainty about the person and form accurate categories for him or her. Thus, similarity may be particularly important during initial encounters with another person. Similarity, then, is a powerful force for attraction and approach tendencies. That is, we are attracted to those whom we perceive as similar, and we are more likely to approach them. But there are lots of ways we can be similar to someone; we might be like someone physically, racially, sexually, demographically, attitudinally, morally, ethically, etc. Some kinds of similarity seem to be more important than others in the establishment of intercultural relationships.

One of the pioneers in the study of similarity is Donn Byrne. Byrne's efforts have focused mainly on attitude similarity and attraction. Byrne's fundamental postulate is that attitude similarity between persons leads to positive affect, which in turn leads to attraction (see Figure 9.4).[33] Byrne has become well-known for his "bogus stranger" experiments, which have relevance for intercultural communication. In these experiments, Byrne asks research participants to indicate their attitudes on a variety of topics and issues. The participants are then paired with a "stranger," who is portrayed as a research participant whose attitudes on the same topics and issues were assessed at an earlier time. Prior to the pairing of the research participants and the stranger, the research participants are shown the stranger's attitude responses. In actuality, however, the stranger is "bogus" because his or her attitude responses are manufactured either to match or to conflict with the research participants' attitude responses. After interacting with the stranger, the research participants then rate the stranger's level of attractiveness. Consistently, those research participants paired with an attitudinally similar stranger provide higher attractiveness ratings than do those paired with an attitudinally dissimilar stranger. Yet in each case, the stranger is the same person.[34]

Figure 9.4   Relationship between similarity and attraction.

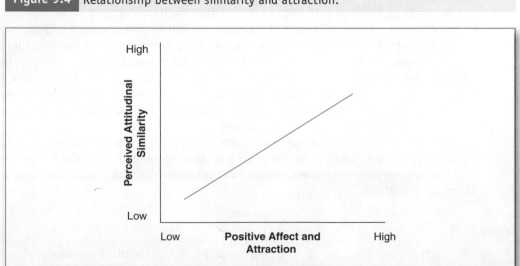

Attitude similarity is only one way people label themselves as like or unlike others. A White student once commented that similarity was not a factor in her relationship with her boyfriend, explaining that he was Black. Upon further questioning, it was discovered that she and her boyfriend were the same age, were studying at the same college, were pursuing the same major, enjoyed similar tastes in music and food, and had similar attitudes on a variety of topics. The point here is that although we may have dissimilarities with others, the people with whom we develop and maintain interpersonal relationships are typically very much like ourselves. Perceived similarity, sometimes called perceived homophily, is perhaps the most dominant force in our motivations to interact with others. But similarity can come in many shapes and sizes. We can be similar to others culturally, attitudinally, linguistically, racially, behaviorally, affectively, and/or physically. The more similar we find ourselves to someone else, the more likely we are to initiate and sustain communication with that person. Although it facilitates interaction and attraction, cultural similarity (which is only one kind of similarity) may not be a necessary ingredient in forming meaningful and lasting relationships. Two persons from radically different cultures may find they have a great deal in common with each other.

PERCEPTIONS OF RELATIONAL INTIMACY ACROSS CULTURES

Although the same types of relationships exist across cultures, the level of intimacy varies considerably. In other words, what it means to be a student in your culture is probably not the same as what it means to be a student in another culture. Moreover, the relationship between student and teacher varies widely across cultures. In the United States, for example, student–teacher relationships at the college level might be perceived as relatively informal and personal compared with student–teacher relationships in China or Korea. Gudykunst and Nishida studied the influence of culture on perceptions of intimacy and communication behavior in the United States and Japan.[35] In each culture, students were asked to rate the level of intimacy (on a scale of 1 to 9, where 1 = intimate, 9 = nonintimate) for 30 different relationships. Gudykunst and Nishida reasoned that because of their collectivistic tendencies, the Japanese students would perceive in-group relationships as more intimate than would the American students, who are individualistic. Gudykunst and Nishida also maintained that because Japan is considered a masculine-oriented culture in which sex roles are clearly differentiated, male–female relationships (e.g., lover, spouse, boyfriend/girlfriend) would be perceived as less intimate than in the United States. Gudykunst and Nishida argued that in cultures such as Japan, where sex roles are strictly distinguished, there is not much informal interaction between males and females. Moreover, when interaction does occur, its content is relatively superficial. The results of their survey are shown in Table 9.1.

When comparing the ratings, American students are often surprised to see that Japanese students rate *close friend* and *best friend* as the most intimate of their relationships. In Japan, even classmates are rated as more intimate than spouses. These results confirm the notion that when you travel to a land with a culture different from your own, your relationship roles in that culture (as student, friend, employee, etc.) could be perceived very differently from when you occupy the same roles in the United States.

Table 9.1   Relationship Terms and Intimacy Ratings

Relationship Type	U.S.*	Japan*
Family		
Spouse (*haigusha*)	1.33	4.32
Father (*chichioya*)	2.75	2.57
Mother (*hahaoya*)	2.35	2.06
Son (*musuko*)	2.59	4.76
Daughter (*musume*)	2.55	4.87
Brother (*kyodai*)	3.12	3.51
Sister (*shimai*)	2.88	3.78
Aunt (*oba*)	4.53	4.99
Cousin (*itoko*)	4.67	4.66
Grandparent (*sofubo*)	3.75	4.15
Uncle (*oji*)	4.55	5.21
Social		
Fiancé (*konyakusha*)	1.29	4.32
Lover (*koibito*)	1.25	2.81
Boy/girlfriend (*otoko/onna tomodachi*)	1.70	3.32
Best friend (*ichiban no shinyu*)	2.51	1.73
Mate (*tsureai*)	1.75	4.45
Steady (*kosai shiteiru hito*)	2.27	2.92
Close friend (*shinyu*)	2.85	1.83
Friend (*tomo*)	3.67	3.42
Date (*detonoaite*)	4.02	3.48
Companion (*tomodachi*)	3.08	3.05
Neighbor (*kinjo no hito*)	5.72	5.92
Acquaintance (*chijin*)	6.79	4.95

Relationship Type	U.S.*	Japan*
Professional/Work		
Cohort (*nakama*)	5.40	2.85
Coworker (*shigato-makama*)	5.76	5.27
Employer (*koyosha*)	6.39	6.86
Colleague (*doryo*)	5.33	4.76
Roommate (*doshukusha*)	3.85	4.88
Classmate (*dokyusei*)	5.72	3.84
Other		
Stranger (*shiranai hito*)	8.35	7.99

SOURCE: Gudykunst, W. B., & Nishida, T. (1986). The Influence of Cultural Variability on Perceptions of Communication Behavior Associated With Relationship Terms. *Human Communication Research, 13,* 147–166.

*In each culture, students were asked to rate the level of intimacy for 30 different relationships on a scale of 1 to 9 (1 = intimate; 9 = nonintimate). Lower scores represent more perceived intimacy.

Eastern and Western Cultures and Relationships

As demonstrated by Gudykunst and Nishida, perceptions of relationships differ widely across cultures. In individualistic cultures such as the United States, relationships are typically viewed from the perspective of the self. As June Ock Yum asserts, individualists see themselves as distinct individuals who participate in relationships to maximize their own self-interests.[36] In many collectivistic cultures, such as South Korea, relationships are guided by Confucianism. According to Yum, the fundamental theme of Confucianism is that proper relationships form the cornerstone of society. Moreover, an individual's conduct in society should be guided by four principles: (a) *humanism,* treating others as one wishes to be treated; (b) *faithfulness,* loyalty rather than personal interest or profit; (c) *propriety,* social decorum and etiquette; and (d) *wisdom.*[37]

Yum points out that three of these four principles have direct implications for how relationships are perceived in East Asian cultures such as China, compared with Western cultures such as the United States (see Table 9.2). First, in contrasting Eastern and Western relationships, Yum alleges that many East Asian cultures practice *particularism*—that is, the belief that particular or unique rules and guidelines apply to each individual relationship. Relational partners are to be sensitive to differences in such factors as status when interacting with others. Most East Asian cultures believe in strict, well-defined social hierarchies in which people are perceived as higher or lower than others. In contrast, persons in Western cultures practice what Yum calls a *universalistic orientation* to relationships. Yum alleges that most Westerners try to treat others as equally as possible, regardless of status or intimacy level of the partners.[38]

Table 9.2	Relationship Principles
Eastern Cultures (e.g., China)	*Western Cultures (e.g., USA)*
Particularism	Universalism
Long-term asymmetrical reciprocity	Short-term symmetrical reciprocity
Clear in-group/out-group distinction with pre-scribed group membership	Blurry in-group/out-group distinction with optional and voluntary group membership
Use of intermediaries	Avoidance of intermediaries
Blending of personal and public relationships	Separation of personal and public relationships

SOURCE: Yum, J. O. (1997). The Impact of Confucianism on Interpersonal Relationships and Communication Patterns in East Asia. In L. A. Samovar & R. E. Porter (Eds.), *Intercultural Communication: A Reader* (8th ed., pp. 78–88). Belmont, CA: Wadsworth.

Yum also contends that relational partners in Eastern cultures engage in *long-term* and *asymmetrical reciprocity*. You may recall from Chapter 3 that reciprocity refers to the give-and-take, or mutual exchange, in interpersonal encounters. According to Yum, in Confucian philosophy, dependence on others is an inevitable and accepted part of relationships. People will always be indebted to others who help or assist them in some way. She states that, "under this system of reciprocity, the individual does not calculate what he or she gives and receives. To calculate would be to think about immediate personal profits, which is the opposite of the principle of faithfulness."[39] Western relationships, on the other hand, are characterized by short-term and symmetrical reciprocity, or even contractual reciprocity. In the United States, for example, some marital relationships begin with premarital legal agreements that carefully spell out expectations, possessions, and obligations for the relational partners.

Another difference between Eastern and Western relationships is that in many Eastern cultures, who is and is not a member of the in-group or the out-group is defined clearly. Yum maintains that Confucian philosophy prescribes that people associate and identify with relatively few, yet very cohesive, groups. Moreover, one's affiliation with in-groups is long-lived, perhaps even lifelong. Group associations in most Western cultures are, for the most part, optional and voluntary. Many of the groups with whom one associates in the United States, for example, are designed to somehow facilitate one's individual development (e.g., "self-help" groups), and one's association with such a group lasts only as long as one benefits from membership.[40]

A fourth difference between relationships in Eastern and Western cultures is the use of intermediaries (go-betweens). For the most part, persons in Western cultures prefer direct, face-to-face contact in interpersonal relationships, including those with business associates. In the United States, for example, the use of intermediaries is typically reserved for formal or legal situations and is usually contractual (as with lawyers or realtors). Yum points out that in

Eastern cultures, because the distinctions between in-groups and out-groups are so well defined, intermediaries are essential and are used even in informal situations—such as introductions, dating, and marital arrangements—and in relatively small business transactions. The principle behind the use of intermediaries is to save face.[41]

A fifth difference in interpersonal relations in Eastern and Western cultures, according to Yum, is that Confucianism's emphasis on faithfulness and loyalty in relationships leads to blending of personal and public relationships. In the United States, people can maintain "strictly business" relationships, whereas many Eastern cultures prefer to do business with trusted associates with whom they have established a strong interpersonal bond. Many U.S. businesses would be well served by initiating frequent contact, establishing mutual interests, and developing shared experiences with their Eastern-culture counterparts.[42]

Interethnic and Interracial Relationships and Marriages

Marital relationships exist in virtually every culture. According to anthropologist Michael Howard, the most common type of marriage practice in the United States and most Western industrialized nations is monogamy—that is, marriage between one man and one woman. In most cases, monogamy is proscribed legally, and acquiring multiple spouses is illegal. In cultures in which marriage is governed legally, people are allowed, by law, to enter into and leave marriages—that is, people can marry, divorce, and marry again. This is called *serial monogamy*. Howard asserts that most cultures prefer not to limit the number of spouses available to a person. These cultures practice polygamy—that is, marriage to more than one spouse. Contrary to popular belief, polygamy is not the practice of a husband's having multiple wives. Actually, there are two types of polygamy: polygyny, in which a man has multiple wives, and polyandry, in which a woman has more than one husband. According to Howard, polygyny is permitted in the majority of societies.[43] Indeed, in their study of cross-cultural differences in family and sexual life among 68 cultures, Gary Becker and Richard Posner report that only 2 of those cultures did not practice polygyny.[44]

Although the number of interethnic and interracial marriages is growing, according to the U.S. Census Bureau, in 2010, 90% of married-couple households in the United States were of the same race/ethnicity. About 82% of opposite-sex (presumably unmarried) couple households were of the same race/ethnicity.[45] In 2010, there were 5.4 million interracial/interethnic married-couple households in the United States, of which 38% were White/Hispanic, 14% were White/Asian, 8% were White/Black, and 5% were White/American Indian or Alaskan Native. To be sure, societal and attitudinal changes about interracial and interethnic marriages and relationships take time. Social sanctions discouraging them remain. In fact, legislation banning interracial marriages still existed in the United States as recently as the year 2000, when Alabama became the last state to remove such laws.

A common assumption is that interethnic and interracial relationships experience more difficulties than intraethnic or intraracial relationships because of the cultural or ethnic differences. And evidence suggests that interracial marriages are more likely to end in divorce than are intraracial marriages. About two thirds of interracial marriages end in divorce, compared with 40% to 50% for all marriages. In their literature review, Adam Troy, Jamie Lewis-Smith, and Jean-Philippe Laurenceau point to research that shows that interracial partners may face obstacles that intraracial partners do not. For example, interracial couples are often stared at in public; are negatively stereotyped; face social-network opposition, including pressure not to marry; are discriminated against by restaurant staff, real-estate agents, hotel managers, and retail clerks; and experience obscene phone calls, hate mail, and vandalized property. Troy and his associates also maintain that ethnic and or racial differences might intensify conflict-management differences. So Troy and his colleagues conducted a study comparing intra- and interracial couples to test the assumption that the relationship quality of interracial couples is lower than for intraracial relationships. In their study, they surveyed more than 100 heterosexual couples, of which 32 were interracial and 86 were intraracial. Surprisingly, their results showed that partners in interracial relationships reported significantly higher relational satisfaction compared with those in intraracial relationships, and no differences were found for conflict or attachment style. That is, interracial couples did not engage in or use conflict techniques differently than did intraracial couples, and they reported being equally as attached to their partners, despite the racial differences. Troy and his colleagues assert that their results contradict the notion that interracial relationships are more dysfunctional than intraracial ones. Their results shed light on the similarity research reported above; that is, while similarity plays an important role in attraction and approach tendencies, some types of similarity (e.g., attitude similarity) may play a larger role than other types of similarity—in this case, racial similarity.[46]

In addition to the growing number of interracial marriages, American attitudes about these relationships are changing. A 2001 survey conducted by *The Washington Post,* the Henry J. Kaiser Family Foundation, and Harvard University found that 86% of Black respondents said their families would welcome a White, Asian, or Hispanic person into their family. Among Whites, 66% said they would accept Hispanics or Asians, but only 55% would accept a Black person. Among Hispanics, 86% would accept Whites, 79% would accept Asians, and 74% would accept Blacks. Among Asians, 77% would accept Whites, 71% would accept Hispanics, and 66% would accept Blacks. Although the percentage of interracial marriages is growing and the attitudes about such relationships are improving, cross-cultural (i.e., racial or ethnic) relationships are susceptible to pressures and strains not present in same-race or same-ethnicity marriages or relationships. For example, results from the same survey reported above show that 65% of White–Black couples said they experienced problems within their families at the start of their relationship, and 24% of White–Asian or White–Hispanic couples reported problems.[47]

Intercultural Relational Maintenance

In the past several decades, a substantial body of literature in the social sciences has emerged focusing on *relational maintenance,* which centers on how relational partners uphold and sustain their established relationships. Many studies in relational maintenance investigate how relational partners keep the relationship in satisfactory condition and/or how they repair relationships that need mending, including use of conflict management. Laura Stafford of the University of Kentucky has worked extensively in this area. In some of her most recent research, Stafford proposes a typology of seven relational maintenance behaviors couples use to sustain their relationships: (a) self-disclosure, where relational partners reveal aspects of themselves to their partners; (b) relationship talk, where couples communicate about the status of the relationship; (c) positivity, which involves interacting with the partner in a cheerful, optimistic, and uncritical manner; (d) understanding, which means feeling understood by the partner; (e) assurances, or messages that stress one's continuation in the relationship; (f) networks, which refers to use of social networks, including interacting with or relying on common affiliations and relatives; and (g) tasks, or attempts to maintain the relationship by performing one's responsibilities, such as household chores.[48]

Relational maintenance researchers generally agree that these seven behaviors are representative of the types of behaviors couples use to sustain their relationships, but little work has been done to identify the types of relational maintenance behaviors employed by partners in intercultural relationships. Michael Reiter and Christina Gee sought to find out if two additional relational maintenance behaviors might affect intercultural relationships. These are open communication and support. Open communication is a maintenance behavior that includes self-disclosure (as defined by Stafford above) but here includes a lack of topic avoidance, meaning that individuals who engage in more open communication tend not to avoid topics. Reiter and Gee believe this is an important issue for intercultural dyads, especially if they tend to avoid communication about cultural differences. Support involves giving advice, offering comfort, and providing reassurance, which appear to overlap with Stafford's maintenance behaviors of assurances and advice. But here, Reiter and Gee extend this to mean relationship-specific support, which likely plays a particularly important role in relational maintenance for intercultural relationships, given the types of societal obstacles these couples face.[49]

Here, Reiter and Gee extend the construct of the relationship-specific support to include support for culture. In their study, Reiter and Gee asked nearly 400 participants to complete measures of open communication and support regarding their romantic relationships. The majority of participants identified their relationships as intracultural, and about one third categorized their relationships as intercultural. The findings of their study indicated that, when compared with intracultural relationships, individuals in intercultural relationships were more likely to report conflict related to cultural differences. However, individuals in intercultural relationships were also more likely to indicate that discussion of these differences facilitated relationship maintenance. Additional results showed that in intercultural relationships, higher levels of open communication about culture and higher levels of cultural support were related to lower levels of relationship distress. Reiter and Gee point out that when compared with intracultural partners, intercultural partners were more likely to report that exchange of cultural values with their partner helped their relationship grow. Here, Reiter and Gee argue that if partners are able to understand, appreciate, and integrate each other's similarities and differences, they will be able to use these differences to maintain their relationship quality. In addition, this result also demonstrates the overall benefit of open communication about culture between partners as a relational maintenance strategy. Finally, for individuals in intercultural relationships, higher levels of open communication about culture and cultural support predicted higher levels of relationship satisfaction.[50]

Stafford has extended her research on relational maintenance to gay and lesbian relationships, arguing that because gay and lesbian couples are not fully accepted in most societies, they may rely on unique maintenance behaviors to sustain their relationships. After surveying a number of gay men and lesbian women, Stafford found that, overall, the maintenance behaviors reported by gay and lesbian couples are quite similar to those reported by heterosexual couples. In addition, Stafford found that gay and lesbian couples also utilize particular relationship maintenance behaviors, including (a) seeking out gay/lesbian supportive environments and (b) being the same as heterosexual couples. Seeking supportive environments refers to the choice to live, work, or socialize in places that are supportive of gay and lesbian relationships. The second new maintenance behavior, being the same as heterosexual couples, included references to how gay and lesbian couples did not see themselves as different from heterosexual couples. Stafford also noted that gay and lesbian couples use a third type of maintenance behavior that has been reported in previous research—that is, social support—but that they use it in a unique way, such that references to support meant being openly gay/lesbian with family, friends, and coworkers in public places.[51]

As we can see from the research reported above, communication plays a principal role in marriage and relational maintenance. Depending on the type of marriage, however, communication within marriages can vary considerably. For example, Howard notes that jealousy and rivalry among wives is common in cultures that practice polygyny. Sororal polygyny, in which a man marries sisters, is one way of getting around the interpersonal problems associated with this practice. Another is restricting the communication among wives—for example, housing each wife in a separate dwelling, as do the Plateau Tonga of Zambia. Rationing communication is another strategy; the Tanala people of Madagascar require that a husband must spend one day with each of his wives in succession. In the Lacandon culture of Southern Mexico, wives are assigned hierarchical positions in which senior-ranking wives have more privileges than junior-ranking wives.[52]

In a recent article, Cynthia Cook argues that polygyny has a positive effect on population growth and fertility but can be harmful to the physical and psychological health of women and children. Cook has observed that some single African American women engage in a kind of polygyny she calls *man-sharing*. According to Cook, the lack of eligible or employable African American men is a key reason for the high incidence of single-parent households among African Americans. Many of these women, she argues, may engage in man-sharing— that is, having a relationship with a man who already has a wife and a job. Cook argues that man-sharing may be an adaptive cultural practice for the African American community in that it stabilizes its birth rate. Ironically, writes Cook, African American women are typically horrified when they learn about African polygamy, since they have been socialized to look forward to a monogamous relationship. Yet many unmarried African American mothers are actually participating in polygyny/man-sharing without being socially and culturally recognized as the second or third wife.[53]

Polyandry, the practice of having multiple husbands, is observed less frequently than polygyny. Howard reports that polyandry is practiced on a regular basis in Tibet and in some parts of India, Nepal, and Sri Lanka. Howard also reports that the most common form of polyandry is fraternal polyandry—that is, a woman who marries brothers.[54]

What are some of the factors that may lead someone to initiate an intercultural, interethnic, or interracial relationship? Shana Levin and her colleagues sought to answer this question. Like others, Levin and her associates recognize the importance of perceived similarity in establishing a relationship. But if intercultural or interracial dating or marriage were solely influenced by similarity, then there would be far fewer intercultural couples than what we see today. In their study, Levin and her colleagues collected data from more than 2,000 students attending a large multiethnic university. Their sample included a sizeable number of White, Asian American, Latino, and African American students. The students completed a number of questionnaires that asked about their demographics, social class, in-group friendships, college dating patterns, in-group bias, intergroup anxiety, and in-group identification. The results show some interesting patterns.[55]

First, consistent with the theory that perceived similarity is a dominant factor in initiating a relationship (i.e., approach tendencies), an overwhelming number of students from all four groups dated members of their own group more than they dated members of other groups. Whites dated Whites, Asian Americans dated Asian Americans, Latinos dated Latinos, and African Americans dated African Americans. Levin and her colleagues also found, however, that many students dated at least one member of another group during their college years. In these cases, Whites were more likely to have dated Latinos and Asian Americans than to have dated African Americans; Asian Americans were more likely to have dated Whites, followed by Latinos, and then African Americans; Latinos were more likely to have dated Whites than to have dated Asian Americans and African Americans; and African Americans were more likely to have dated Latinos and Whites than to have dated Asian Americans.[56]

Availability also plays a role in who dates whom—that is, what options are available to someone when choosing to date someone else. In this study, Asian Americans represented the largest group, followed closely by Whites. Latinos and African Americans were the smallest groups, with half as many Latinos and one sixth as many African Americans. Levin and her associates reasoned that if partner availability were a significant factor in intergroup dating choice, Whites and Asian Americans would date each other with much greater frequency than they date Latinos and African Americans. The results showed that only Asian Americans chose intergroup dating partners consistent with availability. In this study, the researchers found that when Asian American students date outside their group, they date Whites over Latinos and African Americans. Factors other than availability seem to be influencing the intergroup dating choices of Whites, Latinos, and African Americans. One demographic variable also played a role in intergroup dating, where men were more likely to date outside their ethnic group than were women.[57]

Regarding group attitudes, results of this study indicated that students who exhibited more in-group bias were more anxious about interacting with members of other groups, and those who had higher levels of group identification before college were less likely to intergroup date. Yet Levin and her colleagues found that pressure from in-group members not to socialize with or date out-group members before college was not significantly associated with college intergroup dating. Results also indicated that students who engaged in more intergroup dating in college reported less in-group bias at the end of college. Students who dated more outside their group during college also felt less anxious interacting with people of different groups at the end of their fourth year in college. Group identification at the end of college was not significantly associated with college intergroup dating. Students with more college intergroup dating experience did, however, feel significantly more pressure from in-group members not to socialize with or date out-group members at the end of their fourth year in college. Interestingly, Asian Americans with more college intergroup dating experience felt significantly more pressure from in-group members not to socialize with or date out-group members at the end of college. However, this relationship was not seen among either Whites or Latinos.[58]

Overall, Levin and her colleagues conclude that these results demonstrate the generally positive nature of intergroup dating during the college years for Whites, Asian Americans, and Latinos. Specifically, the more they dated members of other groups during college, the less in-group bias students from all three groups showed and the less intergroup anxiety Asian American and Latino students expressed at the end of college. However, Asian American students who dated outside their group more during college also felt more pressure from members of their own group not to socialize with or date members of other groups at the end of college.[59]

The Internet as Relational Maintenance

The Internet has profoundly changed the way humans communicate. Estimates vary, but we can be sure that millions of people (perhaps billions) use the Internet to connect with others. Teresa Correa and her colleagues report that more than 75% of U.S. adults and even more teenagers—about 95%—have been online. Correa notes that, initially, people went online because it offered a unique form of anonymity. But now people use the Internet to socialize with and expand their social networks.[60] One of the primary Internet tools for initiating and maintaining relationships is social networking sites, such as Facebook and Twitter. Ashwini Nadkarni and Stefan Hofmann from Boston University argue that Facebook use is motivated by two primary needs: the need to belong and the need for self-presentation. They also argue that cultural factors, especially individualism and collectivism, mediate these needs. Persons in collectivistic cultures are conditioned to want to belong and may use Facebook to satisfy that need. Although they do not directly test their hypothesis, Nadkarni and Hofmann also predict that members of individualistic cultures are more likely to share private information on Facebook and more likely to raise controversial topics, compared with Facebook users from collectivistic cultures.[61]

In related work, Temple University sociologists Sherri Grasmuck, Jason Martin, and Shanyang Zhao compared the differences in self-presentation on Facebook accounts among five U.S. student groups: Whites and four racial minority groups, including Vietnamese Americans, Indian Americans, Latin Americans/Caribbean Islanders, and African Americans. Their findings indicate that the groups use different strategies in self-presentation constructions on Facebook. Based on their analyses, Grasmuck and her colleagues concluded that

> African Americans, Latinos, and Indian ancestry students project a visual self that is dramatically more social, that they invest more frequently and intensively in displaying a cultural self marked by specific consumer and popular cultural preferences, and they invest more in the direct "about me" narrations than do Vietnamese or

white students. The uplifting and often inspirational quotes related to racial themes of injustice frequently included by the African American, Latino, and Indian students convey a sense of group belonging, color consciousness, and identification with groups historically stigmatized by dominant society. The profiles of white students and Vietnamese students rarely signaled group identification or ethno-racial themes, reflecting "strategies of racelessness" more typically discussed in research focused on white students in offline college contexts. The intensive investments of minorities in presenting highly social, culturally explicit, and elaborated narratives of self in the Facebook profiles are consistent with preoccupations about and heightened awareness of racial identities during this stage of life.[62]

Another study investigated the role of self-expression on Facebook pages. This study compared the Facebook profiles of U.S. Caucasians, African Americans, and Asians attending a Midwestern university. The results indicate that African American student profiles contained more descriptive statements that expressed internal attitudes, beliefs, and values—including the use of personal pronouns—than did those of Caucasian or Asian students. Asian students had more statements reflecting their social affiliations (i.e., group memberships) than did Caucasians or African Americans. Regarding the total amount of self-descriptive statements, African Americans had the most, followed by Caucasians and Asians. The authors of this study contend that these results are reflective of individualism and collectivism; that is, as the authors state, African Americans are "the most individualistic individuals," followed by Caucasians and then Asians, who are more collectivistic than either of the other two groups.[63]

Psychologists J. Patrick Seder and Shigehiro Oishi of the University of Virginia examined the connection between subjective well-being and the ethnic/racial homogeneity of the Facebook friendship networks of several U.S. student groups, including African American, Asian, European American, Latino, and Middle Eastern first-year college students. They found that among European American students, having a homogeneous Facebook friendship network was associated with higher life satisfaction and positive affect, as well as with lower felt misunderstanding. Among non-European American participants, they found no relationship between the homogeneity of Facebook friendship networks and subjective well-being. In explaining their results, Seder and Oishi speculate that European American students may be more likely to form Facebook friendships with others they perceive to be similar to themselves (i.e., homophily) than with their microcultural group counterparts. Seder and Oishi consider that while they may have good intentions to establish friendships with persons from diverse cultures, these students may simply prefer to focus their time and energy on those relationships that require less effort.[64]

The studies cited above focus primarily on U.S. student and U.S. microcultural student groups and their Facebook use. Related research has compared Facebook use across cultures. For example, Katherine Karl, Joy Peluchette, and Christopher Schlaegel compared the types of personal information U.S. and German students posted on their Facebook pages. Their analysis showed that U.S. students were more likely than German students to post problematic information to their Facebook profiles. Examples of problematic information are comments regarding their participation in activities that are in violation of university policy, comments regarding their sexual activities and preferences, comments regarding their use of alcohol and illegal drugs, photos of themselves drinking alcohol, seminude self-photos, and self-photos with firearms. Overall, U.S. students were more likely than German students to post a variety of personal information, including their e-mail address; relationship status; religious beliefs; sexual orientation; photos of romantic partners, pets, family members; and photos of themselves in athletic, traditional, or humorous poses. The authors suggest that these differences may be due to dimensions of cultural variability, specifically that U.S. students are more individualistic and lower in uncertainty avoidance than are German students. They also speculate that because the United States has a much larger population than Germany, U.S. students may feel more anonymous and less responsible for their behavior compared with German students. In some interesting commentary, the researchers caution that U.S. students may be putting themselves at a disadvantage if they pursue employment internationally, especially if German and other international employers are accessing Facebook profiles as part of their employee selection process.[65]

Japan

In early 2013, Facebook had nearly 17 million active users in Japan (13% of the population), surpassing the Japanese social network Mixi. This marks a substantial increase of more than 200% since September 2011. The largest user age group, with 6 million users, is 25- to 34-year-olds. Males slightly outnumber female users in Japan. Rob Gilhooly of *New Scientist* magazine reports that a central reason why Japanese are switching to Facebook is because of Facebook's policy of using real names—as opposed to Mixi, where most users are anonymous. Gilhooly notes that Facebook also gained an increase in Japanese users following the release (in Japan) of the film *The Social Network* in early 2011. Many Japanese businesses also see the value of Facebook in recruiting recent college graduates. Young Japanese job seekers often use their Facebook pages to highlight their education and attract employers.[66]

India

In India, there are nearly 63 million users of Facebook, and 75% of those users are men. Similar to Japan, the largest age group, with more than 30 million users, is currently 18- to 24-year-olds. In addition to using social media to initiate and maintain relationships, many Indian youth are relying on it to start social action movements and protest for their rights. This is especially significant for women, who are muted and face much sex discrimination in India. For women, Facebook functions to do more than initiate and maintain friendships; it gives them a voice to air their grievances and expose the sexual violence inflicted against them in a social system where such violence is often ignored (recall the discussion in Chapter 6 of dowry deaths in India).[67]

Korea

One of South Korea's most popular social networking sites is Cyworld. Kyung-Hee Kim and Haejin Yun, communication professors in South Korea, indicate that the prefix *cy-* stands for *cyber* in English and *relationship* in Korean.[68] Users engage in *cying*, which is the term for managing one's account. Kim and Yun observe that expressions such as *cying* and *cyholic* are widely used among Koreans, even those without Cyworld accounts. Cyworld users' homepages are called *minihompies*, which is pronounced "mini-home-peas," where the *p* stands for page. Recall from Chapter 6 that social order in Korea is based on Confucianism, whose central axiom is obedience to superiors and recognition of one's place or status. In Korea, recognition of one's place in the social hierarchy is paramount and is communicated via special vocabularies. These vocabularies consist of particular terms and phrases for addressing one who is superior, equal, or of lower status. Online terms in Cyworld reflect this Korean value. Cyworld friends are called *ilchons*. Kim and Yun point out that the term *ilchon* (i.e., 1-chon) refers to the relationship between parents and children, 2-chon refers to the relationship between grandparents and children, and 3-chon refers to the relationship between aunts/uncles and nephews/nieces. Cyworld users engage in *ilchon* surfing and visit other Cyworld users' minihompies, and leave messages there. Cyworld users can also par ticipate in an exchange system that uses a sort of cyber-currency, called *dotori,* with which users can purchase decorations for their minihompies. Users can also send virtual gift cards to each other.

Like users of Facebook in the United States, Kim and Yun maintain, Cyworld users have two central reasons for cying: maintaining their existing social relationships and reflecting on themselves. Kim and Yun note that Korea is a high-context culture. Recall from Chapter 2 that in high-context cultures, indirect communication is preferred. Kim and Yun describe a feature in Cyworld where users view and relate to themselves in the third person with minihompy diary-keeping activities. Here they put their own posts about themselves side by side with those of their *ilchon* visitors. This creates the false impression that their own posts came from another visitor. Kim and Yun assert that through cying, users are able to express on their minihompies what they could not say offline. They maintain that minihompies allow an indirect way of communicating personal thoughts and feelings in direct ways.[69]

A general conclusion that most research has supported is that social networking sites are used primarily for social interaction with friends with whom users have a preestablished relationship offline and that they serve mostly to support preexisting social relations within geographically bound communities. That is, as far as we can tell, most users of social networking sites are not implementing social media to initiate new relationships outside their geographical areas.

Mate Selection and Desirability Across Cultures

When you think about getting married or finding a romantic partner, what characteristics do you imagine? Are you looking for someone who is good-looking? Educated? In possession of a good sense of humor? Wealthy? The famed evolutionary psychologist David Buss is interested in the answers to these questions and has investigated mate preferences and opposite-sex desirability across cultures for decades. Before looking at his findings, take a moment to complete the survey in Self-Assessment 9.2.

In some of his most recent research, Buss and his colleague Susan Hill argue that human mate preferences have evolved in response to recurring and different adaptive problems that

Self-Assessment 9.2

Selecting a Mate: Factors in Choosing a Mate

Directions: Below are 18 characteristics of people that you may find either desirable or undesirable. On a scale of 0 to 3, rate each of the characteristics on how important or desirable it is in choosing a mate. A score of 0 = irrelevant or unimportant, 1 = somewhat important, 2 = important, and 3 = indispensable.

_____ 1. Sociability

_____ 2. Similar education

_____ 3. Pleasing disposition

_____ 4. Refinement, neatness

_____ 5. Similar religious background

_____ 6. Good looks

_____ 7. Education and intelligence

_____ 8. Mutual attraction–love

_____ 9. Good cook and housekeeper

_____ 10. Good financial prospect

_____ 11. Desire for home and children

_____ 12. Chastity (no previous experience in sexual intercourse)

_____ 13. Dependable character

_____ 14. Good health

_____ 15. Favorable social status or rating

_____ 16. Similar political background

_____ 17. Emotional stability and maturity

_____ 18. Ambitious and industrious

Preferences Concerning Potential Mates

Directions: Below is a set of 13 characteristics. Please rank them on their desirability in someone you might marry. Give a 1 to the most desirable characteristic in a potential mate, a 2 to the second most desirable characteristic in a potential mate, a 3 to the third most desirable characteristic in a potential mate, and so on until you have ranked all 13 characteristics. No characteristic can receive the same ranking as another.

_____ 1. Easygoing

_____ 2. Healthy

_____ 3. Physically attractive

_____ 4. Good heredity

_____ 5. College graduate

_____ 6. Exciting personality

_____ 7. Intelligent

_____ 8. Creative and artistic

_____ 9. Good housekeeper

_____ 10. Good earning capacity

_____ 11. Religious

_____ 12. Wants children

_____ 13. Kind and understanding

SOURCE: Buss, D. M. (1989). Sex Differences in Human Mate Preference: Evolutionary Hypotheses Tested in Thirty-Seven Cultures. _Behavioral and Brain Sciences, 12,_ 1–49; Buss, D. M. (1994). Mate Preferences in Thirty-Seven Cultures. In W. J. Lonner & R. Malpass (Eds.), _Psychology and Culture_ (pp. 197–202). Boston: Allyn & Bacon.

each sex has had to solve when judging the desirability of someone else. These different mate preferences present men and women with a different set of assessment problems when evaluating the desirability of members of the opposite sex. One source of information about the desirability of another as a romantic partner is how that person is perceived when interacting with same-sex others. Buss and Hill found that women rate men more desirable when the men are shown surrounded by women than when they are shown alone or with other men. They label this the _desirability enhancement effect._ In contrast, men rate women less desirable when they are shown surrounded by men than when they are shown alone or with women. Buss and Hill call this the _desirability diminution effect._ The authors maintain that both effects are reflected in men's and women's judgments of intrasexual rivals, such that women will judge other women depicted with men as being less desirable to men than the same women depicted alone or with other women. Moreover, men will judge other men depicted with women as being more desirable to women than the same men depicted alone or with other men.[70]

In his earlier research, Buss initiated the International Mate Selection Project, consisting of 49 research collaborators from 33 countries located on six continents and five islands.[71] The focus of the project has been to identify people's preferences in choosing a mate. According to Buss, scholars from myriad academic fields are interested in mating practices and mate selection. Evolutionary biologists, for example, believe that mate preference is a central evolutionary force. Sociologists study mating practices because they affect the distribution of wealth in society (e.g., when the rich prefer to mate with the rich). Geneticists understand that mate preferences can affect genetic inheritability estimates. Social psychologists see mate preference as a psychological phenomenon related to interpersonal attraction. Yet, despite all the interest, Buss alleges that very little is known about the types of characteristics people value in potential mates and how these values might vary across cultures—hence, the International Mate Selection Project.

The purpose of his research was to identify (a) which characteristics individuals value in potential mates, (b) similarities and differences among countries in their values, (c) clusters of countries that are similar to one another, and (d) sex differences in the degree of variation in mate selection within each country. Buss and his research collaborators surveyed more than 10,000 people from 33 different countries. In Africa, subjects were from Nigeria, South Africa, and Zambia. Asian countries sampled were China, India, Japan, and Taiwan. In the Middle East, Jewish and Palestinian Israel and Iran were surveyed. European countries studied were Belgium, Bulgaria, Estonia, Finland, France, Germany, Great Britain, Greece, Ireland, Italy, the Netherlands, Norway, Poland, Spain, Sweden, and the former Yugoslavia. In North America, the United States (including Hawaii) and Canada were sampled. South American countries surveyed were Brazil, Colombia, and Venezuela. Oceanic countries were Australia and New Zealand. Participants from Indonesia were also sampled.[72]

In the study, individuals were asked to complete the "Factors in Choosing a Mate" and the "Preferences Concerning Potential Mates" instruments (see Self-Assessment 9.2). After analyzing the completed surveys, Buss found that in spite of the unique cultural variability associated with each sample, there were substantial commonalities among all the samples. Table 9.3 outlines the four top-rated variables. Some of the least preferred characteristics from the rating instruments were "chastity," "similar religious background," "similar political background," and "favorable social status." The lowest-ranked characteristics were "college graduate," "good earning capacity," and "religion."

Table 9.3	Universally Preferred Characteristics

Universally Preferred Characteristics: Ranking Instrument = Preferences Concerning Potential Mates
1. Kind and understanding
2. Intelligent
3. Exciting personality
4. Healthy
Universally Preferred Characteristics: Rating Instrument = Factors in Choosing a Mate
1. Mutual attraction–love
2. Emotional stability and maturity
3. Good health
4. Pleasing disposition

SOURCE: Buss, D. M. (1989). Sex Differences in Human Mate Preference: Evolutionary Hypotheses Tested in Thirty-Seven Cultures. *Behavioral and Brain Sciences, 12,* 1–49; Buss, D. M. (1994). Mate Preferences in Thirty-Seven Cultures. In W. J. Lonner & R. Malpass (Eds.), *Psychology and Culture* (pp. 197–202). Boston: Allyn & Bacon.

Buss noted that although the cultures shared some overall commonalities, each country displayed some unique mate preferences. For example, the highest rated characteristic for Iranian men and women was "refinement and neatness." On the other hand, Chinese men rated "good health" as most important. Chinese women chose "emotional stability" as their top-rated characteristic. Nigerian men rated "good health" the highest, whereas Nigerian women rated "emotional stability" the highest. Buss reported that the largest effect of culture was seen in the variable of "chastity." China, India, Indonesia, Iran, Taiwan, and Palestinian Israel placed the most importance on this characteristic, whereas Sweden, Finland, Norway, the Netherlands, and West Germany ranked it the least important.[73]

Probably the greatest difference among cultures occurred between men and women. In some countries, the sexes differed little in their rankings, whereas in others, they differed greatly. The two countries with the highest degree of sexual dimorphism, Nigeria and Zambia, were also the two that practice polygyny. Moreover, more similarity was found between men and women from the same culture than between men and men or women and women from different cultures. The largest sex difference occurred for the variables of "good financial prospect" and "good earning capacity." Women generally valued these traits more than did men. Men across the globe valued physical attractiveness in marriage partners more than did women. Buss states,

> The importance of good looks is not limited to Western Europe or North America; nor is it limited to cultures saturated with visual media such as television, movies, and videos; nor is it limited to particular racial, ethnic, religious, or political groups. In all known cultures worldwide, from the inner-continental tribal societies of Africa and South America to the big cities of Madrid, London, and Paris, men place a premium on the physical appearance of a potential mate.[74]

Women, on the other hand, place somewhat greater value than do men on "emotional stability and maturity," "favorable social status," "education and intelligence," and "college graduate." In another sex difference, men worldwide prefer wives who are younger than themselves. In polygynic cultures such as Zambia and Nigeria, where men may have multiple wives, men prefer brides who are much younger than themselves. Conversely, women prefer men who are older. In his conclusion, Buss notes that culture appears to exert substantial effects on mate preferences and that, in general, the effects of sex on mate preferences are small compared with those of culture (see Figure 9.5).[75]

Buss's research above shows us that mutual attraction and love are nearly universal factors in choosing a mate. But how people from different cultures define love may differ. In their review of some of the research on love across cultures, Todd Jackson and his colleagues contend that love is conceived differently across cultures. They point to research that has found that students of Asian descent score higher on measures of companionate and pragmatic love styles and lower on erotic love styles compared with their European-descended counterparts.[76]

In related research, Fred Rothbaum and Bill Yuk-Piu Tsang found that, in comparison with U.S. love songs, Chinese love songs focus on love in the natural world and love as a value of Confucianism, Buddhism, and Taoism, with an emphasis on interdependence. U.S. love songs focus on the love partner without regard to context. Other studies have found that Chinese concepts of love typically stress love as related to sadness, jealousy, and betrayal, while U.S. concepts of love equate it with happiness.[77]

Figure 9.5   Although commonalities can be found across cultures, culture is thought to exert great influence over individuals' mate preferences.

To extend this research, Jackson and his colleagues asked American and Chinese couples to complete the Love Stories Scale, an instrument designed to assess preferences for 25 metaphors for love. Examples of love metaphors include *history,* in which love forms an indelible record where partners keep a mental and physical record of their relationship; *war,* in which love is a series of battles in a continuing war; *mystery,* in which love is a mystery where partners do not let themselves be known; *pornography,* in which love is dirty and partners are objectified; *fantasy,* in which love results in couples living happily ever after; *democracy,* in which love is two partners equally sharing power; and so on. Their results showed that fantasy emerged as a prototypical theme for Americans that was missing from the Chinese responses. For the Chinese, democracy and history emerged as themes, where the sharing of power and history between partners was an important ingredient of love. Pornography emerged in both Chinese and American themes.[78]

Shuangyue Zhang and Susan Kline have also studied mate selection across cultures. Their study examined the influence of one's social network on intention to marry and relational commitment to another in both China and the United States. Zhang and Kline point out that the familial network of a potential mate is highly valued in East Asian cultures, particularly in China. To be sure, however, social network support is positively related to relationship development and stability in the United States as well. But Zhang and Kline were interested in finely tuning how and to what extent family and friend networks affect one's decision in the process of mate selection in both China and the United States. Zhang and Kline point to research that has documented that one's social networks significantly influence the initiation, development, maintenance, and dissolution of any given relationship. Noting that personal relationships do not exist in isolation from one another, Zhang and Kline assert that social networks are important because relational partners need validation of their own perspectives regarding their relationship from members of their close networks. In fact, some interesting research shows that one's social network is often better at predicting relationship outcome than are the two individuals involved in the relationship.[79]

Also, other studies have demonstrated that perceived support from one's network positively affects relationship development and stability. For example, Zhang and Kline point to research that shows that romantic partners experience less uncertainty and are less likely to terminate their relationship when they communicate frequently with their partners' social network. In their own study, Zhang and Kline examined the role of social networks in mate selection in China and the United States. They suspected that the cultural orientations of individualism and collectivism may play a role in the impact of social networks and mate selection across these two cultures. Recall from Chapter 2 that filial piety is one of the most salient values in Chinese culture. In China, the family is seen as the basic unit of society. In their study, Chinese and American students completed surveys that measure the role of social networks in mate preferences. Zhang and Kline predicted that (a) family-oriented beliefs would be considered more important for Chinese than for Americans, (b) Chinese would be more likely to comply with their network members regarding their marriage decisions than would Americans, (c) Chinese would be more likely to indicate network disapproval as an obstacle to marrying their dating partners than would Americans, and (d) the influence of family and friends would be a better predictor of one's marriage intentions and relational commitment for Chinese than for Americans. All their predictions were confirmed. In their discussion of the results, Zhang and Kline point to China's collectivistic orientation, and especially filial piety, as accountable for the emphasis on social networks.[80]

Arranged Marriages

In some cultures, an individual's preference in selecting a mate is moot because marriage is arranged by parents or a trusted family friend or mediator. In many instances, the bride and groom of an arranged marriage do not even meet until the day of the wedding. A bride price, similar to a dowry, is an essential ingredient of the arranged marriage in many cultures. Although not as common as they once were, arranged marriages are still practiced in a variety of cultures and within some microcultural groups in the United States, such as the Hmong. Many young persons in the United States find the prospect of an arranged marriage quite frightening and unnerving. Yet Katie Thao, a Hmong woman who emigrated from Laos to the United States when she was young, indicates that the arranged marriage in which she participated was one of the most satisfying events of her life.[81] To Thao, the time and effort associated with searching for a mate represented considerable uncertainty and anxiety. In traditional Hmong culture, arranged marriages are negotiated by the parents. Because Thao had faith and trust in her parents to select the ideal spouse for her, she had little to worry about and very little uncertainty about the match. Although she admits to being nervous on her wedding day, Thao says she loves the man she married very much, and they have three children now. Although it happens infrequently, the woman can reject the arranged match. As Lor notes, however, there are certain situations in which the match cannot be refused. According to Lor, if the groom's family clan has high status, is unusually wealthy, or is related to the bride's family in some way, the match is essentially permanent.[82]

Serena Nanda has written several books about gender and sex roles in India. She writes that just about all marriages in India are arranged. During a year-long field trip to India,

STUDENT VOICES ACROSS CULTURES

Marriage in Saudi Arabia

My name is Mohammad I. Alshaya, and I am from Riyadh, Saudi Arabia. I graduated from St. Norbert College with a major in business administration.

Since Saudi Arabia is heavily influenced by the religion of Islam, marriage is considered holy. This is because Islam encourages its followers to get married and multiply. However, these days, people who are getting married have some concerns. There are, of course, some burdens on both the bride and the groom. The most difficult part of marriage, for example, is the bride wealth (dowry).

The point of marriage is to bring two individuals together. However, there are more important aspects associated with marriage than uniting two people. For example, marriage in Saudi could bring two families together; this is essential in all marriages because those two families could become one family. Another vital reason for marriage is the importance of forming a family that contributes well to society.

Mothers from both the groom's and the bride's sides play a major part in matching two individuals as a wife and a husband. Arranged marriages are very common where I am from. The mother of the groom usually plays the role of matchmaker, for which she will be given the descriptive qualities that the man is looking for in a woman. What most men seek in a wife is not quite the same as in other cultures. Qualities are similar, but the order is different. For Saudi men, reputation is probably ranked first, followed by social status. Attractiveness is very important, but it will never be as crucial as reputation and social status.

Nanda interviewed several women whose marriages were arranged. Like other countries that practice arranged marriage, in India, the parents make the arrangements. Oftentimes, parents will place "matrimonial" advertisements in magazines, describing their sons or daughters and soliciting potential mates for them. The sons and daughters play virtually no role in mate selection. When Nanda asked Indian women why they take such little responsibility in these matters, she found that most women believe that marriage is too important for inexperienced people such as themselves to make the selection and the arrangements. Nanda found that young men and women do not date and have very little, if any, social contact with members of the opposite sex. Moreover, she found that among the women she interviewed, they found the prospect of having to meet a lot of young men and then compete for their attention and affection too anxiety producing. When Nanda asked the women how they could marry a man who was a stranger to them, the women rejected that description, suggesting that because their parents knew the man, the man was not a stranger. In India, the parents typically go to great lengths to find the right spouse for their daughters. Family reputation is more important than love, and marriages are usually arranged between men and women of the same caste.[83]

In China, a grotesque form of arranged marriage has been rekindled: bride trafficking. *Newsweek* correspondent Dorinda Elliot reports that in many of the rural communities of China, crooked marriage brokers offer kidnapped women and girls for sale to prospective buyers. According to Elliot, in recent years, Chinese authorities freed almost 100,000 kidnapped women and children and arrested almost 150,000 bride traffickers for participating in what she calls a virtual slave trade. Ironically, writes Elliot, local Chinese peasants sympathize with men who buy their wives, believing that if a woman takes the bride price and sends it to her parents, the man deserves to have her as his wife.[84]

Marital Dissolution and Divorce Across Cultures

A fact of life for all of us is that some of our relationships will end. Like marriage practices, divorce customs vary across cultures. Although it is relatively easy to calculate the divorce rate in any given culture, understanding why people divorce is a much more difficult task. Communication problems are a main reason for divorce in a number of countries. But in many cultures, social and economic issues often play a role in divorce decisions as well. Factors such as income, sexual dissatisfaction, childlessness, women's equality issues, religion, and the ease with which one can obtain a divorce all vary across cultures.

Divorce Rates Across the World[85]

Sweden	55%
United States, Australia	46%
United Kingdom	43%
Canada, Russia	40%
Israel	26%
Switzerland	25%
China	20%
Greece	17%
Singapore, Poland	17%
Spain	15%
Italy	12%

In general, monogamy is correlated with lower divorce rates than is polygyny.[86] Although the reasons for divorce vary, one trend that seems consistent across most cultures is that the overall divorce rate is on the rise. In Japan, the number of divorce cases in 2009 was about 3.5 times more than 50 years ago. Today in Japan, about one in three marriages end in divorce which is one every 2 minutes and 4 seconds. In India, however, the divorce rate remains low, where only 1 in 100 marriages end in divorce. Pittu Laungani notes that there is a strong stigma against divorce in India, especially on women. Indian women should not even think of divorce, asserts Laungani, lest they face the loss of status, removal of custody of their children, and threat of poverty. So strong are the social consequences of divorce in that country that most married Indian women endure the most appalling domestic conditions to remain married.[87]

In China, the divorce rate is increasing. Since the passage of legislative reforms in the early 1980s and then more reform in 2003, divorce has become much simpler in China and divorce rates have soared. According to a recent article in *China Daily*, more than 5,000 couples divorce in China every day. The article cites Chen Yijun, a sociologist at the Chinese Academy of Social Sciences. Yijun suggests that less communication between spouses and increasing extramarital affairs are the chief reasons for divorce in China. In addition, Yijun suggests that Chinese men and women are becoming more personally and financially independent than ever before.[88]

The divorce rate in Australia hovers at about 45%. According to a report issued by the Australian Institute of Family Studies, the three main reasons for divorce in Australia are communication problems, incompatibility, and extramarital affairs. Communication problems were the most cited reason for divorce among men and women. The report maintains that communication problems are associated with difficulties expressing emotional attrition in the relationship, not being understood by one's spouse, feeling that one's needs are not being met, loss of affection and companionship, and feeling lonely and unappreciated.[89]

Citing increased opportunities for women, the *Women's International Network News* reports that the divorce rate in Russia is rising quickly. Because they are now able to find their own apartments and support themselves financially, more and more Russian women are seeking divorce. The divorce rate in Russia has plateaued at about 40%.[90]

DEVELOPING A SKILL SET: TOWARD INTERCULTURAL COMMUNICATION COMPETENCE

1. As stated at the beginning of the chapter, initiating and maintaining relationships with others is one of the most necessary and challenging functions of human survival. Initiating and maintaining relationships with people from different cultures presents a unique set of circumstances that many people find hard to address. Having read this chapter, keep in mind that beginning a new relationship is fraught with uncertainty, which leads to anxiety. No one likes feeling anxious, but remember that anxiety is perfectly natural. So don't let anxiety prohibit you from initiating a relationship with someone from another culture. In the next week or so, try approaching and interacting with one of your fellow students who is from a culture different from your own.

2. During the early stages of an intercultural relationship, be conscious of the ways you reduce uncertainty, keeping in mind that people from other cultures (e.g., high vs. low context) reduce uncertainty using different kinds of communication strategies. Be flexible and mindful that your way of reducing uncertainty (e.g., asking a lot of questions, making direct eye contact) may actually increase uncertainty for your new intercultural friend. Keep in mind also that your new friend may not ask a lot of questions, may not look at you directly, and may use the nonverbal environment to reduce uncertainty. This does not necessarily mean that he or she is shy or apprehensive.

3. Consider your group of close friends. Notice how similar you are to them (e.g., age, education level, dress habits, music and TV interests). Now consider how similar you may be to your fellow international students. While they come from different parts of the world, you may actually have a lot in common with them. For example, you are probably close in age and education level, and they probably speak English. Although you are different, you may have more in common with them (i.e., similarity) than you think.

CHAPTER SUMMARY

People across the world, in all cultures, initiate, maintain, and dissolve relationships. Reducing uncertainty is a major part of initiating relationships, and one's level of intercultural communication apprehension and sociocommunicative style affect this process. Empathy and similarity are important in maintaining relationships. Perceptions of relationships differ significantly across cultures, particularly between Eastern and Western cultures. Perhaps the most important of all relationships—marriage—varies across cultures in terms of the different types of marriage, mate selection, arranged marriage, and marital dissolution.

Visit the student study site at www.sagepub.com/neuliep6e for e-flashcards, web quizzes, web resources, and more.

DISCUSSION QUESTIONS

1. In thinking about the quote at the beginning of the chapter—"Without others, there is no self"—how do your family, friends, and professors define who you are?

2. What communication strategies do you use to reduce uncertainty when interacting with others?

3. After completing the Sociocommunicative Orientation/Style Instrument (Self-Assessment 9.1) in this chapter, how does your level of assertiveness and responsiveness affect your relationships?

4. In what ways are you similar to your closest friends?

5. What are the primary characteristics you look for in a potential relational partner?

6. Why would you or would you not consider a person from a different culture as a potential mate?

KEY TERMS

anxiety/uncertainty management theory   335

arranged marriage   365

assertiveness   339

empathy   344

polyandry   351

polygamy   351

polygyny   351

relational empathy   344

responsiveness   339

sociocommunicative style   330

third culture   344

uncertainty   331

uncertainty reduction theory   331

NOTES

1. Gergen, K. J. (1991). *The Saturated Self: Dilemmas of Identity in Contemporary Life.* New York: Basic. (Quote on p. 178)

2. Berger, C. R., & Calabrese, R. J. (1975). Some Explorations in Initial Interaction and Beyond: Toward a Developmental Theory of Interpersonal Communication. *Human Communication Research, 1,* 99–112.

3. Ibid. Reproduced with permission of Oxford University Press, Inc. via Copyright Clearance Center.

4. Gudykunst, W. B., & Kim, Y. Y. (2003). *Communicating With Strangers: An Approach to Intercultural Communication* (4th ed.). New York: McGraw-Hill.

5. Gudykunst, W. B. (1983). Uncertainty Reduction and Predictability of Behavior in Low- and High-Context Cultures. *Communication Quarterly, 31,* 49–55; Gudykunst, W. B. (1988). Uncertainty and Anxiety. In Y. Y. Kim & W. B. Gudykunst (Eds.), *Theories of Intercultural Communication* (pp. 123–156). Newbury Park, CA: Sage; Gudykunst, W. B. (1995). Anxiety/Uncertainty Management (AUM) Theory. In R. Wiseman (Ed.), *Intercultural Communication Theory* (pp. 8–58). Thousand Oaks, CA: Sage.

6. Gudykunst, W. B., & Nishida, T. (1984). Individual and Cultural Influences on Uncertainty Reduction. *Communication Monographs, 51,* 23–36.

7. Sanders, J., & Wiseman, R. (1991). *Uncertainty Reduction Among Ethnicities in the United States.* Paper presented at the annual convention of the International Communication Association, Chicago, IL.

8. Gudykunst, W. B., Sodetani, L. L., & Sonoda, K. T. (1987). Uncertainty Reduction in Japanese-American-Caucasian Relationships in Hawaii. *Western Journal of Speech Communication, 51,* 256–278.

9. Berger & Calabrese, Some Explorations in Initial Interaction and Beyond, pp. 99–112.

10. Ibid.

11. Gudykunst & Kim, *Communicating With Strangers.*

12. Gudykunst, W. B. (2005). An Anxiety/Uncertainty Management (AUM) Theory of Effective Communication: Making the Mesh of the Net Finer. In W. B. Gudykunst (Ed.), *Theorizing About Intercultural Communication* (pp. 281–322). Thousand Oaks, CA: Sage.

13. Ibid.

14. Ibid.

15. Ibid.

16. Ibid.

17. Neuliep, J. W. (2012). The Relationship Among Intercultural Communication Apprehension, Ethnocentrism, Uncertainty Reduction, and Communication Satisfaction During Initial Intercultural Interaction: An Extension of Anxiety and Uncertainty Management (AUM) Theory. *Journal of Intercultural Communication Research, 41,* 1–16.

18. Ibid.

19. Neuliep, J. W., & Ryan, D. J. (1998). The Influence of Intercultural Communication Apprehension and Socio-Communicative Orientation on Uncertainty Reduction During Initial Cross-Cultural Interaction. *Communication Quarterly, 46,* 88–99.

20. Berger & Calabrese, Some Explorations in Initial Interaction and Beyond.

21. Neuliep & Ryan, The Influence of Intercultural Communication Apprehension and Socio-Communicative Orientation on Uncertainty Reduction During Initial Cross-Cultural Interaction.

22. Neuliep, J. W., & Grohskopf, E. L. (2000). Uncertainty Reduction and Communication Satisfaction During Initial Interaction: An Initial Test and Replication of a New Axiom. *Communication Reports, 13,* 67–78.

23. McCroskey, J. C., & Richmond, V. P. (1996). *Fundamentals of Human Communication.* Prospect Heights, IL: Waveland.

24. Ibid.

25. Neuliep & Ryan, The Influence of Intercultural Communication Apprehension and Socio-Communicative Orientation on Uncertainty Reduction During Initial Cross-Cultural Interaction.

26. Berger & Calabrese, Some Explorations in Initial Interaction and Beyond; Ibid.

27. Anderson, C. M., Martin, M. M., Zhong, M., & West, D. (1997). *Reliability, Separation of Factors, and Sex Difference on the Assertiveness–Responsiveness Measure: A Chinese Sample.* Paper presented at the annual convention of the International Communication Association, Montreal, Quebec, Canada; Thompson, C. A., Ishii, S., & Klopf, D. W. (1990). Japanese and Americans Compared on Assertiveness/Responsiveness. *Psychological Reports, 66,* 829–830; Thompson, C. A., & Klopf, D. W. (1991). An Analysis of Social Style Among Disparate Cultures. *Communication Research Reports, 8,* 65–72.

28. Broome, B. J. (1991). Building Shared Meaning: Implications of a Relational Approach to Empathy for Teaching Intercultural Communication. *Communication Education, 40,* 235–249. (Quote on p. 240)

29. The concept of third-culture building was initially articulated by Fred Casmir. Broome's approach is based on Casmir's work in this area.

30. Broome, Building Shared Meaning.

31. Klopf, D. W. (1998). *Intercultural Encounters: The Fundamentals of Intercultural Communication.* Englewood, CO: Morton.

32. Duck, S., & Barnes, M. K. (1992). Disagreeing About Agreement: Reconciling Differences About Similarity. *Communication Monographs, 59,* 199–208. (Quote on p. 199)

33. Byrne, D. (1992). The Transition From Controlled Laboratory Experimentation to Less Controlled Settings: Surprise! Additional Variables Are Operative. *Communication Monographs, 59,* 190–198.

34. Ibid.

35. Gudykunst, W. B., & Nishida, T. (1986). The Influence of Cultural Variability on Perceptions of Communication Behavior Associated With Relationship Terms. *Human Communication Research, 13,* 147–166.

36. Yum, J. O. (1997). The Impact of Confucianism on Interpersonal Relationships and Communication Patterns in East Asia. In L. A. Samovar & R. E. Porter (Eds.), *Intercultural Communication: A Reader* (8th ed., pp. 78–88). Belmont, CA: Wadsworth.

37. Ibid.

38. Ibid.

39. Ibid., p. 81.

40. Ibid.

41. Ibid.

42. Ibid.

43. Howard, M. C. (1997). *Contemporary Cultural Anthropology* (5th ed.). New York: Pearson.

44. Becker, G. S., & Posner, R. A. (1993). Cross-Cultural Differences in Family and Sexual Life. *Rationality and Society, 5,* 421–432.

45. U.S. Census Bureau. (2010). *Households and Families: 2010 Census Brief: Interracial and Interethnic Coupled Households Appendix Tables.* Washington, DC: Author. Retrieved from http://www.census.gov/population/www/cen2010/briefs/tables/appendix.pdf

46. Troy, A. B., Lewis-Smith, J., & Laurenceau, J.-P. (2006). Interracial and Intraracial Romantic Relationships: The Search for Differences in Satisfaction, Conflict, and Attachment Style. *Journal of Social and Personal Relationships, 23,* 65–80.

47. Kaiser Family Foundation. (2001, September 1). *Race and Ethnicity in 2001: Attitudes, Perceptions, and Experience.* Menlo Park, CA: Author. Retrieved from http://kff.org/other/poll-finding/race-and-ethnicity-in-2001-attitudes-perceptions/

48. Stafford, L. (2011). Measuring Relationship Maintenance Behaviors: Critique and Development of the Revised Relationship Maintenance Behavior Scale. *Journal of Social and Personal Relationships, 28,* 278–303.

49. Reiter, M. J., & Gee, C. B. (2008). Open Communication and Partner Support in Intercultural and Interfaith Romantic Relationships: A Relational Maintenance Approach. *Journal of Social and Personal Relationships, 25,* 539–559.

50. Ibid.

51. Haas, S., & Stafford, L. (1998). An Initial Examination of Maintenance Behaviors in Gay and Lesbian Relationships. *Journal of Social and Personal Relationships, 15,* 846–855.

52. Howard, *Contemporary Cultural Anthropology.*

53. Cook, C. T. (2007). Polygyny: Did the Africans Get It Right? *Journal of Black Studies, 38,* 232–250.

54. Howard, *Contemporary Cultural Anthropology.*

55. Levin, S., Taylor, P. L., & Caudle, E. (2007). Interethnic and Interracial Dating in College: A Longitudinal Study. *Journal of Social and Personal Relationships, 24,* 323–341.

56. Ibid.

57. Ibid.

58. Ibid.

59. Ibid.

60. Correa, T., Hinsley, A. W., & Gil de Zuniga, H. (2010). Who Interacts on the Web? The Intersection of Users' Personality and Social Media Use. *Computers in Human Behavior, 26,* 247–253.

61. Nadkarni, A., & Hofmann, S. G. (2012). Why Do People Use Facebook? *Personality and Individual Differences, 52,* 243–249.

62. Grasmuck, S., Martin, J., & Zhao, S. (2009). Ethno-Racial Identity Displays on Facebook. *Journal of Computer-Mediated Communication, 15,* 158–188. (Quote on p. 179)

63. DeAndrea, D. C., Shaw, A. S., & Levine, T. R. (2010). Online Language: The Roles of Culture in Self-Expression and Self-Construal on Facebook. *Journal of Language and Social Psychology, 29,* 425–442. (Quote on p. 437)

64. Seder, J. P., & Oishi, S. (2009). Ethnic/Racial Identity in College Students' Facebook Friendship Networks and Subjective Well-Being. *Journal of Research in Personality, 43,* 438–443.

65. Karl, K., Peluchette, J., & Schlaegel, C. (2010). Who's Posting Facebook *Faux Pas*? A Cross-Cultural Examination of Personality Differences. *International Journal of Selection and Assessment, 18,* 174–186.

66. Espinosa, J. (2012, September 13). Facebook overtakes Japanese social network Mixi in Japan. *Inside Facebook.* Retrieved from http://www.insidefacebook.com/2012/09/13/facebook-overtakes-japanese-social-network-mixi-in-japan; Gilhooly, R. (2012, July 25). Why Japan finally fell for Facebook. *New Scientist.* Retrieved from http://www.newscientist.com/article/mg21528756.400-why-japan-finally-fell-for-facebook.html; *Japan Facebook Statistics.* (2013). Retrieved from http://www.socialbakers.com/facebook-statistics/japan

67. *India Facebook Statistics.* (2013). Retrieved from http://www.socialbakers.com/facebook-statistics/india; Ramaswamy, R. (2013, January 12). Social media boon for youth uprising. *Daily News & Analysis.* Retrieved from http://www.dnaindia.com/mumbai/report_social-media-boon-for-youth-uprising_1788197; Thistlethwaite, S. B. (2013, January 8). The "war on women" meets social media. *Washington Post.* Retrieved from http://www.washingtonpost.com/blogs/guest-voices/post/the-war-on-women-meets-social-media/2013/01/08/4a1ad2f8-5915-11e2-88d0-c4cf-65c3ad15_blog.html

68. Kim, K.-H., & Yun, H. (2007). Cying for Me, Cying for Us: Relational Dialectics in a Korean Social Network Site. *Journal of Computer Mediated Communication, 13*(1), 298–318.

69. Ibid.

70. Hill, S. E., & Buss, D. M. (2008). The Mere Presence of Opposite-Sex Others on Judgments of Sexual and Romantic Desirability: Opposite Effects for Men and Women. *Personality and Social Psychology Bulletin, 34*(5), 635–647.

71. Buss, D. M. (1989). Sex Differences in Human Mate Preference: Evolutionary Hypotheses Tested in Thirty-Seven Cultures. *Behavioral and Brain Sciences, 12,* 1–49; Buss, D. M. (1994). Mate Preferences in Thirty-Seven Cultures. In W. J. Lonner & R. Malpass (Eds.), *Psychology and Culture* (pp. 197–202). Boston: Allyn & Bacon.

72. Buss, Mate Preferences in Thirty-Seven Cultures.

73. Ibid.

74. Ibid., p. 200.

75. Ibid.

76. Jackson, T., Chen, H., Guo, C., & Gao, X. (2006). Stories We Love By: Conceptions of Love Among Couples From the People's Republic of China and the United States. *Journal of Cross-Cultural Psychology, 37,* 446–464.

77. Rothbaum, F., & Tsang, B. (1998). Love Songs in the United States and China. *Journal of Cross-Cultural Psychology, 26,* 306–319.

78. Jackson et al., Stories We Love By.

79. Zhang, S., & Kline, S. (2009). Can I Make My Own Decision? A Cross-Cultural Study of Perceived Social Network Influence in Mate Selection. *Journal of Cross-Cultural Psychology, 40,* 3–23.

80. Ibid.

81. This account was provided by Katie Thao in a personal communication in the summer of 1995.

82. Lor, H. (1997). *The Hmong.* Unpublished student manuscript, St. Norbert College, De Pere, WI.

83. Nanda, S. (2000). Arranging a Marriage in India. In P. R. Devita (Ed.), *Stumbling Toward Truth: Anthropologists at Work* (pp. 196–204). Prospect Heights, IL: Waveland.

84. Elliot, D. (1998). Trying to Stand on Two Feet. *Newsweek, 313,* 48–50.

85. Feldstein Family Law Group. (2012). *Divorce Fact Sheet 2012.* Retrieved from www.separation.ca/pdfs/divorcefacts.pdf

86. Gage-Brandon, A. J. (1992). The Polygyny-Divorce Relationship: A Case Study of Nigeria. *Journal of Marriage and the Family, 54,* 285–293.

87. Hays, J. (2013). Divorce in Japan. *Facts and Details.* Retrieved from http://factsanddetails.com/japan/cat18/sub117/item616.html; Laungani, P. (2007). *Understanding Cross-Cultural Psychology.* London: Sage.

88. China: Divorce Increase and Change Affect Women. (1994). *Women's International Network News, 20,* 59; China's Divorce Rate Up 21.2 Percent in 2004. (2005). *China Daily.* Retrieved from http://www.chinadaily.com.cn/english/doc/2005-03/01/content_420456.htm; Over 5,000 couples divorce each day in China. (2011, June 2). *China Daily.* Retrieved from http://www.chinadaily.com.cn/china/2011-06/02/content_12629641.htm

89. Wolcott, I., & Hughes, J. (1999). *Towards Understanding the Reasons for Divorce* (Working Paper No. 20). Melbourne: Australian Institute of Family Studies. Retrieved from http://www.aifs.gov.au/institute/pubs/WP20.pdf

90. Russian Business Women Are Moving Up Slowly. (1998). *Women's International Network News, 24,* 75.

CHAPTER 10

Intercultural Conflict

Honest disagreement is often a good sign of progress.

—Mahatma Gandhi

Imagine yourself in the following situation:

> Akira Abe is an international exchange student from Japan who lives down the hall from you in your dorm. You have interacted with Akira only occasionally and do not know him very well. This morning, Akira approached you to complain that you frequently play your music so loudly that he is unable to study or sleep. Akira then asked if you would please stop playing your music so loudly.

What would you do in this situation? How would you resolve this conflict? Would you comply with Akira's request? Would you argue with Akira?

Conflict, such as the one depicted above, is an inevitable part of living in a society with others. All types of human relationships—from strangers to acquaintances to intimates—experience conflict. Communication plays a paradoxical role in most conflicts, because communication is required both to instigate conflict and to resolve it. Unfortunately, conflict is the source of much relational stress and dissolution; fortunately, the successful resolution of conflict is one of the strongest and most consistent predictors of relational satisfaction. Hence, an understanding of conflict and how to resolve it is an essential part of becoming a competent communicator, especially in your relationships with persons from other cultures.

DEFINITION OF INTERCULTURAL CONFLICT

In the past 25 years, a growing body of theory and research has emerged in the intercultural communication literature regarding the nature of intercultural conflict. Much of this research is based on the work of Stella Ting-Toomey and John Oetzel.[1] They define intercultural conflict as

> the implicit or explicit emotional struggle between persons of different cultural communities over perceived or actual incompatibility of cultural ideologies and values, situational norms, goals, face-orientations, scarce resources, styles/processes, and/or outcomes in a face-to-face (or mediated) context within a sociohistorical embedded system.[2]

Recall from Chapter 1 that a fundamental assumption of intercultural communication is that it is a group phenomenon experienced by individuals. Likewise, during intercultural conflict, one's group membership (i.e., culture) becomes a factor in how conflict is perceived, managed, and resolved. Some of these cultural factors may be unconscious, such as one's degree of individualism or collectivism. Other factors are probably very conscious. Recall your conflict with Akira. The two of you are from different cultural communities, have incompatible goals, and desire different outcomes. You choose to play your music loudly. Akira prefers that you not play your music loudly. From a sociohistorical perspective, you may wonder if all Japanese are quiet and dislike loud music. Perhaps Akira questions if all Americans are rude and insensitive to the wishes of others. Although the conflict between you and Akira could just as easily have occurred between two U.S. students or two Japanese students, the fact that it happened between a U.S. student and a Japanese student complicates the issue.

Ting-Toomey and Oetzel maintain that intercultural conflict involves a certain degree of ethnocentric perception and judgment. Recall from Chapter 1 and Chapter 5 that ethnocentric persons hold attitudes and behaviors about their in-group that are biased in favor of the in-group, often at the expense of out-groups. Ethnocentric persons foster cooperative relations with in-group members while competing with, and perhaps even battling, out-group members.[3] Hence, by virtue of our cultural upbringing, we think we are correct (i.e., loud music is great vs. loud music is disrespectful). To explain intercultural conflict further, three models will be presented next: Young Kim's Model of Intercultural Conflict, Ting-Toomey and Oetzel's Culture-Based Social Ecological Conflict Model, and Benjamin Broome's Model of Building a Culture of Peace Through Dialogue.

Kim's Model of Intercultural Conflict

Well-known intercultural communication scholar Young Yun Kim has developed a model of intercultural conflict. Kim argues that intercultural conflict occurs at three interdependent and interrelated levels, including a micro or individual level; an intermediary level; and a macro or societal level (see Figure 10.1).[4]

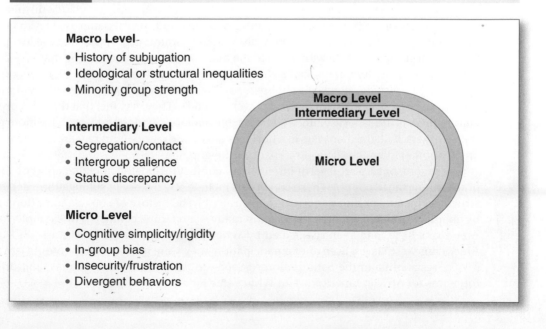

Figure 10.1 Kim's Model of Intercultural Conflict

Macro Level
- History of subjugation
- Ideological or structural inequalities
- Minority group strength

Intermediary Level
- Segregation/contact
- Intergroup salience
- Status discrepancy

Micro Level
- Cognitive simplicity/rigidity
- In-group bias
- Insecurity/frustration
- Divergent behaviors

Macro Level
Intermediary Level
Micro Level

The micro, or *individual,* level of intercultural conflict refers to the unique attitudes, dispositions, and beliefs that each individual brings to the conflict. According to Kim's model, cognitive simplicity/rigidity refers to the degree of inflexibility in the way individuals think about people from different cultures. Rigid, simplistic thinking includes gross categorization and stereotyping (e.g., all Americans are rude; all Japanese are quiet). In-group bias refers to the degree to which the individual is ethnocentric. Recall from Chapter 1 that ethnocentrism is defined as viewing one's own group as being at the center of everything and using the standards of one's own group to measure or gauge the worth of all other groups. Insecurity/ frustration refers to the degree to which the individual has a high level of uncertainty about, and fear of, out-group members (e.g., they will steal our jobs). Divergent behavior refers to the behavioral patterns of the individual that clearly *differentiate* and distance him or her from out-group members. For example, obviously different speech patterns or accents may ostensibly separate groups from one another. During conflict, people will often exaggerate their mannerisms and speech to accentuate their differences compared with out-groups. Because you are upset about Akira's complaint, you may intentionally turn up the volume on your music. Imagine two employees working together, each from a different culture, who have gross stereotypes of each other, are both ethnocentric, fear each other, and have highly divergent behavioral patterns. Kim's model predicts that such a situation is likely to engender conflict.[5]

The *intermediary* level of intercultural conflict refers to the actual location and context of the conflict. Some environments (e.g., neighborhoods, school, work) may be more likely than others to facilitate conflict. Segregation and contact refer to the extent to which the individuals' cultural groups interact on a daily basis. Perhaps the most basic condition for intercultural conflict is contact between diverse cultures or ethnicities on a day-to-day basis. Segregated workplaces or schools do not allow for much interaction, and components at the individual level (e.g., cognitive rigidity, in-group bias) tend to escalate to intolerable levels that facilitate intercultural conflict. Intergroup salience refers to the observable physical and social differences between the conflicting individuals. Such cultural markers include distinct physical and behavioral differences, such as race, language, and speech patterns. As Kim notes, to the extent that the groups are culturally distinct, the communicative skills of the less powerful cultural group will clash with those of the majority group members. The majority group's symbol system is dominant. Status discrepancy refers to the degree to which conflicting parties differ in status along cultural lines. For example, African Americans often argue that U.S. culture practices an asymmetrical power structure. They may feel that the U.S. corporate culture reflects the same asymmetry. On the job, managers and supervisors have more power than workers. If all the managers in a business are of one race or ethnicity and all the workers are of another, then the status discrepancy is heightened.[6]

The macro, or *societal,* level of intercultural conflict includes factors that are probably out of the interactants' control. These conditions include any history of subjugation, ideological/ structural inequality, and minority group strength. The history of subjugation of one group by another is a key environmental factor in many intercultural conflicts. For example, African Americans have long been subjugated by Whites in the United States. Historically, African Americans were slaves. Even after emancipation, they were not allowed to vote. As late as the 1960s, restaurants in the South enforced separate bathrooms, seating areas, and drinking fountains for African Americans and Whites (see Figure 10.2).

Figure 10.2 Segregated drinking fountain in use in the American South.

Often, the tensions expressed today are rooted in the history of one group's subjugation of another group. Ideological and structural inequity refers to societal differences regarding power, prestige, and economic reward. Historically, in the United States, Whites have held most of the power positions and gained most of the economic reward. Hence, there is a vast ideological and structural difference between Whites and other groups. Minority (i.e., microcultural) group strength refers to the amount of power (e.g., legal, political, economic) a particular group possesses. Microcultural groups vary in their ability to rally their members against structural inequalities. Minority group strength varies as a function of the status of the group's language within the society, the sheer number of members in the group, and forms of societal support (e.g., governmental services designed specifically for that group). Relative to other microcultural groups, African Americans, for example, are economically and politically quite powerful. Political scientists argue, for instance, that presidential elections are swung by the African American voting bloc. According to Kim, the greater the ethnic group's strength, the more likely that an individual in that group will take action in intercultural conflict situations.[7]

Taken together, these three levels of conflict merge during any intercultural conflict. To the extent that these individual, intermediary, and societal factors are present, intercultural conflict will likely ignite.

An Intercultural Conversation: Kim's Model of Intercultural Conflict

Mike Fabion is the vice president of Acme Marketing Firm, a company his father founded. Acme is a direct marketing firm for insurance agencies. Mike is 58 years old and White. He was born and raised in Kenilworth, Illinois, a wealthy Chicago suburb. Mike has six directors under him in Acme's organizational hierarchy. These six directors each manage and supervise about seven employees. Thus, Mike supervises about 50 employees. Once a year, Mike has one-on-one meetings with each employee. These meetings are a part of each employee's annual evaluation. Today, Mike is meeting with Nicole Newton. Nicole is a new employee and has worked for Acme for just over a year. She was hired soon after graduating from college with a bachelor's degree in communication. This will be her first evaluation meeting. She was hired as a telemarketer and hopes to move up in the organization soon. She is African American and 23 years old. She was raised in the city of Chicago, in a public-housing district. Their meeting takes place in Mike's office. She and Mike have never met.

Mike:	Good morning, Nicole. Come in and have a seat.
Nicole:	Hi, Mike.
Mike:	Actually, until I get to know my employees, I prefer to be called Mr. Fabion.
Nicole:	Oh, OK, Mr. Fabion (placing emphasis on "Mr.").
Mike:	(Noticing her tone of voice) So, where are you from?
Nicole:	I grew up on the South Side.
Mike:	(Thinks to himself, "She and I have nothing in common.") I'm from Kenilworth.
Nicole:	Yeah, I've heard of that.
Mike:	So, do you have any education beyond high school?
Nicole:	Yes. As my résumé indicates, I have a bachelor's degree. That should be in my file.
Mike:	Oh, yes, here it is. It says here you have a degree in communication? What's that all about? Classes in speech, I guess, or radio and television?
Nicole:	Well, no. I took classes in organizational communication, political communication, intercultural communication . . . courses like that. We discuss and explore how humans interact within a variety of contexts. It's a great major!
Mike:	Well, there was no such major when I went to school. I don't understand. Why not major in business? Anyway . . . I've been reading your manager's monthly assessments of your performance. I can see you need improvement in several areas, including customer service and attitude.
Nicole:	Really? I thought I was doing fine.

Mike:	Well, your manager says you are informal with customers. I think that leaves a bad impression. (Thinks to himself, "I guess that's not taught in communication classes.")
Nicole:	Really? I think they like it. I think it's all right to be a little relaxed once in a while.
Mike:	Well, maybe elsewhere, but not here.
Nicole:	Have any of my customers complained?
Mike:	Not directly, no.
Nicole:	So then, what's the problem? (Thinks to herself, "What's his problem? He thinks he's pretty special. He needs a class in communication.")
Mike:	Look, Nicole, I'm not going to argue with you. I'm telling you to improve your attitude and stop being so informal with the customers.
Nicole:	Whatever you say, Mr. Fabion.

Several of the factors outlined in the Kim model can be applied to this brief conflict exchange between Mike and Nicole. In terms of the micro–individual level, Mike's cognitive rigidity and simplicity are reflected in his inflexible stance about Nicole's informality, which doesn't seem to be an issue with her customers since none of them has complained, and his lack of knowledge about communication degrees. Regarding the intermediary level, that Mike prefers for Nicole to call him "Mr. Fabion" highlights the status discrepancy between them. That Mike meets with his employees only once a year shows that he has little contact with (i.e., is segregated from) them. Moreover, persons in Kenilworth may rarely interact with persons in the inner city. Finally, at a macro–societal level, there is a history of subjugation between their groups, and Nicole's group has demonstrable minority group strength.

A Culture-Based Social Ecological Conflict Model

In a model of conflict that complements the Kim model discussed above, Ting-Toomey and Oetzel have developed what they call a culture-based social ecological conflict model.[8] You will see some similarities between this model and the Kim model. In their model, Ting-Toomey and Oetzel highlight four main factors that come into play during an intercultural conflict episode: primary orientation factors, situational appraisals, conflict processes, and conflict competence. During intercultural conflict, these four factors come together interdependently in a complex formula that defines the specific conflict episode (see Figure 10.3).

The primary orientation factors are what each individual brings to the conflict. This would be similar to Kim's micro level, but with some added variables. Ting-Toomey and Oetzel suggest that each individual brings macro, exo, meso, and micro layers to the conflict—with *macro* meaning "larger than," *exo* meaning "external or outside," *meso* meaning "middle or intermediate," and *micro* meaning "localized or small." Similar to Kim's model, the macro-level primary orientation factors are the larger sociocultural factors, histories, worldviews, beliefs, and values held by each individual. Macro-level variables may be outside

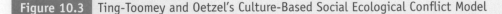

Figure 10.3 Ting-Toomey and Oetzel's Culture-Based Social Ecological Conflict Model

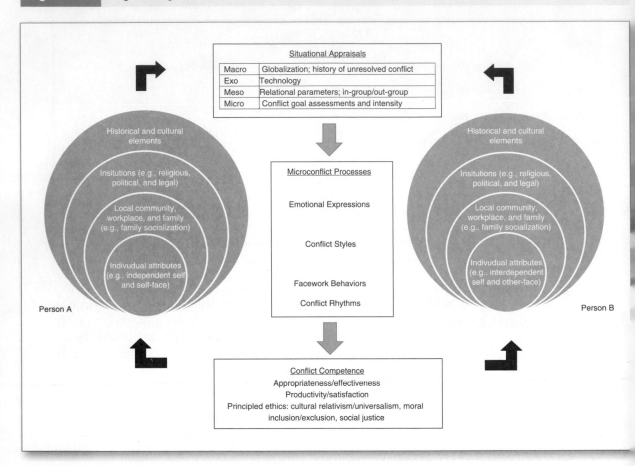

the individual's control but nevertheless affect his or her approach to conflict. Some macro-level variables might include the effects of globalization (i.e., the compression of cultural boundaries) on an individual. Exo factors include the formal institutions present in any culture, including religious institutions, governments, and health care systems, among others that are external to the individual but affect his or her approach. Meso-level factors refer to the more immediate dimensions of a particular culture—for example, the local church group, one's workplace setting, or even one's extended family. Finally, the micro-level factors include the individual's unique intrapersonal attributes, such as his or her level of individualism or collectivism, actual physical location, and personal experiences, among others.[9] For example, Ting-Toomey and Oetzel point out that individualists tend to address conflict through assertiveness, express their emotions, and value personal accountability. Collectivists restrain their emotions and protect the in-group.

While primary orientation factors are the principal influences on conflict, they affect how each individual perceives (appraises) the situation in which the conflict takes place. Macro, exo, meso, and micro levels appear here as well. Macro situational features might include the effects of globalization on this particular situation, such as immigration. Oftentimes, immigrant groups are faced with conflict from the native cultural groups. But, of course, not all conflicts are about immigration. Exo-level variables might include whether the interactants are in-group or out-group members. We tend to use different communication strategies when interacting with the in-group compared with the out-group. Meso-level variables focus on relational dimensions in this particular conflict and might include one's status in the family or organization. Finally, micro-level situational features might include the individual's goal in a given situation (e.g., to ask for a pay raise).[10]

The micro conflict processes include those factors that emerge from the conflict interaction itself. For example, during conflict, the two individuals' conflict interaction styles come into play interdependently. So how does Individual A's competitive style combine with Individual B's avoidance style? Finally, how do the individuals manage their emotions? Are they expressive or restrained?

Last, the model includes conflict competence criteria and outcomes, which include effectiveness/appropriateness, productivity/satisfaction, and principled ethics. Conflict competence refers to the application of intercultural conflict knowledge. In other words, how are we to use what we know about conflict to act competently and produce an effective, appropriate resolution? Appropriateness refers to the degree to which the individuals' behaviors are suitable for the cultural context in which they occur. Effectiveness refers to the degree to which the individuals achieve mutually shared meaning, which leads to intercultural understanding. Productivity/satisfaction refers to the degree to which the individuals are able to create the desired images of themselves, to what extent those images are accepted by the opposing party, and the perception by both parties that a successful resolution has been reached. Ting-Toomey and Oetzel refer to productive resolution as a "win–win" conflict orientation and to unproductive resolution as a "win–lose" conflict orientation. A comparison of the two orientations is presented in Table 10.1.[11]

| Table 10.1 | Win–Lose and Win–Win Conflict Orientations |

Win–Lose Conflict Orientation	Win–Win Conflict Orientation
Ignoring cultural differences	Respecting cultural differences
Insensitivity to conflict context	Sensitivity to conflict context
Arguing and defending self-interest	Uncovering deeper conflict needs
Conflict mode	Compromising mode
Engaging in mindless behaviors	Practicing mindful conflict skills
Rigidity of conflict posture	Willingness to change

SOURCE: Oetzel, J. G., Ting-Toomey, S., Masumoto, T., Yokochi, Y., & Takai, J. (2000). A Typology of Facework Behaviors in Conflicts With Best Friends and Relative Strangers. *Communication Quarterly, 48*, 397–419.

We can apply the Culture-Based Social Ecological Model to the earlier interaction between Mike Fabion and Nicole Newton, as we did the Kim model. Regarding their primary orientation factors, Mike and Nicole have very different macro-level orientations. Race plays a key role here, as Nicole's cultural roots are in subjugation and slavery. Their exo-level factors are also key. Mike and Nicole are probably not members of the same social institutions. Mike is unfamiliar with Nicole's education in communication. They differ in age, and their political affiliations are likely to be different as well. The meso-level factors are particularly relevant here because, within the workplace, Mike carries much higher status than Nicole. Interestingly, their micro-level factors may not differ considerably, as both were raised in the United States and probably carry an individualistic orientation. They likely appraise the conflict situation differently. At the macro level, the issue of race is unresolved, especially in Chicago. At the meso level, Mike's hierarchical status in this organization places him at a distinct advantage. In this scenario, Nicole's goal is to receive a positive evaluation, while Mike's goal is to point out what he sees as a problem (i.e., Nicole's informality). Ironically, Nicole is correct in thinking that Mike needs a course (or two) in communication.

INTERCULTURAL DIALOGUE, CONFLICT RESOLUTION, AND A CULTURE OF PEACE

So how might Mike and Nicole resolve their conflict? Like the other scholars cited in this chapter, Benjamin Broome maintains that conflict is an unavoidable consequence of living in a culturally diverse world. But Broome also believes that among myriad cultural groups, peace is possible. He argues that successful intercultural conflict resolution requires that conflicting interactants engage in *dialogue* and promote a *culture of peace*.[12] Broome asserts:

> To build and maintain peace, we must learn productive ways to handle disagreements, and we must develop norms, mechanisms, and institutions that will guide us toward resolving divisive issues without violence. A central means through which such actions can unfold is *dialogue*.[13]

Broome traces the etymology (i.e., the origins) of the word *dialogue* to ancient Greece, where *dia* means "through or across" and *logos* means "words or reason." Broome contends that via dialogue, conflicting parties can reason with each other using communication as the vehicle toward understanding and eventual conflict resolution. Via dialogue, Broome asserts, conflicting parties become aware of how they each interpret and prescribe meaning to the immediate context. Broome is careful to point out that dialogue does not rule out disagreement. Instead, via dialogue, conflicting parties begin to understand each other's unique perspective on the issue confronting them, which can then lead to peace. Broome's model is presented in Figure 10.4.[14]

According to this model, as conflicting individuals engage in dialogue, a number of processes can result and lead to the possibility of a culture of peace. First, dialogue makes possible sustained contact. Just as in the Kim model and Ting-Toomey and Oetzels's model, Broome maintains that conflict is often ongoing because conflicting parties are segregated or have little contact with each other. To engage in dialogue, conflicting parties must come

Figure 10.4	Broome's Model of Building a Culture of Peace Through Dialogue

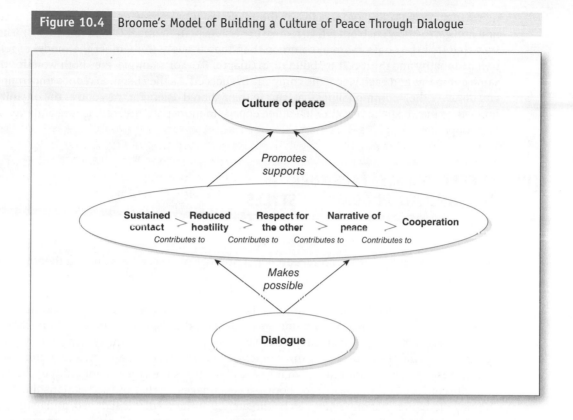

together and interact. Without interaction, it is impossible to understand the other's position. And while Broome admits that sustained contact does not guarantee a resolution, without contact, resolution is unfeasible. Such contact, Broome asserts, can help the conflicting parties reduce uncertainty and become aware of each other's perspectives, which helps reduce hostility. By segregating themselves, the conflicting parties make any kind of empathy between groups impossible. But via dialogue, at least understanding the other's point of view becomes possible, which can then lead to a reduction of hostility. As conflicting parties engage in interaction and begin to reduce hostility, they can begin to develop respect for each other. Broome maintains that as members of each group begin to listen to each other and to understand each other's viewpoints, they will develop a degree of regard and respect for each other. Once again, Broome acknowledges that this does not necessitate agreement but at least can initiate the process of peaceful discussion rather than hostile confrontation. As peaceful discussion continues, interactants are more likely to engage in cooperative rather than competitive and hostile action. This, then, can lead to a culture of peace.[15]

Broome is careful to point out that building a culture of peace is a lengthy and difficult process. He understands that unequal social and economic conditions, beyond either party's control, may prevent conflicting parties from engaging in willful dialogue. He asserts that each party must be a willing participant. Moreover, current societal, national, or international events outside the control of either party may impede progress as well.[16]

So what Mike Fabion and Nicole Newton might try is to engage in more frequent interaction and get to know each other (i.e., reduce uncertainty—remember Chapters 1 and 9?). They may find that they have more in common than they thought (remember the model of relational empathy and third-culture building in Chapter 9?). For example, they both work for the same company, and each wants the company to succeed. As they begin to reduce uncertainty and discover their commonalities—at least in their shared desire for the good of the organization—they may begin to respect each other, engage in more peaceful interaction, and eventually cooperate.

THE CONCEPT OF FACE, FACEWORK, AND COMMUNICATION CONFLICT STYLES

Face

In an effort to explain intercultural conflict, a number of researchers apply a theory called *face-negotiation theory.*[17] According to this view, the concept of *face* explains how people of different cultures manage conflict. Face refers to a person's sense of favorable self-worth or self-image experienced during communicative situations. Face is an emotional extension of the self-concept. It is considered a universal concept; that is, people in all cultures have a sense of face, but the specific meanings of face may vary across cultures. Ting-Toomey and her associates differentiate among three types of face: self-face, other-face, and mutual-face. Self-face is the concern for one's own image, other-face is the concern for another's image, and mutual-face is the concern for both parties' images or that of the relationship. Ting-Toomey maintains that one's face can be threatened, enhanced, undermined, and bargained over both emotionally and cognitively. According to face-negotiation theory, people in all cultures try to maintain and negotiate face in virtually all communication situations. Generally, however, persons of individualistic cultures have a greater concern for self-face and a lesser concern for other-face than do members of collectivistic cultures.[18] The concept of face becomes particularly significant in situations where uncertainty is high, as in conflict situations where the character of the communicators might be called into question.

Facework

In most conflict situations, interactants are required to defend or save their faces when they are threatened or attacked. The various ways one might deal with conflict and face are collectively called *facework*. Specifically, facework refers to the communicative strategies employed to manage one's own face or to support or challenge another's face. Facework can be employed to initiate, manage, or terminate conflict.[19] Oetzel and his colleagues classify three general types of facework strategies used in intercultural conflict: dominating, avoiding, and integrating facework (see Table 10.2). Dominating facework behaviors are characterized by an individual's need to control the conflict situation and defend his or her self-face. Avoiding facework behaviors focus on an attempt to save the face of the other person. Integrating facework allows for the shared concern for self- and other-face and strives for closure in the conflict.[20]

Table 10.2	Facework Behaviors

Dominating Facework Behaviors

1. Aggression: verbally assault the other person
   "I would say nasty things about the other person."
   "I would ridicule the other person."

2. Defend self: reply to a threat
   "I would be firm in my demands and not give in."
   "I would insist my position be accepted."

Avoiding Facework Behaviors

1. Avoidance/pretend: dismissal of the conflict that does not threaten the other's face
   "I would act as though I wasn't upset at all."
   "I would try to ignore it and behave as if nothing happened."

2. Give in: succumb and/or yield to the other
   "I would give in to the other person's wishes."
   "I would let the other person win."

3. Involve a third party: reliance on an outside party to help manage the conflict
   "I would ask another friend to help us negotiate a solution."
   "I would talk with the other person through an outside party."

Integrating Facework Behaviors

1. Apologize: offer an apology for the conflict
   "I would offer an apology even though I didn't do anything wrong."
   "I would say I'm sorry and act as though it didn't happen."

2. Compromise: utilize direct discussion to resolve the conflict
   "I would try to find some middle ground to solve the problem."
   "I would try to combine both our viewpoints."

3. Consider the other: show concern for the other
   "I would listen to the other person and show respect."
   "I would tell the other person I'm aware of their position."

4. Private discussion: engage in relational talk about the conflict in a private setting
   "I would keep our discussions private."
   "I would wait until we were by ourselves to talk about it."

(Continued)

(Continued)

5. Remain calm: stay quiet and unruffled

"I would try to remain calm."

"I would try to listen well."

6. Express emotions: communicate feelings about the conflict

"I would express my feelings in a straightforward manner."

"I would be direct in expressing my feelings."

SOURCE: Oetzel, J. G., Ting-Toomey, S., Masumoto, T., Yokochi, Y., & Takai, J. (2000). A Typology of Facework Behaviors in Conflicts With Best Friends and Relative Strangers. *Communication Quarterly, 48,* 397–419.

Self-Assessment 10.1

Self-Face, Other-Face, and Mutual-Face Concerns

Remember your conflict with Akira Abe at the opening of this chapter? Now try to imagine yourself in a different situation.

You loaned your car, with a full tank of gas, to Akira. Recall that he is an international exchange student from Japan whom you do not know well. After he returned your car, you noticed that half of the gas had been used.

Directions: Take a moment and imagine yourself in the above conflict. What would you do? How would you handle this situation? For the following items, please indicate the degree to which you (5) strongly agree, (4) agree, (3) are neutral, (2) disagree, or (1) strongly disagree in terms of the conflict situation presented above.

_____ 1. I am concerned with respectful treatment for both of us.

_____ 2. My primary concern is saving my own face.

_____ 3. Relationship harmony is important to me.

_____ 4. I am concerned with maintaining the poise of the other person.

_____ 5. Maintaining humbleness to preserve the relationship is important to me.

_____ 6. Helping maintain the other person's pride is important to me.

_____ 7. I am concerned with protecting my self-image.

_____ 8. My concern is to act humble in order to make the other person feel good.

_____ 9. My concern is to help the other person maintain his or her dignity.

_____ 10. I don't want to embarrass myself in front of the other person.

Scoring:

1. Sum your responses to Items 2, 7, and 10. Scores must range from 3 to 15. This is your self-face score. Higher scores, above 12, indicate a high self-face concern.

2. Sum your responses to Items 4, 6, 8, and 9. Scores must range from 4 to 20. This is your other-face score. Higher scores, above 16, indicate a high other-face concern.

3. Sum your responses to Items 1, 3, and 5. Scores must range from 3 to 15. This is your mutual-face score. Higher scores, above 12, indicate a high mutual-face concern.

SOURCE: This scale is an adaptation of the Face Concern Scale used in Oetzel, J. G., Ting-Toomey, S., Masumoto, T., Yokochi, Y., Pan, X., Takai, J., et al. (2001). Face and Facework in Conflict: A Cross-Cultural Comparison of China, Germany, Japan, and the United States. *Communication Monographs, 68,* 235–258; and Ting-Toomey, S., & Oetzel, J. G. (2001). *Managing Intercultural Conflict Effectively.* Thousand Oaks, CA: Sage.

Cross-cultural research has shown that individualists, such as U.S. Americans, tend to prefer facework behaviors that defend the self-face or confront the other (i.e., aggression). Collectivists, such as Taiwanese and Chinese, tend to prefer other-face strategies such as avoiding the conflict, seeking a third party, or giving in to the other. Collectivists also prefer mutual-face facework such as attempting to solve the problem through a third party, having a private discussion, or apologizing.[21]

Conflict Communication Styles

In addition to the facework strategies one might use to manage face during conflict, researchers have studied conflict interaction styles. Whereas facework is employed to manage and uphold face during conflict, conflict interaction styles refer to the ways individuals manage the actual conflict. How people manage communication during conflict differs considerably across cultures.[22]

One's conflict interaction style is based on two communication dimensions. The first is the degree to which a person asserts a *self-face need*—that is, seeks to satisfy his or her own interests during conflict. The second is the degree to which a person is cooperative (i.e., observes an *other-face need*) and seeks to incorporate the interests of the other.[23] The combination of assertiveness, or self-face need, and cooperativeness, or other-face need, defines five primary communication styles and three secondary styles of managing conflict. The five primary styles are dominating, integrating, obliging, avoiding, and compromising.[24] The three secondary styles are emotional expression, third-party help, and neglect (see Figure 10.5).[25]

The degree to which a person asserts a high self-face need while simultaneously discounting the other-face need defines the *dominating* communication style. A person exercising a dominating approach might use his or her authority, expertise, or rank to try to win the conflict. The person who assumes a high self-face need while also attending to the needs of the other-face takes on an *integrating* style. This person might try to collaborate with the opponent or try to find an agreeable solution that fully satisfies both parties. The person who tries

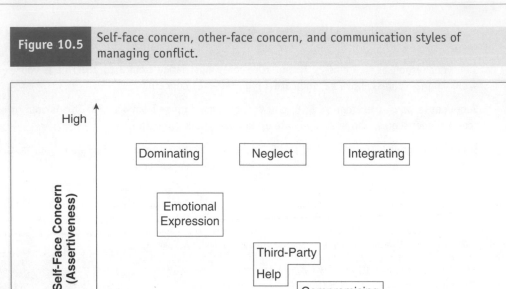

Figure 10.5 Self-face concern, other-face concern, and communication styles of managing conflict.

to balance both self-face and other-face needs takes on a *compromising* style. This person would probably use a "give-and-take" approach and might propose some middle ground for resolving the conflict, understanding that each party may have to give up something to gain something. The person using an *avoiding* style ignores both self-face need and other-face need. This person might keep the conflict to himself or herself and not discuss it. The person who puts the other-face need ahead of self-face need assumes an *obliging* style. This person will try to accommodate the opponent or try to satisfy the needs of the other before satisfying his or her own needs.

Ting-Toomey and Oetzel maintain that the five primary conflict styles overlook some of the subtle, fine distinctions of conflict behavior used across cultures, and so they have added three secondary styles. *Emotional expression* refers to how one might use his or her emotions to guide conflict. This is demonstrated by the type of person who listens to his or her base feelings and proceeds accordingly. *Third-party help* is the extent to which a person is willing to engage an outsider to act as a go-between in the conflict. *Neglect* is the use of a passive-aggressive approach, whereby a person might ignore the conflict but attempt to elicit a response from the other via aggressive acts. For example, this person might insult the other or say things that might damage the other's reputation (e.g., "I would say nasty things about the person to others").[26]

Research in this area has shown that, in general, individualists tend to use more dominating styles during conflict than do collectivists. Collectivists tend to use more integrative, obliging, and avoiding styles during conflict. Such generalizations do not hold for all cultures considered collectivistic, however. For example, in a study comparing five cultures, Ting-Toomey and her colleagues found that Korean, Japanese, and American college students used fewer avoidance-type conflict styles than did Chinese and Taiwanese students. They also found that Korean and American students were less likely to engage in obliging styles than were Chinese, Japanese, and Taiwanese students.[27] In their study, Hyun Lee and Randall Rogan found that Americans were actually less confrontational during conflict than were Koreans, a culture considered to be collectivistic.[28]

AN INTERCULTURAL CONVERSATION: DOMINATING AND THIRD-PARTY CONFLICT STYLES

Kevin, who grew up in Madison, Wisconsin, is a student at the University of Wisconsin. Kevin is enrolled in an introductory communication course. The professor has assigned Kevin and Kokkeong, an international exchange student from Malaysia, to work on a project together. The professor has given them the option of either submitting a paper or giving a presentation. Kevin and Kokkeong disagree on which option to pursue. Kevin prefers the presentation option, while Kokkeong prefers the paper option.

In the following conversation, Kevin asserts himself forcefully. He stresses his experience and expertise on the matter of presentations versus papers. His approach is typical of a dominating conflict style. Kokkeong, on the other hand, tries to convince Kevin that they should seek the advice of a third party, either other students or the professor. Kevin simply refuses.

Kevin:	Well, Kokkeong, I think we should do a presentation. I hate writing papers.
Kokkeong:	Well, what have other students done?
Kevin:	I don't know, probably presentations. Nobody likes writing papers.
Kokkeong:	Well, maybe they might have some advice.
Kevin:	Advice about what?
Kokkeong:	About which assignment is preferred.
Kevin:	But I already know what assignment I prefer.
Kokkeong:	I wonder if we should ask the professor for his advice.
Kevin:	Why? He's already given us the option. Look, I've been a student here for 2 years. I know how these things work. Let's just do the presentation.
Kokkeong:	I think I'll ask some others what they think.
Kevin:	Go ahead, but doing a presentation is the best choice. I know what I'm talking about.

THE INTERCULTURAL CONFLICT STYLE INVENTORY

Mitchell Hammer has developed a model of intercultural conflict based on his Intercultural Conflict Style (ICS) Inventory. Hammer is the founder of several organizations that focus on intercultural communication. He has applied his conflict model in work with the NASA Johnson Space Center, the Federal Bureau of Investigation, and the National Institutes of Health. Hammer's ICS Inventory is a theoretical model and assessment tool used by professional mediators and trainers to diagnose and manage intercultural conflicts. Hammer contends that the dynamics of conflict revolve around two fundamental features of all conflict: disagreement and emotional reaction. Like others, Hammer maintains that a central characteristic of conflict is disagreement. This is consistent with Ting-Toomey and Oetzel's definition, presented earlier in this chapter, which describes conflict as mismatched expectations between individuals from different cultures who perceive an incompatibility between their values, norms, goals, scarce resources, or outcomes. Disagreement would be considered the cognitive component of conflict. A second fundamental feature of conflict is the affective or emotional response to the disagreement. According to Hammer, conflicting parties experience an antagonistic emotional reaction toward each other based on their disagreement and the perception of threat associated with it. So Hammer's conflict model is based on a cognitive and affective component—that is, disagreement and the negative emotional reaction to it.[29]

The focus of Hammer's model is on intercultural conflict style. Like others, Hammer contends that people respond in patterned ways to conflict and that their communication styles are predictable. Conflict style, then, is the behavioral component of conflict that follows from the cognitive (i.e., disagreement) and affective (i.e., negative emotional reaction) dimensions of conflict. Echoing the work of Ting-Toomey and others, Hammer maintains that one's conflict style is learned culturally. But Hammer argues that the five conflict styles based on an individual's concern for self- or other-face have been developed within individualistic, Western cultural conceptions and that these models may not adequately reflect intercultural conflict styles. Take, for example, the avoiding style, where the person ignores both self-face need and other-face need. Consistent with Ting-Toomey's research, Hammer notes that in collectivistic cultures, an avoiding style is used to maintain relational harmony and actually reflects a high concern for self and others. Following his contention that conflicts evolve from disagreement and its resulting negative emotional reactions, Hammer proposes that people, regardless of culture, deal with disagreement either directly or indirectly and that they either openly express or restrain their emotional reactions to conflict. Thus, one's intercultural conflict style is defined by one's direct or indirect communication about disagreements and his or her emotionally expressive or emotionally restrained behaviors.[30]

Recall from Chapter 7 that direct communication includes the use of precise language, where one's intentions are explicitly stated and the sender is responsible for making his or her case known. Indirect communication includes the use of ambiguous language, or hinting, and the burden of understanding rests with both the sender and the receiver. Ting-Toomey's research has indicated that a direct style is often associated with individualistic and low-context cultures, while an indirect style is associated with collectivistic and high-context cultures. Emotionally expressive individuals overtly and visibly (i.e., nonverbally) communicate their feelings through intense facial expressions, frequent gesturing, body posture, and overall active involvement. Emotionally restrained individuals minimize gesturing, mask their emotions both verbally and nonverbally, hold back their sentiments, and control their feelings. Extant research suggests that individualistic and low-context cultures are often emotionally expressive, while collectivistic, high-context cultures are often emotionally restrained.[31]

According to Hammer's model, during conflict, the extent to which an individual is either direct or indirect and emotionally expressive or emotionally restrained defines his or her intercultural conflict style, of which there are four types. Hammer maintains that these styles are independent of culture. The four styles are (a) discussion, (b) engagement, (c) accommodation, and (d) dynamic style (see Figure 10.6).[32]

As the graphic shows, an individual who approaches conflict directly but is emotionally restrained takes on a *discussion* conflict style. This person emphasizes precise language and straightforward communication about the disagreement while withholding his or her emotions. This person is typically comfortable addressing conflict and is calm and collected emotionally. The person who is direct in his or her communication and is also emotionally expressive takes on an *engagement* style. This person is confrontational about the disagreement and forthright with his or her emotions. This is the type of style that "pulls no punches." When a person communicates about conflict indirectly and without emotion, he or she takes on an *accommodation* style. This is the type of person who only hints at the nature of the disagreement and may prefer an intermediary to address the conflict. This person sees emotional outbursts as potentially dangerous. Finally, the person who communicates indirectly about the disagreement but is emotionally expressive takes on a *dynamic* style. Verbally, this person may use exaggeration and repetition of his or her messages while also employing a nonverbal, emotionally confrontational form of expression.

Figure 10.6 Intercultural conflict styles.

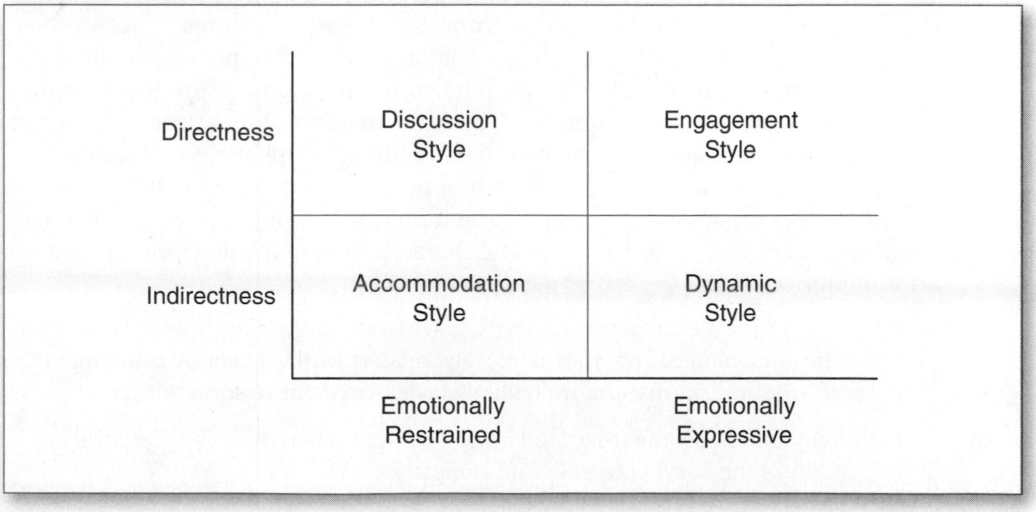

Hammer has developed an instrument that measures these four styles. He maintains that the ICS Inventory is useful in applied settings, such as organizations and even families. Hammer asserts that after the conflicting parties recognize their own style and that of their counterpart, they can better manage conflict. For example, Hammer cites a case in which one of the conflicting parties used an engagement style and the other used accommodation. Hammer points out that a large part of the conflict between the two was the misperceptions each party held about the other. The accommodation-style individual felt that the engagement-style person was rude and aggressive, while the engagement-style party felt that the accommodating-style individual was deceptive and lacking in commitment.

Hammer also notes that, particularly in the United States, many people believe that their conflict style is discussion and that this is the most appropriate style. But after completing his scales, many of these people see that they actually approach conflict with an accommodation, engagement, or dynamic style. Hammer concludes by saying that when persons try to implement a discussion style, thinking it is the most appropriate and having little awareness of the other three styles—particularly their cultural roots—they tend to see the engagement style as callous, the accommodation style as lacking sincerity, and the dynamic style as unstable and disorganized. Knowledge of these various styles is the first step toward successful conflict management and resolution.[33]

INDIVIDUALISTIC AND COLLECTIVISTIC APPROACHES TO CONFLICT

A central theme articulated throughout this book is that whenever individuals from different cultures come together and interact, they bring with them a whole host of different value orientations, cultural expectations, verbal and nonverbal routines, perceptual experiences (e.g., ethnocentrism), and divergent group memberships (e.g., ethnicity) that often lead to communication problems and conflict. A source of intercultural conflict is often a felt need to protect one's group—that is, one's culture. This need may be felt passionately.

In her work, Ting-Toomey maintains that persons from individualistic cultures approach conflict differently than do persons from collectivistic cultures.[34] According to Ting-Toomey, individualists tend to follow an outcome-oriented approach to intercultural conflict. Collectivists, on the other hand, tend to follow a process-oriented approach. The outcome-oriented approach preferred by individualists emphasizes the importance of asserting their self-identity in the conflict and the accomplishment of perceived tangible outcomes or goals. The process-oriented approach preferred by collectivists focuses on mutual-face or group-face interests. These interests are sought prior to, or in lieu of, any tangible outcomes or goals.[35] The specific characteristics of the outcome-oriented approach are summarized below.[36]

1. To the individualist, conflict is closely related to the goals or outcomes. Conflict is "end" oriented, in that the individualist seeks to achieve something.

2. Individualists become frustrated during conflict when their counterparts are unwilling to address the conflict openly and honestly.

3. Individualists see conflict as satisfying when their counterparts are willing to confront the conflict openly and assert their feelings honestly.

4. Conflict is seen as unproductive when no tangible outcomes are negotiated and no plan of action is executed.

5. Conflict is seen as productive when tangible resolutions are reached.

6. Successful management of conflict is defined as when individual goals and the differences between the parties are addressed openly and honestly.

The specific characteristics of the process-oriented approach are summarized below.[37]

1. The significance of the conflict is assessed against any face threat incurred in the conflict; it is also evaluated in terms of in-group versus out-group.

2. Conflict is seen as threatening when the parties move forward on substantive issues before proper facework management.

3. Conflict is seen as satisfying when the parties engage in mutual face-saving and face-giving behavior and attend to verbal and nonverbal communication.

4. Conflict is seen as unproductive when face issues and relational/group feelings are not addressed properly.

5. Conflict is defined as productive when both parties can declare win–win results on facework in addition to substantive agreement.

6. Successful management of conflict means that the faces of both conflict parties are saved or upgraded and each person has dealt with the conflict strategically in conjunction with substantive gains or losses.

Ting-Toomey maintains that the outcome-oriented model preferred by individualists encourages an effective finish to the conflict over the appropriate treatment of the parties involved. The collectivist-preferred process-oriented model emphasizes the appropriate treatment of the parties involved over an effective solution. Moreover, asserts Ting-Toomey, the accomplishment of one criterion may help accomplish the other. For example, as individualists successfully address the core issues in the conflict, appropriate and genial interaction between the parties can follow naturally—that is, face saving. On the other hand, from the collectivist's perspective, acting appropriately in the conflict by engaging in necessary facework eventually brings about effective outcomes. For collectivists, strategic facework is more important than winning or losing a conflict. In fact, collectivists often see losing a given conflict for the moment as gaining key advantages in the long term. In the end, the key to competent intercultural conflict management is *mindfulness,* where each person is mindful of cultural differences, mindful of the different goals, and willing to experiment with different conflict management styles.[38]

CONFLICT RESOLUTION IN HIGH- VERSUS LOW-CONTEXT CULTURES

As we have seen throughout this book, communication is very much dependent on the context in which it occurs. The contextual model guiding the organization of this book includes the cultural, microcultural, environmental, perceptual, and sociorelational contexts and how these contexts affect the choice of verbal and nonverbal messages. And recall from Chapter 2 that the degree to which interactants focus on these contexts while communicating varies considerably from culture to culture. In some cultures, persons choose to focus more on the verbal codes than on the nonverbal elements, while in other cultures, people actively monitor the nonverbal elements of the context. Edward Hall describes the former as low context and the latter as high context.

According to Hall, a high-context culture is one in which most of the information during communication is found in the physical context internalized in the person, while very little is found in the explicit code (see Figure 10.7). A low-context culture is one in which the mass of information is in the explicit code (i.e., the verbal code). Elizabeth Chua and William Gudykunst have compared conflict resolution styles between high- and low-context cultures.[39] They argue that in low-context cultures, such as the United States, individuals are more likely to separate the conflict issue from the persons involved. In high-context cultures, such as China, the conflict issue and the persons involved are typically connected. For example, directly disagreeing with someone may be seen as losing face and is perceived as insulting. Moreover, Chua and Gudykunst assert that persons in low-context cultures tend to be more direct and explicit in their dealings with conflict, whereas persons in high-context cultures prefer implicit communication. In their study of nearly 400 persons from both high- and low-context cultures, Chua and Gudykunst found that persons from low-context cultures preferred solution-oriented conflict resolution styles, whereas persons from high-context cultures preferred nonconfrontational styles.[40]

Figure 10.7 What kind of conflict style might be at play here?

Solution-Oriented Conflict Styles Preferred by Low-Context Cultures

1. Direct communication about the conflict
2. Collaborating behaviors that aim to find a solution for both parties
3. Giving in or compromising
4. Accommodating the other
5. Confronting the issue

Nonconfrontational Styles Preferred by High-Context Cultures

1. Indirect communication
2. Avoiding or withdrawing from the issue
3. Using silence
4. Glossing over differences
5. Concealing ill feelings

Chua and Gudykunst conclude that their results are consistent with other research that has found a similar pattern between high- and low-context cultures. Specifically, research has revealed that Mexicans (i.e., a high-context culture) prefer to deny that conflict exists or to avoid instigating conflict, while U.S. Americans (i.e., a low-context culture) are more direct in their dealings with conflict.[41]

STUDENT VOICES ACROSS CULTURES

Rodrigo Villalobos

I am from Leon, Guanajuato, Mexico, but now reside in the United States. I am a graphic design major.

I do not believe that people from Mexico deal with trouble or stressful situations in the same way as others do. To generalize on a particular set of characteristics that define how a person of Mexican nationality resolves his or her own problems would be almost impossible. The social and economic surroundings of every individual in Mexico are usually completely different, which makes their problem-solving processes much different as well.

However, there are a certain number of behaviors or attitudes that one can expect to see from a Mexican when that person is in a stressful or uncomfortable situation.

As Mexicans are Latinos, our character and personalities are rather warm and heartfelt. We express our feelings, to a certain extent, more than people from other races or ethnicities do. For example, when a situation makes a Mexican person happy, he or she will express it more boldly than someone from Sweden would. In the same manner, when a Mexican person feels uncomfortable, upset, or mad about a specific problem or situation, this person's reaction will be quite volatile (e.g., yelling, screaming, lack of verbal communication, trying to avoid the problem, etc.).

We all know that the shortest way to solve problems is through communication and an open-minded understanding of the situation. Perhaps the slower pace of life in Mexico affects how Mexicans approach their problems (e.g., postponing dealing with problems). Also, pride and lack of will to reconcile might be obstacles a Mexican must confront before considering a possible solution.

Since friendships have a lot of value to persons from Latin America (not to say they don't to people from other places), friends will ask for advice and talk to each other for insight into a problem.

CHAPTER SUMMARY

This chapter began by asking you to imagine yourself in a conflict. All types of human relationships—from strangers to acquaintances to intimates—experience conflict. We cannot avoid or eliminate conflict, but we can manage and reduce it. Communication plays a paradoxical role in most conflicts because communication is required both to instigate conflict and to resolve it. Unfortunately, conflict is the source of much relational stress and dissolution. In this chapter, we have seen that a variety of factors play a role in triggering and escalating conflict. Three models were presented, including Kim's Model of Intercultural Conflict, Ting-Toomey and Oetzel's Culture-Based Social Ecological Model, and Broome's Model of Building a Culture of Peace Through Dialogue. We have seen how the concepts of face and facework contribute to intercultural conflict. Finally, the chapter ended with a model of conflict styles and a discussion of how persons from different cultures manage conflict.

 Visit the student study site at www.sagepub.com/neuliep6e for e-flashcards, web quizzes, web resources, and more.

DISCUSSION QUESTIONS

1. Recall a conflict that you have experienced. How did your cultural background affect how you handled the conflict?

2. What types of intercultural conflicts occur on your college or university campus? What groups or cultures have frequent conflicts? How might you employ Broome's Model of Building a Culture of Peace Through Dialogue?

3. Regarding Question #2 above, how do these groups manage and address their conflict?

4. Do you prefer to handle conflict directly or to avoid it altogether?

5. What irritates you the most about how others handle conflict? Why?

ETHICS AND INTERCULTURAL CONFLICT

1. Your roommate is friends with an international exchange student from China. Recently, your roommate and his Chinese friend have been disagreeing on several issues. Your roommate discloses to you that his Chinese friend typically avoids conflict and uses avoidance facework and conflict styles. Your roommate thinks that this will give him a unique advantage and decides to approach his Chinese friend assertively and engage in dominating facework and a competitive conflict style to win the conflict. Is your roommate's strategy a good one?

KEY TERMS

avoiding facework   384

dominating facework   384

face   384

facework   384

NOTES

1. Oetzel, J. G., & Ting-Toomey, S. (2003). Face Concerns in Interpersonal Conflict: A Cross-Cultural Empirical Test of the Face Negotiation Theory. *Communication Research, 30,* 599–624; Ting-Toomey, S. (1994). Managing Conflict in Intimate Intercultural Relationships. In D. Cahn (Ed.), *Intimate Conflict in Personal Relationships* (pp. 47–77). Hillsdale, NJ: Erlbaum; Ting-Toomey, S. (1994). Managing Intercultural Conflict Effectively. In L. Samovar & R. Porter (Eds.), *Intercultural Communication: A Reader* (7th ed., pp. 360–372). Belmont, CA: Wadsworth; Ting-Toomey, S., & Oetzel, J. G. (2001). *Managing Intercultural Conflict Effectively.* Thousand Oaks, CA: Sage; Ting-Toomey, S., & Oetzel, J. G. (2013). Introduction to Intercultural/International Conflict. In J. Oetzel & S. Ting-Toomey (Eds.), *The SAGE Handbook of Conflict Communication: Integrating Theory, Research, and Practice* (pp. 635–638). Los Angeles: Sage.

2. Ting-Toomey & Oetzel, Introduction to Intercultural/International Conflict, p. 635.

3. Ting-Toomey & Oetzel, *Managing Intercultural Conflict Effectively.*

4. Kim, Y. Y. (1989). Interethnic Conflict: An Interdisciplinary Overview. In J. B. Gittler (Ed.), *Annual Review of Conflict Knowledge and Conflict Resolution* (Vol. 1). New York: Garland; Kim, Y. Y. (1990). *Explaining Interethnic Conflict: An Interdisciplinary Overview.* Paper presented at the annual convention of the Speech Communication Association, Chicago, IL.

5. Ibid.

6. Ibid.

7. Ibid.

8. This discussion of the model is based entirely on Ting-Toomey, S., & Oetzel, J. G. (2013). Culture-Based Situational Conflict Model: An Update and Expansion. In J. G. Oetzel & S. Ting-Toomey (Eds.), *The SAGE Handbook of Conflict Communication: Integrating Theory, Research, and Practice* (pp. 763–789). Los Angeles: Sage. (Figure 10.3 reprinted from page 773.)

9. Ibid.

10. Ibid.

11. Ibid.

12. This discussion of the model is based entirely on Broome, B. J. (2013). Building Cultures of Peace: The Role of Intergroup Dialogue. In J. G. Oetzel & S. Ting-Toomey (Eds.), *The SAGE Handbook of Conflict Communication: Integrating Theory, Research, and Practice* (pp. 737–761). Los Angeles: Sage.

13. Ibid., p. 740.

14. Ibid., p. 751.

15. Ibid.

16. Ibid.

17. This discussion of face-negotiation theory is based on the following sources: Oetzel, J. G., & Ting-Toomey, S. (2003). Face Concerns in Interpersonal Conflict: A Cross-Cultural Empirical Test of the Face Negotiation Theory. *Communication Research, 30,* 599–624; Ting-Toomey, S. (1988). Intercultural Conflict Styles: A Face-Negotiation Theory. In Y. Kim & W. Gudykunst (Eds.), *Theories in Intercultural Communication.* Newbury Park, CA: Sage; Ting-Toomey, S. (2005). The Matrix of Face: An Updated Face-Negotiation Theory. In W. B. Gudykunst (Ed.), *Theorizing About Intercultural Communication.* Thousand Oaks, CA: Sage; Ting-Toomey, S., & Kurogi, A. (1998). Facework Competence in Intercultural Conflict: An Updated Face-Negotiation Theory. *International Journal of Intercultural Relations, 22,* 187–225.

18. Ting-Toomey & Kurogi, Facework Competence in Intercultural Conflict.

19. Oetzel, J. G., Ting-Toomey, S., Masumoto, T., Yokochi, Y., & Takai, J. (2000). A Typology of Facework Behaviors in Conflicts With Best Friends and Relative Strangers. *Communication Quarterly, 48,* 397–419.

20. Ibid.

21. Cocroft, B., & Ting-Toomey, S. (1994). Facework in Japan and the United States. *International Journal of Intercultural Relations, 18,* 469–506; Oetzel et al., A Typology of Facework Behaviors in Conflicts With Best Friends and Relative Strangers.

22. Ting-Toomey, S., & Oetzel, J. G. (2003). Cross-Cultural Face Concerns and Conflict Styles. In W. B. Gudykunst (Ed.), *Cross-Cultural and Intercultural Communication* (pp. 127–147). Thousand Oaks, CA: Sage.

23. The concepts of assertiveness and cooperativeness are found in a number of sources, including Rahim, M. A. (1983). A Measure of Styles of Handling Interpersonal Conflict. *Academy of Management Journal, 26,* 368–376; Thomas, K. W., & Kilmann, R. H. (1974). *Thomas-Kilmann Conflict MODE Instrument.* New York: XICOM, Tuxedo; Ting-Toomey, S. (1988). Intercultural Conflict Styles: A Face-Negotiation Theory. In Y. Y. Kim & W. B. Gudykunst (Eds.), *Theories of Intercultural Communication* (pp. 213–235). Newbury Park, CA: Sage.

24. Rahim, A Measure of Styles of Handling Interpersonal Conflict.

25. Ting-Toomey & Oetzel, *Managing Intercultural Conflict Effectively.*

26. Ting-Toomey & Oetzel, *Managing Intercultural Conflict Effectively;* Ting-Toomey, S., Yee-Jung, K. K., Shapiro, R. B., Garcia, W., Wright, T. J., & Oetzel, J. G. (2000). Ethnic/Cultural Identity Salience and Conflict Styles in Four U.S. Ethnic Groups. *International Journal of Intercultural Relations, 24,* 47–81.

27. Ting-Toomey, S., Gao, G., Trubisky, P., Yang, Z., Kim, H. S., Lin, S. L., et al. (1991). Culture, Face Maintenance, and Styles of Handling Interpersonal Conflict: A Study in Five Cultures. *International Journal of Conflict Management, 2,* 275–296.

28. Lee, H. O., & Rogan, R. G. (1991). A Cross-Cultural Comparison of Organizational Conflict Management Behaviors. *International Journal of Conflict Management, 2,* 181–199.

29. Hammer, M. R. (2005). The Intercultural Conflict Style Inventory: A Conceptual Framework and Measure of Intercultural Conflict Resolution Approaches. *International Journal of Intercultural Relations, 29,* 675–695.

30. Hammer, The Intercultural Conflict Style Inventory; Ting-Toomey, S. (1994). Managing Intercultural Conflicts Effectively. In L. Samovar & R. E. Porter (Eds.), *Intercultural Communication: A Reader* (pp. 360–372). Belmont, CA: Wadsworth; Ting-Toomey, S. (1999). *Communicating Across Cultures.* New York: Guilford; Ting-Toomey et al., Ethnic/Cultural Identity Salience and Conflict Styles in Four U.S. Ethnic Groups.

31. Ibid.

32. Hammer, The Intercultural Conflict Style Inventory.

33. Ibid.

34. Ting-Toomey & Oetzel, *Managing Intercultural Conflict Effectively.*

35. Ibid.

36. Ibid.

37. Ting-Toomey, *Communicating Across Cultures.*

38. Ibid.

39. Chua, E. G., & Gudykunst, W. B. (1987). Conflict Resolution Styles in Low- and High-Context Cultures. *Communication Research Reports, 4,* 32–37.

40. Ibid.

41. Ibid.

CHAPTER 11

Intercultural Communication in Business, Health Care, and Educational Settings

CHAPTER OBJECTIVES

After reading this chapter, you should be able to

1. discuss how dimensions of the cultural context affect organizations across cultures;

2. identify how the environmental context affects doing business in other cultures;

3. identify variables in the perceptual context and how they influence business with other cultures;

4. compare managerial styles of Japanese, Germans, Mexicans, and Chinese;

5. identify and discuss the four lay theories of illness;

6. identify and discuss patient–provider communication in health care settings across cultures;

7. identify and discuss learning style differences across cultures; and

8. identify and discuss teacher immediacy across cultures.

However objective and uniform we try to make organizations, they will not have the same meaning for individuals from different cultures.

—Fons Trompenaars[1]

Recall from Chapter 1 that one dimension of communication is that it is ubiquitous; that is, it is everywhere all the time. Another dimension of communication discussed in Chapter 1 is that it is contextual. The physical, social, and psychological setting in which communication occurs has a dramatic effect on how messages are encoded, decoded, and interpreted. Finally, as we have been discussing throughout this book, another dimension of communication is that it is cultural. Communication is culture bound. When we travel across cultural boundaries, the message sent is usually not the message received. So when you step into a different culture or country, you will be sending, receiving, and interpreting messages all the time in many different settings. If you participate in your college or university study-abroad program, you may spend a semester studying at a foreign college or university. While there, you may become ill or need to interact with that country's health care providers. And during your study-abroad experience, you will become a consumer of goods and services in that country and will interact with people in a variety of business settings. The purpose of this chapter is to apply many of the concepts we have studied so far within three communication settings common to every culture: education, health care, and business. We'll start with the business setting.

Imagine the following scenario:

You have just graduated from college and accepted a management job with Acme Corporation. Acme has placed you in one of its Mexican offices. During your first week in your new job, you decide to schedule a meeting with your Mexican employees. The meeting is scheduled for 9:00 a.m. on Wednesday. On Wednesday morning, you show up a bit early to prepare for your meeting. At 9:00 a.m., not a single employee has arrived for the meeting. At 9:20 a.m., two people finally show up. Not until 9:45 a.m. are all the team members in attendance. What has happened? You are confused, frustrated, and feeling a bit angry.

Doing business in Mexico (and in many other countries) is different from doing business in the United States. Mexican cultural values, such as collectivism and large power distance; Mexican social expectations; and Mexican workplace practices are different from those of U.S. workers and managers. To be sure, they are so different that U.S. managers working in Mexico often find themselves ineffective. The U.S. manager who does not put forth the effort to learn about these differences and adjust his or her managerial style accordingly will end up just as you did in the above scenario—frustrated and disillusioned.

Have you ever shopped at a Wal-Mart? Wal-Mart has more than 4,000 stores in the United States. Of all Americans, 90% live within 15 miles of a Wal-Mart. On average, every American household spends a little more than $2,000 each year at Wal-Mart. In the United States, every 7 days, 100 million people shop at a Wal-Mart. Wal-Mart is also successful internationally. It is the largest retailer in both Canada and Mexico, and the second largest in Britain. Worldwide, more than 7 billion people shop at Wal-Mart every year. So, this year, the statistical equivalent of every person on the planet will shop at a Wal-Mart.[2]

Wal-Mart is clearly a financial success, both nationally and internationally. But as Mark Landler and Michael Barbaro note, in 2006 Wal-Mart closed its stores in Germany. The chain has had difficulty breaking into the Korean and Japanese markets as well. Something is not working in those countries, and many believe that some of Wal-Mart's international problems stem from the company's arrogance and overestimation of its competence. For a company that boasts 7 billion customers a year, a certain degree of confidence is understandable. But in some places, Wal-Mart's attempts to impose its values on the market just do not work—at least not in places such as Germany, Korea, and Japan.

Referring to its failure in Germany, a Wal-Mart international spokesperson commented that it was a good lesson for the company and that they have learned to be more sensitive to cultural differences. For example, many Germans found the idea of a smiling greeter at the door of every Wal-Mart off-putting. In fact, many male shoppers interpreted the friendly greetings as flirting. The company also failed to foster good relations with German labor unions (Wal-Marts in the United States are not union). At one point during its tenure in Germany, Wal-Mart closed the headquarters of one of its chains and moved it to another geographic location—a common occurrence in the United States, usually accompanied by employees packing up and moving with the company. But in Germany, most of the employees quit rather than moving. A major problem was that the American managers in Germany just did not understand the German market or customers.[3]

Landler and Barbaro point out that the conglomerate also has made cultural gaffes in Brazil and Mexico. In Brazil, the company focused a campaign on golf clubs, in a country where many do not play golf. In Mexico, it emphasized ice skates. In Korea, the Wal-Mart product shelves were so tall that customers had to use ladders to reach the products. The point of this account is that the management and sales tactics of one country, no matter how successful they may be in that country, probably are not suitable for another country. Even if you can boast 7 billion shoppers, you still need to be perceptive of cultural differences.[4]

Coordinating and managing people from different cultures within an organizational context represents one of the greatest challenges for the corporate world in the new millennium. Few managers will survive and function effectively without an understanding of the subtleties and complexities of managing others in a multicultural and multinational business environment. Businesses and organizations from virtually every culture have entered into the global marketplace. Given the dramatic cultural transformation in today's marketplace, the relevance of intercultural communication competence cannot be overstated. To compete in the global and U.S. markets, today's managers must possess the skills to interact with people who are different from themselves.

INTERCULTURAL MANAGEMENT

Professor Philip Rosenzweig of Harvard University argues that successful cross-cultural management depends on the ability of managers to communicate effectively. Rosenzweig points out that communication is especially important during the initial stages of a business relationship. Depending on the culture, the process of building trust among business partners may take days, weeks, or even months. Moreover, Rosenzweig asserts, this process cannot be accelerated. Rosenzweig recognizes that many American managers prefer to "get down to business" without spending much time getting to know their business partners. In fact, according to Rosenzweig, many American managers view such relationship building as a waste of valuable time. Rosenzweig argues that investing time and energy into building trust and developing relationships may earn huge benefits in terms of confidence and trust.[5]

Perceptions of time and timing are also important considerations in cross-cultural business exchanges. Rosenzweig recommends that American managers allow the pace of negotiations to develop on its own. He cautions managers not to impose artificial deadlines for the sake of efficiency. How agreement and disagreement are communicated is another important factor during cross-cultural negotiations. Rosenzweig points out that American managers tend to favor forthrightness during negotiations. In many other cultures, such directness may be seen as rude and discourteous.[6]

Most of what you have been exposed to in this textbook can be applied to your role in organizational settings across cultures. The topics and issues discussed in each chapter can guide you in becoming a successful intercultural manager. Most businesses and organizations can be thought of as mini-cultures, each representing a pattern of values held by a recognizable group of people with a common goal that is pursued by means of a collective verbal and nonverbal symbol system (see Figure 11.1). Like cultures themselves, organizations possess value systems, exist in some environmental context, process information with a unique perceptual perspective, develop sociorelational connections with others, and communicate using distinctive verbal and nonverbal codes. As you prepare to conduct business with persons in organizations from different cultures or microcultures, you cannot assume that your business practices will be understood or accepted by your counterparts. Figure 11.2 outlines some of the more salient issues that affect the development of organizational culture in any country.

Figure 11.1   The values of an organization often mirror those of its culture.

Figure 11.2 Dimensions of culture and the organizational culture.

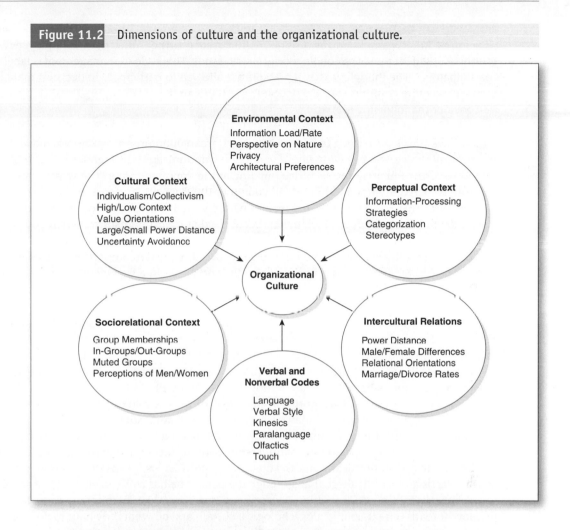

First, consider the cultural context of an organization. Organizational culture often parallels country culture. Hence, if values differ significantly across cultures, then the management practices of those cultures are also likely to differ. When managing people from other cultures, try to ascertain where on the individualism–collectivism continuum an organization falls. Organizations in collectivistic cultures are more likely to emphasize group harmony and teamwork. In this way, the organization may be more like a community than an entity. Individualistic corporations emphasize personal goals and within-organization promotion. Employees often compete for organizational resources and promotions, and the organization is seen more as an entity than as a community.

Power distance is another important cultural influence to assess when dealing with organizations across cultures. Organizations in large–power-distance cultures will be status conscious (e.g., placing emphasis on a person's position, degree), will employ top-down communication, and will be mindful of employee welfare. Formality between employer and employee will be the rule. Employees will not be expected to participate in management decision making. In small–power-distance cultures, such as the United States, employees are routinely asked for their opinion on work-related issues. This style of management is labeled "participatory." The thought is that if workers are allowed to participate in decision making, they will be more committed to the decision.

Consider the following scenario:

> You have traveled to Korea to meet with your Korean counterpart, whom you have never met in person but with whom you have communicated through letters, e-mail, and so forth. You arrive at his office building at the appointed time. The weather in Seoul is incredibly hot and humid. As you enter the floor of your partner's office, you notice that there are no walls separating the various desks. The scene appears relaxed to you. Most of the men are sitting around in their undershirts. When you locate your partner, you find him sitting with his feet up on the desk, in his undershirt, fanning himself. When you introduce yourself, your Korean partner acts as if nothing has happened and puts on a shirt, tie, and jacket in a very matter-of-fact way. Your meeting then begins.[7]

In addition to assessing an organization's cultural context, it is important to assess its environmental context—that is, its perspective on the environment, including such issues as information load, privacy, and the company's overall orientation to nature. Assumptions about privacy are also important to take into account. The scenario presented at the beginning of this section is based on a fascinating discussion by Philip Harris and Robert Moran about privacy in Korea. They report that in Korea, privacy is a luxury few possess or can afford. Because physical privacy may be impossible to obtain, Koreans build imaginary or psychological walls around themselves. A client calling on a Korean on a typically hot and humid day may find this person in his undershirt with his feet on his desk, fanning himself. Because there are no physical walls, the culturally informed visitor coughs to announce his arrival. Harris and Moran allege that although the person he has come to visit is in clear view, the visitor pretends not to "see" him. According to Harris and Moran, to secure some level of privacy, Koreans retreat behind a psychological curtain and do what they have to do, unseen by those who are in plain view. To violate the screen of privacy once it has been created is rude and discourteous.[8]

The perceptual context of the individual, learned through enculturation, often manifests in the organization. Understanding how the organization processes information is crucial to establishing and maintaining effective communication. One information-processing strategy in which people from all cultures engage is categorizing and stereotyping. Before embarking on a business venture with people from a foreign culture, it may be useful to know of the culture's perceptions of Americans and their business practices. As mentioned earlier, Canada is the United States' largest trading partner, yet Canadians hold some of the most negative views of the American people. In most of the Western countries surveyed, perceptions of Americans are positive. Characteristics such as "honest," "inventive," and "hardworking" are typical. But they also associate Americans with negative traits such as "greedy" and "violent." Canadians, in particular, do not view Americans as honest, and Canada is the only Western nation in which the majority regard Americans as rude.[9]

An organization's emphasis on group membership is clearly something that U.S. managers should know about their foreign counterparts. As mentioned in Chapter 6, all people of all cultures belong to groups. One of the primary groups to which all people belong is the family. Recall that Chapter 6 profiled family life across a variety of cultures. Fons Trompenaars employs a family metaphor in describing a particular type of ideal corporate culture seen often in Turkey, Venezuela, Hong Kong, Malaysia, India, Singapore, and Spain. This does not mean that all corporations in these countries are family-like; it simply means that this proto-type is seen more frequently in these cultures than in others. According to Trompenaars, the family corporation culture is simultaneously personal, with close face-to-face relationships, and hierarchical, in the sense that everyone knows his or her place in the rank order. At the top of the hierarchy are the parents (i.e., the chief executives), who are regarded as caring and as knowing better than the children (i.e., the subordinates). The power at the top is perceived not as threatening but as intimate and benign. The philosophy of the employees is to do more than is required contractually to please the older brother or father (i.e., the person of higher rank).[10]

Obviously, understanding the verbal and nonverbal codes of your foreign counterparts is an essential part of a successful business venture. Although it is true that most of your foreign business partners will speak some English, your knowledge and use of their language demonstrates your willingness to meet them halfway and will be much appreciated. When conducting business with your foreign counterparts, be conscious of terms and phrases that may be well understood within your corporation but misunderstood by outsiders. For example, the common American colloquial expression, "See ya later," may be taken literally, such that your counterpart expects to schedule a specific date and time for seeing each other later.

Although knowing your foreign partner's language (and he or she knowing yours) is certainly an advantage, other communication considerations, independent of verbal language, can affect your business propositions—most notably, nonverbal communication. As discussed in Chapter 8, nonverbal communication varies a great deal across cultures. One's kinesic, paralinguistic, olfactory, haptic, and proxemic behaviors can be interpreted differently depending on with whom one is interacting.

MANAGEMENT PRACTICES ACROSS CULTURES

The top 10 countries with which the United States trades, in terms of both imports and exports, are Canada, China, Mexico, Japan, Germany, the United Kingdom, South Korea, France, Taiwan, and Brazil. In 2010, U.S. trade with these countries accounted for nearly $3 trillion (i.e., $3,000,000,000,000).[11] In the following pages, we will profile four of these countries: Japan, Germany, Mexico, and China.

Japanese Management Practices

Richard Grainger and Tadayuki Miyamoto argue that Japanese organizations are essentially social organizations, of which two key features are lifetime employment (*shushin koyo*) and seniority grading (*nenko joretsu*). Based on these principles, the Japanese company is seen as a custodian of employee security and welfare. The lifetime employment system is based on a psychological contract between the employees and the company about the employees' life-time dedication to the company in exchange for lifetime job security from the organization. Japanese organizations also practice a seniority-based wage and promotion arrangement whereby employees are promoted and compensated based on the number of years they have served the organization. The system rewards older and longer-serving employees. Conversely, employees who change their employers are penalized. Grainger and Miyamoto maintain that under these arrangements, employees willingly sacrifice their short-term losses for long-term company success. Hence, employees maintain high morale and loyalty to the company, which enables the company to invest more resources in employee career development.[12]

Ronald Dore, a British sociologist specializing in Japanese economy and society, argues that the nature of the firm in Japan is much more like a community than in other countries. This is probably reflective of Japan's traditional collectivistic orientation. Dore also maintains that the lifetime employment system has survived to a remarkable degree. To be sure, Dore notes, there is a degree of career mobility for young Japanese. But, Dore points out, the pro-portion of young Japanese workers between the ages of 30 and 34 who have been working for one particular company for less than 1 year was 4% in 1985, rose to 5% in 1990, and was back to 3% in 2002. Hence, career mobility among young Japanese remains restricted. The same is true for the Japanese who are moving up by changing firms, which is still quite rare.

Dore notes that one aspect of Japanese business has changed. The majority of Japanese firms now have a kind of performance-based pay, replacing the seniority-based merit system discussed above. But Dore is cautious about whether this change will endure. Many of the Japanese firms that introduced the new system in the mid-1990s have backtracked because of the heavy administration costs and dramatic effects on worker morale. Also, many Japa-nese saw objectively measuring differences in performance as counterproductive.[13]

Some Japanese work groups begin their day by exercising together, an activity called *taiso*. Interestingly, the primary purpose of *taiso* is not for physical benefit but to engage the group members in coordinated activity. After the day's work is finished, businesses encourage their employees to eat and drink together to maintain harmonious group relationships. Though such activities may appear to serve a purely social purpose, the underlying motivation is to aid productivity at work. The number of hours worked in a typical Japanese workweek has declined significantly over the past 20 years. In 1994, according to William Brown, Rebecca Lubove, and James Kwalwasser, the typical Japanese worker spent more than 2,500 hours on the job every year. According to the Japanese Ministry of Labor, that number had decreased to about 1,750 hours per year in 2012.[14]

In most organizations across cultures, managers are in positions of power and influence. As such, they engage in a variety of behavioral strategies to influence the attitudes and behav-iors of their subordinates. Asha Rao, Keiji Hashimoto, and Aruna Rao surveyed Japanese managers regarding their preferences for a variety of influence strategies. Although some of the Japanese managers preferred influence tactics similar to those preferred by U.S. manag-ers, the researchers identified several strategies that appear to be unique to the Japanese. One strategy is labeled *firm's authority*. In contrast to American managers, who may appeal to "higher-ups" to influence their employees, Japanese managers do not appeal to a specific person in the organizational hierarchy but, rather, to the entire organization itself, independent of their superiors. This strategy is probably linked to the Japanese concept of the business organization as a family.[15]

A second type of strategy, called *personal development*, occurs when a Japanese manager convinces his (most managers are men) employees to comply with a request to enhance their careers within the organization. This tactic may be effective because many Japanese remain with a single company for their entire lives. American managers, on the other hand, convince employees that by complying with a request, the employees will develop skills they can take with them when they leave the organization.[16]

Another strategy is labeled *socializing*. With this strategy, Japanese managers ask to spend time with their employees after hours. According to Rao, Hashimoto, and Rao, such a strategy allows for informal interaction between managers and subordinates that is impossible in the context of the formal work environment. Interestingly, they also report that Japanese managers in Canada were disappointed when their subordinates rejected their requests to socialize after work. The Japanese managers felt that this severely limited their influence potential, and they had to resort to using assertive tactics on the job.

Rao, Hashimoto, and Rao report that Japanese managers use a variety of tactics outside the work environment to influence their subordinates. In general, compared with American managers, Japanese managers use influence tactics that are subtle and indirect. For example, if a Japanese manager wants a subordinate to focus on the Canadian market for a specific product, the manager, rather than telling the employee directly, might funnel information about that market to him or her, hoping that the employee will sense the manager's intent. In addition, Japanese managers use strategies that rely on the influence of the organization and group harmony.[17]

AN INTERCULTURAL CONVERSATION: CLASHING CULTURAL CONCEPTS ON THE JOB

In the following conversation, American businessman Jim Neumouth is applying for a job in Japanese businessman Kietaro Matsumoto's corporation, located in Kyoto.

Kietaro:	So, Mr. Neumouth, why would you like to work for our corporation?
Jim:	I believe I have the necessary skills and experience for this position. I'm very independent, I set very high goals for myself, and I believe your company will allow me to pursue them.
Kietaro:	What do you mean by "goals"?
Jim:	I have very high sales objectives. I try to reach the top in whatever I do. One of my goals is to become your leading salesperson. For example, I had the highest percentage of sales of anyone in the company I worked for in the United States. I was named salesperson of the year in 2008.
Kietaro:	I see. That's very impressive.
Jim:	Thanks. Now, I'd like to expand into an international market, and I'd like to bring my experience and motivation to your company. I think I can be the best here, too.

In the above conversation, Jim does a good job of expressing his talents and experience. In the United States, he might appear to be the ideal candidate; however, to Kietaro, he does not seem to be a team player and may disrupt the harmony of the sales teams. When doing business with companies in collective cultures, it may be wise to formulate strategies that are consistent with group unity; strategies perceived to promote the individual within the organization may be frowned on. Also, keep in mind that reaching a decision in collectivistic organizations sometimes takes much longer than in individualistic ones. Often, collectivists go to great pains to win everyone over to achieve consensus.

Richard Lewis maintains that a common attitude among Japanese businesspersons is that foreigners are always outsiders—called *Gaijin*. Many believe the term carries negative connotations. Lewis observes that any effort to speak Japanese will be mildly appreciated but not taken seriously. He also notes that translating and interpreting Japanese behavior can be very difficult (see Table 11.1).[18]

Table 11.1 American Perceptions and Japanese Realities

American Perception	Japanese Reality
The Japanese are really shy.	As a high-context culture, the Japanese do not feel a need to talk. They are comfortable with silence.
Japanese fall asleep a lot during class or presentations.	Many Japanese close their eyes when they are deeply concentrating.
Japanese say yes even when they mean no. Why can't they just say what they mean?	To save face (yours and theirs), Japanese will agree with you in principle.
It takes Japanese forever to make decisions or even to respond to a fax or written correspondence.	Japanese will not make a decision without first consulting relevant others to reach a consensus.
Japanese will never look you in the eye.	Indirect eye contact is a sign of deference in Japan.
When Japanese talk, they seem so ambiguous. I never know what they're trying to say or what they really mean.	Japanese language is vague. But even more than that, to the Japanese, communication is a two-way process. The burden of understanding rests with both the speaker and the listener. Often, the speaker will only hint at what is meant. The listener must be an active participant.

SOURCE: Table adapted from Lewis, R. D. (2006). *When Cultures Collide: Leading Across Cultures,* pp. 515–517. Copyright © 2006, Boston: Nicholas Brealey.

German Management Practices

Although the German economy has fluctuated since reunification, it was growing at a rate of about 3.3% in 2010; it is now the fifth largest economy in the world. The average income per capita in U.S. dollars is $36,000. The U.S. Department of State maintains that the German market, the largest in Europe, is attractive to many U.S. businesses. Germans are drawn to innovative products that display high quality and contemporary styling. They are especially interested in high-tech products, particularly those that assist them in entering the age of the Internet.[19]

Like the United States and Europe in general, Germany is a decentralized collection of states and regions. Many are quite diverse, with unique customs and conventions. The northern and southern regions are particularly different, so generalizing about Germany is difficult and should be approached with some degree of caution. According to intercultural consultants William Drake and Associates, most Germans believe that people are controlled by their own actions, that facts are more important than face (in sharp contrast to the Japanese), and that factual honesty is more important than politeness (again, clashing with Japanese conventions). According to Drake and Associates, German children are taught that useless people amount to nothing and that children are to be quiet and respectful. They are also taught to "save for a rainy day."[20]

Ursula Glunk, Celeste Wilderom, and Robert Ogilvie point out that a unique feature of Germany's economic structure is a state-regulated apprentice system through which young German adults learn a specialized skill, for which they receive a state diploma. According to Glunk and her colleagues, learning is both on the job and theoretical. The curriculum is determined by the government, an employers' association, and German trade unions. During their apprenticeship, students are supervised by local chambers of commerce. This system leads to a remarkably well-trained workforce. According to Glunk and her colleagues, about 70% of German workers have been through this system. They also note that technical knowledge and engineering skills are highly valued in Germany. They maintain that German employees are continuously challenged with new procedures, tools, and techniques.[21]

In addition, German managers are known to be specialists for which a technical background is more typical than a formal education. German foremen, supervisors, and managers typically have professional rather than academic degrees. Hence, quality of skill and amount of experience are the most important promotional considerations in German firms. Finally, Glunk and her colleagues note that many German organizations implement a shadow-worker program whereby managers choose and train their own replacements. Germans believe that this kind of program reduces the politics of promotional ploys and insecurity around who will succeed whom. In this type of program, vacations, illness, and other periods of absence are covered by the designated replacement. Thus, the successor can temporarily experience his or her future position. Glunk and her colleagues maintain that this policy preserves smooth organizational functioning.[22]

Focusing their analysis primarily on West Germans, anthropologists Edward and Mildred Hall contend that compartmentalization is the most prominent structural feature of German culture—that is, that Germans have a tendency to isolate and divide many aspects of their lives into discrete, independent units. Germans are known to compartmentalize their daily schedules, educational system, office buildings, corporations, homes, and even lines of communication. In fact, Hall and Hall argue that on the job, Germans will not share information with others except within their own working groups. Hall and Hall maintain that such a restricted flow of information may be the biggest obstacle in doing business with Germans. One result of German compartmentalization is a culture in which significant events and changes can take place without people knowing about them. Even informal information networks that connect public and private organizational boundaries are rare in Germany.[23] Given this condition, U.S. companies wishing to do business in Germany would be wise to understand that they may not be able to operate out of a centralized location. Instead, they may have to set up multiple sites from which to conduct commerce. German emphasis on compartmentalization manifests in many areas of German life and business, particularly with respect to privacy and specialization. Germans are a private (and formal) people. Most German managers isolate themselves in their offices behind closed doors, contrasting sharply with the open-door policies exercised by many American managers.

Doors are an important cultural symbol to the Germans. According to Hall and Hall, doors provide a protective shield between the individual and outsiders. Upon encountering a closed door in German businesses or homes, an "intruder" should always knock. As Hall and Hall note, closed doors uphold the honor of the space, afford a boundary between people, and eliminate the possibility of eavesdropping, interruptions, and accidental intrusions. Moreover, according to Hall and Hall, within corporations, the closed door indicates that a manager respects the privacy of subordinates and is not looking over their shoulders.[24]

German compartmentalization can also be seen in the overall market strategy of many successful German corporations. Unlike many U.S. or Japanese corporate conglomerates whose global market success is attributable to diversification, many German firms concentrate on specialization—that is, doing one thing and doing it right. German corporations with large shares of specialized markets can focus on design, quality, and service rather than on competitive pricing. Such corporations manufacture a smaller and narrower class of products, sell to fewer consumers, and contract with fewer suppliers than do their less successful competitors. To be sure, many of these exclusive products are expensive, but the Germans believe that specialization leads to quality and profit. German products are known worldwide for their high caliber and quality workmanship (e.g., Mercedes, BMW). Steiner Optik maintains 80% of the global market for military field glasses. Krones manufactures more than 70% of the world's bottle-labeling machines. The Germans seem to be teaching the rest of the world that, at least for them, specialization works.[25]

Like the United States, Germany is considered a low-context, monochronic culture—except even more so. According to Hall and Hall, the German language is quite literal, with individual German words having exact and precise meanings. For example, the Germans have no fewer than eight words for *comfort*, each reflecting a slightly different type of comfort. Having been conditioned by their language, Germans are fairly formal, nitpicky about precision, punctual, and fanatic about facts. All these characteristics carry over into their business relations. On the job and in business dealings, Germans are absolutely obsessed with facts and precision. Lines of authority are carefully observed. Interactions between business partners and friends are reserved and formalized. Germans are conscious of rank and will always refer to someone by his or her appropriate title. Even neighbors who may have lived next door to each other for years address each other with their last names, as in "Herr (Mr.) Schmidt." If a person also carries a degree, such as a PhD or MD, he will be called "Herr Doktor Neulieb," and so forth.[26] Women, however, are typically addressed with their first names, as in "Frau Batina Neulieb."

Even in social situations, Germans often appear unfriendly. They generally will not smile in greeting and are intolerant of small talk. On the job, German workers expect that their managers will respect their privacy and that procedures will be executed precisely. Table 11.2 outlines some features of doing business with Germans that may help Americans transacting business in Germany.

Table 11.2	Interacting Effectively With Germans

1. Be prepared. In business, the Germans will be informed and will expect that you are, too.

2. Engage in only minimal small talk.

3. Be informed about, and use, appropriate titles.

4. Avoid emotional appeals. Emphasize facts and figures. Germans respect quantitative reports.

5. Observe hierarchical seating and order of speaking.

6. Organize your presentation in compartments, and have your specialists present their own areas separately and as distinct parts of the presentation.

7. Be punctual; start and stop as you planned. Follow your agenda closely.

8. Avoid humor. Be frank, direct, and honest. Demonstrate that you have done your homework.

SOURCE: Lewis, R. D. (2006). *When Cultures Collide: Leading Across Cultures.* Copyright © 2006, Boston: Nicholas Brealey.

Mexican Management Practices

Mexico has a free-market economy, with a gross domestic product of $1.3 trillion and a growth rate of 5% in 2010. The Mexican per capita income is $14,000, one third that of the United States. Income distribution remains highly unequal, with more than 45% of the population living in moderate poverty and 18% in extreme poverty. Trade with the United States and Canada has tripled since the implementation of NAFTA (the North America Free Trade Agreement) in 1994. As mentioned earlier, in 2010, Mexico was the United States' third most important trading partner, following Canada and China.[27]

Ned Crouch points out that Mexicans are unusually group oriented. He maintains that they are exceptionally concerned about any behavior that would upset the harmony of their household, church, or workplace. In fact, Crouch argues that on a scale of individual- versus group-oriented work styles, Mexicans and Americans would fall at opposite ends of the continuum. He cautions American managers working in Mexico not to reward individuals within work groups. Generally, Mexican workers do not wish to call attention to themselves for outperforming coworkers and may be ashamed and embarrassed if recognized above others. In Mexico, individual effort and self-starting are met with suspicion. Even arriving early to work requires an explanation to coworkers, because they will think that person is trying to get ahead by showing off. Crouch points out that for a worker to leave his or her workstation to talk to the supervisor about mundane, work-related issues is disquieting to others in the group, unless the employee has explained his or her need to communicate with the supervisor beforehand. Moreover, Crouch asserts that the Mexican worker's attitude toward the boss is virtually never confrontational. Mexican workers value harmony above all else. A manager expressing favoritism to an individual Mexican worker will upset the harmony and shatter the team spirit.[28]

Mexico is considered a large–power-distance culture. Recall that in such cultures, people expect and accept that the power within the culture and its institutions will be distributed unequally. Crouch explains that, historically, Mexicans have never known a world without hierarchy. For example, the Spanish had kings and queens, and the Aztecs had powerful *caciques* (warrior chiefs). To be sure, the Spanish language is replete with words and phrases that communicate hierarchy (e.g., proper titles, salutations, and honorifics) and emphasize the idea that some people hold superior positions over others. Crouch asserts that Mexicans hold to traditional hierarchical roles based on family, education, age, and position. According to Crouch, Mexicans are puzzled and offended by Americans' casual and informal communication style. He maintains that Mexicans find the relaxed and easy communication between people of different hierarchical levels off-putting. The Mexican distinction between superior and subordinate is part of a deeply rooted pattern dating back to Aztec divisions among priest, prince, and peasant, and among the Spanish queen, soldier, and citizen. For small–power-distance Americans, the implications of superior and inferior status that accompany this pattern are unacceptable.[29]

In low (or weak) uncertainty-avoidance cultures such as the United States, employees are encouraged to innovate and take risks. In high (or strong) uncertainty-avoidance cultures such as Mexico, innovative or risk-taking behavior is considered inappropriate. Mexican workers generally prefer close supervision. Likewise, compensation based on incentive is eschewed. Mexican workers prefer to know exactly what they are supposed to do, and they want to be rewarded for doing it.

Chinese Management Practices

In 2010, the People's Republic of China surpassed Japan as the world's second largest economy (following the United States), with a gross domestic product worth an estimated $1.4 trillion. China's economy is also the world's fastest growing major economy, with average growth rates of 10% over the past three decades. Much of this economic power is the result of free-market reforms instituted in 1978. China is the largest exporter and second largest importer of goods in the world. For example, China overtook the United States last year as the biggest automobile market in the world. Indeed, China has now surpassed Germany as the largest exporter of automobiles. Moreover, China is the world's biggest buyer of iron ore and copper and the second biggest importer of crude oil.[30] Out of 183 world economies, the World Bank rates China 79th in terms of ease of doing business. China ranks 151st in terms of starting a business, 65th in terms of getting credit, and 15th in terms of trading across borders.[31]

Several times throughout this book, China has been described as a collectivistic, large–power-distance culture. China's large power distance can be attributed to its Confucian heritage, which results in a hierarchical society. As we saw in Chapter 2, modesty, obedience, and respect for seniors are deeply rooted Chinese values. Confucian ideals form the foundation

STUDENT VOICES ACROSS CULTURES

Doing Business in Sweden

My name is Carl Ekstrom. I was born and raised in Sweden, in a city called Sodertalje, about 45 minutes from Stockholm. Hockey has always been a huge part of my life, and I realized that I had a great opportunity to combine college with my love of hockey. After attending Union College in Schenectady, New York, I transferred to St. Norbert College in De Pere, Wisconsin. I attended school there for about 4 years and recently graduated very satisfied with my experience.

The business climate in Sweden is in some ways similar to the one in the United States, but there are also many differences. One major difference is the formality of the office setting. Swedish people emphasize equality among all employees. Superiors are always addressed by their first names, regardless of the speaker's rank. Even though superiors usually have the final word in a business decision, they are always looking for feedback from their employees. As a result of this decision-making framework, there are always several meetings throughout a business day in which employees can share their opinions.

Swedish business attire is also different from that in many other countries. The attire is more casual; jeans worn with a collared shirt is considered appropriate. There are no suits in the office during a regular workweek. Swedish people are also adamant about maintaining their *fika* breaks every day. These are short breaks during which everyone drinks coffee and has general, non-work-related conversations. *Fika* happens at least three times a day, regardless of where one works. This adds to the casual business climate.

Even though the business climate is more casual in Sweden, employees are expected to complete their tasks on time, and business management is usually strict in this regard.

of Chinese management. China is also considered a high-context culture. As such, China's Confucianism, collectivism, power distance, and high context are ingrained in Chinese management practices. Because of the culture's high-context orientation, the environment in which business is conducted is important. Where the meeting takes place, who is invited, and who is presenting all are critical ingredients in a successful business meeting.

China's Confucian heritage affects how Chinese will approach their business relationships. Recall from Chapter 6 that in Confucian-based societies, great emphasis is placed on harmonious relationships and knowing one's proper place in the social hierarchy. All relationships are seen as unequal, and one's ethics are directed toward observing these inequalities. Contrary to the United States, where business is business and not to be taken personally, the Chinese will go to great lengths to establish trust and a social bond in their international business relationships. When doing business in China, you can expect your Chinese counterpart to invite you to informal gatherings and to discuss topics unrelated to the business at hand, such as politics, the arts, information about your family, etc. The Chinese want to see you as a member of the business family—that is, the group.[32]

Decision making is an important part of management. In the United States, management decision making is often a collaboration between workers and managers, where debate is encouraged (and sometimes legislated via union agreements). Jie Tang and Anthony Ward point out that in Chinese management, the manager is expected to make decisions on behalf of the entire group. This is expected and desired among both the managers and workers. The idea of open communication between managers and workers is not only unheard of but thought of as peculiar. Tang and Ward hypothesize that this style is probably reflective of collectivistic thinking, where workers are a part of one group and managers a part of another. In-group/out-group distinctions are a part of collectivistic thinking. These distinctions are also Confucianistic. Tang and Ward note that this can be an effective and efficient decision-making system, but it can also be time-consuming when a particular question is not asked of the right person and must make its way to the top of the hierarchy before being answered.[33]

Communication between managers and workers is restricted. Tang and Ward note that workers are on a need-to-know basis, and the flow of job-related information is limited. Likewise—and consistent with their collectivistic, large–power-distance, and high-context nature—Chinese workers will probably not initiate communication with a manager, even if they have concerns about the way a job is being handled. While they may discuss it with another worker, they will not address the manager, probably due to their desire not to stand out or be thought of as confrontational. Recall from Chapter 2 that modesty and finding the middle ground are valued in China. In addition, recall from Chapter 10 that collectivists, and particularly Chinese, do not approach conflict but, rather, avoid it in an effort to maintain harmony. Plus, in an effort to save everyone's face—both those of managers and workers—on-the-job conflict is resolved via mediation and compromise.[34]

To make one final point about doing business in China, gift giving was once an important part of Chinese culture. Today, however, Chinese business culture prohibits giving gifts. In fact, gift giving is considered bribery and is technically illegal. But, depending on the specific case, attitudes about giving gifts are relaxing. If you wish to give a gift to an individual, do it privately—in the context of friendship, not business. Your Chinese counterpart will probably decline the gift two or three times before accepting it. Once he or she accepts the gift, express gratitude. Giving a gift to the entire company, rather than to an individual, can be an acceptable alternative. But make sure you present the gift to the appropriate team leader.[35]

CULTURE, INTERCULTURAL COMMUNICATION, AND HEALTH CARE

On January 21, 2013, Dr. Margaret Chan, director-general of the World Health Organization (WHO), in a speech to the WHO Executive Board in Geneva, Switzerland, asserted:

> The climate is changing. Antibiotics are failing. The world population keeps getting bigger, and older. The rise of chronic noncommunicable diseases is relentless. The microbial world continues to deliver surprises.

Public expectations for health care are rising. Budgets are shrinking. Costs are soaring at a time of nearly universal austerity. Social inequalities are at the worst levels seen in half a century. Conflicts are rife. The health consequences, also for civilians, are severe.

The will to relieve human misery is strong but gets blunted by too few resources, too little capacity, and too much uncoordinated aid.[36]

Although advances in health care over the past century have been monumental, the status of the world's health remains in flux. Reflecting on the words of Chan above, consider the following four health care scenarios in four different cultures:

Researchers in Switzerland have developed a new medical device that identifies irregularities in heart rate and can, within seconds, alert doctors and patients via their smartphones. The device consists of four noninvasive electrode sensors attached to the skin and linked to a radio module and computer chip, which clips to the patient's belt. Heart data are then sent to the patient's smartphone, where they can be viewed in real time.[37]

Cao gio, also known as coining or coin rubbing, is a dermabrasive (i.e., skin) therapy thought to alleviate symptoms from a number of illnesses (e.g., headache, body aches and pains). Coining is used by a number of ethnic groups from Southeast Asia. During coining, the skin on the patient's chest and back is lubricated with oils or balms and then rubbed firmly with the edge of a coin. The procedure often generates considerable skin damage (e.g., burning and scarring). In some cases, the oils and balms used are toxic and, if absorbed, lead to camphor intoxication. In these cases, the patient can suffer nausea, vomiting, confusion, tremors, and even convulsions.[38]

The majority of African American women (i.e., more than 80%) are either overweight or obese. These women are at significant risk for a range of serious health issues, including high blood pressure, high cholesterol, arthritis, stroke, gall bladder disease, heart disease, diabetes, and some cancers. The high obesity rates among these women are often attributed to cultural factors, such as a preference for high-fat and high-calorie foods, a distorted frame of reference for normal and healthy body weight, and a lack of physical activity. Societal and environmental factors also contribute, including poverty and limited opportunities for recreational physical activity.[39]

Rural Dominicans often combine folk and professional medicine to manage their health care. One rural Dominican woman took modern antibiotics for a vaginal infection, yet taped garlic to her palm to cure an infection in her hand and relied on prayer to heal an infection in her infant son. In another case, a local faith healer dissolved modern antibiotics in tea, then rubbed the potion on a sick child in a prayer ritual to eliminate the child's fever.[40]

As the above four scenarios suggest, people from diverse cultural backgrounds face different health issues and carry vastly different assumptions about their health. Recall from Chapter 1 that culture is defined as *an accumulated pattern of values, beliefs, and behaviors, shared by an identifiable group of people with a common history and verbal and nonverbal symbol systems.* To be sure, different cultural groups have different beliefs, values, and behaviors associated with their health and health care. These different belief and value systems translate into diverse theories and practices about the causes and treatments of illness (see Figure 11.3). As Hope Landrine and Elizabeth Klonoff note, "The health beliefs of professionals and laypersons alike are structured and informed by a cultural context from which they cannot be separated and without which they cannot be fully understood."[41]

Lay Theories of Illness

In his classic text on culture, health, and illness, Cecil Helman suggests that people from different cultures generally attribute illness to one of four causes: (a) factors within the individual, such as bad eating and exercise habits; (b) factors within the natural environment, such as air and water pollution; (c) societal factors, such as intergroup conflict, poor health care facilities, etc.; or (d) supernatural factors, including religious beliefs, fate, and indigenous beliefs.[42] Helman notes that these attributions for health and illness reflect the particular culture's general value orientations. For example, persons in Western cultures such as the United States, which are often individualistic, generally believe that the origins of illness are rooted in the individual patient. As Helman explains, the responsibility for one's health generally, though not exclusively, rests with the individual. So ill health is often considered to be the result of the individual's bad habits, such as poor diet, lack of exercise, damaging lifestyle choices, poor personal hygiene, alcoholism, drug abuse, or other deviant behavior. Thus, from this perspective, one should feel guilty when faced with ill health. To be sure, persons in this orientation understand that other factors contribute to illness, such as heredity (e.g., cancer, diabetes) and environmental conditions (e.g., pollution, allergens, poisons, food additives, weather).[43] Typically, these cultures rely on a biomedical model of health care, where the fundamental assumption is that diagnosis and treatment of illness should be based on scientific data.

Helman observes that in many non-Western cultures, illness is often attributed to societal and/or supernatural conditions. Societal attributions are based on intergroup or interpersonal conflict within the culture. Here, according to Helman, one of the most common causes of illness is thought to be witchcraft. According to a 2010 Gallup poll, belief in witchcraft is widespread throughout sub-Saharan Africa and affects how believers in witchcraft see their lives and their health. For example, 95% of persons surveyed in Ivory Coast, 80% of those in Senegal, 77% of those in Mali, and 75% of those in Niger personally believe in witchcraft. On average, 55% of persons in the 18 African countries surveyed believe in witchcraft. The study found that believers in witchcraft rate their general well-being lower than do those who do not believe in witchcraft.[44] Helman notes that among believers in witchcraft, certain persons, often women, are thought to possess mystical powers that can harm others. So conflicting families or groups may call on a witch to put a curse (e.g., illness) on their opposition.[45]

Supernatural conditions, such as religion, pure fate, and indigenous belief systems, are also thought among certain cultures to be the origin of illness. Here, one's ill health is believed to be caused by the intervention of a supernatural being. This is also referred to as the *personalistic* approach. Helman explains that persons in such cultures may believe

Figure 11.3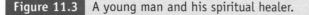

| Figure 11.3 | A young man and his spiritual healer. |

that their illness is God's punishment for their misdeeds, such as not attending church regularly or not saying their prayers. In Western cultures, such as the United States, persons might attribute their illness to *bad luck;* that is, they believe that their illness is the work of fate.[46]

Helman is careful to point out that persons in many cultures make multicausal attributions for illness. So, while persons in Western cultures may rely on the biomedical approach for their health, they may also believe that a supernatural force is responsible in some way.

Health Care and Resources Across Cultures

Health care is clearly one of the dominant forces that people in all cultures must manage. But the available resources to manage health care differ considerably across cultures. One of the biggest challenges facing the world's countries is the monumental cost associated with health care. For example, in 2011, health expenditures in the United States totaled $2.7 trillion (i.e., $2,700,000,000,000).[47] Government expenditure on health care as a percentage of total government expenditures varies considerably across the world, as does the number of physicians available to treat patients (see Table 11.3).

In addition to the disparities in terms of cost, the number of physicians, and life expectancy, to name only a few, the differences in how cultures address health issues are also significant. It is within these contexts where communication plays a key role.

Table 11.3 Government Expenditures on Health Care Across Cultures		
	Government Expenditure on Health Care as a % of Total Government Expenditures	Physicians per 10,000 People
Afghanistan	3.7	2.1
Brazil	6.0	17.2
Canada	17.2	19.1
Central Africa Republic	11.0	0.8
Chad	13.8	0.4
China	10.3	14.2
Cuba	15.5	64.0
France	16.0	35.0
Germany	18.0	35.3
Iraq	3.1	6.9
Kuwait	6.1	17.9
Mexico	15.0	28.9
Nigeria	6.4	4.0
Pakistan	3.1	8.1
Saudi Arabia	8.4	9.4
United Kingdom	15.1	27.4
United States	18.7	26.7

SOURCE: World Health Organization. (2011). *World Health Statistics 2011*. Publications of the World Health Organization can be obtained from WHO Press, World Health Organization, 20 Avenue Appia, 1211 Geneva 27, Switzerland.

HEALTH COMMUNICATION

The study of health communication is relatively young compared with other areas of communication study. Kevin Bradley-Wright and his colleagues point out that the study of health communication began in the mid-1970s. At about that time in U.S. history, professional and social attitudes about health and health care transitioned. Bradley-Wright and his colleagues note that physicians and other health care providers historically have addressed health care

STUDENT VOICES ACROSS CULTURES

Health Care in the Faroe Islands

My name is Viviann Filispdóttir Hansen. I was born and raised on the Faroe Islands, located in the North Atlantic. I am 25 years old and graduated from St. Norbert College in 2013.

Because the Faroe Islands is such a small country, everyone knows one another in some way; so the doctor–patient relationship is much more personal than formal. Physicians are approachable but at the same time keep a professional environment. The majority of physicians practicing medicine on the Faroe Islands are schooled in surrounding Scandinavian countries, but in the past 5 to 10 years, many of our physicians have been educated in Poland because the programs there have a very good reputation.

In the Faroe Islands, we pay an annual fee of about $550 for health care. This covers as many doctor and hospital visits as we need. We start paying this annual fee when we are 16 years old. Before that, we are on our parents' health insurance (the $550 fee does not change).

When making an appointment, we call the doctor's office and get an appointment within 2 days, depending on the seriousness of our situation. We always meet with doctors directly, and they give a diagnosis and send the patient to a specialist if needed. The quality of care is good, but the wait to see the doctor can be a little long (about an hour but, again, depending on severity of the illness). Doctors treat patients with respect and take their opinions into consideration; however, they ultimately give patients the treatment they think fits best.

issues via a biomedical model of medicine that focuses on the scientific method and procedures for treating disease. This approach utilizes physical evidence such as laboratory results, X-rays, MRIs (magnetic resonance imaging), and surgery to diagnose and treat illness. Since about 1970, health care workers have begun to include a psychosocial approach to illness. To be sure, this approach does not ignore the scientific component of health care but expands it to include other variables that affect health, such as a patient's culture, ethnicity, coping abilities, and other socially oriented events. The study of health communication typically focuses on this latter approach to health care.[48]

The Centers for Disease Control and the National Cancer Institute define health communication as "the study and use of communication strategies to inform and influence individual decisions that enhance health."[49] The study of health communication covers a vast array of topics, far too many to address in this chapter. But one area in particular that has direct relevance for intercultural communication is patient–provider communication. The focus here is on the face-to-face interaction between the patient and his or her individual health care provider, which includes physicians, nurses, psychiatrists, psychologists, and counselors, among others.

The late Dr. Julian Wohl, Professor Emeritus of psychology and former director of the Clinical Psychology Training Program at the University of Toledo, wrote that just about all psychotherapy (and by extension health care) is intercultural. Wohl asserted that health care is intercultural whenever cultural differences are present within the four elements of any health care communication context—that is, the health care provider, the patient, the locale or setting, and the method to be employed. He explains that to ignore the cultural differences in any of these elements is to court disaster.[50] Likewise, Tina Carmichael, a registered nurse and registered respiratory therapist at Children's Hospital of Boston, has written: "To become successful practitioners as a body of nurses, we must address the challenges of a nonhomogenous client-centered practice as well as a nonhomogenous work place."[51]

Provider–Patient Communication

Dr. Debra Roter, a professor of health policy and management at the Johns Hopkins Bloomberg School of Public Health, points out that, historically, the relationship between the provider and patient in medical contexts has been asymmetrical. Because of their advanced education and experience, providers (e.g., physicians) hold more power than patients and are responsible for managing the interaction with patients, while the patients are generally passive. This approach, which was dominant throughout the 20th century, is called *paternalism*. In contrast, an approach labeled *consumerism* or *mutual participation* has been the popular model in the 21st century, where the patient sets the agenda and shares responsibility for decision making. As Roter describes, in this model, the provider accommodates patient requests for information and services.[52]

The degree to which paternalism and consumerism are practiced across cultures has been the focus of a number of studies. Theoretically, we would expect that in large–power-distance and collectivistic cultures, a paternalistic approach might continue to dominate provider–patient communication. But several studies have shown that this is not the case. In an oft-cited study, Keith Bennett, David Smith, and Harry Irwin studied patient preferences for participation in medical decisions across several cultural groups, including Hong Kong, Australia, the United States, and China.[53] Their results revealed several interesting and counter-theoretical findings. They found that (a) Hong Kong patients prefer to participate in medical decision making with their physicians instead of deciding for themselves or delegating such decisions to their doctors; (b) students from Australia, China, and the United States overwhelmingly prefer joint decision making with their doctors; and (c) adult participants in three cities in mainland China do not prefer to delegate decisions to doctors when given the opportunity to participate in such decisions. Bennett and his colleagues conclude:

> The outcome is singular, strong, and consistent. Regardless of age, culture, and nationality, patients prefer to take part in joint decision making with their doctors. The convergence of findings on this issue is remarkable. Patients prefer to discuss and participate in decisions regarding their medical care. Chinese participants do not differ from those in Australia, the United States, or the United Kingdom in regard to the part they want to play. What we have found on this matter is cultural similarity, not cultural difference.[54]

In a similar study, Min Sun Kim, David Smith, and Gu Yueguo investigated the influence of patients' individualism (i.e., independent self-construal) and collectivism (i.e., interdependent self-construal) on preferences for medical decision making among patients in Hong Kong and

Beijing, China. In their study, they asked patients to rank four medical decision-making choices: joint decision making, delegation of decision to physicians, deciding alone, and family decision making.[55] Consistent with the findings of Bennett and his colleagues, cited above, their findings showed that participants from both Hong Kong and Beijing preferred joint decision making. However, the patients' level of collectivism and/or individualism affected their ranking of choices. The patients' level of collectivism was predictive of doctor decision making and family decision making. The patients' individualism was not. Individualism was predictive of joint decision making and patient decision making but not of decision making by the family or doctor alone.

In a related study, David and Sarah Jeanne Smith surveyed older individuals in Hong Kong, Beijing, and Suzhou (China) regarding their communication about medicine. Specifically, they asked participants what sources of information and advice about medicine they used most often, what topics were of most importance in terms of communication and medicine, and what roles physicians and patients played in such communication. They then compared the responses with those of U.S. participants.[56] Their results revealed that Chinese participants, both in Hong Kong and mainland China, expressed a marked preference for doctors trained in Western medicine as sources of information and advice. Yet, compared with U.S. participants, Chinese respondents relied more heavily on family and friends for health information and advice. In the United States and Hong Kong, participants were asked to select the source from which they would most like to learn more about medicine. In the United States, 77% chose their U.S. doctor; in Hong Kong, 50% chose the Western doctor, and 12% chose the Chinese doctor. When asked what topics were most important to older patients, participants' concern about the side effects of medicine ranked among the top three in all settings. Finally, physicians in mainland China were described more positively by their patients than were those in either Hong Kong or the United States.[57]

The studies cited above compare provider–patient communication across cultures. Yet one quarter of practicing physicians in the United States who were not U.S. citizens when they entered medical school are graduates of international medical schools. The great majority of them now make up more than 50% of first-year family practice residents. Hence, a significant proportion of provider–patient communication in the United States is truly intercultural.

In one study, Betsy Sleath, Richard Rubin, and Angela Arrey-Wastavino examined the extent to which physicians expressed empathy and positiveness to Hispanic and non-Hispanic White patients during primary-care visits. Their results showed that physicians expressed empathy at equal rates to Hispanic and non-Hispanic White patients. However, when examining only Hispanic patients, physicians were significantly more likely to express empathy to patients whom they knew better. Also, physicians expressed positiveness to non-Hispanic White patients more often than to Hispanic patients.[58]

Researchers in Australia sought to identify communication factors affecting health care for Aboriginal patients from the Yolngu language group of northeast Arnhem Land. In this study, interactions between Aboriginal patients and health care workers (non-Aboriginals) were videotaped and in-depth interviews about perceptions of the interaction were conducted with all participants, in their first language. The authors report that a shared understanding of key health-related concepts was rarely achieved. Moreover, they report that miscommunication between the health care staff and Aboriginal patients often went unrecognized. Sources of problematic communication included a lack of patient understanding of the language, a lack of medical knowledge by the Aboriginals, and marginalization of the Aboriginals by the health care workers. The authors concluded that communication problems were so pervasive that even trained interpreters provided only a marginal solution.[59]

As we saw in Chapter 8 on nonverbal communication, a person's accent plays a role in how that person is perceived by others, especially if the person speaks with a nonnative accent. In one study by Donald Rubin, Pamela Healy, T. Clifford Gardiner, Richard Zath, and Cynthia Partain Moore, participants were exposed to recordings of a physician speaking in an Asian accent and in a standard English accent. Participants then rated the physician's superiority, interpersonal attractiveness, dynamism, professional competence, their (the participants') intent to comply with the physician's instructions, and recall of the physician's instructions. Interestingly, the English-accented physician was rated higher than the Asian-accented speaker on only one of the variables—interpersonal attractiveness (Figure 11.4).[60]

In an intracultural study conducted in the United States, physician Rachel Johnson and her colleagues sought to determine whether the quality of communication during medical visits differed among African American and White patients in terms of the duration of the visit and average speech speed, patient-centered orientation (i.e., physician verbal dominance and physician patient-centeredness), and overall emotional tone (i.e., patient and physician positive affect). Data were collected from 30 White, 21 African American, 9 Asian or Indian American, and 1 other race/ethnicity physicians. The results showed that physicians were more verbally dominant and engaged in less patient-centered communication with African American patients than with White patients. Both African American patients and their physicians exhibited lower levels of positive affect than did White patients and their physicians.[61]

In another study, similar to the one reported above, Johnson and several of her colleagues compared patient–physician communication in same-race and different-race doctor–patient visits and examined whether communication behaviors could explain differences in patient ratings of satisfaction and participatory decision making with their physicians. In the study, African American and White patients received care from 31 physicians (of whom 18 were African American and 13 were White). Patients completed scales designed to measure their perceptions of physician patient-centeredness, physician participatory decision-making styles, and overall satisfaction with their physician. The results showed that same-race patient–doctor visits were longer and had higher ratings of patient positive affect compared with different-race doctor–patient visits. Patients in same-race doctor–patient visits were more satisfied and rated their physicians as more participatory in health care decision making than did those in different-race doctor–patient visits.[62]

While the research cited above is not an exhaustive account of the research done on intercultural communication in health care settings, it does allow us to draw some (tentative) conclusions about health care communication that seem rather counter-theoretical when it comes to culture. For example, theoretically, we might expect that patients in collectivistic, large–power-distance cultures might defer to their health care providers when making decisions about health care treatment options. But the research cited above suggests that patients in these cultures prefer to participate in such decision making. Of course, while these patients indicate that they would like to participate in such decision making, we do not know for sure if they actually do. Decades of research on accents has shown that persons with nonnative accents are perceived differently (i.e., negatively). Yet the study cited above suggests that in health care settings, the provider's nonnative accent has only a minimal effect on patient perceptions of him or her. The one area of research cited above that seems consistent with

Figure 11.4   Physician and patient communication and decision making vary across cultures.

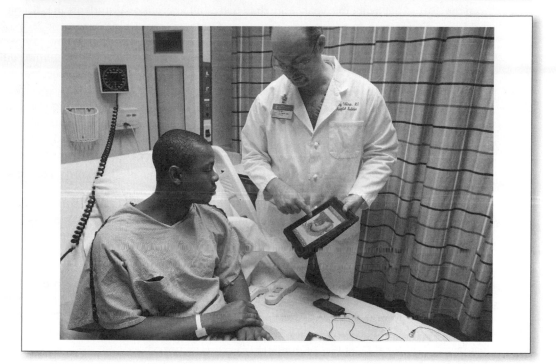

many of the theories discussed in this text is patient–provider communication within the United States, particularly with microcultural groups and health care providers. The research in this area suggests that microcultural group status does affect health care communication between patient and provider.

INTERCULTURAL COMMUNICATION AND EDUCATIONAL SETTINGS

One type of relationship that exists in every culture is the student–teacher relationship. And in all cultures, students learn and teachers teach. Students can learn by seeing, hearing, reflecting, experiencing, reasoning, memorizing, and even intuiting. Teachers can teach by lecturing, demonstrating, discussing, questioning, and applying principles. But *how* students go about learning and teachers go about teaching may vary considerably across cultures.

And, as in the health care context, virtually all the interactions within an educational/classroom setting are face to face (online courses notwithstanding; although, in the United States the majority of prospective students prefer the in-class experience over online courses).[63]

In the United States and abroad, grade school and high school teachers, as well as college professors, are finding their classrooms filled with students from various cultures. According to the Institute of International Education, during the 2011–2012 academic year, there were nearly 800,000 international students attending U.S. colleges and universities, a 6% increase from the 2010–2011 academic year. More than half of all international students in U.S. colleges and universities come from just four countries. Students from China represent 25% of all international students studying in the United States. Students from India represent 13%, South Korea 9.5%, and Saudi Arabia 4.5%. These countries have some significant cultural differences compared with the United States. Interestingly, the United States' closest neighbors geographically—that is, Canada and Mexico—represent only 3.5% and 1.8%, respectively, of international college students studying in the United States. California has the highest number of international students, followed by New York, Texas, Massachusetts, and Illinois.[64]

Just under 300,000 U.S. college students studied abroad for academic credit during the 2010–2011 academic year, which is a modest 1.3% increase from the previous year. But U.S. student participation in study-abroad programs has nearly tripled in the past 20 years. The majority of U.S. college students (i.e., 55%) study abroad in Europe, about 15% in Latin America, and about 12% in Asia. For the top five study-abroad destinations for U.S. students, just over 12% of students choose the United Kingdom, 11% Italy, 9.5% Spain, 6.2% France, and 5.3% China.[65] Given the statistics cited here, it seems safe to say that considerable intercultural communication is occurring in college classrooms across the United States and abroad.

Within the United States, grade schools and high schools are also becoming more intercultural. As the microcultural group population grows, so does enrollment in our nation's schools. In 2011, among all public school students from prekindergarten through 12th grade, almost one in four (i.e., 23.9%) were Hispanic, almost double the percentage from 20 years ago. There will also be about 4 million students of Asian descent attending U.S. schools, or just over 7% of the total student population.[66]

Learning Styles Across Cultures

In Chapter 5, you were introduced to some of the ideas of Richard Nisbett, a distinguished professor at the University of Michigan, who has researched and written extensively about how humans process information. Nisbett points out that, historically, many of the most prominent psychologists in the 20th century strongly believed that basic human cognitive processes are universal (i.e., not cultural), that normal human beings are equipped with the same set of learning procedures, and that human thought processes work in much the same way regardless of the subject matter. Based on his research and that of others, Nisbett now believes that such assumptions may be at least partially incorrect and that culture plays a much more influential role in human learning processes than we once thought.[67]

One area of research in education that has received a substantial amount of attention is the subject of learning styles. Proponents of the learning style approach (e.g., educators, psychologists, sociologists, counselors) maintain that individuals have their own personal learning style—that is, their own unique way of gathering, storing, and retrieving information to solve problems. Many now believe that while learning is a universal feature among humans, specific information-processing abilities (i.e., learning styles) are acquired via culture and the socialization process. If we know and understand how people learn, we can then adapt our teaching methods to accommodate them. For example, might students from a large–power-distance culture be at a disadvantage in a classroom with a teacher who comes from a small–power-distance culture? What about students from a collectivistic culture being asked to work on projects alone, without the cooperation of others? Consider the following scenario from AnneMarie Pajewski and Luis Enriquez:

> When Hispanic students work in a group, not all are expected to do their equal share. A group member who does not happen to be working will not be offensive, while in an Anglo group of students, each is expected to do his/her share. The cooperative tendency of Hispanics can also be seen in sharing material objects and information. Sharing also means helping another student during a test, which is considered cheating in an Anglo culture. Recently, in the co-authors' ESOL class, composed of mostly Hispanics, a student was reprimanded by a non-Hispanic instructor for copying from another student's test. Both students were stunned and offended, because to them, they were helping each other, not cheating.[68]

One theory of learning styles is called experiential learning theory (ELT), developed by David Kolb.[69] Although not accepted by all learning theory scholars, Kolb's ELT model has received a substantial amount of attention in education and psychology and has been applied extensively in cross-cultural and intercultural research (see Figure 11.5).[70] Kolb's ELT model is based on the work of some of the major philosophers, psychologists, and education reformers of the 20th century, including John Dewey, Kurt Lewin, Jean Piaget, and Carl Rogers, among others. Kolb's central thesis is that learning occurs when knowledge is gained via the transformation of experience. In other words, we learn when we take our experiences and transform or convert them into knowledge. He argues that knowledge, and hence learning, results from (1) grasping experience and (2) transforming experience.

Figure 11.5 Kolb's model of experiential learning.

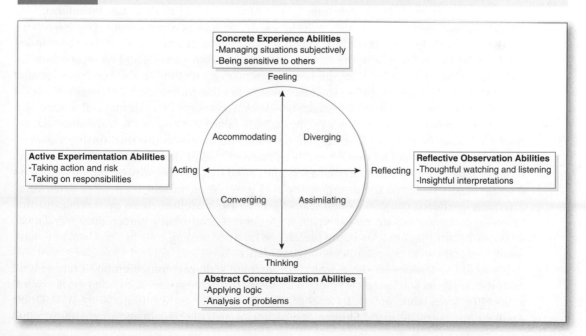

According to Kolb, grasping experience means to seize or take hold of it. This includes concrete experience (CE) and abstract conceptualization (AC). In explaining CE, Kolb argues that in grasping experience, some people take in new information directly via tangible and empirical methods; that is, they need to see, hear, smell, touch, or taste it. For them, experience needs to be real or factual. Others tend to take in new information via symbolic means (i.e., AC). These people think, analyze, and plan abstractly. In transforming experience, some people tend to observe others who are involved in the experience and reflect on it (i.e., reflective observation, or RO). Then, there are those who approach experience and actively participate in it (i.e., active experimentation, or AE).[71]

Kolb maintains that not all learning situations are equal, and learners must select which learning abilities are best suited for the specific learning situation they are facing. For example, Kolb points out that a person learning how to drive a car needs to tap into CE, but when learning via the owner's manual about how the car functions, he or she uses AC. So, when faced with unique learning situations, we choose between one or the other grasping experience options—CE or AC—and one or the other transforming experience options—AE or RO. Over time, Kolb maintains, humans develop a preferred way of learning based on their past experiences and especially their socialization. Specifically, one's choice of grasping experience (i.e., CE or AC) and one's choice of transforming experience (i.e., AE or RO) define that person's preferred learning style, of which there are four: diverging, assimilating, converging, and accommodating.[72]

The person adopting a *diverging* style of learning combines CE and RO. These people view concrete situations from several different points of view. Kolb describes these people as having broad cultural interests, being interested in people, enjoying group work, and tending to be imaginative and creative. The *assimilating* learning style is the combination of AC and RO. These learners prefer to put information into concise logical form. They prefer theories that are logically sound, without much regard for their practicality. They prefer to focus on ideas rather than people. Kolb speculates that persons interested in the sciences might be assimilating types. *Converging* learners combine AC and AE. They find practical uses for information and prefer technical tasks and problems to social and interpersonal issues. These learners experiment with new ideas. Kolb speculates that environmental scientists or economists might prefer this style. Finally, the *accommodating* style combines CE and AE. Accommodating learners prefer "hands-on" experience. They tend to act on intuition rather than logic and prefer to work with others, rather than technology, to solve problems.[73]

Kolb and others in this area of research believe that a variety of factors may influence one's preferred learning style. One factor is culture. Yoshitaka Yamazaki of the International University of Japan conducted an extensive review of literature on the relationship between culture and experiential learning styles. He reviewed studies that investigated the learning styles of Japanese and American managers and found that the majority of, but not all, Japanese managers preferred the diverging learning style, while a slight majority of Americans managers preferred the converging learning style. He attributes these preferences to the Japanese tendency toward collectivism, high context, and strong uncertainty avoidance. Likewise, he attributes the American preference for a converging style to American individualism, low context, and weak uncertainty avoidance.[74]

Yamazaki also reviewed the research on learning style preference among Chinese and American teachers and found that most of the Chinese teachers were distributed more toward a diverging style, while American teachers tended to prefer an accommodating style. Once again, he attributes this to the Chinese orientation toward collectivism and strong uncertainty avoidance. That not all teachers from either culture preferred these styles is important to note, because some teachers in each group preferred other learning styles. For example, Yamazaki reviewed the research on learning style preference among French, German, and Quebecois students of business administration, and while there were differences among the three groups, each group's overall preferred learning style was assimilating. But although a plurality of 43% of German students preferred the assimilating style, nearly 33% preferred a converging style. Among the Quebecois students, 38% preferred assimilating but 25% preferred a diverging style. Among the French students, a plurality of 34% preferred assimilating while 28% preferred a diverging style.[75]

The research cited above tells us that culture seems to play a role in preferences for learning styles. But how much of a role does culture play? Simy Joy and Kolb sought to answer that question. Specifically, they aimed to assess the relative influence of culture on learning style preference in comparison with sex (i.e., male/female), age, level of education (i.e., secondary school, college graduate, graduate degree), and area of specialization (i.e., humanities and fine arts, social professional, basic sciences and mathematics, and applied science professional) of students born in and currently residing in seven nations: the United States, Italy, Germany, Poland, Brazil, India, and Singapore. Although the influence of culture was quite small, Simy and Kolb report that a preference for AC over CE was explained by a combination of culture, gender, level of education, and area of specialization. The variability in preference for AE over RO was accounted for only by age and area of specialization, however. The influence of culture was not significant. When comparing the relative influence across learning styles, area of specialization seemed to carry more influence than did culture. In the second part of their study, they examined the influence of individual culture dimensions on learning style preferences. They found that individuals tend to have a more abstract learning style in cultures that are collectivistic and uncertainty avoidant. Individuals may have a more reflective learning style in countries that are high in collectivism and uncertainty avoidance. In general, their results support the contention that culture affects learning style preference, but its influence is rather small and certainly not unilateral.[76]

Teacher Immediacy in the Classroom and Across Cultures

In the past 30 years, the topic of teacher immediacy has received a great deal of attention in the communication literature. The concept of immediacy stems from the work of psychologist Albert Mehrabian and refers to those verbal and nonverbal behaviors that reduce the physiological and psychological distance between interactants. Researchers in communication have extended the concept of immediacy to the classroom and, specifically, teacher immediacy. Here, teacher immediacy refers to the verbal and nonverbal communication expressed by teachers that reduces the physiological and psychological distance between teachers and students.[77] In the United States, verbal immediacy behaviors include the judicious use of humor, self-disclosure, narration (storytelling), and the prosocial use of certain types of power, such as expert power and referent power. Other verbal immediacy behaviors might include addressing students by their first names, initiating conversation with students before and after class about topics unrelated to class, and encouraging students to ask questions and discuss issues during class. Typical nonverbal immediacy behaviors include smiling, moderate gesturing, moving around the class instead of standing behind a lectern, direct eye contact, and casual dress. To be sure, these might not be the behaviors considered immediate in other cultures.

Figure 11.6   Teacher immediacy varies considerably across cultures.

One of the most consistent findings in the literature is that teacher immediacy has a positive effect on perceived cognitive learning, affective learning, and behavioral intentions of students to engage in the lessons, theories, and behaviors taught in class. But the research has also shown that moderate amounts of immediacy produce more positive learning outcomes than does too much immediacy. So, while using humor in the classroom is considered immediate, students do not want a class that's nothing but one-liners. Of course, to the extent that teacher immediacy is a function of communication, it must be considered a cross-cultural phenomenon (Figure 11.6).[78]

Consider the following description of a typical Chinese classroom, provided by Yuqin Zhao from the Harbin Institute of Technology in China:

> The classroom discourse in China is more oriented towards a hierarchical face system and assumes more respect from students toward the teacher. The teacher would value those who are more obedient and quiet in class, listen to him and follow his instruction with no conditions. He prefers standing in the front of the classroom with more dignity and authority, doing a most noble job of transmitting knowledge and truth to his students. In Chinese classrooms, the atmosphere is usually serious. Students should sit in lines and rows straightly, listen to the teacher and should not interrupt the teacher's talk with questions. Students should show respect to their

teachers both in class and out of class by greeting the teachers first. It is regarded impolite and even rude for students to call their teachers by their name. In a Chinese classroom, students always address their teacher very formally with a title of "teacher" plus his surname, such as "Teacher Zhang." This is the case for students of all ages, from children in kindergarten to doctoral students in universities. No matter where and when, students should always address the people who had ever taught them with "teacher" formally, even outside school and after their graduation. Chinese teachers also address their students in a very formal way, by their full names, never by their given names. In China, the relationship between teachers and students is more hierarchical, formal and distant.[79]

A number of cross-cultural comparisons of teacher immediacy have been conducted. For example, Jim Neuliep found that U.S. college students rated their U.S. professors as more verbally and nonverbally immediate than did Japanese college students in rating their Japanese professors. Neuliep attributed this to the Japanese high-context and large–power-distance tendencies. In this study, Neuliep also found that while U.S. professors were rated as more immediate than Japanese professors, there were strong correlations between teacher immediacy and cognitive, affective, and behavioral learning with each group of students. In other words, as a professor's immediacy ratings increased, both U.S. and Japanese students responded that they learned more from that professor.[80]

In a 2011 study by Kemal Sinan Özmen from Gazi University in Turkey, student teachers in Japan, Turkey, and the United States completed a nonverbal immediacy scale and a questionnaire about its importance in teaching. The findings indicated that U.S. teachers rated their nonverbal immediacy higher than did teachers in Turkey or Japan (in that order) but that each of the three cultures considered nonverbal immediacy as a requisite part of effective teaching and as positively correlated with effective teaching. Incidentally, the study also found that U.S. student teachers believe "touching" to be a critical variable in defining effective teaching.[81]

In 2001, K. David Roach and Paul Byrne conducted a cross-cultural comparison of instructor communication (i.e., nonverbal immediacy and learning outcomes) in German and American classrooms. In their study, U.S. students and German students rated their instructors' nonverbal immediacy and perceived cognitive and affective learning. Their results showed that U.S. instructors were perceived as more nonverbally immediate than German instructors. U.S. students also reported more cognitive learning than did their German counterparts. Interestingly, in each culture, nonverbal immediacy was significantly linked with cognitive and affective learning.[82]

In 2005, Roach and his colleagues compared nonverbal immediacy between French and U.S. instructors. Like the results reported above, U.S. instructors were perceived by U.S. students as more immediate than were French instructors (by French students). In each culture, however, instructor nonverbal immediacy was found to be positively related to student affective learning, positive affect toward instructor, cognitive learning, and ratings of instruction. Instructor nonverbal immediacy, though positively related to these learning outcomes in both cultures, was significantly stronger for American students when compared with French students. Roach speculates that this difference may be linked to power distance, since France is considered to have a larger power distance than the United States. American students expect less power distance between themselves and their instructors than do French students, who recognize the student–teacher status difference. Hence, Roach concludes that French instructors may see no need to exercise nonverbal immediacy.[83]

Scott Johnson and Ann Miller compared teacher immediacy in the United States and Kenya. Students in both countries rated their teachers' verbal and nonverbal immediacy and then rated how much they learned in their classes with these teachers. Their results showed that Kenyan and U.S. students differed significantly on ratings of their teachers' verbal and nonverbal immediacy. U.S. teachers were rated higher in both. However, no significant differences were found between Kenyan and U.S. students regarding the amount of learning they reported as occurring in their classes, although the Kenyan sample scores were lower than those of the U.S. sample on all measures. And, although Kenyan students rated their teachers lower on both verbal and nonverbal immediacy than did U.S. students, there were strong correlations between immediacy and learning among the Kenyans. In other words, to the extent that their teachers were immediate, Kenyan students reported learning more. Johnson and Miller speculate that other cultural variables may mediate the influence of immediacy on learning outcomes. For example, they point out that Kenya is a large–power-distance culture. Students who recognize the high-status role expectations within a large–power-distance culture may not respond as strongly to immediacy displays within high/low-status relationships and yet may still learn a lot.[84]

Jim McCroskey and his colleagues compared teacher nonverbal immediacy and affective learning outcomes across four cultures: Puerto Rico, Finland, Australia, and the United States. Their results showed that the Puerto Rican and U.S. teachers did not differ from each other but were perceived as significantly more nonverbally immediate than teachers in Australia and Finland. The Finnish teachers were perceived as less nonverbally immediate than teachers from the other three cultures. Yet, in each culture, teacher nonverbal immediacy was found to be positively correlated with affect toward the content being taught (i.e., affective learning). In other words, asserts McCroskey, whether the culture favors high or low immediacy, if the teacher is relatively more immediate, the student's affective learning is enhanced.[85]

What the research on teacher immediacy shows us is that while perceptions of teacher immediacy vary across cultures, teacher immediacy is almost always associated with positive learning outcomes. So even in cultures where teachers may not be perceived as immediate—as U.S. teachers are—as immediacy increases, students report that they learn more cognitively, affectively, and behaviorally.

Some Recommendations for the Intercultural Classroom

So we know that students across cultures have different learning styles, and we know that teachers across cultures have different teaching styles. Hence, in an intercultural classroom, students and teachers prefer to learn and teach differently. Richard M. Felder, the Hoechst Celanese Professor Emeritus at North Carolina State University, has authored or coauthored hundreds of papers on engineering and science education. Felder is also the codirector of the National Effective Teaching Institute. In recognizing the differences in learning and teaching styles, Felder offers some recommendations that may be helpful for teachers in an intercultural classroom.[86]

1. *Motivate learning.* Felder recommends that when teaching new material (i.e., material that is new to the students), one should try to teach the material in the context of students' experiences, both past and future.

2. *Balance concrete and conceptual information.* Recall from Kolb's model that concrete thinkers take in new information directly via tangible and empirical methods; that is, they need to see, hear, smell, touch, or taste it. Conceptual thinkers tend to take in new information via symbolic means. These people think, analyze, and plan abstractly.

3. *Balance structured and unstructured activities.* Use teaching approaches that emphasize formal training with open-ended, unstructured activities that emphasize conversation and the students' cultural context.

4. *Make liberal use of visuals.* Use photographs, films, videos, and live dramatizations to illustrate lessons.

5. *Don't just lecture.* In addition to lecturing, provide intervals for students to reflect on what they have learned. Hold discussions, allow students to ask questions, or have them write reflective essays.

6. *Allow students to cooperate on some assignments.* Felder argues that active learners learn best when they interact with others.

CHAPTER SUMMARY

Doing business with and managing people in a work setting; providing health care; and teaching students in a culture other than one's own are daunting tasks indeed. This chapter has discussed how the principles presented throughout the text can be applied across cultures to the business world, the health care context, and the classroom setting. An understanding of the cultural, microcultural, environmental, perceptual, sociorelational, verbal, nonverbal, and relational contexts of the native and host cultures increases the probability of being an effective and productive manager, health care provider, or teacher across cultures. Managers, health care practitioners, and teachers who understand the intercultural context are in a much better position to succeed.

Visit the student study site at www.sagepub.com/neuliep6e for e-flashcards, web quizzes, web resources, and more.

DISCUSSION QUESTIONS

1. How are the dominant cultural values of the United States reflected in U.S. management styles and U.S. company policies?

2. How might the U.S. management style of participative management affect a U.S. manager in Mexico? In China?

3. How might the U.S. emphasis on time (i.e., monochronic) affect how you would do business in Mexico?

4. What considerations would you make in preparing for a presentation in a German or Chinese company?

5. How do patients across cultures prefer to make medical decisions?

6. What are some of the factors that affect patient–provider communication?

7. Are learning styles among students different across cultures?

8. Do teachers across cultures differ in immediacy?

9. How does teacher immediacy affect learning?

KEY TERMS

cultural context   403

environmental context   404

health communication   418

immediacy   427

learning styles   424

organizational culture   403

patient–provider communication   419

perceptual context   404

power distance   403

NOTES

1. Trompenaars, F. (1994). *Riding the Waves of Culture: Understanding Diversity in Global Business.* Burr Ridge, IL: Irwin, p. 14.

2. Fishman, C. (2006). *The Wal-Mart Effect.* New York: Penguin.

3. Landler, M., & Barbaro, M. (2006, August 2). International Business; No, Not Always. *New York Times,* pp. A1, A3.

4. Ibid.

5. Rosenzweig, P. M. (1994). *National Culture and Management* (Teaching Note 9-394-177). Boston: Harvard Business School.

6. Ibid.

7. This scene is adapted from Harris, P. R., & Moran, R. T. (1996). *Managing Cultural Differences.* Houston: Gulf.

8. Harris & Moran, *Managing Cultural Differences.*

9. Pew Global Attitudes Project. (2005, June 23). *American Character Gets Mixed Reviews: U.S. Image Up Slightly, but Still Negative: 16-Nation Pew Global Attitudes Survey.* Washington, DC: Pew Research Center. Retrieved from http://pewglobal.org/files/pdf/247.pdf

10. Trompenaars, *Riding the Waves of Culture.*

11. U.S. Census Bureau. (2010, October). *Top 10 Countries With Which the U.S. Trades.* Retrieved from http://www .census.gov/foreign-trade/top/dst/2010/10/balance.html; U.S. Census Bureau. (2010, October). *Top Trading Partners: Total Trade, Imports, Exports.* Retrieved from http://www.census. gov/foreign-trade/statistics/highlights/top/top1010yr.html

12. Grainger, R. J., & Miyamoto, T. (2003). Human Values and HRM Practice: The Japanese Shukko System. *Journal of Human Values, 9,* 105–115.

13. Dore, R. (2004). *Japanese Style Management: Has it Survived? Will it Survive?* Research Institute of Economy, Trade, and Industry, IAA. Retrieved from http:// www.rieti.go.jp/en/events/bbl/04090801.html

14. Brown, W. S., Lubove, R. E., & Kwalwasser, J. (1994). Karoshi: Alternative Perspectives of Japanese Management Styles. *Business Horizons, 37,* 58–61; Ministry of Health, Labour, and Welfare. (2012). *Provisional Report of Monthly Labour Survey.* Retrieved from http://www.mhlw. go.jp/english/database/db-l/25/2507pe/2507pe.html

15. Rao, A., Hashimoto, K., & Rao, A. (1997). Universal and Culturally Specific Aspects of Influence: A Study of Japanese Managers. *Leadership Quarterly, 8,* 295–313.

16. Ibid.

17. Ibid.

18. Lewis, R. D. (2006). *When Cultures Collide: Leading Across Cultures.* Boston: Nicholas Brealey.

19. Central Intelligence Agency. (2011). *The World Factbook: Germany.* Retrieved from https://www.cia.gov/library/publications/the-world-factbook/

20. William Drake & Associates. (1997). *Managing Business Relationships in Germany.* Retrieved from www.culturebank.com/demo/demogermany/sld001.htm

21. Glunk, U. Wilderom, C., & Ogilvie, R. (1996). Finding the Key to German-Style Management. *International Studies of Management and Organization, 26,* 93–108.

22. Ibid.

23. Hall, E. T., & Hall, M. R. (1990). *Understanding Cultural Differences.* Yarmouth, ME: Intercultural Press.

24. Ibid.

25. German Lessons. (1996). *The Economist, 340,* 59.

26. Drake & Associates, *Managing Business Relationships in Germany;* Ibid.

27. U.S. Census Bureau. (2011). *Foreign Trade Statistics, 2011;* U.S. Central Intelligence Agency. (2011). *The World Factbook: Mexico.* Retrieved from https://www.cia.gov/library/publications/the-world-factbook/

28. Crouch, E. C. (2004). *Mexicans and Americans: Cracking the Cultural Code.* Yarmouth, ME: Intercultural Press; Pelled, L. H., & Xin, K. R. (1997). Work Values and the Human Resource Management Implications: A Theoretical Comparison of China, Mexico, and the United States. *Journal of Applied Management Studies, 6,* 185–199.

29. Ibid.

30. Hamlin, K., & Yanping, L. (2010, August 16). China Overtakes Japan as World's Second-Biggest Economy. *Bloomberg News.* Retrieved from http://www.bloomberg.com/news/2010-08-16/china-economy-passes-japan-s-in-second-quarter-capping-three-decade-rise.html

31. *Doing Business 2011: Making a Difference for Entrepreneurs.* (2011). The World Bank. Retrieved February 19, 2011, from http://www.doingbusiness.org/data/exploreeconomies/china/

32. Laroche, L. (2003). *Managing Cultural Diversity in Technical Professions.* Amsterdam: Butterworth-Heinemann.

33. Tang, J., & Ward, A. (2003). *The Changing Face of Chinese Management.* New York: Routledge.

34. Ibid.

35. Chen, P. P. W. (2004, July 30). China Business Etiquette: Gift Giving. *Executive Planet.*

36. Chan, M. (2013, January 21). *WHO Director-General Addresses Members of the Executive Board.* Retrieved from http://www.who.int/dg/speeches/2013/eb132_20130121/en/index.html

37. Knight, M. (2011, October 24). *Smartphone detects danger in a heartbeat.* Cable News Network. Retrieved from http://www.cnn.com/2011/10/24/tech/mobile/heart-monitor-smartphone-app/index.html

38. Rampini, S. K., Schneemann, M., Rentsch, K., & Bächli, E. B. (2002). Camphor Intoxication After Cao Gío (Coin Rubbing). *Journal of the American Medical Association, 288*(1), 45.

39. Martin, T., Campo, S., & Askelson, N. M. (2012). African American Women and Weight Loss: Disregarding Environmental Challenges. *Journal of Transcultural Nursing, 23*(1), 38–45.

40. Schumacher, G. (2010). Culture Care Meanings, Beliefs, and Practices in Rural Dominican Republic. *Journal of Transcultural Nursing, 21*(1), 93–103.

41. Landrine, H., & Klonoff, E. A. (1992). Culture and Health-Related Schemas: A Review and Proposal for Interdisciplinary Integration. *Health Psychology, 11*(4), 267–276. (Quote on p. 267)

42. Helmen, C. G. (2007). *Culture, Health, and Illness* (5th ed.). London: Hodder Arnold.

43. Ibid.

44. Tortora, B. (2010). *Witchcraft Believers in Sub-Saharan Africa Rate Lives Worse.* Retrieved from http://www.gallup.com/poll/142640/witchcraft-believers-sub-saharan-africa-rate-lives-worse.aspx

45. Helman, *Culture, Health, and Illness.*

46. Ibid.

47. These statistics were taken from the Centers for Medicare & Medicaid, Office of the Actuary, National Statistics Group, U.S. Department of Commerce, Bureau of Economic Analysis, and the U.S. Bureau of the Census. Retrieved from http://www.cms.gov/Research-Statistics-Data-and-Systems/Statistics-Trends-and-Reports/NationalHealthExpendData/Downloads/Proj2011PDF.pdf

48. Bradley-Wright, K., Sparks, L., & O'Hair, H. D. (2013). *Health Communication in the 21st Century.* West Sussex, UK: Wiley-Blackwell.

49. Centers for Disease Control and Prevention. (2011). *Health Communication Basics.* Retrieved from http://www.cdc.gov/healthcommunication/healthbasics/whatishc.html

50. Wohl, J. (1989). Integration of Cultural Awareness Into Psychotherapy. *American Journal of Psychotherapy, 43,* 343–355.

51. Carmichael, T. (2013). Cultural Competence: A Necessity for the 21st Century [Letter to the Editor]. *Journal of Transcultural Nursing, 22,* 5–6.

52. Roter, D. (2000). The Enduring and Evolving Nature of the Patient–Physician Relationship. *Patient Education and Counseling, 39,* 5–15.

53. Bennett, K., Smith, D. H., & Irwin, H. (1999). Preferences for Participation in Medical Decisions in China. *Health Communication, 11*(3), 261–284.

54. Ibid., p. 281.

55. Kim, M. S., Smith, D. H., & Yueguo, G. (1999). Medical Decision-Making and Chinese Patient's Self-Construals. *Health Communication, 11*(3), 249–260.

56. Smith, D., & Smith, S. J. (1999). Chinese Elders' Communication About Medicine. *Health Communication, 11*(3), 237–248.

57. Ibid.

58.   Sleath, B., Rubin, R. H., & Arrey-Wastavino, A. (2000). Physician Expression of Empathy and Positiveness to Hispanic and Non-Hispanic White Patients During Medical Encounters. *Family Medicine, 32*(2), 91–96.

59.   Cass, A., Lowell, A., Christie, M., Snelling, P. L., Flack, M., Marrnganyin, B., et al. (2002). Sharing the True Stories: Improving Communication Between Aboriginal Patients and Healthcare Workers. *Medical Journal of Australia, 176*(10), 466–470.

60.   Rubin, D. L., Healy, P., Gardiner, T. C., Zath, R. C., & Moore, C. P. (1997). Nonnative Physicians as Message Sources: Effects of Accent and Ethnicity on Patient's Responses to AIDS Prevention Counseling. *Health Communication, 9*(4), 351–368.

61.   Johnson, R. L., Roter, D., Powe, N. R., & Cooper, L. A. (2004). Patient Race/Ethnicity and Quality of Patient–Physician Communication During Medical Visits. *American Journal of Public Health, 94,* 2048–2090.

62.   Cooper, L. A., Roter, D. L., Johnson, R. L., Ford, D. E., Steinwachs, D. M., & Powe, N. R. (2003). Patient-Centered Communication, Ratings of Care, and Concordance of Patient and Physician Race. *Annals of Internal Medicine, 139,* 907–915.

63.   Lytle, R. (2012, October 18). Interest in Online Courses Could Be Peaking. *US News & World Report.* Retrieved from http://www.usnews.com/education/online-education/articles/2012/10/18/interest-in-online-courses-could-be-peaking

64.   Institute of International Education. (2012). *Opendoors 2012 "fast facts."* Retrieved from http://www.iie.org/opendoors

65.   Ibid.

66.   Davis, J. W., & Bauman, K. (2011). *School Enrollment in the United States: 2008 Population Characteristics.* Washington, DC: U.S. Department of Commerce, Economics and Statistics Administration, U.S. Census Bureau; Fry, R., & Lopez, M. H. (2012). *Hispanic Student Enrollments Reach New Highs in 2011.* Washington, DC: Pew Hispanic Center.

67.   Nisbett, R. E., & Norenzayan, A. (2002). Culture and Cognition. In D. L. Medin & H. Pashler (Eds.), *Stevens Handbook of Experimental Psychology* (3rd ed., Vol. 2, pp. 561–597). New York: John Wiley.

68.   Pajewski, A. M., & Enriquez, L. (1996). *Teaching From a Hispanic Perspective: A Handbook for Non-Hispanic Adult Educators.* Phoenix: Arizona Adult Literacy and Technology Resource Center.

69.   Joy, S., & Kolb, D. A. (2009). Are There Cultural Differences in Learning Style? *International Journal of Intercultural Relations, 33,* 69–85; Kolb, D. A. (1984). *Experiential Learning: Experience as a Source of Learning and Development.* Englewood Cliffs, NJ: Prentice Hall.

70.   There are several graphic variations of Kolb's model. This one is based on the following sources: Joy, S., & Kolb, D. A. (2009). Are There Cultural Differences in Learning Style? *International Journal of Intercultural Relations, 33,* 69–85; Yamazaki, Y. (2005). Learning Styles and Typologies of Cultural Differences: A Theoretical and Empirical Comparison. *International Journal of Intercultural Relations, 29,* 521–548. Joy, S., & Kolb, D. A. (2009). Are There Cultural Differences in Learning Style? *International Journal of Intercultural Relations, 33,* 69–85.

71.   Kolb's model is described and explained in a variety of sources. The source used here is Kolb, D. A., Boyatzis, R. E., & Mainemelis, C. (2001). Experiential Learning Theory: Previous Research and New Directions. In R. J. Sternberg & L. F. Zhang (Eds.), *Perspective on Cognitive Learning and Thinking Styles* (pp. 227–247). Mahwah, NJ: Lawrence Erlbaum.

72.   Ibid.

73.   Ibid.

74.   Yamazaki, Learning Styles and Typologies of Cultural Differences.

75.   Ibid.

76.   Joy & Kolb, Are There Cultural Differences in Learning Style?

77.   Andersen, J. F. (1979). Teacher Immediacy as a Predictor of Teaching Effectiveness. In D. Nimmo (Ed.), *Communication Yearbook 3* (pp. 543–559). New Brunswick, NJ: Transaction Books; Mehrabian, A. (1971). *Silent Messages.* Belmont, CA: Wadsworth.

78.   Neuliep, J. W. (1997). A Cross-Cultural Comparison of Teacher Immediacy in American and Japanese College Classrooms. *Communication Research, 24,* 431–451.

79.   Zhao, Y. (2007). Cultural Conflicts in an Intercultural Classroom Discourse and Interpretations From a Cultural Perspective. *Intercultural Communication Studies, XVI,* 129–136.

80.   Neuliep, A Cross-Cultural Comparison of Teacher Immediacy in American and Japanese College Classrooms.

81.   Özmen, K. S. (2011). Perception of Nonverbal Immediacy and Effective Teaching Among Student Teachers: A Study Across Cultural Extremes. *International Online Journal of Educational Sciences, 3*(3), 865–881.

82.   Roach, K. D., & Byrne, P. (2001). A Cross-Cultural Comparison of Instructor Communication in American and German Classrooms. *Communication Education, 50*(1), 1–14.

83.   Roach, K. D., Cornett-DeVito, M. M., & DeVito, R. (2005). A Cross-Cultural Comparison of Instructor Communication in American and French Classrooms. *Communication Quarterly, 53*(1), 87–107.

84.   Johnson, S. D., & Miller, A. N. (2002). A Cross-Cultural Study of Immediacy, Credibility, and Learning in the U.S. and Kenya. *Communication Education, 51*(3), 280–292.

85.   McCroskey, J. C., Fayer, J. M., Richmond, V. P., Sallinen, A., & Barraclough, R. A. (1996). A Multicultural Examination of the Relationship Between Nonverbal Immediacy and Affective Learning. *Communication Quarterly, 44*(3), 297–307.

86.   Felder, R. M., & Henriques, E. R. (1995). Learning and Teaching Styles in Foreign and Second Language Education. *Foreign Language Annals, 28*(1), 21–31.

CHAPTER 12

Acculturation, Culture Shock, and Intercultural Competence

CHAPTER OBJECTIVES

After reading this chapter, you should be able to

1. define acculturation,

2. identify and discuss the factors that facilitate or hinder acculturation,

3. define and name the stages of culture shock,

4. recognize and discuss the causes of culture shock,

5. assess your level of culture shock,

6. identify the five personality dimensions linked to success in long-term intercultural encounters,

7. identify and discuss the four components of intercultural communication competence, and

8. assess your intercultural willingness to communicate.

Nothing so sensitizes us to our own culture as living outside it and then trying to return.

—John Condon and Fathi Yousef[1]

————

Having read the previous 11 chapters of this book, you may well be motivated to go out and interact with people from different cultures. Perhaps you are even ready to travel abroad! In either case, remember that intercultural communication assumes the principle of difference. Not all intercultural communication is successful. This chapter focuses on three important features associated with intercultural communication as they relate to traveling abroad to foreign cultures: (a) acculturation, (b) culture shock, and (c) intercultural communication competence. **Acculturation** is the process whereby you adapt to a new culture by adopting its values, attitudes, and practices. **Culture shock** is a multifaceted experience resulting from the stress associated with entering a new culture. **Intercultural communication competence** is defined as the degree to which you effectively adapt your verbal and nonverbal messages to the appropriate cultural context. When you communicate with someone from a different culture, you will have to adjust and modify the kinds of verbal and nonverbal messages you send. This process requires that you have some *knowledge* about the person with whom you are communicating, that you are *motivated* to communicate with him or her, and that you have the appropriate verbal and nonverbal *skills* to encode and decode messages. Each of these variables affects the success rate of your intercultural communication experiences. When individuals or groups enter a new culture, they are faced with a different set of values, different behavioral patterns, and a different verbal and nonverbal communication system. In most (perhaps all) cases, such people are affected by their new cultural surroundings.

ACCULTURATION

Acculturation is the term used to describe what happens when people from one culture enter a different culture. Many years ago, acculturation was defined by Robert Redfield, Ralph Linton, and Melville Herskovits as "those phenomena which result when groups of individuals having different cultures come into continuous first-hand contact with subsequent changes in the original culture pattern of either or both groups."[2] John Berry, well-known for his work on acculturation, argues that in practice, when two different cultural groups engage in continuous contact, one of the two groups will induce more change than the other. For example, when immigrants enter the United States, they are probably going to experience more change than the people already living here. Berry also distinguishes between acculturation at the group level and at the individual level. He contends that the distinction is important because not all members of the group experience the same levels of acculturation.[3]

According to Berry, in pluralistic, diverse societies such as the United States, three factors bring cultural groups together: mobility, voluntariness, and permanence. For example, regarding mobility, some groups experience acculturation because they have moved into a new culture—as is the case for immigrants and refugees such as the Hmong people of Laos, who came to the United States. Other groups experience acculturation because they have had a new culture thrust on them, as is the case for indigenous peoples such as Native Americans. Some groups enter acculturation voluntarily, such as Mexican immigrants to the United States, whereas others experience acculturation involuntarily, as did African slaves brought to the United States. Finally, some groups will experience a relatively permanent acculturation change, as African Americans and Mexican Americans have, whereas others face only temporary acculturation, as do exchange students studying abroad or expatriates in temporary job transfers. Berry maintains that despite the sometimes dramatic differences in circumstances of acculturating groups, the overall acculturation process is universal across groups.[4]

Acculturative Stress

Most people experience a degree of stress and strain when they enter a culture different from their own. Acculturation is often marked by physical and psychological changes that occur as a result of the adaptation required to function in a new and different cultural context. People adapting to new cultures face changes in their diet, climate, housing, communication, role prescriptions, and media consumption, as well as in myriad rules, norms, and values of a new and (relatively) dissimilar culture. Moreover, such persons are isolated from familiar social networks and may experience problems with language, unemployment, and discrimination. The stress associated with such changes, known as **acculturative stress**, is marked by a reduction in one's physical and mental health.[5]

Many immigrant groups in the United States experience acculturative stress. A rather substantial body of research has documented the effects of acculturative stress on America's largest microcultural group, Hispanics. Alexis Miranda and Kenneth Matheny point out that among Hispanics, acculturative stress is related to decreased self-efficacy expectations, decreased career aspirations, depression, and suicidal ideation (especially in Hispanic adolescents).[6] In their work with Hispanics, Julie and David Smart have observed that acculturative stress is associated with fatalistic thinking. They argue that acculturative stress has a lifelong effect on Hispanics' psychological well-being, decision-making abilities, occupational effectiveness, and physical health. They contend that for Hispanic immigrants, the most significant aspect of acculturative stress is the loss of social support from the family. They maintain that this loss is particularly intense for Hispanics because of their collectivistic orientation. In fact, Hispanic women may be more likely than men to suffer from acculturative stress because their roles are clearly prescribed in their native culture. In the United States—an individualistic, equality-based society—women's roles are more open and unspecified.[7] Joseph Hovey, in his work, found that family dysfunction, separation from family, negative expectations for the future, and low income levels were significantly related to higher levels of acculturative stress.[8]

In an interesting line of research, Emeka Nwadiora and Harriette McAdoo investigated acculturative stress among Amerasian refugees in the United States. Amerasians are individuals born of American servicemen and Vietnamese or Cambodian women during the Vietnam War. Because of their mixed racial background, these children were considered half-breeds and social outcasts in their homeland. In 1987, Congress passed the Amerasian Homecoming Act, permitting all Amerasians and their immediate families (including wives, half-siblings, and mothers) to immigrate to the United States. Nwadiora and McAdoo report that Amerasians have faced pervasive prejudice in the United States, often by

Asians, Europeans, and especially African Americans. In their research, they found that the Amerasians experienced acculturative stress in the areas of spoken English, employment, and limited formal education. They also report that gender and race had no significant impact on acculturative stress.[9]

In addition to the above factors, Berry argues that the degree of acculturative stress experienced by people adapting to new cultures varies according to the similarities and dissimilarities between the host culture and the immigrants' native culture. To the extent that the cultures are more similar than different, less stress is experienced. Individual personal traits also play a role in the manifestation of acculturative stress. Berry notes that such characteristics as one's degree of previous exposure to the new culture; one's level of education; one's sex, age, language, race, and income; and one's psychological and spiritual strength all affect acculturative stress.[10] A well-educated woman from the United States may experience more acculturative stress than a well-educated man from the United States when entering a culture that does not recognize sexual equality (either socially or legally).

A Model of Acculturation

Acculturation is not unilateral; it is an interactive process between a culture and groups of people. When individuals or groups of individuals enter a new culture, they are often changed by the culture, but they also impact the culture in return. For example, although Mexican immigrants face challenges imposed on them by the dominant culture, their presence has changed the United States' cultural milieu, especially in places such as Texas and California. Young Kim's model of cultural adaptation takes into account both individual and cultural factors that affect acculturation. Kim argues that acculturation is not a linear, one-way process; rather, an interaction occurs between the stranger and the host culture. Kim argues that the role of communication, the role of the host environment, and the role of predisposition best explain the acculturation process (see Table 12.1).[11]

In terms of the role of communication, personal communication refers to the individual's host communication competence—that is, the degree to which the newcomer can encode and decode verbal and nonverbal messages within the host environment. Kim argues that natives acquire this competence early in life; so it comes to them automatically. Host communication competence also refers to the degree to which the newcomer understands the host language's rules and norms, knows effective and appropriate conflict resolution strategies, and is motivated to initiate and develop host culture relationships. Social communication refers to the actual interaction between the newcomer and host persons. Participating in

Table 12.1   Factors Affecting Cultural Adaptation and Acculturation

Communication	Environment	Predisposition
Personal communication	Host receptivity	Preparedness
Social communication	Host conformity pressure	Ethnicity
Ethnic group strength	Personality	

relationships, engaging in conflict resolution, and exposing oneself to the mass communication of the host culture can enhance and facilitate the acculturation process.[12]

Kim argues that the environment plays a key role in the acculturation process. The degree to which the host culture is receptive to strangers is important. Certain factions in the United States, for example, believe the country should close its borders to immigrants. Given the tensions in the Middle East, Americans sometimes face hostilities when they enter certain countries. Host conformity pressure is another factor. The extent to which natives within the host culture exert pressure on newcomers to conform to their culture's values, beliefs, and practices can facilitate or alienate the newcomers. In the United States, for example, people expect that newcomers will speak English. In fact, some members of the U.S. Congress have introduced legislation that would make English the official language of the United States. Ethnic group strength refers to the amount of influence the newcomer's group wields in the host culture. Clearly, some ethnic groups are more powerful than others politically, economically, and socially. Because of their numbers, Blacks and Hispanics have become powerful ethnic groups in the United States. Kim notes that as ethnic group strength increases, members of the ethnic group may encourage newcomers to maintain their native ethnic heritage and pressure them not to conform to the host culture. Hence, newcomers may feel pressure from the host culture to adapt while simultaneously facing pressure from their native ethnic group to preserve their ethnic heritage.[13]

Predisposition factors also affect acculturation. Kim argues that newcomers enter into their new culture with varying degrees of readiness. How much people know about their new culture, their ability to speak the language, the probability of employment, and their understanding of the cultural institutions will have a dramatic effect on their acculturation process. Newcomers' ethnicity will also play a role in the pace of their acculturation.

Kim uses the term *ethnicity* to refer to the inherited characteristics that newcomers have as members of distinct ethnic groups. Such characteristics include race and language. For example, because of their ethnicity, Japanese may have a more difficult time acculturating to the United States than would a person from Great Britain. Finally, Kim argues that certain personality characteristics affect the individual's acculturation process. Age, for example, has been shown to affect acculturation. Generally, young persons adapt more quickly to new and different modes of behavior than do older persons, who may be set in their ways. Karmela Liebkind found that among Vietnamese refugees in Finland, younger generations maintained much more positive attitudes about acculturation than did older generations. Liebkind explains that the Finnish values and practices of gender equality and egalitarian parent/child relationships contrasted sharply with Southeast Asian values of hierarchical familial relationships and filial piety. In the traditional Southeast Asian family, children are taught to be loyal. They are obligated to show respect and obedience to their parents. Wives are expected to rear the children and serve their husbands. Not having been completely enculturated into Vietnamese society, the younger generations of the refugee Vietnamese families found it much easier than did their parents to acculturate into Finnish society.[14]

Modes of Acculturation

For acculturation to occur, there must be contact between the members of the host culture and the newcomers. Berry argues that such contact needs to be continuous and direct. He maintains that short-term accidental contact does not generally lead to much acculturation.

Moreover, the purpose of contact between the two groups is an important consideration. Berry points out that acculturation effects may vary according to whether the purpose of contact is colonization, enslavement, trade, military control, evangelization, or education. The length of contact is also a factor, as are the social or political policies of the mainstream culture as they relate to the immigrant group (i.e., political representation, citizenship criteria, language requirements, employment opportunities, and so forth).[15]

Berry points out that an individual's level of acculturation depends in part on two independent processes: the degree to which the person approaches or avoids interaction with the host culture (i.e., out-group contact and relations) and the degree to which the individual maintains or relinquishes his or her native culture's attributes (i.e., in-group identity and maintenance). On the basis of these two factors, Berry has identified four modes of acculturation: (a) *assimilation,* (b) *integration,* (c) *separation,* and (d) *marginalization* (see Figure 12.1).[16]

To the extent that the individual desires contact with the host culture (and its various microcultures) while not necessarily maintaining an identity with his or her native culture, assimilation occurs. According to Hardin Coleman, the individual loses his or her original cultural identity as he or she acquires a new identity in the host culture. During assimilation, the individual takes on the behaviors and language habits, and practices the basic rules and norms of the host culture. There is an ongoing effort to approach the dominant culture while discontinuing the values, beliefs, and behaviors associated with the native culture. Coleman argues that the defining property of the assimilation mode is that the individual endeavors to acquire the values and beliefs of a single cultural group, with the ultimate goal of becoming indistinguishable from other members of the host culture. The individual will seek interaction with members of the host culture and build social networks with them.[17]

On the other hand, some people desire a high level of interaction with the host culture while maintaining identity with their native culture. This kind of acculturation is called integration. In this mode, the individual develops a kind of bicultural orientation that successfully blends and synthesizes cultural dimensions from both groups while maintaining an identity in each group. Coleman maintains that people practicing this mode of acculturation take part in activities that allow individuals from different groups to interact without the obstacle of social hierarchies. Presumably, integration is associated with less acculturative stress and conflict. To be sure, an individual's successful integration of cultural skills and norms does not mean that the person relinquishes his or her native cultural identity. In fact, Coleman contends that the development of the bicultural identity is what leads to a successful life in a bicultural context. In other models of acculturation, this mode is called

| Figure 12.1 | Modes of acculturation. |

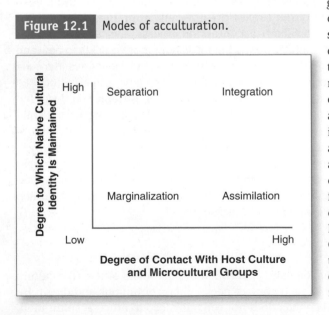

pluralism or *multiculturalism*. This mode of acculturation guides many of the social and legislative efforts in the United States' educational and affirmative action statutes.[18]

When individuals prefer low levels of interaction with the host culture and associated microcultural groups while desiring a close connection with, and reaffirmation of, their native culture, the mode of acculturation is called separation. Here, the individual resists acculturation with the dominant culture and chooses not to identify with the host cultural group. At the same time, the person retains his or her native cultural identity. Coleman argues that people choosing separation may harbor animosity toward the host culture as a result of social or historical factors. Such persons generally focus on the perceived incompatibility between their native culture and the host culture. Although the values and beliefs of the host culture are eschewed, the individual may take on selected behaviors of the host culture for purely functional reasons (e.g., to get a job). Coleman suggests that separated persons communicate almost exclusively with their own group while actively avoiding participation in situations with members of the host culture. Some African Americans and Native Americans, for example, prefer not to identify with the dominant White culture because of past racism and the country's history of slavery. In some models, the separation mode is labeled *segregation*.[19]

The fourth type of acculturation is marginalization. Marginalization occurs when the individual chooses not to identify with his or her native culture or with the host culture. In many instances, marginalized people give up their native culture only to find that they are not accepted by the host culture, to which they would choose to acculturate if given the opportunity. These persons experience alienation from both cultures. Often, they feel a sense of abandonment. Dysfunctional behaviors (e.g., alcoholism or drug abuse) are often seen in marginalized people. African Americans, Asian Americans, and Hispanic Americans often feel marginalized in U.S. culture. Acculturative stress is often found among marginalized groups.[20]

Another possible acculturation mode, articulated by Richard Mendoza, is cultural transmutation. In this mode, the individual chooses to identify with a third cultural group (microculture) that materializes out of the native and host cultural groups. For example, a youth may choose to join a gang or some other kind of microcultural outlet. Although similar to separation, cultural transmutation is different in that a new cultural identity is created. In other models of acculturation, this is called *fusion*. Gay and lesbian groups are a good example of the cultural transmutation mode of acculturation. In this mode, individuals have left their native heterosexual groups and immigrated into homosexual contexts. Religious groups are another example of acculturative transmutation. Many religious communities merge the values, beliefs, and behaviors of diverse religions into a new religion.[21]

Acculturation in the United States

The two largest ethnic populations in the United States are Hispanics and Blacks. For these groups, acculturation refers to the degree to which they participate in the cultural traditions, values, beliefs, and norms of the dominant White society; remain immersed in their own unique cultural customs and conventions; or participate in both. As Hope Landrine and Elizabeth Klonoff comment, some microcultural groups remain highly traditional, whereas others are highly acculturated.[22] Highly traditional Hispanics and Blacks differ significantly from Whites in a variety of values and behaviors, whereas highly acculturated Hispanics and Blacks do not (see Figure 12.2).[23]

Figure 12.2 Hispanics are the largest ethnic population in the United States.

Social scientists are beginning to understand that the degree of acculturation for microcultural groups within the United States is associated with a variety of social and medical problems, such as alcoholism, cigarette smoking, drug abuse, and HIV/AIDS-related knowledge, attitudes, and behaviors.[24] Moreover, microcultural group acculturation is tied to methods of conflict resolution (e.g., belligerent behaviors), willingness to use counseling, career development and work habits, and educational achievement (i.e., increased absences, lower grades). The more marginalized or segregated the group, the more likely its members are to experience physical and mental health problems and the less likely they are to seek out appropriate avenues to handle them. Landrine and Klonoff maintain that ethnic differences observed in the United States might be better understood as degrees of acculturation. According to Landrine and Klonoff, understanding a microcultural group's level of acculturation has the potential to diminish racist beliefs about ethnic differences and to increase our knowledge of such differences as a symptom or exhibition of culture.[25]

In an effort to better understand maladaptive attitudes and behaviors among the various microcultural groups in the United States, researchers have devoted considerable attention to assessing levels of acculturation. The Acculturation Rating Scale for Mexican Americans (ARSMA) was first published in 1980. The scale was recently revised and is used to assess Mexican American acculturation according to Berry's four modes of acculturation—namely, integration, assimilation, separation, and marginalization. It is designed to be completed by persons of Mexican or Hispanic origin.

Self-Assessment 12.1

Acculturation Rating Scale for Mexican Americans II

Directions: In the blank space to the left of each item, place a number between 1 and 5 that best applies to you: 1 = not at all, 2 = very little or not very often, 3 = moderately, 4 = much or very often, and 5 = extremely often or almost always.

_____ 1. I speak Spanish.

_____ 2. I speak English.

_____ 3. I enjoy speaking Spanish.

_____ 4. I associate with Anglos.

_____ 5. I associate with Mexicans and/or Mexican Americans.

_____ 6. I enjoy listening to Spanish music.

_____ 7. I enjoy listening to English language music.

_____ 8. I enjoy Spanish-language TV.

_____ 9. I enjoy English-language TV.

_____ 10. I enjoy English-language movies.

_____ 11. I enjoy Spanish-language movies.

_____ 12. I enjoy reading books in Spanish.

_____ 13. I enjoy reading books in English.

_____ 14. I write letters in Spanish.

_____ 15. I write letters in English.

_____ 16. My thinking is done in English.

_____ 17. My thinking is done in Spanish.

_____ 18. My contact with Mexico has been . . .

_____ 19. My contact with the U.S.A. has been . . .

_____ 20. My father identifies or identified himself as "Mexicano."

_____ 21. My mother identifies or identified herself as "Mexicana."

_____ 22. My friends while I was growing up were of Mexican origin.

_____ 23. My friends while I was growing up were of Anglo origin.

_____ 24. My family cooks Mexican food.

(Continued)

(Continued)

_____ 25. My friends now are of Anglo origin.

_____ 26. My friends now are of Mexican origin.

_____ 27. I like to identify myself as an Anglo.

_____ 28. I like to identify myself as a Mexican American.

_____ 29. I like to identify myself as a Mexican.

_____ 30. I like to identify myself as an American.

_____ 31. I have difficulty accepting some ideas held by Anglos.

_____ 32. I have difficulty accepting certain attitudes held by Anglos.

_____ 33. I have difficulty accepting some behaviors exhibited by Anglos.

_____ 34. I have difficulty accepting some values held by some Anglos.

_____ 35. I have difficulty accepting certain practices and customs commonly found in some Anglos.

_____ 36. I have, or think I would have, difficulty accepting Anglos as close personal friends.

_____ 37. I have difficulty accepting some ideas held by some Mexicans.

_____ 38. I have difficulty accepting certain attitudes held by Mexicans.

_____ 39. I have difficulty accepting some behaviors exhibited by Mexicans.

_____ 40. I have difficulty accepting some values held by some Mexicans.

_____ 41. I have difficulty accepting certain practices and customs commonly found in some Mexicans.

_____ 42. I have, or think I would have, difficulty accepting Mexicans as close personal friends.

_____ 43. I have difficulty accepting ideas held by some Mexican Americans.

_____ 44. I have difficulty accepting certain attitudes held by Mexican Americans.

_____ 45. I have difficulty accepting some behaviors exhibited by Mexican Americans.

_____ 46. I have difficulty accepting some values held by Mexican Americans.

_____ 47. I have difficulty accepting certain practices and customs commonly found in some Mexican Americans.

_____ 48. I have, or think I would have, difficulty accepting Mexican Americans as close personal friends.

Scoring:

1. Sum your responses to the following items: 2, 4, 7, 9, 10, 13, 15, 16, 19, 23, 25, 27, and 30. Divide the sum by 13. This is your Anglo Orientation Score (AOS).

2. Sum your responses to the following items: 1, 3, 5, 6, 8, 11, 12, 14, 17, 18, 20, 21, 22, 24, 26, 28, and 29. Divide the sum by 17. This is your Mexican Orientation Score (MOS).

3. Sum your responses to the following items: 31, 32, 33, 34, 35, and 36. This is your Anglo Marginality (ANGMAR).

4. Sum your responses to the following items: 37, 38, 39, 40, 41, and 42. This is your Mexican Marginality (MEXMAR).

5. Sum your responses to the following items: 43, 44, 45, 46, 47, and 48. This is your Mexican-American Marginality (MAMARG).

Acculturative Types Generated by ARSMA-II:

Traditional Mexican = MOS scores $\geq$ 3.7 and AOS scores $\leq$ 3.24.

Integrated = AOS $\geq$ 3.5 and MOS $\geq$ 2.8.

Marginal = ANGMAR $\geq$ 17.34, MEXMAR $\geq$ 17, and MAMARG $\geq$ 15.

Separation = MEXMAR $\leq$ 11, ANGMAR $\geq$ 15, and MAMARG $\geq$ 15.

Assimilated = MOS $\leq$ 2.4 and AOS $\geq$ 4.

SOURCE: Acculturation Scale for Mexican Americans II, from Cuellar, I., Arnold, B., & Maldonado, R. (1995). Acculturation Rating Scale for Mexican-Americans. *Hispanic Journal of Behavioral Sciences, 17,* 275–305. Copyright © 1995 SAGE Publications. Used by permission of the publisher.

About 13% of the population in the United States is African American. As with other microcultural groups, some African Americans are more acculturated than others. Landrine and Klonoff have developed an instrument designed to measure levels of African American acculturation. They argue that within the microcultural context, acculturation refers to the degree to which microcultural groups (e.g., African Americans, Asian Americans, Native Americans) participate in the traditional values, beliefs, and practices of the dominant White culture, remain immersed in their own cultural traditions, or blend the two traditions.[26]

African Americans who complete the instrument are asked to indicate their preference for things identified as being African American, their religious beliefs and practices, and their experience with traditional African American foods and games, as well as any relevant childhood experiences, superstitions, interracial attitudes and cultural mistrust of the White majority, experiences with "falling out," adherence to Black family values, and family practices. This scale is designed for African Americans in the United States and is not applicable to other microcultural groups. The two scales discussed here are valid indices of acculturation for Hispanics and African Americans and indicate that cultural diversity can be measured reliably. Such measurements give us a better understanding of an individual's perceptual context. The more we know about a person's individual level of acculturation, the better able we are to provide culturally competent services to him or her.

Self-Assessment 12.2

African American Acculturation Scale

Directions: On a scale ranging from 1 to 7, indicate the extent to which you agree or disagree with the statement: 1 = totally disagree, 2 = disagree, 3 = slightly disagree, 4 = don't know, 5 = slightly agree, 6 = agree, and 7 = totally agree.

_____ 1. Most of the music I listen to is by Black artists.

_____ 2. I like Black music more than White music.

_____ 3. The person I admire most is Black.

_____ 4. I listen to Black radio stations.

_____ 5. I try to watch all the Black shows on TV.

_____ 6. Most of my friends are Black.

_____ 7. I believe in the Holy Ghost.

_____ 8. I believe in heaven and hell.

_____ 9. I like gospel music.

_____ 10. I am currently a member of a Black church.

_____ 11. Prayer can cure disease.

_____ 12. The church is the heart of the Black community.

_____ 13. I know how to cook chitlins.

_____ 14. I eat chitlins once in a while.

_____ 15. Sometimes I cook ham hocks.

_____ 16. I know how long you're supposed to cook collard greens.

_____ 17. I went to a mostly Black elementary school.

_____ 18. I went (or go) to a mostly Black high school.

_____ 19. I grew up in a mostly Black neighborhood.

_____ 20. I avoid splitting a pole.

_____ 21. When the palm of your hand itches, you'll receive some money.

_____ 22. There's some truth to many old superstitions.

_____ 23. IQ tests were set up purposefully to discriminate against Black people.

_____ 24. Most tests (such as the SAT and tests to get a job) are set up to make sure Blacks don't get high scores on them.

_____ 25. Deep in their hearts, most White people are racists.

_____ 26. I have seen people "fall out." I know what "falling out" means.

_____ 27. When I was a child, I used to play tonk. I know how to play bid whist.

_____ 28. It's better to move your whole family ahead in this world than it is to be out for only yourself.

_____ 29. Old people are wise.

_____ 30. When I was young, my parent(s) sent me to stay with a relative (aunt, uncle, grandmother) for a few days or weeks, and then I went back home again.

_____ 31. When I was young, I took a bath with my sister, brother, or some other relative.

Scoring: Sum your responses to the above 31 items. Your score must range between 33 and 231.

Scores 33–60 = Acculturated.

Scores 66–85 = Mostly acculturated.

Scores 99–130 = Bicultural (slightly acculturated).

Scores 165–185 = Bicultural (slightly traditional).

Scores 198–200 = Mostly traditional.

Scores 200–231 = Traditional.

SOURCE: The African American Acculturation Scale II, from Landrine, H., & Klonoff, E. A. (1995). The African American Acculturation Scale II. *Journal of Black Psychology*, *21*, 124–153. Copyright © 1995 Association of Black Psychologists. Used by permission of SAGE Publications.

CULTURE SHOCK

When people move to a new culture, they take with them the values, beliefs, customs, and behaviors of their old culture. Often, depending on the degree of similarity between the old and the new culture, the values, beliefs, customs, and behaviors of the native culture clash with those of the new culture. This can result in disorientation, misunderstandings, conflict, stress, and anxiety. Researchers call this phenomenon *culture shock*. Michael Winkelman defines culture shock as a multifaceted experience that results from the numerous stressors that occur when coming into contact with a different culture.[27] Anyone can experience culture shock, although some are more prone to it than others. Winkelman maintains that culture shock can occur with immigrant groups—such as foreign students and refugees, international business exchanges, Peace Corps volunteers, and social workers entering new communities during crises—as well as with members of microcultural groups within their own culture and society. Expatriate professors teaching abroad often describe their experiences using the term *education shock*.

Anthropologist Kalervo Oberg was the first to apply the term *culture shock* to the effects associated with the tension and anxiety of entering into a new culture combined with the sensations of loss, confusion, and powerlessness resulting from the forfeiture of cultural norms and social rituals.[28] Likewise, Winkelman points out that culture shock stems from the challenges associated with new cultural surroundings in addition to the loss of a familiar cultural environment.[29] Culture shock appears to be a psychological and social process that progresses in stages, usually lasting as long as a year. Most models of culture shock include four stages. The first model of culture shock, developed by Oberg nearly 50 years ago, incorporates a medical metaphor and terminology—beginning with the incubation stage, followed by crisis, leading to recovery, and finishing with full recovery.[30] William Smalley's model begins with a fascination stage, and then moves through hostility, adjustment, and biculturalism. Alan Richardson's four-stage model includes elation, depression, recovery, and acculturation. Daniel Kealey's model incorporates exploration, frustration, coping, and adjustment phases (see Table 12.2).[31]

Table 12.2	Culture Shock Models		
Oberg (1954)	**Smalley (1963)**	**Richardson (1974)**	**Kealey (1978)**
1. Incubation	1. Fascination	1. Elation	1. Exploration
2. Crisis	2. Hostility	2. Depression	2. Frustration
3. Recovery	3. Adjustment	3. Recovery	3. Coping
4. Full recovery	4. Biculturalism	4. Acculturation	4. Adjustment

Most models of culture shock describe the process curvilinearly, or by what Sverre Lysgaard called the "U-curve hypothesis."[32] Elaborating on the U curve, Professor Kim Zapf asserts that culture shock begins with feelings of optimism and even elation that eventually give way to frustration, tension, and anxiety as individuals are unable to interact effectively with their new environment. As they develop strategies for resolving conflict, people begin to restore their confidence and eventually recover and reach some level of acculturation.[33]

The initial stage of culture shock, usually called something like the *tourist stage* or *honeymoon stage,* is characterized by intense excitement and euphoria associated with being somewhere different and unusual (see Figure 12.3). Winkelman asserts that this stage is typical of that experienced by people who enter other cultures temporarily during honeymoons, vacations, or brief business trips.[34] The stresses associated with cultural differences are tolerated and may even seem fun and humorous. During the tourist phase, the newcomers' primary interactions with their new cultural environment are through major cultural institutions, such as museums, hotels, Western restaurants, and so forth.

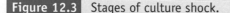

| **Figure 12.3** | Stages of culture shock. |

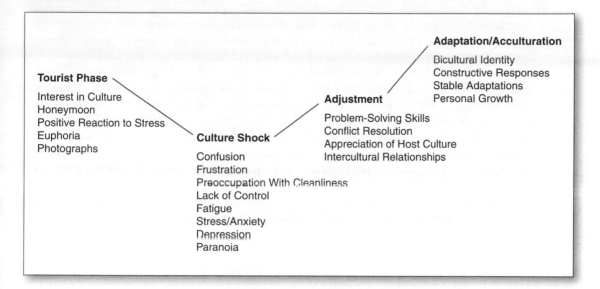

This phase may last weeks or months but is temporary. In some instances, the tourist phase may be very short, as when newcomers are confronted with drastic changes in climate or hostile political environments. Eventually, the fun and excitement associated with the tourist phase give way to frustration and real stress, or active *culture shock*. Failure events once considered minor and funny are now perceived as stressful. Winkelman maintains that culture shock is partially based on the simultaneous effects of cognitive overload and behavioral inadequacy that are rooted in the psychological and physical stresses associated with confronting a new environment. The new environment requires a great deal of conscious energy that was not required in the old environment, which leads to cognitive overload and fatigue. People also experience role shock in that the behaviors associated with their role in their native culture may be dramatically different from the behaviors for that same role in the new culture. Finally, people may experience personal shock in the form of a loss of intimacy with interpersonal partners. In describing the second phase of culture shock, Winkelman notes,

> Things start to go wrong, minor issues become major problems, and cultural differences become irritating. Excessive preoccupation with cleanliness of food, drinking water, bedding, and surroundings begins. One experiences increasing disappointments, frustrations, impatience, and tension. Life does not make sense and one may feel helpless, confused, disliked by others, or treated like a child.[35]

Stephen Rhinesmith notes that during the culture shock phase, people feel helpless, isolated, and depressed. Paranoia—in which newcomers are convinced that their troubles are deliberate attempts by the natives to disrupt their lives—is also a typical response to culture shock. In this phase, people may develop irrational fears of being cheated, robbed, or even assaulted.[36] The degree to which one experiences culture shock varies from person to person. Walt Lonner has identified six factors that affect the nature of culture shock experienced: (a) control factors, (b) interpersonal factors, (c) organismic/biological factors, (d) intrapersonal factors, (e) spatial/temporal factors, and (f) geopolitical factors. Arza Churchman and Michal Mitrani have added three additional factors: (a) the degree of similarity between one's native and new culture, including the physical environment; (b) the degree and quality of information about the new environment; and (c) the host culture's attitude and policies toward immigrants (see Figure 12.4).[37]

Some people never recuperate from the crisis stage of culture shock and return home or isolate themselves from the host culture by restricting their interaction with it, such as by fostering only intracultural relationships (e.g., in a military base or university setting). When the lines of communication with the host culture are severed, there is little hope of acculturation or recovery from the crisis stage. The third phase of culture shock is typically called the adjustment phase, or reorientation phase. Here, people eventually realize that

Figure 12.4   Factors that affect culture shock.

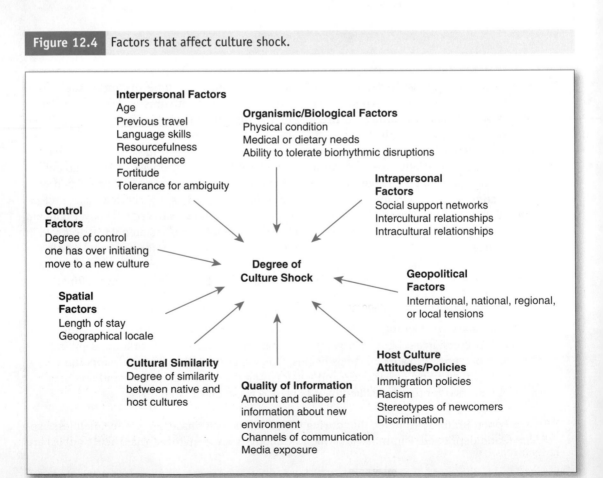

the problems associated with the host culture are due not to deliberate actions by the natives but, rather, to a real difference in values, beliefs, and behaviors. At this stage, people actively seek out effective problem-solving and conflict-resolution strategies. They begin to develop a positive attitude about solving their problems. As Winkelman notes, the host culture begins to make sense, and pessimistic reactions and responses to it are lessened as people recognize that their problems are due largely to their inability to understand, accept, and adapt.[38] Typically, the adjustment phase is gradual and slow, and often people relapse into mini-crisis stages. The final stage of culture shock is labeled the *adaptation* or *acculturation stage.* At this point, individuals actively engage the culture with their new problem-solving and conflict-resolution tools, and experience some degree of success.

Kim argues that to the extent that people acculturate to their new culture, they experience cultural transformation. They possess a degree of functional fitness in which the external demands of the host culture are met with appropriate and consistent internal responses. Moreover, they develop a level of competency in communicating with the natives. As a result of their successes, people also acquire psychological health, take on an intercultural identity, and foster a sense of integration with their host environment.[39]

STUDENT VOICES ACROSS CULTURES

Jessica Bahrke

When I moved to Madrid, I was on a high for about a month. Everything was new and exciting—the people, the food, the culture—everything different and exhilarating. During this time, I took every opportunity to see the sights, visit museums, experience the never-ending night life, and eat as many tapas as possible. This honeymoon period lasted for about 4 weeks before I really started to immerse myself in the Spanish culture. It took that long to realize that I was more or less living as a tourist on an extended vacation. It took about 4 weeks for the culture shock to sink in.

Before I left the States, I thought I had made every preparation I could to prevent culture shock. I honestly thought that I had mentally prepared myself and would be able to avoid the vast majority of the common struggles people go through when entering a new culture. I still feel as though my preparation allowed me to handle the shock better, but I was not able to avoid it altogether. A simple trip to the grocery store would leave me frustrated and upset. How could a country possibly survive without cooking spray? And, more important, how was I to keep my eggs from sticking to the pan? Being from the dairy state of Wisconsin, I would gag at the thought of not refrigerating milk and eggs; however, no one seemed to be getting sick. There was no epidemic of salmonella going around Spain. After speaking with the locals and building up a lot of courage, I was eventually able to stomach these items.

Not only did the differences in food cause me small, daily aggravations, but simple greeting practices put me outside my comfort zone. Every time I met a new friend or acquaintance, I would extend my hand instinctually, expecting to feel a hand grip mine in return. Instead, I would be tugged into an unexpected embrace and kissed once on each cheek before I realized what was going on. It wasn't as if I was unaware that this was customary in Europe—of course I had read about this—but it always went against my nature to do it. Even though this introductory practice became commonplace, it never grew into a natural behavior during my time there.

W-Curve Models of Reentry Culture Shock

As mentioned above, most models of culture shock contain four phases in the U-curve tradition. But many people who have lived outside their native culture argue that they experience a kind of reentry shock when they return home. Adrian Furnham and Stephen Bochner's

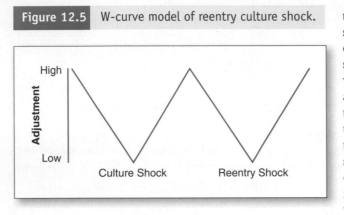

Figure 12.5   W-curve model of reentry culture shock.

"W-curve" model of culture shock contains two U curves—the initial culture shock experienced when the traveler enters a new culture and a reentry shock U curve (see Figure 12.5). In other words, when people return home after an extended stay in a foreign culture, they experience another round of culture shock, this time in their native culture. Furnham and Bochner note that students returning from study abroad often report a reentry-shock phenomenon. Some students fear that they will be treated differently by their "stay-at-home" peers, friends, and parents when they return. In addition, because they have successfully acculturated themselves to a foreign culture, they essentially have to reacculturate to their native culture.[40] Students frequently report that the nature of long-term international travel transforms them. When they return home, they are different; they have taken on new perspectives and see the world through a different lens. Students lament that communicating their experiences abroad to their friends and families at home is often difficult.

Strategies for Managing Culture Shock

If you are traveling to a new culture for the first time, you will likely experience some kind of culture shock. The level of intensity will vary. In addition, the duration of your culture shock will depend on your ability to manage it. Probably the best piece of commonsense advice is to do your homework and be prepared. Successful management of culture shock depends on an awareness of its symptoms and the degree of its severity. Winkelman maintains that sometimes people falsely attribute their problems to sources other than culture shock. He argues that people have a tendency to deny that they are experiencing it. His advice is that one should accept the fact that virtually all atypical problems that occur during acculturation are caused or exacerbated by culture shock.[41] Zapf has developed a questionnaire, called the Culture Shock Profile, to assess the intensity of culture shock an individual is experiencing. Please keep in mind that everyone experiences some degree of culture shock when entering a new culture for some length of time. Zapf recommends that the Culture Shock Profile be taken several times during the first year of one's move—specifically, after the first month, sometime during the fourth or fifth month, and then after 1 year. If managed appropriately, most culture shock is significantly reduced after a year.[42]

STUDENT VOICES ACROSS CULTURES

W-Curve Model Of Reentry Culture Shock

I'm Hillary Hubertz from Walworth, Wisconsin. In my senior year of college, I spent a semester abroad at The University of the Sunshine Coast in Sippy Downs, Queensland, Australia. I majored in communication and, while studying abroad, took many courses that immersed me in the Australian culture.

When I signed up to spend a semester abroad in Australia, I was worried about everything except coming back home to the United States. If anything, I was hoping the 5 months would go fast, because before I even left, I was excited to return home. My preparations for leaving included talking to people about what to pack, what activities to do while there, and what classes were worth taking. Never was I warned about the pain of leaving and the challenges of coming back home.

I blinked, and 5 months were gone. Lifelong friends had been made, kangaroos had been pet, the Great Barrier Reef had been explored, the Sydney Opera House had been seen, and, of course, classes had been passed. The thought of coming home had become a nightmare. Saying goodbye to the amazing people I had met was a form of torture, and getting on the plane was physically and mentally painful. While leaving Australia was a challenge, it was nothing compared with the challenge ahead of me—readjusting to life in the United States.

Home life, social life, and academic life—they had all changed, and for what felt like the worse. Transitioning from an everyday adventure to the same old routine was suffocating. Returning to St. Norbert was thrilling at first, until the nostalgia wore off. Everything that was simple before I left for my semester abroad was now difficult. Getting a cup of coffee was sad without my friends and the ocean feet away from the coffee shop; classes were so different they felt impossible, and walking even proved challenging (in Australia, you walk on the left side, not the right). I had to get used to driving a car and accepting that reliable public transportation was not the norm in the United States. I had to get used to the portions of food. I had to get used to having classes every day versus twice a week. And I had to get used to always needing to be on time and in a rush. It took me a couple of weeks to adjust to the way of life in Australia, but it has been months and I am still struggling to readjust to the way of life in the United States.

In subsequent work, Zapf has created a list of danger signs that indicate when culture shock may be getting out of control:[43]

- You are drinking more.
- You are avoiding people.
- You are subject to uncontrollable emotions.
- You spend too much time texting and e-mailing people from home.
- You constantly complain about your host culture.
- You have adopted very negative attitudes about the local people.
- You feel very alone.
- You constantly think about things.
- You fear you are misunderstood by just about everyone, including your friends and family back home.

Self-Assessment 12.3

Culture Shock Profile

Directions: Below is a list of 33 terms that may or may not describe how you feel about your experiences in your new culture. On a scale of 0 to 3, indicate the frequency with which you experience the feeling: 0 = none, 1 = slight, 2 = moderate, and 3 = great.

I feel:

_____ 1. Enthusiastic

_____ 2. Impatient/irritable

_____ 3. A desire to resign

_____ 4. Happy/content

_____ 5. Energetic

_____ 6. Rejected

_____ 7. Purposeful/directed

_____ 8. Pessimistic/hopeless

_____ 9. Contemptuous of others (natives)

_____ 10. Angry/resentful

_____ 11. A need to complain

_____ 12. Creative

_____ 13. Confident/self-assured

_____ 14. Ready to cry

_____ 15. Challenged

_____ 16. Cynical

_____ 17. A sense of discovery

_____ 18. Helpless/vulnerable

_____ 19. Optimistic/hopeful

_____ 20. Inadequate/self-doubt

_____ 21. Isolated/homesick

_____ 22. Physically ill

_____ 23. I need to "get out"

_____ 24. Confused/disoriented

_____ 25. Excited/stimulated

_____ 26. Accepted

_____ 27. A sense of loss

_____ 28. Overwhelmed/bewildered

_____ 29. Afraid/panic

_____ 30. Depressed/withdrawn

_____ 31. Frustrated/thwarted

_____ 32. Exhausted/sleep difficulty

_____ 33. Apathetic/"I don't care"

Scoring: To determine your level of culture shock, reverse your score for Items 1, 4, 5, 7, 12, 13, 17, 19, 25, and 26. If your original score was a 0, reverse it to a 3. If your original score was a 1, reverse it to a 2. If your original score was a 2, reverse it to a 1, and if your original score was a 3, reverse it to a 0. After reversing the scores for those 10 items, sum the entire 33 items. Scores must range from 0 to 99. The higher your score, the more culture shock you are experiencing, and the more you should engage in some of the strategies listed in this section.

SOURCE: Zapf, M. K. (1993). Remote Practice and Culture Shock: Social Workers Moving to Isolated Northern Regions. *Social Work, 38*, 694–705.

INDICATORS OF SUCCESS IN THE INTERCULTURAL CONTEXT

Considering the warning signs indicated above, there are also keys to success in overcoming acculturative stress and culture shock. Karen van der Zee and her colleague Jan Pieter van Oudenhoven have written extensively about the factors that contribute to an individual's ability to cope with acculturative stress and culture shock.[44] Through their years of study, van der Zee and Oudenhoven have identified five personality dimensions directly linked to success in long-term intercultural encounters. They argue that these five dimensions increase an individual's professional performance, personal adjustment, and social integration during acculturation across a variety of settings, including employee effectiveness on the job, successful immigration, relational satisfaction among expatriates and their families, and the academic performance of students studying abroad. These five dimensions are cultural empathy, open-mindedness, social initiative, emotional stability, and flexibility.[45]

As we learned in Chapter 9, experiencing pure empathy toward another is impossible, but here cultural empathy refers to an individual's sincere attempt to identify with, understand, and sympathize with the feelings, thoughts, and behaviors of the individuals from the new culture with whom he or she is living and interacting. Van der Zee and Oudenhoven point to research indicating that cultural empathy is positively associated with psychological adjustment in a new culture. Open-mindedness refers to the individual's motivation and ability to delay or defer judgment when confronted with the different behaviors or values of a new culture. When confronted with cultural differences, often our initial response is to reject them. Like cultural empathy, open-mindedness is associated with psychological adjustment and also satisfaction with life in the new culture. Social initiative refers to the individual's tendency to approach social situations. Recall from Chapter 1 that intercultural communication is replete with uncertainty, and uncertainty is associated with anxiety, which often leads to avoidance. Individuals who are willing to approach communicative situations tend to integrate better into their host culture than do those who avoid such situations. While maintaining relationships with family and friends from home is absolutely fine, establishing relationships with members of your host culture is one of the best ways to ensure a successful intercultural experience. Emotional stability refers to the individual's ability to remain composed when faced with novel and stressful conditions. To be sure, you will confront many situations that appear unusual and even strange. Your ability to remain calm and poised will serve you well. Finally, flexibility refers to your ability to transition from or replace those thoughts, feelings, and behaviors that have become almost second nature to you, in favor of new strategies to deal with everyday situations. Van der Zee and Oudenhoven assert that rather than fearing new and unknown situations, individuals should try to seek them out and view them as a challenge rather than a threat.[46]

INTERCULTURAL COMMUNICATION COMPETENCE

One of the fundamental goals of this book is to help you become a competent intercultural communicator. *Intercultural communication competence* is defined as the degree to which you effectively adapt your verbal and nonverbal messages to the appropriate cultural context.[47] When you communicate with someone from a different culture, to be interculturally competent, you will have to adjust and modify the kinds of verbal and nonverbal messages you send. This process requires that you have some *knowledge* about the person with whom you are communicating, that you are *motivated* to communicate with him or her, and that you have the appropriate verbal and nonverbal *skills* to encode and decode messages.

Interculturally competent people successfully and effectively adapt their verbal and nonverbal messages to the appropriate cultural context. For the most part, competence is perceived in an individual rather than inherently possessed. In other words, an individual may appear competent to one person but not to another. Moreover, intercultural competence varies from situation to situation. That is, a particular American may be quite competent while interacting with Chinese people and relatively incompetent when interacting with Germans. Verbal and nonverbal appropriateness and effectiveness are two important qualities of intercultural competence. According to Brian Spitzberg, appropriate behaviors conform to the rules, norms, and expectancies of the cultural context.[48] For example, when greeting a Japanese person in Japan, one is expected to bow. The rules associated with bowing are determined by one's status (e.g., age, sex, occupation, education). The person of lower status bows lower and longer than the person with higher status and typically does not make direct eye contact. Effective behaviors are those that successfully perform and accomplish the rules and norms.[49] For example, to the extent you are able to bow correctly, your behavior will be perceived as effective and competent. As we have seen throughout this book, the appropriateness and effectiveness of verbal and nonverbal messages varies considerably across cultures. Behaviors considered appropriate in one culture may not be wholly appropriate in another culture.

A MODEL OF INTERCULTURAL COMPETENCE

Spitzberg and his colleague Bill Cupach argue that there are three necessary and interdependent ingredients of communication competence: (a) knowledge, (b) motivation, and (c) behavior.[50] The model of intercultural competence presented in this text includes these three dimensions along with a fourth component, situational features (see Figure 12.6). In this model, intercultural competence is the potential outcome of four interdependent components of the intercultural communication encounter. Each component influences and is influenced by the other three.

The Knowledge Component

The knowledge component of intercultural competence consists of how much one knows about the culture of the person with whom one is interacting. To the extent that people have knowledge about other cultures, they are more likely to be perceived as competent (although there is no guarantee!). Consider your own general cultural awareness. Self-Assessment 12.4 is a self-report instrument designed to assess your level of cultural awareness.

Figure 12.6	Model of intercultural competence.

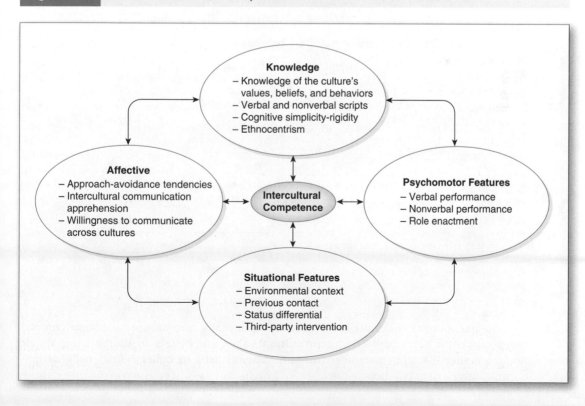

Self-Assessment 12.4

Cross-Cultural Awareness

Directions: The scale consists of 15 items concerning what you know or don't know about other cultures. Respond to each item on a scale of 1 to 5: 1 = definitely no, 2 = not likely, 3 = not sure, 4 = likely, and 5 = definitely yes. Be as honest with yourself as possible in completing the scale.

_____ 1. I can accurately list three countries that are considered collectivistic.

_____ 2. I can accurately identify three countries that have large power distance.

_____ 3. I can conduct business in a language other than my own.

_____ 4. I know the appropriate distance at which to stand when interacting with people in at least two other cultures.

_____ 5. I know the appropriate touch rules in at least two other cultures.

_____ 6. I know in what countries I can use first names when conducting business.

_____ 7. I can name the (political/governmental) leaders of four other countries.

_____ 8. I understand and can practice appropriate gift giving in three other countries.

_____ 9. I can identify some gestures appropriate in the U.S.A. that are considered obscene in other countries.

_____ 10. I understand sex-role differences in at least two other countries.

_____ 11. I can name three countries that are considered polychronic.

_____ 12. I understand the proper protocol for exchanging business cards in at least two other countries.

_____ 13. I understand the business philosophies of Japan and China.

_____ 14. I can name the United States' top three trading partners.

_____ 15. I can name the currencies in four other countries.

Scoring: Sum the 15 responses. Scores must range from 15 to 75. The higher your score, the more culturally aware you are. Scores at or above 50 indicate a relatively healthy degree of cultural awareness.

SOURCE: This scale is loosely adapted from Goodman, N. R. (1994). Cross-Cultural Training for the Global Executive. In R. W. Brislin & T. Yoshida (Eds.), _Improving Intercultural Interaction: Models for Cross-Cultural Training Programs_ (pp. 34–54). Thousand Oaks, CA: Sage.

To be perceived as culturally knowledgeable, minimally, one should have some comprehension of the other person's dominant cultural values and beliefs. In addition, one should know whether the other person is from an individualistic or collectivistic, high- or low-context, large- or small–power-distance, and high- or low–uncertainty-avoidance culture.

In the model of intercultural competence, *verbal and nonverbal scripts* are also a part of the knowledge component. Communication theorist Charles Berger argues that verbal and non-verbal scripts (or plans) guide communication action. Scripts are like blueprints for communication that provide people with expectations about future communicative encounters with others. Berger and Jerry Jordan have argued that knowledgeable communicators develop and maintain a repertoire of scripts that enable them to comprehend and predict their actions and the actions of others. They have demonstrated that people store scripts in long-term memory. According to Berger and Jordan, when anticipating interaction with others, communicators establish goals. They search their long-term memory for instances when they have tried to accomplish similar goals and then access a script or plan that was successful in achieving those goals in the past. The frequency and similarity with which a particular script has been used facilitates access to it. In never-before-encountered situations, people may possess vicariously based scripts. Perhaps one has witnessed a similar event by watching a film or reading a comparable account.[51] The more plans one has, the better equipped one is to enact them.

Cognitive simplicity and rigidity refers to the degree to which individuals process information about persons from different cultures in a simplistic and rigid manner. Kim includes this dimension in her model of intercultural conflict. According to Kim, people with simplistic and rigid cognitive systems tend to engage in gross stereotyping. Moreover, such individuals may have narrowly defined and inflexible categories. Narrow categorizers tend to make more negative and more confident judgments about other people, particularly those from other cultures. Such persons probably think dogmatically (i.e., are narrow-minded). Metaphorically, a person with a simple and rigid cognitive system sees the world with blinders on, like a racehorse. Obviously, the competent communicator would possess an open and flexible cognitive system. The person with a simple and rigid system would not be perceived as competent.[52]

As discussed in Chapter 5, *ethnocentrism* is the extent to which one perceives one's own group as the center of everything and judges other groups with reference to it. Ethnocentrics tend to create and reinforce negative attitudes and behaviors toward out-groups. Judgments about in-groups and out-groups almost always are biased in favor of the in-group at the expense of the out-group. Furthermore, ethnocentric groups see themselves as righteous and exceptional and view their own standards as universal and moral. Out-groups are seen as immoral, subordinate, and impotent. Ethnocentrism is clearly an obstacle to intercultural communication competence. The ethnocentric person most likely possesses narrow categories and a simple and rigid cognitive system.[53] In his research, Rich Wiseman found that ethnocentrism was the strongest predictor of general cultural understanding. That is, higher levels of ethnocentrism were associated with less general cultural understanding. Higher levels of ethnocentrism were also related to less positive regard for other cultures.[54]

The Affective Component

The **affective component** of intercultural communication is the degree to which one approaches or avoids intercultural communication—that is, one's level of motivation to interact with others from different cultures. A central feature here is intercultural communication apprehension (ICA). ICA is defined by Jim Neuliep and James McCroskey as the fear or anxiety associated with either real or anticipated interaction with persons from different cultures.

Persons high in ICA tend to avoid interacting with others from different cultures.[55] As mentioned in Chapter 1, because they are seen as strangers, people from different cultures may seem unusual and novel. This difference can create tension and anxiety, which, in turn, can lead to avoidance. On the other hand, some people may be positively predisposed to initiate intercultural interactions even when they are completely free to choose whether or not to communicate. This predisposition, labeled by Jeffrey Kassing, is called intercultural willingness to communicate.[56] You can assess your individual level of intercultural willingness to communicate by completing the Intercultural Willingness to Communicate Scale.

Kim has argued that one's ability to cope with stress also affects one's approach–avoidance tendencies. Because of the potentially inordinate uncertainty of intercultural communication, anxiety levels may be high as well, leading to increased stress. Some people handle stress well, whereas others do not. William Gudykunst and Kim maintain that to be an effective intercultural communicator, one needs to tolerate ambiguity to a certain degree. The more one is able to manage stress and endure ambivalence, the more likely one is to initiate intercultural communication and to be an effective and competent intercultural communicator.[57]

Self-Assessment 12.5

Intercultural Willingness to Communicate Scale

Directions: Below are six situations in which a person might choose to communicate or not to communicate. Assume that you have completely free choice. Indicate the percentage of times you would choose to communicate in each type of situation. Keep in mind that you are reporting not the likelihood that you would have an opportunity to talk in these instances but, rather, the percentage of times you would talk when the opportunity presented itself. Indicate in the space to the left what percentage of time you would choose to communicate: 0 = never, 100 = always.

_____ 1. Talk with someone I perceive to be different from me

_____ 2. Talk with someone from another country

_____ 3. Talk with someone from a culture I know very little about

_____ 4. Talk with someone from a different race than mine

_____ 5. Talk with someone from a different culture

_____ 6. Talk with someone who speaks English as a second language

Scoring: Your score must range from 0 to 600. Scores below 300 indicate a general unwillingness to communicate interculturally. Scores above 350 indicate a slight willingness to communicate interculturally. Scores above 400 indicate a moderate level, and scores above 500 indicate a high willingness to communicate interculturally.

SOURCE: Adapted from Kassing, J. W. (1997). Development of the Intercultural Willingness to Communicate Scale. *Communication Research Reports, 14*, 399–407.

The knowledge component and the affective component of intercultural competence are interdependent in that the more knowledge one has, the more likely one is to approach situations involving intercultural communication. The increase in knowledge generally leads to an increase in motivation. Likewise, the more motivation one has, the more likely one is to pursue interaction with people from different cultures, thereby learning more about them and their culture and increasing one's knowledge.

The Psychomotor Component

The psychomotor component of intercultural communication is the actual enactment of the knowledge and affective components. The elements of the psychomotor component are (a) verbal and nonverbal performance and (b) role enactment.[58] Verbal performance is how people use language. A person may know a great deal about the language of the host culture but not be able to engage in a conversation. Many foreign exchange students in the United States come here not to learn more about English but to practice using it in actual conversations. An American student who recently returned from a year's stay in Japan reported that she had been paid handsomely for hourly conversations with Japanese. People would come to her apartment and pay her simply to converse in English about trivial subjects for 60 minutes. These Japanese had all the knowledge they needed about English but wanted to sharpen their performance skills. Knowing and being able to use a second language certainly increases one's perceived competence when interacting interculturally. Language scripts and plans that reduce uncertainty are of particular importance. The psychomotor function is where one puts the scripts and plans into action. If one does not speak the language of the host culture, then at the very least, one should know some of the basic greetings, requests, and routines used frequently in that language.

Nonverbal performance is also an important part of the psychomotor component. Here, the individual needs to pay close attention to the nuances of the kinesic, paralinguistic, haptic, olfactic, and proxemic codes of the other culture. As with verbal knowledge and performance, one may have knowledge of a particular culture's nonverbal mannerisms but may not be able to execute them. Hence, before traveling to a foreign country, it might be wise to polish and refine your repertoire of nonverbal skills. For example, before traveling to Japan, you might practice bowing with family members or friends. Keep in mind also that how you smell will affect how others perceive you. Many cultures feel that Americans smell antiseptic because of our frequent use of soaps, perfumes, and so forth. As mentioned in Chapter 8, we have a tendency to mask the natural odor of the human body, and this custom seems strange to many other cultures.

Role enactment refers to how well one executes the appropriate verbal and nonverbal messages according to one's relative position and role in the host culture.[59] The behaviors that professors in the United States enact in the classroom may be misinterpreted or seen as improper in classrooms in other cultures. Managers must be particularly careful about the types of strategies they employ across cultures. Men and women should know how their sex roles vary across cultures. American women returning from abroad frequently comment on how badly they were treated. The freedoms U.S. women have gained throughout this century are not shared by women across the globe. A female student who had recently returned from a semester of study in Southern Italy recounted her experience:

I couldn't believe how the men acted toward me and my friends. When we would walk through town, they would whistle and hiss at us. They would try to touch us and acted like all we wanted to do was sleep with them. It was simply expected. Everyone told us that this was how they treated women and to just get used to it.

As we have seen throughout this text, the verbal and nonverbal behaviors expected for certain sex and occupation roles vary considerably across cultures. In particular, understanding these two role positions is key to becoming interculturally competent.

Situational Features

The fourth component of intercultural competence is the actual situation in which intercultural communication occurs. Remember that a person may be perceived as competent in one situation and not in another. Perceived competence varies with the situation. Some of the situational features that may affect competence include, but are not limited to, the *environmental context, previous contact, status differential,* and *third-party interventions.* Recall from Chapter 4 the influence of the environment on communication. Some situations may have higher information loads than others, which may affect your motivation and ability to enact appropriate verbal and nonverbal behaviors. Highly loaded situations may increase anxiety and reduce your motivation to approach another. In addition, you should have some knowledge of the host culture's perception of time and space. If you are lucky enough to be invited into someone's home, keep in mind that the use of space in homes varies dramatically across cultures. In some of her work, Kim discusses the importance of previous contact and status differences.[60]

Because of the dynamic nature of competence, any previous contact you may have had with a person from another culture may enhance your perception of competence. Competence and trust take time to establish and build, and your competence will grow as you interact more with the people of your host culture. Conversations with persons from other cultures provide a particularly rich source of data for you. The more contact you can have with these people, the more likely you will be to learn about them (knowledge) and feel comfortable (affective) interacting with them, thus enabling you to master your verbal and nonverbal skills (psychomotor).

Although you may have sufficient knowledge about another culture and be motivated to interact, status differences may require you to take on multiple modes of behavior. Certain verbal and nonverbal strategies may be more or less appropriate depending on whether you are interacting with someone of lower, equal, or higher status. In the United States, we have a tendency to minimize status differences. In other cultures, as we learned in Chapter 2, one's status determines the order of speakers and the types of codes to use in a given situation. Because your status may be high in one situation and low in another, you should be mindful of how the communication will vary accordingly.[61]

The addition of a third party may noticeably change the dynamics of the situation and, hence, your competence. All of a sudden, your status may go up or down, as might the status of the person with whom you are interacting. The sex of the third party may also alter the situational features. Topics that were appropriate just a moment ago may now be unfit for discussion. The competent communicator keeps a sharp eye on the changing characteristics of the situation and adapts his or her verbal and nonverbal communication accordingly. The model of intercultural competence provided in Figure 12.6 depicts the knowledge, affective, psychomotor, and situational features as interdependent. This means that as one component changes, the others are affected as well. Generally, as knowledge increases, one's motivation to approach increases. As motivation increases, one is more likely to engage in behaviors. If the behaviors are successful, one learns more about intercultural communication, which serves to further increase motivation. And the cycle continues.

AN INTEGRATED MODEL AND MEASURE OF INTERCULTURAL COMMUNICATION COMPETENCE

For the past 10 years or so, Lily Arasaratnam has been developing what she calls an integrated model and measure of intercultural communication competence. Like others, Arasaratnam maintains that being a competent intercultural communicator involves knowing about other cultures, an approach tendency, and the application of appropriate and effective communication behaviors. Arasaratnam believes that effective and appropriate behavior can be best judged and determined from the perspectives of both the communicator enacting the behavior and the other person with whom intercultural communication occurs. Moreover, Arasaratnam contends that a person who is competent in one type of intercultural exchange probably possesses characteristics that enable him or her to communicate competently in other intercultural exchanges as well.

In related research, Arasaratnam and Marya Doerfel discovered that those who were identified as competent intercultural communicators possessed five qualities in common: (a) empathy, (b) intercultural experience/training, (c) approach tendencies, (d) a global attitude, and (e) listening skills. Arasaratnam and Doerfel arrived at these five characteristics via interviews with persons from 15 different countries who were asked to describe a competent intercultural communicator. Arasaratnam and Doerfel interviewed persons from the United States, Bahamas, Bosnia, Burkina Faso, China, Egypt, Ghana, India, Indonesia, Ivory Coast, Japan, Malaysia, Nigeria, Norway, and the Philippines. Specifically, they wanted to identify those traits in competent intercultural interactants that transcend the cultural context and cultural identity.[62]

Empathy, of course, involves the extent to which one can infer the cognitions and motivations of another. As we saw in Chapter 9, complete empathy is impossible. Here, empathy also includes the ability to sense, accurately perceive, and appropriately respond to one's personal, interpersonal, and social environment. Approach tendencies involve the individual's interest in and effort to talk, understand, and extend help. This includes the anticipation of or actual engagement in intercultural communication. Intercultural experience and training involves the actual study of intercultural communication. Respondents in the study reported that taking a course in intercultural communication led to competence. Regarding the listening aspect, competent intercultural communicators are perceived as such because they are willing to spend time listening and learning and they know about cultural matters and are good at relating to different cultures. The global attitude dimension describes individuals who are open to others, better at communicating, show interest in differences and are aware of them, and have a level of exposure to these differences that makes them able to discern them. For example, are they speaking from their own cultural perspective or trying to communicate in the other's cultural mode or speaking in a cultural mode that is neutral or not specific to either culture? Based on these five characteristics, Arasaratnam developed a scale designed to measure one's intercultural communication competence.[63]

Self-Assessment 12.6

The Intercultural Communication Competence Scale

Directions: The following items may or may not describe how you think, feel, and behave when interacting with people from different cultures. In the space to the left of each item, indicate the degree to which you (5) strongly agree, (4) agree, (3) are neutral, (2) disagree, or (1) strongly disagree with the statement. There are no right or wrong answers. It's best to record your initial response and not think too much about it.

_____ 1. I often find it difficult to differentiate between similar cultures (e.g., Asians, Europeans, Africans, etc.).

_____ 2. I feel a sense of belonging to a group of people based on relationship (i.e., family, friends) instead of cultural identity (i.e., people from my culture, people from other cultures).

_____ 3. I find it easier to categorize people based on their cultural identity than their personality.

_____ 4. I often notice similarities in personality between people who belong to completely different cultures.

_____ 5. If I were to put people in groups, I would group them by their culture rather than by their personality.

_____ 6. I feel that people from other cultures have many valuable things to teach me.

_____ 7. I feel more comfortable with people from my own culture than with people from other cultures.

_____ 8. I feel closer to people with whom I have a good relationship, regardless of whether they belong to my culture or not.

_____ 9. I usually feel closer to people who are from my own culture because I can relate to them better.

_____ 10. I feel more comfortable with people who are open to people from other cultures than with people who are not.

_____ 11. Most of my close friends are from other cultures.

_____ 12. I usually change the way I communicate depending on whom I am communicating with.

_____ 13. When I interact with someone from a different culture, I usually try to adopt some of his or her ways.

_____ 14. Most of my friends are from my own culture.

_____ 15. I usually look for opportunities to interact with people from other cultures.

Scoring: Reverse your responses for Items 1, 2, 7, 8, 9, and 14. For these six items, if your original response was a 5, reverse it to a 1; if your original score was a 4, reverse it to a 2; if your original score was a 3, leave it a 3; if your original score was a 2, reverse it to a 4; and if your original score was a 1, reverse it to a 5. After reversing your scores for these items, sum all 15 items. Your score must range between 15 and 75. Higher scores (above 55) indicate more intercultural communication competence. Lower scores (below 35) indicate less intercultural communication competence.

SOURCE: Arasaratnam, L. (2009, May). The Development of a New Instrument of Intercultural Communication. _Journal of Intercultural Communication, 20._ Published by Elsevier. URL: http://www.immi.se/intercultural/.

CHAPTER SUMMARY

Leaving your native culture for a new one can be one of the most rewarding, yet challenging experiences of a lifetime. Upon relocating to a new culture, everyone goes through a process of acculturation—that is, a process of cultural change that results from ongoing contact between two or more culturally different groups. For some, this process can be particularly difficult, whereas for others, it is relatively easy. Acculturation is in large part a function of how much interaction one chooses to have with members of the new culture and how much of the old culture one desires to maintain. Virtually everyone experiences some degree of culture shock when entering a new culture for an extended period of time. Culture shock results in feelings of disorientation, misunderstandings, conflict, stress, and anxiety. Often, a traveler experiences the same feelings upon returning home. In addition to discussing its causes and symptoms, this chapter has offered several strategies for assessing and managing culture shock. Although culture shock sounds awful, understanding its causes, symptoms, and effects is the first step in alleviating the severity you might experience. Generally speaking, most students who travel abroad experience only minor levels of culture shock.

Finally, one of the foremost goals of this book is to help you become a competent intercultural communicator. As defined in this chapter, _intercultural communication competence_ is the degree to which you effectively adapt your verbal and nonverbal messages to the appropriate cultural context. This chapter has presented a model of intercultural competence that includes knowledge, affective, psychomotor, and situational components. To be a competent intercultural communicator, you must have some _knowledge_ about the person with whom you are communicating, you need to be _motivated_ to communicate with people who are different from you, and you need to engage in appropriate and effective verbal and nonverbal _skills_ to encode and decode messages. You also need to be sensitive to the situational features that influence the verbal and nonverbal messages you send. It is hoped that you, after having read this text, are more knowledgeable about culture, are more motivated to enter into new cultures and establish relationships with persons from different cultures, and have gained some communication skills. Although challenging, intercultural communication is one of the most rewarding life experiences you will ever encounter.

Visit the student study site at www.sagepub.com/neuliep6e for e-flashcards, web quizzes, web resources, and more.

DISCUSSION QUESTIONS

1. What factors do you think would most affect you if you were to travel to another culture?

2. Why do some groups in the United States assimilate more than others?

3. What groups do you think are the most assimilated in the United States?

4. How might the dominant culture of the United States help diverse groups assimilate?

5. Are there good reasons for groups not to assimilate to U.S. culture?

KEY TERMS

acculturation   436

acculturative stress   437

adjustment phase   450

affective component   459

assimilation   440

cultural transmutation   441

culture shock   436

integration   440

intercultural communication
    competence   436

intercultural willingness to
    communicate   460

knowledge component   457

marginalization   441

psychomotor component   461

reentry shock   452

separation   441

situational features   462

NOTES

1.   Condon, J. C., & Yousef, F. (1975). *An Introduction to Intercultural Communication.* Indianapolis, IN: Bobbs-Merrill. (Quote on p. 270)

2.   Redfield, R., Linton, R., & Herskovits, M. (1936). Memorandum on the Study of Acculturation. *American Anthropologist, 38,* 149–152.

3.   Berry, J. W., & Sam, D. T. (1997). Acculturation and Adaptation. In J. W. Berry, M. H. Segall, & C. Kagitcibasa (Eds.), *Handbook of Cross-Cultural Psychology: Social Behavior and Applications* (Vol. 3, pp. 291–326). Boston: Allyn & Bacon.

4.   Ibid.

5.   Nwadiora, E., & McAdoo, H. (1996). Acculturative Stress Among Amerasian Refugees: Gender and Racial Differences. *Adolescence, 31,* 477–488.

6.   Miranda, A. O., & Matheny, K. B. (2000). Sociopsychological Predictors and Acculturative Stress Among Latino Adults. *Journal of Mental Health Counseling, 22,* 306–318.

7.   Smart, J. F., & Smart, D. W. (1995). Acculturative Stress of Hispanics: Loss and Challenge. *Journal of Counseling and Development, 73,* 390–397.

8. Hovey, J. D. (2000). Psychological Predictors of Acculturative Stress in Mexican Immigrants. *Journal of Psychology, 134*, 490–502.

9. Nwadiora & McAdoo, Acculturative Stress Among Amerasian Refugees.

10. Berry, J. W. (1987). *Understanding the Process of Acculturation for Primary Intervention.* Unpublished manuscript, Department of Psychology, Queen's College, Kingston, Ontario. Cited in Nwadiora & McAdoo, Acculturative Stress Among Amerasian Refugees.

11. Kim, Y. Y. (1997). Adapting to a New Culture. In L. A. Samovar & R. E. Porter (Eds.), *Intercultural Communication: A Reader* (8th ed., pp. 404–417). Belmont, CA: Wadsworth.

12. Ibid.

13. Ibid.

14. Liebkind, K. (1996). Acculturation and Stress: Vietnamese Refugees in Finland. *Journal of Cross-Cultural Psychology, 27*, 161–180.

15. Berry, J. W. (1990). Psychology of Acculturation. In R. A. Dienstbier (Ed.), *Nebraska Symposium on Motivation 1989* (pp. 201–234). Lincoln: University of Nebraska Press.

16. Data for Figure 12.1 adapted from Berry, Psychology of Acculturation.

17. Berry, Psychology of Acculturation; Coleman, H. L. K. (1995). Strategies for Coping With Cultural Diversity. *Counseling Psychology, 23*, 722–741.

18. Coleman, Strategies for Coping With Cultural Diversity; Cuellar, I., Arnold, B., & Maldonado, R. (1995). Acculturation Rating Scale for Mexican-Americans II: A Revision of the Original ARSMA. *Hispanic Journal of Behavioral Sciences, 17*, 275–305.

19. Ibid.

20. Cuellar et al., Acculturation Rating Scale for Mexican-Americans II.

21. Coleman, Strategies for Coping With Cultural Diversity; Cuellar et al., Acculturation Rating Scale for Mexican-Americans II; Mendoza, R. H. (1989). An Empirical Scale to Measure Type and Degree of Acculturation in Mexican-American Adolescents and Adults. *Journal of Cross-Cultural Psychology, 20*, 372–385.

22. Landrine, H., & Klonoff, E. A. (1995). The African-American Acculturation Scale II: Cross Validation and Short Form. *Journal of Black Psychology, 21*, 124–153.

23. Acculturation Scale for Mexican Americans II, from Cuellar, I., Arnold, B., & Maldonado, R. (1995). Acculturation Rating Scale for Mexican-Americans. *Hispanic Journal of Behavioral Sciences, 17*, 275–305. Copyright © 1995 SAGE Publications. Used by permission of the publisher.

24. DeLeon, B., & Mendez, S. (1996). Factorial Structure of a Measure of Acculturation in a Puerto Rican Population. *Educational and Psychological Measurement, 56*, 155–166.

25. Landrine & Klonoff, The African-American Acculturation Scale II.

26. Ibid.

27. Winkelman, M. (1994). Cultural Shock and Adaptation. *Journal of Counseling and Development, 73*, 121–127.

28. Oberg, K. (1954). *Culture Shock* (Bobbs-Merrill Series in Social Science, A-329). Indianapolis, IN: Bobbs-Merrill; Oberg, K. (1960). Culture Shock: Adjustments to New Cultural Environments. *Practical Anthropology, 4*, 177–182.

29. Winkelman, Cultural Shock and Adaptation.

30. Oberg, *Culture Shock*; Oberg, Culture Shock: Adjustments to New Cultural Environments.

31. These models are briefly reviewed in Zapf, M. K. (1993). Remote Practice and Culture Shock: Social Workers Moving to Isolated Northern Regions. *Social Work, 38*, 694–705; see also Kealey, D. J. (1978). Adaptation to a New Environment. In Canadian International Development Agency (Ed.), *Pre-Departure Documentation Kit* (pp. 48–55). Hull, Quebec: CIDA Briefing Centre; Richardson, A. (1974). *British Immigrants and Australia: A Psychosocial Inquiry.* Canberra: Australian National University Press; Smalley, W. A. (1963). Culture Shock, Language Shock, and the Shock of Self-Discovery. *Practical Anthropology, 10*, 49–56.

32. Lysgaard, S. (1995). Adjustment in a Foreign Society: Norwegian Fulbright Grantees Visiting the United States. *International Social Science Bulletin, 7*, 45–51.

33. Zapf, Remote Practice and Culture Shock.

34. Winkelman, Cultural Shock and Adaptation.

35. Ibid., p. 122.

36. Rhinesmith, S. (1985). *Bring Home the World.* New York: Walsh.

37. Churchman, A., & Mitrani, M. (1997). The Role of the Physical Environment in Culture Shock. *Environment and Behavior, 29*, 64–87; Lonner, W. (1986). Foreword. In A. Furnham & S. Bochner (Eds.), *Culture Shock: Psychological Reactions to Unfamiliar Environments* (pp. xv–xx). London: Methuen.

38. Winkelman, Cultural Shock and Adaptation.

39. Kim, Adapting to a New Culture.

40. Furnham, A., & Bochner, S. (Eds.). (1986). *Culture Shock: Psychological Reactions to Unfamiliar Environments.* London: Methuen.

41. Winkelman, Cultural Shock and Adaptation.

42. Zapf, Remote Practice and Culture Shock.

43. Zapf, M. K. (1991). Cross-Cultural Transitions and Wellness: Dealing With Culture Shock. *International Journal for the Advancement of Counseling, 14*, 105–119.

44. Van der Zee, K., & Van Oudenhoven, J. P. (2013). Culture Shock or Challenge? The Role of Personality as a Determinant of Intercultural Competence. *Journal of Cross-Cultural Psychology, 44*(6), 928–940.

45. Ibid.

46. Ibid.

47.   Gudykunst, W. B., & Kim, Y. Y. (1997). *Communicating With Strangers: An Approach to Intercultural Communication*. New York: McGraw-Hill; Spitzberg, B. H. (1997). A Model of Intercultural Competence. In L. A. Samovar & R. E. Porter (Eds.), *Intercultural Communication Reader* (8th ed., pp. 379–391). Belmont, CA: Wadsworth.

48.   Spitzberg, A Model of Intercultural Competence.

49.   Ibid.

50.   Spitzberg, B. H., & Cupach, W. R. (1984). *Interpersonal Communication Competence*. Beverly Hills, CA: Sage.

51.   Berger, C. R., & Jordan, J. (1992). Planning Sources, Planning Difficulty, and Verbal Fluency. *Communication Monographs, 59*, 130–149.

52.   Kim, Y. Y. (1990). *Explaining Interethnic Conflict: An Interdisciplinary Overview*. Paper presented at the annual convention of the Speech Communication Association, Chicago, IL.

53.   See, for example, Hewstone, M., & Ward, C. X. (1985). Ethnocentrism and Causal Attribution in Southeast Asia. *Journal of Personality and Social Psychology, 48*, 614–623; Islam, M. R., & Hewstone, M. (1993). Intergroup Attribution and Affective Consequences in Majority and Minority Groups. *Journal of Personality and Social Psychology, 64*, 936–950; Segall, M. H. (1979). *Cross-Cultural Psychology: Human Behavior in Global Perspective*. Monterey, CA: Brooks/Cole; Sumner, W. G. (1906). *Folkways*. Boston: Ginn.

54.   Wiseman, R. L., Hammer, M. R., & Nishida, H. (1989). Predictors of Intercultural Communication Competence. *International Journal of Intercultural Relations, 13*, 349–370.

55.   Neuliep, J. W., & McCroskey, J. C. (1997). The Development of Intercultural and Interethnic Communication Apprehension Scales. *Communication Research Reports, 14*, 145–156.

56.   Kassing, J. W. (1997). Development of the Intercultural Willingness to Communicate Scale. *Communication Research Reports, 14*, 399–407.

57.   Gudykunst & Kim, *Communicating With Strangers;* Kim, Y. Y. (1991). Intercultural Communication Competence: A Systems-Theoretic View. In S. Ting-Toomey & F. Korzenny (Eds.), *Cross-Cultural Interpersonal Communication* (pp. 259–275). Newbury Park, CA: Sage.

58.   Gudykunst & Kim, *Communicating With Strangers*; Spitzberg, A Model of Intercultural Competence.

59.   Gudykunst & Kim, *Communicating With Strangers*.

60.   Kim, Explaining Interethnic Conflict.

61.   Gudykunst & Kim, *Communicating With Strangers*; Ibid.

62.   Arasaratnam, L. A., & Doerfel, M. L. (2005). Intercultural Communication Competence: Identifying Key Components From Multicultural Perspectives. *International Journal of Intercultural Relations, 29*, 137–163.

63.   Arasaratnam, L. A. (2009). The Development of a New Instrument of Intercultural Communication Competence. *Journal of Intercultural Communication, 20*.

Glossary

acculturation: The process of cultural change that results from ongoing contact between two or more culturally different groups

acculturative stress: The degree of physical and psychological stress persons experience when they enter a culture different from their own as a result of the adaptation required to function in a new and different cultural context

adaptors: Mostly unconscious nonverbal actions that satisfy physiological or psychological needs, such as scratching an itch

adjustment phase: Third stage of culture shock, in which people actively seek out effective problem-solving and conflict-resolution strategies

affect displays: Nonverbal presentations of emotion, primarily communicated through facial expressions

affective component: Approach–avoidance tendencies during intercultural communication; the extent to which one experiences intercultural communication apprehension and one's willingness to communicate

affective style: Communication manner where the process of interaction is emphasized, placing the burden of understanding on both the speaker and the listener; relies heavily on nonverbal cues

African Americans: Microcultural group in the United States whose ancestors were brought to the United States as slaves

Amish: A microcultural, religiously oriented group whose members practice simple and austere living

analogic communication: Nonverbal communication: continuous and ongoing

anxiety/uncertainty management theory: A theory developed to explain the interrelationships among uncertainty, anxiety, mindfulness, and communication effectiveness

arranged marriage: Marriage that is initiated and negotiated by a third party rather than by the bride and groom

assertiveness: An individual's ability to make requests, actively disagree, and express positive or negative personal rights and feelings: approach tendencies

assimilation: The degree to which an individual takes on the behaviors and language habits and practices the basic rules and norms of the host culture while relinquishing ties with the native culture

avoiding facework: Communicative behaviors that focus on an attempt to save the face of the other person during communication or conflict

built environment: Adaptations to the terrestrial environment, including architecture, housing, lighting, and landscaping

carpentered-world hypothesis: Learned tendency of those living in industrialized cultures to interpret nonrectangular figures as rectangles in perspective

categorization: Classifying or sorting of perceived information into distinct groups

chronemics: The perception and use of time

collectivism: Cultural orientation where the group is the primary unit of culture. Group goals take precedence over individual goals.

communication: The simultaneous encoding, decoding, and interpretation of verbal and nonverbal messages between people

communication apprehension: The fear or anxiety associated with either real or anticipated communication with another person or group of persons

context: The cultural, physical, social, and psychological environment

contextual style: Role-centered mode of speaking where one's choice of messages is influenced by one's relative status in the conversation

cultural context: An accumulated pattern of values, beliefs, and behavior held by an identifiable group of people with a common verbal and nonverbal symbol system

cultural transmutation: Mode of acculturation in which the individual chooses to identify with a third cultural group (microculture) that materializes out of the native and host cultural groups

culture: An accumulated pattern of values, beliefs, and behaviors shared by an identifiable group of people with a common history and verbal and nonverbal symbol system

culture shock: The effects associated with the tension and anxiety of entering a new culture, combined with the sensations of loss, confusion, and powerlessness resulting from the forfeiture of cultural norms and social rituals

decay: Memory loss due to lack of use

denotative meaning: The literal meaning of a word; the dictionary meaning

dialect: A language variety associated with a particular region or social group

digital communication: Verbal communication

direct style: Manner of speaking where one employs overt expressions of intention

dominating facework: Communicative behaviors characterized by an individual's need to control the situation and defend his or her self-face

dynamic: Something considered active and forceful

Ebonics: From the terms *ebony* and *phonics,* a grammatically robust and rich African American speech pattern whose roots are in West Africa

elaborate style: Mode of speaking that emphasizes rich, expressive language

elaborated code: A cultural context wherein the speakers of a language have a variety of linguistic options open to them to explicitly communicate their intent via verbal messages

emblems: Primarily hand gestures that have a direct verbal translation; can be used to repeat or to substitute for verbal communication

empathy Often defined as the degree to which we can accurately infer another's thoughts or feelings

environmental context: The geographical and psychological location of communication within some cultural context

episodic long-term memory: A component of long-term memory where private individual memories are stored

ethnocentric attributional bias: The tendency to make internal attributions for the positive behavior of the in-group while making external attributions for its negative behavior; also called the ultimate attribution error

ethnocentrism: The tendency to place one's own group (cultural, ethnic, or religious) in a position of centrality and highest worth, and to create negative attitudes and behaviors toward other groups

exacting style: Manner of speaking where persons say no more or less than is needed to communicate a point

face: A person's sense of favorable self-worth or self-image experienced during communicative situations. Face is an emotional extension of the self-concept. It is considered a universal concept.

facework: Communicative strategies employed to manage one's own face or to support or challenge another's face

fixed-feature space: Space bounded by immovable or permanent fixtures, such as walls

gender: A socially constructed and learned creation usually associated with one's sex; masculinity and femininity. People are born into a sex group but learn to become masculine or feminine. The meaning of gender stems from the particular culture's value system.

GENE (Generalized Ethnocentrism) Scale: Self-report instrument designed to measure generalized ethnocentrism

generative grammar: The idea that from a finite set of rules, a speaker of any language can create or generate an infinite number of sentences, many of which have never before been uttered

haptics: The use of touch and physical contact between interactants

health communication: The study and use of communication strategies to inform and influence individual decisions that enhance health

high context: Cultural orientation where meanings are gleaned from the physical, social, and psychological contexts

high load: A situation with a high information rate

Hispanic: Defined by the U.S. government as a person of Cuban, Mexican, Puerto Rican, South or Central American, or other Spanish culture or origin, regardless of race

Hmong: Microculture belonging to the Sino-Tibetan language family, culturally similar to the Chinese. The Hmong, whose name means "free people" or "mountain people," fought for the United States during the Vietnam War, and many have immigrated to the United States since the end of the war.

horizontal collectivism: Cultural orientation where the self is seen as a member of an in-group whose members are similar to one another

horizontal individualism: Cultural orientation where an autonomous self is valued but the self is more or less equal to others

illusory correlation principle: When two objects or persons are observed to be linked in some way, people have a tendency to believe they are always linked (or correlated)

illustrators: Primarily hand and arm movements that function to accent or complement speech

immediacy: The physical and psychological distance/closeness between interactants

indirect style: Manner of speaking wherein the intentions of the speakers are hidden or only hinted at during interaction

individualism: Cultural orientation where the individual is unique and individual goals are emphasized over group goals

informal space: Space defined by the movement of the interactants

information rate: The amount of information contained or perceived in the physical environment per some unit of time

in-group: A membership group whose norms, goals, and values shape the behavior of the members. Extreme in-groups see the actions of an out-group as threatening.

instrumental style: Sender-focused manner of speaking that is goal and outcome oriented. Instrumental speakers use communication to achieve some goal or purpose.

integrating facework: Communicative behaviors that allow for the shared concern for self- and other-face and strive for closure during communication or conflict

integration: Mode of acculturation in which the individual develops a kind of bicultural orientation that successfully blends and synthesizes cultural dimensions from both groups while maintaining an identity in each group

intentionality: During communication, the voluntary and conscious encoding and decoding of messages

intercultural communication: Two or more persons from different cultures or microcultures exchanging verbal and nonverbal messages

intercultural communication apprehension: The fear or anxiety associated with either real or anticipated communication with a person from another culture or microculture

intercultural communication competence: The ability to adapt one's verbal and nonverbal messages to the appropriate cultural context

intercultural conflict: The implicit or explicit emotional struggle between persons of different cultures over perceived or actual incompatibility of cultural ideologies and values, situational norms, goals, face orientations, scarce resources, styles/processes, and/or outcomes in a face-to-face context

intercultural willingness to communicate: Predisposition to initiate intercultural interaction with persons from different cultures even when completely free to choose whether or not to communicate

interference: During recall, when new or old information blocks or obstructs the recall of other information

involuntary membership groups: Groups to which people belong and have no choice but to belong, such as sex, race, and age groups

involuntary nonmembership groups: Groups to which people do not belong because of ineligibility

kinesics: General category of body motion, including emblems, illustrators, affect displays, and adaptors

knowledge component: The extent of one's awareness of another culture's values and so forth; also, the extent to which one is cognitively simple, rigid, and ethnocentric

language variety: The way a particular group of people uses language

languages: Systematic sets of sounds, combined with sets of rules, for the sole purpose of communicating

learning styles: An individual's unique way of gathering, storing, and retrieving information to solve problems

LGBT: Persons who consider themselves lesbian, gay, bisexual, or transgender

long-term memory: Cognitive storage area where large amounts of information are held relatively permanently

low context: Cultural orientation where meanings are encoded in the verbal code

low load: A situation with a low information rate

marginalization: A mode of acculturation where an individual chooses not to identify with his or her native culture or with the host culture: sometimes involuntarily

membership groups: Groups to which people belong and where there is regular interaction among members who perceive themselves as members

memory: The storage of information in the human brain over time

microculture: An identifiable group of people who share a set of values, beliefs, and behaviors and who possess a common history and a verbal and nonverbal symbol system that is similar to but systematically varies from the larger, often dominant cultural milieu

monochronic time orientation: Cultural temporal orientation that stresses the compartmentalization and segmentation of measurable units of time

morphemes: Smallest meaningful units of sound; combinations of phonemes

muted groups: Microcultures whose members are forced to express themselves (e.g., speak, write) within the dominant mode of expression

mutual-face: Concern for both parties' images or the image of the relationship during communication, especially conflict

nonmembership groups: Groups to which people do not belong

nonverbal expectancy violations theory: Theory that posits that people hold expectations about the nonverbal behavior of others. When these expectations are violated, people evaluate the violation positively or negatively, depending on the source of the violation.

occulesics: The study of eye contact

olfactics: The perception and use of smell, scent, and odor

organizational culture: An organized pattern of values, beliefs, behaviors, and communication channels held by the members of an organization

other-face: Concern for another's image during communication, especially conflict

out-group: A group whose attributes are dissimilar from those of an in-group and that opposes the realization of in-group goals

out-group homogeneity effect: The tendency to see members of an out-group as highly similar while seeing the members of the in-group as unique and individual

paralanguage: Characteristics of the voice, such as pitch, rhythm, intensity, volume, and rate

patient–provider communication: Face-to-face interaction between the patient and his or her individual health care provider

perception: The mental interpretation of external stimuli via sensation

perceptual context: The attitudes, emotions, and motivations of the persons engaged in communication and how they affect information processing

perceptual filters: Physical, social, and psychological processes that screen and bias incoming stimuli

Personal Report of Communication Apprehension (PRCA-24): Self-report instrument designed to measure communication apprehension

personal style: Manner of speaking that relies on the use of personal pronouns and stresses informality and symmetrical power relationships

phonemes: Smallest units of sound, as in consonants or vowels

physical context: The actual geographical space or territory in which the communication takes place

polyandry: The practice of having multiple husbands

polychronic time orientation: Cultural temporal orientation that stresses the involvement of people and completion of tasks as opposed to strict adherence to schedules; time not seen as measurable

polygamy: The practice of having multiple spouses

polygyny: The practice of having multiple wives

power distance: The extent to which members of a culture expect and accept that power is unequally distributed

process: Anything ongoing, ever changing, and continuous

proxemics: The perception and use of space, including territoriality and personal space

psychomotor component: The extent to which one can translate cultural knowledge into verbal and nonverbal performance and role enactment

reentry shock: The effects associated with the tension and anxiety of returning to one's native culture after an extended stay in a foreign culture

reference group: A group to which a person may or may not belong but with which the person identifies in some way in terms of values and goals

regulators: Nonverbal acts that manage and govern communication between people, such as stance, distance, and eye contact

relational empathy: Shared meaning and harmonization that is the result of the interaction of two people

responsiveness: An individual's ability to be sensitive to the communication of others, including providing feedback, engaging in comforting communication, and listening

restricted code: A cultural context wherein the speakers of a language are limited as to what they can say or do verbally; a status-oriented system

role: One's relative hierarchical position or rank in a group. A role is a prescribed set of behaviors that is expected to fulfill the role. Roles prescribe with whom, about what, and how to interact.

self-face: The concern for one's own image during communication, especially conflict

semantic long-term memory: A part of long-term memory where general information such as how to read and write and the meanings of words is stored

semifixed-feature space: Space bounded by movable objects, such as furniture

sensation: Gathering of visual, auditory, olfactic, haptic, and taste stimuli/information

sensory receptors: Eyes, ears, nose, mouth, and skin

separation: A mode of acculturation where individuals prefer low levels of interaction with their host culture while maintaining a close connection with their native culture

sex: A designation of people based on biological genital differences

sex role: A prescribed set of behaviors assigned to different sexes

short-term memory: Cognitive storage area where small amounts of information are held for short periods of time, usually less than 20 seconds

situational features: The extent to which the environmental context, previous contact, status differential, and third-party intervention affect one's competence during intercultural communication

social identity: The total combination of one's group roles; a part of the individual's self-concept that is derived from the person's membership in groups

social stratification: A culture's organization of roles into a hierarchical vertical status structure

sociocommunicative style: Degree of assertiveness and responsiveness during communication

sociorelational context: The roles one assumes within a culture; the role relationship between interactants (e.g., brother/sister), defined by verbal and nonverbal messages

Spanglish: Hybrid language combining the phonological features (i.e., sounds) and syntactic structures (i.e., grammar) of English and Spanish

Standard English: The variety of English spoken in the United States that is considered correct

Stereotype Content Model: A model that proposes that all stereotypes are based on social perceptions of warmth and competence

stereotype threat: When a stereotyped group believes the stereotype about them may be true

stereotypes: Usually negative but sometimes positive perceptions we have of individuals based on their membership in groups

succinct style: Manner of concise speaking often accompanied by silence

symbol: An arbitrarily selected and learned stimulus representing something else

terrestrial environment: The physical geography of the Earth

third culture: That which is created when a dyad consisting of persons from different cultures comes together and establishes relational empathy

transactional: The simultaneous encoding and decoding process during communication

uncertainty: The amount of unpredictability during communication

uncertainty avoidance: The degree to which members of a particular culture feel threatened by unpredictable, uncertain, or unknown situations

uncertainty reduction theory: Theory whose major premise is that when strangers first meet, their primary goal is to reduce uncertainty

universal grammar: The idea that all languages share a common rule structure or grammar that is innate to human beings, regardless of culture

vertical collectivism: Cultural orientation where the individual sees the self as an integral part of the in-group but the members are different from one another (e.g., status)

vertical individualism: Cultural orientation where an autonomous self is valued and the self is seen as different from and perhaps unequal to others

voluntary membership groups: Membership groups to which people belong by choice, such as a political party or service organization

voluntary nonmembership groups: Membership groups to which people do not belong by choice

Photo Credits

The photographs appearing in the Student Voices Across Cultures feature are used by permission and courtesy of the following individuals:

Page 30: Jennifer Seidemann

Page 52: Pengfei Song

Page 84: Ahmed I. Alshaya

Page 128: Stephen Rupsch

Page 165: Sebastian Friedemann

Page 190: Amanda Garrity

Page 193: Morgan Leah Johnson

Page 236: Ala Aldahneem

Page 250: Chen Chen

Page 303: Anna Shircel

Page 306: Lindsey Novitzke

Page 313: Hussam Almoharb

Page 336: Karen Margarita Henao Carbonell

Page 366: Mohammad I. Alshaya

Page 395: Rodrigo Villalobos

Page 413: Carl Ekstrom

Page 419: Viviann Filispdóttir Hansen

Page 451: Jessica Bahrke

Page 453: Hillary Hubertz

The following chapter opening photos are used by permission:

Chapter 1, page 1: Digital Vision/Digital Vision/ Thinkstock

Chapter 2, page 47: Buena Vista Images

Chapter 3, page 97: Boston Globe via Getty Images

Chapter 4, page 135: © iStockphoto.com/John Sigler

Chapter 5, page 173: Michael Blann/Lifesize/ Thinkstock

Chapter 6, page 215: © David H. Wells/Corbis

Chapter 7, page 245: Jupiterimages/ThinkStock

Chapter 8, page 279: © iStockphoto.com/ Karen Moller

Chapter 9, page 329: © iStockphoto.com/leaf

Chapter 10, page 373: © iStockphoto.com/ Willie B. Thomas

Chapter 11, page 399: Digital Vision/ ThinkStock

Chapter 12, page 435: © iStockphoto.com/ philsajonesen

The following photos appearing within the chapters are used by permission:

Figure 1.2, page 16: Science PR

Figure 1.3, page 21: © iStockphoto.com/ Shmulitk

Figure 1.4, page 22: AP Photo/Gail Burton

Figure 2.3, page 83: © iStockphoto.com/ Juanmonino

Figure 2.4, page 87: LIU JIN/AFP/Getty Images

Figure 3.1, page 111: David Freund

Figure 3.2, page 119: MCT via Getty Images

Figure 3.3, page 123: Photos by Sonja

Figure 4.1, page 144: AP Photo/CHINATOPIX

Figure 4.2, page 148: © 2012 John S. Lander

Figure 4.5, page 153: © James W. Neuliep

Figure 5.1, page 177: Jupiterimages/Photos .com/Thinkstock

Figure 5.2a, page 178: John Foxx/Stockbyte/ Thinkstock

Figure 5.2b, page 178: Jupiterimages/Photos .com/Thinkstock

Figure 5.2c, page 178: Brand X Pictures/Brand X Pictures/Thinkstock

Figure 5.7a, page 189: © Trinette Reed/Corbis

Figure 5.7b, page 189: © moodboard/Corbis

Figure 5.8, page 192: © Daniel Lainé/Corbis

Figure 6.1, page 218: Robert Ginn

Figure 6.2, page 221: © iStockphoto.com/ Izabela Habur

Figure 6.4, page 234: Chad Baker/Jason Reed/ Ryan McVay

Figure 7.2, page 251: © iStockphoto.com/ Marina_Di

Figure 7.3, page 253: © James W. Neuliep

Figure 7.5a, page 272: Time & Life Pictures/ Getty Images

Figure 7.5b, page 272: © Bureau L.A. Collection/Sygma/Corbis

Figure 8.1, page 286: © iStockphoto.com/ stockstudioX

Figure 8.2, page 288: © James W. Neuliep

Figure 8.3, page 288: © James W. Neuliep

Figure 8.4, page 289: © James W. Neuliep

Figure 8.5, page 289: © James W. Neuliep

Figure 8.6a, page 292: © Can Stock Photo Inc./3650308

Figure 8.6b, page 292: © iStockphoto.com/ zilli

Figure 8.7, page 296: Jupiterimages/Brand X Pictures/Thinkstock

Figure 9.5, page 364: Stockbyte/Stockbyte/ Thinkstock

Figure 10.2, page 377: © Bettmann/Corbis

Figure 10.4, page 394: © iStockphoto.com/ killerb10

Figure 11.1, page 402: © iStockphoto.com/ Photomorphic

Figure 11.3, page 417: AFP/Getty Images

Figure 11.4, page 423: Boston Globe via Getty Images

Figure 11.6, page 428: The Washington Post/ Getty Images

Figure 12.2, page 442: © Sollina Images/Blend Images/Corbis

Index

About the Author

James W. Neuliep (PhD, University of Oklahoma) conducts research and teaches courses in intercultural communication, interpersonal communication, small-group communication, communication theory, communication apprehension, ethnocentrism, and research methods. Along with Jim McCroskey, he has developed a number of assessment scales used throughout the discipline. In addition to this intercultural communication textbook, he has also written a communication theory textbook (*Human Communication Theory: Applications and Case Studies*, Allyn & Bacon), and his research has appeared in the following journals: *Communication Education; Communication Quarterly; Communication Reports; Communication Research Reports; Human Communication Research; Journal of Intercultural Communication Research; Journal of Social Behavior and Personality;* and *Communication & Language*. He is the immediate past edito r of *the Journal of Intercultural Communication Research* and has served or is serving on the editorial boards of *Communication Monographs, Communication Quarterly, Communication Reports, Communication Research Reports, Communication Studies, Human Communication, Journal of Applied Communication Research, Journal of Communication, Journal of International and Intercultural Communication,* and *Journal of Social Behavior and Personality*.

$SAGE researchmethods

The essential online tool for researchers from the world's leading methods publisher

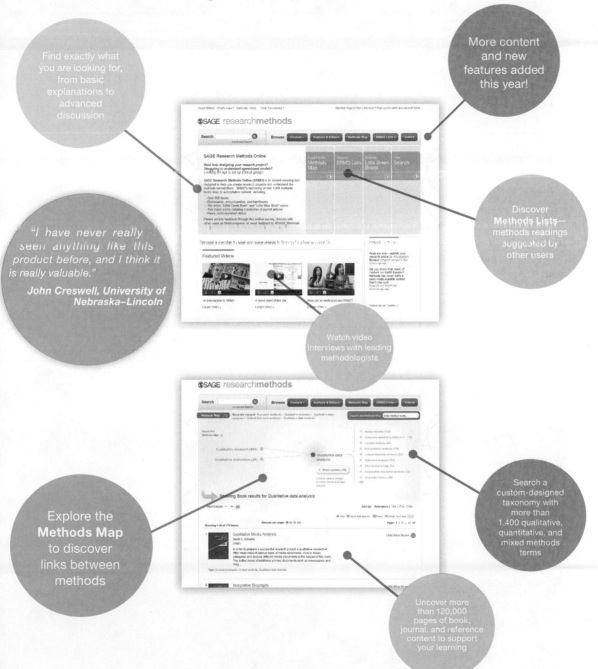

Find exactly what you are looking for, from basic explanations to advanced discussion

More content and new features added this year!

"*I have never really seen anything like this product before, and I think it is really valuable.*"

John Creswell, University of Nebraska–Lincoln

Discover **Methods Lists**—methods readings suggested by other users

Watch video interviews with leading methodologists

Explore the **Methods Map** to discover links between methods

Search a custom-designed taxonomy with more than 1,400 qualitative, quantitative, and mixed methods terms

Uncover more than 120,000 pages of book, journal, and reference content to support your learning

Find out more at
www.sageresearchmethods.com